THE CHINESE COMMUNIST PARTY

A 100-YEAR TRAJECTORY

THE CHINESE COMMUNIST PARTY

A 100-YEAR TRAJECTORY

Edited by Jérôme Doyon
and Chloé Froissart

ANU PRESS

Published by ANU Press
The Australian National University
Canberra ACT 2600, Australia
Email: anupress@anu.edu.au

Available to download for free at press.anu.edu.au

ISBN (print): 9781760466237
ISBN (online): 9781760466244

WorldCat (print): 1416783106
WorldCat (online): 1416782338

DOI: 10.22459/CCP.2024

Cover design and layout by ANU Press

This book is published under the aegis of the China in the World editorial board of ANU Press.

Publication of this book has been supported by the ANU vice-chancellor's strategic funds for flagship titles at ANU Press.

Contents

III. China's Path to Modernisation and Its Challenges

IV. Territorial Control and Nation-Building

Abbreviations

AFIC	All-China Federation of Industry and Commerce
APAP	Action Plan for Air Pollution Prevention and Control
CCP	Chinese Communist Party
CDIC	Central Discipline and Inspection Commission
CICPA	China Institute of Certified Public Accountants
CLO	Central Liaison Office
CMC	Central Military Commission
CPES	China Private Enterprise Survey
CPPCC	Chinese People's Political Consultative Conference
DIC	discipline inspection commissions
DPP	Democratic Progressive Party
EIA	environmental impact assessment
ENGO	environmental non-government organisations
EPB	Environmental Protection Bureaus
EPIL	Environmental Public Interest Litigation
EPL	Environmental Protection Law
FYP	Five-Year Plan
GLF	Great Leap Forward
GMD	Guomindang
HAB	Home Affairs Bureau
HKMAO	Hong Kong and Macau Affairs Office
IAC	Islamic Association of China
MEE	Ministry of Ecology and Environment
MEP	Ministry of Environmental Protection

MoCA	Ministry of Civil Affairs
NCNA	New China News Agency
NDRC	National Development and Reform Commission
NGO	non-governmental organisations
NPC	National People's Congress
PB	Politburo
PBSC	Politburo Standing Committee
PITO	East Turkestan Islamic Party
PLA	People's Liberation Army
PP	preferential policies
PPTO	People's Party of East Turkestan
PRC	People's Republic of China
PwC	PricewaterhouseCoopers
RAB	Religious Affairs Bureau
ROC	Republic of China
SAR	Special Administrative Region
SEPA	State Environmental Protection Administration
SEPB	State Environmental Protection Bureau
SOE	state-owned enterprises
SOMB	Social Organisations Management Bureau
TVE	township and village enterprises
UFWD	United Front Work Department
URCM	Ministry of Urban and Rural Construction and Environmental Protection

Contributors

Shaun Breslin, professor, University of Warwick

Kerry Brown, director of the China Lau Institute, King's College London

Jean-Pierre Cabestan, emeritus professor, Hong Kong Baptist University

Rémi Castets, associate professor, co-director of the D2iA research unit, Bordeaux Montaigne University

Timothy Cheek, professor and Louis Cha Chair in Chinese Research, Institute of Asian Research, University of British Columbia

Edmund W. Cheng, professor, City University of Hong Kong

Alexander F. Day, associate professor, Occidental College

Jérôme Doyon, junior professor, Sciences Po

Chloé Froissart, professor, Inalco

Giuseppe Gabusi, assistant professor, University of Turin

Coraline Goron, assistant professor, Duke Kunshan University

Gilles Guiheux, professor, Université Paris Cité

Vanessa Frangville, professor in China Studies, Université Libre de Bruxelles

Emmanuel Jourda, associate researcher, EHESS

Genia Kostka, professor, Freie Universität Berlin

Frank N. Pieke, professor, Leiden University

Gunter Schubert, chair professor, University of Tübingen

Patricia M. Thornton, associate professor, University of Oxford

Long Yang, postdoctoral researcher, University of Freiburg

Samson Yuen, associate professor, Hong Kong Baptist University

Introduction

Jérôme Doyon and Chloé Froissart

Centenary of the Chinese Communist Party

The small grouping of intellectuals who gathered in July 1921 in the French concession of Shanghai has magnified into one of the largest and most formidable political parties in history. Created with fewer than 60 members, the Chinese Communist Party (CCP) now numbers more than 95 million. From a revolutionary party that emerged in the aftermath of the collapse of the Chinese Empire and World War I, it became, in 1949, a political regime in its own right, a party-state dominating the world's most populous country. Almost every aspect of Chinese people's lives has changed under the Party's rule, and its influence is now global.

The CCP led China's path to modernisation from a rural and underdeveloped country torn apart by warlordism, civil war, and European and Japanese imperialism, to the second largest world economy and a global superpower. The Party survived not only more than a decade of civil war, in spite of being repeatedly driven close to extinction in the 1920s and 1930s, but also the end of the revolutionary process. It endured self-inflicted disasters, ranging from the Great Famine (1959–61) to the destructions of the Cultural Revolution (1966–76), and overcame the transition from a planned to a market-based economy. The economic reforms initiated in the late 1970s brought new challenges linked to the urbanisation of a chiefly rural society, the privatisation of state resources that were the basis of social welfare for millions, and the globalisation of Chinese society and the economy, accelerated by China's accession to the World Trade Organization in 2001 and the surge of outgoing investments that followed the launch of the Belt and Road Initiative in 2013.

The Party adapted to the new social and economic environment its reforms created. Going counter to the idea that wealth brings democratisation, greater prosperity has strengthened rather than weakened the CCP's power. Its ability to modernise the country, rather than to represent it, contributes to its popular support. The Party's own narrative of China's path to modernisation, which is encapsulated today in the idea of a 'China Dream', also boosts nationalistic sentiments and contributes to holding the nation together despite the decreasing importance of Maoist ideals and the social changes brought by the reforms. Moreover, the country's modernisation, and enrichment of the party-state, facilitate the CCP's monitoring of citizens, now technologically enhanced, to ensure it remains the only game in town.

At the same time, adopting a dichotomous perspective that contrasts a vibrant liberalised economy with an ossified Leninist party-state, and, in-between, a society trying to find ways to resist or gain autonomy, misses the evolution of the Party itself and its interactions with social forces, which have oscillated between inclusive tendencies and 'totalitarian refluxes'.[1] For most of its history, the CCP has been an engine of change and cannot be simply seen as a relic of a foregone past. The Party not only made possible the triumph of 1949 but also provided the ideological and organisational bases for the continuation of the power of the People's Republic of China (PRC) since then, surviving the 'Leninist extinction' of the 1990s (Jowitt 1992). The structures that permitted military mobilisation during the civil war became the basis for its governing, monitoring and repression of the Chinese population after 1949. The CCP is the product of clandestine struggle and violence, which explains its hierarchical structure, its culture of secrecy and control, as well as its cohesion based on an 'us–them' logic (Saich 2021). This guerrilla heritage has also contributed to the CCP's decentralised and adaptive features, making it adept at embracing uncertainty and dealing with various challenges, ranging from widespread unrest to global epidemics (Heilmann and Perry 2011). It translates into an extraordinary capacity to experiment, learn from the West and from its own experience, and adapt and systematise what works on the ground. With branches extending to every corner of Chinese society, the CCP has an extraordinary monitoring capacity, but is also more exposed to society than most political parties. The CCP has learned from the collapse of other Communist regimes (Shambaugh 2008), approaching reforms gradually as well as developing, albeit constantly challenged, institutions of leadership succession.

1 Geremie Barmé, '"Ugh, Here We Are"—Q&A with Geremie Barmé', *SupChina*, 8 April 2022, supchina.com/2022/04/08/ugh-here-we-are-qa-with-geremie-barme/.

Its adaptability, and ruthlessness, has allowed the CCP to maintain its power monopoly over a huge and diverse population. It has developed territorial policy experiments that can take many forms, ranging from the opening of coastal special economic zones to foreign investments in the 1980s, to the establishment in the 2010s of camps in the north-western parts of the country to forcibly re-educate millions of China's Muslim population. It has also made and unmade alliances depending on circumstances. The CCP organisation itself metamorphosed in the post-Mao period from a party of the revolutionary classes to a white-collar party, embracing the elite of the liberalised economy and broadening its social bases (Gore 2011; Dickson 2003). From making up the vast majority of the CCP's membership during the Mao era, workers and peasants now constitute only a third. The CCP's united front policy, which aims at cultivating allies among social forces outside the Party, has also transformed. From the partnership with the Nationalist Party that helped the CCP to present itself as a champion of the fight against Japan in the 1930s, it has become an institutionalised platform allowing it to coopt social forces while always refusing them an equal standing.

This fluidity of the CCP is also evident on the ideological front, in contrast to the sense of continuity that the CCP wants to promote about itself with the current leadership's call for members to 'remain true to the [Party's] original aspirations'.[2] After adapting the principles of the Soviet state economy to Chinese realities, the Party took advantage of market practices to 'let some get wealthy first', as was the stated goal in the early years of reform, and now aims at more redistribution and 'common prosperity'. A recent volume published by ANU Press, in the same series as the present volume, testifies to the malleability, as well as persistence, of the Maoist heritage (Franceschini, Loubere and Sorace 2019). Similarly, after presenting itself as a break from the past, the CCP draws more and more on continuities with imperial repertoires (Shue 2022).

It is impossible to encapsulate in one volume the essence of such a changing political organisation. Yet the CCP's centenary has prompted vivid discussion, with several books by veteran analysts of CCP politics greatly enriching our grasp of what holds the CCP together and explains

2 'Resolution of the CPC Central Committee on the Major Achievements and Historical Experience of the Party over the Past Century', adopted at the Sixth Plenary Session of the Nineteenth Central Committee of the Communist Party of China, 11 November 2021, *Xinhua*, 16 November 2021, www.news.cn/english/2021-11/16/c_1310314611.htm.

its longevity. Tony Saich's *From Rebel to Ruler* adeptly captures the tension between unity and diversity throughout the history of the Party, providing an outline to better understand its nature and trajectory (Saich 2021). Bruce Dickson's *The Party and the People* dives into the most recent discussions in understanding the CCP's relation to the Chinese people and how it can be responsive without being accountable to the population (Dickson 2021). David Shambaugh's *China's Leaders* traces the history of the PRC through its figureheads, stressing that despite largely sharing the common goal of making their country rich and powerful they had very different approaches to foreign policy, political language and institutions (Shambaugh 2021). Also focusing on elite politics, Joseph Fewsmith's *Rethinking Chinese Politics* introduces us to the tumultuous world of inner-party power struggles in the post-Mao period, challenging the commonly held view of a gradually institutionalising political process (Fewsmith 2021). Complementary to these works focusing on the organisation and its leaders, the collective volume edited by Timothy Cheek, Klaus Mülhahn and Hans van de Ven traces the CCP's history in 10 lives – 10 biographies illustrating the many perspectives that exist *in* and *on* the CCP (Cheek, Mühlhahn and van de Ven 2021). In recent years, other edited volumes have also provided important discussions on various aspects of the CCP contemporary evolution, be they its practices of power (Shue and Thornton 2017), its modes of action (Zheng and Gore 2019), its operating methods and policies (Lam 2017) or the influence of its revolutionary origins (Franceschini, Loubere and Sorace 2019).

The present volume aims to contribute to this ongoing discussion by providing a thematic analysis of, and multidisciplinary approach to, the Party's trajectory over a century. It finds its origin in a conference convened in Paris and online in June 2021 by Inalco University, the European Institute for Chinese Studies and the Oxford School of Global and Area Studies. The conference brought together a team of scholars from different disciplines (history, sociology, political science, political economy, anthropology and Chinese studies) and continents (Europe, North America and Asia) with the aim of covering the many facets of the CCP's 100-year trajectory. Some of the chapters are revised versions of previously published journal articles.[3]

3 Previous versions of Chapters 1, 2, 3, 5 and 7 have been published by the *Journal of Current China Affairs* as part of a special issue titled 'The Chinese Communist Party at 100'. An earlier version of Chapter 15 was published by *Communist and Post-Communist Studies* under the title 'Deepening the State: The Dynamics of China's United Front Work in Post-Handover Hong Kong'. They are reprinted with permission.

The book departs from previous volumes by combining a level of historical depth mostly found in single-authored monographs with the thematic and disciplinary breadth of an edited volume. It attempts to grasp the CCP's trajectory through the development of its two core features – organisation and ideology – and also its two main historical missions: modernising the country and unifying it through a Party-led, nation-building project. This volume, hence, embodies a rare attempt at investigating the CCP's 100 years of existence, examining both the nature and functioning of the party-state, but also its relationship with society and its policies. Its originality lies in the diversity of its approaches, combining chapters offering synthetic overviews of the state of the art with others exploring new research perspectives. While far from comprehensive (we regret, in particular, not being able to include specific contributions on religion, gender or workers), the present volume stands out for its long-term and multiscale approach, offering complex and nuanced insights, eschewing any Party grand narrative, and unravelling underlying trends and logics, composed of adaption but also contradictions, resistance and sometimes setbacks that may be overlooked when focusing on the short term. Rather than putting forward an overall argument about the nature of the CCP, the many perspectives presented in this volume highlight the complex internal dynamics of the Party, the diversity of its roles in relation to the state, as well as in its interaction with society beyond the state.

Beyond 'Eras' and 'Resilience'

Pointing to the CCP's adaptability and resilience can become a cliché, and the CCP itself does not refrain from relying on that narrative. For the Party's current leader, Xi Jinping: 'A hallmark that distinguishes the Communist Party of China from other political parties is its courage in undertaking self-reform.'[4] A specificity of this official narrative is to present this adaption in a linear and deterministic fashion, always going in the direction of the Party's betterment and China's rise.

The 'Resolution of the Central Committee of the Communist Party of China on the Major Achievements and Historical Experience of the Party over the Past Century', issued in 2021, is a good illustration of this view of

4 'Speech by Xi Jinping at a Ceremony Marking the Centenary of the CPC', *Xinhua*, 1 July 2021, www.xinhuanet.com/english/special/2021-07/01/c_1310038244.htm.

history. This is the third historical resolution issued by the CCP after those in 1945 and 1981. While the first one unified the Party around 'Mao Zedong Thought', the second solidified Deng's position as paramount leader of the reform era by maintaining a balance between criticising and preserving the Maoist heritage. The 2021 resolution likewise aims at solidifying the power of the leader in place, but without closing a period of internal struggle for power or revising previous official views on history. Contrary to recent propaganda materials targeting a broader public, such as the 2021 re-edition of the *Short History of the Chinese Communist Party*, which largely sanitises official history by removing discussion of the excesses of the Mao period, the 2021 resolution largely adopts the 1981 resolution's language on the Mao era. While focusing on glorifying the current leadership's successes and objectives, the resolution also solidifies the leadership's role as the custodian of the *correct* historical view.

According to the 2021 resolution, the PRC's history is divided into three 'eras': the first one (1949–76) laid the foundations for 'socialism with Chinese characteristics' under Mao Zedong's leadership; the second one saw the 'reform and opening of China' under Deng Xiaoping and his successors; the third one paves the way for the 'great rejuvenation of the Chinese nation' under Xi Jinping. This division is very much to Xi Jinping's advantage, positioning him in the continuity of the two great men of the PRC, and relegating other leaders such as Jiang Zemin and Hu Jintao to secondary roles. The official narrative provides a sense of history underpinned by both the affirmation of the necessity of what happened and a constant sense of progress that eventually culminates in the epiphany of the Xi Jinping era. The current era, in fact, takes up more than half of the resolution's text and is presented, in a Marxist view of history, as the synthesis of the previous phases and a 'new breakthrough in adapting Marxism to the Chinese context'.[5] This view is overall deterministic, presenting the CCP's trajectory as proceeding from one victory to the next, downplaying trials and errors, setbacks, and contradictions, while overall erasing the price paid by the Chinese people for these transformations.

Scholarly research tends to share with this official focus on leader-centric 'eras' a tendency to overstress the unity within the eras, and differences between them, as well as the role of supposedly farsighted leaders. Many social scientists have described the evolution of Communist regimes as going

5 'Resolution of the CPC Central Committee'.

through phases, which include, paraphrasing Kenneth Jowitt's terminology, the *transformation* of the old society, the *consolidation* of the revolutionary regime and the *inclusion* of a diversifying society (Jowitt 1992; Huntington 1970; Dimitrov 2013). While presented as a logical evolution, these phases are also generally seen as brought about by the political decision of transformative leaders. This conceptualisation is very enlightening when it comes to comparing Communist regimes' trajectories and how they differ or not. Yet, such an approach may lead, sometimes against the authors' own warnings, to a linear and deterministic reading of history, with the demise of these Communist systems seen as the logical consequence of the *inclusion* phase, when the gap between the founding ideology and the pluralistic society they aim at embracing becomes too large to manage. The idea that demise is the natural horizon of Communist regimes remains central to the field of Chinese politics, feeding both the literature announcing the coming 'crackup' of the Chinese party-state[6] as well as the research explaining the mechanisms behind its surprising survival (Nathan 2003). In both cases, the expected demise of the regime, or its current state of survival, then become a necessary *point of arrival*, from which everything that came before is reinterpreted (Dobry 2009).

Although its findings may prove relevant to this issue, this volume is not driven by the puzzle of the CCP's survival in the face of predicted demise. Rather, it highlights how the CCP concretely developed through leaps and bounds, setbacks and unexpected moves. Looking at a variety of institutions, policy areas, discourses and relations of domination and cooption, this volume stresses that (dis)continuities do not always follow the official division of history, and that change is far from linear: it takes many forms depending on the focus of the enquiry, sometimes echoing the successive fluxes of *fang* (letting go) and *shou* (tightening) characteristic of the early years of reform and opening (Shirk 1993; Baum 1996), or recalling a dialectical logic in which the CCP initiates transformations to which it then has to adapt, including to consequences that appear unexpected and beyond its control (Shue and Thornton 2017). The richness of this volume resides in highlighting this fluidity. Far from following a unified view imposed on them, this volume's different parts and chapters illustrate different forms of the CCP's mutations, hence offering a more complex and diverse picture of its resilience and adaptability.

6 David Shambaugh, 'The Coming Chinese Crackup', *Wall Street Journal*, 6 March 2015, www.wsj.com/articles/the-coming-chinese-crack-up-1425659198.

The CCP's Trajectory through Four Lenses

This volume considers the CCP's 100-year trajectory through four lenses. The first two parts focus on the two pillars of the Party as a political entity, respectively its organisation and ideology (Schurmann 1968). The first part examines the different aspects of the CCP's organisational adaption and expansion. The second part dives into the ideological tensions between the CCP's revolutionary heritage and recent developments, and the discursive bricolage the Party develops in an attempt to reconcile the two. The third and fourth parts explore two central historical missions of the CCP: modernisation and nation-building. While the third part explores the CCP's attempts to modernise the country, and how, in turn, it compels the CCP to adapt to a diversifying society, the fourth part delves into its efforts, from subtle cooption to forced assimilation, to build a unified nation despite ethnic and territorial diversity.

Organisational Trajectory

The three chapters of the volume's first section explore how the Party has been able to adapt and expand its organisation throughout its 100 years of history, without fundamentally transforming its core structure. Liberalising tendencies towards more transparency, diversity and democracy within the CCP have coexisted and alternated with tightening tendencies in favour of widespread control and centralised governance. The chapter by Jean-Pierre Cabestan highlights the permanence of the CCP's Leninist political structure despite the reformist pushes it experienced. In particular, it highlights the under-studied venture under Hu Jintao to introduce more 'intra-party democracy', which was eventually rolled back by Xi Jinping.

Permanence does not, however, equal stasis, and the contributions by Patricia M. Thornton and Frank N. Pieke show how the CCP has been able to rely on its basic Leninist structure to expand its reach towards society and the Chinese state, as well as globally. A century after the CCP's founding, its expanding role in penetrating, regulating and reshaping grassroots social organisations at the expense of the state embodies, for Thornton, a decisive shift in the balance of power within the 'party-state-society trichotomy'. Exploring the contemporary expansion beyond Chinese borders of the CCP's organisational power, Pieke stresses how it contrasts with both China's earlier efforts to export Maoist ideology and revolution as well as China's current much-maligned strategy of influencing and interfering in the society and politics of other countries. The principal aim of the CCP's global extension is not to meddle in the affairs of other countries, but rather to tie Chinese people, goods, money, business and institutions that have ventured abroad back into the strategy and domestic system of China and the CCP.

Ideological Bricolage

This volume's second section highlights the Party's pragmatic efforts to rely on ideological tools and techniques to strengthen its esprit de corps as well as legitimise its rule over society. The continuous reliance on revolutionary references and agitprop practices appears contradictory to the impermanence of the CCP's proclaimed ideological goals, from Mao's continuous revolution to aiming for a moderately prosperous society. Emmanuel Jourda and Kerry Brown, in their respective chapters on the united front policy and the reliance on emotion as a mobilisation tool, show how such practices of power are recycled and revamped for new purposes. Emmanuel Jourda analyses how the concept of 'united front' was defined at different stages in the CCP's history, and shows how the evolution of this framework to handle alliances pragmatically reflects fundamental changes to the CCP's approach to society. This united front concept, initially imported to China by the Comintern, was transformed and repurposed by Mao in the late 1930s as a 'magic weapon' contributing to his power takeover. It then became an essential framework that helped the CCP meet various challenges, from building the PRC as a Communist yet semi-pluralistic regime, to avoiding the political banalisation of the CCP-led system of government by harnessing the Party to its revolutionary past. Kerry Brown explores the role played by the articulation of emotions in the rational, calculating function of Party behaviour, in particular the Mao and Xi eras characterised by high aspirations. As the social and economic transformation of Chinese society has changed how feelings are expressed between these two eras, the terminology of dreaming that emerges in the Xi era is particularly revealing of the CCP's evolving discursive techniques, in that it is part of an overall narrative linked to rejuvenating the Chinese nation and fulfilling its historic mission, but also grants space to personal agency and subjectivity.

At the same time, the emphasis on the proletarian and Leninist features of the CCP has repeatedly clashed with its need to become more inclusive and, in particular, to integrate the country's educated elite. This tension is central to Timothy Cheek's chapter as well as the one by Jérôme Doyon and

Long Yang. The relationship between the CCP and the intellectuals has been defined by a contradiction: the Party's enduring need for ideologues and the Party's suspicion that intellectuals cannot be sufficiently loyal to its goals. Timothy Cheek sheds light on this contradiction from the point of view of the intellectuals. Investigating the reasons why some of them, at various times, choose to join and speak for the Party, Cheek proposes a nuanced view: for some intellectuals, it was about serving the new regime, for others it was onerous subordination, and for yet others it was a noble vocation. Jérôme Doyon and Long Yang stress that, from the Party's perspective, these tensions led it to change its understanding of 'loyalty' throughout its 100 years of history. Detached from a purely ideological approach these evolutions accompanied changes in its recruitment needs, and, paradoxically, it is during periods of expansion that the CCP became more politically demanding with its members.

China's Path to Modernisation and Its Challenges

The CCP's success in retaining power is closely linked to its capacity to modernise China and overcome subsequent challenges threatening social stability. This section investigates the tension between the CCP's monopolistic and often top-down approach to governance, and its need for flexibility as it faces challenges such as the transition from a rural to an urban society, economic modernisation and their social and environmental consequences. Among these principles, the authors outline the enduring yet malleable Marxist core of its ideology (Breslin and Gabusi); the remarkable continuity of the discourse on modernisation underpinning the CCP's changing relation to the environment (Goron and Kotska); the local, functionalist and stratified social citizenship (Froissart), according to which no one has the same entitlements; and an adaptative form of governance towards entrepreneurs (Guiheux). In other words, whereas this part is the one in which we would have expected the most change, each chapter actually stresses continuities.

Following China's unique path to modernisation, the CCP has faced the challenge of forging a lasting alliance with an ever-changing society and, in turn, has been transformed by this endeavour. Three chapters (Day, Guiheux and Froissart) also address the consequences of modernisation on the CCP's alliances with its key social bases, be they peasants, capitalists or, albeit in a more allusive manner, the proletariat, as discussed in Froissart's chapter on migrant workers. All chapters point to the social heterogeneity of these three categories and to the creation of new social classes within them, partly induced by Party social and developmental policies. Day and Froissart highlight the Party's alliance with the wealthy (those most able to contribute to economic development among peasants and migrants) and question the very exitance of social policies to support the poor. At the same time, Guiheux stresses the party's instrumentalist approach, as the current development of Party cells in private enterprises is also meant to compel entrepreneurs to participate in philanthropic activities and become 'agents of social justice'. The CCP has moved away from its role as the vanguard of the proletariat and peasantry and now sees itself as representing the interests of the Chinese population in general, yet, as these three chapters reveal, this claim embodies contradictory trends in CCP policies.

Territorial Control and Nation-Building

This volume's last section focuses on what the CCP perceives as its national margins. Two chapters, by Vanessa Frangville and Rémi Castets, focus on the issue of national minorities and how the CCP has endeavoured to establish its authority over a country that is extremely diverse linguistically, ethnically and religiously. Examining key concepts and debates that have shaped the CCP's vision and construction of the Chinese nation over the past century, Frangville shows that different, and sometimes antithetical, visions of China's national identity have coexisted within the CCP, creating tensions and a longstanding oscillation between integration and assimilation. Considering recent developments in Tibet, Xinjiang and Inner Mongolia, the author argues that, even though the CCP's policy after 1949 tried to use a socialist affirmative strategy towards its minorities under Soviet influence, the legacy of China's imperial occupation of non-Han borders has remained its main drive. Rémi Castets analyses the range of strategies implemented by the Party in Xinjiang since the turn of the 1950s to eradicate forces antagonistic to its modernisation and nation-building project based on an essentialist and unitary Chinese nation. Those tactics have evolved with the political and ideological inflections that have marked the Party's history. Under Xi Jinping, the CCP increasingly approaches alternative worldviews through a security lens, and it now relies on a totalistic surveillance system to reshape representations of national minorities in Xinjiang into 'loyal' Chinese citizens.

Focusing on Hong Kong and Taiwan, the two remaining chapters by Samson Yuen and Edmund Cheng and by Gunter Schubert engage with the issue of the political expansion of the party-state. They highlight how, since 1921, the CCP's discourse and tactics have evolved in territorial matters as the party-state has reshaped the country's political map, re-established its political sovereignty over Hong Kong and Macau, and significantly increased its insistence on 'reunifying' with Taiwan. Samson Yuen and Edmund Cheng examine how the CCP has, since its foundation, been exercising political influence in Hong Kong through united front work. Previously based mainly on cooption tactics, its influence strategies have, in the post-handover period, involved a steady organisational proliferation of social organisations coupled with their increasingly frequent interaction with the mainland authorities and the Hong Kong government. United front work has become more decentralised and multilayered in its structure, including through the steady organisational proliferation of social organisations. Its objectives have diversified beyond elite cooption to include proactive counter-mobilisation against pro-democracy threats. Gunter Schubert seeks to explain China's fluctuating impatience towards reunification with Taiwan through two lenses: China's perception of both Taiwanese domestic politics and Taiwan's China policy, and, conversely, its perception of the US–Taiwan relationship. Taiwan arguably embodies one of the most severe contemporary challenges to CCP legitimacy, as the Party has failed to adequately understand and constructively respond to Taiwan's rising national identity. In the context of what Gunter Schubert terms 'China's neo-imperial rise', all the chapters point to a toughening of the CCP's attempts to establish control over its perceived margins, grounded in a more rigid and unequivocal conception of the Chinese nation under Xi Jinping that reflects the failures of the nation-building process launched after 1949.

As the next step to discuss the CCP's trajectory is set for 2049, for the centenary of the PRC's foundation, the editors of this volume, in line with their contingent approach to history, do not presuppose anything about China's political future. If change necessarily occurs, its nature and timing always remain uncertain. Another cycle of liberalisation/adaption may take place, or the regime may reach a breaking point, which will not necessarily lead to democratisation. To be sure, the CCP today faces new kinds of vulnerabilities. Just as the Party's shrewd play on its contradictory organisational and ideological principles has been a critical driver of its capacity to adapt, the current reabsorption of these contradictions and the emphasis on the Party's omnipotence may be signs of its atrophy. Likewise, the diminishing space for the dialectical exchange between the party-state and the economic and social spheres also demonstrates its fragility. Finally, Xi Jinping's emphasis on his glorious successes may prompt the Party to seek to overcome too hastily the many challenges it still faces, at its expense.

References

Baum, Richard. 1996. *Burying Mao: Chinese Politics in the Age of Deng Xiaoping.* Princeton, NJ: Princeton University Press.

Cheek, Timothy, Klaus Mühlhahn and Hans J. van de Ven, eds. 2021. *The Chinese Communist Party: A Century in Ten Lives.* Cambridge: Cambridge University Press. doi.org/10.1017/9781108904186.

Dickson, Bruce J. 2003. *Red Capitalists in China: The Party, Private Entrepreneurs, and Prospects for Political Change.* Cambridge: Cambridge University Press, 2003. doi.org/10.1017/CBO9780511510045.

Dickson, Bruce J. 2021. *The Party and the People: Chinese Politics in the 21st Century.* Princeton: Princeton University Press. doi.org/10.1515/9780691216966.

Dimitrov, Martin K., ed. 2013. *Why Communism Did Not Collapse: Understanding Authoritarian Regime Resilience in Asia and Europe.* New York: Cambridge University Press. doi.org/10.1017/CBO9781139565028.

Dobry, Michel. 2009. 'Critical Processes and Political Fluidity: A Theoretical Appraisal'. *International Political Anthropology* 2 (1): 74–90.

Fewsmith, Joseph. 2021. *Rethinking Chinese Politics.* Cambridge: Cambridge University Press.

Franceschini, Ivan, Nicholas Loubere and Christian Sorace, eds. 2019. *Afterlives of Chinese Communism: Political Concepts from Mao to Xi*, illustrated edition. Canberra: ANU Press. doi.org/10.22459/ACC.2019.

Gore, Lance. 2011. *The Chinese Communist Party and China's Capitalist Revolution: The Political Impact of the Market.* Abingdon: Routledge. doi.org/10.4324/9780203838952.

Heilmann, Sebastian and Elizabeth Perry, eds. 2011. *Mao's Invisible Hand: The Political Foundations of Adaptive Governance in China.* Cambridge: Harvard University Asia Center. doi.org/10.2307/j.ctt1sq5tc6.

Huntington, Samuel P. 1970. 'Social and Institutional Dynamics of One-Party Systems'. In *Authoritarian Politics in Modern Society: The Dynamics of Established One-Party Systems*, edited by Samuel P. Huntington and Clement Henry Moore, 3–47. New York: Basic Books.

Jowitt, Kenneth. 1992. *New World Disorder: The Leninist Extinction*. Berkeley: University of California Press. doi.org/10.1525/9780520913783.

Lam, Willy Wo-Lap, ed. 2017. *Routledge Handbook of the Chinese Communist Party*. London: Routledge. doi.org/10.4324/9781315543918.

Nathan, Andrew J. 2003. 'China's Changing of the Guard: Authoritarian Resilience'. *Journal of Democracy* 14 (1): 6–17. doi.org/10.1353/jod.2003.0019.

Saich, Tony. 2021. *From Rebel to Ruler: One Hundred Years of the Chinese Communist Party*. Cambridge: The Belknap Press of Harvard University Press. doi.org/10.4159/9780674259638.

Schurmann, Franz. 1968. *Ideology and Organization in Communist China*. Berkeley: University of California Press. doi.org/10.1525/9780520311152.

Shambaugh, David. 2008. *China's Communist Party: Atrophy and Adaptation*. Washington: Woodrow Wilson Center Press.

Shambaugh, David. 2021. *China's Leaders: From Mao to Now*. Cambridge: Polity.

Shirk, Susan. 1993. *The Political Logic of Economic Reform in China*. Berkeley: University of California Press. doi.org/10.1525/9780520912212.

Shue, Vivienne. 2022. 'Regimes of Resonance: Cosmos, Empire, and Changing Technologies of CCP Rule'. *Modern China*. doi.org/10.1177/00977004211068055.

Shue, Vivienne and Patricia M. Thornton, eds. 2017. *To Govern China: Evolving Practices of Power*. Cambridge: Cambridge University Press. doi.org/10.1017/9781108131858.

Zheng, Yongnian and Lance Gore, eds. 2019. *The Chinese Communist Party in Action: Consolidating Party Rule*. China Policy Series 59. Abingdon: Routledge. doi.org/10.4324/9780429243950.

I.
ORGANISATIONAL TRAJECTORY

1

Organisation and (Lack of) Democracy in the Chinese Communist Party: A Critical Reading of the Successive Iterations of the Party Constitution

Jean-Pierre Cabestan

Introduction

According to the Constitution (*zhangcheng* 章程) of the Chinese Communist Party (CCP), all decisions are democratically made whatever their nature. Cadres and leaders are elected and other decisions, such as policies or regulations, are adopted on the basis of a vote following extensive consultation with party members and party grassroots organisations. Likewise, China's four successive state constitutions (*xianfa* 宪法) at first glance look very democratic, claiming to protect all fundamental political rights and to base political appointments and decisions on the principle of election and majority votes (Diamant 2022). These procedures were confirmed in December 2021 in a white paper that presented China's democracy as a 'whole-process people's democracy' (*quanguocheng renmin minzhu* 全过程人民民主).[1] But does the CCP operate on the basis of democratic principles?

Actually, as with other ruling Communist parties, the CCP is a highly top-down and secretive organisation. Secrecy, opacity and the need to keep party secrets are structural, being closely intertwined with 'democratic centralism' (*minzhu jizhongzhi* 民主集中制), a principle introduced by Vladimir Lenin in the Bolshevik Party at the beginning of the twentieth century.

In order to move away from this entrenched opacity and verticality, former CCP secretary-general Hu Jintao (胡锦涛) attempted in 2007–09 to enhance 'intra-party democracy' (*dangnei minzhu* 党内民主). This was not the first time that the CCP had tried to instil more democracy, but it was the most ambitious. After Xi Jinping (习近平) came to power in 2012, instead of intra-party democracy, his CCP has given priority to 'consultative democracy' (*xieshang minzhu* 协商民主), a new form of socialist democracy aimed at consulting more often with the society at large, while strengthening at the same time the leading role of the Party.

Since its foundation, the CCP has faced two major organisational contradictions: 1) between top-down leadership and intra-party democracy and 2) between the leading role of the Party and the principle of democracy (Cabestan 2019c). Neither Hu Jintao nor Xi Jinping has been able, or willing, to overcome these contradictions. The Party has adapted to the new economic and social environment that it created. It has also maintained its reliance on, and expanded, informal institutions that have introduced more flexibility in the actual operation of the CCP (Tsai 2006, 2007). But this is not the focus of this chapter, which rather explores the CCP's formal rules. It attempts, in particular, to demonstrate that the CCP has remained strongly attached to its Leninist principles, because they have, in the author's view, demonstrated their efficacy as the best tools to develop the economy, keep the society stable and under control, empower the nation, as well as protect the country and the Party from any unwelcomed external influence.

1 The State Council Information Office of the People's Republic of China, '"Chinese Democracy" White Paper (Full Text)' (《中国的民主》白 皮书 (全文)), 4 December 2021, www.scio.gov.cn/zfbps/32832/Document/1717206/1717206.htm. See also the English version: 'China: Democracy that Works', *Xinhuanet*, 4 December 2021, www.news.cn/english/2021-12/04/c_1310351231.htm. All website sources in this chapter were accessed on 19 January 2023.

Yet, this reality raises questions about the CCP's own definition of democracy and what the CCP means by democratic centralism or, since 1949, people's democratic dictatorship and today's whole-process people's democracy? To fully understand these concepts and address the unsolvable contradictions mentioned above, the most appropriate method is to start by going back to the original documents. Among them, the successive party constitutions adopted by the CCP since its establishment in 1921 are some of the best indicators of these tensions. The first objective of this article, therefore, is to compare successive iterations of the CCP's constitution over the last 100 years and analyse the changes related to organisation and democracy. But this is not enough. Going further, this work analyses the various attempts, especially Hu Jintao's, to introduce more 'intra-party democracy': this is the second objective of this chapter. Finally, to comprehend why Xi Jinping overturned Hu's reforms, this chapter attempts to explain why the CCP cannot reform and democratise as long as it remains a party-state and China remains a one-party system: this is the chapter's final objective.

It should be noted that this chapter discusses China's CCP constitution, not its state constitution. Some authors have tried to demonstrate the relationship between the two (Backer 2009; Jiang 2014). Since the Party leads the state and the people, there is an 'organic unity' between Party norms and state norms, even more so under Xi Jinping (Smith 2018). Both sets of norms demonstrate the CCP's 'power to proclaim and promulgate falsehood' – or what Neil Diamant calls 'useful bullshit' (Diamant 2022, 193). Nonetheless, and contrary to what Diamant argues, they also legitimise the one-party system. However, the Party and state constitutions contain two very different sets of norms, with very different names in Chinese, leading to confusion, especially when their English translations are used. Thus, in this chapter, I focus on the former, not the latter.

The Successive Iterations of the CCP Constitution

There is a vast literature on the CCP and its history prior to and after 1949 (Brødsgaard 2020; Saich 2021; Saich and Hearst 2017). Nonetheless, save for a few exceptions (Brødsgaard and Chen 2018; Brødsgaard and Zheng 2004; Lam 2020; Li Jingtian 2011; Li Junru 2011; Saich 1996), most authors have not put much emphasis on the CCP Constitution, the rationale for its successive changes or the way it has been implemented. This chapter aims to help fill this gap in the literature.

The CCP Constitution includes the CCP's basic ideology, major objectives and selected formal organisation rules. It does not tell us much about how the Party operates, how members are recruited, how leaders are appointed, how policies are adopted or how decisions are made. Its length and content have varied over the years. The first constitution, adopted at the Second National Congress of the CCP in 1922, included only 29 short articles; by contrast, the latest one, adopted at the Twentieth Congress in 2022, is much longer and more formalised, comprising a long introduction called a 'general programme', 11 chapters and 55 articles. It even defines the party's emblem and flag (see below). A brief overview of successive CCP constitutions and the changes introduced over the years reveals much about the gradual establishment of institutions and adoption of concepts that the Party wants to prioritise and publicise. All the documents used in the following discussion, except the latest CCP Constitution adopted at the Twentieth Congress, can be found on the official CCP news website.[2]

The Party Constitutions before 1949

At the First National Congress of the CCP in July 1921, a party 'programme' (*gangling* 纲领) was adopted by two-thirds of the congress members (*quanguo daibiao dahui* 全国代表大会).[3] At that time, the CCP comprised just 57 members. It joined the 'Third International' or Lenin's Comintern (Communist International) created in 1919 and led by the Russian Communist Party. While it adopted the 'Soviet management system' (soviet means committee in Russian), neither the concept of democracy nor the notion of election was present in the document.[4] Its objective was to establish a 'dictatorship of the proletariat' – a concept introduced by Marx to describe the political organisation of the socialist transition from capitalism to communism and later adopted by Lenin to justify the leading role of the Russian Communist Party as the vanguard of the proletariat. This notion would not be enshrined in the CCP Constitution, except during the Cultural Revolution (see below). However, the importance of keeping Party secrets was emphasised (point 6). Power was exercised by 'executive committees' (*zhixing weiyuanhui* 执行委员会), a structure borrowed from

2 'Database of Previous National Congresses of the Chinese Communist Party' (中国共产党历次全国代表大会数据库), *CPC News*, cpc.people.com.cn/BIG5/64162/64168/index.html.

3 'Brief Presentation of the First National Congress of the Chinese Communist Party' (中国共产党第一次全国代表大会简介), cpc.people.com.cn/BIG5/64162/64168/64553/4427940.html.

4 'Chinese Communist Party Programme (Translated from Russian)' (中国共产党纲领(俄文译稿)), 1921, cpc.people.com.cn/BIG5/64162/64168/64553/4427945.html.

the Guomindang (GMD), both at the central and the local levels. Although recent reports about this congress refer to elections, including the election of Chen Duxiu (陈独秀) as secretary (*shuji* 书记), these bodies were chosen (*xuan* 选) rather than properly elected by Party members.[5] The word 'election' appeared in 1922 in the first CCP Constitution – or, to be more accurate, in the 'statutes' (*zhangcheng* 章程) adopted at the Second National Congress.[6] But, at the same time, this constitution gave much power to the Central Executive Committee in which five members and three alternate members were elected for just one year, a short term that would altogether disappear in 1927 when the Party had to hide or move to the countryside. The following congresses (the third and fourth, held in 1923 and 1925, respectively) kept empowering the Central Executive Committee without extending its term.[7]

It was only in 1927 that the CCP fully adopted the Leninist model. The concept of 'democratic centralism' was formally introduced into the CCP Constitution, which was endorsed by a meeting of newly created Politburo (*zhengzhiju* 政治局, PB), in June 1927, two months after the Fifth CCP Congress.[8] Summarised by Lenin ([1906] 1965) as 'freedom in discussions, unity in action', democratic centralism includes the principle of party leaders' election and accountability to the people, a conception of democracy that, on the surface, is not different from liberal democracy. But, since 1921, the Bolshevik Party and, as a result, other Communist parties had banned factions and clearly privileged discipline and subordination to the higher level over democracy. At the same time, a Central Committee, a Politburo and a Central Standing Committee (*zhongyang changwu weiyuanhui* 中央常务委员会), the last also called in English a 'Secretariat' in article 27 of the constitution, as well as a network of central and provincial control commissions (*jiancha weiyuanhui* 监察委员会) (articles 61–4), were instituted. The CCP was clearly moving towards centralisation and formalisation.

5 'Brief Presentation of the First National Congress of the Chinese Communist Party'.

6 'Constitution of the CCP' (中国共产党章程), 1922, cpc.people.com.cn/BIG5/64162/64168/64554/4428163.html.

7 'The First Revision of the Constitution of the Chinese Communist Party (中国共产党章程第一次修改), July 1923, cpc.people.com.cn/BIG5/64162/64168/64555/4428213.html; 'The Second Revision of the Constitution of the Chinese Communist Party' (中国共产党章程第二次修正案), February 1925, cpc.people.com.cn/BIG5/64162/64168/64556/4428256.html.

8 'Resolution on the Third Revision of the Chinese Communist Party Constitution' (中国共产党第三次修正章程决案), 1 June 1927, cpc.people.com.cn/BIG5/64162/64168/64557/4428293.html.

The Sixth CCP Congress, held in Moscow in 1928, introduced several changes in the constitution that were not very consequential since the CCP was then divided and had two centres, the second one being formed around Mao Zedong (毛泽东) and Zhu De (朱德) in Hunan and later in the Jiangxi Soviet Republic (1931–34). Nonetheless, it is worth mentioning that, at that time, as the CCP decided to refer to its constitution as *dangzhang* (党章), the principle of election became more deeply enshrined into the CCP Constitution (it appeared 23 times).[9] However, as in all other CCP constitutions, this text did not spell out any election procedures, giving, in reality, much discretionary power to the leadership to manipulate elections. This document also consolidated the relationship between the CCP and the Comintern of which the CCP was now a branch. Its article 1 states: 'The Chinese Communist Party is a branch of the Comintern' (*zhongguo gongchandang wei gongchan guoji zhi yi bufen* 中国共产党为共产国际之一部分). More importantly, the 1928 constitution fleshed out 'democratic centralism', with article 7 stating: 'Organisational Principles: The Chinese Communist Party, as other branches of the Comintern, is organised on the principle of democratic centralism' (*zuzhi yuanze: zhongguo gongchandang yu gongchan guoji de qita zhibu yiyang, qi zuzhi yuanze wei minzhu jizhong zhi* 组织原则：中国共产党与共产国际的其他支部一样，其组织原则为民主集中制). This compelled all party members to implement instructions coming from the top of the CCP or the Comintern, even if they disagreed with them.

The notion of democracy as such was mentioned for the first time in the constitution adopted at the Seventh Congress in 1945, four years before the CCP came to power.[10] It was associated with the 'New Democracy system' (*xin minzhuzhuyi zhidu* 新民主主义制度), the anti-GMD alliance 'led by the proletariat', actually the CCP, which gave the illusion to many 'third force' groupings and individuals – non-Communists critical of the GMD government – that the latter was more democratic than the former. As theorised by Mao (Schram, Hodes and Van Slyke 2005), this democracy referred to the CCP's ambition to build an 'independent, free, democratic, united, prosperous and strong … republic' together with many other forces, including the 'small bourgeoisie and other democrats'.[11] In addition,

9 'Constitution of the Chinese Communist Party' (中国共产党党章), July 1928, cpc.people.com.cn/BIG5/64162/64168/64558/4428362.html.

10 'Constitution of the Chinese Communist Party' (中国共产党党章), 11 June 1945, cpc.people.com.cn/BIG5/64162/64168/64559/4442095.html.

11 Ibid.

the new constitution enhanced what would later be called 'intra-party democracy' in introducing for the first time rules on Party members' rights and obligations, especially protections to the exercise of their democratic rights, as the principles of election and eligibility or the right to 'criticise any party personnel at party meetings' (*zai dang de huiyi shang piping dang de renhe gongzuo renyuan* 在党的会议上批评党的任何工作人员) (article 3 of the 1945 CCP Constitution).

At the same time, as is well known, the CCP, then controlled by Mao and his followers, enshrined in its constitution 'Mao Zedong Thought' (*maozedong sixiang* 毛泽东思想), not as its guiding ideology, which remained Marxism–Leninism, but as its 'working compass' (*gongzuo de zhizhen* 工作的指针). It also gave Mao much more power in creating for him the position of chairman (*zhuxi* 主席) of the Central Committee, and in making sure that the leader who held this position was also chairman of the PB and of the newly created Central Secretariat (*shujichu* 书记处), different in name in Chinese from the one set up in 1927.[12] While the Central Committee was supposed to meet at least once every three years, the PB met only every six months, transferring most of its competencies to the five-member Secretariat headed by Mao: the other members were Zhu De, Liu Shaoqi (刘少奇), Ren Bishi (任弼时) and Chen Yun (陈云).

It was also in the 1945 constitution that 'democratic centralism' was fully defined: 'democratic centralism is centralism based on democracy and democracy under centralised leadership' (*minzhu de jizhongzhi, jishi zai minzhu jichu shang de jizhong he zai jizhong lingdao xia de minzhu* 民主的集中制，即是在民主基础上的集中和在集中领导下的民主). Repeated in all subsequent CCP constitutions, this approach to democracy within the Party is fundamental because it clearly indicates that centralised leadership prevails upon democracy – or, to be more accurate, defines both what democracy is and its limits – and that under no circumstances should members' democratic rights challenge the Party leadership.

Like the previous ones, the 1945 CCP Constitution did not reveal much in practical terms about how decisions were made. For example, in this constitution, there was no mention of the Central Military Commission (CMC), a crucial power locus, which Mao took control of from Zhou

12 Article 34 of the 1945 CCP Constitution states: 'The Chairman of the Central Committee is the Chairman of the Politburo of the Central Committee and the Chairman of the Secretariat of the Central Commitee' (中央委员会主席即为中央政治局主席与中央书记处主席).

Enlai (周恩来) at the famous Zunyi Conference in 1935, a power locus that allowed him to more easily sideline his rivals, especially the pro-Moscow faction: Wang Ming (王明), Li Lisan (李立三) and others (Guillermaz 1968).

All in all, before coming to power and becoming a party-state, the CCP was already very secretive and undemocratic. Fighting against the GMD government and, later, the Japanese occupation army, it needed, for the sake of survival, to protect itself from spies and possible infiltrations. That was the rationale of the 1942 'Rectification Movement', a campaign that, ironically, was presented as promoting intra-party democracy, at least in its initial stage, and, more importantly, Mao's 'mass line'. However, the campaign also highlighted the repressive side of the CCP, especially the role of the Social Affairs Office and its then head, Kang Sheng (康生), who came to the fore during the Cultural Revolution (Gao 2019). How could intra-party democracy have flourished in such circumstances?

Changes in the Constitution after the Party Becomes the State in 1949

In 1949, the CCP took over the state. Party secrets then turned into state secrets and the need for opacity became much stronger, to protect the newly established People's Republic of China (PRC) against its enemies, first the GMD and the 'imperialist' camp led by the United States, and later the Soviet Union and all the 'revisionist' forces, both outside and inside the country and the Party.

The first CCP Constitution issued after the Party came to power was adopted by its Eighth Congress in September 1956. Its Chinese name moved back to *zhangcheng* (章程) or 'statutes', a more formal term that is still used today.[13] While the document did not reactivate the concept of a 'dictatorship of the proletariat', it did confirm what the state constitution had stated two years earlier: namely, that the PRC was a 'people's democratic dictatorship' 'led by the working class and based on the alliance between the workers and the peasants' (Diamant 2022). Kept until recently, except during the Cultural Revolution, this notion highlights the basic contradiction on which the regime has always been based. How can a dictatorship be democratic?

13 'Constitution of the Chinese Communist Party' (中国共产党党章), 26 September 1956, cpc.people.com.cn/BIG5/64162/64168/64560/65452/6412169.html.

Yet, thanks to de-Stalinisation in the Soviet Union and the socialist camp as a whole, the CCP Constitution promoted, if not actual transparency, a collective approach to leadership and a willingness to normalise the Party's modus operandi (MacFarquhar 1974). The well-known formula borrowed from Leninist handbooks and included in the CCP Constitution was 'collective leadership and individual responsibility' (*jiti lingdao he geren fuze* 集体领导和个人负责). Mao Zedong's thoughts disappeared from the CCP Constitution. The Central Committee, elected for a five-year term, met once a year as a rule and a National Congress could be convened any time if one-third of the Party congress delegates or one-third of the provincial-level organisations required it.[14] Borrowed from Khrushchev's Soviet Union but never used in practice, this rule would only be partly restored in 1982. A Politburo Standing Committee (PBSC) chaired by Mao and CCP vice-chairmans (including Liu Shaoqi and Zhou Enlai) was instituted within the Central Secretariat. It was headed by a general secretary (*zongshuji* 总书记), initially Deng Xiaoping (邓小平), who was put in charge of the Party's 'daily work' (*richang gongzuo* 日常工作) under the leadership of the PB and the PBSC. Decision-making at the top of the CCP was clearly becoming more collective, even if Mao kept the last word for himself (Teiwes 2015). Aligning here again with the Soviet model, the constitution was moving power, especially regarding domestic policies, to the Secretariat and its members, to the detriment of the PB and the State Council (the central government) headed by Zhou Enlai. Moreover, the constitution introduced the possibility of the Central Committee creating the position of 'honorary chairman' (*mingyu zhuxi* 名誉主席), clearly preparing for Mao's retirement. All this would rapidly become a source of friction that would intensify after the launch of the Great Leap Forward in 1958. Actually, this new power organisation was one of the causes of the Cultural Revolution and Mao's decision to purge Liu and Deng (MacFarquhar 1999). Nonetheless, not every rule became formal: the CMC, chaired by Mao until his death, did not get into the constitution.

14 Article 31 of the 1956 CCP Constitution states: 'If one third of the delegates or one third of the regional organisations request it, the Central Committee must convene a National Congress' (如果有三分之一的代表的要求，或者有三分之一的省一级组织的要求，中央委员会必须召开全国代表大会会议).

As a direct outcome of the Cultural Revolution launched by Mao in 1966, the CCP Constitution adopted at the Ninth Congress in 1969 was much shorter (12 instead of 60 articles in 1956).[15] It was centred around Mao Zedong, both the leader and the thought, as well as his designated successor, Lin Biao (林彪), whose name was mentioned. The Marxist concept of 'dictatorship of the proletariat' replaced the PRC's people's democratic dictatorship. This clearly signalled a return to Marxist–Leninist ideological purity, a growing disregard for the state constitution and a power concentration in the Party to the detriment of the state. But this CCP Constitution tells us very little about how power was exerted, let alone about members' rights. Under the leadership of the CCP chairman, vice-chairman and the PBSC, it planned, in article 9, paragraph 4, to 'establish a number of necessary and capable organs to handle party, government and military daily work in a unified manner' (*zai zhuxi, fuzhuxi he zhongyang zhengzhi ju changwu weiyuanhui lingdao xia, sheli ruogan biyao de jinggan de jigou, tongyi chuli dang, zheng, jun de richang gongzuo* 在主席、副主席和中央政治局常务委员会领导下，设立若干必要的精干的机构，统一处理党、政、军的日常工作). The main duty of Party members was to study and implement Marxism–Leninism and Mao Zedong Thought. Holding a meeting of Party national congress delegates every five years and local congress delegates every three years were the only rules kept in the constitution. The CCP Constitution (12 articles) adopted at the Tenth Congress in 1973 was very similar to the previous document; its main change was to remove Lin Biao and the idea of designating a successor to Mao.[16]

Changes to the Party Constitution since 1977

Things started to change after Mao's death in 1976, but only gradually. The CCP Constitution (19 articles only) adopted by the Eleventh Congress in August 1977 was still influenced by the Cultural Revolution, declaring its successful completion but keeping a reference to the dictatorship of the proletariat and the continuation of the revolution.[17] Despite Deng Xiaoping's recent return to power, the Party was still dominated by Hua Guofeng (华国锋), Mao's handpicked successor, and the so-called Whateverist faction

15 'Constitution of the Chinese Communist Party' (中国共产党党章), 14 April 1969, cpc.people.com.cn/BIG5/64162/64168/64561/4429444.html.

16 'Constitution of the Chinese Communist Party' (中国共产党党章), 28 August 1973, cpc.people.com.cn/BIG5/64162/64168/64562/65450/4429427.html.

17 'Constitution of the Chinese Communist Party (中国共产党党章), 18 August 1977, cpc.people.com.cn/BIG5/64162/64168/64563/4441865.html.

(*fanshipai* 凡是派), which was portrayed by its detractors as defending whatever Mao had said or done (Teiwes 1984; Teiwes and Sun 2011). At the same time, the constitution started to restore some of the norms challenged by Mao and his closest followers, especially the principle of 'collective leadership and individual working responsibility' (*jiti lingdao he geren fengong fuze* 集体领导和个人分工负责)[18] and the role of the Party committees at each level.[19] It also established local discipline inspection commissions (DICs) at the county level and above. Heir to the Central Control Commission established in 1945, which had ceased to operate at the beginning of the Cultural Revolution, the Central DIC (first chaired by Chen Yun) would be set up at the famous Third Plenary Session of the Eleventh Central Committee in December 1978.

The Third Plenum was a turning point in the history of the CCP. It was there that the Party decided to abandon class struggle, rehabilitate or 'reverse the verdict' (*pingfan* 平反) of many victims of the Maoist campaigns, reform the economy and open the country up to the outside world. As a result, the CCP fundamentally changed its modus operandi, laying the ground for the adoption of a deeply revised constitution in 1982. In late 1978, the consensus was not only to restore the institutions set up in the sixth decade of the twentieth century – that is, a Party organisation close to one that presided after 1956 and a state constitution similar to the 1954 one – but also to go further to prevent the return of a strong man with unlimited powers and personality cult.

At the Third Plenum, reformist leader Hu Yaobang (胡耀邦) was put in charge of the Party apparatus with the title of Central Committee secretary-general (*mishuzhang* 秘书长). Fourteen months later, as Liu Shaoqi was rehabilitated post-mortem, the Central Secretariat was fully restored and Hu became general secretary of the Central Committee. The ambition was

18 Article 11, paragraph 1 of the 1977 CCP Constitution states:

> Party committees at all levels implement the principle of combining collective leadership with individual division of labour and responsibility. Relying on political experience and collective wisdom, all important issues should be decided collectively, while allowing individuals to play their due role (党的各级委员会实行集体领导和个人分工负责相结合的原则。要依靠集体的 政治经验和集体的智慧，一切重要问题都由集体决定，同时使个人发挥应有的作用).

19 Article 12, paragraph 12 of the 1977 CCP Constitution states:

> Party committees at all levels should regularly report their work to congresses of party members, often listen to the opinion of the masses inside and outside the party, and accept supervision (党的各级委员会要定期向代表大会或党员大会报告工作，经常听取党内外群众的意见，接受监督).

then to put into place a central power organisation similar to the one set up by the Eighth Congress, moving responsibilities in a number of sectors (ideology, economy, industry and foreign trade) to the Secretariat. But this reform rapidly led to gridlocks and tensions; consequently, the role of the Secretariat was downgraded in 1987 (Cabestan 2014, 147–50).

Yet, the constitution adopted at the Twelfth CCP Congress in 1982 heralded an important organisational change.[20] Much longer (50 articles) and more comprehensive, it aimed first at restoring the prestige of the Party by turning Party members into 'ordinary members of the working people' (*laodong renmin de putong yiyuan* 劳动人民的普通一员) and Party cadres into 'servants of the people' (*renmin de gongpu* 人民的公仆). Held for one year by Hu Yaobang after Hua Guofeng was forced to step down in June 1981, the position of Party chairman was abolished; the official top leader of the Party was to be the general secretary, but his power stemmed from the six-member PBSC (including four elderly leaders). For the first time, the CMC was mentioned, its chair, then Deng Xiaoping, being required to be a member of the PBSC (article 21). However, this latter rule was dropped in 1987 to accommodate Deng who was then retiring from the PBSC but not the CMC. To date, it has not been restored although it has been a rule in practice since Jiang Zemin (江泽民) succeeded Deng as CMC chair in November 1989 (see below). This power distribution clearly weakened Hu's status and laid the ground for Hu's dismissal in January 1987 and later the Tiananmen crisis.

Yet, many new rules introduced in 1982 moved the Party towards reform. Collective leadership was re-emphasised and the cult of personality openly denounced; leaders were asked to avoid 'arbitrariness' (*geren zhuanduan* 个人专断) and submit themselves to the organisation. Meeting every year, the Central Committee could exceptionally convene a National Congress if one-third of provincial-level organisations required it (then article 18, today article 19).[21] To date, this procedure has never been used. An important article was added (then article 37, today article 38), which stated that:

20 'Constitution of the Chinese Communist Party' (中国共产党党章), 6 September 1982, cpc.people.com.cn/BIG5/64162/64168/64565/65448/6415129.html.

21 English version: Twentieth CPC National Congress, 'Constitution of the Communist Party of China', 22 October 2022, english.news.cn/20221026/d7fff914d44f4100b6e586372d4060a4/c.html; Chinese version: 中国共产党章程, www.gov.cn/xinwen/2022-10/26/content_5721797.htm.

> Party leading cadres at every level, whether elected through democratic procedures or appointed by a leading body, do not hold posts for life and can be transferred from or relieved of their posts.

Party members' and Party committees' democratic rights, particularly minority and election rights, were also strengthened. Elder Party leaders were invited to retire and join the newly created central or local advisory committees (*guwen weiyuanhui* 顾问委员会). More importantly, the Party leadership was then conceived as 'mainly political, ideological and organisational', delegating more economic and social responsibilities to the government. This formula would be dropped from the constitution in 2017 (see below); in previous constitutions, the approach to Party leadership was much more holistic – for example, in 1977, the emphasis was still on 'leading the proletarian and revolutionary masses'. Moreover, in 1982, the Party was asked to operate within the boundaries of the state constitution and laws. The priority was to restore state institutions, introduce a new division of labour between the Party and the state (*dangzheng fengong* 党政分工) and establish a 'highly democratic socialist country' (*gaodu minzhu de shehuizhuyi guojia* 高度民主的社会主义国家).

Partly inspired by reformist thinkers such as Liao Gailong (廖盖隆) and his 1980 reform ideas, this evolution opened the door in 1986 to the debate about reforming political structures (*zhengzhi tizhi gaige* 政治体制改革). Supported by Deng, this debate led to a reform plan that was adopted by the Thirteenth Party Congress in September 1987, despite the purge, a few months before, of Hu Yaobang, accused of liberal tendencies (Wu 2013).

Presided over by General Secretary Zhao Ziyang (赵紫阳), the Thirteenth Congress is remembered for its ambitious and courageous political reform plan aimed at not only separating the Party and the government (*dangzheng fenkai* 党政分开) but also establishing a professional civil service and expanding the powers and the representativeness of the state's elected bodies – for example, the people's congresses. At the same time, some articles of the CCP Constitution were amended, mainly those aimed at expanding intra-party democracy.[22] The introduction of a competitive election for local and national delegations to Party congresses, with the number of candidates being higher than the number of positions to be filled, known as 差额选举 (*cha'e xuanju*) in Chinese, was authorised. In case of disagreements

22 'Amendments to Some Articles of the Constitution of the Chinese Communist Party' (中国共产党章程部分条文修正案), 1 November 1987, cpc.people.com.cn/BIG5/64162/64168/64566/65447/4441815.html.

within a Party organ, a vote was required on major issues. The other change worth mentioning was related to the role of the Central Secretariat, which was reduced from being responsible for 'central daily work' (*zhongyang richang gongzuo* 中央日常工作) under the leadership of the PBSC to a 'working organ' of the PBSC (*banshi jigou* 办事机构), concentrating only on Party affairs, and political–ideological work in other institutions, such as the government and the military. However, a key problem for Zhao and the reformists was that the real power holders were retired or 'semi-retired' (*ban tuixiu* 半退休) leaders, such as Deng Xiaoping, then CMC chairman, and Chen Yun, who would take back power and transfer it to more obedient leaders such as Jiang Zemin after the Tiananmen crisis.

The Tiananmen massacre sounded the death knell to all attempts at transparency and intra-Party democracy. After 1989, the Party abandoned any attempt to open its 'black box' and returned to its old, entrenched penchant for secrecy, especially as far as decision-making processes and intra-Party mechanisms were concerned. In the 1992 constitution, adopted at the Fourteenth CCP Congress, the plan to establish a 'highly democratic socialist country' was abandoned. Lessons had been drawn from the collapse of the Soviet Union.[23]

Yet, there are few differences between the 1987 and the 1992 Party constitutions in terms of power organisation, procedures and members' rights. For example, the principle of competitive elections was kept and would be kept in all future constitutions, including the current one. Similarly, fixed terms of office for leading cadres were maintained. And more duties were imposed on leading cadres, now required to 'attend democratic meetings held by the party committee or leading party member's groups' (*dangyuan lingdao ganbu hai bixu canjia dangwei, dangzu de minzhu shenhuohui* 党员领导干部还必须参加党委、党组的民主生活会). This addition to article 8 is still in place today.[24]

The major changes to the constitution introduced at the Fourteenth Party Congress had to do with recognising that China was still in the 'early stage of socialism' and abolishing the central and local advisory commissions after 10 years of operation, many of their members, most of them retired leaders, having already died. This was also part of Deng's plan to clear the way for

23 'Constitution of the Chinese Communist Party' (中国共产党党章), 18 October 1992, cpc.people.com.cn/BIG5/64162/64168/64567/65446/6415682.html.
24 'Constitution of the Communist Party of China', 22 October 2022.

Jiang Zemin and allow him to consolidate his power as general secretary, chairing the (probably weekly) PBSC meetings and deciding on their agenda; CCP (and state) CMC chairman, a position that Deng transferred to him in November 1989; and president of the republic after March 1993.

This 'three powers in one person' (*sanweiyiti* 三位一体) formula[25] has been in place since then, with the exception of the 2002–04 period when Jiang remained CMC chairman after stepping down from and transferring his two other posts (CCP secretary-general and head of state) to Hu Jintao. But it remains an informal rule: after 1987, the CCP Constitution has not stated that the general secretary should also be the CMC chairman, let alone the president of the republic (see Constitution of the CCP [1992], article 22 and 23; Constitution of the CCP [2022], article 23 and 24).

The next two congresses, the fifteenth in 1997 and the sixteenth in 2002, did not change much in the CCP constitution either, except to add to the ideological tenets of the Party; namely, 'Deng Xiaoping Theory' and Jiang Zemin's 'Three Represents', a coded formula allowing the Party to recruit capitalists.[26] In 2002, Party members' duties and the DICs' powers were strengthened, but these measures did not have a big impact on the CCP operation: corruption kept growing (Ang 2020).

It was at the Sixteenth CCP Congress in 2002 that the concept of 'intra-party democracy' was resurrected. In his report, Jiang Zemin qualified it as the 'lifeblood of the party' (*dang de shengming* 党的生命).[27] Nonetheless, it was only at the 2007 Congress, once Hu Jintao had consolidated his power, that the CCP decided to move forward, the general program declaring that 'the Party must fully expand intra-Party democracy and safeguard [the] democratic rights of its members', adding that 'the Party must practice democratic and scientific decision-making'.[28] Article 30 was revised to open

25 Xinhua Net Review, '"Trinity" Leadership System Is a Successful Experience' (新华网评: "三位一体"领导体制是成功经验), 1 March 2018, m.xinhuanet.com/comments/2018-03/01/c_1122469831.htm.

26 'Constitution of the Communist Party of China' (中国共产党党章), 18 September 1997, cpc.people.com.cn/BIG5/64162/64168/64568/65445/4429244.html; 'Constitution of the Communist Party of China' (中国共产党党章), 14 November 2002, cpc.people.com.cn/BIG5/64162/64168/64569/65444/4429114.html.

27 'Jiang Zemin's Report at 16th Party Congress', 8 November 2002, China.org.cn, www.china.org.cn/english/2002/Nov/49107.htm; Chinese version: www.gov.cn/test/2008-08/01/content_1061490.htm.

28 'Constitution of the Communist Party of China' (中国共产党党章), 21 October 2007, cpc.people.com.cn/BIG5/64162/64168/106155/106156/6439183.html; 'Hu Jintao's Report to the 17th Party Congress', China.org.cn, 15 October 2007, www.china.org.cn/english/congress/229611.htm; Chinese version: www.npc.gov.cn/zgrdw/npc/zggcddsbcqgdbdh/2012-11/06/content_1742192.htm.

the door to the competitive election of Party committee leaders.[29] The CCP leadership also began showing a more general intention to improve the country's socialist democracy, especially 'people's democracy' and 'grassroots democracy' (Yu 2009). These three forms of democracy operate under the uncontested leadership of the CCP (Cabestan 2019c). People's democracy refers to elections of the people's congresses, and grassroots democracy refers to village and urban community elections. The proposal was based on various experiments launched in a few localities in the last decade of the twentieth century and the first decade of the twenty-first century. However, as will be shown below, this did not really democratise the internal operation of the CCP. Instead, Hu's reforms contributed to deepening party cadres' corruption and fragmenting the CCP leadership, especially the divided and ill-coordinated nine-member PBSC, feeding Xi Jinping's plan as soon as he took power in 2012 to recentralise power and rein in intra-party democracy experiments.

As such, the CCP Constitution has not changed much since 2007. In 2012, at the Eighteenth Congress, Hu Jintao's 'scientific outlook of development' and the 'theory of socialism with Chinese characteristics' were added.[30] The most important change was not, and did not have to be, included in the constitution: this was the decision, made by the Party leadership, to cut from nine to seven the membership of the PBSC, facilitating Xi's subsequent plan to concentrate power in his own hands by creating new CCP leading small groups and central commissions (Cabestan 2019a).

The major amendments to the CCP Constitution at the Nineteenth Congress in 2017 had to do with the role of the Party and Xi. Instead of limiting its leadership to political, ideological and organisational work, today the Party, presented as 'the most essential attribute of socialism with Chinese characteristics', must keep strengthening its power and overall leadership position by supervising and managing more directly and more tightly the economy and the society. Moreover, not only did 'Xi Jinping Thought on Socialism with Chinese characteristics for the new era' become the Party's major ideology, but Xi, as leader, was elevated in the constitution

29 'Resolution of the 17th Congress on the Revision of the CCP Constitution' (十七大关于《中国共产 党章程(修正案)》的决议), 21 October 2007, www.gov.cn/ztzl/17da/content_781170.htm.

30 'Constitution of the Communist Party of China' (中国共产党党章), 14 November 2012, dangshi.people.com.cn/BIG5/n/2012/1119/c234123-19618241.html.

to the status of 'core of the Party leadership'.[31] A few months later, in March 2018, Xi managed to revise the state constitution to remain president of the republic beyond the 10-year limit. However, it should be noted that the term of office of the top CCP leaders, especially PB and PBSC members, has, to date, never been limited by any CCP Constitution.

The current CCP Constitution, revised at the Twentieth Congress in 2022, goes further in promoting Xi Jinping's thought as the great adaption of Marxism to China's needs today. It has also enshrined the 'Second Centenary Goal' – that is, building a great modern socialist country in all respects by 2049 – and 'common prosperity' (*gongtong fuyu* 共同富裕).[32] Yet, in many respects, especially in terms of leading bodies and members' rights, the current CCP Constitution remains very much based on the 1982–87 ones, save the few additions introduced later and mentioned above.

What do these successive iterations of the CCP Constitution tell us about the Party's genuine modus operandi? Actually, very little and probably less today, under Xi Jinping, than in the Hu era, let alone in the ninth decade of the twentieth century, as the level of secrecy surrounding the CCP's internal operation has arguably intensified. Debates within the Party have been almost totally silenced, and the unity of the Party and the unity of truth have been prioritised.

Yet, these constitutions are good indicators of the Party's founding principles and changing priorities. First, they reflect the 100-year history of a Party modelled on Lenin's and, even more, Stalin's Soviet Communist Party, paying lip-service to elections and democracy but not practising them. Second, they tell us the story of a Party that has turned into a party-state and stuck all along to the same organisational principles of democratic centralism and secrecy. Third, they highlight the story of a party-state that, in order to avoid atrophy (Shambaugh 2008), has tried hard to adapt itself to the new economic and social environment it has created, adding new layers to the ideological mille-feuille and normalising its mechanisms: for example, holding regular congresses every five years and Central Committee meetings every year since 1977; and stabilising the CCP's leadership bodies,

31 'Constitution of the CCP' (中国共产党党章), 24 October 2017, *CPC News*, cpc.people.com.cn/BIG5/n1/2017/1029/c64094-29614515.html; 'Constitution of the Communist Party of China', 24 October 2017, www.xinhuanet.com/english/download/Constitution_of_the_Communist_Party_of_China.pdf.

32 'Constitution of the Communist Party of China', 22 October 2022, english.news.cn/20221026/d7fff914d44f4100b6e586372d4060a4/c.html.

which rarely change between two congresses. Finally, the various versions of the constitution also underscore the CCP's hesitation, particularly after the beginning of the reform era, in terms of the organisation of its leading bodies and internal democracy, as well as its relationship with the state that it leads and the state constitution that it drafts and enacts (Diamant 2022). For a short period during the Cultural Revolution, the CCP seemed to be willing to wither away the state; yet, in another short period, it strengthened the state while redefining the leading role of the Party. Since the early 1990s, and even more since Xi came to power, the Party has clearly reaffirmed its control and domination of the state and state norms.

Hu Jintao's Failed Attempt to Expand Intra-Party Democracy

Hu Jintao's intention to develop intra-party democracy signalled a willingness to both take stock of the experiments conducted by some local Party committees in the last decade of the twentieth century and move the reform forward. In the early first decade of the twenty-first century, more localities tested this reform. As a result, when Hu Jintao announced in 2007 his plan to expand intra-party democracy, it was positively received by many observers (Li 2009).[33] Hu's report to the Party congress, as well as the new CCP Constitution, provided reason to be optimistic about China's gradual democratisation. As a matter of fact, in his report, Hu stated:

> Intra-Party democracy provides an important guarantee for improving the Party's creativity and reinforcing its solidarity and unity. We will expand intra-Party democracy to develop people's democracy and increase intra-Party harmony to promote social harmony.[34]

At the time, the development of intra-party democracy was conceived as the first step towards an expansion of people's democracy and grassroots democracy: both reforms were closely linked to each other. These three forms of democracy were to operate under the uncontested leadership of the CCP (Cabestan 2019c). Hu's report and the CCP's new constitution

33 'Hu Jintao's Report to the 17th Party Congress'.

34 Ibid.

did not give much detail about the content of the reforms. Nonetheless, the plan was fleshed out two years later in a resolution adopted in September 2009 by the Fourth Plenum of the Seventeenth Central Committee.[35]

In this resolution, developing intra-party democracy was understood as expanding competitive elections of Party leading cadres, increasing the number of decisions based on a vote (*piaojuezhi* 票决制) and enhancing transparency. This reform was also aimed at expanding some of the more restrictive rules regarding the tenure, transfer and regional allocation of major leading cadres, which had been introduced in 1993 by Jiang Zemin, by generalising the avoidance system (*huibi zhidu* 回避制度) according to which officials cannot serve in their province of origin, and enhancing the fight against corruption by introducing a more comprehensive supervision system.

The expansion of competitive elections of local CCP leaders by Party committees was probably the most visible development of intra-party democracy. Based on some genuine experiments conducted in the last decade of the twentieth century and first decade of the twenty-first century in Sichuan (Fewsmith 2010) – by Li Yuanchao (李源潮) in Jiangsu before he became director of the Central Organisation Department in 2007 (Li 2007) and, later, by Wang Yang (汪洋) in Guangdong (Li 2008) – it introduced here and there a certain degree of uncertainty all the way to the election of the Central Committee. It also increased the public's level of information, since local candidates for promotion, at least in Shenzhen, were asked to submit statements of purpose and to take part in public debates (Li 2009).

However, the list of candidates was compiled by the higher level in a totally opaque manner and the degree of publicity of the 'election campaigns' was questionable. Most often, the higher level voted to select lower-level officials. For example, in Nanjing, it was up to the 34 municipal CCP committee members to choose four district heads out of eight candidates (Li 2007). And, in most cases, the chances of not being elected remained very low. This was even truer at the central level, where not much change has taken place under Hu. While *cha'e xuanju* of Central Committee members by the

35 'Decision of the Central Committee of the Communist Party of China on Several Major Issues Concerning Strengthening and Improving Party Building under the New Situation' (中共中央关于加强和改进新形势下党的建设若干重大问题的决定(全文)), *China News*, 27 September 2009, www.chinanews.com.cn/gn/news/2009/09-27/1889756.shtml; 'Communiqué of the 4th Plenary Session of the 17th Central Committee of the CCP' (中国共产党第 十七届中央委员会第四次全体会议公报), *Xinhua*, 18 September 2009, cpc.people.com.cn/GB/64093/64094/10080626.html.

2,000-plus Party delegates to the Congress started in 1987, the margin of choice has always remained very small, even after the Seventh Congress: 5 per cent in 1987, 10 per cent in 1992 and 1997, 5.1 per cent in 2002, 8.3 per cent in 2007 and 9.3 per cent in 2012 and 2017. In 1987, because of this new rule, Deng Liqun (邓力群), the arch-conservative former head of the Propaganda Department failed to get elected to the Central Committee. For alternate members, it is a little bit higher, but not much: 11.1 per cent in 2012 and 9.6 per cent in 2007 against 5.7 per cent in 2002. And delegates to the congress, then as today, have always been selected on the basis of a 'large consultation' that included some 33,500 cadres in 2007 (Cabestan 2014, 110–13; Cabestan 2019b, 20; Fewsmith 2018). Consultation is not election; the centre, together with the leading organs at each level, has always remained in control of the selection of delegates to Party congresses.

It was reported in 2007 that Central Committee members were asked to choose future PB members on a list of 200 candidates of ministerial rank established by the 'centre', probably Hu Jintao and the PBSC. In 2012, they were also able to elect PBSC members. But the detail of these elections was never made public. In 2017, Xi Jinping put an end to this innovation. He himself consulted around 300 retired or in-office leaders before selecting the PB and PBSC members. In other words, the principle of cooption was then fully restored, a principle that was never really questioned for selecting the key leaders of the Party and allowing its major factions to negotiate behind closed doors for their share of power (Brødsgaard 2018; Cabestan 2019b, 20; Fewsmith 2021).

One of the reasons invoked by Xi to put an end to this 'democratic' experiment was the Sun Zhengcai (孙政才) affair. Sun was close to Hu and a member of the sixth generation of leaders promoted to the PB in 2012 and later to the position of Chongqing secretary. He was suddenly purged and jailed in July 2017 after having been accused of buying votes and rigging his election to the PB in 2012 (Cabestan 2019b, 20–1). It is very likely that this case was utilised by Xi to sideline Hu's reforms. Nevertheless, it raises a fundamental issue or contradiction.

The issue is that generalising CCP leading cadres' election would have questioned a deeply entrenched 'principle' according to which 'the party manages the cadres' (*dang guan ganbu de yuanze* 党管干部的原则), meaning recommends (*tuijian* 推荐) and appoints (*renming* 任命) them: in other words, the *Nomenklatura* system (Cabestan 2014, 75–83). In such an organisational setting, an election is a formality that pays lip-service to the principle of democracy but cannot challenge the principle of centralism, let alone the *Nomenklatura* system. Underscoring this tension, Fewsmith (2010) noted that 'the Fourth Plenum decision is clear that cadres should be selected with regard to both "integrity and ability, with priority for integrity"' (*decai jianbei, yide weixian* 德才兼备，以德为先) – integrity meaning, of course, political alignment with the Party leadership of the time.

Submitting important decisions made by Party leaders at every level to a vote has been more difficult. The intention was to reduce the discretionary powers of the Party secretary or no. 1 leader (*diyibashou* 第一把手) of each jurisdiction or constituency and promote collective leadership, giving more say to Party committees or at least their standing committee (*changweihui* 常委会). The main problem is that there are very few records of this reform's achievements, except, for instance, in Zhejiang (Li 2009). Moreover, given career imperatives – the secretary would be considered responsible for all the achievements and misdeeds of his jurisdiction before promotion – there was not much incentive to implement the reform. After he came to power, Xi moved in the opposite direction; the concentration of power at the top was imitated by the whole apparatus, giving even more power to the Party secretaries at each level and in every constituency (Doyon 2018).

Enhancing the transparency of Party affairs (*dangwu gongkai* 党务公开) was the third major objective of Hu's reforms.[36] It included the right of ordinary CCP members to access information and to know better what the Party was doing (*zhiqingquan* 知情权). For one thing, this objective underlined how badly informed the rank and file of the Party was and what was expected of them: namely, getting mobilised and propagating the Party's instructions (see below).

True, the reform was supposed to facilitate the evaluation of leading cadres of the higher level by grassroots (or lower-level) Party organisations as well as the organisation of 'democratic consultation meetings' (*minzhu kentanhui* 民主恳谈会) between leading cadres and ordinary Party members. But this has not really materialised: for example, consultations taking place in Wenling municipality (Zhejiang) were only organised between the government or the Party and the society. Nor has much materialised of the proposal to give delegates to Party congresses at various levels a five-

36 'Communiqué of the 4th Plenary Session of the 17th Central Committee of the CCP'.

year tenure (*changren zhi* 常任制), allowing them to continue to exert a role after the congress for which they had been chosen to represent their constituency, except perhaps at the local level, for instance in Shenzhen.[37]

Actually, what the Party managed to achieve was to improve communication at each level of the apparatus about its policies and decisions, not only vis-a-vis its members but also the public in general. As a result, local Party committees have appointed spokespersons and started to issue annual work reports.

In any event, the unrealistic idea that the rank and file of the Party would help the central leadership supervise cadres and ferret out corruption was rapidly killed after Xi came to power. Instead, since 2012, to successfully catch both corrupt 'flies and tigers', Xi has relied on a more centralised Party DIC network headed, until 2017, in Beijing by his close ally Wang Qishan (王岐山) (Ang 2020).

The problem with Hu's reform plan was that it pursued two contradictory objectives: expanding democratic mechanisms and, conversely, introducing appointment rules of leading cadres aimed at promoting the ablest of them, ameliorating their performance and reducing the temptation of corruption. Consequently, it could only fail.

It is true that some CCP leaders, such as Prime Minister Wen Jiabao (温家宝), a former aide of Zhao Ziyang, seemed inclined to revive political reform, emphasising the importance of elections, judicial independence and supervision based on checks and balances (Li 2009). But these good intentions bumped directly against the basic principles of any ruling Communist party: its leading role, democratic centralism and opacity.

Besides, contrary to what Li (2009) expected, it is hard to believe that any CCP leadership would have accepted and legalised the very existence of factional competition. The Bo Xilai (薄熙来) affair and Xi's decision to recentralise the Party under his leadership have shown that, if such a danger did exist, the Party could not tolerate its perpetuation.

37 Guo Yonghang (郭永航), 'The Tenure System of Party Congress Delegates: Exploration and Breakthrough. Thoughts on the Practice of the Permanent System of Party Congress Delegates in Yantian District, Shenzhen' (党代会常任制:探索与突破. 深圳市盐田区党代会常任制的实 践思考), *CPC News*, 15 December 2014, dangjian.people.com.cn/n/2014/1215/c391437-26211810.html.

Xi Questions Hu's Reforms

Xi Jinping did not put an end altogether to the development of intra-party democracy. He still believes that a small dose of competition can help the Party promote more competent leading cadres and, as a result, improve governance (Brødsgaard and Chen 2018, 17). Village elections had tested this system since the ninth decade of the twentieth century. Nonetheless, the formula encouraged, and recently generalised, by the CCP since Xi came to power has been a much more hands-on method of candidates' selection by the township or town Party committee. Now the CCP wants to make sure, with a lot of arm twisting, that villagers will vote for the position of both Party committee secretary and village chief that it has selected (Ma 2021). At a higher level, organisation departments rely on opinion surveys before making recommendations for promotion (Zeng 2016). However, competition is minimal. Party committee members do vote, but the range of choices for principal positions tends to be non-existent, and for deputy position is very limited and uneven. In the 2015 CCP resolution on problems within the Party, a cautious expansion of the scope of the election of leading bodies of grassroots Party organisations was promoted.[38] Nevertheless, emphasis was clearly placed on the CCP leadership, its centralisation and the verticality of power.

Since 2012, a new form of socialist democracy has been promoted: 'consultative democracy' within as well as outside the CCP.[39] According to the authoritative 2021 white paper entitled 'China: Democracy that Works':

> whole-process people's democracy is a complete system with supporting mechanisms and procedures, and has been fully tested through wide participation. It integrates two major democratic models – electoral democracy and consultative democracy.[40]

38 'Decision of the Central Committee of the Communist Party of China on Several Major Issues Concerning Strengthening and Improving Party Building under the New Situation' (中共中央关于加强和改进新形势下党的建 设若干重大问题的决定), *Communist Party Member Net*, 29 October 2015, news.12371.cn/2015/10/29/ARTI1446106246577858.shtml.

39 'Democratic Talks Help Grassroots Social Governance. Exploration and Practice of Deliberative Democracy in Wenling City, Zhejiang Province' (民主恳谈助力基层社会治理. 浙江温岭市开 展协商民主的探索与实践), *Communist Party Member Net*, 17 July 2019, www.12371.cn/2019/07/17/ARTI1563330975171858.shtml.

40 'China: Democracy that Works'.

This white paper offers multiple examples of consultations by the Party and various government organs: consultations can be at the national or local level; based on opinion surveys; or be related to government decisions, specific reforms or draft laws. Consultative democracy is aimed at better reaching not so much Party members but the society at large, particularly its coopted elites (e.g. people's congresses and the members of consultative political conferences). Therefore, it does not threaten the Party leadership (Cabestan 2019c). In other words, 'socialist democracy' remains a democracy under the sole and comprehensive leadership of the CCP – or, to be more accurate, of the party-state that has controlled mainland China since 1949. More importantly for this analysis, the procedures and outcomes of intra-party consultations have remained particularly opaque. More generally, the climate of fear that Xi has instilled with his Anti-Corruption Campaign and his request for 'political discipline' has not been conducive to a more animated and pluralistic democratic life in the Party.

Among the 97 million CCP members, only around 650,000 leading cadres of the departmental level and above (*chuji yishang* 处级以上) may claim to have a say in decision-making (Shih 2017). The rest are foot soldiers mobilised to propagate the Party's gospel and keep an eye on the society. As the COVID-19 crisis has demonstrated, Party members can be activated to help the government carry out national decisions (e.g. localised lockdown and health checks). But their power and access to confidential intra-party information are closely related to their position and status in the organisation.

Conclusions: Why the CCP Cannot Democratise

In such an organisational and ideological environment, can the CCP democratise? Can its democratisation lead to China's democratisation? The answer is no to both questions, for the following reasons.

The first issue is the CCP's opacity. It is true that its level of secrecy is intimately linked to the existence as well as the number of enemies that it needs to fight against. In the reform era, the CCP has been more open about its rules, its congresses and its official functions. Nonetheless, on many issues related to its internal mechanisms and operation, it has remained what I have called elsewhere a 'secret society' (Cabestan 2019b). The political culture that has fed this penchant for secrecy and opacity goes back to its Soviet heritage and the civil war. On a deeper level, it is closely linked to the stability and the legitimacy of the regime itself. Without these rules, the CCP would collapse: *jianguangsi* (见光死) or 'see the light would make it die', as the Chinese would say. It is clear that the level of secrecy has increased under Xi Jinping; this is not only because of the Party's centralisation drive but also because of its higher degree of paranoia in the context of an intensified ideological and geostrategic rivalry, and to some extent cold war, between China and the United States (and the West).

With such constraints, can intra-party democracy develop? Can it become the first step towards China's democratisation? Probably not, unless a top-down political reform plan is imposed on the apparatus by a Party leadership that, in its majority, is ready to take the risk to democratise the country and is able to keep the military and the security organs on its side.

Otherwise, how can any slow progress of intra-party democracy be of interest to the rest of the society? Although CCP membership has gradually increased in the last two decades to reach nearly 7 per cent of the population (against less than 5 per cent in 2000), 93 per cent of Chinese society is out and reduced to being passive spectators of the political life that the CCP puts on stage every day.[41]

This brings us to the last point: 'socialist democracy' is the opposite of democracy (Cabestan 2019c). Indeed, how can a 'people's democratic dictatorship' led by the CCP turn into a democracy without jeopardising the foundation of the political regime? The Party continues to argue that this concept means democracy within the 'people' and dictatorship on the enemies of the people, echoing Mao's famous distinction between non-antagonistic and antagonistic contradictions. As we know, only the Party leadership can delineate the contours of the 'people', and only the Party leadership has the power to identify and target the enemies of the 'people', which are actually just the enemies of the Party. Today, under Xi, the CCP has more enemies than under Hu.

All in all, to stay in power, the CCP needs to remain Leninist, opaque and undemocratic. As the analysis of successive iterations of the CCP Constitution has shown, it also needs to maintain a low degree of institutionalisation to survive.

41 'Update: CPC Membership Exceeds 96.7 Million', *Xinhua*, 29 June 2022, english.news.cn/20220629/82c2acd9187d43c6b0db8cdea00d91b8/c.html.

References

Ang, Yuen Yuen. 2020. *China's Gilded Age: The Paradox of Economic Boom and Vast Corruption.* Cambridge: Cambridge University Press. doi.org/10.1017/9781108778350.

Backer, Larry Cata. 2009. 'The Party as Polity, the Communist Party and the Chinese Constitutional State: A Theory of State-Party Constitutionalism'. *Journal of Transnational Law and Contemporary Problems* 16 (1): 29–102. doi.org/10.2139/ssrn.1325792.

Brødsgaard, Kjeld Erik. 2018. 'China's Political Order under Xi Jinping: Concepts and Perspectives'. *China: An International Journal* 16 (3): 1–17. doi.org/10.1353/chn.2018.0022.

Brødsgaard, Kjeld Erik. 2020. 'The Chinese Communist Party since 1949'. *Oxford Bibliography*. www.oxfordbibliographies.com/display/document/obo-9780199920082/obo-9780199920082-0057.xml.

Brødsgaard, Kjeld Erik and Chen, Gang. 2018. 'The Chinese Communist Party since 1949: Organisation, Ideology and Prospect for Change'. *Brill Research Perspectives in Governance and Public Policy in China* 3 (1–2): 1–60. doi.org/10.1163/24519227-12340004.

Brødsgaard, Kjeld Erik and Zheng Yongnian, eds. 2004. *Bringing the Party Back In: How China is Governed.* Singapore: Eastern Universities Press.

Cabestan, Jean-Pierre. 2014. *Le Système Politique Chinois: Un Nouvel équilibre Autoraire.* Paris: Presses de Sciences Po. doi.org/10.3917/scpo.cabes.2014.01.

Cabestan, Jean-Pierre. 2019a. 'Political Changes in China since the 19th CCP Congress: Xi Jinping Is Not Weaker but More Contested'. *East Asia* 36 (1): 1–21. doi.org/10.1007/s12140-019-09305-x.

Cabestan, Jean-Pierre. 2019b. *China Tomorrow: Democracy or Dictatorship?* Lanham, MD: Rowman & Littlefield.

Cabestan, Jean-Pierre. 2019c. 'The Contradictions of Xi Jinping's Socialist Democracy'. In *Party Watch Annual Report 2019: Scrambling to Achieve a Moderately Prosperous Society*, edited by Julia G. Bowie, 24–34. Washington: Center for Advanced China Research.

Diamant, Neal J. 2022. *Useful Bullshit: Constitutions in Chinese Politics and Society.* Ithaca: Cornell University Press. doi.org/10.7591/cornell/9781501761270.001.0001.

Doyon, Jérôme. 2018. 'Clientelism by Design: Personnel Politics under Xi Jinping'. *Journal of Current Chinese Affairs* 47 (3): 87–110. doi.org/10.1177/186810261804700304.

Fewsmith, Joseph. 2010. 'Inner-Party Democracy: Development and Limitations'. *China Leadership Monitor* 31 (Winter). www.hoover.org/sites/default/files/uploads/documents/CLM31JF.pdf.

Fewsmith, Joseph. 2018. 'The 19th Party Congress: Ringing Xi Jinping's New Age'. *China Leadership Monitor* 55 (Winter). www.hoover.org/sites/default/files/research/docs/clm55-jf-final.pdf.

Fewsmith, Joseph. 2021. *Rethinking Chinese Politics*. Cambridge: Cambridge University Press. doi.org/10.1017/9781108923859.

Gao, Hua. 2019. *How the Red Sun Rose: The Origin and the Development of the Yan'an Rectification Movement*. Hong Kong: The Chinese University of Hong Kong Press.

Guillermaz, Jacques. 1968. *A History of the Chinese Communist Party*. London: Methuen.

Jiang, Shigong. 2014. 'Chinese-Style Constitutionalism: On Backer's Chinese Party-State Constitutionalism'. *Modern China* 40 (2): 133–67. doi.org/10.1177/0097700413511313.

Lam, Willy Wo-Lap. 2020. *The Routledge Handbook of the Chinese Communist Party*. London: Routledge.

Lenin, V. I. (1906) 1965. 'VIII. The Congress Summed up' and 'Report on the Unity Congress of the R.S.D.L.P. A Letter to the St Petersburg Workers'. In *Lenin Collected Work,* 10: 317–82. Moscow: Progress Publisher. Accessed 12 May 2021. www.marxists.org/archive/lenin/works/1906/rucong/viii.htm#v10pp65-376.

Li, Cheng. 2007. 'China's Two Li's: Frontrunners in the Race to Succeed Hu Jintao'. *China Leadership Monitor* 22 (Fall). www.hoover.org/sites/default/files/uploads/documents/CLM22CL.pdf.

Li, Cheng. 2008. 'Hu's Southern Expedition: Changing Leadership in Guangdong'. *China Leadership Monitor* 24 (Spring). www.hoover.org/sites/default/files/uploads/documents/CLM24CL.pdf.

Li, Cheng. 2009. 'Intra-Party Democracy in China: Should We Take It Seriously?' *China Leadership Monitor* 30 (Fall). www.hoover.org/sites/default/files/uploads/documents/CLM30CL.pdf.

Li, Jingtian (李景田), ed. 2011. *Dictionary of the History of the Chinese Communist Party, 1921–2011* (中国共产党历史大辞典, 1921–2011). Beijing: Central Party School Press.

Li, Junru (李君如), ed. 2011. *Do You Know the Chinese Communist Party?* (你了解中国共产党 吗?). Beijing: Foreign Languages Press.

Ma, Ming. 2021. 'The Institutionalization of Primary-Level Party System in Rural China: Managing the Unintended Consequences of Grassroots Democracy'. PhD thesis, Hong Kong Baptist University.

MacFarquhar, Roderick. 1974. *The Origins of the Cultural Revolution. Vol. 1: Contradictions among the People, 1956–1957*. New York: Columbia University Press.

MacFarquhar, Roderick. 1999. *The Origins of the Cultural Revolution. Vol. 3: The Coming of the Cataclysm, 1961–1966*. New York: Columbia University Press.

Saich, Tony, ed. 1996. *The Rise to Power of the Chinese Communist Party: Documents and Analysis*. Armonk: M. E. Sharpe.

Saich, Tony. 2021. *From Rebel to Ruler. One Hundred Years of the Chinese Communist Party*. Cambridge: Harvard University Press. doi.org/10.4159/9780674259638.

Saich, Tony and Nancy Hearst. 2017. 'The Chinese Communist Party to 1949'. *Oxford Bibliographies*. Accessed 12 May 2021. www.oxfordbibliographies.com/view/document/obo-9780199920082/obo-9780199920082-0013.xml.

Schram, Stuart R., Nancy J. Hodes and Lyman P. Van Slyke, eds. 2005. *Mao's Road to Power: Revolutionary Writings, 1912–1949. Volume 7: New Democracy, 1939–1941*. Armonk: M. E. Sharpe.

Shambaugh, David. 2008. *China's Communist Party. Atrophy and Adaptation*. Berkeley: Berkeley University Press.

Shih, Lea. 2017. 'Centralised Leadership – Heterogeneous Party Base. Changes in the Membership Structure of the Chinese Communist Party'. *Merics China Monitor*, 16 August. merics.org/sites/default/files/2020-05/Centralized%20leadership%20%E2%80%93%20Heterogeneous%20party%20base.pdf.

Smith, Ewan. 2018. 'The Rule of Law Doctrine of the Politburo'. *China Journal* 79 (January): 40–61. doi.org/10.1086/694693.

Teiwes, Frederick C. 1984. *Leadership, Legitimacy, and Conflict in China: From Charismatic Mao to the Politics of Succession*. London: MacMillan Press.

Teiwes, Frederick C. 2015. *Politics and Purges in China. Rectification and the Decline of Party Norms, 1950–1965*. 2nd ed. Abingdon: Routledge.

Teiwes, Frederick C. and Sun Warren. 2011. 'China's New Economic Policy under Hua Guofeng: Party Consensus and Party Myths'. *China Journal* 66: 1–23. doi.org/10.1086/tcj.66.41262805.

Tsai, Kellee. 2006. 'Adaptive Informal Institutions and Endogenous Institutional Change in China'. *World Politics* 59 (1): 116–41. doi.org/10.1353/wp.2007.0018.

Tsai, Kellee. 2007. *Capitalism without Democracy: The Private Sector in Contemporary China*. New York: Cornell University Press.

Wu, Wei (吴伟). 2013. *Stage and Backstage of China's Political Reform in the 1980s* (中国80年代 政治改革的台前幕后). Hong Kong: New Century Press.

Yu, Keping. 2009. *Democracy Is a Good Thing: Essays on Politics, Society and Culture in Contemporary China*. Washington: The Brookings Institution Press.

Zeng, Qingjie. 2016. 'Democratic Procedures in the CCP's Cadre Selection Process: Implementation and Consequences?' *China Quarterly* 225: 73–99. doi.org/10.1017/S0305741015001587.

2

Decoupled State, Hollowed Civil Society: The Shifting Party-State-Society Nexus

Patricia M. Thornton

In December 2022, a high-stakes decision to delist nearly 200 Chinese companies from US stock exchanges was shelved at the eleventh hour, after months of intense negotiations that kept a trillion dollars' worth of market capital held by American pension and other investment funds hanging in the balance. At the heart of the dispute was a 2020 law requiring companies to delist from US stock exchanges if they failed to permit US regulators to inspect the work of their principal audit firms. The Holding Foreign Companies Accountable Act, signed into law with bipartisan support after China's Luckin Coffee chain defrauded NASDAQ investors in an accounting scandal that caused the loss of approximately $11 billion in shareholder wealth, pits US regulators against Chinese authorities who have repeatedly claimed that the mandated audit inspections violate its national sovereignty and put state secrets at risk (Bu 2021). The mandatory delisting was successfully forestalled when China agreed to allow US regulators to conduct inspections of audit work 'without interference' for eight state-owned Chinese companies, provided by the mainland China affiliate of KPMG and the Hong Kong affiliate of PricewaterhouseCoopers (PwC). Yet critics remain highly sceptical. In a 2021 letter addressed to the chair of the House Committee on Financial Services, the whistleblowing short-seller who exposed Luckin Coffee's systemic fabrication of financial data and operating numbers charged that, even if US regulators were able to inspect China-based auditors:

> there is no reason to believe that such inspections would be free of CCP manipulation and interference ... China has sought to exploit what it perceives as weaknesses in its strategic competitors' systems. So long as the Communist Party governs China, China will never be what we want it to be.[1]

As another specialist testified to the congressional committee, the 'key aspect of potential risk' for US investors arises from the blurring of the roles of the Chinese state, the Chinese Communist Party (CCP) and the People's Liberation Army in China's business ecosystem: the CCP's influence within firms has been strengthened immeasurably under Xi Jinping:

> through the establishment and reinvigoration of corporate Party committees with individual firms, changes to companies' Articles of Association, and influence through supervisory boards and trade unions that fall under state control.[2]

Senator Marco Rubio was considerably more direct, charging that: 'Under pressure from Wall Street, the Biden Administration struck a bad deal with the Chinese Communist Party.'[3]

Central to the delisting decision is the role played by the CCP, not only in the mainland China-based branches of the Big Four accountancies, but also in the China Institute of Certified Public Accountants (CICPA), the certifying authority for public accountants in China. The State Council's initial 2009 plan to press CICPA to accelerate development of the sector, underpinned by a 'solid political guarantee', resulted in the formation of a central Party committee within the CICPA's national office, the creation of CCP branches in accountancies, and Party cells in specific audit engagement teams the following year. By the end of 2010, Party branches had been

1 Michelle Celarier, 'Muddy Waters' Carson Block Says Wall Street Is "Thoroughly Compromised by China Money"', *Institutional Investor*, October 2021, www.institutionalinvestor.com/article/b1v6npyvs3343d/Muddy-Waters-Carson-Block-Says-Wall-Street-Is-Thoroughly-Compromised-by-China-Money.

2 'Statement of Karen M. Sutter before the U.S. House of Representative's Committee on Financial Services' Subcommittee on Investor Protection, Entrepreneurship, and Capital Markets', 26 October 2021, *Congressional Research Service* 7-5700, 3–4, www.govinfo.gov/content/pkg/CHRG-117hhrg46245/html/CHRG-117hhrg46245.htm.

3 Senator Marco Rubio, 'Biden Strikes a Bad Deal on Chinese Audits', Press Release, 15 December 2022, archive.ph/17eH6.

established in 4,985 accounting firms, or nearly 100 per cent of China's accountancies, up 80 per cent from the previous year (Wen, Humphrey and Sonnerfeldt 2021, 662).

A decade later, in December 2020, a leaked database containing the personal details of some 1.95 million CCP members revealed the extent to which CICPA's Party-building had succeeded. The China-based branches of the Big Four accountancies – PwC, KPMG, Deloitte and Ernst & Young – collectively employed more than 2,000 CCP members, including at least one partner in every firm. One KPMG partner was celebrated on a Party-building website for announcing that her chief goal in the workplace was 'making the red gene take root in KPMG and passing that on through generations'. Another CCP member at a Big Four accountancy admitted that, with the help of the local Party branch: 'We often organise to learn the spirit of the Party and Xi Jinping thought to improve and arm ourselves.'[4] At PwC Guangzhou, Senior Partner Chen Jianxiang (陈建翔) serves as the secretary of its internal Party organisation. In 2018, Chen told reporters that, at his branch, the Party-building activities focused mainly on developing more positive interactive relationships with the state-owned enterprises among their clients. PwC Guangzhou account auditors who are Party members, Chen said, are encouraged to:

> take the initiative in revealing their identities to state-owned enterprise clients in their work. Using the Party organization as a link, they draw closer to each other, [developing a] relationship that surpasses that of ordinary clients and auditors.[5]

Intensive Party-building efforts have targeted professional associations and chambers of commerce since the beginning of the Xi era, particularly since the 2015 'decoupling' reforms that removed these organisations from state management and oversight. Numbering only a few hundred in the initial stage of market reform, by 2019 there were more than 70,000 such associations covering every sector and level of the Chinese economy.[6] Once regarded as 'transmission belts' of state authority, by the mid-1990s private business associations were technically classified as 'non-governmental',

4 Ben Gartside, Jack Hazlewood and Juliet Samuel, 'Big Four Auditors Employ Hundreds of Chinese Communist Party Members', Telegraph, 15 December 2020, 3, www.telegraph.co.uk/business/2020/12/15/big-four-auditors-employ-hundreds-chinese-communist-party-members/.

5 'Promoting Business through Party-Building' (通过党建来促进业务), *Sina.com*, 20 July 2018, archive.ph/heoa7.

6 'Professional Associations Have Been Called "Official-Coloured" for a Long Time' (行业协会商会去'官色'呼唤已久), *Fazhi Ribao* 19 June 2019, archive.is/5u46y.

despite acting as the 'close cousins of the "mass" organisations with which students of Leninist systems are so familiar … closely integrated with, and function[ing] under, the leadership of institutions of the Party-state' (Nevitt 1996, 28). Pearson (1994) characterised their role with respect to the party-state as 'socialist corporatism', whereas Unger (1996) drew a distinction between the overtly 'state corporatist' professional associations and more 'social corporatist' chambers of commerce, which, he argued, had a capacity for 'bottom-up' interest articulation and limited autonomy during Jiang Zemin's rule.

Given this history, the State Council's February 2021 announcement that 728 national and 67,491 local professional associations and chambers of commerce – 92 per cent and 96 per cent of all such organisations, respectively – had successfully 'decoupled' from state control might appear a significant step towards securing their independence. However, since a 'top priority' of the decoupling process was the establishment of primary Party organisations in those organisations,[7] external oversight by state authorities was replaced with more intrusive control by internal Party committees, with regulations mandating disciplinary sanctions for failing to observe democratic centralism and protect the Party's 'core'. As Li (2018, 361) demonstrated, whereas close state ties do not correlate to a loss of autonomy for social organisations, Party-building is far more transformative for such groups by 'affecting their agenda-setting, and even their internal activities'.

Taking the decoupling reforms applied to professional associations and chambers of commerce as a bellwether for the voluntary sector as a whole, I argue that the recent Party-building push alongside the simultaneous rolling back of state management signals an important shift in the balance of power within the 'party-state-society trichotomy' (Shen, Yu and Zhou 2020) strongly in the Party's favour under Xi. Moreover, this expansion of the Party's power and presence is occurring at the expense of the autonomy of *both* the state apparatus *and* the voluntary sector, through both organisational and legal means.[8] Organisationally, as Huang (2020) noted, the CCP's relationship to the state apparatus has undergone three distinct phases of development: from an 'integrated' or 'unitary' party-state

7 'Notice on Doing a Good Job in Pushing Forward the Reform of Decoupling Local Trade Associations and Chambers of Commerce from Administrative Organs' (关于做好全面推开地方行业协会商会与行政机关脱钩改革工作的通知), Joint Organisation Office, 21 June 2019, archive.ph/wDbk2.

8 'Decision on the Deepening the Reform of Party-State Institutions' (深化党和国家机构改革方案), Central Committee of the Chinese Communist Party, 21 March 2018, archive.ph/AzweY.

model during the Mao era, to an attempted separation during the 1980s, to the current 'embedded' party-state model characterised by exclusive 'Party groups' and separate 'Party committees' internal to the state apparatus. This embedded Party model is now being extended beyond the state into private firms, non-profit enterprise units, charitable foundations and even sports teams and clubs – in other words, across both the economy and the voluntary sector (Thornton 2012). At the same time, the Party's 'core leadership' is reshaping the state's role with respect to the voluntary sector from a managerial to a more distant, regulatory one. Efforts 'to deepen and accelerate the separation of the state from enterprises, from government funds, from public affairs, and from social organisations' (*zhengqi fenkai, zhengzi fenkai, zhengshi fenkai, zhengshe fenkai* 政企分开、政资分开、政事分开、政社分开)[9] are thus scaling back the state apparatus in operational terms while also enhancing the Party's control over both the state *and* social forces.

New legal and quasi-legal instruments accompany these organisational shifts under Xi, who has stressed the paramount importance of 'constraining [political] power within a cage of institutions' (*ba quanli guanjin zhidu longzi* 把权力关进制度笼子)[10] to vigorously 'advance building a socialist "rule-of-law country"' (*jianshe shehui zhuyi fazhi guojia* 建设社会主义法治国家).[11] Existing laws aimed at the voluntary sector were revised and new rounds of legislation drafted at a feverish pace to meet the central leadership's aspiration of producing 'a system of social organisations with a separation between state and society, clear powers and responsibilities, and legal autonomy' by 2020.[12] However, in practical terms, Xi has been accused of 'weaponising the rule of law' (Trevaskes 2017) to more tightly constrain both state agents and social associations, while at the same time carving out an expanding extra-legal space for the Party to exercise greater influence and control.

9 Hu Jintao, 'Hu Jintao's Report to the Eighteenth Party Congress' (胡锦涛在党的十八大上的报告), 19 November 2012, archive.ph/39tCs.

10 'Communiqué and Explanation of the Resolution of the Chinese Communist Party 18th Central Committee's Third Plenum' (十八届三中全会《决定》、公报、说明), 18 November 2013, archive.ph/FsPrA.

11 'Constitution of the Chinese Communist Party', revised by the Nineteenth Party Congress (中国共产党章程, 中国共产党第十九次全国代表大会部分修改), 24 October 2017, archive.ph/pDFsG.

12 'Opinion on Reforming the System of Managing Social Organisations to Promote the Healthy and Orderly Development of Social Organisations' (关于改革社会组织管理制度促进社会组织健康有序发展的意见), Central Committee of the Chinese Communist Party and the General Office of the State Council, 1 September 2016, archive.ph/aZYFt.

A close reading of major policy decisions and new legislation concerning the voluntary sector informed by an historical-institutionalist approach demonstrates that, instead of breathing 'new vitality' into China's third realm, as promised by Xi's predecessors,[13] these developments may have already begun to 'hollow out' social organisations. Caught between proliferating laws and regulations, and the Party's demands to engage in political study and Party-building activities, smaller and less well-resourced social organisations are increasingly straightjacketed by a tightening regulatory environment and are struggling to cope.

The Rise of the Integrated Party-State

Like any new political party, the CCP was but one in a diverse field of social and political organisations. Its early survival depended upon its ability to build alliances with, and harness, other social forces in pursuit of its aims. Chen Yung-fa (1986) detailed how early Party activists relied on mass line tactics, filtered through a dense web of social organisations, to mobilise popular support. Sworn brotherhoods and secret societies in rural base areas were tapped as 'parochial mobilisers' and exploited for tactical gains, only to be later discarded or ruthlessly eliminated.

The provisional government of the rural Soviets supervised CCP engagement with social organisations, according to a May 1931 decree that formalised the 'single united, dual body' (*yiyuan erti* 一元二体) (Zhu 2019, 31) of the party-state in the making. The Sixth Party Congress in 1928 called for the establishment of internal Party committees 'in every non-Party mass organisation and in all administrative bodies [such as in the government and in workers' and peasants' unions] if there are more than three CCP members' so as to 'increase the influence of the Party', 'implement Party policies among the non-Party populace' and 'supervise the activity of Party members working in non-Party organisations'.[14] Despite the instability of

13 Hu Jintao, 'Hu Jintao's Report to the Eighteenth Party Congress' (胡锦涛在党的十八大上的报告), 19 November 2012, archive.ph/39tCs; Li Liguo (李立国), 'Reform the System of Managing Social Organisations to Stimulate and Release the Vitality of Social Development' (改革社会组织管理制度,激发和释放社会发展活力), *Qiushi* 10, 2014, accessed 10 May 2021, theory.people.com.cn/n/2014/0516/c40531-25025298.html.

14 'Constitution of the Chinese Communist Party' (promulgated by the Sixth Party Congress) (中国共产党党章1928年7月10日中共六大通过), 10 July 1928, archive.ph/EI5Ce.

the civil war period, an estimated 26,126 social organisations – including guilds, study societies and religious groups – persisted in Nationalist-controlled areas (White, Howell and Xiaoyuan 1996).

Once in power, the Party extended its reach over the state apparatus, as well as over existing social organisations. Although both enjoyed degrees of autonomy during the initial 'New Democracy' period when the CCP adopted an integrated or unitary party-state model (*dangzheng heyi*, 党政合一) (Huang 2020), by the mid-1950s, social organisations were either absorbed into the state structure as 'mass organisations' or repressed. The 1950 Interim Measures for the Registration of Social Organisations stipulated that the Ministry of Internal Affairs and the Council of State Administration would register and manage social associations;[15] however, in the absence of a centralised system to do so, implementation was irregular. Nevertheless, as Lin (2007, 4) noted, the measures 'fundamentally "hollowed out" the non-governmental nature of the various surviving bodies', remaking them in the administrative model of Party and state organisations.

As Ma (2002, 119–20) documented, Mao-era social organisations fell into one of three categories: private organisations inherited from pre-revolutionary times, newly created apolitical professional and charitable groups, and mass organisations established and managed by the state apparatus. Although most social organisations were banned after 1949, a handful of scholarly and professional associations were permitted to continue operating. For example, the Chinese Medical Association and the Chinese Red Cross were used to co-opt educated, technical and managerial elites under the CCP's 'united front'. Mao-era social organisations of the second type included newly created professional and charitable groups, such as friendship associations, cultural agencies and a small handful of transnational research exchange associations relied upon by the new People's Republic of China government to maintain international scientific and cultural ties. Finally, so-called national people's and mass organisations representing workers, peasants, women and youth operated throughout most of the Mao era. Despite their rather different historical backgrounds, all three types were either transformed into, or established as, government-organised non-governmental organisations during the 1950s and 1960s. By 1965, roughly 100 remained at the national level and another 6,000 at the local level, all under direct party-state control (Xie 2004, 26).

15 'Central Government State Council Interim Measures for the Registration of Social Organisations' (中央政务院社会团体登记暂行办法), 29 September 1950, *Fujian Zhengbao* 10: 67–8.

The Party's institutional absorption of state and social forces peaked in the mid-1960s, when the unitary party-state model evolved into an even more extreme pattern of the 'Party substituting for the state' (Zhu 2019, 34). This extraordinary concentration of power in the CCP's hands arguably facilitated the radical Cultural Revolution practice of 'kicking out the [old] Party committees to make revolution', resulting in the 'triple combination' revolutionary committees beginning in 1967. These supplanted the established local Party and state organisations with a joint committee of revolutionary cadres, revolutionary masses and People's Liberation Army forces. It was only after the death of Lin Biao in 1971 that Party organisations gradually began to be re-established at the local level (Zhu 2019, 32), although all 29 provincial-level governments housed 'interlocking directorates' under which the first secretary of a provincial Party committee served concurrently as the head of the provincial revolutionary committee between 1970 and 1971, a practice that survived into the early post-Mao era (Zheng 1997, 148, 196).

The Reformist Interregnum

Deng Xiaoping's interest in party-state reform preceded his rise to power by several decades. As early as 1941, Deng warned that 'the malady of ruling the country through Party institutions was the best way to paralyse, corrupt, and sabotage our Party, and separate it from the masses'. At a preparatory work conference for the Third Plenum in 1978, Deng condemned the practice of the Party substituting itself for the state apparatus. At the National Science Conference a few months later, he warned that the Party should be relied upon only to provide political leadership, and to ensure that the state was implementing the Party's line, principles and policies; any internal Party committee or branch 'should be acquainted with government work and check up on it, but should not attempt to take it over'. In 1986, with the progress of market reforms stalling under the weight of overlapping management by both Party and state officials, serious discussions about clearly delineating separate roles and responsibilities for each were initiated. At a meeting of the Central Finance and Economic Leading Group, Deng stressed that the goal of political reform ought to be 'to motivate and raise the people's initiative, and eliminate bureaucratism. The key should be the separation of the Party and the state' (Chen 1995, 135–50). Zhao Ziyang's political report to the Thirteenth Party Congress in October 1987 lamented that 'the long-standing problems of the lack of a separation between the Party and the state, and of the Party substituting for the state, have not been fundamentally resolved':

> The Party led the people in establishing state power, mass organizations and various economic and cultural organizations. The Party should ensure that [these] organs of political power can fully perform their functions, and should absolutely respect but not underwrite the work of mass organizations, enterprises and public institutions.[16]

Although abandoned following the 1989 Tiananmen demonstrations in favour of re-embedding Party core groups within state offices, the original 1987 reform program also proposed separating the Party from mass organisations such as the Women's Federation, the Communist Youth League and the Federation of Trade Unions. In 1988, these organisations had also briefly enjoyed a degree of autonomy from the Party while still being overseen by the state (Chen 1995, 150) before the window closed in 1989.

Mass organisations aside, the General Principles of Civil Law of 1986[17] recognised social organisations as legal persons – along with enterprises, independently funded official organs (including national and local government offices) and public institutions engaged in public service.[18] The State Council issued further regulations in 1988 concerning foundations,[19] and, in 1989, regulations mandating the registration and management of social associations[20] as well as temporary measures regulating foreign chambers of commerce.[21]

16 'Zhao Ziyang's Report to the 13th Congress of the Chinese Communist Party' (赵紫阳在中国共产党十三次全国代表大会上的报告), 1 July 2008, archive.ph/E4eQy.

17 'General Principles of the Civil Law of the People's Republic of China' (中华人民共和国民法通则), 12 April 1986, www.pkulaw.com/en_law/4202520b3be0ae24bdfb.html.

18 所有制企业, 机关, 事业单位, 社会团体.

19 Foundations were defined as 'social organisational entities', which were 'non-governmental and non-profit institutions established and operated through the voluntary donations made by domestic and foreign social associations, other organisations and individuals'. 'Methods for Managing Foundations' (基金会管理办法), 27 September 1988, www.pkulaw.com/chl/4d238979fd67c5adbdfb.html.

20 'Regulations on the Registration and Management of Social Associations' (社会团体登记管理条例), 25 October 1989, www.pkulaw.com/chl/d8c234aa5baab8a9bdfb.html.

21 'Interim Regulations Managing Foreign Chambers of Commerce' (外国商会管理暂行规定), 14 June 1989, www.pkulaw.com/chl/ea4c8b4b4b14b66dbdfb.html.

The 1989 regulations introduced a system of dual management that required social organisations to find a sponsoring government department before registering with the state Ministry of Civil Affairs (MoCA). In return, the sponsoring agency was responsible for carrying out annual inspections of the organisation's accounts and receiving work reports. Dual registration posed significant barriers, particularly for groups without historic relationships with the state, and those working in politically sensitive areas. MoCA frequently refused to register a social organisation working in a particular field if another was already registered in the same jurisdiction. In some cases, state officials purportedly established and registered social associations themselves to prevent other grassroots groups from attempting to do so (Deng 2010). Although larger municipalities, such as Beijing, Guangzhou and Shanghai, enacted local regulations to manage social organisations, legal and regulatory control prior to 1989 was patchy and uneven (Yan 2007), allowing some groups to evade registration altogether.

Managing Social Organisations under the Embedded Party-State

The aftermath of the 1989 Tiananmen crackdown saw the return of Party core groups to the state structure, many of which had only been dismantled the year before, and the revival of the interlocking directorates of the Mao era (Li and Zhou 2019). However, unlike the system of interlocking directorates that existed under Mao, the deepening of market reform in the 1990s necessitated new legal and regulatory regimes, creating two parallel governing logics. Within the CCP, the majority of Party meetings had long been taken up by the reading, studying and ratifying of policy decisions conveyed by official documents, driven by what Wu (1995) calls 'documentary politics'. As Zhang (2017) observed, the Party's 'rule by document' historically originated as a means of achieving a more responsive and efficient form of governance: policies issued by decree have the advantage of avoiding a prolonged and cumbersome process of public consultation and collective deliberation, particularly when an urgent decision or policy shift is required. However, since the Fifteenth Party Congress affirmed its intention to 'rule the country according to law' in 1997,[22] legal frameworks,

22 'The Communiqué of Fourth Plenum of the Chinese Communist Party's Eighteenth Congress' (中国共产党第十八届中央委员会第四次全体会议公报), 23 October 2014, archive.ph/C6w59.

rules and regulations have increasingly emerged as a system operating in parallel to – and sometimes in competition with – the CCP's 'rule by document', leaving social organisations caught between the two.

Most local governments prior to 1997 had practised a policy of 'no recognition, no banning, no intervention' – the so-called Three Noes Policy – with respect to unregistered social organisations. The origins of this practice apparently lie in a 1988 internal-circulation document issued by MoCA to Shanghai municipal authorities who had requested specific advice on how to deal with foreign NGOs. Although issued internally in response to a request for clarification, other local governments quickly followed suit, allowing unregistered domestic social organisations to exist so long as they did not threaten state security or social stability (Deng 2010, 190–1). As Spires (2011) observed, this 'contingent symbiosis' between local governments and the voluntary sector proved adaptive for overstretched and under-resourced authorities because charitable groups relieved public welfare pressures and demands. According to Snape and Wang (2020, 16):

> State non-implementation was the norm; sporadic implementation was a supplementary habit. Unable or unwilling to register, an estimated 8 million social organisations existed in this grey social space beyond state control.

The Party's Expansion into the Voluntary Sector

Confronted with the lax implementation of existing laws and regulations, central CCP leaders in 1994 began probing the possibilities of Party-building directly within social organisations (Yan 2007). In July 1996, the Politburo Standing Committee carried out a special investigation of social organisations that culminated in the issuing of its 'Notice on Strengthening the Management of Social Organisations and Private Non-enterprise Units',[23] which was released the following month. This notice flagged for urgent attention the possibility that social organisations operating within China were, in fact, 'supported and manipulated by Western hostile forces'. Targeted with particular scorn was that handful of civic associations that

23 'Notice on Strengthening the Management of Social Associations and Private Non-Enterprise Units' (关于加强社会团体和民办非企业单位管理工作的通知), 28 August 1996, www.cecc.gov/resources/legal-provisions/circular-of-the-general-offices-of-the-communist-party-central-committe-0.

claimed as their 'backbone members' 'those "elites" who were behind the turbulence during the spring and summer of 1989'. In a pattern that would often be repeated in the coming years, the notice called for an overall 'clean-up and rectification' of all non-governmental social organisations to be carried out in stages, as well as the revision of existing regulations concerning the registration and management of social organisations and private non-enterprise units 'as soon as possible'. The rectification and review process quickly became the norm during the 1990s and 2000s, beginning with local test runs to hone techniques before being rolled out in stages keyed to particular deadlines, across the whole of the voluntary sector (Dillon 2011).

In February 1998, the balance of power within the party-state-society trichotomy began shifting more notably in the CCP's favour. A 1998 notice[24] called upon registered social organisations with three or more CCP members in good standing to establish separate internal Party organisations, pending the approval of either their sponsoring organisations or the state agency with which they were registered. At the same time, in the wake of the Fifteenth Party Congress's 1997 call to 'govern the country according to law', the state's persistent non-compliance began to be brought to heel. Regulations on the registration and management of social associations, and 'civil non-enterprise units' – defined as civil non-commercial organisations – were promulgated in 1998,[25] followed by new laws governing the management of charitable foundations in 2004.[26] The 1998 regulations provided a far more rigorous set of requirements for social organisations and private non-enterprise units to meet before they would be eligible for registration, including (for social organisations) a stipulated level of membership, a fixed address and a minimum financial requirement that made smaller and less well-resourced groups ineligible to register. Fieldwork surveys conducted in 2002–03 in Shenzhen and Anhui found that only 8–13 per cent of grassroots social organisations in the areas surveyed met the requisite standards for registration; self-help associations for farmers and migrant workers, temporary mutual aid organisations and short-term

24 'Notice on Issues Related to the Establishment of Party Organisations in Social Associations' (关于在社会团体中建立党组织有关问题的通知), 1998, www.pkulaw.com/chl/6a5c4729abd8b7bbbdfb.html.

25 'Regulations on the Registration and Management of Social Associations' (社会团体登记管理条例), 25 September 1998, www.pkulaw.com/chl/27a3f9458bf5b865bdfb.html; 'Provisional Regulations on the Registration and Management of Civil Non-Enterprise Units' (民办非企业单位登记管理暂行条例), 25 October 1998, archive.ph/wip/MkeVF.

26 'Regulations on the Management of Foundations' (基金会管理条例), 2004, www.pkulaw.com/chl/9a3d4693158e4fc7bdfb.html.

groups – for example, teams organised to plan celebratory or other such events – were deemed ineligible for registration and were therefore rendered technically illegal under the new framework (Xie 2004, 20).

The irony of this dilemma was captured, but by no means resolved, in the November 1999 Notice on Further Strengthening the Management of Non-Governmental Organisations,[27] jointly issued by the State Council and the CCP's Central Committee. The notice decried the fact that 'illegal civic organisations' were still on the rise, despite the apparent success of three years of rectification that had reduced the number of social organisations from 200,000 in 1996 to 165,000. Nonetheless, problematic organisations remained. The notice named the Laid-Off Workers Association, the Veterans Association and the Migrant Workers Association as 'illegal social organisations with quite complicated international backgrounds'. It also sounded the alarm over the Falun Dafa Research Association,[28] which had organised the largest outdoor mass protest since 1989 outside the Zhongnanhai leadership compound a few months before. In addition to reiterating the commitment of the Fifteenth Party Congress to build a 'rule of law country', the 1999 notice stressed the importance of not only strengthening the management of social organisations of all types in accordance with law, but also in developing new legal instruments to manage the voluntary sector as a whole.

Equally noteworthy was the notice's observation that 'Party organisations have not yet been widely established in civil society organisations'. The notice labelled the problem of illegal social organisations 'a serious political struggle that concerns the destiny of the Party, the success or failure of socialism, and the fundamental interests of the people', and called for an accelerated development of laws and regulations on the one hand, and a strengthening of the political leadership of social organisations through Party-building on the other. Social organisations with three or more Party members were required to establish separate internal Party organisations no later than 30 June 2000. A few months later, the Organisation Department

27 'Notice on Further Strengthening the Management of Non-Governmental Organisations' (关于进一步加强民间组织管理工作的通知), 1 November 1999, www.pkulaw.com/chl/4ba582a602ef85a1bdfb.html.

28 'Interim Measures on the Banning of Illegal Civic Organisations' (取缔非法民间组织暂行办法), Ministry of Civil Affairs, 6 April 2000, www.pkulaw.com/chl/28f06207d5934d20bdfb.html; 'NPC Standing Committee Resolution on Banning Heretic Cult Organisations, Guarding against and Punishing Heretic Cult Activities' (全国人民代表大会常务委员会关于取缔邪教组织、防范和惩治邪教活动的决定), 30 October 1999, www.pkulaw.com/en_law/4133beb3bd5dbb79bdfb.html.

followed with its detailed 'Views Regarding the Strengthening of Work of Establishing the Party in Social Organisations', which repeated the call for accelerated Party-building to ensure that the voluntary sector 'adheres to a correct political orientation', carries out 'political thought work', and complies with national laws and regulations.[29]

By the time the Sixteenth Central Committee's Fourth Plenum issued its 2004 call to 'strengthen the Party's governing capacity',[30] a nationwide Party-building drive was already well underway. Aimed at 'comprehensive coverage' across so-called two new organisations (i.e. new economic and social organisations established since the adoption of market reforms), by 2008, the Party-building drive had resulted in the creation of new Party branches in 53.5 per cent of eligible social associations, 55 per cent of eligible private non-enterprise units and 51 per cent of eligible foundations nationwide (Sun 2009, 204–5), which had also just come under the purview of newly promulgated regulations.[31]

Decoupling State and Society

Under Xi Jinping's leadership, the Party has unquestionably become more assertive in countering and constraining the power and prerogative of the state and its agencies 'within a cage of institutions'. In redressing the perceived persistent non-compliance of state authorities with respect to the voluntary sector, as well as concerns that state offices might actually be benefiting (financially or otherwise) from their sponsorship of various associations, the Party under Xi has scaled back the state's responsibilities, an approach that has been characterised as the 'the state's retreat and the Party's advance' (Li 2005; Thornton 2013; Shen, Yu and Zhou 2020, 71), and has begun instituting mandatory decoupling of social organisations from the state administration. At the same time, particularly in the wake

29 'Notice Concerning "Opinion on the Work of Strengthening Party Organisations Established in Social Associations"' (关于加强社会团体党的建设工作的意见的通知), 21 July 2000, www.pkulaw.com/chl/24797de1dd9b0084bdfb.html; 'Notice Concerning the Problems of Building Party Organisations in Social Associations' (关于在社会团体中建立党组织有关问题的通知), 16 February 1998, www.pkulaw.com/chl/6a5c4729abd8b7bbbdfb.html; 'Notice Concerning "Opinion on the Work of Strengthening Party Organisations Established in Social Associations"' (关于加强社会团体党的建设工作的意见的通知), 21 July 2000, www.pkulaw.com/chl/24797de1dd9b0084bdfb.html.

30 'Chinese Communist Party Central Committee Decision on Strengthening the Governing Capacity of the Party' (中共中央关于加强党的执政能力建设的决定), 2004, archive.ph/AMr1X.

31 'Foundation Management Regulations' (基金会管理条例), 8 March 2004, www.pkulaw.com/chl/9a3d4693158e4fc7bdfb.html.

of the 2008 financial crisis, the Party has firmly steered social associations at all levels through the deployment of 'strategic' incentives and 'modular' patterning in the direction of what Teets (2013) recognises as a form of 'consultative authoritarianism', encouraging a 'civil society' that enjoys a degree of autonomy but is still subject to indirect control from central officials. Whereas, under Hu Jintao (胡锦涛), social associations were able to advocate more or less actively for limited policy change, Xi Jinping's robust efforts to recentralise control has left the voluntary sector with considerably less political space within which to operate (Teets and Almen 2018). Howell (2019) documented the transformation of the Hu–Wen-era welfarist incorporation in the direction of securitisation under Xi, who has overseen the most sustained and severe crackdown on rights-based and other advocacy groups since 1989.

In March 2013, the State Council announced broad plans for institutional reform,[32] including a shift from the state's management of the voluntary sector to a more distant regulatory role. Concluding that one reason for the persistently high number of illegal social groups was that the requirements for registration remained too high, the new scheme floated the idea of abolishing the dual management requirement for certain categories of social organisations, including for business and professional associations. The 2013 plan called for the decoupling of state agencies from social organisations and the introduction of competitive pressures to boost efficiency across the sector. The dual management requirement was partially lifted from private non-enterprise organisations, allowing them to register directly with MoCA as 'social service organisations'; the state's role was trimmed back to the tasks of registering them and monitoring their compliance with existing laws and regulations.

Two years later, in 2015, the CCP Central Committee issued an ambitious opinion (for trial implementation)[33] laying out a bold new model for the party-state-society trichotomy that placed the Party at the centre of all social organisations. While reasserting 'the self-governance of social organisations according to law', the opinion also called for '*merging* the Party's work with the operations and development process of the social organisation', with 'social organisations and their staff closely united around the Party, constantly

32 'State Council Plan for Institutional and Functional Reform' (国务院机构改革和职能转变方案的决定), 10 March 2013, archive.ph/nDR8Y.

33 'Opinion on Strengthening the Work of Party Building in Social Organisations (for Trial Implementation)' (关于加强社会组织党的建设工作的意见（试行）), 29 September 2015, www.pkulaw.com/chl/46330ba443668dd2bdfb.html.

expanding the influence of the Party in social organisations'. Within a few months, the Party Central Committee issued further new regulations that extended the Party group system across every possible organisational sphere, including the voluntary sector. Revised in 2019, the regulations explicitly applied the principle of democratic centralism to Party groups in social organisations, requiring them to implement all the decisions and policies of the Party's central leadership or face disciplinary sanctions.[34]

Read together, the new scheme reworks the obligations of state agents dealing with social organisations such that they are now responsible for registering and certifying Party-building at the point of application. State agencies serving as the registering authority certify the compliance of social organisations with the requirement that they build and maintain an internal Party organisation, as well as a Party group composed of the leading full-time staff members and officers of the social organisation in question. Successful Party-building has been added to the key performance indicators for cadres within the registering authority. Party organisations within the registering authority are tasked with sharing office space and resources with the social organisation's internal Party committee if necessary, whereas the social organisations are permitted to deduct the costs associated with Party-building from their taxable income allowances, in essence shifting assets and resources away from the state to support Party-building (Snape and Wang 2020, 17).

Under the new regime of 'rigid embedding' (Xu 2017) in eligible social organisations, Party-building responsibilities have become part of the annual evaluation process, with results reported regularly to the registering state authority. However, surveys show considerable disparities in the achievement of these goals. In Guangdong, which ranks second nationwide in terms of its number of social organisations and a CCP penetration rate of 86.6 per cent in 2015, Party-building work accounts for 30 of a possible total of 1,000 points, with 950 points required to attain the 5A rating needed to bid for government contracts as social service providers.[35] In Sichuan, where social organisation formation lags behind, less than 6 per cent of existing social organisations – or fewer than 100 – attained

34 'Regulations (for Trial Implementation) on the Work of CCP Party Groups' (中国共产党党组工作条例(试行), 11 June 2015, www.pkulaw.com/chl/c957d20e2888712ebdfb.html (emphasis added); '2019 Revised Regulations Concerning the Work of CCP Party Groups' (中国共产党党组工作条例(2019修订)), 6 April 2019, www.pkulaw.com/chl/5eadbd866965793bbdfb.html.

35 'Guangdong Provincial Social Organisation Party-Building Work Investigation Report 2015' (广东省社会组织党建工作调研报告), *China Social Organisations* 1 (2016): 25–7.

a 3A rating or higher, the minimum qualification to allow for the transfer of responsibility for some social services. Few social organisations assisting vulnerable populations in Sichuan were thus able to meet the minimum requirements for registration: less than 25 per cent had three or more CCP members as employees or volunteers, inhibiting the establishment of independent internal Party organisations. Of those with internal CCP branches and committees, many hosted Party 'organisations without activities, and activities without value' (Li 2017, 24–6).

Other obstacles abound: turnover rates are high for NGO staff and volunteers alike, making it difficult to maintain stable internal Party branches. Some social organisations, such as chambers of commerce, are populated chiefly by economic migrants who may be registered Party members back home and are reluctant to transfer their memberships to their current place of residence (Xu 2017). Most charitable organisations are too resource-poor to build a Party branch (Chen 2012). Many Party members in social organisations are reluctant or unwilling to take on the burden of Party-building, regarding it as a distraction; some are contemptuous of, or repelled by, such demands to the extent that they even conceal their Party membership rather than participate (Li 2016; Chen 2017). Likewise, registering authorities tend to 'take economic development as the unyielding aim, and Party-building as a soft target' (Yang and Hu 2018), prompting widespread 'organisational idling' in which requisite Party branches are established in name only to meet annual performance targets. One 2007 survey in Changsha found that 41 per cent of grassroots Party branches in the voluntary sector carried out few to no activities; in Shenzhen, a 2008 MoCA survey found that while only 19.8 per cent of Party branches in social organisations carried out activities 'frequently', 19.8 per cent of members found the events 'dull, boring, and unimaginative' (*daiban, fawei, quefa xinyi* 呆板、乏味、缺乏新意) (Chen 2012, 38).

Despite mounting evidence that the compulsory embedment of Party cells in social organisations has produced reactions ranging from 'indifference' and 'perfunctory acquiescence' to 'antipathy to the extent of resistance' (Chen 2012, 38), the 2015 decoupling reforms[36] nonetheless called for state agencies to end their sponsorship of all professional and industry associations and chambers of commerce, which are to host internal Party

36 'Overall Plan for Decoupling Professional Associations and Chambers of Commerce from State Administration' (行业协会商会与行政机关脱钩总体方案), Chinese Communist Party Central Committee and State Council General Office, 8 July 2015, archive.ph/B0MeC.

branches instead. Building upon the CCP Central Committee's 2013 decision on comprehensively deepening reform[37] and the State Council's 2013 institutional reform program, the Overall Plan ordered state agencies to delink from professional and industry associations and chambers of commerce by 'five separations and five norms' (*wu fenli, wu guifan* 五分离、五规范), separating institutions, functions, financial assets, personnel and Party-building, while protecting the same standards or norms of conduct for both state offices and social associations across all five realms. The plan was piloted in two rounds, involving 148 national-level associations in 2015 and 144 in 2017 (Ma 2020, 36–7).

To be clear, the 2013 Overall Plan did not end state oversight altogether: to the contrary, it called upon the state to strengthen a more circumscribed form of supervision by ensuring compliance with existing regulations working through those agencies responsible for taxation, finance, audit and public security. Its release was accompanied by a flurry of media reports detailing state corruption and failure in managing associations, which were said to have fallen 'captive' to the local officials supervising them. For example, in 2015, the Chinese Calligraphers Association either expelled or suspended 18 members, 16 of whom were either current or retired state employees receiving generous sinecures for serving as officers in the association. Media reports that appeared on the heels of the Overall Plan decried the 'widespread' practice of state officials receiving 'hats' from social organisations in exchange for facilitating their registration and management, leading to the forced withdrawal of 887 state cadres in Shaanxi in 2014 from such duties. In addition, in the case of the Shaanxi branch of the Calligraphers Association, a central inspection team found that calligraphic scrolls produced by state cadres were being sold through the association at greatly inflated prices to further pad their modest state salaries. One provincial inspector observed:

> Once these officials took on roles within the association, the price of their works rose rapidly, not because their calligraphy had increased in artistic value, but because their power and official status boosted their worth.[38]

37 'Chinese Communist Party Central Committee Decision on Several Major Issues in Comprehensively Deepening Reform' (中共中央关于全面深化改革若干重大问题的决定), 12 November 2013, www.pkulaw.com/chl/f15519466307ef03bdfb.html.

38 Zheng Henan 郑赫南, 'Decoupling Whether or Not 'Corruption Involving Associations' Can Be Eradicated' (脱钩, 能否根治'涉协会腐败), *Jiancha ribao*, 26 April 2016, archive.ph/LMa04.

In other cases, state officials were accused of embezzling membership fees from industry associations, misappropriating public funds in the name of supervising such organisations, or exerting undue influence over the setting of industry or environmental standards in return for generous kickbacks.[39]

Yet, decoupling was by no means uniformly welcomed, either by state agencies or by the professional associations and chambers of commerce themselves, many of whom were reliant on state subsidies and administrative support. One 2014 survey of the full-time staff of chambers of commerce and professional associations had respondents pre-emptively complaining that 'decoupling is dumping the burden [on us]' and that 'decoupling means losing our status'. Others lamented: 'After decoupling, how will the Party Committee and state guarantee our survival and development?' And: 'How can we operate without higher-level supervision?' (Ma 2020, 41). In one city in Jiangsu, of the 440 professional associations and chambers of commerce that underwent mandatory decoupling in 2016, 188 were unable to establish internal Party organisations two years later: 75 because the CCP members within their organisations were already registered elsewhere, and 42 because they had no CCP members at all within their ranks. Building new Party organisations proved so complicated for the municipal authority that the task had to be 'triple-subcontracted' out to various state agencies, causing 'serious disconnection problems and a hollowing-out of the Party building process' (Cheng and Xu 2018, 39). Another survey of 11 professional associations and chambers of commerce in one Shanghai district found that only one-third managed to adapt after decoupling from the state and building Party branches, whereas the majority found it difficult to proceed without the resources and administrative support previously supplied by their supervising agencies. A few within the sample indicated that they would likely cease operations once their extant surplus funds had been exhausted (Zhao and Zhou 2020), a clear sign that the new Party-building requirement is serving to extinguish, rather than to stimulate, the vitality of the local voluntary sector.

39 'Industry Associations: Some Have Been Infected with "Hidden Power Corruption"' (行业协会：有的已染上'隐性权力腐败), *Jiancha Ribao*, 3 November 2015, archive.ph/zhvLT.

Party Supremacy

Nie and Wu (2022) confirm that Xi Jinping's new Party-Building Campaign has proved 'unprecedentedly resolute and compelling' across the voluntary sector. Shortly after the 2015 CCP Central Committee's declaration that it aimed to 'effectively cover' all social organisations, the CCP appointed MoCA's Social Organisations Management Bureau (SOMB) with overseeing Party-building across the sector. SOMB routinely conducts investigations of social organisations, provides training and support for Party organisations within NGOs, and regularly publishes lists of illegal and non-compliant social organisations. Its successes earned SOMB's former director Zhan Chengfu a promotion to vice minister of MoCA in 2018; shortly thereafter, MoCA issued a new directive requiring all social organisations to revise their articles of association to include a commitment to establish a Party organisation, carry out regular Party-building activities and uphold socialist core values.[40] As recently as March 2021, MoCA introduced a new campaign to 'cleanse the social organisation ecological space' by orchestrating ministerial initiatives across 22 functional systems – including education, public security, state security, justice, finance, housing and foreign exchange – to deprive non-compliant social organisations of access to the space and resources they need to operate and to strip away the 'cloak of legality' beneath which some organisations have continued to operate (Snape 2021). Thus, the 'legal grey zone' (Froissart 2018) that once allowed both local state authorities and unregistered charities and NGOs to quietly coexist and function with a certain degree of autonomy is rapidly being erased.

The state's role in China's voluntary sector has been significantly rolled back and reshaped under Xi Jinping, reduced to facilitating registration, auditing and clearing the way for the Party's further advance. The requirements of Party-building are transforming the voluntary sector by shrinking the scope for autonomous action and discretion on the part of social organisations. Internal CCP branches have been found to police compliance with the Party's political line (Wang 2017), divert organisational resources away from the organisational goals in favour of Party tasks (Lin 2007) and encroach heavily on the 'agenda-setting' process from within (Xiang 2017).

40 'Notice of the Ministry of Civil Affairs on Adding Content Pertaining to Party Building and Socialist Core Values to the Charters of Social Organisations' (民政部关于在社会组织章程增加党的建设和社会主义核心价值观有关内容的通知), 28 April 2018, www.pkulaw.com/chl/7d7500bef3791d8ebdfb.html.

Unfortunately, early evidence suggests that Party-building requirements are rapidly instituting isomorphism across a once highly varied and heterogenous field, thereby 'hollowing-out' the sector as a whole (Nie and Wu 2022). The growing presence and visibility of internal Party groups in national-level professional associations, like the CICPA, as well as in high international profile entities like the Big Four accountancies, is raising serious questions about the reliability and quality of China-based firms, and therefore eroding the confidence of foreign investors. The narrowly averted delisting of some of China's largest and most lucrative firms from US stock exchanges may only serve to delay, rather than reverse, a deeper process of economic decoupling that is already underway.

These are worrying signs as Xi embarks on his third term in power. As early as 2016, Ross and Bekkevold warned that the 'most fundamental contradiction' underpinning Xi's style of governance was that 'between the interests of the Chinese Communist Party and the Chinese state'. They predicted that the Party's increasing reliance on confrontational and nationalistic policies would produce 'increasingly uncertain prospects' that could undermine the fundamental interests of the state in furthering economic trade, cooperation and development (Ross and Bekkevold 2016, 277–8). If such trends continue, it is difficult to envision how Xi might conceivably deliver on his initial promise of the 'China Dream'.

References

Bu, Qingxiu. 2021. 'The Anatomy of Holding Foreign Companies Accountable Act (HFCAA): A Panacea or a Double-Edge Sword?' *Capital Markets Law Journal* 16 (4): 503–27. doi.org/10.1093/cmlj/kmab022.

Chen, Jiaxi (陈家喜). 2012. 'Party-Building in China's New Social Organisations: Models, Difficulties and Directions' (我国新社会组织党建:模式、困境与方向). *Journal of the CCP Central Party School* 16 (4): 36–40.

Chen, Yizi. 1995. 'The Decision Process behind the 1986–1989 Political Reforms'. In *Decision-Making in Deng's China*, edited by Carol Lee Hamrin and Suisheng Zhao, 133–152. Abingdon: Routledge. doi.org/10.4324/9781315286617-12.

Chen, Yun (陈韵). 2017. 'Realistic Dilemmas of Building Party Branches in Social Organisations and Ways Forward' (社会组织党建的现实困境及其彼解路径). *Party and Government Forum* 1: 20–2.

Chen, Yung-fa. 1986. *Making Revolution: The Communist Movement in Eastern and Central China, 1937–1945*. Berkeley: University of California Press. doi.org/10.1525/9780520335707.

Cheng, Kunpeng (程坤鹏) and Xu Jialiang (徐家良). 2018. 'Structural Analysis of Party Building Leading Social Organisations in the New Era – Take S City as an Example' (新时期社会组织党建引领的结构性分析 – 以S市为例). *New Horizons* 2: 37–49.

Deng, Guosheng. 2010. 'The Hidden Rules Governing China's Unregistered NGOs: Management and Consequences'. *China Review* 10 (1): 183–206.

Dillon, Nara. 2011. 'Governing Civil Society: Adapting Revolutionary Methods to Serve Post-Communist Goals'. In *Mao's Invisible Hand: The Political Foundations of Adaptive Governance in China*, edited by Sebastian Heilmann and Elizabeth J. Perry, 138–64. Cambridge: Harvard University Asia Centre. doi.org/10.1163/9781684171163_006.

Froissart, Chloé. 2018. 'Changing Patterns of Chinese Civil Society: Comparing the Hu–Wen and Xi Jinping Eras'. In *Routledge Handbook of the Chinese Communist Party*, edited by Willy Wo-Lap Lam, 352–71. Abingdon: Routledge Press. doi.org/10.4324/9781315543918-22.

Howell, Jude. 2019. 'NGOs and Civil Society: The Politics of Crafting a Civic Welfare Infrastructure in the Hu–Wen Period'. *China Quarterly* 237: 58–81. doi.org/10.1017/S0305741018001236.

Huang, Long (黄龙). 2020. 'The Problem of the Party-State Relationship since the Founding of New China' (新中国成立以来我国党政关系问题). *Southern Journal*, 21–4.

Li, Jingpeng (李景鹏). 2005. 'Civil Society in the Post-Totalitarian Age' (后全能主义时代的公民社会). *China Reform* 11: 37.

Li, Ling and Wenzhang Zhou. 2019. 'Governing the Constitutional Vacuum: Federalism, Rule of Law and Politburo Politics in China'. *China Law and Society Review* 4.1: 1–40. doi.org/10.1163/25427466-00401001.

Li, Mingzhong (李明忠). 2016. 'Thoughts on Strengthening the Party Building Work in Social Organisations' (加强社会组织党建工作的思考). *Reform and Opening* 19: 120–2.

Li, Rui (李睿). 2017. 'Investigatory Report on Sichuan Social Organisation Development and Party-Building Work' (四川省社会组织发展及党建工作调研报告). *Chinese Social Organisations* 20: 24–6.

Li, Shuoyan (李朔严). 2018. 'The Power of Party Integration: The Development of Party, Political Capital and Grassroots NGOs Based on a Comparative Study of Multiple Cases in Z Province and H City' (政党统合的力量: 党、政治资本与草根NGO的发展 基于Z省H市的多案例比较研究). *Society* 1: 160–85.

Lin, Shangli (林尚立). 2007. 'Two Types of Social Construction: The Chinese Communist Party and NGOs' (两种社会建构: 中国共产党与非政府组织). *China Non-Profit Review* 1.

Ma, Qingyu (马庆钰). 2020. 'Key Issues Urgently Needed to Be Solved in the Decoupling Reform of Trade Associations Administrative Management Reform' (行业协会商会脱钩改革急需解决的关键问题). *Administration Reform* 12: 36–42.

Ma, Qiusha. 2002. 'Defining Chinese Nongovernmental Organisations'. *VOLUNTAS: International Journal of Voluntary and Nonprofit Organisations* 13: 113–30. doi.org/10.1023/A:1016051604920.

Nevitt, Christopher Earle. 1996. 'Private Business Associations in China: Evidence of Civil Society or Local State Power?' *China Journal* 36: 25–43. doi.org/10.2307/2950371.

Nie, Lin, and Jie Wu. 2022. 'Strategic Responses of NGOs to the New Party-Building Campaign in China'. *China Information* 36 (1): 46–67 doi.org/10.1177/0920203X21995705.

Pearson, Margaret. 1994. 'The Janus Face of Business Associations in China: Socialist Corporatism in Foreign Enterprises'. *Australian Journal of Chinese Affairs*, 31 January: 25–36. doi.org/10.2307/2949899.

Ross, Robert S. and Jo Inge Bekkevold. 2016. 'Conclusion: New Leaders, Stronger China, Harder Choices'. In *China in the Era of Xi Jinping: Domestic and Foreign Policy Challenges*, edited by Robert S. Ross and Jo Inge Bekkevold, 659–93. Washington: Georgetown University Press.

Shen, Yongdong, Jianxing Yu and Jun Zhou. 2020. 'The Administration's Retreat and the Party's Advance in the New Era of Xi Jinping: The Politics of the Ruling Party, the Government, and Associations in China'. *Journal of Chinese Political Science* 25 (1): 71–88. doi.org/10.1007/s11366-019-09648-5.

Snape, Holly. 2021. 'Cultivate Aridity and Deprive Them of Air: Altering the Approach to Non-State-Approved Social Organisations'. *Made in China* 6 (1): 54–9. doi.org/10.22459/MIC.06.01.2021.06.

Snape, Holly and Weinan Wang. 2020. 'Finding a Place for the Party: Debunking the "Party-State" and Rethinking the State-Society Relationship in China's One-Party System'. *Journal of Chinese Governance*. doi.org/10.1080/23812346.2020.1796411.

Spires, Anthony J. 2011. 'Contingent Symbiosis and Civil Society in an Authoritarian State: Understanding the Survival of China's Grassroots NGOs'. *American Journal of Sociology* 117 (1): 1–45. doi.org/10.1086/660741.

Sun, Weilin, ed. (孙伟林). 2009. *The Management of Social Organisations* (社会组织管理). Beijing: Zhongguo shehui chubanshe.

Teets, Jessica C. 2013. 'Let Many Civil Societies Bloom: The Rise of Consultative Authoritarianism in China'. *China Quarterly* 213: 19–38. doi.org/10.1017/S0305741012001269.

Teets, Jessica C. and Oscar Almen. 2018. 'Advocacy under Xi: NPO Strategies to Influence Policy Change'. *Nonprofit Policy Forum*. doi.org/10.1515/npf-2017-0028.

Thornton, Patricia M. 2012. 'The New Life of the Party: Party-Building and Social Engineering in Greater Shanghai'. *China Journal* 68: 58–78. doi.org/10.1086/666580.

Thornton, Patricia M. 2013. 'The Advance of the Party: Transformation or Takeover of Urban Grassroots Society?' *China Quarterly*, 1–18. doi.org/10.1017/S0305741013000039.

Trevaskes, Susan. 2017. 'Weaponising the Rule of Law in China'. In *Justice: The China Experience*, edited by Flora Sapio, Susan Trevaskes, Sarah Biddulph and Elisa Nesossi, 113–40. Cambridge: Cambridge University Press. doi.org/10.1017/9781108115919.005.

Unger, Jonathan. 1996. 'Bridges: Private Business, the Chinese Government and the Rise of New Associations'. *China Quarterly* 147: 795–819. doi.org/10.1017/S0305741000051808.

Wang, Yang (王杨). 2017. 'Realizing the Functional Mechanism of Party Organisations Embedded in Social Organisations from the Perspective of Structural Functionalism: A Case Study of Party Building in Social Organisations' (结构功能主义视角下党组织嵌入社会组织的功能实现机制 – 对社会组织党建的个案研究). *Socialism Studies* 2: 119–26.

Wen, Wenjun, Christopher Humphrey and Amanda Sonnerfeldt. 2021. 'The Strategic Significance of the CICPA in the Making of a Chinese Home-Grown Public Accounting Profession'. *Accounting and Business Research*. doi.org/10.1080/00014788.2021.1935684.

White, Gordon, Jude Howell and Shang Xiaoyuan. 1996. *In Search of Civil Society: Market Reform and Social Change in Contemporary China*. Oxford: Oxford University Press.

Wu, Guoguang. 1995. '"Documentary Politics": Hypotheses, Process, and Case Studies'. In *Decision-Making in Deng's China*, edited by Carol Lee Hamrin and Suisheng Zhao, 24–38. Abingdon: Routledge. doi.org/10.4324/9781315286617-3.

Xiang, Chunling (向春玲). 2017. 'Some Thoughts on Innovative Party Building in Social Organisations' (关于社会组织党建创新的几点思考). *Scientific Socialism* 3: 69–73.

Xie, Haiding (谢海定). 2004. 'The Legitimacy Problems of China's Citizens' Organisations' (中国民间组织的合法性困境). *Legal Research* 2: 17–34.

Xu, Yushan (徐宇珊). 2017. 'Rigid Embedding and Flexible Integration: Exploration of the Party Building Work Path of Social Organisations – Taking the Party Building Work of Social Organisations in Shenzhen as an Example' (刚性嵌入与柔性融入: 社会组织党建工作路径探索—以深圳市社会组织党建工作为例). *Journal of the Fujian Provincial Committee CCP Party School* 4: 47–53.

Yan, Dong. (2007). 'The Relationship between CCP and NGOs during China's Reform Era' (改革开放以来中国共产党与民间组织的关系). *Modern China Studies* 14, no. 3. www.modernchinastudies.org/us/issues/past-issues/97-mcs-2007-issue-3/1020-2012-01-05-15-35-22.html.

Yang, Xiaowei (阳晓伟) and Hu Shasha (胡莎莎). 2018. 'The Difficulties Faced in Party-Building Work in Social Organisations, and Policy Solutions' (社会组织党建工作面临的困境与破解之策). *Ningbo Economy* 6: 46–8.

Zhang, Xuebo (张学博). 2017. 'Observing the History of "Rule by Document": 1982–2017' (文件治国的历史观察: 1982–2017). *Academe* 9: 224–31.

Zhao, Xiaocui (赵晓翠) and Zhou Jun (周俊). 2020. 'The Process Model of the Organisational Transformation of the Trade Association and Chamber of Commerce in the New Type of Political-Member Relationship' (新型政会关系中行业协会商会组织转型的过程模型). *Governance Review* 36 (1): 33–42.

Zheng, Shiping. 1997. *Party vs. State in Post-1949 China: The Institutional Dilemma*. Cambridge Cambridge University Press.

Zhu, Ganwei (竺乾威). 2019. 'Government Structure and the Party-State Relationship' (政府结构与党政关系). *Ji'nan Xuebao* 246: 30–6.

3

The Chinese Communist Party as a Global Force

Frank N. Pieke[1]

Introduction: Beyond Soft, Hard and Sharp Power

Interest in and concern over Chinese influence abroad have grown exponentially in recent years. The greater significance of China is a matter of much more than the growth of its economy. Under President Xi Jinping (习近平), the country is emerging as a superpower with global ambitions and a rapidly escalating rivalry with the United States. In this new geopolitical climate, facts or suspicions of Chinese influence or even interference abroad feature very prominently. In these discussions, the whole gamut of influence, interference and even sabotage is often lumped together. Chinese 'soft power', 'public diplomacy' (e.g. Confucius Institutes, Chinese cultural centres, support for Chinese-language media) and the activities and expressions of Chinese embassies and diplomats are certainly not always innocent. However, they are of a different order than the

1 I am very grateful to Nána de Graaff and to the research assistants who helped me collect and make sense of the materials that this article is based on. Due to the (at times) sensitive nature of the topic, the research assistants must remain anonymous. I would also like to acknowledge the support of the East Asian Institute in Singapore, the Leiden Asia Centre and the China Knowledge Network in the Netherlands, and the Swedish Collegium for Advanced Study in Uppsala. I am also grateful to Michael Watts, André Gerrits, Jérôme Doyon and Chloé Froissart who read and commented on drafts, and to the participants at the conferences or seminars in France, Sweden, the Netherlands and Singapore where this paper was presented.

genuinely disruptive activities that China engages in, such as disinformation ('fake news') campaigns, cyberattacks, bribery or threats against politicians, espionage, and the theft of civil, military or 'dual use' technology.

The concept of soft power in international relations was developed as the opposite and counterpart of hard power (Nye 2004). The latter involves methods to coerce foreign actors to submit to a country's wishes – against their will if necessary. By contrast, the original thrust of the concept of soft power focused on the influence of culture, values and contact in positively shaping opinions and attitudes regarding a country. However, when the Chinese authorities discovered this American concept of soft power in the early 2000s, they made it an instrument of statecraft and public diplomacy: the party-state develops the narratives, dominates and directs the actors involved, and attempts to control the content and flow of information. This approach is intended to enable China to develop and transmit long-term, well-coordinated and comprehensive public diplomacy policies and unified messages (Cao and Zhao 2013; d'Hooghe 2014).

More recently, in the context of the alarmist debate on Chinese influencing, the concept of 'sharp power' has come into vogue. Sharp power occupies the space between soft and hard power, referring to activities aimed at 'piercing, penetrating or perforating the political and information environments in targeted countries' (Walker and Ludwig 2017, 13). Even more than soft power, Chinese sharp power is state-driven, seeking to exploit the openness and free flow of information in democratic countries to abuse and even undermine the target country's values and policies (Benner et al. 2018; Brady 2017; Diamond and Schell 2018; Joske 2020; Sahlins 2015).

Presenting China's growing international impact as influence, influencing and interference abroad frames its rise as a disruptive force, and implicitly or even explicitly in breach of the international order and rules. Such a representation fails to recognise that the rise of any major power will, to a greater or lesser degree, upset the apple cart, and that the behaviour of such a disruptive new power to a large extent mirrors that of other major powers that came before it. British colonialism in the nineteenth century and American hegemony in the twentieth and twenty-first centuries were also violently disruptive. Britain and the US only came to be seen as bearers of the legitimate world order *after* they had set the rules and created the institutions that other, lesser powers had to live by.

This chapter is intended as a small contribution towards viewing the changing world order from a Chinese rather than an American, or more broadly Western (including Australia and New Zealand), perspective. Other countries may see certain of China's actions as examples of its unwillingness to play by the rules, but these same actions often look very different when viewed from a Chinese perspective. Focusing on a hugely important aspect of China's global impact that the Chinese Communist Party (CCP) calls its 'organisational capacity' (*zuzhili,* 组织力), and what I call its *organising power*, I will show that the CCP does not simply seek to disrupt and meddle in other countries' affairs, but to create enclaves abroad that are drawn back into China's own system. The CCP as a global force is not simply destructive; rather, it intends to remould the world to its own image. I argue that denunciations of Chinese influencing and interference largely miss (or dismiss) this point, and, as a result, only see China as a force that has to be resisted, contained and, if possible, rolled back. Instead, other powers are well advised to try to make smart decisions – while it is still possible – about how to direct and shape this emerging reality in ways that serve their interests and minimise the damage.

Rather than being a part of the CCP's foreign influencing or interference strategy, the CCP's overseas organisational power is driven principally to counter the dangers of what Ruben Gonzalez has termed the 'decentred internationalization of the Chinese state'– that is, processes of localisation of Chinese state agents under the impact of China's global footprint and interests (Gonzalez-Vicente 2011: 403; see also Hameiri and Jones 2016).

As Chinese actors are increasingly present abroad, and as China constitutes a growing slice of the world economy, the CCP is confronted with challenges compelling it to extend the reach of its system abroad. The global reach of the CCP's own organisation is not a devious plan to rule the world or make the world socialist, Chinese or both. It is an evolving response to, and aspect of, the requirements of the specific pattern of 'Chinese globalisation' and China's emerging superpower role that quite literally and naturally makes the world more Chinese, just as, in the twentieth century, US hegemony made the world more American. For the CCP, China's role in the world no longer provides incentives for convergence to liberal norms and institutions. Instead, the impact of its globalisation and superpower pulls China away from them, strengthening its own 'neo-socialist' order not only domestically but also, as we will see in this chapter, abroad (Pieke 2016; see also Economy 2018; McGregor 2019).

The extension of the CCP's organisational power is very different from earlier efforts to export Maoist ideology and revolution. This was most obviously the case during the Korean War in the early 1950s, in Vietnam in the 1960s and 1970s, and in Cambodia after the Vietnamese invasion in 1978. The CCP also materially supported Communist movements in Malaysia, Burma and Indonesia, and was a source of inspiration and ideological and strategic guidance for revolutionary movements across the world. Leaders of India's Naxalites and Peru's Shining Path, for instance, visited China and often stayed for extended periods of training (Cook 2014; Lovell 2019).

Overseas Party-building is also different from the established foreign practices of the CCP's United Front Work Department (*Tongyi zhanzheng gongzuo bu*, *Tongzhan bu* 统一战争工作部、统战部) and International Liaison Department (*Duiwai lianluo bu* 对外联络部). The United Front Department's responsibility for Chinese people overseas makes it a vital plank for China's access to the capital and knowhow of foreign countries and markets (Groot 2004; Sapio 2019). More recently, united front work has become more pervasive both in China itself and among overseas Chinese communities, emphasising not just alliance and support, but insisting on the unity of the Chinese nation, loyalty to China and support for China's system, model and politics (Pieke 2021).

The Party's International Liaison Department, now more commonly referred to as the International Department, focuses on relations with foreign political parties and elites across the political spectrum. Under Xi Jinping, the department has further stepped up its work, for instance by organising major events in Beijing where members of the Politburo or even Xi Jinping himself have met with foreign delegates. The department is particularly active in Belt and Road countries, where its global goodwill strategy is complemented by the active dissemination of the experience and governance model of the CCP. This effort is not limited to countries ruled by an autocratic party, but also includes democracies or nominal democracies like Malaysia, South Africa, Fiji and Uganda. Together with these countries, the International Department coordinates training courses, visits and other exchange events. In 2022, the CCP and six sister parties in southern Africa opened the Mwalimu Julius Nyerere Leadership School where members of foreign partner parties are taught the CCP's organisation, Party-building, discipline inspection, and, more generally, about China's model of governance and development (on the International

Liaison Department, see Brady 2003; Eisenman and Heginbotham 2020, 302–3; Hackenesch and Bader 2020; Lovell 2019; Ngeow 2017, 2020; Shambaugh 2007).[2]

Recently, the United Front Department has taken on increasingly direct responsibility for China's foreign influencing strategy as part of its overseas Chinese work (Joske 2020). In speeches given in 2015 and 2016, Xi explicitly connected the overseas Chinese work of the united front with his Belt and Road Initiative. Moreover, Xi Jinping imagines the overseas role of the United Front Department to be complementary to the work of the International Department (Sapio 2019).

However, overseas Party-building work takes place quite separately from the United Front and International departments, and is best seen as an open-ended process rooted in the domestic organisational practices of the Party. The logic behind this process is pretty consistent and driven by a combination of established Leninist principles and the CCP's view of its leading role in Chinese politics and society (Koss 2021a).

The research for this chapter consists of a systematic search of Chinese-language academic literature and other Chinese written sources (e.g. CNKI Chinese-language publications database, Chinese media databases, policy documents, blogs, reports and other documents on WeChat official accounts).[3] In 2020 and 2021, Nána de Graaff of the Free University in Amsterdam and I carried out interviews with Chinese-invested enterprises in the Netherlands in which we also asked about Party influence and Party-building work (Pieke and De Graaff 2022).

WeChat official accounts have unique added value. Managed by media outlets, academic institutions, governmental bodies and companies, their content is specifically targeted at subscribers rather than the general public. We found numerous sources on Party-building overseas on such accounts

2 The observations on the department's conferencing activities in Beijing under Xi Jinping are based on my own experiences at these events in Beijing between 2014 and 2017. See also Qian Hongshan, 'Deeply Comprehend Xi Jinping's Diplomatic Thought and Create a New Situation for the Party's Foreign Work in the New Era' (深刻领悟习近平外交思想开创新时代党的对外工作新局面), *Xuexi shibao*, 24 August 2022, cn.chinadiplomacy.org.cn/2022-08/24/content_78386423.shtml. The latter is one of my sources on the department's promotion of China's model and experience. On the Nyerere School, see 'Mwalimu Julius Nyerere Leadership School Holds This Year's Seminar for Middle-Aged and Young Cadres of Six Parties in Southern Africa', 25 May 2022, www.idcpc.org.cn/english/news/202205/t20220527_149032.html. It is at present quite unclear exactly what this academy actually entails and whether it has any material presence and location beyond a website and events.

3 All WeChat postings used for this article have been archived and are available upon request.

maintained by Chinese state-owned enterprises (SOEs) that were intended for the use of Party members among their employees or as references for career Party members from their or other companies or organisations. WeChat official accounts provide information on Party-building considered inappropriate for the general public, which turned out to be invaluable for this research.

Our research used the Sogou WeChat (*sougou weixin* 搜狗微信) search engine to perform systematic searches of WeChat official accounts. We started our search using general terms such as '国外党建' (*guowai dangjian* Party-building abroad) and '海外党建' (*haiwai dangjian*, Party-building overseas). Then, narrowing down further, we continued with more specific searches focusing on two categories: 1) specific means and ways of Party-building overseas ('互联网+' (*hulianwangjia*, internet+), '海外党建6+1' (*haiwai dangjian 6+1*, overseas Party-building 6+1), '企业文化' (*qiye wenhua*, corporate culture)); 2) large SOEs that emerged as advanced examples of Party-building overseas, such as Sinopec or the China State Construction Engineering Corporation.

Many of the sources we used were written by Party cadres from SOEs abroad and almost certainly overstate the extent and successes of overseas Party work. Their authors have an obvious incentive to boast of their successes and hide their failures. However, we also found some publications based on Chinese publicly funded academic research projects on overseas Party-building. Much less bullish, these served as an important corrective (Feng 2020; Guo and Sun 2011a, 2011b; Ma 2017).

In addition, we also reviewed recent versions of the CCP Constitution, and general Party regulations, directives and guiding opinions related to Party-building, especially from the Central Organisation Department (*Zhongyang zuzhi bu* 中央组织部), to uncover the development and current trends of Party-building, both domestically and abroad.

Organising Power: Building the CCP Abroad

In 2017, Western media exposed the presence of a number of CCP 'cells' (branches) at universities abroad.[4] Surprisingly, some Chinese newspapers also openly reported on this.[5] The immediate consequence of these 'revelations' was simply that the CCP stopped publicising overseas Party work without any intention of actually putting an end to it. Nevertheless, in the Chinese literature, it is still not difficult to find ample evidence of the continued existence of active Party branches at foreign universities. In particular, Chinese universities with many student exchanges abroad often set up temporary Party branches among their students at foreign universities.[6]

According to Guo and Sun (2011b), Party-building work among Chinese students abroad goes back to at least 2006, when Beijing Union University (*Beijing lianhe daxue* 北京联合大学) established a Party branch for the 12 Party members among its students who went to study at the University of Paisley (now the Paisley Campus of the University of West Scotland). In 2011, such 'basic party organisations' had already been established at more than 10 other colleges and universities overseas.

Foreign Party branches among Chinese students function, to a large extent, using what is called the 'internet+' (*hulianwangjia*, 互联网+) method, which includes the use of social media, online meetings, and online teaching materials and courses. It remains an open question whether this kind of Party work among students has much substance. Guo and Sun's (2011) research of a (small) sample of Party members among returned students in the Nanjing area showed that, even where overseas Party branches existed, daily Party organisational work almost never took place. Only 22 per cent of their respondents reported that their Party branch had relatively strong 'cohesion and charisma' (*ningjuli he ganzhaoli* 凝聚力和感召力; Guo and Sun 2011a, 2011b; see also Feng 2020). Conversely, it must be said that, for

4 Bethany Allen-Ebrahemian, 'The Chinese Communist Party Is Setting Up Cells at Universities across America', *Foreign Policy*, 18 April 2017, foreignpolicy.com/2018/04/18/the-chinese-communist-party-is-setting-up-cells-at-universities-across-america-china-students-beijing-surveillance/.

5 Zhang Yu, 'CPC Members Encounter Obstacles While Trying to Establish Party Branches Overseas', *Global Times*, 28 November 2017, www.globaltimes.cn/content/1077619.shtml (site discontinued).

6 'The Overseas Party Branch at Our College Held a Summary Meeting in Its Work' (我院海外党支部举行工作总结), Tongji University School of Architecture and Urban Planning Graduate Network, 1 December 2018, gs-caup.tongji.edu.cn/9a/eb/c11126a105195/page.htm.

an institution such as the University of Defence Technology (*guofang keji daxue* 国防科技大学), Party branches help to ensure that travelling students return to China with the knowledge they have acquired (Joske 2018).[7]

The concept of Party-building (*dang de jianshe* 党的建设, *dangjian* 党建) is inherently political and strategic. In his 1939 essay 'Introducing *The Communist*', Mao Zedong (毛泽东) called for building a 'Bolshevised Chinese Communist Party which is national in scale, has a broad mass character, and is fully consolidated ideologically, politically and organisationally' (Mao [1939] 1967: 285).[8] As one of the CCP's three 'magic weapons' (*san da fabao* 三大法宝) for defeating the enemy in the Chinese Revolution, Party-building is the process by which the mass of Party members and cadres is transformed into a tool of the revolution.

In 1988, a Central Party-Building Work Leading Group (*Zhongyang dang de jianshe gongzuo lingdao xiaozu*, 中央党的建设工作领导小组) of the Politburo was established. Two of the deputy leaders of the leading group were the heads of the Central Discipline Inspection Commission (*Zhongyang jilü jiancha weiyuanhui* 中央纪律检查委员会) and the Central Organisation Department. The importance of this work is evidenced by the fact that both Hu Jintao (胡锦涛) and, later, Xi Jinping acted as head of the leading group in the years immediately preceding their elevation to CCP general secretary, the highest office in the land.[9]

Party-building refers to self-improvement activities undertaken to maintain what the Party considers to be its own unique nature. Party-building includes the full range of propaganda, education and training, organisational work, discipline inspection, mass organisations and united front work.[10] Party-building also involves teaching, research and theory building, and is even a discipline at Party schools throughout the country.

7 Wang Huowen 王握文, 'National University of Defence Technology Has Established an Overseas Party Branch among Foreign Students' (国防科技大学在留学人员中设立海外党支部), *Jiefangjun bao*, 10 May 2013, dangjian.people.com.cn/n/2013/0510/c117092-21439870.html.

8 In Mao's reinterpretation, Bolshevisation was equated with ideological and political conformity to the centre and strict Leninist organisational principles, which ultimately translated into the Yan'an Rectification Campaign of 1942–44 (Benton 1996).

9 See, for example, Xi Jinping 'Advancing the Great New Project of Party Building Must Be Consistent' (推进党的建设新的伟大工程要一以贯之), speech given on 5 January 2018, *Qiushi* (求实), 2 October 2019, cpc.people.com.cn/n1/2019/1002/c64094-31383736.html.

10 These principles are laid down in the general section of the CCP Constitution. See 'Constitution of the CCP' (中国共产党章程), partially revised at the Nineteenth CCP Party Congress on 24 October 2017, www.12371.cn/2017/10/28/ARTI1509191507150883.shtml.

Party-building specifically deals with the presence of the Party at the grassroots of society. Most importantly, Party work lifts the 'party spirit' (*dangxing* 党性) and strengthens 'party discipline' (*dangji* 党纪), thus aligning the Party's members and cadres with the methods, work style, vision, goals and ideology of the centre. Party-building operates at the nexus of the Party's external role and functions ('the work of the Party', *dang de gongzuo* 党的工作) on the one hand, and routine internal 'party affairs work' (*dangwu gongzuo* 党务工作) on the other. Party-building is how 'the Party must manage the Party' (*dang yao guan dang* 党要管党), bringing together ideology, organisation and political practice.[11] Party-building is, thus, where the Party becomes an instrument not just of governance, but also of political transformation in the pursuit of its ultimate goals and mission.

Over the past 15 years, Party-building efforts have been made to increase and strengthen the Party's presence across Chinese society (Li 2019; McGregor 2010; Shambaugh 2008; Thornton 2012; Thornton, Chapter 2, this volume). Xi Jinping has further accelerated this process, increasing the direct political and administrative role of the Party, strengthening its presence and grip on government, the army, the judicial system, civil society and business (Economy 2018; Grünberg and Drinhausen 2019; Koss 2021b; McGregor 2019; Yan and Huang 2017). A key aspect of this approach is the principle of 'strictly governing the Party' (*cong yan zhi dang* 从严治党) in order to enhance the 'organisational capacity' (*zuzhili* 组织力) of the Party's branches, strengthen the political function of branches and develop their role as a 'battle fortress' (*zhandou baolei* 战斗堡垒) in the consolidation of the Party's long-term governance.[12]

The same principle and approach apply overseas. China's increasing globalisation presents a number of particular challenges to the Party's ambition to strengthen its grip. This includes not only the presence and activation of Party members within foreign organisations and companies present in China itself, an issue that recently has vexed a great many commentators on China,[13] but also necessitates the management of Party members residing outside China. The number of Chinese students abroad

11 'How to Distinguish between Party Affairs Work, Party Work, and Party Building' (如何区分党务工作、党的工作、党的建设), CCP Members Net (共产党员网), 25 December 2018, www.12371.cn/2018/12/25/ARTI1545723916215501.shtml.

12 'Trial Regulations for the CCP Branch Work' (中国共产党支部工作条例(试行)), promulgated in October 2018, www.cjh.com.cn/article_2086_222091.html.

13 For instance, 'Major Leak "Exposes" Members and "Lifts the Lid" on the Chinese Communist Party', *Sky News Australia,* 13 December 2020, www.skynews.com.au/details/_6215946537001.

has increased rapidly. State-owned institutions and companies increasingly have projects or investments outside China and send large numbers of their staff abroad. Recruitment agencies often send large groups of Chinese workers abroad on temporary contracts. In all these cases, Party members are among them.

Party-building work explicitly concerns members who, in principle, temporarily go abroad and not those who have emigrated permanently. The latter have to give up their membership or at least deactivate membership of their original branch in China, after which they become subject to the Party's overseas Chinese policies run by the United Front Department. Party work abroad focuses particularly on members who work abroad for SOEs or large projects, and Chinese students on government scholarships and university programs or exchanges. There is, at present, little mention of Party work among those who have gone abroad under their own steam – that is, self-funded students and private businesspeople. However, private enterprises and their subsidiaries abroad have already been included in the CCP's Party-building drive. In my most recent research on Party-building in the Netherlands and elsewhere in Europe, I have found evidence that, since 2017, some of China's larger private enterprises have been compelled to both commit to Party-building abroad and to work with representatives of the Ministry of Commerce at Chinese embassies and consulates to promote Party-building among other Chinese enterprises abroad (Pieke and De Graaff 2022, ch. 6).

In the Chinese literature, the focus on Party work abroad is presented as following from the requirements of China's 'system'. SOEs and state-coordinated projects are seen as foreign extensions of China's domestic economy and society and are, therefore, 'part of the system' (*tizhinei* 体制内) of the Party and the state, in which the private sector is increasingly incorporated as well. An article on building branches posted on the CCP members' website (*gongchandangyuan wang* 共产党员网) formulated this as follows:

> Although there are particularities in overseas party-building work, it is not treated differently (*jingwai dangjian gongzuo sui you teshuxing, dan wu teshuhua* 境外党建工作虽有特殊性、但无特殊化). Strengthening party building in overseas institutions of Chinese-

> funded enterprises is an inevitable requirement for promoting the institutionalisation and standardisation of overseas party-building work.[14]

Among Chinese-invested companies, the CCP's explicit goal is to achieve 'full coverage' (*quan fugai* 全覆盖) and 'no exception abroad' (*haiwai wu liwai* 海外无例外) to Party-building work.[15] During our research in the Netherlands in 2022, De Graaff and I found references to a commitment to overseas Party-building work for one-third (18 of 54) of the companies that were members of ACIEN, the most important Chinese business association in the country. Most, but not all, of these companies were state-owned or formerly state-owned, showing that foreign Party-building has indeed started to enter the privately owned sector (Pieke and De Graaff 2022, ch. 6).

The Ministry of Commerce plays an important role in foreign Party-building among Chinese-invested enterprises abroad. The ministry does so directly through its foreign trade and investment sections at Chinese embassies and consulates, and indirectly through organisations associated with it, in particular, the China Council for the Promotion of International Trade and the China Chamber of International Commerce. In those countries where it has an office or is otherwise active, the China Council for the Promotion of International Trade is responsible for facilitating the setting up of associations of Chinese enterprises and may even serve as a member of the management board of such organisations. Its work with such associations includes Party-building among firms that are members of particular associations (Pieke and De Graaff 2022, ch. 6).

In foreign contexts, the normal separation in China itself of Party leadership from operational leadership is often impractical. Abroad, a Party committee normally assumes direct operational responsibility, with the leader of a project or unit also acting as its Party secretary, although, in some large SOEs, career Party cadres are also stationed abroad. The Party committee leadership ensures the implementation of the decisions and requirements of the Party committee of the company headquarters.

---

14 Liu Xinjun (柳新军), 'Exploration and Practice of Overseas Grassroots Party Building Work – Taking the Kazakhstan Company of Sinopec International Petroleum Exploration and Development Co., Ltd. as an Example' (境外基层党建工作的探索与实践 – 以中国石化集团国际石油勘探开发有限公司哈萨克斯坦公司为例), CCP Members Net, 12 June 2018, news.12371.cn/2018/06/12/ARTI1528785322774381.shtml.

15 'Strengthen the Supervision of Overseas Institutions of Central-Level SOEs: There Is No Overseas Exception for the Management of the Party' (加强央企境外机构监督：管党治党海外无例外), *Renminwang*, 13 September 2018, news.12371.cn/2015/03/12/ARTI1426131063462262.shtml.

Party members abroad will, in principle, remain members of the Party committee to which they belong in China. The committees of universities and companies are required to involve their members abroad as far as possible in their activities and, if possible, to organise activities abroad for them. In addition, members abroad must also remain locally involved in the Party. In theory, the Party committee of the local Chinese embassy or consulate is responsible for the members among the students and employees of companies and institutions. For workers sent abroad by recruitment agencies, the Party committee of the agency's foreign representation is responsible for the members among them.[16]

In practice, these arrangements that date from 1984 do not appear to work properly. The great distance from China makes it very difficult for Party committees in China to involve their members abroad in their activities taking place in China. The Party committees of embassies and consulates often lack the necessary staff and, perhaps, also the incentive to keep in touch with members dispersed throughout their jurisdiction.

Party organisations often fail to adapt to the very different circumstances abroad, and as a result they atrophy. Due to frequent cross-border rotation, it is difficult to carry out Party member education or build branches systematically. In addition, members are affected by a 'different social and cultural environment, resulting in different ways of living, thinking, and values' (Jiang 2019).

From the Party's point of view, there are a number of major problems with this. Without an active connection to a local branch, 'only those party members with strong ideals and beliefs can resist the temptation' of the 'sugar-coated bullets' (*tangyi paodan* 糖衣炮弹) of a Western lifestyle and 'international hostile forces'.[17] With the erosion of Party spirit and Party discipline, the Party is in danger of losing control of its own members. This can also be a problem for the members themselves. Party members who have to reactivate membership in their branch upon returning to China have been put behind by their time abroad. As a result, their careers and further development as Party members might suffer (Feng 2020).

16 'Notification from the Organisation Department of the CCP Central Committee on Measures to Improve the Organisation Relations of Party Members among Students and Workers Transferred Abroad (Organisation Department Document 1984 no. 15)' (中共中央组织部关于改进接转出国留学、劳务人员中党员组织关系办法的通知(组通字〔1984〕15号), 1984, lxy.usst.edu.cn/_t86/2018/0424/c2330a40229/page.htm.

17 'Sugar-coated bullets' is a CCP phrase that was used in the early 1950s during the Three-Anti and Five-Anti Campaigns that targeted party members who had been corrupted by capitalist influences.

To ensure that the Party does not lose control of its members abroad, other, more recent regulations or opinions have appeared that also refer to overseas Party work. The more general regulations on Party organisation in SOEs of 2004 include the observation that:

> enterprises stationed abroad must establish party organisations and carry out party work in accordance with the number of party members, the local environment, and the actual situation of the enterprise, and *the requirements of flexibility, simplicity, safety and confidentiality*.[18]

A genuine increase in the emphasis on overseas Party work happened in 2016 with the issuance of a 'leading opinion' (*zhidao yijian* 指导意见) specifically on Party work among central enterprises abroad. Although this opinion has remained confidential, we have been able to piece together its gist from some of the articles that we have read.[19]

According to the Chinese literature, the opinion was issued to incorporate new models and methods of Party-building abroad that were already being experimented with. For example, the opinion authorises setting up a network of regional Party branches for which the Party committee of the local establishment of a large Chinese SOE is then responsible and takes on the coordination. This reduces the pressure on the staff of the local embassy and makes it possible to organise Party members dispersed across institutions that do not themselves have a Party organisation (Qiang 2018).

According to the 2016 regulations, Party work abroad should be based on five principles. The first is 'upholding the general principle of the unwavering leadership of the Party' (*jianchi dang de lingdao bu dongyao yuanze* 坚持党的领导不动摇原则). This principle provides the ideological motivation and political guarantee that the achievements of the overseas development of SOEs and institutions serve the construction and development of the cause of socialism with Chinese characteristics (Liang 2019).

18 'Opinion of the Central Organisation Department and the Party Committee of the State-Owned Assets Supervision and Administration Commission of the State Council on Strengthening and Improving the Party-Building Work of Central Enterprises' (中央组织部、国务院国资委党委关于加强和改进中央企业党建工作的意见), 31 October 2004, article 22, www.fnlzw.gov.cn/showLaw.aspx?id=5479&fID=86&pid=73&lid=73 (emphasis added).

19 Reportedly, these regulations bear the crisp title 'Guiding Opinions of the Central Organisation Department, the Party Committee of the State-Owned Assets Supervision and Administration Commission of the State Council, the Party Committee of the Ministry of Foreign Affairs, and the Party Group of the Ministry of Commerce on Strengthening Party Building Work in Overseas Units of Central Enterprises' (中央组织部、国务院国资委党委、外交部党委、商务部党组关于加强中央企业境外单位党建工作的指导意见).

Overt Party activities are often not possible, especially in situations where, for example, employees of a Chinese company frequently work with non-Chinese colleagues. Moreover, many countries do not allow CCP activities. Covert Party activities are, therefore, often necessary, and methods based on the internet or social media must be used more than in China. Such activities take place on the basis of the second principle of overseas Party work, namely the 'principle of the "five non-disclosures"' (*'wu bu gongkai' yuanze* '五不公开'原则): non-disclosure of Party organisation, internal Party positions, Party member status, internal Party documents and internal Party activities in overseas Party-building activities. The five non-disclosures help overseas Party activities avoid 'local political, economic, cultural, and religious risks', and 'provide protection against the long-term and stable development of overseas party building' (Jiang 2019; Party Committee of China Electronics Import and Export 2018; Liang 2019).

In practice, the five non-disclosures mean that Party activities and discussion of Party work must never be held in the presence of foreign employees or visitors, nor should Party activities take place in public places outside the company premises and work sites. For the consumption of foreign employees and visitors, Party activities should be presented as a part of the company's 'corporate culture and team-building' (*qiye wenhua he tuandui jianshe* 企业文化和团队建设; Liang 2019).

The CCP is aware of the security issues that come with the internet, particularly in times of increased geopolitical rivalry.[20] Facebook, Twitter and other foreign social media should be avoided. Instead, the company's intranet and WeChat official account should be used. This has several other advantages, most importantly that their paperless nature facilitates compliance with the 'five non-disclosures'.[21] Further, foreign Party-building apps, such as *Haiwai dangjian 6+1* (海外党建6+1, overseas Party-building app 6+1), help the Party to monitor whether individual Party members complete their daily Party work tasks, such as reading recent Party documents.[22]

20 Gao Lei (高磊), '[Experience] Party Building 1+6' (【心得】党建1+6), posted on the Party Flag is Fluttering (党旗飘飘) WeChat account, 25 February 2019.

21 N.a., 'Case | Excellent Case of Sinopec's Grassroots Party-Building Work – Exploring the Implementation of Overseas "Party-Building +"'(案例 | 中国石化基层党建工作优秀案例 – 探索实施海外'党建+'工作模式), posted on the Sinopec (中国石化) WeChat account, 29 August 2017.

22 Li Helei (李贺雷), 'Highest Attention | Overseas Party-Building "6+1" Is Fully Launched! Let the Party Flag Fly on the "Belt and Road"!' (最关注 | 海外党建'6+1'全面启动! 让党旗在'一带一路'上飘扬!), posted on the China Construction Eighth Engineering Co. Ltd. (中建八局一公司) WeChat account, 27 May 2020.

Covert practices are by no means limited to the operations of Chinese SOEs abroad. Among Chinese students, too, Party activities are carried out under other guises to avoid arousing suspicion or even censure. A recent academic article on foreign Party-building among students abroad observes that, 'due to the special political environment overseas, some party members have kept "invisible" for a long time'. They:

> rely on international student organisations to integrate the training of party members into [other] activities, such as Chinese cultural promotion and exchanges, international volunteer work, speech contests, debate contests, etc. (Feng 2020, 98)

This is confirmed by the earlier research of Guo and Sun, who write that:

> grass-roots student party organisations (party branches or party groups) in foreign countries take into account the special and complex international environment of foreign countries when conducting activities. Most of them publicise, organise, and apply for venues and funds in the name of ordinary student associations. (Guo and Sun 2011a, 102)

The Party organisation of a SOE abroad is subject to the joint leadership of the Party committee of the headquarters of the company back in China and the Party committee of the Chinese embassy of the host country. This third 'dual-leadership principle' (*gongtong lingdao yuanze* 共同领导原则) stipulated in the 2016 confidential regulations goes back to 1984 (see note 19 above). The Party organisations of the headquarters back in China are responsible for the education, management and supervision of Party members and cadres abroad, and bear the costs of this and other Party-building work abroad. The Party committee of the embassy or consulate provides 'political guidance in view of China's foreign policies'. The embassy also carries out ideological and political work in case of 'special situations or emergencies' and facilitates exchanges on Party-building work with other locally present Chinese companies and units (Liang 2019).

The fourth principle of overseas Party work is 'the principle of focusing on the centre and serving the overall situation' (*weirao zhongxin, fuwu daju yuanze* 围绕中心、服务大局原则). This principle follows from article 33 of Chapter V of the CCP Constitution, which stipulates that the primary Party organisations in SOEs and collective enterprises shall carry out their work around the production and operation of enterprises. SOEs abroad face heavy responsibilities and high pressure in an even more complex market operation environment with higher risk than in China itself. Improving corporate efficiency, enhancing corporate competitiveness, and maintaining and increasing the value of state-owned assets are 'the starting point and the end point' of Party organisation work in enterprises abroad (Liang 2019).

The fifth and final principle of the 2016 regulations is the 'principle of adapting measures to local conditions and being pragmatic and efficient' (*yin di zhi yi, wushi gaoxiao yuanze* 因地制宜、务实高效原则). When Party organisations carry out Party-building work abroad, they should fully consider the actual situation and innovate Party organisation and member education and management methods, and, where needed, simplify operating procedures (Liang 2019).

The Party is concerned that the appeal of living abroad will alienate some of its members such that when they return to China they no longer prove reliable, and, moreover, that foreign operations should fit the overall plan and aims of the Party. The Party is well aware that Chinese companies and projects abroad have their own strategic objectives. If left unchecked, the Party believes that foreign operations will make Chinese companies increasingly global and less Chinese. Party-building and Party work in these companies and projects is intended to ensure that they do not stray too far from the plans of the CCP and its vision for the Chinese nation (Ma 2017).

Very interestingly, the final two principles of Party work abroad outlined above seem, at least partially, to negate this heavy-handed emphasis on politics and submission to the Party authorities back in China. They emphasise operational work, profitability and flexible adaption to local conditions. These two principles present Party work as a means of combating corruption and coordinating the activities of the Chinese embassy and other Chinese companies and institutions in a particular region. This is considered particularly important in less developed countries. Yet, even there, Party work is not intended as an instrument of interference in the affairs of other countries, but as a way to make Chinese companies and projects abroad more competitive and better run, operating according to the law and in tune with local circumstances (Ma 2017).

The importance of practical and operational considerations and the primacy of growing assets and making a profit is strongly borne out by the interviews with managers and directors of Chinese-invested firms that De Graaff and I conducted in the Netherlands. Our interviewees emphasised that commercial incentives and criteria (such as key performance indicators, annual targets, promotion opportunities and bonuses) guided the behaviour of company management. Strategies and control from the headquarters were repeatedly said to be issued predominantly or solely on that basis, rather than on the basis of any political or ideological considerations.

Nevertheless, SOEs and banks have one side that focuses on the business and another that focuses on the political; private companies, too, increasingly have to pay lip-service to politics. The tension in the 2016 regulations of political conformity and business success is visible in the incentives and behaviour of at least some SOEs and their Party committees. However, this duality mainly plays out at the corporate headquarters in China and does not concern the daily operational decisions of managers and directors of overseas subsidiaries. We have to conclude that, at least in the Netherlands, overseas Party-building is still very minimal and has, as yet, had little impact on strategy. Where Party-building happens, it mainly concerns the Party life of Party members themselves (Pieke and De Graaff 2022, chs 4, 6).

Overseas Party-Building in Practice

Party members abroad working together in a joint branch are often drawn from several different departments of a company or even from different companies. They, moreover, tend to travel frequently. Members of such a joint overseas branch participate in its study and education activities, but do not need to transfer their Party relationship to the overseas branch. Instead, the branch in their original unit conducts the management and evaluation of these members and collects their membership fee. This helps to organise members scattered over many projects and sites abroad without jeopardising the integrity of the CCP's organisation and its grip over its members.

Online Party work plays an essential role abroad. Some Party committees distribute e-readers to their members with updates of the CCP Constitution and Party-building classics. Through the use of Party-building information apps and WeChat official accounts, foreign grassroots branches get access to the latest developments in the Party and national policies.

In addition to these explicitly political and organisational goals, foreign Party-building work has three further operational goals: 1) keeping Chinese and foreign employees happy and in line; 2) enhancing the competitiveness and management of foreign operations and projects; and 3) presenting a positive image of the company and China to the outside world. The ways that these goals play out in practice are often highly diverse, and the connection with Party work is not necessarily instinctively obvious. Indeed, Party-building often seems to serve as a shorthand or index that points to all that is good and reassuring about China, its system and – increasingly – its culture.

Enterprise Party organisations enforce Party discipline and rules, in the process also reducing the financial risks of their own external operations and the possible loss of state-owned assets. Party branches conduct education and promotion of 'clean government' to fight corruption and excessive lifestyles.

The Party is also involved in labour relations and management. This includes disease and safety management in high-risk countries. One article even reports on mundane facilities for workers and staff as the Party's work:

> In order to enrich the lives of employees, the regional company's party committee has set up a staff food committee, life service station, fitness equipment room, leisure viewing room, shared book room, and a secretary's chat room. (Liang 2019)

Party work also caters for the emotional needs of homesick employees, providing them with more opportunities to be involved with China, their hometown and relatives.

The relevance of Party-building work extends far beyond the company or project and is presented as a magic wand to strengthen China's presence and impact abroad. Party work ensures that Chinese actors do not alienate foreign partners, governments or publics, creating a positive impression of China and Chinese enterprises among the local population (Gao 2020).

The composition of workers and staff on overseas projects is often very complex, with different cultures, beliefs and languages among local employees, high crime rates and conflicts between Chinese and local workers. In order to deal with these problems, Party work must focus on external relations, labour management and, more generally, on a 'good external environment'. By establishing effective leadership and organisation, the Party can ensure the 'smooth flow of internal government orders and orderly organisation' and promote 'the unity and vitality' of overseas employees within the enterprise. Corporate Party organisations can also build 'social and environmentally friendly corporate and community relationships' (Gao 2020: 139; see also Ma 2017).

Overseas Party work therefore explicitly concerns itself with China's larger aims in international politics, especially those that concern China's public diplomacy and soft power strategies. The key concept here is 'corporate culture' (*qiye wenhua* 企业文化). As 'the carrier of party-building work' (*dangjian gongzuo zaiti* 党建工作载体), corporate culture is presented as having 'the same effect as the Party's role in stabilising the team and uniting people and is an effective entry for party-building work to serve production and operation' (Liang 2019). Moreover, the label 'corporate culture' enables a Chinese company to carry out Party work overseas under the 'five non-disclosures' principle and avoid restrictions imposed by foreign governments on overt Party work (Zhang 2017).

Party-building as corporate culture is presented as an approach to tie Chinese and foreign employees together and to the company. Party work enhances the company's 'organising power' and is used 'as the core of team building' of Party members, Chinese employees and foreign employees (Party Committee of China Electronics Import and Export 2019).

This use of Party-building is largely apolitical, aiming to use the Party's organisational power to boost productivity. Concrete examples of how foreign employees are involved in Party work in Chinese companies are dumpling-making competitions, cultural and sports competitions, and other activities that enhance the integration of Chinese and foreign employees, such as regularly praising outstanding foreign employees and selecting foreign employees to visit or study in China.[23] Chinese companies now sometimes even give foreign employees the honorary title of 'excellent employee' (*youxiu yuangong* 优秀员工).[24]

Only in a very few cases is mention made of the recruitment of Party members abroad. In 2012, the CCP deputy secretary of the China Metallurgical Group Corporation Committee required the whole corporation to encourage outstanding overseas employees to join the CCP.[25]

23 N.a., 'Case | Excellent Case of Sinopec's Grassroots Party-Building Work – Exploring and Implementing the Overseas "Party-Building +" Work Model' (案例｜中国石化基层党建工作优秀案例—— 探索实施海外'党建+'工作模式), posted on the Sinopec party member WeChat account, 29 August 2019.

24 For instance, '10 Outstanding Foreign Employees Commended by China Communications Group' (10名优秀外籍员工获中交集团表彰), 13 January 2020, SIDC (State Development & Investment Corp. Ltd.), www.sdic.com.cn/cn/rmtzx/xwzx/gzdt/yqlb/webinfo/2020/01/1580474929071012.htm.

25 China Metallurgical Group Corporation 中冶集团, 'Guo Wenqing Presided over the Meeting of the Party Committee Oof Subordinate Agencies' (国文清主持召开机关党委会议), 21 June 2012, www.mcc.com.cn/mcc/_132154/_132564/183659/index.html.

At Shandong Luqiao Group, 16 people – presumably Chinese staff who had developed themselves overseas – were accepted as members of the CCP.[26] In Cambodia, the China Communications Construction Company's Third Harbour Engineering Co. accepted several probationary members to the CCP.[27] In the UK, Party committees at Chinese-invested firms sometimes attempt to recruit members among locally hired Chinese employees, but tend to concentrate their recruitment efforts on expatriate employees from China. Proving their worth and loyalty to the Party in the relative shelter of a foreign posting, these younger Party members are groomed for a future Party-led career at the headquarters or perhaps elsewhere in China (Makarchev et al. 2022).

Another area where Party work involves foreign employees is corporate social responsibility. Foreign employees have a better understanding of the local situation, and can help with the corporate social responsibility strategy of Chinese companies and projects overseas. Corporate social responsibility involves the image of Chinese companies and their Chinese 'brand'. Here, too, overseas Party work serves as a 'red engine' (*hongse yinqing* 红色引擎) that 'transforms the political advantage of party building into a development advantage of participating in world market competition', ensuring that this remains in tune with the objective of improving the image of Chinese companies abroad and the general thrust of China's soft power strategy (Wu 2020, 19).

One company, China Construction Bridge (中建桥梁), openly argues that:

> the project's party branch has infused the 'China Construction Bridge creed' with traditional Chinese culture, while at the same time taking into account the restricted and concealed nature of overseas party-building activities.[28]

This example also shows that the fusion of corporate culture and Party-building easily spills over into the use of the much broader concept of Chinese culture. Corporate culture is a vehicle 'to tell the Chinese story well'

26 Wu Yonggong (吴永功), 'How to Advance Party Building Overseas?' (海外项目党建怎么抓?), *Dazhong ribao*, 9 November 2020, www.163.com/dy/article/FR0FH7A20530WJTO.html.

27 China Communications Construction Company Third Harbor Engineering Co. (中交三航), 'Work Department of the Party Committee of Xing'anji Corporation' (兴安基公司党委工作部), 16 June 2020, mp.weixin.qq.com/s/L3-KmUGoRDttnT6b5_venQ.

28 China Construction Bridge (中建桥梁), '"Family" Culture Enhances the Hard Power of Overseas Party-Building ('家'文化提升海外党建硬实力), posted on the China Construction Bridge WeChat account, 23 November 2018.

(*jiang hao zhongguo gushi* 讲好中国故事) and persuade foreign employees and others abroad that 'the Chinese way' (*zhongguo daolu* 中国道路) is why China achieved its economic success (Ma 2017). The connection between Party-building and corporate culture thus also serves a more generally positive appraisal of Chinese culture and the fusion of the Party's legitimacy with Chinese civilisation.

Conclusion

Party-building is a crucial component of extending China's system abroad. Party-building ensures that Chinese actors do not stray too far from the interests, plans and objectives of the CCP and its vision for the Chinese nation. Where overseas Party work is discouraged or even forbidden, the Party is happy to operate covertly or under the guise of team building and corporate culture.

Leninist principles of Party-building (e.g. cell-based, hierarchical, strict discipline and democratic centralism) increasingly shape Chinese globalisation. The same can be said of the covert nature of Party-building, which harks back to the Party's roots as the secretive vanguard of a revolutionary movement. A century ago, in the first few years after the founding of the CCP in 1921, Leninism did not come ready-made, but had to be learned, adapted and then imposed upon an often intransigent, motley crowd of Party members and groups across China (van de Ven 1991). Now that the Party extends its reach across the globe, some of the same processes are at work again, albeit on a much larger, vastly better-funded, less-violently contested and much more professional basis.

However, it is important not to stretch the comparison with the CCP's past too far. The overseas extension of the Party principally follows the globalisation of Chinese capital and serves a national agenda that sees China becoming a superpower and equal of the US by 2050. This is not the same as the military conquest and revolutionary takeover of China in 1949. It is also not the same as spreading Communist revolution across the world, as Mao's China periodically, selectively and often half-heartedly attempted to do in the 1950s, 1960s and 1970s.

Overseas Party-building has been born from finding solutions to a range of often contradictory, practical problems arising from China's globalisation. The Party is learning by doing. Its overseas work varies vastly between countries and contexts and is rife with inconsistencies, chiefly because overseas Party work must cater to three quite different agendas. First, Party-building work helps Chinese businesses in their local operations. Second, Party-building work ties Chinese actors abroad to the system back home and the strategic interests of the CCP. Third, Party-building work contributes to China's foreign policy strategy in promoting the 'Chinese story', the 'Chinese way', the 'Belt and Road' and the 'shared community of mankind'.

A key tactic to combining these agendas is connecting Party-building work with 'culture'. The specific characteristics of Party work are presented as an expression of what makes not just the Party, but China as a whole, different and competitive in the global arena. Depending on the context, 'culture' is read as either the 'corporate culture' of a Chinese company, the 'national brand' of Chinese businesses or, more generally, China's modern culture and system or even China's traditional civilisation.

Party-building as 'corporate culture' is, among other things, a method of neo-socialist corporatist labour management, principally of Chinese employees, but also spilling over among foreign employees. As part of the neo-socialist symbiosis of capitalism and socialism in China itself, the Party's power monopoly keeps labour cheap, disciplined and abundant. Similarly, Party-building abroad serves global China's version of corporatist labour relations that overcomes class struggle and unifies management, Chinese employees and foreign workers. The irony of Leninist principles being put to work to obscure class differences, avoid class struggle and facilitate the global expansion of Chinese capital is so thick it needs no further elaboration.

Party-building/Chinese culture is deployed as an organic part of the foreign extension of the Chinese system: Chinese projects, Chinese enterprises and Chinese people. As we saw at the start of this chapter, these are treated as being 'inside the system' – Chinese enclaves organised along Chinese principles, serving Chinese interests and dealing with their foreign environment on (hybridised) Chinese terms. Despite the CCP's profession of the principle that Chinese SOEs and projects should abide by local laws and regulations, the extension of China's system abroad has at least some of the makings of a new type of extraterritoriality, a state of exception that Chinese Nationalists and Communists fought so hard to abolish in China itself a century ago.

The foreign extension of Chinese Party-building culture also has a certain similarity with the global expansion of earlier great powers. The symbiosis of Party work and Chinese culture is an aspect, vector and instrument of

Chinese globalisation, extending crucial parts of China's system, society and economy across the world. As with European imperial powers in the nineteenth century and the US and Soviet Union hegemons of the twentieth century, global expansion presents its agents with a whole range of practical and principled challenges. Institutions, beliefs, concepts and strategies rooted in their own culture and society had to be transplanted into a world that they not merely wished to accommodate, but also wanted to make their own.

In contrast to the colonial or hegemonic practices of these earlier great powers, exporting Communist ideology or the imposition of China's system of Party-led governance beyond the foreign enclaves of China's system are all conspicuously absent. This, I believe, is neither an oversight of the sources used for this article nor an artefact of Chinese censorship. China does not want to rule the world or make the world Chinese. It wants to ensure that its interests are served – against those of other great powers if need be – and, as such, it does not hesitate to project its system, power and influence abroad to do so. This might be enough of a threat to many countries caught up in Chinese globalisation as it is; there is no need to imagine ulterior motives that are even worse.

References

Benner, Thorsten, Jan Gaspers, Mareike Ohlberg, Lucrezia Poggetti and Kristin Shi-Kupfer. 2018. *Authoritarian Advance: Responding to China's Growing Political Influence in Europe*. Berlin: MERICS and GPPI.

Benton, Gregor. 1996. 'Bolshevizing China: From Lenin to Stalin to Mao, 1921–44'. *Journal of Communist Studies and Transition Politics* 12 (1): 38–62. doi.org/10.1080/13523279608415300.

Brady, Anne-Marie. 2003. *Making the Foreign Serve China: Managing Foreigners in the People's Republic*. Lanham: Rowman & Littlefield Publishers.

Brady, Anne-Marie. 2017. *Magic Weapons: China's Political Influence Activities under Xi Jinping*. Washington: Wilson Center.

Cao, Wei (曹玮) and Zhao Ke (赵可). 2013. 'Legitimacy Shaping and China's Public Diplomacy' (合法性塑造及中国 公共外交). *Guoji zhengzhi kexue* 2: 62–93.

Cook, Alexander C. 2014. *Mao's Little Red Book: A Global History*. Cambridge: Cambridge University Press. doi.org/10.1017/CBO9781107298576.

d'Hooghe, Ingrid. 2014. *China's Public Diplomacy*. Leiden: Brill.

Diamond, Larry and Orville Schell, eds. 2018. *China's Influence & American Interests: Promoting Constructive Vigilance*. Stanford: Hoover Institution.

Economy, Elizabeth. 2018. *The Third Revolution: Xi Jinping and the New Chinese State*. Oxford: Oxford University Press.

Eisenman, Joshua and Eric Heginbotham. 2020. 'China's Relations with Africa, Latin America, and the Middle East'. In *China & the World*, edited by David Shambaugh, 291–312. New York: Oxford University Press. doi.org/10.1093/oso/9780190062316.003.0014.

Feng, Liujian (冯留建). 2020. 'The Dilemma and Exploration of Overseas Party-Building Work in the New Era' (新时代海外党建工作的困境及探索). *Renmin luntan* 669 (May).

Gao, Zhe (高哲). 2020. 'Discussion on Strengthening the Ideological and Political Work of Party-Building in Overseas Projects' (加强海外项目党建思想政治工作探讨). *Xiandai shangmao gongye* 13: 138–9.

Gonzalez-Vicente, Ruben. 2011. 'The Internationalization of the Chinese State'. *Political Geography* 30 (7): 402–11, doi.org/10.1016/j.polgeo.2011.09.001.

Groot, Gerry. 2004. *Managing Transitions: The Chinese Communist Party, United Front Work, Corporatism, and Hegemony*. New York: Routledge.

Grünberg, Nis and Katja Drinhausen. 2019. *The Party Leads on Everything: China's Changing Governance in Xi Jinping's New Era*. Berlin: MERICS.

Guo, Qiang (郭 强) and Sun Xiucheng (孙秀成). 2011a. 'Research on the Current State and Innovation Model of Overseas Students' Party-Building Work from the Perspective of Informatization: A Case Study of the Overseas Education College of Nanjing University of Posts and Telecommunications' (信息化视阈下海外学生党建工作的现状与创新模式研究：以南京邮电大学海外教育学院为例). *Nanjing youjian daxue xuebao (shehui kexue ban)* 13 (3): 100–5.

Guo, Qiang (郭 强) and Sun Xiucheng (孙秀成). 2011b. 'An Analysis of the Party-Building Work for Overseas Students in Colleges and Universities in the New Era – A Case Study of Some Colleges and Universities in Nanjing' (新时期高校海外留学生党建工作探析 -- 以南京部分高校为例). *Sheke zongheng* 26 (10): 145–8.

Hackenesch, Christine and Julia Bader. 2020. 'The Struggle for Minds and Influence: The Chinese Communist Party's Global Outreach'. *International Studies Quarterly* 64: 723–33. doi.org/10.1093/isq/sqaa028.

Hameiri, Shahar and Lee Jones. 2015. 'Rising Powers and State Transformation: The Case of China'. *European Journal of International Relations* 22 (1): 72–98. doi.org/10.1177/1354066115578952.

Jiang, Haijun (江海军). 2019. 'Analysis of Strengthening Overseas Party Building Work' (加强海外党建工作探析). *Xiandai guoqi yanjiu* 12: 307.

Joske, Alex. 2018. *Picking Flowers, Making Honey: The Chinese Military's Collaboration with Foreign Universities*. Canberra: ASPI.

Joske, Alex. 2020. *The Party Speaks for You: Foreign Interference and the Chinese Communist Party's United Front System*. Canberra: ASPI.

Koss, Daniel. 2021a. 'Globalising Leninist Institutions: Trends in Overseas Party Building'. *China Brief* 21 (12): 222–43. jamestown.org/program/globalizing-leninist-institutions-trends-in-overseas-party-building/.

Koss, Daniel. 2021b. 'Party Building as Institutional Bricolage: Asserting Authority at the Business Frontier'. *China Quarterly* 248: 1–22. doi.org/10.1017/S0305741021000692.

Li, Yao. 2019. *Role of Chinese Communist Party's Grass-Roots Organisation in Enterprises since the 1990s*. East Asian Institute Background Brief No. 1446. Singapore: East Asian Institute. research.nus.edu.sg/eai/wp-content/uploads/sites/2/2019/04/BB1446.pdf.

Liang, Tao (梁涛). 2019. 'The Angolan Model of Foreign Party Building in State-Owned Enterprises' (国有企业境外党建的安哥拉模式). *Modern Enterprise Culture*. November.

Lovell, Julia. 2019. *Maoism: A Global History*. London: Bodley Head.

Ma, Zhengli (马正立). 2017. '"One Belt One Road" and the Internationalisation of Corporate Party Building' ('一带一路'与企业党建国际化). *Qianyan* 406: 40–8.

Makarchev, Nikita, Chelsea Chunwen Xiao, Ga-Young So and Duy Anh Le. 2022. '"One Step Forward, One Leap Back": Chinese Overseas Subsidiaries under Changing Party-State Sector Relations'. *Journal of Contemporary China* 31: 1–19. doi.org/10.1080/10670564.2022.2030995.

Mao, Tse-tung (Mao Zedong). [1939] 1967. 'Introducing *The Communist*'. In *Selected Works of Mao Tse-tung*, volume II. Beijing: Foreign Language Press, 285-296.

McGregor, Richard. 2010. *The Party: The Secret World of China's Communist Rulers*. New York: Harper.

McGregor, Richard. 2019. *Xi Jinping: The Backlash*. Penguin Random House Australia.

Nye, Joseph S. 2004. *Soft Power: The Means to Success in World Politics*. New York: PublicAffairs.

Ngeow, Chow-Bing. 2017. 'Barisan Nasional and the Chinese Communist Party: A Case Study in China's Party-Based Diplomacy'. *China Review* 17 (1): 53–82.

Ngeow, Chow-Bing. 2020. 'The CPC's International Department and China's Party-Based Diplomacy'. In *China's Search for 'National Rejuvenation'*, edited by Jabin T. Jacob and Hoang The Ang, 157–68. Singapore: Palgrave Macmillan. doi.org/10.1007/978-981-15-2796-8_11.

Party Committee of China Electronics Import and Export Co. Ltd. (中国电子进出口有限公司党委). 2019. 'Taking the "Four Alls" as the Goal to Do a Good Job in Overseas Party Building' (以'四全'为目标抓好海外党建工作). *Sixiang zhengzhi gongzuo yanjiu* 5: 54–5.

Pieke, Frank N. 2016. *Knowing China: A Guide for the Twenty-First Century*. Cambridge: Cambridge University Press. doi.org/10.1017/CBO9781316452097.

Pieke, Frank N. 2021. *Chinese Influence and the Chinese Community in the Netherlands*. Leiden: Leiden Asia Centre. leidenasiacentre.nl/en/publicaties/.

Pieke, Frank N. and Nána de Graaff. 2022. *Chinese Influence and Networks among Firms and Business Elites in the Netherlands*. Leiden: Leiden Asia Centre.

Qiang, Ge (强舸). 2018. 'Four Forms of Overseas Party Building within State-Owned Enterprises against the Background of the "Belt and Road"' ('一带一路'背景下国有企业境外党建的四种模式). *Dangjian xinlun* 6: 49–55.

Sahlins, Marshall. 2015. *Confucius Institutes: Academic Malware*. Chicago: Prickly Paradigm Press.

Sapio, Flora. 2019. 'The United Front Principle: Expansion and Adaptation'. *European Journal of East Asian Studies* 18: 133–64. doi.org/10.1163/15700615-01802001.

Shambaugh, David. 2007. 'China's "Quiet Diplomacy": The International Department of the Chinese Communist Party'. *China: An International Journal* 5 (1): 26–54. doi.org/10.1142/S0219747207000039.

Shambaugh, David. 2008. *China's Communist Party: Atrophy & Adaptation*. Washington: Woodrow Wilson Center Press. www.wilsoncenter.org/article/chinas-communist-party-atrophy-and-adaptation.

Thornton, Patricia M. 2012. 'The New Life of the Party: Party-Building and Social Engineering in Greater Shanghai'. *China Journal* 68: 58–78. doi.org/10.1086/666580.

van de Ven, Hans. 1991. *From Friend to Comrade: The Founding of the Chinese Communist Party, 1920–1927*. Berkeley: University of California Press. doi.org/10.1525/9780520910874.

Walker, Christopher and Jessica Ludwig. 2017. 'From "Soft Power" to "Sharp Power": Rising Authoritarian Influence in the Democratic World'. In *Sharp Power: Rising Authoritarian Influence*, 8–25. Washington: National Endowment for Democracy.

Wu, Fubao (吴付宝). 2020. 'Consolidate the "Commonality" of the Organisational Foundation and Demonstrate the "Individuality" of Overseas Party Building – On the Thinking of Overseas Party Building' (夯实组织基础'共性', 彰显海外党建'个性'——试论海外党建工作思路). *Shidai baogao* 8: 19–21.

Yan, Xiaojun and Jie Huang. 2017. 'Navigating Unknown Waters: The Chinese Communist Party's New Presence in the Private Sector'. *China Review* 17 (2): 37–63. www.jstor.org/stable/44440170.

Zhang, Baosen (张保森). 2017. 'Relying on Corporate Culture to Promote Overseas Party Building' (依托企业文化促进海外党建). *Xiandai qiye wenhua lilun ban* 7.

II. IDEOLOGICAL BRICOLAGE

4

Intellectuals and Ideological Governance of the Chinese Communist Party

Timothy Cheek

Scholars have long noted, and debated, the close but troubled relationship between China's educated elite and its modern political parties in general, and between modern intellectuals and the Chinese Communist Party (CCP) over the century of its existence since 1921. Founded as an outgrowth of study societies convened by radical professors and students, the leadership of the Party was composed almost totally of individuals that most social scientists would describe as intellectuals or as military elites who chose, at one point or another, to take on the trappings of learned governance. And yet, intellectuals have been the subject of brutal repression by all modern Chinese governments, but especially the two Bolshevik parties, the Guomindang (GMD) or Nationalist Party and the CCP. The sufferings of intellectuals under Mao's regime are widely known, from the Yan'an Rectification Movement of 1942–44 through the various campaigns of the 1950s and most especially in the decade of the Cultural Revolution (1966–76/78). Indeed, Eddy U (2019), based on considerable research, has concluded that, by the 1950s, intellectuals had become a despised class in the People's Republic of China (PRC). Tani Barlow traces the identity of China's thinkers and writers from an 'intellectual class' in 1905 to 'enlightened scholars' in the 1920s to 'intellectuals' (*zhishifenzi* 知识分子) ever since. Barlow (1991, 216) identifies a tension between the social power of these knowledge specialists and their dangerous dance with the state in which they succumbed under both Nationalist and Communist regimes, offering a service role to power, a 'category of the state'. Nonetheless, Hung-yok Ip (2004) has traced the attractions of Party service for intellectuals in the Republican period as leaders, heroes and sophisticates. The definition of 'intellectual' not only developed over the twentieth century but also became significantly confounded with the category of Party cadre (*ganbu* 干部) under both the GMD and CCP. Hamrin and Cheek (1986) concluded that 'establishment intellectuals' from the Mao period onward were both high-level intellectuals and high-level cadres.

What do we make of this troubled relationship between China's cultural and technological elites and the Leninist parties of China (and, in particular, the CCP)? I will argue that the CCP's Leninist nature as an ideological organisation requires transformational bureaucrats to implement its form of rule – ideological governance. And intellectuals have been perfect for this role. Legitimated not by elections or by divine right but by ideology as well as performance, the Party needs ideologists to tell its story and mobilise popular support (including, as Kerry Brown has noted in his chapter in this volume, the management of emotions). Stalin called for 'engineers of the soul' and Chinese Communists have embraced the call. Over the century of its existence, a good number of intellectuals have chosen to serve or to speak for the Party as revolutionaries (*gemingjia* 革命家), thought workers (*sixiang gongzuozhe* 思想工作者) and, in more recent decades, experts (*zhuanjia* 专家). It is this fundamental political need – to implement ideological governance – that explains both the irreducible need of the Party for intellectual service and its constant vigilance to ensure that these self-regarding savants stay in line. In fact, the distinction between intellectuals and the party-state should not be reified because many Party leaders *have been* intellectuals. Susanne Weigelin-Schwiedrzik noted this in the 1980s: 'In China, conflicts we normally regard as being conflicts between the Party and intellectuals are conflicts amongst intellectuals' (quoted in Hamrin and Cheek 1986, 20). Likewise, Eddy U (2019, 11) contends 'that the intellectual and Chinese communism were mutually constitutive'.

What motivates some intellectuals to take on service to, and even struggle for leadership in, the Party; and what exactly does the Party want them to do? In this chapter, we will meet a half dozen examples from three moments in the Party's life: the years of war and revolution at mid-century, the Mao years and the most recent decades of reform and opening. Thoughtful scholars turned to Party service, both in the case of the journalist Chen Bulei with the GMD and the noted Ming historian Wu Han with the CCP.

In the new People's Republic, Yue Daiyun, a literature professor at Peking University, committed her life to the Party despite harsh setbacks; Zhang Chuqiao parlayed his expertise in Marxist ideology to high office by the 1970s; and Wang Ruoshui, a junior editor at *People's Daily* who caught Mao's admiring eye in the 1960s, survived the Cultural Revolution to become a rueful reformist promoting 'socialist humanism' in the 1980s. Finally, we will meet divergent responses to the challenges of reform: Wang Yuanhua, another ardent leftist intellectual who, by the 1990s, was offering a trenchant internal critique of his Party; and Jiang Shigong, a Peking University professor of a younger generation who embraced Xi Jinping thought enthusiastically. Why has this relationship continued for a century and why, despite indications of very real alienation from, and resistance to, the ideological rule of the Party today, does this 'deal' between the church and this priesthood still attract minds like Wang Huning's (who, like Zhang Chunqiao 50 years earlier, has risen to the top Politburo Standing Committee of the CCP) and pens like Jiang Shigong's?

I have addressed the idea of ideological governance in modern Chinese political thought and practice elsewhere (Cheek 2021a). Here, I will only briefly recap the longer history of this style of political life and its seminal articulation under Mao and other Party leaders in Yan'an. I want to spend more time looking at some examples of Party intellectuals over the century to see if this perspective helps make sense of their aspirations, their service and their resistance. Finally, I would like to reflect on what this history might portend for today's style of political life under Xi Jinping and what the relationship between China's intellectuals and power can possibly be in the future.

Ideological Governance in Modern China

It is worthwhile defining the key term in this analysis: *ideological governance*. Ideological governance asserts a role for the government as a pedagogical state that has the responsibility to provide order and prosperity through civilising its citizens according to the superior insights of certified transformational bureaucrats learned in a body of thought that, when applied properly, will bring great harmony to all under its sway, and that therefore requires and deserves freedom from competition from alternate (and presumed lesser) forms of political activity.

The resonance between this model of service and these cadres with late-imperial scholar officials in general, and GMD cadres under Sun Yat-sen and Chiang Kai-shek in particular, will be noted in passing; however, we will focus on what has gone on in the CCP where we see the sinews of what John Fitzgerald (2021) has identified as the 'cadre nation'.

Ideological governance can be identified in the 'Sacred Edicts' of the Ming and Qing emperors and village-level propagation of this wisdom through 'Community Compacts' (*xiangyue* 乡约). This style of political life continued apace in the varying regimes of twentieth-century China. The core approach shared by all governments in China down to today is political tutelage (*xunzheng* 训政). This was Sun Yat-sen's explanation for putting democracy off for another day and the primary expression of the pedagogical state under his Nationalist Party. The founding father of China's Republic, Sun came to feel by the 1920s that the Chinese people were not ready for democracy and required instead a period of political education or tutelage during which his one-party state would inculcate the masses in modern civility. This 'Tutelary State', as John Fitzgerald calls it in his study of Sun's political model,[1] was meant to awaken the Chinese people and teach them how to be modern citizens (Fitzgerald 1996). Chiang Kai-shek echoed these pedagogical aspirations in his 1943 *China's Destiny* (*Zhongguo zhi mingyun* 中國之命運) (Chiang 1947, 112).

The proximate and specific tradition that has defined Party practice since the 1940s is *rectification politics*, which dates most notably from the Yan'an Rectification Movement of 1942–44 and the nearly continuous set of political campaigns under the CCP since then. Generally considered a Maoist form of governance and associated with disruptive political campaigns, rectification owes as much to Liu Shaoqi and other less chiliastic Party leaders as it does to Mao. And, more importantly, it characterises regular politics in the Party as much as it does its many disruptive mass movements (Teiwes 1993). The core of rectification politics is the primacy of the human will when it is tempered, reformed and regulated by a superior doctrine and implemented by a capable cadre of trained administrators. It does not require democracy in the electoral sense; it requires a rectified political leadership. These claims, and the promise of Party service as a noble vocation, are famously articulated in the rectification documents of 1942 that became the 'bible' for the Yan'an Rectification Movement.

1 Articulated in Sun Yat-sen, 'Fundamentals of National Reconstruction', 1923, see Fitzgerald (1996, 79).

The key voice, of course, was Mao Zedong's in much studied texts such as 'Reform Our Study' and 'Talks at the Yan'an Conference on Literature and Art'. But much more detailed instructions and management techniques were articulated in the rectification documents by Liu Shaoqi, Chen Yun and other Party leaders.[2]

Liu's lectures on 'Cultivation of the Communist Party Member' offer the *locus classicus* for the Party's claim for the ideological service of intellectuals. Liu begins by noting 'why Communists must undertake self-cultivation'. Personal reform is necessary for a Communist since one's upbringing in the 'old society' generally contradicts the goals of communism. The key to this reform is the thought, or the 'ideological consciousness' (*sixiang yishi* 思想意识), of each individual. Indeed, says Liu: 'The cultivation of ideology is the basis of all other forms of cultivation.' This is all necessary, Liu continues, because 'the Communist Party is the political party of the proletariat and has no interests of its own other than those of the emancipation of the proletariat'. In fact, this noble image is central to Liu's vision: 'Unless the proletariat emancipates all working people and all nations – unless it emancipates humanity as a whole – it cannot fully emancipate itself' (Liu 1981, 130; Liu 1947, 74–5). This is the clarion call to transformational bureaucrats who will implement the Party's ideological governance.

Chinese Intellectuals' Response to the Party's Call

How have Chinese intellectuals responded to these calls? It makes sense to begin with what intellectuals in Yan'an and after have made of this call to take part in the ideological governance of the CCP. A surprisingly large number of intellectuals found this call attractive enough to engage their energies. However, that engagement was neither simple nor uniform. We can think of intellectual engagement with the Party in terms of a continuum from those who sincerely embraced the cultivation Liu Shaoqi offered in 'The Cultivation of the Communist Party Member', to those who did so with ambivalence or reservations, to those who were compelled to go through the motions, to those who resisted passively, to those who actively

2 I give a close reading in the Sinological style of Liu Shaoqi's 'Cultivation of the Communist Party Member' (which is translated in Liu's (1986) English-language *Selected Works* as 'How to Become a Good Communist' (劉少奇,论共产党员的修養) in *On the Party*. See Cheek (2021b).

criticised the whole endeavour or just ran away. To this we should add those who embraced Liu's cultivation cynically for self-promotion and to gain political power. Indeed, most of these responses are itemised by Liu himself in 'Cultivation'! (Liu 1981, 136–48; Liu 1947, 83–98). By the 1930s, Party intellectuals mostly served as cadres (*ganbu* 干部), intellectual cadres.

I have studied the cases of Deng Tuo (邓拓) and Wang Shiwei (王实味). Deng Tuo embraced what became the Yan'an orthodoxy before it was fully formulated and saw intellectual service to the Party (beginning in the Jin-Cha-Ji base area) as a noble vocation. Around the same time, Wang Shiwei, an established translator and Party theorist in Yan'an's Central Research Institute, made a trenchant critique of the abuses of power in the Party and offered a Marxist alternative to Mao's version of rectification (Cheek 1997, 2021c). Both saw themselves as revolutionaries and thought workers. Over the years I have looked further to see if these patterns hold for other intellectuals who took up the Party's call.

To begin with, we have some reports of what the experience of the Yan'an rectification itself was like for 'ordinary' cadres in 1942–44. Tony Saich and David Apter included a fair number of reminiscences of Yan'an cadres they interviewed in the 1980s. Focusing on Party political culture, they reported particularly on experienced CCP cadres' view that the Yan'an *zhengfeng* (整风) was a lot milder than the murderous campaign to suppress counter-revolutionaries (*sufan* 肃反) of the early 1930s in Jiangxi (Apter and Saich 1994, 147–58). More recently, scholars in China have been mining diaries and reflection reports from the 1940s. Huang Daoxuan (黄道炫) at Peking University, for example, has focused on the 'interior worlds' of more ordinary cadres, including intellectuals, from the perspective of *xinling shi* (心灵史), something between the history of emotions and intellectual history. He cites the diary notes of Shen Xia (沈霞), the 20-year-old daughter of the famous writer Mao Dun, who had come to Yan'an with his family in 1940. At the end of 1943, the rectification training class organised by the East Gansu sub-bureau of the Party set its cadres to studying what Huang describes as two 'foundational texts': Mao's 'Combat Liberalism' and Liu's 'Cultivation'. Huang cites Shen Xia's diary from 1943 to show how an intellectual could internalise the challenge to subordinate oneself to the Party as a 'screw in the revolutionary machine', an ideal laid out in Liu's 'Cultivation'. Shen writes:

> Even on sleepless nights, the corners of my lips slide upwards and a genuine smile, though rare in daytime, appears on my face whenever I think about myself being a useful screw – even a very, very tiny one.[3]

But, is the Yan'an experience exceptional? On the attraction of intellectual service, we will consider the seven intellectuals introduced at the start of this chapter in the context of war, revolution and reform.

The examples below reflect the agency intellectuals found in service to the Party. In them we can identify three themes that help us make sense of Chinese intellectuals and the Party in terms of participation in the ideological governance of China:

1. the *attractiveness* of intellectual service to an ideological regime – a chance to save China, rebuild China and to preserve and extend Chinese civilisation; to be teachers of the nation
2. the *agency* of intellectual cadres – service was not necessarily submission
3. the *enduring tensions* (different views of what service to an ideological regime can require of an individual) and *variant exegeses* of what the doctrine means; different levels of engagement, some 'critical' and some 'organic' (in Gramsci's sense).

Loyalty to the Leader: Chen Bulei and Wu Han

Chen Bulei (陈布雷) (1890–1948) was a classic New Culture intellectual and mid-level modern intellectual. His life exemplifies the challenges of state service for intellectuals in China's Republic. After years of dispiriting warlord rule, the completion of the Northern Expedition in 1927 and its nationalist revolution offered the prospect of a real national revolution and a government worth serving. Although Chen was a successful journalist in Shanghai and embraced the professional identity of an independent intellectual, clearly part of him hankered to get beyond the world of words, to make a difference and to belong to something bigger than himself.[4] He passed on the Communists when they came calling in 1925; class struggle did not seem right to Chen. When Generalissimo Chiang Kai-

3 Shen Xia, *Four Years in Yan'an* (延安四年), Daxiang chubanshe, 2009, entry for 27 January 1943, 71, as cited in Huang (2020, 7). Dayton Lekner and Nathan Gan are preparing a formal translation of this text, see *Revisiting the Revolution* at prchistory.org. Recently, Ishikawa Yoshihiro also engaged Shen Xia's diary and offers more reflections in his lecture for the Heidelberg series, 'Living as a Cog in the Organization: A Way of Life in the 1940s', translated by Joshua A. Fogel.

4 A fine literary study of Chen Bulei and his suicide is Ho (2007).

shek sent feelers two years later, Chen's newspaper had disappointed him (by cosying up to the local warlord, Sun Chuanfang). A personal meeting with Chiang clinched the deal. Indeed, Chen's two decades of service to the Nationalist Party was really personal service to Chiang Kai-shek, a leader he deeply admired and for whom he felt great loyalty. Chen wrote brilliantly as Chiang's speech writer, ghostwriting, for example, Chiang's famous account of his December 1936 capture in Xi'an, *Fortnight in Sian*, that led to the second united front with the Communists.

However, Chen Bulei experienced service to his great leader as an unreconcilable tension between his identity as a professional journalist and his service to the Party. In the end, it wore him down. In his suicide note in November 1948, Chen wrote:

> Ever since I left journalism, I have not been free to use my pen to express my own words. In truth, I am nothing more than a scribe, at most a secretary. (quoted in Ho 2007, 22)

And yet, those who worked within the Nationalist Party in the 1940s conceded that Chen Bulei, as the grand secretary in Chiang's cabinet, was a powerful gatekeeper and a major influence on the generalissimo. In Chen's case, he could not reconcile identity and service. However, as the biographer of his suicide, Dahpon Ho, notes:

> [Chen] sheds light on the mundane world of functionaries … probably closer to the experience of most literate Chinese who served the multitude of parties, factions, warlords, or governments through the decades of war and revolution. (Ho 2007, 48)

Liberals turned to the Communist Party, as well. The case of Wu Han (吳晗) (1909–1969) shows both the attraction of state service under the Communists for a Chinese liberal and the personal charisma of Mao Zedong for some intellectuals. Wu Han was a liberal historian, a noted specialist on the Ming dynasty (1368–1644) and a wunderkind professor at Tsinghua University in Beijing.[5] Wu became a leading member of the Democratic League – the effort of liberals to form a 'third road' in Chinese politics. His criticisms of the Nationalists and his apparent sympathies for the Communists got Wu Han on the Nationalist's blacklist. He just managed to escape arrest when police swept Beijing's university campuses in August 1948 by fleeing south. On his way, he accepted a league request to carry

5 Material on Wu Han comes from the excellent biography by Mary G. Mazur (2009).

a letter to the Communist authorities in their 'liberated area' in the Hebei city of Shijiazhuang, about 170 miles southwest of Beijing. He went to the Communist area with some 55 other league and independent democratic figures invited by the CCP to talk about China's future. As was the case with Chen Bulei and Chiang Kai-shek in 1927, so it was for Wu Han in 1948 that two personal meetings with Mao Zedong convinced him that he wanted to serve. 'Wu Han left the sessions with Mao exhilarated by the charismatic leader,' says his biographer, Mary Mazur, 'and inspired to study Lenin's and Mao's writings' (Mazur 2009, 347). It was a case of loyalty to a leader and a revolution that seemed to Wu Han to be worthy. It was also a case that Mao had flattered Wu Han, asking for and reading the historian's writings. Mao called on Wu Han's sense of loyalty to the cause of saving China but also offered him a respected role as an intellectual leader and teacher of the people. Wu Han was so impressed he immediately wrote to Mao asking to join the Party.

But the Party had other plans for Wu Han. Wu Han was asked to serve the Party that had attracted his loyalty as a leader of the Democratic League, but not as a Communist Party member. This Wu Han did, serving as chair of the league's Beijing branch from 1949 until 1966. In the new PRC, Wu Han became vice-mayor of Beijing and was active in the confidential meetings of the city's Party committee and received classified documents, although publicly he was a league official and serving as such in the municipal government under the auspices of the united front. Privately, Wu Han was known among Party leaders as a 'key party member outside of the party' (Mazur 2009, 377). Wu Han was finally allowed to join the CCP in March 1957, though even then his membership was kept secret (until all was revealed in the Cultural Revolution).

Wu Han's service was not nearly as tortured as Chen Bulei's. Wu Han continued his professional identity as academic historian and served as a high-ranking public official of some considerable prestige. It was not, however, a service without tribulations. Wu Han had to cope with the many political campaigns of the 1950s and 1960s. His was a moderate voice, but in the 1957 Anti-Rightist Campaign, Wu Han was an enthusiastic participant and willingly criticised his old league comrades Zhang Bojun and Luo Longji, claiming to preserve the league for another day. By 1957, Wu Han could say that he had balanced intellectual integrity and political service as a liberal. But if he had joined the CCP by then, how could he say that? A careful reading of Wu Han's many writings since 1949, according to Mazur:

> does not substantiate characterizing him as having adopted Communist ideology across the board ... He was selectively influenced by Marxism–Leninism and Mao Zedong's Thought in thinking about China ... Wu was loyal to Communism *as he chose to understand it*, not because the powerful central authority decreed it. (Mazur 2009, 393, original emphasis)

Yue Daiyun, Zhang Chunqiao and Wang Ruoshui

These were older intellectuals, born around the turn of the century. During these same years, a new generation came of age while people such as Chen Bulei and Wu Han were in the midst of their careers. Yue Daiyun would show how a provincial girl could become a noted professor and Party activist, Zhang Chunqiao rose from Shanghai labour work to top leadership in Beijing and Wang Ruoshui embraced Communist journalism and rethought Marxism in the post-Mao era.

For Yue Daiyun (乐黛云) (b. 1931), the CCP was her hope and her pathway to success. From a provincial family of modest means, by the mid-1950s she had a brilliant career as a promising young literature professor at Peking University: Party branch leader in her department, married to a prominent philosophy professor, Tang Yijie, two children and a pleasant house on campus (Yue and Wakeman 1985). Yue loyally supported the revolution in which she believed, moved cautiously through the Hundred Flowers agitations and served with her branch committee in designating rightists in the ensuing Anti-Rightist Campaign. Her life was turned upside down when she herself was pegged as a rightist in a resurgence of the campaign in 1958 for some mild comments she had raised the previous year (Yue and Wakeman 1985). She endured life as a second-class citizen in the 1960s until the Cultural Revolution got both herself and her husband sent to the rural areas of Jiangxi Province. Yue and Tang were back on campus in the early 1970s, but were in need of showing their loyalty. Thus, when her husband was invited to join the radical writing group Liangxiao to help criticise the recently deposed Lin Biao, Yue was pleased and relieved. The Liangxiao scholars were given access to all sorts of restricted materials, and even a field visit to Lin Biao's opulent Beijing residence, Maojiawan (to gather evidence against him).

> This kind of access to inside information in a society dominated by secrecy contributed crucially to Liangxiao's prestige and ensured that the pieces they wrote, collective efforts often published in *People's*

> *Daily* or *Red Flag* and signed with one of the group's pen names, were automatically accepted as definitive. (Yue and Wakeman 1985, 323, 326)

What could be more satisfying for a revolutionary scholar?

Meanwhile, Yue spent much of her time trying to save her two children from the worst of the chaos and the rigours of life under rustication, particularly her teenage daughter. Such considerations, and being reduced to humiliating pleading and petty bribery, were hardly the revolution that had inspired Yue Daiyun when she arrived at Peking University in 1948. Neither was the tortured scholarship that Tang Yijie contributed to Liangxiao the glorious resurgence of Chinese civilisation under socialism that had inspired him. Yue and Tang were paying the price for their engagement in Mao's revolutions, but the full bill was not yet in. After further twists and turns, in 1978, Yue Daiyun's conviction as a rightist was overturned and she was offered the opportunity to rejoin the CCP. Yue hesitated:

> But I still could not forget all those who had died for its cause, sacrificing their lives for the ideals of Liberation. Surely the hardships, the losses suffered together, would not be redeemed unless we strove to keep that flame alive. I would join in the efforts to rebuild the Party. (Yue and Wakeman 1985, 385–7)

Zhang Chunqiao (张春桥) (1917–2005) was among those who took Mao's call to radical policies as a ticket to advancement; he was ready to 'continue the revolution'. Zhang rose to national prominence in the early years of the Cultural Revolution in Shanghai. In bitter factional fighting in 1966, Zhang appeared to play a leading role in ending the street violence (Walder 1977). This successful 'cleansing of the Party' in China's most important commercial and industrial city emphatically got the attention of Chairman Mao and the Cultural Revolution Group. Zhang Chunqiao was 'helicoptered up' to national leadership.

In January 1975, at the peak of his Party career on the standing committee of the CCP Central Committee Politburo, Zhang Chunqiao made what would be the last major defence of radical faith Maoism. Zhang made his case for continuing the radical politics of the Cultural Revolution. 'Politics is the concentrated expression of economics', Zhang declared, 'and whether the ideological and political line is correct or incorrect, and which class holds the leadership, decides which class owns those factories in actual fact.'

He cited Lenin chapter and verse on the need to exercise dictatorship.[6] Zhang then made his case for defining who the enemy is – his competitors inside the CCP:

> These people generally have a good class background; almost all of them were brought up under the red flag; they have joined the Communist Party organisationally, received college training and become so-called red experts. However, they are new poisonous weeds engendered by the old soil of capitalism.[7]

How did good Party cadres become agents of bourgeois restorationism? By adopting incorrect thought, declared Zhang. The unfortunates have betrayed their class by doing 'exactly what Khrushchev and Brezhnev have done … [putting] forward the revisionist programme of "the state of the whole people" and "party of the entire people"'. What is to be done? Zhang outlined his mission:

> so long as the few hundred members of our Party Central Committee and the several thousand senior cadres take the lead and join the vast numbers of other cadres and the masses in reading and studying assiduously, carrying on the investigation and analysis and summing up experience, we can certainly translate Chairman Mao's call [to exercise dictatorship over the bourgeoisie] into reality.[8]

Zhang had, after all, 'applied' Mao's revolutionary ideology successfully to corral his competitors in Shanghai in 1967, parlaying knowledge into political power.

The post-Mao period after the tribulations of the Cultural Revolution was a challenging time for the Party faithful. Zhang Chunqiao was purged in 1976 as a member of the 'Gang of Four', was tried and imprisoned. The leadership set about reinstating Leninist norms and rehabilitating loyal cadres purged over previous decades. Under these conditions, reformist Party intellectuals sought to address deeper causes for the excesses of Mao's later revolutions. Among the most prominent was Wang Ruoshui.

Wang Ruoshui (王若水) (1926–2002) had become an intellectual cadre in the Communist system. He had prospered during the early years of the PRC and survived the Cultural Revolution. He was a government servant

---

6 Chang Ch'un-ch'iao (Zhang Chunqiao 张春桥), 'On Exercising All-Round Dictatorship over the Bourgeoisie' (论对资产阶级的全面专政), in *Hong Qi*, no. 4 (1975) and translated by Foreign Languages Press in Beijing in a pamphlet in the same year.

7 Ibid.

8 Ibid.

and a teacher of the people in the Communist system. He was not a fiction writer or poet, but a theorist, more in the mould of his mentor at *People's Daily*, Deng Tuo. As a guilty member of the generation that partially supported and partially endured the Cultural Revolution, Wang was among those who sought to set things right in the years after Mao died. By the early 1980s, Wang was famous as the voice for 'socialist humanism'. In the early 1980s, reform intellectuals backed by one or another Party leader pushed for a latitudinarian interpretation of Maoism that focused on the need to protect individual and collective rights against the abuses of those in power (Goldman, Cheek and Hamrin 1987; Brugger and Kelly 1991). The bottom line of advocates of Marxist humanism was to push for some form of accountability and to strengthen the norms of inner-Party democracy. These theorists were not dissidents; they were Party members and in positions of influence, several working for the Party's reformist general secretary, Hu Yaobang, and to a lesser degree for the head of the state administration, Premier Zhao Ziyang.

Wang Ruoshui's signal service was to provide the philosophical justification for the most daring ideological reforms of the post-Mao period, reforms that promised to create 'communism with a human face'. Since he was a theorist for the Party, Wang wrote theory, but it was theory for a general reader (including Party leaders), not for professional philosophers. The key term in Wang's reformist Marxist analysis was 'alienation'. In Marxist theory, the 'alienation' of labour that workers experience under capitalism commonly referred to as 'exploitation' – drives their struggle for socialist revolution. Under Stalin and Mao, the Communists declared that this alienation was a thing of the past under the glorious rule of the Party. Wang spoke for a generation of Party theorists who survived the Cultural Revolution, and they disagreed. Wang wrote:

> In the past, we did many stupid things in economic construction due to our lack of experience … and in the end, we ate our own bitter fruit; this is alienation in the economic realm … [T]he people's servants sometimes made indiscriminate use of the power conferred on them by the people, and turned into their masters; this is alienation in the political realm, also called the alienation of power. As for alienation in the intellectual realm, the classic example is the personality cult.[9]

9 Wang Ruoshui, 'Talking about alienation' (谈谈异化问题), *Xinwen zhanxian*, 1980, no. 9, quoted in Kelly (1987, 173). See also Kelly's introduction and bibliographic note to his translations of Wang's essay in *Chinese Studies in Philosophy* (New York), vol. XVI:3 (1985). For details on and writings by Wang, see www.wangruoshui.net/.

Wang's critique of the 'personality cult', of course, pointed to Mao. Wang saw the personality cult as the willing transfer to the leader of powers and dignities that rightfully belonged to 'the people'. Referring to the Cultural Revolution adoration of Mao, Wang confessed: 'Many people, including myself, also propagated the superstition, out of adoration, totally out of adoration then' (quoted in Kelly 1987, 167). Wang Ruoshui was no dissident at this time. He was part of what Peter Ludz called the 'counter-elite', in-house critics within Communist parties in Eastern Europe in the 1980s (Lutz 1972, 62). Indeed, as David Kelly notes, Wang Ruoshui and his colleagues were aware of developments in Eastern Europe and cited the writings of Eastern Europeans (Kelly 1987). We often think of communism as monolithic, but this was demonstrably not the case. Nonetheless, Wang's humanistic approach did not prevail and he was purged in 1987. Yet the Party, still under Deng Xiaoping, took on board some of the ideas of this counter-elite in the ongoing policy of 'reform and opening'.

Into the Twenty-First Century: Wang Yuanhua's Reflections and Jiang Shigong's Triumphalism

How to capture the changes in ideological governance and intellectual service once the massive economic and social changes of 'reform and opening' gained critical mass in the post-Tiananmen 1990s? Here, I merely choose two opposing forms of engagement with the Party's evolving orthodoxy: the critical reflections and cosmopolitan mindset of the senior Party intellectual Wang Yuanhua in the 1990s and early 2000s, and the post-2012 triumphalism and unrepentant nationalism of Jiang Shigong. Ironically, Wang was a homegrown intellectual who never left China but loved nineteenth-century European literature, while Jiang is quite international, has engaged with Western academics, is widely read in Western theory (from Carl Schmitt to Michel Foucault), but embraces the new China-centrism of Xi Jinping.

Writing in the 1990s and early 2000s, after the social impact of economic reform began to be apparent, Wang Yuanhua (王元化) (1920–2008) offered a series of cogent reflections on the Party's and his own history of revolution. Wang had joined the Communist Party in 1938 and worked in the realms of propaganda, thought, art and culture. After the revolution, he served in the Shanghai Writers Association and did editorial work for different newspapers and magazines. He was caught up in a major purge in 1955 against Hu Feng (胡风), who had dared to argue that Mao Zedong's theories of art and literature were too narrow and repressive. Wang was incarcerated and interrogated for some time, and was not finally rehabilitated until 1981, which meant that he had 16 years to reflect on his thought and experiences. Once rehabilitated, he published a series of books – often composed of notes, commentaries and brief essays – that have been immensely influential among Chinese intellectuals because of his willingness to use his personal experience to question received wisdom.[10] In order to make sense of the political turmoil he has lived through, Wang turned to an earlier debate between two Chinese scholars of the early twentieth century, Du Yaquan and Jiang Menglin, over the role of attitude in thought (*sixiang* 思想). Wang's account focused on *taidu* (态度 correct attitude), that complex blend of thought and feeling that is usually translated as 'attitude' (Cheek 2016). For Wang, the *taidu* approach to Chinese politics was the root cause of the troubles that had bedevilled China's revolution in general and the Party's efforts in particular.[11]

In the 1990s, Wang Yuanhua recounted this earlier debate as an object lesson:

> This discussion is of universal significance. Many people still think that thought (*sixiang*) is determined by a correct attitude (*taidu*) … This is precisely what Max Weber calls the 'ethic of ultimate ends.' We know all too well the nature and the danger of this ethic of intentions. It causes scholarship to be based not on the search for truth but to become a tool for various intentions. Theory articles that serve as such intentional tools overflow with arbitrary and factional prejudice and reduce what should be a scholarly sense of responsibility to a factional mentality. (Wang 2004, 24–5, 7–8)

Wang Yuanhua invoked the dangers of the *taidu* approach that his readers in the 1990s and 2000s in China (the text is widely available on the Chinese web) '[knew] all too well' – that is, the abuses of Maoist politics. He wrote as a Party intellectual, but citing Weber as a theoretical resource signalled his cosmopolitan thinking.

10 Xu Jilin offers an overview of Wang Yuanhua's life in 'I Am a Child of the 19th Century – The Last Two Decades of Wang Yuanhu' (我是十九世纪之子' – 王元化的最后二十年), *Dushu*, 2008, 8, www.aisixiang.com/data/20738.html. An updated version in English appears in Xu (2021).

11 See Wang Yuanhua, 'Du Yaquan and the Debate over Eastern and Western Culture' (杜亚泉与东西文化问题论战), accessed November 2012, www.aisixiang.com/data/3728.html, which draws from Wang Yuanhua, *Speculations* (思辨录) (Shanghai: Shanghai guji chubanshe, 2004), 24–5, 7–8.

While such doubts and cosmopolitan thinking continue to engage China's establishment intellectuals, by no means all or even the most prominent are affected.[12] An essay published in China in January 2018 that created a great deal of buzz illustrates this. The essay is by Jiang Shigong (强世功) (b. 1967) and titled 'Philosophy and History: Interpreting the "Xi Jinping Era" through Xi's Report to the 19th National Congress of the CCP'.[13] Here, Jiang is clearly operating as an organic intellectual speaking for the Party, and his appreciation of the lessons of Party history is a far cry from that of Wang Yuanhua.

Jiang Shigong himself is no mere propagandist; he is a well-respected legal scholar and professor at Peking University Law School, focusing on constitutional law.[14] His academic work has attracted the attention of international China scholars, culminating in a special 2014 issue of the research journal *Modern China*, in which Western scholars engaged Professor Jiang on his ideas about Chinese constitutionalism. He is also a well-known defender of China's position on the proper management of the Hong Kong question, and in 2017 published an English-language book entitled *China's Hong Kong: A Political and Cultural Perspective*.

Jiang seeks to systemise Xi Thought. His argument is basically historical, providing a new periodisation of modern and contemporary Chinese history that restores the Party to its central role: China 'stood up' under Mao Zedong, 'got rich' under Deng Xiaoping and is 'becoming powerful' under Xi Jinping. The three pillars of Jiang's argument are: first, the living value of Chinese Marxism, or socialism with Chinese characteristics, as an analytical system or political theory; second, the fundamental role of traditional Chinese cultural resources in the creation of Chinese socialism; and, finally, the creative role played by Xi Jinping, China's current and future 'supreme leader'. Jiang's defence of Marxist state ideology is likely the most robust we have seen since Zhang Chunqiao made the case for his quite different reading of Mao Zedong Thought in 1975. Jiang's argument is, of course, very different from Zhang's (and both are partial and incomplete). Jiang emphasises history, not class struggle, and his goal is essentially conservative

12 A selection reflecting something of the range of Chinese intellectual debate are presented in the translation collection by Cheek, Ownby and Fogel (2020).

13 强世功，'哲学与历史—从党的十九大报告解读'习近平时代' 开放时代，2018年第1期. Translated by David Ownby under the title: Jiang Shigong, 'Philosophy and History', *Reading the China Dream*, www.readingthechinadream.com/jiang-shigong-philosophy-and-history.html. Discussion here draws from our joint introduction to that translation.

14 See Jiang's Peking University website, www.law.pku.edu.cn/sz/zzjs/hl/1910.htm.

and constructive. Still, Jiang employs the tools of dialectical materialism with great skill and rewrites modern Chinese history as the product of the ongoing dialectical relationship between theory and practice in the context of state-building and world-building.

Jiang Shigong's confidence could not contrast more strongly with Wang Yuanhua's self-critical reflections:

> 'Socialism with Chinese Characteristics' is not adding Chinese characteristics to an already defined 'socialist framework'. Rather, it uses China's lived experience to explore and define what, in the final analysis, 'socialism' is … For this reason, the report of the Eighteenth National Congress correctly talked about 'self-confidence in the path', 'self-confidence in the theory', and 'self-confidence in the institutions' involved in the construction of Socialism with Chinese Characteristics.[15]

Jiang's fulsome paean to Xi Jinping Thought (still in its longer, awkward phrasing) reflects the latest change in the relationship between the party-state and intellectuals in China. Increasingly over the past six years we have seen greater censorship, enforced orthodoxy and repression of dissenting voices in public – be they academic and theoretical or social and activist, from university professors, lawyers, ethnic minorities or women. These are perhaps the most perilous days for China's loyal and critical intellectuals since the Cultural Revolution. How long they will have to endure Xi Jinping's demand for 'unity' is open to question.

Conclusion

This review of the relationship between Chinese intellectuals and the CCP from a long-term perspective has suggested that both the Party and some intellectuals have shared the same assumptions about governance in China in which the state is a pedagogical state uplifting a population not yet ready to speak for itself nor yet qualified to be active political subjects in a constitutional polity. All share the fundamental assumptions – if not the details – of Sun Yat-sen's 'political tutelage'.

15 Jiang Shigong, 'Philosophy and History'.

As we are focusing on the history of the CCP in this volume, another reflection from the world of state socialism is appropriate. Both the Bolshevik Party and participating intellectuals contributed to a directed culture. China's propaganda state used the propaganda system as this 'directed public sphere' in which the Party directly manages the public arena and controls public associations of 'civil society' (Cheek 1998). The concept of 'directed' comes from Victor Serge's description of 'directed culture' in Stalin's Soviet Union in which the state controls the arts, ethics and ideas 'for the good of the people'. Miklós Haraszti has shown the appeal of directed culture for intellectuals under state socialism in Hungary. In his ironic novel *The Velvet Prison*, Haraszti's cynical censor concludes:

> Socialism, contrary to appearances, does not suppress the artists' Nietzschean desires but satisfies them … The state prevents my art from becoming a commodity, and it guarantees my status as a teacher of the nation.[16]

Clearly, the intellectual attraction to Party service was not limited to the Chinese.

In China, the propaganda under the CCP provided the venue for this service. The propaganda system came to include the arts and universities, as well as the media. Writers, professors, researchers, as well as journalists – indeed, all *professions* – were incorporated into the propaganda and education system under the direct management of the Propaganda Department of the CCP.[17] But a 'unified' or shared view of the pedagogical mission of intellectuals and the Party is not all. As Kuhn noted for eighteenth-century China, so, too, twentieth-century Chinese political culture and today's have not been homogeneous (Kuhn 1990, 223).[18] There have been significantly different responses within that unified field of the pedagogical state and the transformational bureaucrat. We have seen significant variations from the strident faith in the Party policies of the day – from Zhang Chunqiao to Jiang Shigong (never mind that the content of the orthodoxy is significantly different for each), to the Marxist critiques or revisions raised by Wang Shiwei, Wang Ruoshui or Wang Yuanhua. Across these variations we see our three themes: the *attractiveness* of the 'deal' offered to intellectuals by the

16 Victor Serge's ideas on 'directed' thought and culture are developed by the Hungarian poet and sociologist Miklós Haraszti (1987, 24, 94).

17 This *xuanjiao xitong* is described in Lieberthal (1995, 198–208).

18 Kuhn concludes: 'Chinese culture was unified but not homogeneous. That is why there could occur a society-wide experience such as the soul-stealing crisis, even while different social groups represented that experience in different ways' (Kuhn 1990, 223).

Party (staffed, as Susanne Weigelin-Schwiedrzik and Eddy U have noted, by many fellow intellectuals); the *agency* various intellectuals demonstrated in their practice as transformational bureaucrats; and the *variation and tensions* within that relationship, often managed by divergent exegeses of the current orthodoxy. Since it is the Party line today at the centenary of the CCP to emphasise the continuities or connections with traditional Chinese culture, it may be acceptable to note that a similar conclusion has been made about the relationship between Confucian 'scholars' (*shi* 士) and the imperial state, at least from Song times. Chinese scholars have long noted the echoes of the 'scholar official' (*shidaifu* 士大夫) social role and personal identity in the public lives of twentieth-century Chinese intellectuals (Xu 1999, 2015; Yü 2016). Peter Bol has traced intellectual service to the state and its tensions since the Tang, and Joseph Levenson has concluded that when a tradition no longer evinces such internal tensions, it is dead, 'museum-ified' (Bol 1994; Levenson 1968). So, continuing tensions in intellectual service in China today should satisfy Xi Jinping with this contribution to his Four Histories (*sishi* 四史) by China's divergent and debating establishment intellectuals.[19] The pedagogical state lives.

References

Apter, David E. and Tony Saich. 1994. *Revolutionary Discourse in Mao's Republic.* Cambridge: Harvard University Press.

Barlow, Tani. 1991. 'Zhishifenzi [Chinese Intellectuals] and Power'. *Dialectical Anthropology* 16 (3/4): 209–32. doi.org/10.1007/BF00301238.

Bol, Peter. 1994. *This Culture of Ours: Intellectual Transitions in T'ang and Sung China.* Stanford: Stanford University Press.

Brugger, Bill and David Kelly. 1991. *Chinese Marxism in the Post-Mao Era.* Stanford: Stanford University Press.

Chang, Ch'un-ch'iao (Zhang Chunqiao 张春桥). 1975. 'On Exercising All-Round Dictatorship over the Bourgeoisie' (论对资产阶级的全面专政). In *Hong Qi*, no. 4, and translated by Foreign Languages Press in Beijing in a pamphlet in the same year.

19 'Four Histories' deals with the history of the CCP, the PRC, the reform and opening up, and socialist development in the world.

Cheek, Timothy. 1997. *Propaganda and Culture in Mao's China: Deng Tuo and the Intelligentsia*. Oxford: Clarendon Press.

Cheek, Timothy. 1998. 'From Market to Democracy in China: Gaps in the Civil Society Model'. In *Market Economics and Political Change: Comparing China and Mexico*, edited by Juan D. Lindau and Timothy Cheek, 236–45. Lanham, MD: Rowman & Littlefield.

Cheek, Timothy. 2016. 'Attitudes of Action: Maoism as Emotion in Political Theory'. In *Chinese Thought as Global Theory: Diversifying Knowledge Production in the Social Sciences and Humanities*, edited by Leigh Jenco, 75–100. Albany: NY: SUNY Press.

Cheek, Timothy. 2021a. 'Xi Jinping's Counter-Reformation: The Reassertion of Ideological Governance in Historical Perspective'. *Journal of Contemporary China* 30 (132): 875–87. doi.org/10.1080/10670564.2021.1893554.

Cheek, Timothy. 2021b. 'Revisiting Yan'an Maoism: Reading Liu Shaoqi's "On the Party" 論黨 (1946)'. Presentation at the University of Leipzig, 26 April.

Cheek, Timothy. 2021c. 'Wang Shiwei's Rectification'. In *The Chinese Communist Party: A Century in Ten Lives*, edited by Timothy Cheek, Klaus Mühlhahn and Hans van de Ven, 51–70. Cambridge: Cambridge University Press. doi.org/10.1017/9781108904186.

Cheek, Timothy, David Ownby and Joshua A. Fogel, eds. 2020. *Voices from the Chinese Century: Public Intellectual Debate in Contemporary China*. New York: Columbia University Press.

Cheek, Timothy, Klaus Mühlhahn and Hans van de Ven, eds. 2021. *The Chinese Communist Party: A Century in Ten Lives*. Cambridge: Cambridge University Press.

Chiang, Kai-shek. 1947. *China's Destiny and Chinese Economic Theory*. New York: Roy Publishers.

Fitzgerald, John. 1996. *Awakening China: Politics, Culture, and Class in the Nationalist Revolution*. Stanford: Stanford University Press. doi.org/10.1515/9780804779319.

Fitzgerald, John. 2021. 'Cadre Nation: Territorial Government and the Lessons of Imperial Statecraft in Xi Jinping's China'. *China Journal* 85: 26–48. doi.org/10.1086/710372.

Goldman, Merle, Timothy Cheek and Carol Hamrin, eds. 1987. *China's Intellectuals and the State: The Search for a New Relationship*. Cambridge: Harvard Contemporary China Series. doi.org/10.1163/9781684171095.

Hamrin, Carol and Timothy Cheek, eds. 1986. *China's Establishment Intellectuals*. Armonk: M. E. Sharpe.

Haraszti, Miklós. 1987. *The Velvet Prison: Artists under State Socialism*. New York: Basic.

Ho, Dahpon D. 2007. 'Night Thoughts of a Hungry Ghostwriter: Chen Bulei and the Life of Service in Republican China'. *Modern Chinese Literature and Culture* 19 (1): 1–59.

Huang, Daoxuan (黄道炫). 2020. 'A History of *xinling* from the Yan'an Rectification Movement' (整风运动的心灵史). *Modern History Research* 2. English translation by Dayton Lekner and Nathan Gan in *Revisiting the Revolution*. prchistory.org/revisiting-the-revolution-landing-page/.

Ip, Hung-yok. 2004. *Intellectuals in Revolutionary China, 1921–1949: Leaders, Heroes and Sophisticates*. Abingdon: Routledge. doi.org/10.4324/9780203009932.

Kelly, David. 1987. 'The Emergence of Humanism: Wang Ruoshui and the Critique of Socialist Alienation'. In *China's Intellectuals and the State: The Search for a New Relationship*, edited by Merle Goldman, Timothy Cheek and Carol Hamrin, 159–82. Cambridge: Harvard Contemporary China Series. doi.org/10.2307/j.ctt1sq5th8.10.

Kuhn, Philip A. 1990. *Soulstealers: The Chinese Sorcery Scare of 1768*. Cambridge: Harvard University Press.

Levenson, Joseph R. 1968. *Confucian China and Its Modern Fate: A Trilogy*. Berkeley: University of California Press.

Lieberthal, Kenneth. 1995. *Governing China: From Revolution through Reform*. New York: W. W. Norton.

Liu, Shaoqi (劉少奇). 1947. 'On the Self-Cultivation of the Communist Party Member' (論共產黨員的修養) in *On the Party* (論黨).

Liu, Shaoqi. 1981. *Selected Works of Liu Shaoqi* (刘少奇选集). 2 vols. Beijing: People's Press.

Liu, Shaoqi. 1986. *Selected Works of Liu Shaoqi*. 2 vols. Beijing: Foreign Languages Press.

Lutz, Peter C. 1972. *The Changing Party Elite in East Germany*. Cambridge: MIT Press.

Mazur, Mary G. 2009. *Wu Han, Historian: Son of China's Times*. Lanham, MD: Lexington Books.

Teiwes, Frederick C. 1993. *Politics and Purges in China: Rectification and the Decline of Party Norms, 1950–1965*. 2nd edtion. Armonk: M. E. Sharpe.

U, Eddy. 2019. *Creating the Intellectual: Chinese Communism and the Rise of a Classification*. Berkeley: University of California Press. doi.org/10.1525/luminos.68.

Walder, Andrew. 1977. *Chang Ch'un-ch'iao and Shanghai's January Revolution*. Anne Arbor, MI: Michigan Papers in Chinese Studies, University of Michigan.

Wang, Yuanhua. 2004. *Sibianlu* (Speculations). Shanghai: Shanghai guji chubanshe.

Xu, Jilin (许纪霖). 1999. *Another Kind of Enlightenment* (另一种启蒙). Guangzhou: Huacheng chubanshe.

Xu, Jilin (许纪霖). 2015. *China's Intellectuals: Ten Essays* (中国知识分子十). Revised ed. Shanghai: Fudan daxue chubanshe.

Xu, Jilin. 2021. 'Wang Yuanhua: A Party Intellectual Reflects'. In *The Chinese Communist Party: A Century in Ten Lives*, edited by Timothy Cheek, Klaus Mühlhahn and Hans van de Ven, 175–90. Cambridge: Cambridge University Press. doi.org/10.1017/9781108904186.

Yü, Ying-shih. 2016. *Chinese History and Culture, Vol. 2: Seventeenth Century through Twentieth Century*. New York: Columbia University Press.

Yue, Daiyun and Carolyn Wakeman. 1985. *To the Storm: The Odyssey of a Revolutionary Chinese Woman*. Berkeley: University of California Press.

5

Shades of Red: Changing Understandings of Political Loyalty in the Chinese Communist Party, 1921–2021

Jérôme Doyon and Long Yang

As the Chinese Communist Party's (CCP) one-hundredth anniversary approached, General Secretary Xi Jinping (习近平) called on Party members to 'not forget their original aspirations and firmly remember their mission' (*bu wang chuxin, laoji shiming* 不忘初心，牢记使命). This slogan illustrates the current leadership's focus on Party members' devotion and loyalty to the Party.[1] Regarding party-state officials more specifically, various researchers have noted the increased importance of political criteria in cadre recruitment and discipline under Xi (Li 2018; Snape 2019; Brødsgaard 2019; Doyon 2019).

How to interpret the CCP's focus on 'original aspirations' and devotion to the organisation? For some, the current emphasis on virtue and loyalty contrasts with the declining importance given to political criteria in recruiting Party members and officials in post-Mao China (Snape 2019). Until recently, many viewed the Chinese party-state as moving away from being a 'virtuocracy' (Shirk 1982), a promotion system based on one's

1 'Opinion on Deepening and Consolidating the Results of the "Do Not Forget the Original Aspirations and Firmly Remember the Mission" Educational Subject' (关于巩固深化'不忘初心、牢记使命'主题教育成果的意见), Central Office of the Chinese Communist Party, 15 September 2020.

political virtue understood as the conformity to ideological ideals, and towards a meritocracy or technocracy (Lee 1991; Nee and Lian 1994; Bell 2018). Similarly, surveys conducted by Bruce Dickson (2014) show that while 'working for Communism' was one of the main incentives during the Mao era (1949–78), it has been replaced by less ideological motives in the post-Mao era, such as advancing one's career. By contrast, some research has stressed the continuity between Mao and post-Mao China regarding the mobilisation and disciplining of Party members and cadres (Heilmann and Perry 2011; Koss 2018; Luo 2021). Speaking to the issue of political loyalty more specifically, Andrew Walder (1985) has noted that, while it has taken different forms over time in response to political and economic circumstances, Party members and cadres' political loyalty has always been central to Party leaders, and the 'redness', or virtue, of Party members and officials was never replaced by expertise, or ability, as a recruitment criterion.

Despite the rich literature on the red and expert debate, the actual meaning of 'redness' remains elusive. This chapter contributes to this debate by exploring how the Party's understanding of political loyalty has changed over its 100-year history. Challenging the tendency to treat the CCP's definition of loyalty as a monolithic and unchanging concept, we stress the complex and pluri-dimensional aspects of the Party's understanding of this notion. At different times, the question of who must be loyal, emphasising cadres or members more broadly, and how to show it, has changed drastically. When studying the relationship between the Party and the individuals who populate it, amounting now to more than 95 million members[2] and more than 7 million officials (Chan and Gao 2019), a whole branch of literature is dedicated to better understanding how the CCP did and does think about ability and performance, and how this understanding has changed over time. Previous studies have analysed how work performance, understood in various ways, influences political recruitment and promotion (Li and Zhou 2005; Shih, Adolph and Liu 2012; Landry, Lü and Duan 2018). There is, by contrast, very little research on how the CCP understands political loyalty, despite the impact it may have on the Party's ability to maintain cohesion among its ranks as well as to expand and diversify its membership – key aspects of its resilience (Shambaugh 2008).

2 'Report on Internal Chinese Communist Party Statistics' (中国共产党党内统计公报), *Xinhua*, 5 June 2021, www.12371.cn/2021/06/30/ARTI1625021390886720.shtml.

To better understand what 'red' means, we focus on how the CCP itself has discussed loyalty and political virtue throughout its history. We rely on a corpus of central documents, the most critical intra-party documents (Lieberthal 1978; Snape and Wang 2021), spanning 1921–2021: they contain all the Party regulations, orders and directives issued by the CCP Central Committee, focusing explicitly on issues of organisational development and the recruitment and appointment of Party members and officials. While various departments of the CCP, and, in particular, the Central Organisation Department in charge of human resources, have published hundreds of documents on recruitment issues, the central documents issued by the CCP Central Committee are the more authoritative, encapsulating the perspective of the Party leadership at a given time (on the importance of Party rules, see Smith 2021). To historicise and contextualise these central regulations and orders, we also rely on a range of other Party documents and leader speeches.

Throughout this corpus, we focus on three critical notions the Party uses to describe its relationship with its members: 'loyalty' (*zhong* 忠), 'virtue' (*de* 德) and 'Party spirit' (*dangxing* 党性). This chapter not only highlights the close links between these notions as well as their centrality in the CCP's organisational culture, but also stresses their malleability, which has allowed the CCP to interpret and operationalise them in different ways throughout its history, depending on its needs and objectives. As detailed below, the Party started using the term loyalty at its founding in 1921 and put forward its goal to recruit virtuous (as well as competent) members in the 1930s. We stress that, by the late 1930s, these two notions started to be fused in the CCP's discourse. In other words, a loyal member is fundamentally a virtuous one. The concept of 'Party spirit', understood as an unconditional dedication to the Party also embodies this merging of loyalty and virtue. In line with Kenneth Jowitt's argument that a unique feature of Communist parties is that they are political organisations based on 'charismatic impersonalism' (Jowitt 1992, 23), the notion of 'Party spirit' implies a member's devotion to the organisation itself rather than its cause or leaders. 'Party spirit', popularised through Liu Shaoqi's (刘少奇) famous *How to Be a Good Communist* written in 1939, emerged in the context of the CCP's struggle against the Guomindang (GMD) and Japan (Sorace 2016; Pieke 2018).

With this long-term survey, we trace not only the changes in the Party's understanding of loyalty at different points in time but also what drove these evolutions. Our central argument is that the Party changed its definition of political loyalty when it aimed at expanding and/or diversifying its membership in response to new social, economic and political circumstances. The first dimension of variation is between ascriptive understandings of loyalty, giving more importance to one's background and personal connections, and behavioural ones, based on one's actions (Walder 1985). Early on, the CCP became reliant on an ascriptive understanding of loyalty based on class labels to ensure its survival as a small, clandestine group in a hostile environment. Yet, this ascriptive definition of loyalty was superseded by a behavioural one when the Party needed to expand its recruitment beyond the so-called revolutionary classes of workers and peasants. For instance, 'Party spirit' emerged in the late 1930s and 1940s as a behavioural approach to political loyalty, when membership went from 25,000 in 1936 to close to 5 million in 1949, and the ratio of members not from a worker or peasant background doubled (Gore 2011). The ascriptive definition of loyalty based on class labels was then abandoned in the early years of the reform era as the Party expanded its recruitment among technocrats and burgeoning economic elites to implement the economic reforms.

The second dimension of variation, focusing on the behavioural element, is tied to the level and form of activism expected from Party members and cadres. While, in some cases, a heightened focus on activism may be accompanied by extreme rectification campaigns and a sharp, albeit short-term, decrease in Party recruitment, we show that overall it is paradoxically at the outset of periods of Party expansion that the CCP becomes more demanding. As we will see in the remainder of the chapter, such insistence on activism can take many forms depending on the historical context, but, all in all, it can be understood as a willingness to mould new recruits whose loyalty remains partially questionable, and to deal with enemies from within – intellectuals seen as close to the GMD in the 1930s, the 1989 'rebels' or, more recently, Party members who would challenge the authority of Xi Jinping as the core leader. More broadly, the political virtue of its membership is a way to maintain the Party's vanguard and charismatic status while it becomes increasingly inclusive (Jowitt 1992).

This chapter is structured in a chronological manner. It traces the evolution of the Party's understanding of loyalty, focusing on turning points, and explores how it interacts with the CCP's recruitment trends. During its early years (1921–35), the CCP developed an ascriptive understanding of the loyalty of its ranks in order to survive the GMD's continuous repression. The notion of 'Party spirit' later emerged as a behavioural approach to loyalty in the context of the post–Long March organisational developments (1935–48). After the establishment of the People's Republic of China (PRC) in 1949 and until Mao Zedong's (毛泽东) death in 1976, the CCP oscillated between periods of intense activism and membership expansion, and other periods focused on economic planning. Under Deng Xiaoping's (邓小平) leadership, the Party moved to a behavioural definition of political loyalty, tied initially to one's actions during the Cultural Revolution. As the Party opened its doors to entrepreneurs in the early 2000s with Jiang Zemin's (江泽民) 'Three Represents', the demand for loyalty became increasingly focused on cadres. At the same time, in the context of rising corruption, the CCP's definition of political virtue and Party spirit expanded into the realm of morality, asking officials to be loyal but also exemplary in their personal and familial ethics. Finally, as the CCP under Xi Jinping's leadership further diversifies its membership, we see a push towards activism: the morality and ethics of both Party members and cadres are being increasingly monitored to ensure their loyalty to the Party is genuine.

Class Status as an Initial Answer to the Party's Difficulties in Guaranteeing Loyalty (1921–35)

In its first charter (1921), the CCP stipulated that people who wanted to join the Party had to show their willingness to become 'loyal and honest members' (*zhongshi dangyuan* 忠实党员).[3] However, the Party had difficulties implementing this requirement. The CCP's founding members recruited 'intellectuals' through Marxist study societies or their regional connections at universities. These recruits were mainly loyal to the members they were personally tied to, rather than the organisation as a whole (van de Ven 1992; Bianco 1971). Due to its lack of funds to support its members

3 'The First Program of the Chinese Communist Party' (中国共产党第一个纲领), *Selected Central Committee Documents of the Chinese Communist Party* (中共中央文件选集), vol. 1 (Beijing: Zhonggong zhongyang dangxiao chubanshe, 1989), 4.

as professional revolutionaries, the CCP had to allow them to work in government or companies. What is more, in 1923, one year after the CCP joined the Third International, which was under the de facto leadership of the Soviet Union, it received instructions from the latter to cooperate with the GMD (Saich 2020). Accordingly, its members automatically qualified for GMD membership, which further complexified where, exactly, their allegiance lay.[4]

Against this background, the CCP developed organisational tools to solve this issue. In 1923, it standardised the screening process for recruiting members. Since then, a recruit has to be introduced by two Party members and remain a 'candidate member' (*houbu dangyuan* 候补党员) for months of screening before becoming a full member.[5] Yet, as its membership expanded from around 50 in 1921 to about 50,000 in 1927, the Party lacked the financial means and ideological support to shape members' loyalty in a complex environment (van de Ven 1992, 181). Facing this challenge, the Party could not do much more than ask its new members to read Karl Marx's work.[6]

In 1927, the breakup of the cooperation between the CCP and the GMD led to a reduction of about 80 per cent of the CCP's membership, with many members finding themselves at odds with the Party.[7] This pushed the CCP to investigate why they betrayed the organisation and how to ensure its members' loyalty.[8] To solve this issue, and following the Third International's orders, the CCP increasingly relied on its members' class status to assess their loyalty. The investigation into the breakup with the GMD revealed that most of those who betrayed the Party were 'petty intellectuals' and their actions were said to have led many local Party organs to be destroyed by the Nationalist government. In response to this, the CCP put a great deal of effort into replacing Party secretaries, from the provincial to the county levels, with members labelled as 'workers' and 'poor peasants'.[9] For example,

4 'Resolution on the National Movement and the Guomindang' (关于国民运动及国民党问题的决议案), *Selected Central Committee Documents of the Chinese Communist Party*, vol. 1, 147.

5 'First Amendment to the Statute of the Chinese Communist Party' (中国共产党第一次修正章程), *Selected Central Committee Documents of the Chinese Communist Party*, vol. 1, 158.

6 'Decision on Organisation Problems' (组织问题决议案), *Selected Central Committee Documents of the Chinese Communist Party*, vol. 1, 472–7.

7 'Comrade An Ziwen of the Central Organisation Department's Report about the General Situation of Party Organisation to Chairman Mao' (中央组织部安子文同志关于党的组织概况向毛主席的报告), *Construction* 32, 1949. For a detailed survey of the break-up, see Yang (2008).

8 'Decisions on Party Organisation Problems' (党的组织问题决议案), *Selected Central Committee Documents of the Chinese Communist Party*, vol. 3, 304.

9 'Resolution on the Important Task of Organisation Issues' (最近组织问题的重要任务决议案), *Selected Central Committee Documents of the Chinese Communist Party*, vol. 3, 468–72.

Mao Zedong was instructed to reshuffle the Hunan Provincial Committee he headed. Among its nine new committee members, at least three had to be selected from among workers and poor peasants, and three had to be specifically responsible for mobilising workers and peasants.[10] In 1930, the Third International ordered the CCP to further reduce the proportion of intellectuals among its members: more than 80 per cent of its members had to be workers and poor peasants. The Third International's view, which the CCP adopted, was that the 'proletarianisation' of the CCP could help the Party maintain its members' loyalty.[11]

This ascriptive approach to loyalty, relying on class status as a proxy, resulted in a great purge in the Jiangxi revolutionary base. Between late 1930 and 1934, many members labelled as 'rich peasants' were arrested and executed for spreading rumours against Mao Zedong and complaining about his military decision-making (Chen 1994). According to the CCP, the Nationalist government's military operations had shaken their faith in the Party, and the rumours they spread were meant to subvert the Party from the inside.[12] The CCP then ordered the examination of the class status of all members in an attempt to further purge intellectuals and rich peasants. The official view was that members with the correct class background (i.e. workers or poor peasants) would never waver in their determination to support the Party.[13] This examination of members' class status ended as the Nationalist government destroyed the Communist bases in Jiangxi. The CCP's Central Committee had to evacuate from Jiangxi in 1934, and its membership plummeted from 300,000 to 40,000 after the Long March in late 1935.[14]

10 'Party Centre's Letter to the Hunan Provincial Committee' (中央致湖南省委信), *Selected Central Committee Documents of the Chinese Communist Party*, vol. 3, 309.

11 'Resolution on the Development of the Party Organisation' (关于发展党的组织决议案), *Selected Central Committee Documents of the Chinese Communist Party*, vol. 6, 163–6.

12 'Party Centre's Resolution on the Cadre Question' (中央关于干部问题的决议), *Selected Central Committee Documents of the Chinese Communist Party*, vol. 6, 338.

13 'Political Bureau's Directive on Decision by the Twelfth Plenary Session of the Executive Committee of the Comintern' (中共中央政治局关于共产国际执委第十二次全会决议的决定), *Selected Central Committee Documents of the Chinese Communist Party*, vol. 8, 571–9; 'Resolution of the Central Bureau of the Soviet Areas on the Strength of Party Organisation and Leadership' (苏区中央局关于巩固党的组织与领导的决议), *Selected Central Committee Documents of the Chinese Communist Party*, vol. 9, 14.

14 'Comrade An Ziwen of the Central Organisation Department's Report about the General Situation of Party'.

After the Long March (1935–48): The Emergence of 'Party Spirit'

As the CCP reflected on its failure in Jiangxi, its understanding of loyalty took a behavioural turn. In December 1935, the CCP convened a Politburo meeting to review the Third International's policy concerning recruiting members (Sheng 1992). The resulting resolution stated that members' class status should not be the primary criterion for assessing their loyalty and that intellectuals could be faithful 'allies' (*tongmeng zhe* 同盟者). The result was that intellectuals could join the Party again, and their behaviour and work performance became the basis for demonstrating their loyalty.[15] In the following years, the CCP managed to expand its territory and set up a new power base in these areas. As it did not have enough capable Party members and cadres (Lee 1991, 26), it indeed pushed to recruit many university students and leftist intellectuals.[16] Mao Zedong also realised the importance of intellectuals in mobilising villagers to support the Party and its military. He said that if intellectuals were 'relatively loyal and honest' (*bijiao zhongshi* 比较忠实) to the Party, they were qualified to be Party members.[17] In Mao's words, these Party members should be 'both virtuous and expert' (*decai jianbei* 德才兼备).[18] Among these intellectuals, schoolteachers, in particular, played a crucial role in the Chinese Communist revolution. They helped the CCP take root in the countryside and to further create and sustain base areas in central and north China (Liu 2009).

Along with this practical turn regarding its views on loyalty, a certain distrust of intellectuals, particularly recent recruits, emerged in the late 1930s and early 1940s when the CCP claimed to have discovered the infiltration of traitorous members into its organisations. All members came under examination and their class backgrounds and connections with the GMD were checked (Lee 1991, 36). As per the Nationalist government's

15 'Party Centre's Resolution on the Current Political Situation and the Party's Tasks' (中央关于目前政治形势与党的任务决议), *Selected Central Committee Documents of the Chinese Communist Party*, vol. 10, 605–21.

16 'Party Centre's Resolution on the Recruitment of Large Numbers of Members' (中央关于大量发展党员的决议), *Selected Central Committee Documents of the Chinese Communist Party*, vol. 11, 466–7; 'Party Centre's Resolution on the Recruitment of Large Number of Intellectuals' (中央关于大量吸收知识分子), *Selected Central Committee Documents of the Chinese Communist Party*, vol. 12, 207.

17 Mao Zedong, 'Recruiting Large Numbers of Intellectuals', 1939, accessed 18 April 2023, www.marxists.org/chinese/maozedong/marxist.org-chinese-mao-19391201.htm.

18 Mao Zedong, 'The Current Situation and the Party's Tasks', 10 October 1939, www.marxists.org/reference/archive/mao/selected-works/volume-2/mswv2_21.htm.

regulations on the release of prisoners, between 1934 and 1935 more than 60 per cent of Party members were said to have filed statements of repentance, renouncing their membership in the Party and opposing communism (Liu 2004). While some of them later managed to reinstate their CCP membership, and even take up important positions within Party organs, their loyalty was always under suspicion. Recently recruited intellectuals, in general, were also suspected of working for the GMD.[19]

As the CCP's membership significantly increased during the war with Japan (1937–45), intellectual members again accounted for a substantial proportion of its membership, and the Party viewed them as self-interested. Hence, the Party attempted to remould them and cultivate their loyalty to consolidate its strength. Liu Shaoqi's *How to Be a Good Communist* (1939) exemplified this turn towards a behavioural understanding of loyalty. According to Liu, being loyal required members to subordinate their interests to those of the organisation, whatever the circumstances, and even sacrifice their life for the Party. Self-sacrifice, self-cultivation and a shared acceptance of the Party's centrality were seen as crucial in forging a suitable morality among members. Consequently, 'morality' increasingly meant being loyal to the Party and serving its interests. In Liu's words, when Party members have 'only the Party's interests at heart', their unwavering 'Party spirit' is established.[20] As stressed by Timothy Cheek in his chapter in this volume, undertaking self-cultivation in the decades that followed shaped the relationship between the Party and intellectual cadres in particular.

The Yan'an Rectification Movement (1941–45) was launched based on this understanding of loyalty, aiming at rectifying Party members and cadres, and remoulding them into loyal servants of the organisation, as well as consolidating the centrality of Mao's leadership.[21] While this behavioural take on loyalty and Party spirit was still merged with ascriptive elements – the 'proletariat' being seen as reliable and loyal – these efforts to remould members through political education, criticism and self-criticism meant that even disloyal ones could be transformed into 'the awakened vanguard fighters of the proletariat'.[22] To ensure that Party organs remained under

19 'Party Centre's Instruction Concerning Cadre Examination' (中央关于审查干部问题的指示), *Selected Central Committee Documents of the Chinese Communist Party*, vol. 12, 444–7.

20 Liu Shaoqi, 'How to Be a Good Communist', July 1939, www.marxists.org/reference/archive/liu-shaoqi/1939/how-to-be/.

21 'The Party Centre's Decision on Strengthening Party Spirit' (中央关于增强党性的决定), *Selected Central Committee Documents of the Chinese Communist Party*, vol. 13, 144–6.

22 Liu Shaoqi, 'How to Be a Good Communist'.

the management of 'loyal, honest, and reliable' (*zhongshi kekao* 忠实可靠) members,[23] the Party initiated the Cadre Examination Campaign in 1943. This first massive inner-party rectification campaign aimed at remoulding unreliable individuals deemed to have infiltrated its organs. Through this campaign, the CCP's members and cadres had to demonstrate their unwavering loyalty to the Party. As the historian Gao Hua suggested, the campaign used 'ideological persuasion and coercion to forge an ideal Communist "New Man" who combined loyalty and obedience' (Gao 2018, 326). In the CCP's words, these members had 'two hearts' (*liangtiao xin* 两条心): one was towards the Party in public, and the other was towards the GMD under the cloak of secrecy. The campaign thus aimed to transform members with 'two hearts' into ones with 'one heart'.[24] As a result, many intellectual members were investigated due to their past relationships with members of the GMD when studying at university. As the historian Chen Yung-fa argues, the investigation was also accompanied by the re-education of these intellectuals to ensure their loyalty to Mao and the Party (Chen 1990, 4–5). But Mao realised that this radical practice could lead to new great purges: he ordered local Party leaders not to kill any intellectual members and initiated a Re-examination Campaign to investigate their cases.[25] In the end, the CCP proclaimed that the re-examination in Yan'an had shown that only 20 per cent of intellectual members were, to different degrees, unreliable or disloyal.[26] In parallel, the CCP also institutionalised cadre evaluation to avoid adverse selection by strengthening the organisational departments at each level and institutionalising 'virtue' as a key criterion in the recruitment and promotion of officials. This overall move to a partly behavioural view on loyalty, and the Rectification Campaign that accompanied it, set the basis for the expansion of the CCP. In 1945, when the war with Japan ended, CCP membership increased to more than 1.2 million, paving the

23 'Decision by the Politburo Concerning Strengthening the Party' (中央政治局关于巩固党的决定), *Selected Central Committee Documents of the Chinese Communist Party*, vol. 12, 157–8.

24 'Decision by the Chinese Communist Party Central Committee Concerning Cadre Examination' (中共中央关于审查干部的决定), *Selected Central Committee Documents of the Chinese Communist Party*, vol. 14, 93.

25 'Central Secretariat's Instruction on the Work of Cadre Examination and Anti-Spy to Shanxi-Chahar-Hebei Sub-Bureau' (中央书记处关于审干反奸工作给晋察冀分局的指示), *Selected Central Committee Documents of the Chinese Communist Party*, vol. 14, 402–3.

26 'Central Secretariat's Instruction to Deng Xiaoping, Rao Shushi, Lin Feng, and Cheng Zihua on the Work of Re-examining Confession Elements' (中央书记处关于对坦白分子进行甄别工作给邓小平, 饶漱石, 林枫, 程子华的指示), *Selected Central Committee Documents of the Chinese Communist Party*, vol. 14, 159.

way to seizing national power.[27] Over the following three years, the Party's membership increased 3.5 times, and the CCP continued relying on the cultivation of members' loyalty as a source of its cohesiveness.[28]

The Mao Era (1949–76): Expertise, Activism and the Display of Loyalty

Between 1949 and 1976, the CCP membership increased from 4.48 to 35 million and its understanding of its members and cadres' loyalty changed along with the Party's political agenda. The issue of CCP members' and cadres' loyalty also became increasingly entangled with their behaviour and job performance, oscillating between periods of intense activism and others focused on economic planning. These oscillations marked changes in recruitment strategies, as reflected in Figure 5.1, with activism being underscored when the Party expanded.

Figure 5.1: Trends in CCP Recruitment (1949–66).

Source: *Compilation of Internal Statistical Material of the Chinese Communist Party (1921–2010)* (中国共产党党内统计资料汇编 [1921–2010]), Organisation Department of the Chinese Communist Party, Beijing: Dangjian duwu chubanshe, 2011.

27 Mao Zedong, 'Resolution on Certain Historical Questions' (关于若干历史问题的决议), 1945, *Selected Works of Mao Zedong* (毛泽东选集), vol. 3 (Beijing: Renmin chubanshe, 1991), 952–1003.

28 Liu Shaoqi, 'Liu Shaoqi's Speech at the Chinese Communist Party's First National Organisational Work Conference' (刘少奇在中国共产党第一次全国组织工作会议上的报告), 1951, *Reference and Educational Material on the History of the Chinese Communist Party* (中共党史教学参考资料), vol. 19 (Beijing: Neibu chuban, 1986), 260–9.

During the early years of the PRC, particularly before 1951, the lack of CCP members and cadres to administer the country and manage industries compelled the Party to change its criteria for defining its members' loyalty, leaning towards a behavioural approach. Loyalty increasingly had to do with members' ability.[29] To demonstrate their loyalty, members had to acquire the scientific knowledge and skills necessary to serve the Party's new political agenda (Schurmann 1971, 5). In early 1949, An Ziwen (安子文), then deputy director of the CCP's Central Organisational Department, reported to Mao that the Party was in dire need of recruiting new members who could manage industries and cities.[30] The existing members, coming mainly from a rural background, lacked the knowledge and skills to establish economic stability and carry out industrialisation (Gao 2004). The Party's organisation departments at different levels focused on recruiting individuals with higher education or technical skills, and existing members had to show their political zeal by undergoing further training. As shown in Figure 5.1, this led to a decrease in CCP admissions because the total number of experts and intellectuals was small compared to the rural population that constituted the bulk of the membership.

To counter this trend, the CCP started expanding again in the early 1950s, while closely monitoring the recruits' political loyalty. The CCP recruited intellectuals, yet it still distrusted their loyalty in the Cold War context and initiated political campaigns to examine their virtue and loyalty (Oksenberg 1968). In early 1950, the CCP launched a rectification campaign among Party members and cadres to secure their loyalty by cultivating their 'virtue'.[31] Two years later, Liu Shaoqi said it was wrong to prioritise members' expertise over their virtue and loyalty. In Liu's analysis, many educated members had studied and worked under the Nationalist government, which put their dedication to the Party in doubt. They might be in touch with officials of the Nationalist government in Taiwan. Liu thus ordered organisation departments to cultivate their political virtue through criticism and self-criticism sessions.[32] In that context, the Central Organisation Department

29 'Party Centre's Decision on the Preparation of 53,000 cadres' (中共中央关于准备五万三千个干部的决议), *Selected Central Committee Documents of the Chinese Communist Party*, vol. 17, 426–31.

30 'Comrade An Ziwen of the Central Organisation Department's Report about the General Situation of Party'.

31 'Party Centre's Instruction on Developing and Strengthening the Party Organisation' (中央关于发展和巩固党的组织的指示), *Selected Documents on Organisational Work* (组织工作文件选编), 1949–52 (Beijing: Neibu chuban, 1980), 221–3.

32 Liu Shaoqi, 'Struggling for Becoming Better Communists' (为更高的共产党员的条件而斗争), 1953, *Liu Shaoqi's Writings since the Founding of the People's Republic of China* (建国以来刘少奇文稿), vol. 3 (Beijing: Zhongyang wenxian chubanshe, 2005), 245–64.

standardised 'virtue' and 'expertise' as the critical criteria in Party member and cadre recruitment. Here virtue referred to the acceptance of the Party's ideology and regulations and was, therefore, indistinguishable from political loyalty.[33] Expertise meant that members should learn the necessary scientific knowledge and skill to perform their duty effectively. Meanwhile, the new technical cadres were instructed to work under the supervision of 'old revolutionaries' to ensure their virtue and loyalty towards the Party.[34] The CCP thus ordered local units to cultivate these new Party members: if they were relatively loyal, provincial authorities had to promote them, even if it bypassed the normal promotion process.[35]

Starting from 1955, the CCP's top leaders became increasingly concerned about collusion between the American camp and the alleged Chinese domestic 'enemies'.[36] Against this background, the mid-1950s witnessed both high levels of recruitment and the purge of allegedly disloyal Party members. The Party initiated a campaign to examine the individual histories of its members, ranging from the rank and file to provincial Party secretaries.[37] According to official statistics, between 1955 and 1960, more than 51 million cadres, Party members and public sector staff members were investigated. Around 630,000 of them were identified as 'hidden enemies' (*yincang de diren* 隐藏的敌人), most of them intellectual Party members.[38]

The Party's distrust of intellectuals peaked with the Anti-Rightist Campaign of 1957–58 and the Great Leap Forward (1958–61). More than half a million intellectuals were forced into manual labour or banished to frontier regions. Living a life of hardship became a means for them to show their willingness to subordinate their individual interests to the socialist cause

33 'Party Centre's Decision on Strengthening Cadre Management' (中央关于加强干部管理的决定), *Selected Documents on Organizational Work*, 1953–54 (Beijing: Neibu chuban, 1980), 101–6.

34 An Ziwen, 'Struggling for Removing Negative and Unhealthy Phenomena in the Party's Organisation' (为消除党组织内的消极的和不健康的现象而斗争), *People's Daily*, 12 February 1953.

35 'Party Centre's Decision on the Unified Allocation of Cadres, the Reforming of the Technicians, and the Cultivation and Training of a Large Number of Cadres' (中央关于统一调配干部,团结,改造原有技术人员及大量培养, 训练干部的决定), *Selected Documents on Organisational Work*, 1953–54, 98–101.

36 Mao Zedong, 'Speech at the Chinese Communist Party's National Congress' (在中国共产党全国代表会议上的讲话), 1955, www.marxists.org/chinese/maozedong/marxist.org-chinese-mao-195503.htm.

37 Zhongyang pizhuan, 'Central Organisation Department's Report Concerning the Situation of Cadre Examination Conference' (中央组织部关于审干工作会议的情况的报告, *Selected Documents on Organisational Work*, 1957, 323–9.

38 'Party Centre's Summary Report Concerning the Campaign to Wipe Out Hidden Counterrevolutionaries' (中共中央十人小组关于肃清暗藏反革命分子运动的总结报告), *Collection of Documents from the Campaign to Wipe Out Hidden Counterrevolutionaries* (肃清暗藏反革命分子运动文件汇编) (Jinan: Neibu chuban, 1961), 32.

(Cheek 2015). Cadres with intellectual class status were said to have become a privileged class as they had indulged in a 'bourgeois lifestyle'. In the early 1960s, millions of cadres were sent to villages to live, work and eat together with villagers.[39] Making them more like villagers and cultivating their sense of the 'proletariat' became one of the main ways of ensuring they would be loyal to the Party.[40] To showcase their political loyalty, they had to share the villagers' daily routine.[41] While the emphasis on monitoring the behaviour of Party members and cadres to ensure their loyalty took place at a time when the CCP membership was increasing rapidly (1951–60), as shown in Figure 5.1, the extreme form taken by the Anti-Rightist Campaign led to a disruption of recruitment in 1957.[42] The following years saw a decrease in recruitment as the CCP blamed rural cadres for the failure of the Great Leap Forward and curtailed its expansion in the countryside.[43]

CCP recruitment started to pick up again in 1964 and peaked in 1966 in the wake of the Socialist Education Movement and the beginning of the Cultural Revolution. Once again, CCP urban Party members and cadres were sent to the countryside to change their lifestyle to resemble that of villagers, their ability to adopt a 'proletarian' lifestyle being a sign of their loyalty.[44] About 3.5 million officials and university students were sent to the countryside to carry out the Socialist Education Movement (1962–66) (Perry 2019, 552).

The Cultural Revolution (1966–76) was a unique period as personal loyalty to Mao Zedong was placed above loyalty to the Party. With the Party apparatus virtually collapsing, Mao sustained his reign through a personality cult (Wu 2014). While Party spirit as an organisational view

39 'Central Organisational Department's Notification Concerning Sending Cadres at the Central Level Down to Villages' (中央组织部关于从中央一级抽调干部下放农村基层的通知), *Selected Documents on Organisational Work*, 1960, 360–1.

40 'Party Centre's Notice on the Methods of Cadre Work in the Future' (中央关于今后干部工作方法的通知), *Selected Documents on Organisational Work*, 1957, 290–4.

41 'Central Organisational Department's Notification Concerning Sending Cadres at the Central Level Down to Villages'.

42 'Party Centre's Instruction on the Work of Recruiting Members during the Second Five-Year Plan' (中央关于第二个五年计划时期接收新党员工作的通知), *Selected Documents on Organisational Work*, 1957, 259–61.

43 'Party Centre's Urgent Instruction Letter Regarding the Current Policy Problem of People's Communes' (中共中央关于农村人民公社当前政策问题的紧急指示信), *Selected Important Documents since the Founding the People's Republic of China* (建国以来重要文献选编), vol. 13 (Beijing: Zhonggong zhongyang wenxian chubanshe, 1996), 675–6.

44 'Party Centre's Instruction on the Control and Priority of Recruiting New Members' (中共中央关于领导有控制有重点地接受新党员的指示), *Selected Documents on Organisational Work*, 1964, 102–7.

of loyalty became less relevant, it was during this period that a behavioural approach to loyalty became central within the CCP. Mao's personality cult translated into repeated and ritualistic demonstrations of loyalty that pervaded everyday life, art and culture (Leese 2011). While Figure 5.1 shows a net increase in CCP recruitment in 1966, the disruption of the CCP bureaucracy and the lack of data or archival material make it impossible at this point to systematically analyse how this personalised view on loyalty was operationalised in the Party's recruitment policy in subsequent years.

The Deng Xiaoping Era (1978–97): Party Spirit against Factionalism and Rebellion

After the beginning of the reform and opening following Mao Zedong's death, the Party's approach to political loyalty changed drastically, moving away from ascriptive criteria. Class labels gradually disappeared as a criterion to join the Communist Youth League and the CCP and to enter school or receive job assignments. Individuals were no longer to be referred to by their earlier class designation (Lee 1991). The CCP also changed its policy concerning individuals' overseas connections, as such links were no longer a legitimate reason to bar someone from joining the Party (Lee 1991, 191). Overall, one's family background or social relations became less important in evaluating one's loyalty when admitting them into the Party or getting them promoted.

The implementation of economic reforms required technically skilled individuals and, as a result, educational qualifications became increasingly important in recruiting CCP members and officials (Lee 1991). In 1980, Deng Xiaoping called for the recruitment and promotion of individuals who were 'revolutionary, younger, more educated, and more technically specialised' (*geminghua, nianqinghua, zhishihua, zhuanyehua* 革命化、年轻化、知识化、专业化).[45] The 'productive forces standard' (*shengchan li biaozhun* 生产力标准) became central in cadre management as recruiting and promoting officials was increasingly based on their technical skills and work performance (Takahara 2018). Yet, Deng still emphasised revolutionary qualities, referring to CCP members' and cadres' adherence to the current Party line and their behaviour during the Cultural Revolution.

45 Deng Xiaoping, *Deng Xiaoping Selected Works* (邓小平文选), vol. 2 (Beijing: People's Publishing House, 2014), 316.

The Party line was defined by the 'Several Principles of Political Life in the Party', a landmark central document of the reform era issued in 1980.[46] It criticised the previous poor implementation of collective leadership and stressed the leadership's opposition to 'personal arbitrary rule'. It called on Party members to 'study diligently, be both red and expert', and revived the notion of 'Party spirit' after it was set aside during the Cultural Revolution, presenting it as a remedy against factionalism.

This definition of Party spirit directly targeted the individuals who had advanced their political careers under the protection of the 'Gang of Four':

> There are still a number of cadres and Party members relatively deeply influenced by Lin Biao (林彪) and the 'Gang of Four' that are still factionalist, and are even still conducting factionalist activities … 'there are no visible mountains but there are hidden rocks'.[47]

A notice on the selection of cadres more specifically was issued in 1986, calling for a careful investigation of their behaviour during the Cultural Revolution and since the Third Plenum of the Eleventh Central Committee held in December 1978. Against this background, a rectification campaign was implemented (1983–87) to deal with the 'three kinds of people' who obtained Party membership and advanced their political careers during the Cultural Revolution (Ch'i 1991; Baum 1994).

In line with what we have seen during previous periods, this turn to a definition of loyalty based on members' current and past behaviour took place at a time of Party expansion. As shown in Figure 5.2, the number of yearly Party recruits started to increase again in the early 1980s after a decade of overall stagnation and decrease, and it peaked during the Rectification Campaign.

The definition of political loyalty based on members' behaviour during the Cultural Revolution became obsolete once the Party had weeded out what it perceived as factionalist elements. As a result, Party recruitment progressively became routinised and procedural in the late 1980s. Figure 5.2 in fact shows a clear drop in recruitment after 1985–86. In addition to the decrease in recruitments, widespread inactivity among Party members has been widely seen as a sign of political decay, leading to the 1989 movement (Ch'i 1991; Rosen 1990).

46 'Several Principles on Political Life in the Party' (关于党内政治生活的若干准则), Central Committee of the Chinese Communist Party, 1980.
47 Ibid.

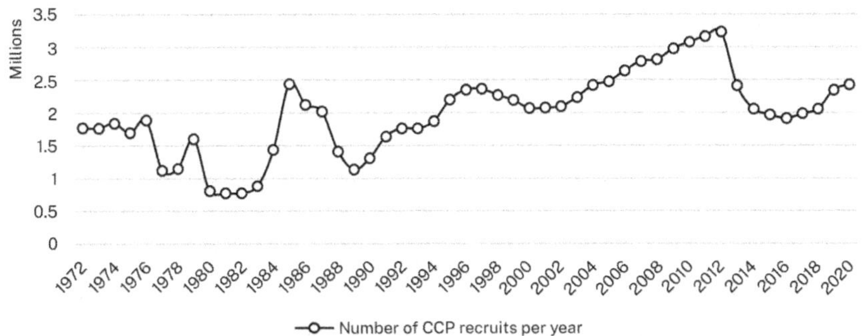

Figure 5.2: Trends in CCP Recruitment (1972–2020).

Source: *Compilation of Internal Statistical Material of the Chinese Communist Party (1921–2010)* (中国共产党党内统计资料汇编 [1921–2010]), Organisation Department of the Chinese Communist Party, Beijing: Dangjian Duwu Chubanshe, 2011; 'Internal Chinese Communist Party Statistical Reports', 2012–21, accessed on 12 April 2022, news.12371.cn/dzybmbdj/zzb/dntjgb/.

The June 1989 mobilisations, in which many CCP members took part, pushed the Party to rethink its approach to recruitment. A central notice published in August 1989 criticised the low quality of Party members and the tendency to rely mainly on age and diplomas in appointing and promoting cadres. It noted that the Party could not rely on 'the productive forces' standard as a substitute for the principle of having both virtue and talent, and that recruiters 'must be prevented from paying more attention to talent and less to virtue'.[48] In 1990, the Party drafted, for the first time, a separate central document dedicated to the process of recruiting CCP members.[49] To limit adverse selection, it stressed the screening and training of individuals before their admission to the Party. It set a minimum training requirement of 40 hours for new recruits and a compulsory biannual evaluation of every cell's recruitment work. The political education of Party members and cadres to strengthen their Party spirit was further stressed by a 1994 central decision on Party-building.[50] This emphasis on loyalty and political education was accompanied by another wave of Party expansion, as shown in Figure 5.2. This post-1989 recruitment drive has been widely documented and was particularly strong among students: the Party wanted to ensure they developed a stake in the regime's survival (Rosen 2004; Gore 2011).

48 'Notice on Strengthening Party Construction' (关于加强党的建设的通知), Central Committee of the Chinese Communist Party, 1989.

49 'Chinese Communist Party's Working Rules for Recruiting Members (Provisional)' (中国共产党发展党员工作细则 (试行)), Central Committee of the Chinese Communist Party, 1990.

50 'Decision on Few Important Issues Regarding the Strengthening of Party Building' (关于加强党的建设几个重大问题的决定), Central Committee of the Chinese Communist Party, 1994.

The 'Three Represents' (2000): A Moral Turn in the Party's Understanding of Loyalty

As China further liberalised its economy, Jiang Zemin initiated the Three Represents policy to coopt an emerging middle class within the Party. Jiang Zemin first introduced this policy during an inspection tour of Guangdong Province in February 2000. In practice, the policy lifted the ban on recruiting private entrepreneurs into the CCP (Dickson 2003), as the Party was to represent not only the three revolutionary classes – workers, farmers and soldiers – but also the 'advanced productive forces' (*xianjin shengchanli* 先进生产力), the 'advanced culture' (*xianjin wenhua* 先进文化) and the 'interest of the vast majority of the Chinese people' (*zhongguo zui guangda renmin de genben liyi* 中国最广大人民的根本利益).[51] This policy was included in the Party charter in 2002. This change was accompanied by a new push in Party recruitment after 2002, as shown in Figure 5.2. It also accelerated the sociological transformation of the CCP towards a middle-class Party: while workers and peasants still represented more than 50 per cent of its membership in 1997 (Gore 2011, 19), they represented less than 35 per cent in 2019.[52]

Due to high levels of corruption (Wedeman 2012), which resulted in the masses increasingly objecting to Party members' morality,[53] discussions of members' and cadres' ethics became increasingly important in the late 1990s and 2000s. A 2001 central document called for the improvement of the Party's 'workstyle' (*zuofeng* 作风) to limit 'formalism', 'bureaucratism' and 'hedonism', and to prevent disconnection from the masses. The issue of 'workstyle' is directly linked to the Party's image, and therefore political loyalty: 'Some cadres do not have excellent moral integrity, and their behaviour is not checked carefully, which impacts the image and prestige of the Party.'[54] This expanded definition of what constitutes virtue, and by extension loyalty, became the norm in the early 2000s, and remained so under Hu Jintao (胡锦涛). Issues of workstyle and Party spirit were effectively

51 Jiang Zemin, 'Comrade Jiang Zemin's Work Report at the 16th Party Congress' (江泽民同志在党的十六大上所作报告), 8 November 2002, www.mfa.gov.cn/chn/pds/ziliao/zyjh/t10855.htm.

52 'Chinese Communist Party Internal Statistics 2019 Report' (2019年中国共产党党内统计公报), Organisation Department of the Chinese Communist Party, June 2020.

53 Li Yuanchao, 'Uphold the Standard of Being Equipped with Both Virtue and Talent but Virtue Comes First in Choosing People' (坚持德才兼备以德为先用人标准), *Qiushi*, 16 October 2008.

54 'Party Centre's Decision on Strengthening and Improving Workstyle Building' (中共中央关于加强和改进党的作风建设的决定), Central Committee of the Chinese Communist Party, 2001.

conflated in a 2009 central document on Party-building: 'strengthening the cultivation of Party spirit provides important foundations and impetus for developing a fine workstyle'.[55]

In that context, Party cadres became the main focus of attention, instead of mere members. In a 1995 speech, Jiang asked cadres to 'pay attention to politics', study ideological texts and exemplify Party spirit.[56] As the Party increasingly fused the question of political virtue with personal and family ethics, Jiang Zemin also asked cadres to 'take the lead in establishing a good family style'.[57] The educational campaign of the 'three stresses' launched in 1998 also called on Party cadres to 'stress study, stress politics, stress righteousness' (Luo 2021).

Beyond such campaigns, it was through the institutionalisation of recruitment, evaluation and promotion mechanisms that cadres were to be kept in check. This process started under Deng Xiaoping, as central regulations structured an assessment system based on the cadres' 'virtue' (*de* 德), 'ability' (*neng* 能), 'diligence' (*qin* 勤) and 'achievement' (*ji* 绩).[58] The Party regularly reviewed cadres' behaviour and performance, asking them to conduct criticism and self-criticism sessions focusing on their behaviour, ideology and adherence to Party policies and regulations (Manion 1985; Lee 1991, 315). Jiang Zemin went one step further with the issuance in 1995 of the first complete and systematic central document on the management of leading cadres, specifying that they were to be held responsible for the performance of their units.[59] These mechanisms were further defined as the 1995 provisional document was replaced in 2002 by the full-blown 'Regulations on the Promotion and Appointment of Leading Party and Government Cadres' (for an analysis of the different versions of this document, see Doyon 2019).

55 'Party Centre's Decision on Some Important Issues Related to Strengthening and Improving Party Building under New Circumstances' (中共中央关于加强和改进新形势下党的建设若干重要问题的决定), Central Committee of the Chinese Communist Party, 2009.

56 Jiang Zemin, 'Leading Cadres Must Pay Attention to Politics' (领导干部一定要讲政治), 27 September 1995, www.reformdata.org/1995/0927/4391.shtml.

57 Jiang Zemin, 'Leading Cadres Must Take the Lead in Establishing a Good Family Style' (领导干部要带头树立好的家风), 21 July 1998, www.reformdata.org/1998/0721/5758.shtml.

58 'Notice on Selecting and Appointing Cadres Strictly According to Party Principles' (关于严格按照党的原则选拔任用干部的通知), Central Committee of the Chinese Communist Party, 1986.

59 'Provisional Work Regulations for the Promotion and Appointment of Leading Party and Government Cadres' (党政领导干部选拔任用工作暂行条例), Central Committee of the Chinese Communist Party, 1995.

New cadre management regulations adopted the expanded definition of loyalty mentioned above, fusing political virtue and personal ethics. Contrasting with the Deng era's understanding of virtue as 'upholding socialism and Party leadership',[60] the 2007 Provisional Regulations on Civil Service Assessments defined virtue as 'referring to political and ideological quality as well as displays of personal integrity, professional ethics and social virtue' (quoted in Snape 2019). This trend is in line with Jowitt's argument regarding the evolution of Communist systems: as they become more inclusive in dealing with society, Communist party-states must maintain discipline among their officials so as not to lose their charismatic impetus and legitimacy (Jowitt 1992). In parallel to the widespread cooption of social actors through Party membership, it implies the training and mobilisation of officials to maintain their 'Party spirit' (Pieke 2009; Sorace 2016) as well as the standardisation and expansion of the discipline apparatus to ensure the cadres' compliance (Brødsgaard 2012; Li 2018).

The Xi Jinping Era (Post-2012): Combating *Fake Loyalty*

The domain of political virtue and Party spirit expanded under Xi Jinping in the context of a massive anti-corruption drive (Fu 2014). Not only has the meaning of virtue further expanded into the realm of ethics and personal relationships, but also, and by contrast to what has been the norm under his two predecessors, Party members are once again the focus of the CCP's calls for loyalty, alongside cadres.

As we have seen, political criteria never disappeared from cadre selection and promotion in the reform era. They have, however, become increasingly crucial under Xi Jinping as his administration has criticised the tendency to select cadres based on artificial indicators of ability, such as GDP growth (Doyon 2019). Virtue is once again seen as more important than ability in selecting officials. The 2014 and 2019 versions of the Work Regulations for the Promotion and Appointment of Leading Party and Government

60 Deng Xiaoping, 'Reform of the Party and State Leaders System' (党和国家领导制度的改革), 18 August 1980, *Deng Xiaoping Selected Works*, vol. 2.

Cadres put forward 'political quality' (*zhengzhi suzhi* 政治素质) and 'political standard' (*zhengzhi biaozhun* 政治标准) as essential criteria for cadre recruitment and evaluation.[61]

The emergence of these vague notions of political quality or standard go hand in hand with an extensive understanding of virtue and Party spirit. Going one step further in the direction of fusing political virtue and personal ethics, recent regulations ask for the 'strengthening of (cadre) monitoring outside of the workplace, inquiring about (their) social morality, professional ethics, family virtue, personal integrity etc'.[62] Confirming the fusion of the two notions that emerged under Jiang Zemin, for Xi Jinping, 'workstyle issues are fundamentally Party spirit issues'.[63] Moreover, cadres' relationships, particularly with family members, have become increasingly important in judging their loyalty. Official criticisms of 'naked officials' (*luoguan* 裸官) illustrate this tendency well. As officials whose immediate families live abroad, they are perceived as at risk of defecting or using their overseas connections to facilitate corrupt behaviour.[64] Interestingly, this broadening of the definition of virtue does not concern only cadres: according to the revised Party disciplinary regulations, both cadres and members can be sanctioned for violating social or family morals.[65]

Against this background, cadres, as well as mere Party members, must be increasingly active in performing their political loyalty. According to the 'Several Principles on Political Life in the Party under the New Situation', a revised version of the landmark document of 1980 discussed above, Party members must 'unswervingly implement the Party's basic line' and they cannot have an 'ambiguous', 'aloof or indifferent' stance on ideological issues. These guidelines also note that:

61 'Work Regulation for the Promotion and Appointment of Leading Party and Government Cadres' (党政领导干部选拔任用工作条例), Central Committee of the Chinese Communist Party, 2014; 'Work Regulation for the Promotion and Appointment of Leading Party and Government Cadres' (党政领导干部选拔任用工作条例), Central Committee of the Chinese Communist Party, 2019.

62 'Work Regulation for the Promotion and Appointment of Leading Party and Government Cadres' (党政领导干部选拔任用工作条例), Central Committee of the Chinese Communist Party, 2019.

63 Xi Jinping, 'Steadfastly Promoting the Construction of the Party's Integrity and the Fight Against Corruption' (坚定不移推进党风廉政建设和反腐败斗争), 12 January 2016, theory.people.com.cn/n1/2018/0103/c416126-29743028.html.

64 'Notice Regarding Improving the Reporting of Leading Cadres' Personal Matters' (关于进一步做好领导干部报告个人有关事项工作的通知), Organisation Department of the Chinese Communist Party, December 2013.

65 'The Chinese Communist Party's Disciplinary Regulations' (中国共产党纪律处分条例), Central Committee of the Chinese Communist Party, August 2018.

> when the people's interests are harmed, when the image of the Party and the state is damaged, or when the Party's ruling position is threatened, one must stand up for them with a clear stance and take the initiative to wage the struggle resolutely.[66]

Party members who do not actively show their loyalty risk being accused of being 'two-faced individuals' (*liangmian ren* 两面人). This term, reminiscent of the 'two hearts' intellectuals of the 1930s–40s, did not appear in the 1980 version of the document. According to a central document on Party-building issued in 2019, the term refers to individuals who challenge the authority of the leadership by 'complying in public with the centre's orders while opposing them in private'.[67] Along these lines, Party members are forbidden to 'openly express viewpoints and opinions that run counter to the lines of theories, guiding principles and policies, as well as the implementation of major decisions of the Party Centre'.[68]

These different forms of unsanctioned behaviour fall under the umbrella term of 'fake loyalty' (*wei zhongcheng* 伪忠诚).[69] As detailed by a provincial Party school team, fake loyalty can take a variety of forms, illustrating the Party's encompassing definition of loyalty:

> First, the ones who pay lip service to Marxism, while in reality they have faith in Feng Shui masters and have only personal promotion and wealth in their hearts. Second, the ones who look diligent on the surface but eat, drink and are merry in private. Third, the ones who pretend to focus on economic development but abuse their power for personal gain behind the Party's back. … Fourth, the ones who behave like they are dedicated to the public but under the table mix up officialdom and business … Fifth, they are Party members or leading cadres on the surface but … they see foreign countries as escape routes and are always preparing to 'jump ship'.[70]

66 'Guidelines on the Political Life within the Party under the New Situation' (关于新形势下党内政治生活的若干准则), Central Committee of the Chinese Communist Party, 27 October 2016.

67 'Opinion on Strengthening the Party's Political Construction' (关于加强党的政治建设的意见), Central Office of the Chinese Communist Party, 31 January 2019.

68 'The Chinese Communist Party's Regulations on the Protection of Party Members' Rights' (中国共产党党员权利保障条例), Central Committee of the Chinese Communist Party, 4 January 2021.

69 'Opinion on Strengthening the Party's Political Construction' (关于加强党的政治建设的意见), Central Office of the Chinese Communist Party, 31 January 2019.

70 'Firmly and Clearly Oppose "Fake Loyalty"' (旗帜鲜明反对'伪忠诚'), *Qiushiwang*, 25 January 2018, www.qstheory.cn/dukan/hqwg/2018-01/25/c_1122313690.htm.

The Xi Jinping administration relies on encompassing definitions of political virtue and Party spirit as tools to strengthen Party cohesion, with issues of corruption and disloyalty being closely monitored and sanctioned by the Party disciplinary apparatus. Going beyond the institutional checks on cadres developed in the past 40 years, Party cadres and members have been asked since the Mass Line Education Campaign launched in 2013 to take part in criticism and self-criticism sessions, called 'democratic life meetings' (*minzhu shenghuohui* 民主生活会) (Doyon 2014). They should also join regular training sessions, on CCP history or the CCP's charter, for example, to rectify their workstyle and strengthen their Party spirit.[71] The explicit willingness to rectify Party cadres, but also members, through education and self-criticism is reminiscent of Liu Shaoqi's views on the relationship between the Party and its members, as exposed in *How to Be a Good Communist* (Liu 1939), and of practices of the Mao era. They are, however, more about ensuring organisational discipline and obedience to the leader than instilling a revolutionary ideology within the Party ranks. This is reflected in the slogan of the 'Two Safeguards', included in the Party's charter in 2022 at the occasion of the Twentieth National CCP Congress: to safeguard the 'core' status of General Secretary Xi Jinping within the CCP and to safeguard the centralised authority of the Party.

The emphasis on rectification and active loyalty of Party members has been accompanied by a change in recruitment policy. A revised version of the Working Rules for Recruiting Members was published in 2014, giving more weight to the screening and education of recruits and calling on recruiters to stress quality over quantity.[72] While we see in Figure 5.2 a clear drop in the number of annual CCP recruits between 2012 and 2016, numbers have risen again since then. The turn to a voluntaristic take on political loyalty has, in fact, gone together with the growth of Party cells in social organisations and private businesses, further expanding beyond the CCP's traditional support bases and among potentially less reliable publics (Koss 2021; Doyon 2021).

The pressure put on Party cadres and members has the potential to create adverse effects. Cadres appear reluctant to take new initiatives for fear of being disciplined, leading to bureaucratic inaction (Ang 2020). Also,

71 'Opinion on Deepening and Consolidating the Educational Results of the "Do Not Forget the Original Aspirations and Firmly Remember the Mission" Theme' (关于巩固深化'不忘初心、牢记使命'主题教育成果的意见), Central Office of the Chinese Communist Party, 15 September 2020.

72 'Chinese Communist Party's Working Rules for Recruiting Members' (中国共产党发展党员工作细则), Central Committee of the Chinese Communist Party, 11 June 2014.

despite the increase in Party recruitment, the emphasis on activism further limits debates within the Party. While diverse views still coexist within the CCP under Xi Jinping, they have less space to be expressed (Cai 2021): the limited venues for political competition within the CCP, or 'intra-party democracy', have been curtailed (see Jean-Pierre Cabestan, Chapter 1, this volume), and channels for internal communications are also increasingly controlled.[73] Over time, this may further restrict the Party's capacity to attract new recruits and lead to its elite being increasingly disconnected from what goes on at the grassroots.

Conclusion

With the objective of contributing to a better understanding of the CCP's evolution, this chapter draws on a corpus of central documents spanning the 100 years of the CCP to show the malleability of the CCP's understanding of its members' and cadres' loyalty. Far from monolithic and unchanging, the CCP has shown its adaptability and ability to rethink its relationship with its membership in response to the evolving political, social and economic circumstances.

Tracing these evolutions, we show that the CCP's understanding of political loyalty has evolved mainly along two dimensions. First, it fluctuated between ascriptive interpretations of loyalty and behavioural ones. While, in its early years, the CCP primarily relied on an ascriptive view of loyalty linked to class labels, it quickly realised the importance of recruiting more intellectual members to expand its territory and influence. It is in that context that the Party popularised the notion of 'Party spirit', as developed in Liu Shaoqi's *How to Be a Good Communist*. Beyond the question of class background, Party members' loyalty could be cultivated by transforming their 'two hearts' into having 'one heart' towards the Party. In that context, the issue of political loyalty became fused with that of virtue to justify the necessity of subordinating their individual interests to those of the Party's. This behavioural approach to political loyalty continued to play an essential role in the following decades. It became hegemonic with the disappearance of class labels in the early years of the reform era and with the policy of the Three Represents that marked the end of the Party's class nature.

73 Dave Kang, 'In Xi's China, Even Internal Reports Fall Prey to Censorship', Associated Press, 31 October 2022, apnews.com/article/health-china-beijing-covid-wuhan-3c199e3f1a084013da18fc9e6061e775.

Second, as part of the behavioural approach to loyalty, the level of activism expected from CCP members and cadres varied drastically over time. This activism took the relatively narrow form of a personality cult under Mao; however, as the CCP's understanding of virtuous behaviour expanded to personal and family ethics in the later reform era, it also assumed more encompassing ones. The Party's call for activism at times focused specifically on CCP cadres – seen as the key political elite whose loyalty really matters – as was the case under Jiang Zemin and Hu Jintao. At different times, this extended to the broader CCP membership to ensure the organisation's mobilisation capacity, as under the Xi administration.

This chapter also shows that the CCP emphasises behavioural notions of loyalty and, in particular, high levels of activism when it wants to expand and diversify its membership. Rather than a pure sign of atrophy, emphasising political activism is, hence, part of the CCP's inclusion strategy, as it aims at ensuring the loyalty of new and diverse members and can contribute to the adaptability and resilience of the CCP as an organisation (Shambaugh 2008; Nathan 2003; Saich 2021). This push for Party expansion can, however, be disrupted by extreme rectification campaigns when the leadership becomes highly suspicious of new members and tries to govern every aspect of their lives. In line with Liu Shaoqi's approach to loyalty and Party spirit, every element of Party members' behaviour must then reflect their dedication to the organisation. We saw that CCP recruitment dropped during the Anti-Rightist Campaign of the 1950s and during the anti-corruption and mass line campaigns of the early 2010s. Beyond limiting its inclusiveness, such campaigns can also limit internal debates, preventing the CCP from tapping into the diversity of its membership to ensure its adaption to changing social developments.

References

Ang, Yuen Yuen. 2020. *China's Gilded Age: The Paradox of Economic Boom and Vast Corruption*. New York: Cambridge University Press. doi.org/10.1017/9781108778350.

Baum, Richard. 1994. *Burying Mao: Chinese Politics in the Age of Deng Xiaoping*. Princeton: Princeton University Press. doi.org/10.1515/9780691186399.

Bell, Daniel. 2018. *The China Model: Political Meritocracy and the Limits of Democracy*. Princeton: Princeton University Press.

Bianco, Lucien. 1971. *Origins of the Chinese Revolution, 1915–1949*. Stanford: Stanford University Press.

Brødsgaard, Kjeld Erik. 2012. 'Cadre and Personnel Management in the CPC'. *China: An International Journal* 10(2): 69–83. doi.org/10.1353/chn.2012.0016.

Brødsgaard, Kjeld Erik. 2019. 'China's Political Order under Xi Jinping: Concepts and Perspectives'. *China: An International Journal* 16(3): 1–17. doi.org/10.1353/chn.2018.0022.

Cai, Xia. 2021. 'The Party That Failed'. *Foreign Affairs* 100, no. 1.

Chan, Hon S. and Jie Gao. 2018. 'The Politics of Personnel Redundancy: The Non-Leading Cadre System in the Chinese Bureaucracy'. *The China Quarterly* 235: 622–43. doi.org/10.1017/S0305741018000565.

Cheek, Timothy. 2015. *The Intellectual in Modern Chinese History*. Cambridge: Cambridge University Press, 2015. doi.org/10.1017/CBO9781139108874.

Chen, Yung-fa. 1990. *Yan'an's Shadow* (延安的阴影). Taipei: Institute of Modern History, Academia Sinica.

Chen, Yung-fa. 1994. 'The Futian Incident and the Anti-Bolshevik League: The "Terror" in the CCP Revolution'. *Republican China* 19(2): 1–51. doi.org/10.1080/08932344.1994.11720232.

Ch'i, Hsi-sheng. 1991. *Politics of Disillusionment: The Chinese Communist Party under Deng Xiaoping, 1978–1989*. Armonk: M. E. Sharpe.

Dickson, Bruce J. 2003. *Red Capitalists in China: The Party, Private Entrepreneurs, and Prospects for Political Change*. Cambridge: Cambridge University Press. doi.org/10.1017/CBO9780511510045.

Dickson, Bruce J. 2014. 'Who Wants to Be a Communist? Career Incentives and Mobilized Loyalty in China'. *China Quarterly* 217: 42–68. doi.org/10.1017/S0305741013001434.

Doyon, Jérôme. 2014. 'The End of the Road for Xi's Mass Line Campaign: An Assessment'. *China Brief* 14, no. 20 (October).

Doyon, Jérôme. 2019. 'Clientelism by Design: Personnel Politics under Xi Jinping'. *Journal of Current Chinese Affairs* 47 (3): 87–110. doi.org/10.1177/18681026 1804700304.

Doyon, Jérôme. 2021. 'Influence without Ownership: The Chinese Communist Party Targets the Private Sector'. *Institut Montaigne*, 26 January. www.institutmontaigne.org/en/blog/influence-without-ownership-chinese-communist-party-targets-private-sector?_wrapper_format=html.

Fu, Hualing. 2014. 'Wielding the Sword: President Xi's New Anti-Corruption Campaign'. University of Hong Kong Faculty of Law Research Paper 30. doi.org/10.2139/ssrn.2492407.

Gao, Hua. 2018. *How the Red Sun Rose: The Origin and Development of the Yan'an Rectification Movement, 1930–1945*. Hong Kong: Chinese University Press. doi.org/10.2307/j.ctvbtzp48.

Gao, James. 2004. *The Communist Takeover of Hangzhou: The Transformation of City and Cadre, 1949–1954*. Honolulu: University of Hawai'i Press.

Gore, Lance. 2011. *The Chinese Communist Party and China's Capitalist Revolution: The Political Impact of the Market*. Abingdon: Routledge. doi.org/10.4324/9780203838952.

Heilmann, Sebastian and Elizabeth Perry, eds. 2011. *Mao's Invisible Hand: The Political Foundations of Adaptive Governance in China*. Cambridge: Harvard University Asia Center. doi.org/10.2307/j.ctt1sq5tc6.

Jowitt, Kenneth. 1992. *New World Disorder: The Leninist Extinction*. Berkeley: University of California Press. doi.org/10.1525/9780520913783.

Koss, Daniel. 2018. *Where the Party Rules: The Rank and File of China's Communist State*. New York: Cambridge University Press. doi.org/10.1017/9781108354981.

Koss, Daniel. 2021. 'Party Building as Institutional Bricolage: Asserting Authority at the Business Frontier'. *China Quarterly* 248.S1 (November): 222–43. doi.org/10.1017/S0305741021000692.

Landry, Pierre F., Xiaobo Lü and Haiyan Duan. 2018. 'Does Performance Matter? Evaluating Political Selection along the Chinese Administrative Ladder'. *Comparative Political Studies* 51 (8): 1074–105. doi.org/10.1177/0010414017730078.

Lee, Hong Yung. 1991. *From Revolutionary Cadres to Party Technocrats in Socialist China*. Berkeley: University of California Press. doi.org/10.1017/CBO9780511664250.008.

Leese, Daniel. 2011. *Mao Cult: Rhetoric and Ritual in China's Cultural Revolution*. Cambridge: Cambridge University Press. doi.org/10.1017/CBO9780511984754.

Li, Hongbin and Zhou Li-An. 2005. 'Political Turnover and Economic Performance: The Incentive Role of Personnel Control in China'. *Journal of Public Economics* 89, no. 9–10 (September): 1743–62. doi.org/10.1016/j.jpubeco.2004.06.009.

Li, Ling. 2018. 'Politics of Anticorruption in China: Paradigm Change of the Party's Disciplinary Regime 2012–2017'. *Journal of Contemporary China*, July, 1–17. doi.org/10.1080/10670564.2018.1497911.

Lieberthal, Kenneth. 1978. *Central Documents and Politburo Politics in China.* Ann Arbor: University of Michigan. doi.org/10.3998/mpub.20021.

Liu, Chang. 2009. 'Prometheus of the Revolution: Rural Teachers in Republican China'. *Modern China* 35 (6): 567–603. doi.org/10.1177/0097700409337249.

Liu, Shousen. 2004. 'Zhao Yimin: A Legendary on the CCP's Propaganda Front' (赵毅敏: 中共宣传战线上的传奇人物) *Party History Panorama* (党史博览) 6: 18–21.

Luo, Zhifan. 2021. 'Discipline the Party: From Rectification Campaigns to Intra-Party Educational Activities in China'. *China: An International Journal* 19 (4): 52–74. doi.org/10.1353/chn.2021.0041.

Manion, Melanie. 1985. 'The Cadre Management System, Post-Mao: The Appointment, Promotion, Transfer and Removal of Party and State Leaders'. *China Quarterly* 102: 203–33. doi.org/10.1017/S030574100002991X.

Nathan, Andrew J. 2003. 'Authoritarian Resilience'. *Journal of Democracy* 14 (1): 6–17. doi.org/10.1353/jod.2003.0019.

Nee, Victor and Peng Lian. 1994. 'Sleeping with the Enemy: A Dynamic Model of Declining Political Commitment in State Socialism'. *Theory and Society* 23 (2): 253–96. doi.org/10.1007/BF00993817.

Oksenberg, Michel. 1968. 'The Institutionalisation of the Chinese Communist Revolution: The Ladder of Success on the Eve of the Cultural Revolution'. *China Quarterly* 36: 61–92. doi.org/10.1017/S0305741000005610.

Perry, Elizabeth. 2019. 'Making Communism Work: Sinicizing a Soviet Governance Practice'. *Comparative Studies in Society and History* 61 (3): 535–62. doi.org/10.1017/S0010417519000227.

Pieke, Frank N. 2009. *The Good Communist: Elite Training and State Building in Today's China.* Cambridge: Cambridge University Press. doi.org/10.1017/CBO9780511691737.

Pieke, Frank N. 2018. 'Party Spirit: Producing a Communist Civil Religion in Contemporary China'. *Journal of the Royal Anthropological Institute* 24 (4): 709–29. doi.org/10.1111/1467-9655.12913.

Rosen, Stanley. 1990. 'The Chinese Communist Party and Chinese Society: Popular Attitudes toward Party Membership and the Party's Image'. *Australian Journal of Chinese Affairs* 24 (July): 51–92. doi.org/10.2307/2158889.

Rosen, Stanley. 2004. 'The Victory of Materialism: Aspirations to Join China's Urban Moneyed Classes and the Commercialization of Education'. *China Journal* 51: 27–52. doi.org/10.2307/3182145.

Saich, Tony. 2020. *Finding Allies and Making Revolution: The Early Years of the Chinese Communist Party*. Leiden: Brill. doi.org/10.1163/9789004423459.

Saich, Tony. 2021. *From Rebel to Ruler: One Hundred Years of the Chinese Communist Party*. Cambridge: The Belknap Press of Harvard University Press. doi.org/10.4159/9780674259638.

Schurmann, Frans. 1971. *Ideology and Organisation in Communist China*. Berkeley: University of California Press.

Shambaugh, David. 2008. *China's Communist Party: Atrophy and Adaptation*. Washington, DC; Berkeley: Woodrow Wilson Center Press.

Sheng, Michael. 1992. 'Mao, Stalin, and the Formation of the Anti-Japanese United Front, 1935–37'. *China Quarterly* 129: 149–70. doi.org/10.1017/S0305741000041266.

Shih, Victor, Christophe Adolph and Mingxing Liu. 2012. 'Getting Ahead in the Communist Party: Explaining the Advancement of Central Committee Members in China'. *American Political Science Review* 106 (1): 166 87. doi.org/10.1017/S0003055411000566.

Shirk, Susan L. 1982. *Competitive Comrades: Career Incentives and Student Strategies in China*. Berkeley: University of California Press. doi.org/10.1525/9780520315969.

Smith, Ewan. 2021. 'On the Informal Rules of the Chinese Communist Party'. *China Quarterly* 248, no. S1 (November): 141–60. doi.org/10.1017/S0305741021000898.

Snape, Holly. 2019. 'A Shifting Balance between Political and Professional Responsibility: Paradigmatic Change in China's Civil Servant and Cadres Management Systems'. *Mapping China Journal* 3: 1–24.

Snape, Holly and Weinan Wang. 2021. 'Finding a Place for the Party: Debunking the "Party-State" and Rethinking the State-Society Relationship in China's One-Party System'. *Journal of Chinese Governance* 5 (4): 477–502. doi.org/10.1080/23812346.2020.1796411.

Sorace, Christian. 2016. 'Party Spirit Made Flesh: The Production of Legitimacy in the Aftermath of the 2008 Sichuan Earthquake'. *China Journal* 76 (1): 41–62. doi.org/10.1086/685844.

Takahara, Akio. 2018. 'The CCP's Meritocratic Cadre System'. In *Routledge Handbook of the Chinese Communist Party*, edited by Willy Wo-Lap Lam, 606–51. London: Routledge. doi.org/10.4324/9781315543918-10.

van de Ven, Hans. 1992. *From Friend to Comrade: The Founding of the Chinese Communist Party, 1920–1927*. Berkeley: University of California Press.

Walder, Andrew G. 1985. 'The Political Dimension of Social Mobility in Communist States: China and the Soviet Union'. *Research in Political Sociology* 1: 101–17.

Wedeman, Andrew. 2012. *Double Paradox: Rapid Growth and Rising Corruption in China*. Ithaca: Cornell University Press. doi.org/10.7591/cornell/9780801450464.001.0001.

Wu, Yiching. 2014. *The Cultural Revolution at the Margins: Chinese Socialism in Crisis*. Cambridge: Harvard University Press. doi.org/10.4159/harvard.9780674419858.

Yang, Kuisong. 2008. *Guomindang: Unity with Communists and Anti-Communism* (国民党的联共与反共). Beijing: Shehui kexue wenxian chubanshe.

6

The United Front: The Magic Weapon of the Chinese Communist Party's Metamorphoses

Emmanuel Jourda

Introduction

The united front (*tongyi zhanxian* 统一战线) as a concept is closely linked to the history of Chinese communism. However, it still barely figures as a research subject. During the revolutionary period, few authors made it their main concern (Van Slyke 1967; Armstrong 1977). Since the beginning of the twenty-first century, the subject has been examined by only a small number of researchers, most notably Gerry Groot, although more recent works (Lulu 2019; Joske 2022; Brady 2017) demonstrate that it is increasingly present in the politics of the Xi Jinping era. The former lack of interest can be explained by the fact that the united front with Chinese characteristics is, in general, absent from the historical corpus of international political concepts. Yet, its pertinence and its function became clear during Mao Zedong's revolutionary march towards power and rejection of Soviet influence, and in the attitudes of his successors to his legacy in post-revolutionary China.

This article aims to take stock of the development of the united front concept in the Chinese context, from its designation by Mao as a 'magic weapon' to its reshaping under Xi Jinping (De Giorgi 2019). In contrast to works that examine the united front through the prism of its practices or institutional framework, which remain insufficient and often overemphasise its permanence,[1] the proposed discursive approach relies on official Chinese sources to demonstrate how the use of the united front, as a conceptual and malleable tool of power, is an ideological–institutional indicator of the Chinese Communist Party (CCP) regime's transformations. To develop this approach, this chapter follows changes to the united front's terminology. The parts on the revolutionary period are mainly based on secondary sources in French and English as cited in the text, with added insights provided by the use of Stuart Schram' work (cf. *infra*). For the post-revolutionary period, the main sources are two periodicals – *Chinese Communist Party* (*Zhongguo gongchandang* 中国共产党) and *China Politics* (*Zhongguo zhengzhi* 中国政治) – which provide a useful illustration of the official discourse throughout the period.

When it comes to defining the united front based on its practices, for many years such characterisation was the prerogative of the services of the Chinese Nationalist Party (Guomindang, GMD), as a result of GMD–CCP cooperation (*guogong hezuo* 国共合作) during the rather chilly phases of their civil war. In the GMD's anti-Communist terminology, the united front corresponded to a designation describing any action targeting a potential adversary in order to infiltrate (*shentou* 渗透), divide (*fenhua* 分化), persuade (*lalong* 拉拢) or conquer (*zhengqu* 争取) by negotiation (*tanpan* 谈判) or fomenting (*cefan* 策反) in order to isolate (*guli* 孤立) using methods (*fangfa* 方法) and expedients (*shouduan* 手段) covering the agitprop spectrum: dissimulation (*weizhuang* 伪装), propaganda (*xuanchuan* 宣传) and provocation (*gudong* 鼓动), either directly or via auxiliaries (Wu Caiguang 1996). From then on, this vocabulary was also used by those in opposition to the irredentist aspirations of the CCP, notably with regard to Taiwan and Hong Kong (Jourda 2019b).[2] More broadly, united front work is presently described as synonymous with interference by the CCP in the public space, with the intent to produce a context favourable to its political, cultural or economic interests, outside or within its frontiers (e.g. Hong Kong, Taiwan, Tibet, Xinjiang, the diaspora, Confucius Institutes, silk

1 Samson Yuen and Edmund Cheng, Chapter 15, this volume, provide, by contrast, a welcome illustration of how United Front practices have changed over time in the context of Hong Kong.

2 The acronym *tongzhan* 统战, for *tongyi zhanxian*, disconnected in this context from any conceptual aspect, signifies nothing more than, word for word, *battle for unification*.

roads, etc.). United front practices can, therefore, be summarised as a combination of influence, interference and counter-interference (Charon and Jeangène Vilmer 2021; Brady 2017; Liao and Tsai 2019).

Institutionally, the united front consists primarily of the political 'work' carried out by the United Front Work Department (*tongyi zhanxian gongzuo bumen* 统一战线工作部门) (UFWD), directly reporting to the Central Committee of the CCP.[3] However, the CCP discourse is evasive on what 'united front work' means, as much on the selected targets (*duixiang* 对象) – potentially all non-Communists – as on the concrete actions carried out and the results achieved. Further, this definition is reductive in that it does not provide an understanding of why and how the united front became, above all, a component of the party-state, figuring in the preamble to the Constitution of the People's Republic of China (PRC).[4] It serves as a framework for political consultation (*zhengzhi xieshang* 政治协商), notably with the eight democratic parties (*ba ge minzhudang* 八个民主党) present at the Chinese People's Political Consultative Conference (CPPCC) (*Zhongguo renmin zhengzhi xieshang huiyi* 中国人民政治协商会议). Hence, the united front presents three clear facets; it is at once an institution, an apparatus and an action directed at targets.

However, these definitions of the united front based on its practices or institutional framework remain unsatisfactory. They cannot explain how and why the united front has been assimilated into the history of the revolution, as part of the theory and the myth, particularly through its qualification as a 'magic weapon'. To unveil the united front in all its complexity and malleability, it should be historicised, beginning with Franz Schurmann's ([1966] 1968) reflections on the ideology and organisation of the CCP.[5] This approach allows us to consider it as belonging not in a register of pure theory (*lilun* 理论), but as political thought (*sixiang* 思想) – an organisational notion dedicated to the implementation of a grassroots politico-ideological practice for the entire CCP, the state and their respective offshoots. The united front can then be considered cumulatively as both a structure and

3 A first official version of a united front entity was established in December 1937 representing the CCP in Wuhan with the Guomindang. It then evolved into its definitive form in the 1940s.

4 Constitution of the People's Republic of China, 1982, china.usc.edu/constitution-peoples-republic-china-1982.

5 Schurmann does not go into detail about the united front, but he influenced the work of Van Slyke, as indicated by the latter's acknowledgements.

an ideology, a mode of action and the codification of action, and a historic process of implementation of the Communist revolution and an element of its myth.

Therefore, I have chosen not to address the united front through its practices, which are well documented by the existing literature (Van Slyke 1967; Armstrong 1977; Groot 2004, 2012, 2016, 2019, 2021; Brady 2017; Liao and Tsai 2019; Lo, Hung and Loo 2019), but through a discursive approach to determine its political function in the CCP organisation and discourse since its Maoisation. This fresh approach is possible thanks to Stuart Schram's (2004, 2005) work on Mao's writings, which have never been exploited from the united front angle. It provides an opportunity to reconsider the significance of opaque official terms, such as the united front's status as a 'magic weapon' or 'science', formulated by Mao and his successors. To this end, this chapter starts with how the concept and the characteristics of the united front, as formulated by its Soviet initiators, were sinicised and systemised by Mao in the late 1930s. We will then see how the concept was both institutionalised and relegated to become an abstraction after 1949 and until the end of the Maoist era. The final sections provide a new reading of the evolution of the concept in post-revolutionary PRC, from a reformist lever to an instrument to re-ideologise the regime, in particular under Xi Jinping.

At a fundamental level, the inclusion of the united front in the Chinese system is not based on the extensively documented difficulties of the first united front (Chevrier 1983), ending in 1927,[6] but on its appropriation by Mao, implicitly from 1927 to 1936 and explicitly in the late 1930s. This allowed Mao to invent political properties for the concept, to the point of turning it into an infallible ideological weapon, leading inexorably to the consolidation of the Party's hegemony, whatever the context. The result was a hybrid notion – an operational attribute of Communist power – that included elements of discourse, organisation, power and myth. This can be traced through the history of the 'magic weapon' label attached to the idea of the united front.

6 The first united front was formed on Maring's initiative, with Sun Yat-sen in the 1920s. The Communist International (Comintern) had requested that recalcitrant Chinese Communists take out individual membership in the GMD. Chiang Kai-shek put a stop to this in spring 1927.

After the end of the first united front, Mao created, progressively and tentatively, his own practice of the concept. This started covertly and pragmatically among the bandits of the Jingganshan and the Gelaohui secret societies of Northern Shaanxi (Jourda 2023), an approach that contrasted with the inconsistent way the CCP had been dealing with such groups (Park 2002). These initial steps in the sinicisation of the united front are generally overlooked as they did not lead to the development of specific political concepts and do not have their place in the well-defined narrative of Moscow's overall approach to relying on the united front to counter the Japanese invasion.

It was only long after the Japanese invaded northern China in 1931 that the second united front was formed between the GMD and the CCP. At first, neither Chiang Kai-shek (Jiang Jieshi) nor Mao Zedong were in favour of it; Chiang saw it (rightly so) as a stepping-stone for Mao in the direction of power, and Mao wanted to build a strong united front without Chiang, because of the civil war climate. The rapprochement nevertheless took place under pressure from Moscow, which hoped to make China a buffer zone from the Japanese threat, with Chiang as the key player in armed resistance. In 1932, Mao, as a prudent tactician in a CCP in which he was still far from dominant, stressed that an end to the united front would lead to the failure of the revolution. It remained to be decided what form the front should take. Action from the base was preferred to alliances at the top in order to recruit, undermine and infiltrate the supposed popular level of the Nationalist structure (Roux 2009). But the CCP radicalised its action. It planned vain urban uprisings and peasant unrests in areas held by the GMD, in conjunction with military offensives, to achieve a hypothetical mobilisation of the masses. Mao stood aside and became marginalised in 'his' soviet when the leaders of the CCP had to retreat there (1931–32). In 1932, the game changed when the Comintern ordered the end of the 'class against class' strategy and the return of the united front (from then on 'anti-Fascist'). In late 1935, the pro-Comintern wing of the CCP tried to impose the idea of a united front led by the Nationalists, against Mao's opinion (Esherick 2022). This course of action was supposed to gain ground in the towns and thus to revive a failing urban strategy. These discussions were set aside while the CCP had no permanent base and while Chiang pursued his eradication policies. It was only the game of bluff played at the Xi'an Incident in December 1936 that enabled the 'alliance' between the two parties, providing a stage for their enmity (Tsang 2015).

Following the arrest of Chiang by Zhang Xueliang, the Nationalist general in command of the troops that had been ordered to liquidate the remainder of the Long March in North Shaanxi, Mao hoped for the trial and elimination of Chiang. Stalin decided otherwise. Mao, submitting reluctantly to the wishes of Moscow, and Chiang, only too pleased to escape lightly, both agreed half-heartedly to cooperate against Japan. The alliance they formed was only symbolic in that each occupied different and distinct territories (Mitter 2013). Unlike during the period of integration of the 1920s, the CCP continued to carry out autonomous structural and military consolidation. However, this theoretical reconciliation did bring about the end of the civil war and allowed for the eventuality of a coalition government (*lianhe zhengfu* 联合政府). This was a coalition whose statist potential for the CCP was enhanced by a central political role and implantation in urban centres, on the condition of positions in territories held by the GMD. The Japanese invasion in July 1937 still did not produce concerted resistance (Paulès 2019). Chiang Kai-shek's best forces were decimated while Mao Zedong preserved his. Wang Ming was sent by Moscow to improve the effectiveness of a unified military front under the authority of Chiang. So began a new phase in the struggle for hegemony within the CCP, which was undecided for several months from late in 1937 onwards until the military situation led Stalin to favour Mao.

Mao entered the political fray armed with a theory of practice (*shijian lun* 实践论) legitimising action on the ground in preference to dogma and disconnected abstract decisions. Mao skilfully positioned this autonomy in the context of a Chinese operational particularism. He was careful to avoid theorising any break with Moscow. The other side of the coin was that this autonomy depended on success on the ground (Chevrier 2022). His synthesis of the ideas garnered during the 1930s would have remained theoretical if Wang Ming's strategic pretensions had not been destroyed by action on the ground. Wang's failure at Wuhan in summer 1938 disqualified him and incited Stalin to play the Mao card.

Mao emerged from the struggle officially established as the CCP's number one, recognised as the leader of an independent party within a political alliance where he could control his own position. The laurels of patriotism lost by the CCP in the 1930s were regained by virtue of the alliance; participation in the alliance spared the Communist forces from facing Japan on the frontline, which would have been unavoidable if the GMD had capitulated. Mao was keen to occupy the space on the political stage provided by the legalisation of the CCP and other parties in the name of the united resistance movement. From September 1937, the united front existed officially through the establishment of the Consultative Council for National Defence (*guofang canyihui* 国防参议会), which was yet to become active (Fairbank and Feuerwerker 2008). Against this background, Mao continued to appropriate the revolutionary values of Sun Yat-sen, increasingly relying on Nationalist references and his demand for democracy in China. With the launch in March 1938 of the People's Political Council (*guomin canzhenghui* 国民参政会), the avatar of the tortuous process of institutionalisation of the Nationalist regime during the 1930s, the united front was put in place, further associating the CCP with values of resistance, liberty, pluralism and moderation. However, the question of unification of the CCP was still to be finalised in order to accentuate the struggle against the GMD in an unfavourable context in which the Communist forces were marginalised on the ground, their urban presence was at its lowest point and Chiang had regained his popularity (Chevrier 2022).

Mao achieved this in just a few years by structuring, normalising and expanding the system of action characterised by the 'three magic weapons' (*san ge fabao* 三个法宝) formula, in which the united front, previously destined to be relegated to the margins of the revolution, became central. While this terminology is well known, its intellectual origin has long remained unclear. Relying on the work of Stuart Schram, never analysed from the united front angle, it is now possible to propose a brand-new genealogy of the concept that refreshes the perspective of Mao's rise to power at the heart of a communism in the process of 'sinicisation' (*Zhongguohua* 中国化).

A Chinese 'Magic Weapon'

On 1 April 1938, addressing pupils at the Northern Shaanxi Public School directed by Cheng Fangwu, Mao mentioned that every Communist should behave in an exemplary manner and put his words and commitments, both political and military, into action, because the CCP did not have in its ranks 'an elder Party member living on a mountain, training disciples to master the use of magic weapons and then sending them down the mountain in batches'.[7] This reference is taken from the *Investiture of the*

7 'Speech at the Opening Ceremony for the Second Session of the Northern Shaanxi Public School' in Schram (2004, 275–9).

Gods (*fengshen yanyi* 封神演义), a sixteenth-century work attributed to Xu Zhonglin (许仲琳) that shaped Daoist myths and legends (Xu 2002). Yuanshi Tianzun (元始天尊), the Celestial Venerable of the Primordial Beginning, the immortal of the Kunlun mountains, gave three magic weapons to his disciple and great strategist Jiang Ziya (姜子牙), who was destined to carry out the will of the gods by putting an end to the reign of the Shang dynasty, which had lost the celestial mandate to the Zhou (eleventh century BCE): an apricot-yellow banner (*xinghuangqi* 杏黄旗) to erase all difficulty, a supernatural steed in the form of a chimeric version of Père David's deer (*elaphurus davidianus* – *sibuxiang* 四不像) and a whip to lash spirits (*dashenbian* 打神鞭).

In May 1939, Mao, on his road to power, engaged the Party in a prolonged conflict (*chijiu zhan* 持久战) with Japan and the Guomingdang. On 9 July, in the same school, he reiterated the historical-heroic-Daoist reference, but delivered in person three contemporary magic weapons to the young people who were about to leave for the front, so that they could destroy 'demons, ghosts, and monsters'. The triptych included the united front, 'armed struggle' (*wuzhuang douzheng* 武装斗争) and 'Party-building' (*dang de jianshe* 党的建设). Between April 1938 and July 1939, Mao transformed himself into the demiurge of combat communism; to accomplish the destiny of China, he prepared the levers of a triple asymmetrical war against political, military and ideological systems greater than himself: sinicisation of communism and control of the Party; guerrilla warfare against the Japanese troops and armed conflict with the GMD; and political infighting on the ground held by the Nationalist regime to win the favour, or at least the neutrality, of the nation's various elements. The reference to the three weapons was undoubtedly intended to galvanise the young recruits by using an explicitly Chinese popular mythical-heroic cultural reference that they could probably master far better than Communist rhetoric. This origin story was overlooked for many years, however, because the truncated, brief and largely forgotten text taken from the speech[8] mentions only the united front and makes it the only modern magic weapon, a counterpart to the anti-demon whip offered to this army of young recruits.[9]

8 'Persist in Long-Term Cooperation between the Guomindang and the Communist Party' in Schram (2005, 148–54).

9 The chronology presented here rests on the fact that the texts in question are the versions closest to the originals we have at hand today.

It was not until 4 October 1939, in his introduction to the new journal the *Communist* (*Gongchandangren* 共产党人), that Mao again used the three pillars of the magic devices to enable a heroic CCP to 'storm and shatter the enemy's positions' for the revolution.[10] The reference to the Daoist legend was omitted, probably because the journal was intended to bolshevise a party in constant need of unifying and edifying. As it became better known than the July speech, this text contributed to obscuring the cultural origins of the idea. It demonstrates, however, the scope of the program of sinicisation of Maoist action: bolshevisation and acculturation of the available Communist concepts in one move, to have them at hand.

Mao's changes of position between these different registers, and his apparent hesitation as to the content of the 'weapons',[11] have left observers confused and in danger of seeking coherence (Armstrong 1977) at the price of a multidimensional practice that was still in a tentative and uncertain phase.

This rediscovery of the origins of the magic weapons terminology allows us to better understand its impact. Although excluded from the history of political ideas because of its picturesque aspect, the notion nevertheless demonstrates how Mao constructed his communism. It was not the united front itself that was sinicised, as that belonged in the framework provided by Moscow, but the way in which it was used and closely linked to the establishment of the CCP as the priority expressed in the October article.[12] Party construction, as inscribed in the rewriting of the history of the Party, was made cohesive around the leader in a triple temporal approach: in the past, the magic weapons ensured the continuity of the struggles undertaken by the CCP since its foundation; in the present, they imposed a continuum of action on three fronts, as the domination of the CCP must emerge from the interconnection between the three 'weapons' affecting the whole revolutionary process and leading the Party to victory; for the future, the formula becomes a form of incantation, announcing a supposedly ineluctable victory in a context of great uncertainty. In this way, in the space of a few months, Mao transformed an anecdotal but easily accessible cultural reference into hyperbole that could be applied to *his* CCP.

10 'Introducing the Communist', in Schram (2005, 244–54).

11 Mao also uses the term 'magic weapons' for the Japanese when they are 'hitting hard' and 'winning over'. Cf. 'Please Take a Look and See Whose Realm Our Land Is Today', 18 May 1941, in Schram (2005, 745).

12 For Stuart Schram, the naming of the three magic weapons was intended specifically as a tool for building the Party. See Schram (2005, xvii).

Many years would pass before this discursive bricolage would have a widespread impact. At the time, the CCP was under great pressure. Chiang Kai-shek, on his side, also used political weaponry against the Communists to restore the reputation of his regime (and himself personally), while disputing the battleground of public opinion. He acted slowly but surely and delayed calling for a constituent assembly until 1940, thus reviving the democratic opposition, although the latter was still far from leaning towards the Communist side (Fairbank and Feuerwerker 2008). However, here Mao could use the 'New Democracy' to exploit this opportunity, adding it to the three magic weapons. Combining them into a triple central ensemble provided the possibility of sliding from one module to another, whatever the mode, open or closed, moderate or radical, at anytime, anywhere, whatever the circumstance, on a global or local scale. In other words, on a symbolic level, the *magic* represented the Maoist revolution in motion, at once autonomous and orthodox with regard to Moscow.

From this perspective, it is possible to represent the united front as a balance point in the framework of Maoist action. It allows the one who wields its discursive power to accuse anybody to be either too dogmatic or too opportunistic, depending on the state of the CCP's internal struggle. It also allows moving towards political pragmatism without appearing as heterodox. However, on the ground, the exercise was a double-edged sword: the cadres had to reduce their intransigence (and that of the 'base') concerning exactions, hoarding and collectivisation of land, at least for the moment, as the interests of the allies had to be preserved. But these compromises might have exposed them to accusations that could lead to 'rectification' if they damaged the ideological purity of the Party.

In the Maoist struggle for hegemony, the united front concept may be viewed not as a simple import, but as a political appropriation adapted to the Chinese context and the transformation of the CCP in its quest for power. It allowed, even beyond the simple tactical level, to fight the enemies of the revolution (at a particular moment) – the so-called first rank of enemies (e.g. imperialism, big business, the invading Japanese, Nationalists, etc.) – by seeking alliances with the second-rank enemy sociopolitical groups (e.g. progressive parties, the middle classes, Nationalists, activists, etc.), acceptable in the first instance but likely to be eventually included in the first category. The united front became a way to rank adversaries, using potential checks and levers to strategically advance the revolution at several different speeds. This approach always implies isolating the enemy (of the first rank) by clearly displaying the points common to the Communists and to the targets (of the second rank) (Van Slyke 1967; Armstrong 1977). However, in Maoist practice, it should only be seen as a starting point. The political action consisted in reinforcing the union – by delegitimising and marginalising elements within the so-called friendly camp (the rest of society), the hesitant, the critics and the potential adversaries of the CCP – by letting it appear to be the product of a consensus seemingly achieved by autonomous forces (Groot 2004). The work of the united front should then be interpreted as bringing about the social structuring intended for its transformation, according to the needs and political ambitions of the Party. This structuring is represented by multiple units (associations, organisations, etc.), apparently self-governed but, in practice, proxy Communist cells. From then on, the process should no longer be seen as consistent with forming a consensus achieved through alliances. On the contrary, it aimed to produce a consensus by removing all dissent, notably by occupying the public domain (Chevrier 2022). This way, the CCP was reassured in its ecumenical self-representation as being the avant-garde not of a class but of the 'people' made up of allied classes.

Establishing an Institutional Parenthesis

After it first appeared, the 'magical' symbolic became part of the revolution for as long as the Party was aiming for power. Its use did not, however, cease with the founding of the PRC. On the contrary, the united front was used to institutionalise the political order of a 'people's democracy'. It became a module that established an institutional parenthesis that ended with the 'New Democracy' and the launching of the 'grand disorder' desired by Mao.

Following the launch of the Rectification Movement (*zhengfeng yundong* 整风运动) (1942–44) (Cheek 2016), the Maoist party built up coherence during July 1943 around Mao Zedong Thought (*Mao Zedong sixiang* 毛泽东思想). The united front then served to structure a national union against the GMD. It, therefore, quit the register of the purely material and provisional, and tactical or strategic, alliance. It became an overall and effective device for social organisation, contributing (according to Mao) to the freeing of energies favouring the overriding ambition of the Party. Seen from this angle, it was not autonomous forces that were enrolled in the adventure, but structured and formatted energies produced and engendered by the system that they were supposedly producing and engendering (Chevrier 2022).

From an institutional angle, appearances had been saved. In January 1946, the Political Consultative Conference (*zhengzhi xieshang huiyi* 政治協商會議) ended the exclusive control of the GMD over the nation and opened the way towards the 'coalition government' instalment desired by the Roosevelt administration. Pluralism disappeared with the return to civil war (1946). In 1948, while Chiang's regime promulgated a democratic constitution in the hope of staunching the flow of democrats moving over to the CCP camp, Mao thought up the idea of long-term democratic coexistence with his allies. In September 1949, a common program (*gongtong gangling* 共同纲领) was set up structuring the CPPCC, a constituent assembly of the PRC (Bonnin 2007).

In the following years (in different regions), the united front was still useful. The CCP, which asserted itself into the military sphere, was still far from being able to 'hold' the towns and needed proxies to manage urban society and take control in the quietest possible way. It was presented as a useful tool to maintain some political plurality around the CCP by liaising with intellectuals (Vidal 2008) or with gangsters (Wong 1997) to bide time for the Party to structure itself and develop the means to squash any resistance, especially in rural areas (Xu and Billingsley 2013; Wang Di 2018). As for rhetoric, the combination of the three 'weapons' was always necessary. In Party writings, they were still described as important because they had helped to conquer the enemy during the revolution from a position of weakness (Van Slyke 1967; Armstrong 1977). This new status doubtless explains why observers chose to translate *fabao* alternatively as three fundamental questions, three principal elements, three main weapons (Van Slyke 1967) or three magic wands (Tsou 2000). The 'eight character' concept from the 1950s, 'long-term coexistence and mutual supervision' (*changqi gongcun, huxiang jiandu* 长期共存、互相监督),[13] describing the relationship between the CCP and the eight democratic parties illustrates this renewed united front discourse. However, this outreach was already little more than window dressing. The allies were entrenched in a dissolving united front space. Mao sped up the march towards the socialist revolution, which could only sweep away the institutionalisation of the New Democracy and its attributes. This change was evident in the evolution of the triptych formed of the united front, the Red Army and Marxism–Leninism (Van Slyke 1967).

13 Mao, Zedong, 'On the Correct Handling of Contradictions Among the People', 27 February 1957, www.marxists.org/reference/archive/mao/selected-works/volume-5/mswv5_58.htm.

At the end of the 1950s, Mao broke away from the political apparatus of the conquest by devitalising the united front, no longer required since the generalisation of collectivism, the struggles and the 'contradictions within the People', and until the start of the struggle against the 'new bourgeoisie'. The united front was doubly neutralised as a lever for tactical or strategic action (Van Slyke 1967). On the one hand it was included in the preamble to the constitution in 1954, a non-binding niche in a legal framework relegated to the shadows of Maoist ideology. On the other hand, it was included in Mao Zedong Thought and became an abstraction (Van Slyke 1967). Thus, the united front was no longer a vector of the struggle for hegemony. With the Cultural Revolution, it was Mao Zedong Thought that was brandished as an invincible and 'all-powerful magic weapon' (*wanneng fabao* 万能法宝) (Chuang 1967), able to overcome all the difficulties and all the enemies in a war taking place in China and abroad. The irony is that this action enshrined the concept and made it available to Mao's successors, who, with perfect fidelity to dogma, would be able to use it as a tool for reform and the Party's *statisation*.

Shield against the Maoist Momentum and Lever for Reform

Often seen as a remnant of Maoist rhetoric, Gerry Groot's seminal work on the evolution of the united front in the post-Maoist era showed how it became a tool for the CCP to 'manage transitions' (Groot 2004) by providing some leeway for the regime to recreate, even artificially, some sort of dialogue with society. Going one step further in analysing the evolution of the concept, I stress in the remainder of this chapter how it was refashioned to allow for the invention of a post-revolutionary China without changing its Communist framework.

In 1975, the first signs of a way out of Maoist chaos can be seen in the call by Zhou Enlai for a much-needed 'democratic consultation' (*minzhu xieshang* 民主协商) (Zhan 1986). In 1977, after Mao's death, Hua Guofeng attempted the improbable conciliation of a Maoist relaunch and the rehabilitation of the old targets of the united front who had been purged. The Hua Guofeng interlude and the 'Four Modernisations' only lasted until late 1978. In order to be disruptive without being labelled a Chinese Khrushchev, Deng Xiaoping chose a strategy of skirting around the main obstacles in his way (Chevrier 1985). To do this, Deng, like Mao, reset the ideological superstructure and its organisational embodiment. He reinstated the political characteristics of the New Democracy in the name of pre–Cultural Revolution institutional Maoism.

The united front could thus be presented as a political attribute linked to the first era of the Party under Mao. It provided the opportunity for a pragmatic leap over the Maoism of the Cultural Revolution, meaning that it no longer needed to follow the revolution while continuing to refer to its Maoist heritage (Jourda 2012). From the Communist journals mentioned above, one can see that, on an institutional level, invoking the united front enabled the relaunch of the CPPCC. Multiparty cooperation was reinforced and extended from eight to 16 characters by adding 'sincere collaboration' (*gandan xiangzhao* 肝胆相照) and 'common destiny' (*rongru yu gong* 荣辱与共) to long-term coexistence and reciprocal supervision[14]. At a social and economic level, Deng reached out to those who had been repressed over the previous 30 years and whose skills were required for the relaunch. At the Party core, this reference contributed to countering both the guardians of the Maoist momentum as much as the reform purists. Providing autonomy for the ideological referential was vitally important. To this end, Deng relaunched the Maoist 'magic weapon' aspect, which would therefore be inappropriate to contest. To complement this, he raised the united front to the rank of 'science'; it was said to be contributing to scientific socialism at a high level as a purely Chinese 'independent science', and this science was also considered as a part of the Marxist–Leninist united front's 'theoretical heritage' (*lilun baoku* 理论宝库) (Zhang 1986). In doing so, one should note, Deng was careful, like Mao in the 1930s, not to theorise the change. One can even observe his optimisation of the method, presenting himself as orthodox via a double conceptual tutelage, both Maoist and Marxist, that legitimised his search for autonomy. Once again, the disadvantage was that the scheme depended on success on the ground. This synthesis and sinicisation of Marxist and Maoist invocations in order to redirect them towards reform would have remained theoretical if the practical implementation had not proved Deng right. As for Mao, these shields provided little cover, either in power games between factions or among the old targets of the united front who had learned from their experience. Within the CCP, there was much

14 'Some Understandings on the Principles of "Long-Term Coexistence and Mutual Supervision" and "Sincere Collaboration, Common Destiny"' (对"长期共存,互相监督","肝胆相照,荣辱与共"方针的几点认识), *People's Daily*, 4 November 1982, cn.govopendata.com/renminribao/1982/10/4/3/#607575.

criticism of the incongruousness of a regeneration that lacked consistency (Jourda 2012). However, Deng managed to retain it as a lever in his hand in internal Party struggles.

In 1987, having emerged unscathed from dissent within the Party, Deng Xiaoping openly launched a general movement of reform with Zhao Ziyang. As neither the Party nor Deng himself fully acknowledged a distancing from the revolutionary referential, rhetoric enabled them to use to their advantage the temporal dilatation that the united front had favoured continuously since its introduction in China (Jourda 2012): in the past, the Cultural Revolution was constantly being encrypted and relegated to a historical parenthesis in the ongoing construction of PRC institutions; in the present, it was used to disguise all manner of hesitancy; in the future, it accompanied the 'initial phase of Socialism' (*shehui zhuyi chuji jieduan* 社会主义初级阶段), which must lead in the long term to revolution, once the material conditions created by economic development had been achieved (Fan 1988).

A Tool for the Re-Ideologisation of the Regime

In 1989, the Tiananmen crisis interrupted the reform movement. A new chapter in the use of the united front began, a chapter once again expressed in slogans, their development demonstrating the ideological–institutional frame underlying the regime's transformations. In late June 1989, Jiang Zemin began liaising with the democratic parties to reassure them. This meant explaining that repression by the statist and authoritarian CCP in no way signified a return to limitless revolutionary violence that could affect the united front objectives or the reforms that had taken place (Jourda 2012). Thenceforth, the Party, assuming its transformation from revolution to state via the Communist route (Chevrier 2001), accelerated the march towards state-building using the revolutionary referential. In official publications, the magic weapon is recycled to this end, solely in its 'triumphant' (*zhansheng* 战胜) and 'victorious' (*shengli* 胜利) aspect in the face of all obstacles. In an offensive and de-ideological approach, the united front was used as a rhetorical lever offering 'enormous superiority' (*juda youshi* 巨大优势) to the CCP in order to 'make an ally of adversity' (*huaxian weiyi* 化险为夷). Again, it was success on the ground that boosted this terminology, which was more proactive than conceptual.[15]

After a decade of rapid economic growth, the CCP, becoming the party of the state (rather than the party of the revolution), carried out its Copernican revolution via the Three Represents (*san ge daibiao* 三个代表) (Cabestan 2018). Their purpose was to openly recognise the existence of social sectors previously considered non-revolutionary (such as businesspeople) and place the CCP above them, eliminating the eventuality of a future struggle. This development weakened the notion of the united front, as society no longer needed to be classified in different groups in preparation for the revolution.

Under Hu Jintao, the authorities felt obliged to provide a framework for this social recognition by the CCP and its metamorphosis to party-state in the face of a de-ideologised future. To consolidate the gains and correct the excesses of Jiang Zemin's reform, Hu focused on stabilising the regime rather than pushing the reform drive forward. Hu was seeking middle-of-the-road governance, situated at a point between justice and political stability so as to avoid not only a proletarian revolution (a return to Mao) but also a democratic revolution (Jourda 2012). The united front action was launched to this end. It created consensus at the service of a governance presented as pluralist via 'multiparty cooperation' (*duodang hezuo* 多党合作) (Liu 2000) for the benefit of a 'harmonious society' (*hexie shehui* 和谐社会) (Su 2006).

But the new framework was still a constraint for the CCP. In light of Xi Jinping's restructuring of the system that followed, it would appear to be the collegial nature of the leadership, as well as the 'judiciarisation' (*fazhihua* 法制化) of the country's governance and the growing distancing of the population from its revolutionary culture, that constrained the Party. In a Weberian paradox of unintended consequences, the party of the state, in the de-ideologising country it is shaping, is in danger of finding its hegemony contested because of its growing position as a party-state confined to non-ideological governance. The institutional provision of the united front can be useful in this case as a sounding board for the discordant voices at the heart of democratic consultation (Tong 2007).

15 'Overview of the 17th National United Front Work Conference' (第十七次全国统战工作会议概况), 1990, accessed 5 January 2005, cpc.people.com.cn/GB/64107/65708/65722/4444530.html.

In reaction to this, the end of Hu Jintao's mandate was characterised by a defensive quest for checks. As in Mao's case, putting 'Chinese characteristics' (*Zhongguo tese* 中国特色) to the forefront allowed Hu to counter a form of political universalism, from then on Western democracy (Wang Xingdao 2003). To close the ranks politically, 'the common interest' (*gonggong liyi* 公共利益) was put forward as the sum of the particular interests of united front targets: in the wider sense, all non-Communists who submit to or tolerate the authority of the Party (Jiangsu UFWD and Joint Research Group of Jiangsu Academy of Social Sciences 2007). The alliance between the CCP and democratic parties was re-injected into participation in 'public affairs' (*hezuo gongshi* 合作共事) in the name of 'harmony-cooperation' (*hehe* 和合) (He and Zhao 2021) intended to produce a 'collective victory' (*gongying* 共赢) (Jourda 2012). Theoretical research on the united front was resumed to create cohesion, showing early signs of ideology returning to the stage (Wu Baotong 2008). As previously, the resulting slogans did not attract much attention, only appearing pertinent after the fact.

In spite of these protective shields, the trivialisation of CCP ideology opened the door for top cadres wishing to take over the political apparatus by appropriating revolutionary values. After the challenge by Bo Xilai (Broadhurst and Wang 2014), Xi Jinping followed the same path but with a view to restoring order and restarting the regime. From as early as 2012, the new leadership pushed forward with remedying the 'situation in the ideological sphere' (*dangqian yishi xingtai lingyu qingkuang* 当前意识形态领域情况) to build the 'grand renewal of the Chinese nation' (*Zhonghua minzu weida fuxing* 中华民族伟大复兴).[16] This ambition only being possible by repositioning a dynamic Party at the centre of a reactivated political life, Xi reinstated the symbols of the Maoist revolutionary myth (Lam 2012). The goal was not to return to the revolution, but to reset the CCP's political drive.

As the legatee of Maoist communism, Xi paired ideological adjustment with ad hoc restructuring. The united front rhetoric was immediately included in a 'concentric' (*tongxin* 同心) movement with a 'core leadership' (*lingdao hexin* 领导核心) producing 'dynamic stability' (*dongtai wending* 动态稳定) as opposed to the 'stationary stability' (*jingtai wending* 静态稳定) of the previous period (Yang, Xu and Zhang 2010). To this end, the united

---

16 Cao, Guoxing (曹国星), 'Full Left Turn? The Central Committee of the Chinese Communist Party Issued a "Bulletin on the Current Situation in the Ideological Field"' (全面左转?中共中央下发'关于当前意识形态领域情况的通报'), RFI, 13 May 2013.

front was to nourish an 'organic combination' (*youji jiehe* 有机结合) (Wang Puqu 2013) of society, state and Party; in other words, a space in which there would be no dissent, but that would not smother social initiative and would be a substitute for the role played by democracy in modern societies.

Several recent works (Groot 2021; Joske 2019, 2020; Lulu 2019; Smith 2018; Wang and Groot 2018) show that, from 2012 onwards, institutionally, the implementation of this ambition took the form of strengthening the united front apparatus. A group supervising the work of the united front was created within the Central Committee (*Zhongyang tongzhan gongzuo lingdao xiaozu* 中央统战工作领导小组) to restart the entire apparatus in a coordinated manner. The UFWD recruited 40,000 new cadres, and the number of offices was increased and reorganised to include all the issues in Chinese politico-social life. The united front extended its hold on the CPPCC and the democratic parties. Its bureaux were to be active in Xinjiang, Tibet, Hong Kong, Taiwan and the diaspora, concerning all areas (e.g. religion, private enterprise, internet, etc.) (Groot 2016). From then on, the state services and departments in charge of such questions (religion, diaspora, ethnic issues) would be bypassed in favour of the UFWD. In this way, Xi Jinping made the united front a tool intended to exercise coordinated action against any dissent between the Party and society by circumventing the state.

These institutional changes go together with a broadening of united front practices both at home and abroad, as documented by recent studies. In the context of the Belt and Road Initiative, the united front becomes the magical weapon to lobby and suppress any discordant voice that could weaken the harmonious hegemony the CCP aims to establish (Brady 2017). This willingness to make friends by any means necessary (Liao and Tsai 2019) takes the form of an influence war (Charon and Jeangène Vilmer 2021) comparable to the infiltration strategies involving every element of the party-state (Joske 2022). These practices have been described in-depth for Australia and New Zealand (Brady 2017), but they are also visible in Hong Kong (Lo, Hung and Loo 2019; see Yuen and Cheng, Chapter 15, this volume), among diaspora circles in France (Jourda 2019a) and in Taiwan where the united front aims at politicising small political parties' extreme elements linked to the triad world (Jourda 2019c).

The broadening of its scope and the creation of this organic whole has also transformed the united front's relationship with its targets. Thenceforth the aim is not simply to superficially win them over, but to 'attract' (*xina* 吸纳) (Wang and Li 2017) them in order to 'include/contain' (*baorong* 包容) (Zhou and Sun 2011) them by 'incorporating' (*zhenghe* 整合) (Yang 2014), 'fusing' (*zonghe* 综合) (Zhang and Zhu 2009), 'encasing' (*qianru* 嵌入) (Xiao and Yuan 2010) and 'regulating' (*tiaozheng* 调整) (Shi and Cui 2012) their aspirations in the only possible version considered 'consensual' (*gongshi* 共识) (Li 2012) of the China Dream embodied exclusively by the CCP.[17]

The study of these evolving practices should not, however, make us lose sight of the role played by the united front in shaping the Chinese regime from the inside, and organising it based on the CCP's ambitions. The broadening of the united front that is taking place under Xi Jinping is accompanied by a new rhetoric, which can only really find its true meaning if and when grassroots action succeeds. The new triptych – magic weapon, harmony/cooperation and 'balance' (*pingheng* 平衡) – forms the 'thought essence' (*sixiang de jingsui* 思想的精髓) of the united front (He and Zhao 2021). This innovation engenders a new, murky terminology, in which the work of the united front has morphed from an 'art of governance' (*zhishu* 治术) and a simple 'instrumental strategy' (*gongju celue* 工具策略) into the 'path of governance' (*zhidao* 治道): in other words, a 'national systemic model' (*guojia zhidu moshi* 国家制度模式) (He and Zhao 2021). The united front thus becomes a tool at the service of the re-ideologisation of the Chinese regime, integrated around a CCP intended as inclusive, authoritarian and ideological. It remains to be seen whether this holistic framework can provide sufficient impetus for Xi Jinping to succeed in his hegemonic ambitions, despite the pandemic and the economic crisis that goes with it.

Conclusion

For the last 100 years, the united front, as a device promulgated and enacted according to circumstances, has represented a thread that can be followed to decrypt the metamorphoses and developments of the CCP. The concept should be seen as the product of the confrontation between revolutionary momentum and the principle of reality (Chevrier 1983). In a world where dogma guides action, the united front can function as a dispensatory framework to pursue action when the revolutionary drive is missing. It was first an imported and provisional political instrument, injected

17 On the emergence of the China Dream discourse, see Kerry Brown, Chapter 7, this volume.

pragmatically into the ideological superstructure of the CCP to prepare for the Chinese Revolution. Under Mao's impetus, it became a framework to take over the country and to build the PRC, but that framework was later dismantled and put aside in the name of the socialist revolution. Deng Xiaoping used it as a prop to move on from Maoism and as a screen to protect his reforms. Once the united front was free of its revolutionary guise, Jiang Zemin made it a part of the structure of the party-state itself. Hu Jintao and especially Xi Jinping revived its old revolutionary basis; the latter made it an essential element of his system of integrated ideological governance. Whatever the constraints of the Communist march towards revolution and statism, the united front is a practical costume with which to dress the necessary arbitration to avoid issues of compromise, reversal, delay or failure. The united front, therefore, serves as a 'theoretical sliding screen' for the adjustment of discourse and action to fit the theory of the proletarian revolution and its Communist direction.

References

Armstrong, J. D. 1977. *Revolutionary Diplomacy, Chinese Foreign Policy and the United Front Doctrine*. Berkeley: University of California Press.

Bonnin, Michel. 2007. 'Servante, épouvantail ou déesse: la démocratie dans le discours du pouvoir et dans celui de la dissidence'. In *La Chine et la démocratie*, edited by Pierre-Étienne Will and Mireille Delmas-Marty, 493–516. Paris: Fayard.

Brady, Anne-Marie. 2017. 'Magic Weapons: China's Political Influence Activities under Xi Jinping'. Wilson Centre, 18 September. www.wilsoncenter.org/article/magic-weapons-chinas-political-influence-activities-under-xi-jinping.

Broadhurst, Roderic and Peng Wang. 2014. 'After the Bo Xilai Trial: Does Corruption Threaten China's Future?' *Global Politics and Strategy* 56 (3): 157–78. doi.org/10.1080/00396338.2014.920148.

Cabestan, Jean-Pierre. 2018. *Demain la Chine : démocratie ou dictature?* Paris: Gallimard.

Charon, Paul and Jean-Baptiste Jeangène Vilmer. 2021. 'Chinese Influence Operations. A Macchiavellian Moment'. IRSEM. www.irsem.fr/report.html.

Cheek, Timothy. 2016. 'Making Maoism: Ideology and Organization in the Yan'an Rectification Movement, 1942–1944'. In *Knowledge Acts in Modern China: Ideas, Institutions, and Identities*, edited by Robert Culp, Eddy U and Wen-hsin Yeh, 304–27. Berkeley: Institute of East Asian Studies.

Chevrier, Yves. 1983. 'Mort et transfiguration: le modèle russe dans la révolution chinoise'. *Extrême-Orient, Extrême-Occident* 2: 41–108. doi.org/10.3406/oroc.1983.887.

Chevrier, Yves. 1985. 'Les réformes en Chine ou la stratégie du contournement'. *Politique étrangère* 50 (1): 119–38. doi.org/10.3406/polit.1985.3446.

Chevrier, Yves. 2001. 'De la révolution à l'État par le communisme'. *Le Débat* 117: 92–113. doi.org/10.3917/deba.117.0092.

Chevrier, Yves. 2022. *L'empire Terrestre, Histoire du politique en Chine aux XXème et XXIème siècles*. Paris: Seuil.

Chuang, H. C. 1967. 'The Great Proletarian Cultural Revolution: A Terminological Study'. *Studies in Chinese Communist Terminology* 12: 1–72.

De Giorgi, Laura. 2019. 'United Front'. In *Afterlives of Chinese Communism, Political Concepts from Mao to Xi*, edited by Christian Sorace, Ivan Franceschini and Nicholas Loubere, 303–8. Canberra: ANU Press. doi.org/10.22459/ACC.2019.

Esherick, J. W. 2022. *Accidental Holy Land: The Communist Revolution in Northwest China*. Oakland: University of California Press. doi.org/10.1515/9780520385337.

Fairbank, John K. and Albert Feuerwerker, eds. 2008. *The Cambridge History of China 13. Republican China 1912–1949*. Part 2. Cambridge: Cambridge University Press.

Fan, Zhengfu (范征夫). 1988. 'On the Characteristics of the United Front in the initial phase of Socialism' (试论社会主义初级阶段统一战线的特点). Zhengdang luntan. Published in Zhongguo zhengzhi 6.

Groot, Gerry. 2004. *Managing Transitions: The Chinese Communist Party, United Front Work, Corporatism and Hegemony*. New York: Routledge.

Groot, Gerry. 2012. 'A Self-Defeating Secret Weapon? The Institutional Limitations of Corporatism on United Front Work Effectiveness in 21st Century China'. In *The Chinese Corporatist State: Adaptation, Survival and Resistance*, edited by Jennifer Hsu and Reza Hasmath, 41–73. New York: Routledge.

Groot, Gerry. 2016. 'The Expansion of the United Front under Xi Jinping'. *The China Story*. www.thechinastory.org/yearbooks/yearbook-2015/forum-ascent/the-expansion-of-the-united-front-under-xi-jinping/.

Groot, Gerry. 2019. 'The CCP's Grand United Front Abroad'. *Sinopsis*, 24 September. sinopsis.cz/en/the-ccps-grand-united-front-abroad/.

Groot, Gerry. 2021. 'The CCP's United Front Work Department: Roles and Influence at Home and Abroad'. In *The Routledge Handbook of Chinese Studies*, edited by Chris Shei and Weixiao Wei, 41–55: New York: Routledge. doi.org/10.4324/9780429059704-5.

He, Husheng (何虎生) and Zhao Wenxin (赵文心). 2021. 'The Essence of the United Front Thought of the Communist Party of China: Magic Weapon, Harmony and Balance' (中国共产党统一战线思想的精髓要义: 法宝、和合与平衡). *Journal of Renmin University of China* 35 (1): 123133.

Jiangsu United Front Work Department (中共江苏省委统战部) and Joint Research Group of Jiangsu Academy of Social Sciences (江苏省社会科学院联 合课题组). 2007. 'Research on New Social Stratification and Discussion on United Front Work Mechanism' (新的社会阶层研究及统战工作机制探讨), *Jiangsusheng shehui zhuyi xueyuan xuebao* 6: 53–8.

Joske, Alex. 2019. 'Reorganizing the United Front Work Department: New Structures for a New Era of Diaspora and Religious Affairs Work'. *China Brief* 19 (9). jamestown.org/program/reorganizing-the-united-front-work-department-new-structures-for-a-new-era-of-diaspora-and-religious-affairs-work/.

Joske, Alex. 2020. 'The Party Speaks for You: Foreign Interference and the Chinese Communist Party's United Front System'. Australian Strategic Policy Institute's International Cyber Policy Centre, Policy Brief 32. www.aspi.org.au/report/party-speaks-you.

Joske, Alex. 2022. *Spies and Lies: How China's Greatest Covert Operations Fooled the World.* Melbourne: Hardie Grant Books.

Jourda, Emmanuel. 2012. 'Les usages postrévolutionnaires d'un canon orthodoxe: le Front Uni et l'invention politique de l'après-révolution en Chine (1978–2008)'. PhD thesis, EHESS.

Jourda, Emmanuel. 2019a. 'The Ram Union: Emergence of an International NGO Supported by the Party-State'. *China Perspectives* 2: 47–55. doi.org/10.4000/chinaperspectives.9150.

Jourda, Emmanuel. 2019b. 'Le Parti communiste chinois, le Front Uni et les triades: patriotisme, business et crime organisé'. *Sociétés politiques comparées* 47. www.fasopo.org/sites/default/files/varia3_n47.pdf.

Jourda, Emmanuel. 2019c. 'Inventions et récupérations du mythe politique des sociétés secrètes, de la révolution de 1911 à Hong Kong 2020'. *Études chinoises* 38 (1&2): 97–167.

Jourda, Emmanuel. 2023. 'Mao et les bandits: L'enrôlement des brigands et des sociétés secrètes dans la révolution chinoise (1919-1954)'. Sociétés politiques comparées 60. www.fasopo.org/sites/default/files/varia2_n60.pdf.

Lam, Willy. 2012. 'The Maoist Revival and the Conservative Turn in Chinese Politics'. *China Perspectives* 2: 5–15. doi.org/10.4000/chinaperspectives.5851.

Li, Dexin (李德新). 2012. 'Contemporary Demand and Effective Construction of Political Consensus' (政治共识的时代需求与有效构建), *Zhongguo zhengzhi* 2.

Liao, Xingmiu, and Tsai Wen-Hsuan. 2019. 'Clientelistic State Corporatism: The United Front Model of "Pairing-Up" in the Xi Jinping Era'. *China Review* 19 (1): 31–56.

Liu, Yandong (刘延东). 2000. 'Deeply Understand the Great Political Significance of Upholding and Improving the Multiparty Cooperation System' (深刻认识坚持和完善多党合作制度 的重大政治意义). *Zhongyang shehui zhuyi xueyuan xuebao*. Published in *Zhongguo zhengzhi* 9.

Lo, Sonny Shiu-Hing (盧兆興), Steven Chung-Fun Hung (洪松勳) and Jeff Hai-Chi Loo (盧海馳). 2019. 'China's New United Front Work in Hong Kong: Observation of Cooptation and Winning the Hearts and Minds of the People' (中國新統一戰線工作在香港: 籠絡人心工程的觀察). *Mainland China Studies* 62 (4): 25–74.

Lulu, Jichang. 2019. 'Repurposing Democracy: The European Parliament China Friendship Cluster'. *Sinopsis*, 26 November. sinopsis.cz/en/ep/.

Mitter, Rana. 2013. *China's War with Japan, 1937–1945: The Struggle for Survival.* London: Allen Lane.

Park, Sang-Soo. 2002. 'La révolution chinoise et les sociétés secrètes : l'exemple des Shaan-Gan-Ning et du Nord Jiangsu (années 1930–1940)'. PhD thesis, EHESS.

Paulès, Xavier. 2019. *La République de Chine (1912–1949).* Paris: Les Belles Lettres.

Roux, Alain. 2009. *Le Singe et le Tigre: Mao, un destin chinois*. Paris: Larousse.

Schram, Stuart R. 2004. *Mao's Road to Power: Revolutionary Writings 1912–1949.* Vol. VI. New York: M. E. Sharpe.

Schram, Stuart R. 2005. *Mao's Road to Power: Revolutionary Writings 1912–1949.* Vol VII. New York: M. E. Sharpe.

Schurmann, Franz. [1966] 1968. *Ideology and Organization in Communist China.* 2nd ed. Berkeley: University of California Press. doi.org/10.1525/9780520311152.

Shi, Xuehua (施雪华) and Cui Heng (崔恒). 2012. 'On the Adjustment of the Core Function of the CPPCC' (论中国人民政治协商会议功能重心的调整). *Zhongguo zhengzhi* 6.

Smith, Graeme. 2018. 'Xi Jinping Gives China's United Front a Bureaucratic Boost'. *War on the Rocks*, 1 May. warontherocks.com/2018/05/xi-jinping-gives-chinas-united-front-a-bureaucratic-boost/.

Su, Haitao (苏海涛). 2006. 'The Role of the United Front in Building a Harmonious Society' (统一战线在构建和谐社会中的作用). *Renmin zhengxiebao*. Published in *Zhongguo zhengzhi* 3.

Tong, Yi (佟一). 2007. 'Since the Third Plenary Session of the Eleventh Central Committee of the Communist Party of China, the National Multiparty Cooperation Theory, Policy Innovation and Development' (中共十一届三中全会以来我国多党合作理论, 政策的创新与发展). *Zhongyang shehui zhuyi xueyuan xuebao*. Published in *Zhongguo zhengzhi* 4.

Tsang, Steve. 2015. 'Chiang Kai-shek's "Secret Deal" at Xian and the Start of the Sino-Japanese War'. *Palgrave Communications* 1, 14003. doi.org/10.1057/palcomms.2014.3.

Tsou, Tang. 2000. 'Interpreting the Revolution in China: Macrohistory and Micromechanisms'. *Modern China* 26 (2): 205–38. doi.org/10.1177/009770040002600205.

Van Slyke, Lyman P. 1967. *Enemies and Friends: The United Front in Chinese Communist History.* Stanford: Stanford University Press.

Vidal, Christine. 2008. 'D'un régime à l'autre: les intellectuels ralliés au pouvoir communiste, 1948–1952'. *Études chinoises* 27: 41–86. doi.org/10.3406/etchi.2008.916.

Wang, Bingquan (王炳权) and Li Haiyang (李海洋). 2017. 'The Historical Progress of Recruiting Chinese Political Elites and Its Transforming Logic' (中国政治精英吸纳模式的历史演进与转换逻辑). *Zhongguo zhengzhi* 4.

Wang, Di. 2018. *Violence and Order on the Chengdu Plain: The Story of a Secret Brotherhood in Rural China, 1939–1949*. Stanford: Stanford University Press. doi.org/10.1515/9781503605336.

Wang, Puqu (王浦劬). 2013. 'The Consultative Governance and the Realization of Human Rights in China' (中国的协商治理与人权实现). *Zhongguo zhengzhi* 2.

Wang, Ray and Gerry Groot. 2018. 'Who Represents? Xi Jinping's Grand United Front Work, Legitimation, Participation and Consultative Democracy'. *Journal of Contemporary China* 27: 1–15. doi.org/10.1080/10670564.2018.1433573.

Wang, Xingdao (王行道), ed. 2003. *Party System with Chinese Characteristics* (中国特色的政党制度). Beijing: Huawen.

Wong, Man Fong. 1997. *China's Resumption of Sovereignty over Hong Kong*. Hongkong: The David C. Lam Institute for East-West Studies.

Wu, Baotong (吴宝通). 2008. 'On United Front Thought' (论统战思维). *Zhongyang shehui zhuyi xueyuan xuebao*. Published in *Zhongguo zhengzhi* 8.

Wu, Caiguang (吳彩光). 1996. *Research on the Communist Party's United Front and Countermeasures. General Education Textbooks for Military Academies of the National Army* (中共統戰及對策研究 國軍軍事院校通識教育教材). Taipei: Liming wenhua.

Xiao, Cunliang (肖存良) and Yuan Feng (袁峰). 2010. 'The Construction and Embedding of the Party System of New China' (新中国政党制度的建构与嵌入). *Zhongguo zhengzhi* 3.

Xu, Youwei and Philip Billingsley. 2013. 'Listen to What the Bandits Have to Say: Voices from the Post-"Liberation" Suppression Campaign in Guangxi'. *Intercultural Studies* 47: 139–69.

Xu, Zhonglin (许仲琳). 2002. *Tales of the Teahouse Retold: Investiture of the Gods*. Adaption by Katherine Liang Chew. New York: Writers Club Press.

Yang, Aizhen (杨爱珍), Xu Jiapeng (许家鹏) and Zhang Liang (张亮). 2010. 'The Social Value of the Multi-Party Cooperation System: Discussing the System's Function on Protecting Social Stability' (多党合作制度的社会性价值-论多党合作制度在维护社会稳定中的作用). *Zhongguo zhengzhi* 9.

Yang, Yuanhao (杨渊浩). 2014. 'Political Integration Mechanism in Contemporary China' (试论当代中国政治整合机制). *Zhongguo zhengzhi* 7.

Zhan, Qing (詹清). 1986. 'A Model of Upholding the Spirit of Democracy – Read "Selected Works of Zhou Enlai on the United Front"' (坚持民主精神的楷模 – 读 "周恩来统一战线文选"). *Xuexi yu yanjiu*. Published in *Zhongguo gongchandang* 2.

Zhang, Bin (张彬) and Zhu Guanglei (朱光磊). 2009. 'Deepening the Study on Governmental Processes of China from the Point of "Interest Aggregation": A Technique Analysis of the Development of Chinese Politics in the Past 30 Years' (从"利益综合"环节入手深化中国政府过程研究 - 对近三十年中国政治发展的一个技术性分析). *Zhongguo zhengzhi* 4.

Zhang, Chengzong (张承宗). 1986. 'The Patriotic United Front in the New Era' (新时期的爱国统一战线). *Huadong shifan daxue xuebao*. Published in *Zhongguo gongchandang* 4.

Zhou, Shuzhen (周淑真) and Sun Lin (孙林). 2011. 'The Inclusiveness of Party System with Chinese Characteristics and Its Development' (中国特色政党制度包容性及其发展). *Zhongguo zhengzhi* 8.

7

Knowing and Feeling the 'China Dream': Logic and Rhetoric in the Political Language of Xi's China

Kerry Brown

Officials in the People's Republic of China (PRC) no longer speak in the cautious, restrained way they once did. In the era of Wolf Warrior Diplomacy from 2020 and the COVID-19 pandemic, prominent figures in the government have been accused by some commentators of using language that indicates anger, scorn or indignation. This is particularly targeted at those in the outside world who are seen as criticising the legitimacy of its governance system. Phrases used by government representatives like Ministry of Foreign Affairs spokesperson Zhao Lijian are a good example. His Twitter account since around 2018 has deployed increasingly colourful and strident language attacking those framed as enemies of the state he serves. Both the ways in which this communication is undertaken (on non-Chinese social media platforms) and the content (invective-laden, aggressive and confrontational) mark a change that has merited close attention by analysts and commentators.

Is this a generic issue, showing that China is undergoing the same changes in public language and communication that other places have also experienced (such as the US or in Europe) because of the widening use of social media? Some analysts have argued that it is more than this, and that the language and style of delivery from an official figure like Zhao is indicative of something more strategic and worthy of attention. In particular, it is seen as revealing an increasingly nationalistic, autocratic mindset, and one determined not just to tell its own citizens how to think, but also how they should feel. This language has been characterised as deliberately emotional and unreasonable (Brandy and Schafer 2020; Martin 2021).[1] It is, in essence, evidence of a China that not only feels powerful but also wishes to act powerfully and manifest that through its language.

The argument in this chapter focuses on the strategic use of emotion and how this relates to what language means in contemporary China. Far from being spontaneous, intemperate and uncontrolled, the 'wolf warrior' language and its ilk is the precise opposite – the result of a highly deliberative process that recognises that a key component of meaning is not just intellectual or rational understanding but also feeling and evaluation. In this new situation, the carriers and generators of emotion, such as narratives and the key phrases and terms conveying them, are linked to an underlying acceptance that, in Xi's China, it is no longer enough to simply *know* that the country is doing as well as the government says. It is also necessary to feel this too. Both must be understood as part of an epistemological process that involves thinking, albeit in different ways.

There is wide acknowledgement that feelings have been on the rise in recent decades in China. The country has grown increasingly nationalistic. A more emotionally loaded discourse is something that has grown clearer in Chinese-language material. The patriotic education campaigns of the 1990s have inculcated in Chinese school children a narrative of modern history that builds on feelings of resentment and anger about the treatment of their country by outside powers in their modern history. This process has been well studied (Callahan 2008; Wang 2012). Vocabulary about 'heroic' (*yingxiong* 英雄) and 'great' (*weidai* 伟大) 'struggle' (*douzheng* 斗争, a term in use since the Maoist era), along with more negative notions, such as 'national humiliation' (*guochi* 国耻), 'sacrifice' (*xisheng* 牺牲) and 'pain' (*tongku* 痛苦), are key terms in this pedagogical discourse. These terms (and others) provide a palette on which dramatic word pictures can be produced of the country's 'life and death struggle' (*shengsidouzheng* 生死斗诤), which then arouses appropriate emotional responses in the audience. Emotions are not alien to Chinese political communication. However, as this chapter argues, rather than two discreet strands of communication, one factual and

1 See also Lindsay Gorman, 'Do China's "Wolf Warrior" Diplomats Really Have Any Bite?' *Financial Times*, 14 April 2021, www.ft.com/content/7e508af8-0b35-4610-b52d-8c9e3e888a91.

empirical and the other emotive and concerned with feeling, the two are part of one complex discursive strategy. To think is to feel, and to feel is to think in the discourse of the PRC under Xi. And, while that may have been *implicitly* recognised in the past, now it is *explicitly* accepted.

The narratives of nationalism under Xi Jinping, leader since 2012, as the country progresses towards what he calls its great 'rejuvenation' (*fuxing* 复兴) and 'renaissance' (*wenyi fuxing* 文艺复兴) exemplify how this works in practice. With a host of economic (China becoming the world's largest economy in gross terms perhaps by 2030), military (China having the world's largest navy in vessel terms) and social (the country eradicating what it defines as absolute poverty in 2020) data, the Chinese audience (and those listening in from the outside world) are both informed about empirical issues and made to believe that only certain feelings are appropriate in response. As will be argued a little later, in this context, emotions are seen not as something outside of rationality and beyond language or intellectual evaluation, but as an integral and crucial part of human thinking. In Xi's China, therefore, presenting the facts and how to feel about the facts is a coherent and legitimate communicative practice.

The 'China Dream' (*zhongguo meng* 中国梦) and 'dreaming' are important examples of this. They have played a core role in official language since their first appearance in late 2012. What is striking is that these specific terms have not appeared in this way before. They did not figure in the language of the Mao era, or in that of Deng Xiaoping, Jiang Zemin or Hu Jintao, the four 'core leaders' before Xi. These particular phrases about dreaming indicate something new. They show that politicians are now using a form of language that clearly is not just about instructing, or ordering, but also about appealing to more complex motivations.

This is not to say that the leadership of the PRC in previous eras has not tried to speak to the emotions of the Chinese people and sought to find forms of power and persuasion in emotion. From 1949 to 1976, in the Maoist era, the use of hyperbole, stirring vocabulary and narratives of victory by good over evil was common in leaders' speeches – from Mao himself to Jiang Qing, Lin Biao and Kang Sheng, all radical leaders in the Cultural Revolution. As one phrase from the time went, words were meant to 'touch people's souls', rousing attitudes from anger and indignation to joy, which assisted people in prosecuting revolution. In classic speech act fashion, to say in a certain, intense, powerful way in Mao's era was to do (Searle 1969). For the politics of this time, acts of speech were as important as physical acts. Uttering while feeling the right way about what one was uttering was a core component of revolutionary behaviour, and a sign of fidelity and conviction to the Party cause.

The difference between then and now is one of context. The China of the Xi era, economically, socially and geopolitically, differs dramatically from that of the Mao era. And while Chinese nationalism still prevails, along with ideas of mission, struggle, rejuvenation and greatness, the stage for these today when the country is so much stronger economically and geopolitically is vaster in scale. It therefore arouses far bolder thoughts and emotions. The nationalism of the PRC in the twenty-first century has matured, grown and transformed as the country has materially prospered. So, while the principal idea of all Chinese people being part of a joint historic mission through the guidance and leadership of the Chinese Communist Party (CCP) to achieve renaissance and rejuvenation has remained dominant and unchanged, the reality is that, today, this is a far more exciting prospect than it was under Mao simply because so much more of it has been achieved. In the 1960s, many Chinese did not dare to dream. Today, not only is the government inviting them to do so, but also it is telling them they have to. That is the difference between these two eras.

Dialectic and Rhetoric: The Language of Thinking and the Language of Feelings

The distinction between these uses of language – appealing to rational argument versus arousing emotional attitudes – was recognised by Aristotle. He argued in *Rhetoric* 2,500 years ago that, for persuasion, one looked first at the character of the speaker, second at 'putting the audience into a certain frame of mind' and third at 'the proof, or apparent proof, provided by the words of the speech itself'. On the second point, Aristotle stated that 'persuasion may come through the hearers, when the speech stirs their emotions'. This can be done through the use of stirring symbols, or powerful kinds of language forms. Unlike logical persuasion, in which the effect of influencing a listener is achieved through proving 'a truth or an apparent truth by means of the persuasive arguments suitable to the case in question', rhetoric aimed at producing or impacting feelings follows a more complex pattern (Aristotle 350 BCE).

What is different today compared to Aristotle's time is the deeper understanding of emotions and the ways in which they are entwined with all forms of thinking and persuasion, even the most seemingly logical ones. Logical and empirical thoughts are not neatly separated from emotional feelings. Rather, they are different intellectual processes of trying to evaluate and understand issues. The key difference is the ways in which they are prompted by different kinds of facts and situations.

In a recent study of the physiology and sociology of emotions, Leonard Mlodinow presents a framework in which the fact that there are emotional responses that are seen as right or wrong shows that emotions have a logic (Mlodinow 2022). The American philosopher of emotions Richard Solomon, in a similar vein, argued that emotions are rational evaluations, albeit about issues different from the kinds of assessments one might make when describing a physical fact like whether a cup of coffee is hot or cold, for instance. Emotional language and thinking involves a deeper and more complex interplay between the speaker and what is being spoken about. In this interplay between subject and object, the act of evaluation comes to the fore. In essence, to say 'I am angry' is to infer 'I am an agent, and I am experiencing a situation or a set of facts that create in me the disposition whereby I need to be annoyed, dissatisfied and frustrated and to consider doing something about that'.

Emotional responses on this model can be judged right or wrong. It would be strange for someone to experience a negative act, like being hit or insulted by someone else, and to evaluate the situation as one in which they should respond happily or positively. To be angry in these circumstances would be regarded as rational and correct. Solomon argued strongly against what he called the idea of 'raw emotion', something akin to a pressure cooker simmering uncontrollably under the surface and then exploding unguided when prompted. He showed that even the most powerful emotions could be articulated and defined in rational, intellectual categories. In essence, to feel anything one has to verbalise, and that involves an immediate need to categorise and perform other rational actions. It is not that strong emotions, like hate or love, have non-linguistic, non-rational raw material that gets clothed in language afterwards. These arise from a process of rational evaluation, or misevaluation, of situations in which the words are present from the start and constitute, to some degree, the feeling (Solomon 1977, 139). The core insight here is that the structure of emotions, like the structure of thinking, is a highly intellectual process.

We can gain further insight into this division between kinds of discourse from the thinking of the philosopher Jérôme Bruner. His work focused on differences between what he called argument and storytelling in narratives. Both, he stressed, were ways of thinking. But they showed thought undertaken in different ways. In 'Actual Minds, Possible Worlds', Bruner (1986, 11) wrote:

> There are two modes of cognitive functioning, two modes of thought, each providing distinctive ways of ordering experience, of constructing reality. The two (though complementary) are irreducible to one another. Efforts to reduce one mode to the other or to ignore one at the expense of the other inevitably fail to capture the rich diversity of thought. Each of the ways of knowing, moreover, has operating principles of its own and its own criteria of well-formedness. They differ radically in their procedures for verification. A good story and a well-formed argument are different natural kinds. Both can be used as means for convincing another. Yet what they convince of is fundamentally different: arguments convince one of their truth, stories of their lifelikeness. The one verifies by eventual appeal to procedures for establishing formal and empirical proof. The other establishes not truth but verisimilitude.

Bruner's distinction between 'argument' and 'storytelling' aligns well with the two Aristotelian categories of 'dialectic' and 'rhetoric'. They also show the kinds of mental processes in which the role of emotions and feelings is more pronounced in one than the other. And yet, through their mutual need for persuasion and well formedness, both clearly *are* ways of thinking and both involve thought. To feel is to think, though in a different way and with different dynamics to that focused on what could be categorised as factual or rational argument.

The PRC, since 1949, is a place where this division between what Aristotle called the 'dialectic' rational register and the 'rhetorical', and what Bruner calls 'argument' and 'storytelling', is strongly in evidence. For the former, we can see the language of technocratic instruction and report, found in documents like the various five-year economic plans from 1953 and government work reports and statements. Against this sits the language of angry attack or patriotic pride that figure as part of the 'rhetoric' and 'storytelling' function used by leaders like Mao and Xi referred to above. These two sorts of discourse, as we will see later, can sound very different. They are clearly aimed at having a different kind of impact on the audience. Nor is this something that is unique to public political language in China.

The existence of these two prime registers in discourse, and the way they relate to each other, is universal. This is something made powerfully clear by the sociologist Manuel Castells who argues, in the post-modern era, how complex social, cultural and economic global changes have brought about a situation in which:

> the relentless rationalist efforts of the last two centuries to proclaim the death of God and the disenchantment of the world mean we are in again – if we ever left – an enchanted world, where the way we feel determines what we believe and how we act. (Castells 2010, xviii)

The division between the discourse of argument and the discourse of feeling, and how they relate to each other, matters everywhere. It is just that in China, as ever, this has occurred with Chinese characteristics!

The use of 'dream' as a key term since 2012 by Xi is significant because it sits between the dialectical and the rhetorical, the argumentative and the storytelling. It is constructed partly on a set of recognised facts – the country's material and social transformation in the last half a century, its current status economically and geopolitically in the world, and a host of separate economic data, all of which attest to China being a certain kind of success. 'Dream' also, as will be argued later, acknowledges the profound process of individualisation that has been ongoing in Chinese society over this period. At the same time it permits a specific set of feelings – pride, confidence, hope and expectation verging on excitement – that are clearly aimed for by the Xi leadership and regarded as critically useful for its overall nationalist political mission. Therefore, to argue for the 'Chinese Dream' is to recognise both a set of empirical facts and the story they are embedded in, wherein it is not just permissible but also almost mandatory to feel the emotions listed above. In this way, Xi's China has created a language in which thinking and feeling can be melded together – and Castells's 'feeling determining acting' can occur – in ways that the party-state mandates, authorises and (most importantly of all) controls.

Political Language in China Post-1949

That political language in China has a performative and propagandistic function has been conceptualised by a number of scholars since the 1960s. But the ways in which feelings relate to thinking has been less attended to. Much of the existing work has focused on the specific political vocabulary used in China after the Communist victory in 1949 when an official state creed came into existence. The interest here was the ways in which this demonstrated ideological and intellectual control. Franz Schurmann wrote of the ways in which the adoption of Marxism–Leninism as the official ideology meant the importation of a series of new terms into the Chinese language to convey the key ideas of this new belief system (Schurmann 1966, 61–2). This, he claimed, was to create a new way of thinking that accorded with the goals of the new leadership. Michael Schoenhals, over two decades later, looked at how official editorials in the *People's Daily* were crafted and refined by key propagandists like Hu Qiaomu to continue to promote core Maoist ideological beliefs and political programs (Schoenhals 1994). The core aim here was to control the ways language conveyed ideological messages.

Emerging from the use of critical discourse theory from the 1980s, the relationship between language and power structures in China has received wide attention (e.g. Tsung and Wang 2015). The excellent China Media Project and, in particular, the work of Qian Gang, while not overtly theoretical, has concentrated on keywords and their links to specific strategies to exercise political influence – again through informing, conveying ideas and communicating facts rather than looking at strategies to generate a parallel emotional narrative.[2] The rise and fall of terms like 'harmonious society', for instance, can be directly linked to the replacement of one leader (in this case Hu Jintao) by another (Xi Jinping). Kerry Brown and Una Bērziņa-Čerenkova (2018) analysed the key words of the Xi era that are designed to convey core socialist values and the impact these are meant to have on people's conduct.

However, very little has been explicitly written about language and emotion as they relate to each other when used in political, power related discourse, particular emanating from elite leaders. The extant studies either concentrate on language and politics or on emotions – never on both as part of the same reality. Works like Elizabeth Perry's (2002) 'Mobilizing the Masses', which addresses the function of propaganda to rouse people's feelings, exemplifies this. Mainly focused on the Mao era, it describes very well how core messages and ideas are promoted to a Chinese audience to get their compliance and acceptance by arousing and inciting them to feel anger and rage at enemies and class struggle targets. But it does not look

2 'The China Media Project Website', accessed 20 April 2023, chinamediaproject.org/.

more deeply at the ways in which feeling and thinking might be intimately and dynamically linked in this process, nor does it range more widely than highly inflammatory mass campaigns (Perry 2002, 111–28). Perry Link comes a little closer to attending not just to how Chinese political language tries to instruct but also how it generates emotions and feelings as a matter of course. But his focus is on the role of metaphor and symbolism and the links between China's current political discourse and its relationship to other Chinese literary traditions (Link 2013). Neither of these works look very deeply at how rationalising and feeling might be understood in the same discourse. In essence, what they lack is any sense of an epistemology in which feelings are acknowledged as a fundamental part of all knowledge rather than an occasional phenomenon.

Sticking to the Facts: Technocratic Discourse from Deng to Hu

As argued above, in the Mao era, class struggle and dramatic mass mobilisation campaigns like the Cultural Revolution or the Great Leap Forward in the late 1950s were accompanied by language that, in tone, content and delivery, was clearly highly charged and, in many cases, was meant to incite and arouse people rather than just to inform them. However, from the late 1970s and the onset of the Deng era, things changed. For Deng, Jiang and Hu, a technocratic discourse was dominant, one driven more by ordering specific economic and social changes to carry through reform and opening, and reporting on the success of this through specific empirical facts like economic growth or tangible evidence of China's material development. This started with the Deng Xiaoping–led project from the late 1970s that saw the whole operation of governance change, as the work of Teiwes and Sun (2007, 2016) shows. This intermediary period can be called the consolidation era. Administrative performance became important, delivering specific targets like GDP growth, rising import and export figures, and the implementation of policies that were meant to have a demonstrable impact on people's material living standards. Practice, as the popular slogan then put it, became the sole criterion of truth. The aggressive, Utopian and often provocative language of the Mao era in this new discourse and governance was not just jettisoned – in some respects it was held up as a model of failure.

We can seek an explanation for this once more in context. The Mao and Xi eras at either side of these periods can be categorised as ones in which the situation was and is amenable to high emotional charge and where the 'storytelling' function was and is more of a priority: for the first, because it witnessed the struggle to found and stabilise the new country, with all the effort that involved, and emotions of pride, expectation and, initially at least, hope this gave rise to; for the second because it has framed itself as the 'new era' in which national rejuvenation is at a particularly important moment and great nation status is imminent. For the Xi period, it is an era of fruition and realisation. The meaning of a phrase like 'historic mission' for national renaissance, which has been used since the 1990s, is now far clearer, because the aim being aspired to is far more obviously within reach; consequently, the excitement and hope arising from this is more intense and rational. It would have been hard to feel intense hope of China becoming the world's top economy in the Mao era. But under Xi, that aim is no longer fanciful. It is, in fact, a very rational thing to expect (whether in fact it happens or not).

Greater acceptance of the link between thinking and emotions can be attributed to the work of the chief ideologue Wang Huning. Indeed, Wang Huning has been key to this process. Under Jiang in the mid-1990s, he constructed a series of slogans and memes in which the core idea of Chinese people needing to be proud of their identity, culture and unique intellectual and cultural assets were placed at the centre of the overall political communication strategy. The Chinese people were invited to not just know they were Chinese and to define this in a certain way (e.g. 5,000 years of history, Confucian heritage, etc.) but also to feel confident and proud about being Chinese. 'China Dream' is the key term that has come from this development in the Xi era. To refer back to Castells's point, in Xi's China, it is clear that feeling is as important as thinking or believing, to such an extent that they must almost be simultaneous – two aspects of one complex response. To intellectually recognise the country's great material progress is not enough. One must also have the appropriate emotional attitude: pride, happiness and even joy. Far from being simply about economic success, conveyed in technocratic, statistical language, politicians like Xi have stressed the importance of having clear messages and answers on the thorny issue of what Chinese identity means and how feelings (particularly pride and happiness) play a role in this identity. And while Chinese identity involves emotions of pride, confidence or happiness, it is also about more than this. It means having a sense of authenticity and conviction, whereby people know that these are not just positive feelings but the *right* feelings – that is, the *correct* emotional responses (just like one has the correct rational response to 'one plus one' when one replies that it equals two) to the situation the country says it is in. Identity is not just about facts (what makes you who you are in terms of your material and physical circumstances) but involves a far more complex evaluation of what the facts of daily existence and circumstance mean in terms of the larger context and the (right) feelings a citizen should have about them. Wang Huning's contribution has been both to accept the need for this imperative to go beyond facts and to assert that there is a correct emotional response to these – one that the party-state under Xi must speak to and shape.

Preparing for the Dream: Elite Leaders Speak at Party Anniversaries

'China Dream' is where the language of fact and feeling come together. This can be illustrated by many different kinds of events and examples from the Xi era (post 2012). One of the most striking was the celebration by the CCP of its one-hundredth anniversary on 1 July 2021. On that day, Xi spoke with confidence and assertiveness of the CCP leading a country that had delivered modernity on its own terms. The CCP was now able to face the world as at least an equal, and perhaps even a superior. Clearly, this achievement needed not just intellectual acknowledgement but also an appropriate emotional response.[3] On this anniversary, Xi was addressing a national Chinese audience, most of whom may not have cared much about the formal ideology of the Party and its specific doctrines and technical ideas, but they were nevertheless invited to respond to the increasing evidence that nationalistic feelings were a valid emotional response to the situation that China, the entity the CCP represented, was in. The 'rejuvenated nation' spoken of that day, rather than the CCP itself, could arouse people's pride and affection because it was a worthy object of admiration and love due to the size of its economy, its geopolitical impact, the size of its military and the physical transformation of its modernised landscape, along with its lauded cultural attributes. Inevitably, these were what Xi spoke of that day.

3 Xi Jinping, 'Xi Jinping's Full Speech from the 100th Anniversary of the Communist Party', *Quartz Magazine*, 1 July 2021, qz.com/2028306/xi-jinping-speech-transcript-for-the-ccps-100th-anniversary/.

Xi's performance showed where his era and earlier times differed. Past elite leaders did not have the vast array of assets that Xi could deploy to trigger happy, proud, nationalistic feelings in order to 'sell' the CCP's core message. For Mao, speaking at the very genesis of the PRC over seven decades earlier, the sources of happiness and the cultivation of love towards the new country were spoken of more in terms of hope than current reality:

> We are proclaiming the founding of the People's Republic of China. From now on our nation will belong to the community of the peace-loving and freedom-loving nations of the world and work courageously and industriously to foster its own civilization and well-being and at the same time to promote world peace and freedom. Ours will no longer be a nation subject to insult and humiliation. We have stood up. Our revolution has won the sympathy and acclaim of the people of all countries. We have friends all over the world.[4]

The language here is about the future, of what 'will' happen, and of how China 'will no longer' be a certain thing. China may have 'stood up' and won sympathy, but the onus is on how things will happen going forward, and how the 'insult and humiliation' of the recent past will now be consigned to history.

In 2001, in a far more institutionalised context, Mao's successor and core leader Jiang Zemin could speak in stirring ways as Party secretary and president. His confidence came from the fact that the 80-year-old party, having enjoyed half a century in power, had tangible evidence of its successes and contributions to draw on. While Jiang Zemin used the occasion to promote the main ideology associated with his era – the Three Represents (in which private business entrepreneurs were eventually allowed to become CCP members) – he did so in language that was also aspirational and future oriented, like Mao's:

> In the new century, the great historical tasks for our Party are to continue the modernization drive, accomplish the great cause of the reunification of our motherland, safeguard world peace and promote common development. Facing the profound changes in the domestic and international situations, our Party should follow closely the progressive trends of the world and unite and lead people of all ethnic groups throughout the country in seizing the opportunities

4 Mao Zedong, 'The Chinese People Have Stood up', USC US-China Institute, 21 September 1949, china.usc.edu/Mao-declares-founding-of-peoples-republic-of-china-chinese-people-have-stood-up.

> and taking up challenges to accomplish the three major historical tasks successfully. To this end, we must unswervingly fulfil the requirements of the 'Three Represents'.[5]

This is the language of a great project, a work in progress. It is pragmatic, realistic and almost humble in tone. Ten years later, Hu Jintao, marking his own ideological innovation, 'Scientific Development', in a speech celebrating the ninetieth anniversary of the CCP, tied everything to the hope and desire for national rebirth:

> In contemporary China, only development counts, and this calls for pursuing scientific development. We should take scientific development as the goal and give priority to accelerating the shift of model of economic development … We will promote fairness and justice; long-term, steady and rapid economic development; and social harmony and stability. We will continue to make new and greater achievements in pursuing civilized development that leads to increased production, better lives for the people, and a sound ecosystem, and thus lay a more solid foundation for building a moderately prosperous society in all respects and realizing the great rejuvenation of the Chinese nation.[6]

In all of these, the sense of aspiration – of bringing something about in terms of China's recreation – is clear, whether they be conveyed through Mao and the sense of victimisation and of China standing up; or by Jiang's notion of historic tasks, reunification and modernisation; or by Hu and the construction of a rejuvenated, better society. Each of the elite leaders spoke as much about their hopes for the future as they did about the present reality the country was in. Each was implicitly saying that good things, which their listeners would like and feel happy about, were going to happen because of changes in the current situation. Hope and desire are fundamental emotions. They contain evaluations of one of the most complex and unknowable things – the future. Yet none of these leaders deployed the word 'dream' – surely one of the most frequent terms used when thinking, and feeling, about the future.

5 Jiang Zemin, 'Jiang Zemin's Speech at the Meeting Celebrating the 80th Anniversary of the Founding of the CPC', *China Daily*, 7 July 2001, www.china.org.cn/english/2001/Jul/15486.htm.

6 Hu Jintao, 'Speech at a Meeting Commemorating the 90th Anniversary of the Foundation of the Communist Party of China', China.org.cn, 1 July 2011, www.china.org.cn/china/CPC_90_anniversary/2011-07/01/content_22901507.htm.

Dreaming Together – Or Dreaming Alone

One of the reasons for this can be found in the ways that 'dreaming' links to the notion of an individual and a person. One can imagine that, even for an idealist and utopian such as Mao, using a word like 'dream' would have raised uncomfortable echoes of the ultimate capitalist ideal – the 'American Dream'. Dreaming was something private, self-centred and indulgent. The collectivist ethos underpinning Mao's, Jiang's and Hu's statements is powerfully present. For instance, in each of the statements above, there was recognition that they were speaking in a moment when all Chinese people had worked together, committed to a common enterprise, either of national foundation, national reconstruction or national economic reopening. Although emotions are clearly stirred in this language, and through the ambitions alluded to, they are more on the social rather than the individual level.

Despite the underlying similarities in terms of the encouragement of key positive public emotions built on a shared concentration on China the great nation, as well as a shared narrative and understanding about its modern history, the context in which each of these statements was delivered was changing and evolving. This created a quandary for Xi when he became the core of the 'fifth generation of leaders' from 2012. The Maoist society dominated by collectivist social organisation, mass campaigns and strict enforcement of CCP norms and economic behaviour had dramatically changed after 1978. Economic liberalisation alone had resulted in a transformed society, where, as Kleinman et al. (2011) recognised, by the end of the Hu era, there was often rampant individualism, some of it verging on almost pathological hedonism.

The rise of this new form of individualism can be seen in the radical changes to the country's material circumstances. From 1980 onwards, the new economic policies started to have an impact. Specific results could be witnessed, measured, spoken about and offered as evidence of success. These had tangibility. This is not to say that in the Mao era there were no material improvements in people's lives. But these occurred in a complex situation in which they stood beside crises from the famines of the early 1960s and widespread social instability from 1966 onwards. Under Deng, a commitment was made to simplify the CCP. Its elite leaders' key message, and the CCP's main mission, was to make China materially wealthy while preserving the one-party system. Dense deployment of economic data became a key means of getting this message across, embodying the changes happening in people's lives and conveying success. The dialectic/argument function dominated. People needed to be persuaded to engage in this practical process of national material enrichment, rather than aroused to feel a certain way about larger, longer-term abstract national goals. The audience for elite leaders was one that did not have to principally feel happy, angry, indignant or bitter – but to simply produce. Language such as that conveyed by Hu Jintao in 2003 epitomises this, showing that statistics had taken control:

> I know you are all interested in China's current economic situation and future trends of development … From 1978 to 2002, China registered an average annual GDP growth rate of 9.4%. In 2002, when [the] world economy experienced a growth slowdown, [the] Chinese economy grew by 8%. In the first half of this year, China's GDP went up by 8.2% despite the interruption by SARS. At present, China's economy remains in good shape with a strong momentum for expansion. The 7% increase target set for this year is well within reach.[7]

This is the message of the prudent accountant, not the leader of a party historically committed to revolutionary change. But it does display a communication strategy in which the audience is offered empirical evidence that can speak for itself about how the country is progressing and growing. This is indeed the discourse of 'seeking truth from facts' in which there is an unproblematic relationship between what is described and what conclusions can be drawn.

What linked Hu's language to that of Jiang and Mao was the sharing of an historic narrative of positive progressive development, and the commitment to stimulating excitement about the future. The latter was where the strongest emotional energy was generated through a sense of expectation and direction. In the 'Cultural Contradictions of Capitalism', Daniel Bell (1976) wrote about how capitalist societies were frequently infected by a fetishisation of the future. The future would always be better, things would be faster, easier more luxurious. This offers a common point with socialism with Chinese characteristics – a hunger for tomorrow not only being better but also being seen to be better – showing this, for example, in GDP figures

7 Hu Jintao, 'Speech by President Hu Jintao of China at APEC CEO Summit', Permanent Mission of the People's Republic of China to the United Nations and other International Organisation, 19 October 2003, www.fmprc.gov.cn/ce/cgvienna/eng/xw/t127528.htm.

that always went up, never into recession. During the early Mao years, that there was a tomorrow at all (given the horrific levels of death and destruction that had occurred during the civil war and the Sino-Japanese War) was, in itself, a positive and unifying message. The promise of a new China would, as Mao said in 1949:

> lead the people of the whole country in surmounting all difficulties and undertaking large-scale construction in the economic and cultural spheres to eliminate the poverty and ignorance inherited from the old China.[8]

As the PRC proceeded, expectations changed. The message was no longer about simply surviving, though that remained important through many of the hardest Mao years, but, eventually, after 1978, became about prospering. Indeed, by the time of Hu it started to be about even more than that – about thriving and somehow dealing with the excesses of wealth and material goods that had been created.

Xi Jinping: Dreaming about Feeling Together

Clearly, between the Hu and Xi eras there was a rethink of how the Party was managing its public messaging. The dense and impersonal Hu-era style was no longer adequate. There needed to be recognition that, while promoting strong collective narratives and accepted facts and interpretation of the Party's achievements was important, this was happening in a context in which individualism in China was an unchangeable new reality. The Party, therefore, had to create at least some kind of register where, despite this profound change, it could still mobilise and motivate people and create a language that did not just instruct but also inspired and engaged both on a public, collective level, and down to the individual. The era of the rhetoric/storytelling function had returned.

From 2012, Xi deployed a different kind of language, often using his own life story, something Hu, Jiang and Deng had never done, and conveying the China story in a more concrete, less technocratic language. Speaking in Seattle during a visit to the US in 2015, Xi stated:

8 Mao Zedong, 'Long Live the Great Unity of the Chinese People', Marxist.org, 30 September 1949, www.marxists.org/reference/archive/mao/selected-works/volume-5/mswv5_02.htm.

> Towards the end of the 1960s when I was in my teens, I was sent from Beijing to work as a farmer in a small village of Liangjiahe near Yan'an of Shaanxi Province, where I spent seven years. At that time, the villagers and I lived in 'earth caves' and slept on 'earth beds'. Life was very hard. There was no meat in our diet for months. I knew what the villagers wanted the most. Later I became the village's party secretary and began to lead the villagers in production. I understood their needs. One thing I wished most at the time was to make it possible for the villagers to have meat and have it often. But it was very difficult for such a wish to come true in those years. At the Spring Festival early this year, I returned to the village. I saw blacktop roads. Now living in houses with bricks and tiles, the villagers had Internet access. Elderly folks had basic old-age care and all villagers had medical care coverage. Children were in school. Of course, meat was readily available. This made me keenly aware that the Chinese dream is after all a dream of the people. We can fulfil the Chinese dream only when we link it with our people's yearning for a better life.[9]

The statistics of the Hu era largely disappeared. In its place was storytelling. But not just any storytelling: a specific form in which Xi figured as an individual – albeit one with a strongly representative and symbolic function – came to the fore. Alongside this, more complex issues have been recognised, such as the need for cleaner governance within the Party, the desire to address inequality through common prosperity and the notion that China is seeking greater autonomy through its 'dual circulation' policy. Nationalistic pride has also grown stronger, because, through economic growth and geopolitical developments, the country has more to feel proud about. The political challenge for Xi and his colleagues was how to find the best language to encourage, and exploit, this pride, and to allow Chinese people to feel, rather than just know about, their country's achievements.

This question of audience is a key one for any communication practice and strategy. It is striking that, for all the changes in people's daily lives, and the rise of individualism and social differentiation, both Mao and Xi talked of their serving, and speaking directly to, their core audience – a very generic notion of 'the People'. This term has remained remarkably static, despite all the changes going on around it. On 15 November 2012, when Xi emerged on the stage of the Great Hall of the People as the key leader, he stated: 'It is the people who create history.' The Party, he explained, '[maintain] close ties

9 Xi Jinping, 'Full Text from President Xi Jinping's Speech', National Committee on US China Relations, 22 September 2015, www.ncuscr.org/content/full-text-president-xi-jinpings-speech.

with the people'.[10] That was its task. This echoed Mao's celebrated speech of September 1944, 'Serve the People', when he had talked of 'the common revolutionary objective' – to lift the suffering of the Chinese people.[11]

That they both said they were talking to this group is one thing. But what did they signify by this term? Surely conceptualisation of it had not remained unchanged over the decades: or had it? In fact, of all the terms in modern Chinese political discourse, few can be more contentious than that of the 'people' (*renmin* 人民). The contemporary Chinese writer Yu Hua noted that '*renmin*' was 'remote, but … so familiar too' (Yu 2012, 3). His work provides insight into how and why Xi's use of the term was so different to Mao's. Once upon a time, Yu explained, 'during the Cultural Revolution, the definition of "the people" could not have been simpler', namely 'workers, peasants, soldiers, scholars, merchants'. But, after that:

> new vocabulary started sprouting up everywhere – netizens, stock traders, fund holders, celebrity fans, laid-off workers, migrant labourers and so on – slicing into smaller pieces the already faded concept that was 'the people'. (Yu 2012, 6)

The 'people' had become atomised, complex and diverse.

For Mao, there were clear and elemental moral distinctions between 'good' and 'bad' people, and that was all. You were an enemy or a friend. For Xi, the 'people' – the audience he spoke to – might have been figured as though they were still one great collective. But his tone of almost deprecation and respect to this great mass, and the fact that Chinese people were clearly socially, culturally and economically more diverse than ever before, marked a massive difference. As Xi stated:

> During the long process of history, by relying on our own diligence, courage and wisdom, Chinese people have opened up a good and beautiful home where all ethnic groups live in harmony and foster an excellent culture that never fades.[12]

The use of 'we' is rhetorically crucial here. Xi was speaking as one of those he was addressing. He was on the podium, for sure. But he was also asserting he was in the crowd listening too.

10 'China's New Party Chief Xi Jinping's Speech', BBC, 15 November 2012, www.bbc.com/news/world-asia-china-20338586.

11 Mao Zedong, 'Serve the People', Marxist.org, 9 September 1944, www.marxists.org/reference/archive/mao/selected-works/volume-3/mswv3_19.htm.

12 'China's New Party Chief Xi Jinping's Speech'.

Moving the people while recognising the vast complexity contained within them; trying, despite this, to speak directly to them, as one of them; recruiting them into a narrative carrying clear evaluations that will lead to emotional responses – these have been major objectives of the Xi era. But, as the occasion of the one-hundredth anniversary of the foundation of the Communist Party made clear, when Xi spoke once more to his audience he used a crucial new term. The Party, at 100 years of age, was not just in the business of thinking, or planning, or doing, but also 'dreaming' – and it was doing so with confidence, Xi stated:

> To realize national rejuvenation, the party has united and led the Chinese people in pursuing a great struggle, a great project, a great cause, and a great dream through a spirit of self-confidence, self-reliance, and innovation, achieving great success for socialism with Chinese characteristics in the new era. We Chinese are a people who uphold justice and are not intimidated by threats of force. As a nation, we have a strong sense of pride and confidence. We have never bullied, oppressed, or subjugated the people of any other country, and we never will. By the same token, we will never allow any foreign force to bully, oppress, or subjugate us. Anyone who would attempt to do so will find themselves on a collision course with a great wall of steel forged by over 1.4 billion Chinese people.[13]

'Dream' is a profoundly significant term here. This issue of Chinese people being invited by their leaders to dream is a new development. It says something important about the evolution of the role of aspiration in contemporary China, and the space now being granted to it by political leaders – something that has grown from the language of previous elite leaders but which is now located in a very different context and with a different kind of content and usage. It also marks a deeper acceptance of the individualism of the people being spoken to, and of there needing to be acknowledgement of their having the agency to take this offer to 'dream' and shape it to their own unique circumstances.

The act of dreaming as it occurs in Chinese literary and historical traditions is a well attested one, and something that the contemporary discourse of a national and personal dream calls on. In his excellent book on the *Chinese Dreamscape* during the era 300 BCE – 800 CE, Robert Ford Campany writes of the importance given to dreams through divination and a complex set of interpretative tools by Chinese writers and thinkers. But, looking at

13 Xi Jinping, 'Xi Jinping's Full Speech from the 100th Anniversary of the Communist Party'.

this history today, one thing is certain: dreams have always been regarded as carrying meaning. Indeed, as Campany (2020, 67) observes: 'Questions about dreaming were inextricable bound up with questions about how best to live.'

Despite this, Mao seldom if ever mentioned dreams to address this issue of capturing aspirations, hopes and desires about the future. None of his significant statements or slogans referred to dreams. For much of the post-reform era, most elite Party leaders refrained from speaking in an emotional register, instead keeping to the business of informing, ordering and quantifying. Using the language of dreams, therefore, bespeaks an important shift – an acknowledgement that the Party needs to get back into the business of arousing and inspiring emotions and using these as part of its political strategy.

Deploying the language of dreams opens up interesting new spaces for political discourse in contemporary China. It goes some way towards solving the conundrum of how to accept the rise of individualism in society and addresses the need to have language that can arouse people's feelings in a way that is controllable by the party-state and hitched to its own agenda. Appealing to dreams – a very open and vague term – allows plenty of space for different sorts of evaluations of different kinds of reality. As used by Xi, the one thing that is certain is that the qualities of being individual, varied and almost worldly are regarded as positives. Unlike in the Mao era, the Party knows that it cannot command so easily but needs to carry at least some elements of persuasion. Inviting the people to dream is an uncontentious thing to do, especially as the invitation does not specify what the dream should be about beyond better living standards and a great, powerful and strong country. The main thing is to ensure that the dream itself can be shared. This is how Xi spoke when he first deployed the term in 2013: 'Everyone has an ideal, ambition and dream.' But then, in an act of Party appropriation, he went on to say: 'In my opinion, achieving the rejuvenation of the Chinese nation has been the greatest dream of the Chinese people since the advent of modern times.' This was not just a thing shared by people at a particular time:

> This dream embodies the long-cherished hope of several generations of the Chinese people, gives expression to the overall interests of the Chinese nation and the Chinese people, and represents the shared aspirations of all the sons and daughters of the Chinese nation. (Xi 2014, 38)

This reminder of the aspirations and emotions of past elite leaders, and the context of a China that, after four decades of economic and material enrichment could now allow itself the luxury to dream and to stand a chance of seeing those dreams come to reality, creates the peculiar sub-discourse within Xi-speak for this term. In May 2013, Xi declared that 'the Chinese dream pertains to the past and the present, but also the future'. This idea of dreaming about the past belongs more to the traditional use of the term – much as people often dream in their sleep about what has happened to them. But the second definition of dreaming, which is closer to the sense of hoping, aspiring and wishing, is also important here – as a nod to the future. So is the sense of tangibility:

> The Chinese dream is the dream of the country and the nation but also of every ordinary Chinese. One can only do well when one's country and nation do well ... The great renewal of the Chinese nation will eventually become a reality in the course of the successive efforts of youth. (Xi 2014, 53)

For Xi, the situation of China today is best seen as a dream fulfilled. We often hear that people of the Maoist era who survived into the current one feel that they would never have dreamed of China being in the position it is today, with the levels of development it has. But for a politician sitting at the top of the CCP, this is a complex story to gather into one phrase that can then generate positive emotions to go beyond simple intellectual acknowledgement. To compound the challenge, the status of the party, the diversity of the audience and the complexity coming from different technological platforms all mean that it is very difficult to say one thing that will reach and speak to everyone and make them feel the way the Party wants them to. The idea of dreaming – a state of emotional receptivity, but without any overt emotions necessarily linked with it – achieves this goal. One can dream and be happy, fulfilled, ecstatic, pleasantly confused, satiated, thrilled – the choice is yours. The main thing is just to dream. The feelings start to flow after that.

Conclusion

The use of language to communicate instructions, interpretations and facts and also to promote a set of emotional responses has been and continues to be an essential part of political life in contemporary China – as it is in any community. The CCP's five core elite leaders since 1949 have all used a mixture of language in their main communications to instruct, command and inform; such language also aims to inspire, to mobilise and to create emotions in people ranging from love to hate, fear to pride. This does not mean that these kinds of language uses are utterly distinct from each other. As Solomon argues, emotions are evaluations of situations and circumstances, albeit complex ones, and they have a logic of their own.

The CCP's leadership, through the language used at core public occasions such as celebrations of Party anniversaries, illustrates the evolution of the relationship between language to inform and language to inspire and talk to people's emotions over the last 80 years. While Mao deployed terms laden with reference to victimisation, standing up and the need for pride and hope, for Deng, Jiang and Hu, the commitment to a more prosaic politics of building better material lifestyles meant that, while a sense of nationalism was present in their language, their principal aim was to direct, report (tangible economic success) and show (evidence that China was indeed modernising and growing stronger).

These political and social changes have resulted in a society in which there are far higher levels of individualism and self-expression than in the Maoist era. Even so, under Xi Jinping, the CCP elite leadership has used 'dream' as a term that can at least address the strong feelings of satisfaction and love of the strong Chinese nation that has resulted from the economic and material changes in the country since the 1980s. That 'dreaming' is a key part of the Xi-era discourse reveals not only how important actions, information and the presentation of facts are in terms of what the Party wants the people to accept, but also how important feelings are, arising from the evaluation of those facts. Just as there are clear right and wrong ways to regard policy and political options in contemporary China, so there are also right and wrong ways to feel about these things. This shows the ambition of the Xi era – that it is willing not just to assert its own reality, but also to assert its own account of whether the people should feel happy or sad about that reality.

References

Aristotle. 350 BCE. *Rhetoric.* Translated by W. Rhys Roberts. www.documentacatholicaomnia.eu/03d/-384_-322,_Aristoteles,_17_Rhetoric,_EN.pdf.

Bell, Daniel. 1976. *The Cultural Contradictions of Capitalism.* New York: Basic Books.

Brandy, Jessica and Bret Schafer. 2020. 'How China's "Wolf Warrior" Diplomats Use and Abuse Twitter'. Brookings, 28 October. www.brookings.edu/techstream/how-chinas-wolf-warrior-diplomats-use-and-abuse-twitter/.

Brown, Kerry and Una A. Bērziņa-Čerenkova. 2018. 'Ideology in the Era of Xi Jinping'. *Journal of Chinese Political Science* 23: 323–39. doi.org/10.1007/s11366-018-9541-z.

Bruner, Jérôme. 1986. *Actual Minds: Possible Worlds*. Cambridge: Harvard University Press. doi.org/10.4159/9780674029019.

Callahan, William. 2008. *China: The Pessoptimist Nation*. Oxford: Oxford University Press.

Campany, Robert Ford. 2020. *The Chinese Dreamscape 300 BCE–800 CE*. Cambridge: Harvard Yencheng Monographs.

Castells, Manuel. 2010. *The Power of Identity*. Revised edition. Chichester: Wiley-Blackwell.

Kleinman, Arthur, Yunxiang Yan, Jing Sun, Sing Lee, Everett Zhang, Pan Tianshu, Wu Fei and Gao Jinhua. 2011. *Deep China: The Moral Life of the Person*. Berkeley: University of California Press.

Link, Perry. 2013. *An Anatomy of Chinese: Rhythm, Metaphor, Politics*. Cambridge: Harvard University Press. doi.org/10.4159/harvard.9780674067684.

Martin, Peter. 2021. *China's Civilian Army: The Making of Wolf Warrior Diplomacy*. New York: Oxford University Press.

Mlodinow, Leonard. 2022. *Emotional: The New Thinking about Feeling*. London: Allan Lane.

Perry, Elizabeth J. 2002. 'Moving the Masses: Emotion Work in the Chinese Revolution'. *Mobilization: An International Quarterly* 7 (2): 111–28. doi.org/10.17813/maiq.7.2.70rg70l202524uw6.

Schoenhals, Michael. 1994. *Doing Things with Words in Chinese Politics*. Berkeley: University of California Press.

Schurmann, Franz. 1966. *Ideology and Organisation in Communist China*. Berkeley: University of California Press.

Searle, John. 1969. *Speech Acts: An Essay in the Philosophy of Language*. Cambridge: Cambridge University Press. doi.org/10.1017/CBO9781139173438.

Solomon, Richard C. 1977. *The Passions: The Myth and Nature of Human Emotions*. New York: Anchor Books.

Teiwes, Frederick and Warren Sun. 2007. *The End of the Maoist Era: Chinese Politics during the Twilight of the Cultural Revolution 1972–1976.* New York: Routledge.

Teiwes, Frederick and Warren Sun. 2016. *Paradoxes of Post-Mao Rural Reform: Initial Steps toward a New Chinese Countryside 1976–1981.* New York: Routledge. doi.org/10.4324/9781315719498.

Tsung, Linda and Wei Wang, eds. 2015. *Contemporary Chinese Discourse and Social Practice in China.* Amsterdam: John Benjamins.

Wang, Zheng. 2012. *Never Forget National Humiliation: Historical Memory in Chinese Politics and Foreign Relations.* New York: Columbia University Press.

Xi, Jinping. 2014. *The Governance of China.* Vol. 1. Beijing: Foreign Languages Press.

Yu, Hua. 2012. *China in Ten Words.* New York: Pantheon Books.

III.
CHINA'S PATH TO MODERNISATION AND ITS CHALLENGES

8

'Whatever It Takes': The Political Economy of the Chinese Communist Party

Shaun Breslin and Giuseppe Gabusi

Providing an overview of 100 years of the political economy of the Chinese Communist Party (CCP) is not an easy task. This is not, however, because a century is an excessively long era to study. On the contrary, the problem is how short the period is. Or, more correctly, the problem is how quickly and how many times things have changed – and often rather dramatically – in such a relative short time scale. Studying all the changes in the post-Mao era alone would be enough to fill the pages of a number of books. But, if anything, the pace and extent of change in the first decade of the People's Republic of China (PRC) was even faster and more dizzying. And, as we are studying the CCP and not just the PRC, we should not forget that over a quarter of this century had passed before it even came to power.

Nevertheless, while it entails providing a broad-brush and, at times, stylised analysis of different eras, we argue that it is possible to identify unifying strands that cut across all of these 100 years (albeit at times in different ways). We do this by focusing on three fundamental issues that have been at the heart of the political economy of Chinese Marxism. The first is how the Party dealt with the missing (more or less) industrial base that Marx and Engels thought would be the determinant of the ideational change that would bring about a Communist revolution. The second is the Chineseness of Chinese Marxism. Since its very birth, the CCP incorporated in its DNA a nationalistic approach: the emphasis on the Party delivering China back to its rightful place in the world provides a thread that runs through the years. Moreover, rather than seeing the writings of Marx and Engels as providing a blueprint that had to be followed, there has instead been an emphasis on the need to treat Marxism as a rather flexible and malleable guiding theory. It is the specifics of the Chinese case that should dictate exactly what can and should be done at any moment in time and not the revolutionary expectations of the original Marxist texts. Our third constant is the importance of identifying the 'primary contradiction' facing the Party and the revolution at any given time.

We combine these three in a single emphasis on 'Whatever It Takes'. This, in part, refers to an overarching objective to do what it takes to regain full sovereignty (that had been stolen by the colonial powers) and to 'catch up' with the West by turning China into a major modern(ised) economy. All China's leaders have shared these goals.

But there is more to Whatever It Takes than just national rejuvenation. Once the primary contradiction has been established, then anything and everything is justified in dealing with it and warding off the potential existential threat to the Party and the regime. In the earlier years of the CCP, the revolutionary and then state consolidation goals of the Party resulted first in a rather pragmatic, results-driven political economy epitomised by the idea of a 'New Democracy', and then conflicting ideas over how best to move forward in the 1950s. But once Mao identified class conflict as the primary contradiction threatening the regime, this justified whatever it took to eliminate those counter-revolutionaries.

In Deng's era, the identification of underdevelopment as the primary contradiction resulted in a dramatic shift from politics to economics in command, and doing whatever it took to spur development. In the 1990s, as Jiang Zemin promoted growth at all costs (but not at the expense of the CCP's monopoly of power), the economy became unbalanced. Addressing overinvestment, indebtedness and inequality was the main focus of the Hu Jintao-Wen Jiabao era. Finally, Xi Jinping has been concerned more with the contradiction between unsustainable growth and satisfying the people's needs for a better quality of life. Here, while Xi is trying to move on and do something new, he justifies innovation by explaining that he is repeating what his predecessors did when they applied Marxism–Leninism to China's specific conditions in earlier eras. In the differing emphasis on being more 'Communist' or more 'Chinese' at any moment in time, we find evidence both of change and continuity at the same time.

Revolution and (Pre-)Industrialisation

From the outset, Chinese Marxism faced three significant political economy problems that generated the need to focus on whatever it took. The first was capacity: what could be realistically achieved given the nature of the Chinese economy at the time, the extent of support for the Party and the nature of the international order. The second was survival. This was a party, after all, that spent much of the period from 1927 to 1949 in various forms of internal exile, trying to repel both domestic and foreign threats to its existence. After 1949, the challenge shifted to existential threats to the new People's Republic. How best to fend off external threats was a challenge for all China's leaders; how best to fend off and defeat domestic challenges to the revolution was a particular focus for Mao.

And both of these are effectively a function of the third and, in our view, more important problem: underdevelopment and the lack of industrialisation. The Marxism of Marx and Engels was a (materialist) revolutionary ideology of post-industrialisation. How was the CCP meant to lead a revolution in a country where industrialisation was still in its very early stages (at best) and the industrial working class represented a tiny percentage of the population?[1] And if a revolution was possible (as it turned out to be), then how was such industrialisation to be subsequently generated without fostering the very oppression, alienation and revolutionary class consciousness that Marx and Engels thought were the inevitable consequences of this shift in the dominant mode of production, particularly as much of the population did not share the Party's ideological goals, and, as Johnson (1962) argues, even many of the people who actively supported the Party were inspired by national liberation goals rather than Marxist ones?

Of course, the CCP was not the first Communist party to face this dilemma. By the time the CCP was formed, Marxism had already been modified to become a revolutionary ideology for a pre-industrialised society in the still new Soviet Union. Indeed, Gregor argues that it was Lenin, not Mao, who first 'compromised' Marxism by having to 'fabricate the entire missing industrial base', thus detaching Marxism from its original post-industrial origins (Gregor 1995). Gregor's observations formed part of a broader conversation over whether Mao's ideas were so far removed from

1 Scholars disagree over the specific figures, but a figure of less than 10 per cent for the entire urban population covers most of the evaluations, which was, in turn, still only 10.6 per cent of the total in 1949. See Chan and Xu (1985).

the Marxist original that they represented an entirely new theory rather than, as claimed by Mao and the CCP, a modification of it (Knight 2007). Many might agree. But this justification has been a foundational principle of the nature of Chinese Marxism. Even before Mao formally called for the 'sinification of Marxism' in 1938 (Wylie 1979), one of China's foundational Marxist thinkers and activists, Li Dazhao, had already argued for the need to develop a distinctive Chinese form of Marxism. He also saw no contradiction between being a Marxist and being a patriot (Meisner 1967). While Marxism–Leninism provides the theoretical foundational guiding principles and the basic mode of analysis, it needs to be applied to the specifics of the Chinese case to provide a framework for effective political action. Real world and contemporary practice (rather than dogmatic adherence to the original texts) has to be the sole criterion of truth. So Chinese Marxism simply had to be as much about China – at the very least – as it was about the writings of Marx and Engels.

As Knight (2005, 1–2) explains, when Marxism was first being debated within China and formalised into the guiding ideology of the CCP, one of the key debates (and contestations) was the emphasis on economic determinist understandings of revolution on the one hand, and the agency of humans to bring about change on the other hand. The former could potentially result in what he calls 'passivity' – waiting for the inevitable progress of history to unfold – while the latter instead pointed to humans' ability to 'accelerate the momentum of history' through revolutionary activism and mobilisation. Influenced by the Soviet Union and the Communist International, many members of the newly founded party in, and after, 1921 believed that a Marxist revolution was neither imminent nor feasible. The initial emphasis was on working with and within the Guomindang (GMD) to bring about a much-needed national liberation revolution that was an inevitable precursor to a (distant) socialist one (Liu 2000). It was as part of this alliance with the GMD that Mao was asked to investigate the peasant uprisings in Hunan Province in the midst of the Northern Expedition that 'unified' China under GMD rule. As Schram (1989, 39–41) notes, Mao was not alone in thinking about the revolutionary potential of the peasantry, but he certainly went further than others in shifting his revolutionary focus away from the cities and to the countryside. According to Schwartz (1951, ch. XII), this investigation left Mao convinced that the peasants (and particularly poor peasants), if correctly organised and mobilised, could form a revolutionary class that would overthrow the imperialists, warlords, corrupt officials, 'local tyrants, and evil gentry'.[2] The mode of analysis was a Marxist one, but the guide to action came from the specifics of the Chinese case study at the time.

The extent to which principles and preferences dictated the political economy of those areas under CCP control in the revolutionary period is questionable. As Saich (1997) argues, collectively, academic research on this period shows that the main task was survival, and what *should* be done was less important than what *could* be done given the nature of political alliances and political economies in the different rural areas that the CCP found itself controlling. Even after the adoption of a formal 'land to the tiller' policy in 1946, there was no overall pattern, but rather an 'anything goes' environment and 'considerable opportunism within the Party'. In some areas, landowners only had to sell land that was not essential to support themselves to the local authorities; however, in others, 'the landlords and rich peasants lost their lives as well as their property to mobs' (Klein 1961, 62).

The more moderate approach emphasising the need to work with non-Communist groups was outlined by Mao in 'On New Democracy' long before the CCP looked likely to become a ruling party (in 1940). This was both a theory of Marxist revolution and an idea of how a post-revolutionary political system and political economy might function. Given the nature of China at the time, elements of the bourgeoisie could become allies with the working classes (including the peasantry) in overthrowing feudalism and colonialism. These were the major forces of oppression in China at the time rather than, for example, the oppression of a capitalist bourgeois system, as was the case in more advanced industrialised economies in America and Europe. After the revolution, while it would be important, Mao noted, that the private sector could not 'dominate the livelihood of the people', this did not mean the end of the private sector per se. Major enterprises and banks would be brought under state control, but otherwise the private sector would be allowed to contribute to economic reconstruction and development. This might not be a true socialist revolution, but neither was it a European-style transition from feudalism to capitalism; it was something distinct and different and a result of China's distinct and specific circumstances.[3]

2 Mao Zedong, 'Report on an Investigation of the Peasant Movement in Hunan', 1927, www.marxists.org/reference/archive/mao/selected-works/volume-1/mswv1_2.htm.

3 Mao Zedong, 'On New Democracy', January 1940, www.marxists.org/reference/archive/mao/selected-works/volume-2/mswv2_26.htm.

Defining a Political Economy for the New People's Republic

Capacity, pragmatism and existential threats combined to provide the basis for China's new political economy after 1949 as well (Brugger 1981, ch. 2). This was a country that had suffered governance deficiencies since at least the arrival of the British in 1839. The evolution of the national economy had been distorted by confrontation with foreign powers, the economic priorities of external colonial powers, uprisings and rebellions, a fractious and unstable transition from empire to republic, the fragmented and competing development strategies of different warlords and the GMD regime in Nanjing, civil war(s) and war with (and partial occupation by) Japan.

And even this does not tell the full story. Add on the US-led economic and diplomatic embargo on China and the only partial nature of the victory in the civil war,[4] as well as the uneven distribution of support for the CCP across the country, and the challenge for China's leaders becomes clearer. It was not long, of course, before the outbreak of the Korean War further highlighted the importance of building the economic means of ensuring national defence and regime survival.

This helps explains why 'leaning to one side' (i.e. the Soviet Union) for a security umbrella made immense sense. It also helps explain why New Democracy principles seemed to be adopted after 1949, with the private sector not only tolerated, but, in some places, actively encouraged to grow; China's leaders seemed to be philosophically quite happy with the 'compatibility between the private economy and a state-owned and command economy' (So 2002, 684). Land reform was also conducted in different ways in different places; for example, there was a rather zealous and violent implementation of land reform in northern China (where the CCP had a history of control before 1949) but a more moderate policy in the newly liberated areas (where the CCP had not previously had extensive control or influence) (Kung 2008).

4 With fighting continuing in Tibet and the south-west beyond 1949 and the GMD ensconced on Taiwan.

The original expectation was that this phase would be a relatively long-lived one, allowing for extensive national economic reconstruction. All this changed with the large-scale nationalisation of the industrial economy after the outlining of the 'General Line for the Transition to Socialism' in October 1953. As Li (2006) argues, it was at this point that China moved to what he calls the 'Economic Stalinisation of China' as Mao sought to not just emulate the Soviet experience, but to make an even faster transition than the Soviet one. The First Five-Year Plan contained the sort of large industrial projects establishing the basic heavy industrialisation deemed necessary for laying the foundations for future growth and providing for national defence. It also signalled the end of the private sector – or at least the end of the private sector for roughly three decades.

Political Economy, Existential Threats and Class Struggle

With the benefit of hindsight, there appears to be a distinction between those who focused on doing whatever it took to win the class war on the one hand, and those who focused on doing whatever it took to grow the economy on the other. However, it is wrong to draw such a distinction for two reasons. First, because Mao thought that his approach would result in even faster economic growth than alternative proposals (Gray 2006, 662). It was not a case of either ideational or economic progress, but that getting the former right would then get the latter right as well. Second, it is wrong because there was not just one alternative to Maoist preferences/convictions. Wang Ning (2015), for example, points to two very different approaches on the non-Maoist side of the divide: a more statist, Soviet-influenced, centrally planned political economy, and one that allowed a greater role for market forces and incentives, including not just the toleration but also the promotion of some forms of private ownership.

Such a 'two-line' approach, though, reflects the way that Mao saw – or at least, explained – the world in black-and-white terms. It was essential to identify 'who are our enemies and who are our friends'[5] and then to defeat the enemies. To be sure, there should be a distinction between mistaken and

5 Mao Zedong, 'Directives Regarding the Cultural Revolution', 1 June 1967. This part of the selected works is a list of various short statements made between 1966 and 1969, see www.marxists.org/reference/archive/mao/selected-works/volume-9/mswv9_84.htm.

misguided positions, and malign and deliberately counter-revolutionary ones. But it was essential to take whatever action was necessary to defeat an enemy that would otherwise defeat you. The most significant, violent and chaotic of these justified actions was, of course, the Cultural Revolution. But it was far from the only one (Teiwes 1979).

At the Eighth Party Congress in 1956, the Party formally stated that classes had disappeared as everybody now had the same relationship to the newly socialised means of production. But in Mao's writings, his understandings of class began to change, becoming more like a state of mind than anything else. This included what we might call attitudinal hangovers in which 'reactionary thought … inherited from the past, still exists in the minds of a considerable number of people … even after the socio-economic system has been transformed'.[6] It also came to include the idea that Party members themselves might become agents of oppression. The routinisation and bureaucratisation of the revolution, as had occurred in the Soviet Union, could result in the Party exercising a form of dictatorship over the people, rather than with and for them.[7]

Mao's thinking on class and class struggle evolved over the early years of the PRC as he struggled with his colleagues to assert his views and witnessed the consequences of early policy initiatives (Starr 1971). Despite the initial success of the land reform movement in giving land to the tiller (if not always totally successful under other definitions), this was just the first step – and, crucially, not necessarily a socialist one. Indeed, Mao came to argue that land reform could potentially lead *away* from socialism. Changes that were based on giving peasants what could be conceived of as private property could generate ideational consequences that ran against the CCP's ambitions.[8]

To counter this, it was important to keep persuading and educating the people about why socialism and the CCP's agenda were in their best interests. It was also essential that the pace of revolutionary change was maintained to prevent the emergence of new relationships and certainties that could generate new unequal power dynamics. As a result, in the space

6 Mao Zedong, 'Directives on the Cultural Revolution', 26 August 1967, www.marxists.org/reference/archive/mao/selected-works/volume-9/mswv9_84.htm.

7 Mao Zedong, 'Twenty Manifestations of Bureaucracy', February 1970, www.marxists.org/reference/archive/mao/selected-works/volume-9/mswv9_85.htm.

8 Mao Zedong, 'Talk on Questions of Philosophy', 18 August 1964, www.marxists.org/reference/archive/mao/selected-works/volume-9/mswv9_27.htm.

of five or six years, most of the rural population underwent three major transformations. The initial process of land reform was quickly followed by a push to build on some of the organic self-help mutual aid teams that were forming in parts of the countryside. But even before this transition had been completed in all of the country, a further move to cooperatives had begun. Mao then favoured a further transition to collectives, which were not just bigger than the cooperatives, but were also based on socialist distribution principles of 'from each according to his deeds'. Mao's views were opposed by key figures within the Party elite who argued that without modern inputs from the industrial sector, cooperatives could not flourish.[9] The priority had to be production, and this meant that the pace of collectivisation should be gradual.

This opposition was enforced in an official State Council directive in March 1955, which called for a cautious approach. Mao's preferences were again put to one side at the Party congress the following year. So what became the Great Leap was not formally sanctioned by the Party through its institutionalised decision-making system. It was through more ad hoc ways that Mao's ideas prevailed: a tour of the country in an attempt to build a wide base of support for his ideas among local leaders.[10] That said, while MacFarquhar (1983) sees the Great Leap as a primarily Mao-driven strategy, he also notes the relative lack of opposition from other leaders once it began to unfold, with even those who were later vocal critics playing at least some role in its implementation.

In theory, not only would the Great Leap show the superiority of socialism and Marxist thinking, but also would generate more rapid growth than any other strategy under consideration. Further, it would break down some of the key divisions in society and the economy that could result in the re-emergence of oppression and alienation, such as divisions between town and county, cleavages between factory managers and workers, and the separation of the experts from the masses. Another theme of the Great Leap was the importance of self-sufficiency. This was very much related to concerns about national defence and survival. With communes and the countryside providing for themselves, this would create a form of cellular communism, which meant that the country could survive an invasion or foreign attack in ways that it could not if industrial production was concentrated in the

9 Notably by Liu Shaoqi, Chen Yun, Ma Yinchu and Li Fuchun.

10 And initially also via a special ad hoc meeting in Beijing in July 1955. For detailed accounts of elite competition and Mao's goals before and during the Great Leap, see Teiwes and Sun (1999) and Bachman (1991).

cities. The same logic subsequently inspired what became known as Third Front industrialisation. Fearing that tactical nuclear strikes could quickly and easily destroy China's entire industrial capacity, the decision was made to establish 'a strategic defence in the rear' by moving industrial capacity and manpower away from supplies and markets in the more developed regions of the east to the safer havens of the west (Liu 1987, 258). The economic costs were enormous (Naughton 1988) but were considered a price worth paying because the calculation was that some sort of major military conflict was not only possible but also inevitable.

With the Great Leap resulting in mass famine and economic collapse in many areas, revolutionary goals gave way to what MacFarquhar (1997, 23) calls a series of 'emergency measures' based on 'seat-of-the-pants decision-making'. By 1961, the ideas that Chen Yun had been advocating five years earlier as an alternative to Mao's came back to the fore. Under this pragmatism that turned a deaf ear towards Maoist ideology, planning was revitalised, targets vastly reduced, rural industry scaled back, some power recentralised and the communes more or less reverted back to collectives, even though the name 'people's commune' continued until 1982. Whereas Mao wanted to mobilise the peasants through revolutionary zeal, Chen thought that material incentives were more important. Where Mao put his faith in the initiative of local cadres, Chen thought that only through central control – viewing the country as a single chessboard – could the Party ensure measured and logical development. Managers and experts were brought back into positions of influence, and academic ability and the correct political background became increasingly important for gaining university entrance.

Chen's ideas are often referred to as the 'birdcage' theory (Naughton 1995). The bird is the free market and the cage is the state system. Without the cage, the bird would fly away, but if the bars of the cage were too restrictive, then the bird would be unable to move and would die. The challenge, then, was to ensure that the cage was strong enough to keep the bird in and large enough for it to flourish. Private activity and the market were entirely legitimate as long as they did not dominate the economy and do things that the state and the collective sectors could not do (or could not do as well). If the private sector started doing things that the Party did not like, including reducing the Party's ability to control the economy as a whole, then its legitimacy to act could be and would be curtailed. While the scope for the private and the market has increased significantly in the post-Mao era, this basic philosophy remains more or less in place today.

The limits of space and the focus on political economy here do not allow for an in-depth investigation into the causes and evolution of the Cultural Revolution.[11] The extent of the political and societal chaos in 1967 and 1968 would surely have been enough in itself to highlight the need to bring the chaos under control. But the economic decline witnessed in 1967 and 1968 must have also been worrying, following as it did not long after the famine and decline brought about by the Great Leap. Thanks to the military, a form of order was restored across the country, and for the final years of Mao's life, two conflicting visions of political economy vied for predominance: on the one side, the more pragmatic approach now supported and promoted by Deng,[12] and on the other, a reformed Maoist approach associated with the Gang of Four. The former wanted to place economics and economic reconstruction as the main priority, while the latter still argued that politics and political struggle should be in command.

Opening Up and Reform

After Mao's death in 1976, it took two years before Deng Xiaoping emerged from the succession struggle within the CCP as its prominent and charismatic leader.[13] Deng put forward a policy of economic reform that was officially adopted by the Party at the Third Plenum of the Eleventh Central Committee in December 1978. However, neither Deng nor anybody within the CCP elite had in mind a coherent strategy for China's economic development. There was a very clear idea of what China needed to transition *from*. What Deng knew was that the Cultural Revolution had destroyed the country's social fabric and capital, and that the CCP was striving to gain a new legitimacy; indeed, this was implicitly acknowledged by the CCP in its 1981 'Resolution on Party History' condemning Mao's 'grave left errors'. Consequently, Deng would do whatever it took to increase productivity and raise the standards of living of the population. Rather than class struggle, economic modernisation and growth became an absolute priority. In 1981, during a trip to Japan, Deng set the target of quadrupling the country's per

11 Joseph, Wong and Zweig (1991) contains a number of chapters that assess different aspects of China's political economy during the Cultural Revolution.

12 Over the years, Deng's pragmatism has become a myth that he himself contributed to creating. See Naughton (1996).

13 For the often forgotten or swiftly dealt with interim years, see Weatherley (2010).

capita gross national product by the year 2000 (Yeh 1996, 11), and this goal became a CCP commitment at the Twelfth Party Congress at Party Secretary Hu Yaobang's suggestion.[14]

Addressing underdevelopment as the primary contradiction in Chinese politics meant pursuing a 'reorientation of development strategy' (Naughton 1995, 76–7) that would 'involv[e] a dramatic reduction in industrial investment and a shift of resources toward the household sector' (Naughton 1995, 59). But Deng did not have a clear blueprint for the economy, and it was this lack of vision that made him let economic experiments unfold (Naughton 1995; White 1984; Hamrin 1990). After all, he was not new to reform attempts. Although he had initially been a Mao loyalist, between 1962 and 1965 he tried to introduce incentives within the economic system aimed at improving the low performance of enterprises. While Mao was interested in mass (macro) mobilisation projects, Deng insisted on the (micro) link between incentives, delegation of authority and individual motivation (Naughton 1995, 83). From his personal experience in the 1960s, he learnt two lessons: economic suffering would bring politically dangerous consequences for the CCP's (socialist) legitimacy, and market incentives could set off powerful dynamics of growth. It was time to try again, without dismantling the command system of the economy and the CCP monopoly of power. Undoubtedly, state institutions were rationalised and modernised (Zheng 2004; Peerenboom 2007), but bureaucracy was actually strengthened and party-state capacities (the 'Leninist *apparat*') enhanced (Naughton 1996, 68).

Reforms were introduced gradually – in agriculture, industry and in international trade and foreign investment. Ex-post, key to reforms was the implementation of 'responsibility systems' across economic sectors, whereby the government partially and progressively delegated authority to economic and even institutional actors (provinces, local governments, firms, managers, cadres, households and even individuals), who were made responsible for their decisions regarding expenses, savings and investment.

The desire to create a more efficient and sustainable economy was accompanied by serious concerns about the consequences of any transition on unemployment and social stability. Therefore, the willingness to use market forces was constrained by the necessity to control them. The CCP

14 See Zhao Ziyang, 'Advance along the Road towards Socialism with Chinese Characteristics', *People's Daily*, 4 November 1987.

had to strike a balance between growth-enhancing market economic reforms and the political necessity to protect those who might suffer from the introduction of these reforms; at least until 1994, and with the partial exception of the period immediately before Tiananmen (see below), the CCP quite succeeded in generating 'growth without losers' (Lau, Qiang and Roland 2000). That is the reason why reforms implemented a 'dual-track system' in which market elements coexisted with the plan: had experiments failed, it could have been possible to return to the old economic pattern, without causing any existential disruption of the system. Experimentalism and 'seeking truth from facts' were in line with the CCP's longstanding adaption of Marxism–Leninism to China's actual conditions. As times had changed, what the Party should do had to be rethought by once more applying the guiding theoretical principles to concrete circumstances. That much was clear and agreed. But which specific policies could best serve China's need to grow remained the subject of considerable internal debate.[15]

For Deng, plan and market were just economic means: deprived of their ideological meaning, market incentives were new instruments that could be utilised even in a socialist context (the white cat/black cat story). Once incentives were introduced to the system, they followed a capitalist logic, but it was contingent capitalism, as Deng never put into question the supremacy of the Party. The whole point was doing whatever worked to attain centrally mandated goals – which revolved around the rate of GDP growth. If the private sector could achieve results that the state sector could not, then it would be encouraged. Private actors were increasingly allowed to pursue their own economic objectives as long as they conformed with 'higher' party-state goals, but their freedom to act and the parameters of action could be and were changed if they were deemed to not be doing what the party-state wanted them to do. The CCP drew the 'red lines', which economic actors knew they could not cross without suffering serious consequences. In this sense, China can be defined as a peculiar form of developmental state (in line with the experiences of Japan, Korea and Taiwan), in which the CCP has been the developmental agency in charge of economic policies (Gabusi 2017). Economic nationalism and a certain obsession with the necessity of 'catching-up' with industrialised countries have always been among the main features of East Asian developmental states, and China is no exception.

15 The intra-party discussion in those years is often portrayed as a struggle between reformists and conservatives, see, for instance, Howell (1993). However, we should always bear in mind that this binary distinction is a simplification, as neither group is a coherent bloc.

The reform process was given a new boost in 1982–83, with the first significant removal of price controls on more than 500 small consumer goods. In September of the same year, Prime Minister Zhao Ziyang wrote a letter to the Politburo Standing Committee members and to the three most important elders (Deng Xiaoping, Chen Yun and Li Xiannian). The main point in his message was that the Party would maintain 'a planned commodity economy with public ownership', moving away from command planning to guidance planning, the latter allowing economic actors to choose the means to reach set targets (Naughton 1995, 178). But targets had to be met, implying a state preparedness to intervene when the market could not deliver what it was meant to. In other words, the state would retain the commanding heights of the economy: officially, the 1984 'Decision on the Reform of the Economic Structure' was still characterising China as a planned 'socialist commodity economy' (*shehuizhuyi shangpin jingji* 社会主义商品经济).

Zhao Ziyang himself made an ex-post justification of the use of private capital and private entrepreneurship as a means to an end in his speech on the primary stage of socialism at the Thirteenth Party Congress in 1987. With at least some echoes of Mao's conception of New Democracy from nearly five decades before, Zhao argued that:

> China [had to] go through an extremely long primary stage so that it [could] achieve the industrialisation and the commercialisation, socialisation, and modernisation of production that other countries have secured through capitalistic means.[16]

In this primary stage, non-state actors could help expand productive forces and build socialism. More than 40 years of the 'reform era' have not yet revealed how long this primary stage will last, whether it will ever end and, in the affirmative case, what the secondary stage will consist of.

Of course, such reforms had the same negative effects as any market reform in a transition economy: (limited) laid-off workers in the state sector,[17] rising inflation and rampant corruption. The protests that culminated in the bloody repression in Tiananmen Square in June 1989 had much to do with post-reform economic insecurity as well as with post-Mao youth aspirations

16 Zhao Ziyang, 'Advance along the Road of Socialism with Chinese Characteristics', Speech at Thirteenth Party Congress, 4 November 1987, *Beijing Review* 30, no. 45: 1–27.

17 'In 1989, 423,000 permanent and contract state workers (0.5% of the total) were laid off, quit, or were on contracts that were not renewed' (Naughton 1995, 212).

to a freer political environment. From 1989 to 1990, and in line with Premier Li Peng reintroducing elements of state control at the Third Plenum of the Thirteenth Central Committee in September 1988, the Central Committee tried to reverse the marketisation of the economy by adopting preferential policies for state-owned enterprises (SOEs), and planning was given renewed consideration. The cost of slowing down reforms nevertheless proved to be higher than the benefits of accelerating them: macroeconomic austerity brought recession because agents were already responding to price signals, and conservatives faced political resistance (especially from the CCP coastal elite) to proposals of discriminating against township and village enterprises (Naughton 1995).

Probably feeling threatened by the spectres of economic failure and by the collapse of the Soviet Union and its satellites in Europe, and sensing that conservatives were being weakened by the economic stalemate, in January 1992 Deng relaunched his reform campaign during a 'Southern inspection tour' (*nanxun*) that included the success stories of the Shenzhen and Zhuhai special economic zones and Shanghai. In the same year, the Fourteenth CCP Congress would declare the construction of a 'socialist market economy' as the objective of the reforms – an economy where public ownership would still dominate. Since then, and probably until Xi Jinping seemed to solve the dilemma, China was in transition from socialism, 'crossing the river by feeling the stones', but not knowing where the other bank of the river was and what it would look like. How long would Zhao Ziyang's 'primary stage of socialism' last?

In the meantime, the 1993 Third Plenum resolution on the 'Establishment of a Socialist Market Economic System' marked a 'consensus' in the elite to offer society a social pact: more economic freedoms in exchange for absolute loyalty to CCP rule and guidance. Under the policy of 'grasping the large, letting go the small' (*zhuada fangxiao* 抓大放小), the state was to consolidate and corporatise large SOEs, while different bureaucracies were encouraged to reorganise their industrial apparatus and to get rid of the most unprofitable enterprises. Private businesses were allowed to emerge and thrive in most sectors, international trade was increasingly liberalised and foreign investors were invited to contribute to China's new economic bonanza. Jiang Zemin consolidated Deng's reforms, including the process (which had started in 1991) of transforming SOEs in big conglomerates: a new policy directive selected 65 large enterprises to form a 'national team' (Sutherland 2003, 11, 39). Also, Jiang sealed the corporatist alliance with private entrepreneurs in his Three Represents theory at the Sixteenth

Party Congress in 2002, allowing them to join the CCP rank and file. Zhu Rongji, Jiang's premier, convincingly led the negotiations that would lead China to join the World Trade Organization in 2001. To the eyes of the West, this was the event that would definitively confirm that Beijing was set on a path of capitalist transformation that would one day cause China to finally embrace democracy and free its market from state interference. After a period of *interregnum*, the end of the liberal illusion would become evident with Xi Jinping's rise to power.

Addressing Imbalances

While it was Xi Jinping who formally changed the primary contradiction at the Party congress in 2017, previous leaders had already acknowledged that the rapid growth mode of the 1990s was reaching the end of its useful life, and that a new direction was needed. Hu Jintao had first signalled the importance of a greater focus on what was done with growth (rather than just generating it) by 'putting people first' (*yi ren wei ben* 以人为本) and building a harmonious society (*hexie shehui* 和谐社会). There was a recognition that the previous emphasis on going all out for growth could not solve all of China's socioeconomic problems; indeed, more than that, it had actually exacerbated a number of tensions, such as growing inequality and environmental damage.

A number of steps were taken to start the shift to a new set of policies, or, at the very least, to try to draw back from the rush for growth. From 2004 until quite late in 2008, macroeconomic policy focused on slowing the growth in fixed assets investment (which had been exceeding GDP growth) and reducing the problem of overcapacity in a number of industries. Steps were also taken to reduce China's competitive advantage as a cheap export production platform in an attempt to emphasise higher quality value-added exports.[18]

18 Including the reduction of the export tax rebates, the firm implementation of labour laws, and the appreciation of the RMB by around 20 per cent in the three years from the end of the currency peg in July 2005.

The problem for the leadership was that these measures worked. One consequence of them working was complaints from provincial leaders in coastal provinces (where the processing export trade was concentrated) about an increase in laid-off workers. And, in fact, many of the policies that had been implemented were subsequently reversed.

This episode demonstrates the key dilemma between doing what is thought to be right and logical for economic sustainability in the long run, and what is deemed to be politically acceptable in the short term. Top of the list of politically unacceptable – or at least risky – outcomes was a large increase in unemployment. This dilemma became more evident when the impact of the global financial crisis saw Chinese exports collapse,[19] with as many as 26 million migrant workers in export industries being laid-off. Perhaps ironically, the Chinese response, while highly successful in its own right in ensuring that growth was maintained and a crisis of the real Chinese economy averted, actually exacerbated many of the problems that the pre-crisis policy was trying to overcome: overcapacity increased as did the reliance on debt-funded investment to generate growth.

The response to the global crisis was, perhaps, the prime example of doing Whatever It Takes to address China's economic weaknesses in the dialectic spirit of the CCP's conception of Marxism–Leninism. It was a case of doing things in the short term that the leadership had previously identified as being the source of the problem, not the solution. It was a case of acting to avert a short-term crisis, and worrying about the long term later. And it was a case of Wen Jiabao handing over an economy to Li Keqiang that he called 'unbalanced, uncoordinated and unsustainable', in part because of what had come before the Hu–Wen era, and in part because of what happened in, and after, 2008.

Xi Jinping: Making the CCP Great Again

Upon coming to power in 2012, Xi Jinping adopted a nationalistic narrative, arguing that the time had come for the 'rejuvenation of the Chinese nation' and for the fulfilment of the 'Chinese Dream'. At the beginning, nobody knew what 'Chinese Dream' meant, but it increasingly became clear that 'the need to confirm a sense of national identity seemed to call for a clear developmental choice: affirming socialism' (Dittmer 2021a, 5). The literature

19 When totalled up, exports in 2009 as a whole were down 16 per cent on 2008.

has long argued over whether China owes its economic success to the state presence and guidance in the economy or whether China has developed because markets have been working *despite* inefficiencies and distortions created by state meddling in resource allocation, credit, and both private and public companies' production choices. The epitome of the latter voices – all praising Dengist policies – is Huang Yasheng, who in 2011 argued that earlier marketisation and liberalisation, not state intervention, had laid the ground for China's development (Huang 2008; Coase and Wang 2012; Nee and Opper 2012). Along the same lines, Nicholas Lardy (2014) wrote that China was not an example of state capitalism, but rather that the private sector was 'the major driver of growth'. Later, Lardy (2019) would take note of the increasing support of the state sector, arguing that the retreat of markets would, in the end, undermine the long-term sustainability of the economy.

In essence, state capitalism directs the market to 'further empower government' (Bremmer 2010, 179). Although China's economic rise undoubtedly strengthened Xi Jinping's claim to the superiority of 'socialism with Chinese characteristics in the new era' (a label first introduced at the Nineteenth Party Congress), this definition can be misleading, because state and markets in the post-1978 PRC have never been separate entities: they interact with each other in a symbiotic way, empowering both bottom-up entrepreneurial activities and a top-down steering of the economy, unleashing a peculiar form of 'Sino-capitalism' (McNally 2012). If 'patrimonial capitalism' has been defined in the 'varieties of capitalism' literature as a system in which the boundary between the state and firms is not clearly defined and the economic environment is highly politicised (Becker 2009, 2014), perhaps this definition would define today's China even better. It is the combination of state and markets, in a mutually reinforcing dynamic, that has driven China's growth. But it was the CCP that set the boundaries within which the markets could operate.

In recent years, this principle has become increasingly evident in finance. Controlling credit is, in fact, another way to govern markets in the 'right', regime-friendly direction. For decades, financial repression has been the norm in China, rewarding investment at the expense of savings. Not only have reforms strengthened the four largest and oldest state banks (they are now ranked among the largest 50 companies in Global Fortune 500),[20] but

20 See 'Global 500', accessed 12 June 2021, fortune.com/global500/2020/search/.

also they have made it clear that the national interest must prevail in all banking activities, private or public. Article 34 of the Chinese Commercial Bank Law, while stating that banks should make commercial considerations before adopting loan decisions, requires them to 'conduct their business of lending in accordance with the needs of the national economic and social development and under the guidance of the industrial policies of the State' (Szamosszegi and Kyle 2011). Within an institutional setting characterised by the absence of the rule of law, rules and regulations can be interpreted, swiftly changed or selectively implemented to obtain an outcome in line with CCP wishes and interests.

The CCP firmly believes that markets cannot be completely trusted. In particular, finance is subject to conformity with CCP goals. For instance, the 2014–16 ups and downs on the Shanghai stock market prompted the state to rein in further development of private capital markets, as they had become an evident source of instability. The logic was the same in August 2015, when capital flight followed the partial liberalisation of capital accounts, pushing up the value of the RMB: the government simply backtracked (Dittmer 2021a, 29). Private actors must be controlled and put into line, especially if they have become too big, too powerful or too (relatively) dissenting; the regulatory takeover of Anbang Insurance or the last-minute and financially devastating stop to the multi-billion dollar Shanghai IPO of Ant Financial, a company of the Alibaba Group (whose founder, worldwide celebrity Jack Ma, had criticised the sclerotic banking system just a week before), are cases in point.[21]

Thus, what to make of Xi Jinping's announcement at the Third Plenum of the Eighteenth Party Congress in 2013 that the market would play a 'decisive role' in China's future evolvement of the economy? The gap between rhetoric and reality reflects the dilemma that the CCP has always faced in its existence, especially in the post-1978 era: what if markets are needed for growth but they move China into a direction not compatible with social stability – a prerequisite for the persistence of the CCP's monopoly of power? What if the 'new normal' announced by Xi Jinping at the Eighteenth Party Congress – a new attention to 'growth quality', trying to escape from the excesses of 'GDPism' and from the post-2008 debt trap – implies *less* growth along with job losses? This dilemma forces the

21 Katie Canales, 'Jack Ma Hasn't Been Seen in Public since Ant Group's IPO was Pulled. Here's How Chinese Regulators Slammed the Brakes on the Firm's Would-Be Record-Breaking $37 Billion IPO', *Business Insider*, 4 January 2021.

CCP to continue to experiment with new ways to reconcile the apparently irreconcilable forces in the economy: while announcing the 'decisive role' of the market, Xi did not miss the opportunity to restate the 'dominance' of the public sector. Thus, the system features what Dittmer calls:

> an adaptive Chinese form of state socialism, with limited (and closely monitored) capitalist characteristics … a theoretically inconsistent hybrid (e.g. socialism as end, capitalism as means, or socialist rhetoric, capitalist practice), its future systemic identity *in statu nascendi*. (Dittmer 2021a, 8)

But the CCP has, since its very birth, adapted Marxism–Leninism to China's historical conditions – its state socialism has always been fluid and managed according to the (national and international) constraints of any given time, which shaped the identification of different primary contradictions. To many, this 'inconsistent hybrid' of doing 'Whatever It Takes' to develop China *and* save the regime at the same time cannot be called Marxism–Leninism, but this is the kind of Marxism–Leninism the CCP has always identified itself with.

Both 'dual circulation' and 'common prosperity' are manifestations of the new variant of the Whatever It Takes attitude of the CCP to pursue a form of development that sustains its legitimacy and does not put into question the logics of Marxist–Leninist state control of the economy. The former stresses the need to rely more on domestic supply and demand than before as an engine of growth, and the latter has a focus on dealing with the worst excesses of inequality, addressing the problems faced by poorer groups and regions, and promoting fairness and a sense of national common purpose. Politics – that is, the CCP – has always been in charge of the fundamental trajectories of the economy throughout the PRC's history, and the idea that, under Deng, 'economics took command' (Dittmer 2021b, 368) might be grounded in the liberal illusion the West had long nurtured about China. Undoubtedly, with Xi Jinping's current emphasis on 'enhancing the Party's leadership over the SOEs',[22] this illusion has now faded away.

SOEs are indeed the 'jewels in the crown' of the CCP, dominating strategic sectors of the economy (Chen 2021, 44). When Xi Jinping came to power, the elite was well aware that the state sector was largely inefficient – even

22 'On strengthening the Party's leadership over SOEs' (论加强党对国有企业的领导), *Red Flag Document*, 2017.

though at that point industrial policies had created several global giants.[23] The 'decisive role of the market' narrative also advocated injecting private and foreign capital into SOEs, accepting forms of mixed ownership (*hunhe suoyouzhi* 混合所有制). However, this further step in liberalisation never truly materialised, for reasons related to the CCP's fears of losing control of the economy and representing another side of the same dilemma haunting the Party since 1949. In fact, previous rounds of corporatisation had turned many SOEs into autonomous centres of personal powers and wealth (Brødsgaard 2012), often enriching managers and their families in both legal and illegal ways and without giving much back to the state coffers. Far from giving SOEs more clout, leverage or influence by engaging private capital, the CCP had to rein in their ambitions and reassert its extractive capacity. In what Chen (2021) labels 'State Capitalism 2.0', and in a reversal of Deng's policy on the matter, Party committees and Party groups are now 'embedded in the corporate governance structure' and involved in daily management operations, ensuring that SOE strategies and decisions are in line with CCP preferences and also with Xi's personal campaign against corruption.

Conclusion

In June 2021, almost 100 years after the foundation of the CCP, the *People's Daily* published two articles celebrating the achievements of the Party entitled 'Socialism Has Not Let Down China' and 'China Has Not Let Down Socialism'. The articles emphasised how the Party has made an original contribution to Marxism by adhering to the principle of scientific socialism and by promoting the sinicisation of Marxism, thus giving birth to a 'socialist culture with Chinese characteristics'. The articles also celebrated the economy's resilience in bouncing back from the impact of COVID-19 lockdowns. This celebration turned out to be rather premature, as China's zero-COVID strategy, personally associated with Xi Jinping, instead saw many parts of the country subsequently being placed under various forms of restrictions as other major economies were returning to something like normal. Added to this was an increasingly tense set of international relations with a range of Western states (and others too) and the already difficult task of shifting the economic model to deal with the new primary

23 In 2002, only six SOEs were listed in the Global Fortune 500, but in 2002 that number had risen to 65 (Chen 2021, 49).

contradiction. The CCP might have finished its first centenary celebrating its achievements, but it started its second with Xi cautioning the people to be 'more mindful of potential dangers, be prepared to deal with worst-case scenarios, and be ready to withstand high winds, choppy waters, and even dangerous storms'.[24]

As we have shown in this chapter, the 'Communist' and the 'Chinese' elements have always been present in the design and implementation of the Party's political economy. True, we have seen waves of change over the decades, including periods of liberalisation and privatisation and then greater state control, but the basic philosophy and identification of the dilemmas seems to be constant. In fact, Mao, Deng and Xi all share the view that markets must serve China's economic catching-up and reinforce the Party's legitimacy. Of course, if markets and market incentives threaten the Party's firm grip on power, liberalisation will be halted, regardless of the long-term economic consequences. So what really changes in the political economy of the Party is the way it deals with the dilemmas and the means activated to attain the desired goals. The logic of doing 'Whatever It Takes' to lift China out of poverty and to keep the monopoly of power has always been the same, going back to the foundational logic of the Party's own reading of Marxism–Leninism.

References

Bachman, David. 1991. *Bureaucracy, Economy, and Leadership in China: The Institutional Origins of the Great Leap Forward.* Cambridge: Cambridge University Press. doi.org/10.1017/CBO9780511664144.

Becker, Uwe. 2009. *Open Varieties of Capitalism: Continuity, Change and Performances.* Basingstoke: Palgrave Macmillan.

Becker, Uwe. 2014. 'Institutional Change in the BRICs, Eastern Europe, South Africa and Turkey, 1998–2008'. In *The BRICs and Emerging Economies in Comparative Perspective: Political Economy, Liberalisation and Institutional Change*, edited by U. Becker, 27–52. Abingdon: Routledge.

Bremmer, Ian. 2010. *The End of the Free Market: Who Wins the War Between States and Corporations?* New York: Portfolio.

24 Xi Jinping, 'Report to the 20th National Congress of the Communist Party of China', 16 October 2022, www.fmprc.gov.cn/eng/zxxx_662805/202210/P020221025833535574835.doc.

Brugger, Bill. 1981. *China: Liberation and Transformation*. London: Routledge.

Chan, Kam Wing Chan and Xu Xueqiang. 1985. 'Urban Population Growth and Urbanization in China since 1949: Reconstructing a Baseline'. *China Quarterly* 104: 583–613. doi.org/10.1017/S0305741000033324.

Chen, Gang. 2021. 'Consolidating Leninist Control of State-Owned Enterprises: China's State Capitalism 2.0'. In *China's Political Economy in the Xi Jinping Epoch: Domestic and Global Dimensions*, edited by L. Dittmer, 43–60. Singapore: World Scientific. doi.org/10.1142/9789811226588_0002.

Coase, Ronald and Ning Wang. 2012. *How China Became Capitalist*. Basingstoke: Palgrave Macmillan. doi.org/10.1057/9781137019370.

Dittmer, Lowell. 2021a. 'Transformation of the Chinese Political Economy in the New Era'. In *China's Political Economy in the Xi Jinping Epoch: Domestic and Global Dimensions*, edited by L. Dittmer, 3–40. Singapore: World Scientific. doi.org/10.1142/9789811226588_0001.

Dittmer, Lowell. 2021b. 'Where is China Going and Why?' In *China's Political Economy in the Xi Jinping Epoch: Domestic and Global Dimensions*, edited by L. Dittmer, 349–80. Singapore: World Scientific. doi.org/10.1142/9789811226588_0013.

Gabusi, Giuseppe. 2017. '"The Reports of My Death Have Been Greatly Exaggerated": China and the Developmental State 25 Years after *Governing the Market*'. *Pacific Review* 30 (2): 232–50. doi.org/10.1080/09512748.2016.1217254.

Gray, Jack. 2006. 'Mao in Perspective'. *China Quarterly* 187: 659–79. doi.org/10.1017/S0305741006000294.

Gregor, A. James. 1995. *Marxism, China and Development: Reflections on Theory and Reality*. New Brunswick: Transaction Books.

Hamrin, Carol. 1990. *China and the Challenge of the Future: Changing Political Patterns*. Boulder: Westview Press.

Howell, Jude. 1993. *China Opens Its Doors: The Politics of Economic Transition*. Hemell Hempstead: Harvester Wheatshef.

Huang, Yasheng. 2008. *Capitalism with Chinese Characteristics: Entrepreneurship and the State*. New York: Cambridge University Press.

Johnson, Chalmers. 1962. *Peasant Nationalism and Communist Power: The Emergence of Revolutionary China, 1937–1945*. Stanford, CA: Stanford University Press. doi.org/10.1515/9781503620582.

Joseph, William, Christine Wong and Christine Zweig, eds. 1991. *New Perspectives on the Cultural Revolution*. Cambridge: The Council on East Asian Studies, Harvard University.

Klein, Sidney. 1961. 'The Land Reform Policies of the Chinese Communist Party, 1928–1958: A Brief Economic Analysis'. *Agricultural History* 35 (2): 59–64.

Knight, Nick. 2005. *Marxist Philosophy in China: From Qu Qiubai to Mao Zedong, 1923–1945*. Dordrect: Springer.

Knight, Nick. 2007. *Rethinking Mao: Explorations in Mao Zedong's Thought*. Lanham: Lexington Books.

Kung, James Kai-sing. 2008. 'The Political Economy of Land Reform in China's "Newly Liberated Areas": Evidence from Wuxi County'. *China Quarterly* 195 (September): 675–90. doi.org/10.1017/S0305741008000829.

Lardy, Nicholas R. 2014. *Markets over Mao: The Rise of Private Business in China*. Washington: Peterson Institute for International Economics.

Lardy, Nicholas R. 2019. *The State Strikes Back: The End of Economic Reform in China?* Washington: Peterson Institute for International Economics.

Lau, Laurence J., Qian Yingyi and Gérard Roland. 2000. 'Reform without Losers: An Interpretation of China's Dual-Track Approach to Transition'. *Journal of Political Economy* 108 (1): 120–43. doi.org/10.1086/262113.

Li, Hua-yu. 2006. *Mao and the Economic Stalinization of China, 1948–1953*. New York: Rowman and Littlefield.

Liu, Guoguang, ed. 1987. *China's Economy in 2000*. Beijing: New World Press.

Liu, Jianyi. 2000. 'The Origins of the Chinese Communist Party and the Role Played by Soviet Russia and the Comintern'. PhD thesis, University of York.

MacFarquhar, Roderick. 1983. *The Origins of the Cultural Revolution. Vol. 2: The Great Leap Forward, 1958–1960*. Oxford: Oxford University Press for the Royal Institute of International Affairs.

MacFarquhar, Roderick. 1997. *The Origins of the Cultural Revolution. Vol. 3: The Coming of the Cataclysm, 1961–1966*. Oxford: Oxford University Press for the Royal Institute of International Affairs. doi.org/10.1093/acprof:oso/9780192149978.001.0001.

McNally, Christopher A. 2012. 'Sino-Capitalism: China's Reemergence and the International Political Economy'. *World Politics* 64 (4): 741–76. doi.org/10.1017/S0043887112000202.

Meisner, Maurice. 1967. *Li Ta-chao and the Origins of Chinese Marxism*. Cambridge: Harvard University Press. doi.org/10.4159/harvard.9780674180819.

Naughton, Barry. 1988. 'The Third Front: Defence Industrialization in the Chinese Interior'. *China Quarterly* 115: 351–86. doi.org/10.1017/S0305741 00002748X.

Naughton, Barry. 1995. *Growing Out of the Plan: Chinese Economic Reform, 1978–1993*. Cambridge: Cambridge University Press. doi.org/10.1017/CBO97805 11664335.

Naughton, Barry. 1996. 'Deng Xiaoping: The Economist'. In *Deng Xiaoping: Portrait of a Chinese Statesman*, edited by D. Shambaugh, 83–106. New York: Oxford University Press.

Nee, Victor and Sonja Opper. 2012. *Capitalism from Below: Markets and Institutional Change in China*. Cambridge: Harvard University Press. doi.org/10.4159/ harvard.9780674065390.

Peerenboom, Randall. 2007. *China Modernizes: Threat to the West or Model for the Rest?* Oxford: Oxford University Press.

Saich, Tony. 1997. 'Uncertain Legacies of Revolution'. In *New Perspectives on State Socialism in China*, edited by T. Cheek and T. Saich, 303–20. Armonk: Sharpe.

Schram, Stuart. 1989. *The Thought of Mao Tse-tung*. Cambridge: Cambridge University Press. doi.org/10.1017/CBO9780511521454.

Schwartz, Benjamin. 1951. *Chinese Communism and the Rise of Mao*. Cambridge: Harvard University Press.

So, Bennis Wai-yip. 2002. 'The Policy-Making and Political Economy of the Abolition of Private Ownership in the Early 1950s: Findings from New Material'. *China Quarterly* 171: 682–703.

Starr, John Bryan. 1971. 'Conceptual Foundations of Mao Tse-Tung's Theory of Continuous Revolution'. *Asian Survey* 11 (6): 610–28. doi.org/10.2307/ 2642773.

Sutherland, Dylan. 2003. *China's Large Enterprises and the Challenge of Late Industrialisation*. London: Routledge Curzon. doi.org/10.4324/97802035 11749.

Szamosszegi, Andrew and Cole Kyle. 2011. 'An Analysis of State-Owned Enterprises and State Capitalism in China'. US–China Economic Security Review Commission Report, 26 October. www.uscc.gov/sites/default/files/Research/ 10_26_11_CapitalTradeSOEStudy.pdf.

Teiwes, Frederick. 1979. *Politics and Purges in China: Rectification and the Decline of Party Norms 1950–1965*. New York: Sharpe.

Teiwes, Frederick and Warren Sun. 1999. *China's Road to Disaster: Mao, Central Politicians and Provincial Leaders in the Great Leap Forward, 1955–59*. New York: Routledge.

Wang, Ning. 2015. 'The Chinese Economic System Under Mao'. *Man and the Economy* 2 (2): 153–93. doi.org/10.1515/me-2015-6002.

Weatherley, Robert. 2010. *Mao's Forgotten Successor: The Political Career of Hua Guofeng*. Basingstoke: Palgrave. doi.org/10.1057/9780230282926.

White, Gordon. 1984. 'Changing Relations between State and Enterprise in Contemporary China: Expanding Enterprise Autonomy'. In *China's Changed Road to Development*, edited by Neville Maxwell and Bruce McFarlane, 43–60. Oxford: Pergamon. doi.org/10.1016/B978-0-08-030849-4.50009-7.

Wylie, Raymond. 1979. 'Mao Tse-tung, Ch'en Po-ta and the "Sinification of Marxism", 1936–38'. *China Quarterly* 79: 447–80. doi.org/10.1017/S0305741000038273.

Yeh, K. C. 1996. 'Macroeconomic Issues in China in the 1990s'. In *The Chinese Economy under Deng Xiaoping*, edited by R. F. Ash and Y. Y. Kueh. New York: Oxford University Press.

Zheng, Yongnian. 2004. *Globalization and State Transformation in China*. Cambridge: Cambridge University Press.

9

From War on Nature to War on Pollution: Continuity and Change in the Chinese Communist Party's Ecological Agenda

Coraline Goron and Genia Kostka[1]

Introduction

A growing body of research has studied environmental management and governance in China, ranging from top-down vs bottom-up measures, to environmental laws and regulations, to the use of policy instruments, to different forms of citizen participation, to China's model of authoritarian environmentalism. The consensus is that there has been incremental but significant progress to address many of China's environmental issues. Over the years, China's environmental bureaucracy has gradually been reformed and strengthened, and top-down signals have now clearly made the environment a high-priority issue. In this discussion, however, relatively little attention has been paid to the role of the Chinese Communist Party (CCP). While there are good reasons for considering the party-state as a single entity (Li and Shapiro 2020), we argue that there is distinct merit

1 We would like to acknowledge the help of Ms Rachel (Weijun) Rong in gathering data for this chapter.

in looking at the CCP's approach to environmental governance, including how it has decided to (not) use the institutions of the Party and the state to govern the environment.

This chapter addresses this gap by examining how the CCP and related structures have shaped environmental management in the Mao era (1949–78), the reform and opening-up era (1978–2013) and the Xi Jinping era (2013–). How has the CCP exercised its political power over the environment, and how has this shaped the development of China's environmental governance? Based on analysis of various documents and secondary sources, we examine the CCP's approach to the environment through the lens of three core vectors of its power: the CCP's key developmental and environmental concepts and doctrines and its diffusion in society through propaganda; the gradual upgrading of the environmental bureaucracy; and its choice of governance tools, techniques and technologies.

We find that, alongside major changes to the level of attention paid to the environment, the CCP's approach to environmental governance has also changed. While in the reform and opening-up era, following the chaos of the Cultural Revolution, the environment was regarded as a symbol of state modernisation with an emphasis on building regulatory capacity and embracing marketisation, in the Xi era, the CCP has resorted to governing the environmental field directly and has considerably politicised its governance by making it a marker of Xi's doctrinal contribution to socialism with Chinese characteristics, and a political priority task for Party cadres and local leaders. Since 1949, the Party has relied on ideology and personalised leadership, using doctrine and control over local cadres' performance and career development as key vectors of power for dealing with challenging environmental crises. However, the modus of implementation has changed over time: in the reform and opening-up era, the party-state experimented with various regulatory and market mechanisms, but in the Xi era, the CCP has taken greater control of environmental issues by increasingly using Party structures and the CCP's propaganda machine to push through environmental protection measures. The CCP has also increasingly drawn on technology and (albeit to a limited extent) citizen feedback.

The chapter is structured as follows: the next section analyses the evolution of CCP doctrines and propaganda towards the environment from Mao to Xi. The third section looks at the progressive upgrading and politicisation of the environmental bureaucracy. The fourth section summarises a general shift from a defeat of the regulatory environmental state to the resilience of authoritarian environmentalism. The chapter concludes that CCP organs and methods have increasingly been employed in the field of the environment.

From Mao to Xi: Pollution to Ecological Civilisation as the Beacon of Modernisation in the CCP Doctrine

To understand environmental politics and what is shaping the political agenda in China, a focus on ideology and the CCP's interpretation of key developmental and environmental concepts is important. Although it has retained some key fundamentals, the vision of the environment in the CCP ideology has changed a lot since the Mao era.

The Mao era did not have a very elaborate doctrine regarding the environment, but some key elements of the political discourse epitomised the leaders', especially Mao's, attitude towards the environment. As summarised by Liebman (2019), the language of 'war against nature' (*zhan tian dou di* 战天斗地) and seeing chimneys as 'modernisation'[2] coexisted with the idea and practice that frugality and waste reutilisation were key socialist virtues; according to Mao, 'wasting attitudes were as bad as corruption' (*langfei de xinwei he tanwu Yiyang zui'e* 浪费的行为和贪污一样罪恶). For instance, Lei Feng, the archetypal 'good citizen' who was presented as a model for all to emulate across China, was praised during the Mao era and early reform era for his extreme frugality (Tian 2011). Lei Feng was used to support the 'mass line ascetism that aimed to incentivize people living in a poor nation forged after decades of war to work hard collectively with minimal resources to create a modern, socialist China' (Jeffreys and Xuezhong 2016). However, the official line was that industrial pollution and waste were scourges of capitalism and that socialist countries like China were, therefore, immune to them (Chen and Zhou 2015; Zhang 2020).

There was a big shift in the 1970s. The first expressions of a modern Chinese environmental discourse were made at the United Nations Conference on the Human Environment, held in Stockholm in 1972. At the conference, the Chinese delegation sent by Zhou Enlai promoted two core ideas: global injustice and the imperative of development. There

2 Mao Zedong is quoted as saying that 'looking out from Tiananmen, I wish to see chimneys everywhere, (从天安门望出去，应该处处都有烟囱).

were two sub-components: a claim to a 'right to pollute' and a new openness to international cooperation, considered necessary for modernisation. The 'right to pollute' was advanced in reaction to the Club of Rome's influential *Limits to Growth* report issued in 1972, which exhorted governments to control industrialisation and population growth. China, India and many other developing countries opposed the characterisation of their economic development as a global environmental threat. They demanded and, with the adoption of the 'sustainable development' concept in 1992, succeeded in including development in the emerging global environmental agenda (Bernstein 2000). Openness to international cooperation became a key element of China's environmental discourse, mirroring Deng Xiaoping's general reform and opening-up doctrine.

Domestically, Zhou Enlai pushed for recognition that socialist China was facing industrial pollution issues (Zhang 2010). Henceforth, the official propaganda portrayed China's efforts to address environmental problems as exemplary, while Western demands were often portrayed as hypocritical and imperialist (Zhang and Barr 2013). The official discourse boasted that China, unlike the West, would pursue economic development and simultaneously protect the environment. In the 1990s, the official discourse began to reflect the international concept of 'sustainable development'.

Nonetheless, these earlier environmental discourses and policies were mere lip-service, and the imperative of development and modernisation prevailed until the late 2000s. Environmental protection itself was framed as a *development issue*. This frame was enshrined in the interim Environmental Protection Law (EPL) in 1979 and the first Central Environmental Policy Document adopted in 1981.[3] Another official script unambiguously prioritised *economic* development over environmental protection. By the mid-1990s, Deng Xiaoping's maxim of 'development is the hard truth' (*fazhan cai shi ying daoli* 发展才是硬道理) became hegemonic in the Party and in society (Jahiel 1998). Urban but especially rural industrialisation was the order of the day despite rapidly apparent environmental ravages.[4] The role of markets and governments in environmental protection was absent from the official environmental discourse. The very few dissonant voices

3 'Decision on Reinforcing Environmental Protection in the Process of Reforming the National Economy' (国务院关于在国民经济调整时期加强环境保护工作的决定), Document No. 27, State Council, 24 February 1981.

4 'Speech by Premier Li Peng When Meeting with the Council Members', 1997 Annual Conference of the CCEICD, 3 October 1997, www.cciced.net/ccicedPhoneEN/Events/AGMeeting/1997_4009/meetingplace_4010/201609/t20160922_89438.html.

that did speak up were repressed. For instance, Bo Hechuan's *China on the Edge: The Crisis of Ecology and Development*, which attributed environmental problems to misguided expansionary economic policies, was summarily banned in mainland China (Bo 1992).

The need to update the CCP ideology on economic development and modernisation only began to take hold in the 2000s amid an increase in serious pollution incidents and social protests. The number of petitions registered with the State Environmental Protection Administration (SEPA) grew tenfold between 1995 and 2005, and social movements related to environmental claims were rising by 29 per cent every year, to the point that SEPA's director, Zhou Shengxian, publicly called it a serious threat to social stability.[5] When Hu Jintao and Wen Jiabao took office in 2002, their political response to this looming threat to the CCP's legitimacy (Wang 2013, 2018) was to propose a 'scientific approach to development concept' (*kexue fazhan guan* 科学发展观), which claimed to be people-centred, comprehensive, coordinated and sustainable. By 2004, ideas around 'scientific development' generated intense 'political thought work' within the Party and the government. Eventually, it was added to the official roots of socialism with Chinese characteristics (i.e. Marxism–Leninism, Mao Zedong Thought, Deng Xiaoping Theory and Jiang Zemin's 'Three Represents') and was cited as a guiding principle for the fifth strategic document on environmental protection issued by the State Council in 2005. In October 2007, the Seventeenth Party Congress incorporated the concept into the CCP Constitution. At the same congress, Hu Jintao's work report introduced the objective of building an *ecological civilisation*.

In the wake of the 2008 global economic crisis, Chinese leaders' official discourse began to focus on maintaining growth while investing more in 'green growth'. Despite a push to achieve environmental targets in 2010–11, Hu and Wen's second term ended amid rising environmental unrest and severe criticism that they had failed to transform China's economic development model (Wang 2018). However, instead of being considered a sub-section of Hu Jintao's thought, ecological civilisation was elevated to become one of the fundamental missions of the party-state through a revision of the CCP Constitution by the Eighteenth Party Congress in December 2012, which characterised its mission as the 'Five-in-One' (*wu wei yi ti* 五位一体) goal of 'economic, political, cultural, social, and ecological civilisation construction'. When he took

5 Li Fenshao, 'Environment Issues to be Addressed More Urgently', *China Daily*, 4 May 2006, www.chinadaily.com.cn/china/2006-05/04/content_582574.htm.

office in 2013, President Xi Jinping insisted even more on linking ecological civilisation to his 'economic new normal' advocacy (characterised by slower GDP growth and large-scale industrial transformation). Under his leadership, ecological civilisation became a pillar of the official doctrine of 'socialism with Chinese characteristics'. In 2018, the doctrine of ecological civilisation was further mainstreamed in the Constitution of the People's Republic of China.

To push the ecological civilisation agenda, Xi Jinping became the main original producer of this political discourse, which was disseminated throughout the party-state apparatus and to every corner of Chinese society by CCP propaganda. Unlike his predecessors, who had viewed the environmental crisis as a social and political threat, Xi turned ecological civilisation into a positive narrative associated with the realisation of the 'Chinese Dream' (*Zhongguo meng* 中国梦) and the 'New Era' (*xin shidai* 新时代). Xi's ecological civilisation claims that environmental problems are solvable and will be solved under the leadership of the CCP (Wang 2018). It also represents a promise that the attainment of the right balance between humans and nature will enable prosperity forever, as captured in Xi's most-quoted ecological civilisation aphorism: 'Lucid waters and lush mountains are invaluable assets' (*lüshui qingshan jiu shi jinshan yinshan* 绿水青山就是金山银山). In line with the historical materialism that characterises the doctrine of socialism with Chinese characteristics (Foster 2017), ecological civilisation has been presented as the next step in the evolution of human civilisation (Ke 2013). This approach enshrines ecological civilisation in the CCP's teleological modernisation discourse, which is 'characterised by a normative, prescriptive, and also deterministic connotation of progress' (Marinelli 2018, 368). The pathway to transformation that this discourse points to relies on 'top-level design' (*dingceng sheji* 顶层设计) and is strictly implemented by the CCP,[6] whose main task is to correct the attitude and values of local officials and citizens. This vision is captured in the term *daobi* (倒逼), a synonym for structural coercion,[7] which environmental leaders have used extensively to express the goal of toppling the dominant logic focused solely on economic growth.[8]

6 'National Working Conference on Environmental Protection Held in Beijing', Ministry of Ecology and Environment, 23 January 2017, english.mee.gov.cn/News_service/Photo/201701/t20170123_395162.shtml.

7 Chao Bai, '"Daobi" Means "Being Compelled"' ('倒逼'意味着'被动'), *Southern Daily*, 1 February 2013, theory.people.com.cn/n/2013/0201/c107503-20399929.html.

8 Wu Xiaoyan, 'The Climate Change Targets "daobi" Force China to Embrace Green and Low Carbon Development' (应对气候变化目标倒逼我国向绿色低碳发展转型), *China Reform Daily*, 25 November 2014.

There are clear ideological shifts over time, from little environmental doctrine in the Mao era to 'right to pollute' narratives in the early reform and opening-up era to the ideological push for an ecological civilisation in the late reform and opening-up era and early Xi era. However, despite the dramatic ideological shifts in the development of the CCP's doctrine, there are also several elements of continuity. First, the emphasis on modernisation and development was never undermined. The ecological civilisation discourse is still very much a modernisation discourse (Pan 2016). There is also this very strong continuity in the narrative of history as a continuum, where things are like they are because this is the trend of history that guides the CCP and is the only right path of development. Finally, the portrayal of China against the West has remained prominent, though more pronounced in the Mao and Xi eras. As noted above, the very premises of environmental policy in China in the 1970s were promoted as a way to avoid 'following the road of Western capitalist countries'. It is interesting to see that this framing is still being used today after years of unchecked economic development and environmental devastation.

Upgrading and Politicisation of the Environmental Bureaucracy

Following the chaotic state-building efforts of the Mao era, the development of an environmental bureaucracy in the state apparatus resembling that of industrialised economies was a major endeavour of the reform era. However, since the 2000s, in parallel with the spread of a greener doctrine and the desire to change the growth-focused political culture of the party-state, the CCP has re-politicised the environmental bureaucracy by intensifying personalised leadership and oversight of local cadres to enable the CCP to exercise control over environmental management.

Bureaucratic Upgrading

It has been a protracted, incremental process to strengthen and upgrade China's environmental bureaucracy. In the Mao era, there were no dedicated environmental institutions in the government until 1974, when Zhou Enlai set up an informal Environmental Protection Leading Small Group (*guowuyuan huanjing baohu lingdao xiaozu* 国务院环境保护领导小组) under the State Council. Earlier, the ministries in charge of related matters, such as the Ministry of Health and the Ministry of Forestry, had been marginalised in personnel matters and lacked stability as they were frequently reshuffled and disbanded during the tumultuous Cultural Revolution. As a result, there was no systematic approach to environmental management until the reform and opening-up era.

It was with the launch of the reform and opening-up era that the CCP started building a specialised regulatory system in the state to handle environmental protection. Step by step, China set up a vertical bureaucratic structure with Environmental Protection Bureaus (EPBs) at provincial, municipal and county levels, independent from other industrial ministries such as the ministries of coal, power and metallurgical industries. Initially, the environmental bureaucracy's primary task was to monitor industrial pollution, but it had to work within the planned economy system and slowly adapt to its chaotic and uneven dismantlement.

In 1982, the Ministry of Urban and Rural Construction and Environmental Protection (URCM 城乡建设环境保护部) was created with an EPB (环保局). However, the EPB occupied a very minor position inside the large URCM. In 1984, the central leadership decided that environmental protection was a 'basic state policy' (*jiben guoce* 基本国策), which led the leading small group to be upgraded into a National Environmental Protection Commission (*Guowuyuan huanjing baohu weiyuanhui* 国务院环境保护委员会) and the EPB into a State Environmental Protection Bureau (SEPB 国家环境保护局). Importantly, even though it remained formally under the URCM, this change in status allowed the SEPB to receive funds from the Ministry of Finance and begin to establish its own vertical bureaucracy with a provincial and sub-provincial system. By 1988, this project was well underway. Under the impetus of larger governmental reforms supported by General CCP Secretary Zhao Ziyang, the SEPB was upgraded to the better-staffed, higher-ranking (vice-ministerial grade) and independent SEPA under the State Council. Noticeably, SEPA was maintained through the dismantlement and sharp reduction of the state administration serving the planned economy in the 1990s. By 1996, 2,500 local EPBs and 2,223 environmental monitoring stations had been created throughout the country, mostly at the county level, with a total staff of around 88,000 (Jahiel 1998).

This rank and the new identity as a regulatory agency (Zeng et al. 2000) provided more political clout to China's environmental bureaucrats. Nevertheless, in the 1990s, SEPA and local EPBs, which were often low-ranking, 'non-indispensable administrations', remained in a difficult position to supervise the two dominant types of industrial actors in China at the time: state-owned enterprises (SOEs) and the township and village enterprises (TVEs). On the one hand, SOEs mainly followed orders from their industrial branches, which had their own environmental offices and local leaders with their own developmental priorities (Chang and Wang 2010). On the other hand, local EPBs could not control the rapidly growing number of TVEs. In 1998, the industrial ministries were disbanded and the National Environmental Protection Commission, which had supported dialogue between them and SEPA, was also dismantled. SEPA became the sole authority in charge of environmental pollution and was upgraded to a ministerial rank. While this resolved some fragmentation problems, it also impacted the ability of local EPBs to monitor enterprises. This difficulty was compounded by a lack of funding. For the most part, EPBs relied on the pollution fees they were able to collect from local industries, which made them functionally dependent on continued pollution (Jahiel 1997). Meanwhile, the funds redistributed from the centre were scarce and irregular. It was not until 2007 that SEPA got a fixed budget line in the National Budget (Wu and Ma 2011).

SEPA's responsibilities remained primarily circumscribed to environmental pollution issues, with nature and resource conservation, sustainable development, energy conservation and climate change largely beyond its reach. In time, this fragmentation led to increasingly severe bureaucratic turf wars. For instance, in the 1980s and 1990s, the industrial ministries implemented energy conservation in their respective domains. Only loose coordination was achieved via a cross-ministerial joint-meeting system for energy conservation from 1985 to 1990, and then by a powerless Energy Conservation Office (节能处). However, this weak organisation excluded TVEs, and it fell apart when the industrial ministries were abolished in the late 1990s. Climate change was also not added to SEPA's responsibilities. SEPA was only one of the participants in the loose National Climate Change Coordination Group (NCCCG 国家气候变化协调小组) that was set up in 1990 to coordinate China's participation in international climate negotiations (Zou 2008). In 1998, the office of this group was transferred from the Meteorological Agency to the State Planning and Development Commission and then, in 2003, to the National Development and Reform Commission (NDRC). This move resolutely defined climate change as an economic development issue. In sum, despite the upgrading of the environmental bureaucracy, its mandate remained narrow with limited financial capacity.

In the 2000s, the adoption of the doctrine of Scientific Development and Ecological Civilisation led to major institutional changes. First, in 2008, SEPA was upgraded to the Ministry of Environmental Protection (MEP), a full ministerial-level ministry, and became a department of the State Council. Second, the Climate Change Office was upgraded to a department of the NDRC. Third, the National Commission on Climate Change was merged with the newly established Energy Conservation Leading Group into a 'double-hatted' National Leading Group on Climate Change, Energy Saving and Emissions Reduction (*Guojia yingdui qihoubianhua ji jieneng jianpai gongzuo lingdao xiaozu* 国家应对气候变化及节能减排工作领导小组) chaired by Premier Wen Jiabao to resorb the coordination issues derived from the bureaucratic fragmentation, though it never quite succeeded. This group kept enlarging in the subsequent decade and reached 31 members in 2018. Local governments were encouraged to follow suit (Qi et al. 2008).

The latest step in this progressive upgrading and centralising process occurred a decade later, in 2018. Following the inclusion of ecological civilisation in the People's Republic of China (PRC) Constitution, the MEP was dismantled and replaced by a revamped and potentially more powerful Ministry of Ecology and Environment (MEE *shengtai huanjing bu* 生态环境部). Given greater authority over policies touching on climate change, it was hoped that the new MEE would finally resolve the problems of coordination and fragmentation of authority (Ran 2013; Kostka and Zhang 2018). However, while the MEE appears to have solved some problems, in 2021, the portfolio for climate change, reframed as carbon neutrality, was largely reverted to the NDRC, and coordination with the new Ministry of Natural Resources over nature conservation has remained complicated.

An element of continuity throughout this bureaucratic restructuring and upgrading has been that the environment was considered a specialised, non-political portfolio and a dead-end for promotion in the cadre evaluation and promotion system.[9] This started to change under the second mandate

9 Cao Xiaojia, 'Who Will Be the Leader of Environmental Protection?' (谁来配强环保一把手?), *China Environment Network*, 17 December 2014, www.chinanews.com.cn/ny/2014/12-17/6884996.shtml.

of Xi's ecological civilisation era. Some exemplary promotions at the central level after 2013 started to signal to other leading cadres that accepting environmental leadership positions could be career enhancing. For instance, as illustrated in Table A9.1, two recent environmental ministers, former Tsinghua University president Chen Jining (2015–17) and long-term MEP administrator Li Gangjie (2018–20), were rapidly promoted into very important positions: Chen became the mayor of Beijing and Li became vice-secretary and governor of Shandong Province, both very attractive career posts in China.[10] Some evidence at the provincial level further suggests that local environmental bureau leaders have also begun to be promoted to important positions.[11] The fact that a career or passage in the environmental bureaucracy is now a promotion pathway signals the elevation of the ecological civilisation agenda, and that the CCP has adjusted its organisation to reward those who help in implementing it.

Recentralisation and Personalised Responsibility

Fragmentation and lack of capacity were key problems in China's environmental bureaucracy during the reform era. The reason was not only the limited scope but also the influence of local governments over local EPBs. Under Xi Jinping, the introduction of a bureaucratic reform that transferred more powers from local to provincial governments marked an important step to address this problem. In October 2015, the Fifth Plenary Session of the Eighteenth National Congress of the CCP launched a direct management system of municipal EPBs by the provincial EPB (and of county EPBs by municipal EPBs). Before this reform, although guidelines had been sent vertically from superior EPBs, the local government made final decisions, especially on budget and personnel matters. As local leaders often prioritised the economy over the environment, this organisation gave rise to problems of 'local protectionism' and lax enforcement of environmental regulations (Kostka and Mol 2013; Lorentzen, Landry and Yasuda 2014). Under the new 'vertical management' system, provincial EPBs have acquired the authority to nominate and pay the salaries of the director and vice-director positions of municipal EPBs (and municipal EPBs have the

10 However, it is unlikely that the current environmental minister, Huang Runqiu, who is not a CCP member, will be able to follow the same path.

11 'From Chen Jining to Li Ganjie, What's behind Environmental Protection Officials Governing Localities' (从陈吉宁到李干杰 环保官员主政地方的背后), *China News Weekly*, 6 May 2020, huanbao.bjx.com.cn/news/20200506/1068817.shtml.

same authority over county-level EPB leaders). In addition, environmental monitoring and inspections, previously the responsibility of municipal and county EPBs, have been brought up to the provincial level (Ma 2017).

However, while the outcomes of this reform were still unclear in 2022, scholars have observed that similar vertical management reforms in the fields of quality and technology supervision and land management had stalled or even reverted to a horizontal-based management system after failing to bring significant improvements in enforcement (Ma 2017). Moreover, the experience of EPB recentralisation pilots in 12 provinces between 2016 and 2020 indicated that, while the reform might have increased their independence from local governments, it also showed pronounced disadvantages. Some observers noted that the pilots became isolated in their localities, as local government officials no longer viewed EPB leaders as 'their' agents. This reform has also not addressed the problem of 'central protectionism' whereby local regulators face tremendous difficulties in regulating the activities from higher-ranked central-level state-owned enterprises in their jurisdictions (Eaton and Kostka 2017). Importantly, this isolation not only restricted their access to information critical to their regulatory work but also could shrink the promotion opportunities for local EPB staff, making it difficult to attract competent personnel (Ma 2017). Thus, it is unclear whether this reform can solve the longstanding dilemmas faced by the EPB in the complex politics of the local state.

The increasing use of ad hoc working groups and reliance on the personalised responsibility of leading Party cadres at different administrative levels point to the efforts to concentrate environmental management. Xi has appointed his closest collaborators to head critical environmental CCP leading small groups, signalling the importance he places on environmental issues. For instance, upon taking power in 2013, Xi created the Task Force for the Promotion of Economic Development and Ecological Civilisation (*Zhongyang jingji tizhi he shengtai wenming tizhi gaige zhuanxiang xiaozu* 中央经济体制和生态文明体制改革专项小组),[12] led by Liu He, who was also director of the General Office serving the Communist Party's Leading Group for Financial and Economic Affairs and a close adviser to Xi. In 2019, this task force was seemingly replaced by a more important Central

12 'The Central Leading Group on Deepening Economic Reforms Establish Small Leading Group for the Promotion of Economic Development and Ecological Progress, Eco-Civilisation Is Guaranteed by the Top' (中央全面深化改革领导小组下设经济体制和生态文明体制改革专项小组 生态文明建设有了顶层组织保障), *Xinhuanet*, 24 January 2014.

Ecological Environmental Protection Supervision Work Leading Group (*Zhongyang shengtai huanjing baohu jiandu gongzuo lingdao xiaozu* 中央生态环境保护督察工作领导小组), which was entrusted to CCP Central Committee Politburo Standing Committee Member and Vice Premier Han Zheng. Local Party committees were encouraged to follow suit to strengthen their supervision over the ecological and environmental protection work of lower Party committees and governments and their relevant departments.[13] In 2021, following the announcement of the Carbon Peaking and Carbon Neutrality goals, a Leading Group on Carbon Peaking and Neutrality (*Tan dafeng zhonghe gongzuo lingdao xiaozu* 碳达峰中和工作领导小组) was established jointly by the Party Central Committee and the State Council, also chaired by Han Zheng, which may replace the State Council National Leading Group on Climate Change, Energy Saving and Emissions Reduction and upgrade it by placing it under the CCP Central Committee rather than the State Council. The increasing reliance on ad hoc working groups under Xi, which has been observed in other sectors as well, may have allowed the CCP to shift its environmental priorities (from pollution to climate change) but may also signal the persistent weakness of the MEE.

Perhaps the most typical illustration of how the CCP has used personalised leadership (by which responsibility for environmental issues is nominally assigned to individual local leaders, rather than specialised departments) is the new River Leader system (*hezhang zhi* 河长制) deployed across the country during the Thirteenth Five-Year Plan (FYP) (2016–20). In December 2016, the CCP Central Committee and the State Council established a four-level River Leader system (provinces, cities, counties and townships),[14] which was enshrined as the Water Pollution Prevention and Control Law in June 2017. Building on decades of experimentation, the system requires that the responsibility for all the lakes and rivers in any given jurisdiction must be individually assigned to the leaders of its Party committee or government, who, through their cadre rank, concentrate decision-making power in their jurisdiction. These River Leaders sign dedicated responsibility contracts that make them responsible for achieving specific goals related to the quality of rivers and lakes. They are expected to deploy their political authority to

13 'Regulations on the Central Ecological Environmental Protection Supervision Work' (中共中央办公厅 国务院办公厅印发《中央生态环境保护督察工作规定》), General Office of the Central Committee of the Communist Party of China and the General Office of the State Council, 17 June 2019, www.gov.cn/zhengce/2019-06/17/content_5401085.htm.

14 'Opinions on the Full Implementation of the River Chief System' (中共中央办公厅 国务院办公厅印发《关于全面推行河长制的意见》), General Office of the Central Committee of the Communist Party of China and General Office of the State Council, 10 December 2016.

mobilise resources, organise relevant departments and supervise the River Leaders at the administrative level directly below them (Chien and Hong 2018). Their performance is evaluated based on detailed criteria put in the responsibility contracts, and incentivised by financial bonuses as well as severe penalties, including a lifelong political (and penal) responsibility for any damage caused to the ecological environment of the river or lake during their mandate.[15] Figure 9.1 summarises a typical River Leader coordinating system for river and lake governance.

This system aims specifically at breaking the bureaucratic and jurisdictional fragmentation that has plagued transboundary water basins in China. However, many observers have highlighted its shortcomings, including the (notorious) defects of the top-down and non-transparent cadre evaluation system, compounded by a lack of public participation, despite the institution of so-called Civilian or Folk River Leaders (Wu et al. 2020).

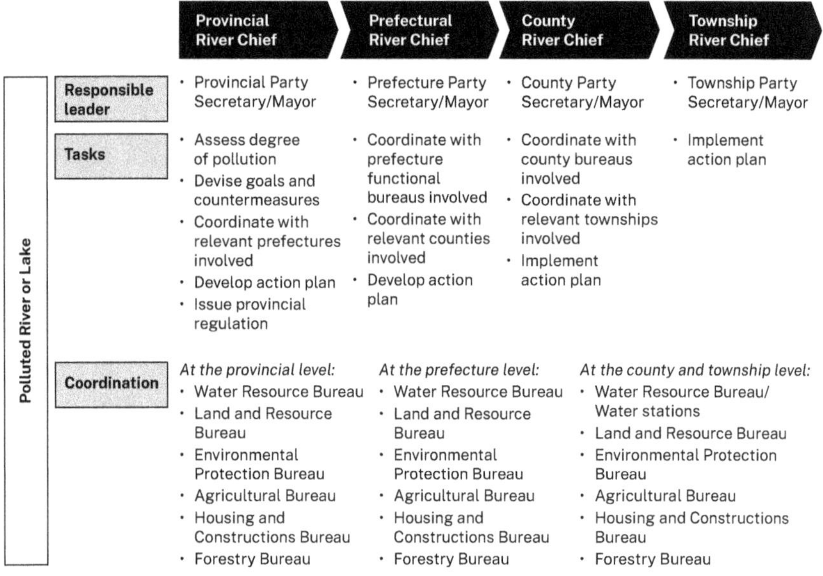

Figure 9.1: The River Leader System Coordinating River and Lake Governance.

Source: Author's research.

15 Ibid.

The Emergence of Authoritarian Environmentalism and Retreat of Participatory Governance

The choice of environmental governance tools and instruments has mostly followed the dominant ideological and institutional setup of the particular era. Whereas the Mao era relied on campaigns, the reform and opening-up era promoted the use of regulatory, market-based and participatory governance approaches, even though planning was always important. By contrast, under Xi Jinping, the use of command-and-control instruments such as planning, campaigns and crackdowns has been given renewed impetus as a means to achieve rapid and tangible results. While official central documents present the combination of top-down control supported by innovative data technologies and public supervision as the model of China's 'modern environmental governance',[16] critics have denounced an emerging authoritarian model that is inefficient, socially costly and detrimental to civil liberties (Li and Shapiro 2020).

Environmental Campaigns and Attempted Policy Interventions in the Mao Era

During most of the Mao era, the main vector of party-state action in society was campaigns and mass mobilisation, such as the 1952 'Patriotic Health Movement' (*aiguo weisheng yundong* 爱国卫生运动), which campaigned for the removal of garbage and the building and rebuilding of public toilets and water wells. Some of these campaigns are infamous for their severe repercussions on nature, and others directly targeted environment-related projects. An example of a campaign with severe repercussions is the campaign to eliminate the four pests (*chu si hai yundong* 除四害运动): rats, flies, mosquitoes and sparrows. Examples of specific environment-related projects include the large-scale 'greening the motherland' (*lühua zuguo* 绿化祖国) tree-planting campaign in 1956, for which Mao enlisted the country, especially the youth, as well as the massive deforestation campaigns during the Great Leap Forward (1958–62). During the early years of the Cultural

16 'Guiding Opinions on Building a Modern Environmental Governance System' (中共中央办公厅 国务院办公厅印发《关于构建现代环境治理体系的指导意见》), State Council and Central Committee of the Communist Party of China, 3 March 2020, www.gov.cn/zhengce/2020-03/03/content_5486380.htm.

Revolution (1966–76), projects and campaigns affecting the environment were driven less by utopianism than by the coercion and chaos from erratic class struggle mass mobilisation campaigns.

Shortly after the PRC was established, the new ministries in charge of forestry and health started introducing some preliminary environmental guidelines. For instance, in 1951, the Ministry of Forest Reclamation issued the first Interim Regulations on Forest Protection, and the first nature reserve, the Dinghushan Nature Reserve, was established in 1956. In 1963–65, new forest protection policies were issued, and more natural reserves were created in an attempt to reverse the disaster of the Great Leap Forward. Similarly, in the 1950s, the Ministry of Health introduced the first policy mandating the comprehensive utilisation of industrial waste, management of the 'three wastes' (*san fei* 三废) – gas exhaust, water sewage and waste residues – and, particularly, management of the toxic effluents from industrial and mining enterprises. A national Conference on Industrial Wastewater Treatment and Comprehensive Utilisation of Wastewater held in late 1959 further emphasised the prevention of industrial harm and flagged the 'three simultaneous' (*san tongshi* 三同时) concept requiring that new projects install facilities to prevent and control pollution and other hazards at the same time as the main project.

Most environmental regulation efforts stalled when the state collapsed during the Cultural Revolution. They only resurfaced when the country emerged from chaos in the early 1970s. The first National Environmental Protection Conference convened by Zhou Enlai in 1972 proclaimed a landmark '32-Character Environmental Policy Order' that paved the way for the adoption of a series of environmental regulations, including the first environmental document of the State Council on the Provisions on Protecting and Improving Environment and the industrial 'three wastes' emissions standards, jointly issued by the State Planning Commission, State Capital Construction Commission and Ministry of Health. These new provisions and standards helped to lay the groundwork for the inclusion of environmental protection rules and environmental harm prevention principles in the PRC Constitution in 1978 and the adoption of the interim EPL in 1979.

Modernising Environmental Governance in the Reform Era: Promotion of the Law, Markets and Civil Society Participation

In the reform era, the newly established environmental regulators pursued significant changes to environmental governance, from issuing comprehensive environmental plans, regulations and laws to introducing market-based instruments. During this period, civil society participation was also relatively welcome in the environmental field, which encouraged the growth of environmental non-government organisations (ENGOs) and new public participation channels, although environmental awareness remained low.

In the early period of opening up, environmental administrators relied mainly on traditional planning instruments by introducing environmental plans. The first 10-year plan for environmental protection was produced by the State Council's Environmental Protection Leading Group in 1975 for the Fifth FYP (1976–80). This plan promoted the overall goal of 'controlling environmental pollution within five years and solving environmental pollution within 10 years'. In 1982, environmental protection was, for the first time, included as an independent chapter in China's Sixth FYP (1981–85), which set the goals of preventing new pollution, treating pollution from old enterprises, improving the 'three wastes' treatment capacity, and strengthening legislation and law enforcement. The Seventh FYP (1986–90) included an independent five-year environmental protection plan focused on urban pollution, industrial pollution and environmental capacity constraints.

In parallel, there was a build-up of regulatory and legal tools to implement environmental plans and policies. Inspired by foreign legislation and written in cooperation with international partners, the legal and regulatory corpus for environmental protection developed rapidly. In 1993, an Environment Protection and Resources Conservation Committee was established in the National People's Congress, and Qu Geping was appointed to chair it. Both he and Xie Zhenhua, who was trained as a lawyer and had replaced him as chair of SEPB in 1988, strongly advocated environmental legislation. These efforts led China to sign more than 30 multilateral environmental agreements to catch up with the adoption of environmental standards and regulations before and after China's accession to the World Trade Organization (Jahiel 2006). However, these laws were more often a list of general principles rather than precise rights and obligations (Wang, He and Fan 2014). Moreover, the institutional basis for enforcing these laws was weak.[17] Penalties were often insignificant and violators could hardly be sued for damage in court (Stern 2013). Enforcement relied on the EPBs, but their ability to enforce environmental regulations and deter polluters was very limited.

In the 2000s, learning from its counterparts in Western countries, the Chinese environmental bureaucracy sought to expand its capacity by outsourcing environmental protection services to third-party organisations. This was most notably the case with the environmental impact assessment (EIA) agencies, which had to be remunerated for delivering the certificates required to approve industry projects. Unsurprisingly, however, these agencies rapidly turned into a hub for corruption and malpractice.[18] To address this, between 2005 and 2007, the MEP cancelled numerous projects that had been approved without valid EIAs. However, the problems persisted, and many instances of corruption were uncovered during the Anti-Corruption Campaign launched by Xi Jinping in 2014–15.[19]

In the 2000s, influenced by international partners and development agencies such as the World Bank, SEPA introduced several market economy instruments and market-based approaches to alleviate the lack of budget, leading Carter and Mol (2006) to praise a convergence with OECD practices and a 'shift away from a rigid hierarchical command-and-control system of governance'. For instance, during the Tenth FYP, with foreign assistance from the United States and the OECD, there was experimentation with emissions trading to reduce SO_2 emissions. However, they did not yield good results. In a still poor legal environment with a lack of independent third-party regulators, it turned out to be impossible to organise a system based on companies' self-reporting and voluntary trading. Moreover, there were no markets or price-based systems on which the economic incentives underlying compliance with such a system could operate. One of the experts sent by the OECD to assist with the project strongly criticised the advocates of market-based policy instruments who had 'written their prescriptions without first doing a physical examination of the patient' and had 'first

17 Wang Jin, 'Environmental Rule of Law for 30 Year, Why Is Pollution Intractable?' (环境法治30年为何难治污染?), *Green Tencent*, 18 August 2010, chem.vogel.com.cn/c/2010-09-08/532552.shtml.

18 Ibid.

19 Ministry of Environmental Protection, '2015 Report on the State of the Environment in China' (2015年环境状况报告), 20 May 2016, www.gov.cn/xinwen/2016-06/02/5078966/files/9ab14b4ce3294d5ab212bc83d3d31b7b.pdf.

recommended environmental instruments and secondarily tried to bend institutions to support the already identified cure' (Bell 2003). During this period, the MEP further experimented with 'green GDP' accounting and various environmental tax schemes.

Notwithstanding the failure of SO_2 emissions trading pilots, the idea that 'command-and-control' policies were inefficient and that the market had to 'play a bigger role in resource allocation' gained traction within the NDRC, which was tasked with tackling climate change.[20] Following the successful introduction of renewable energy projects in China through the Kyoto Protocol's 'clean development mechanism', foreign and domestic policy advocates successfully pushed for the introduction of a carbon emission trading scheme as the principal policy instrument to mitigate climate change. From 2011 onwards, emissions trading became a significant symbol of China's openness to international cooperation, featuring prominently in China's joint declarations with the US and the EU (Biedenkopf, Van Eynde and Walker 2017). At the same time, the carbon emissions trading pilots served China's ambition to be seen as a global rule-maker, even though their implementation was fraught with difficulties and their impact on domestic carbon emissions reduction was limited (Goron and Cassisa 2017). The official narrative around the need to use the market instead of commands has regained momentum with the commitment of Xi Jinping to develop a national emissions trading scheme and with the pressure to use market-based mechanisms in many other environmental sub-fields, including energy and water uses, as a more cost-effective alternative to using blunt-force enforcement of environmental targets.

Another important development of the 2000s was the unprecedented support for civil society and for promoting consultative decision-making.[21] This new emphasis on public participation came largely in response to the growing number of environmental protests. For instance, a specific petition system was introduced for environmental governance in 1991 and further institutionalised with a national '12369' petition hotline in 2001, which was subsequently upgraded and made accessible directly through the environmental ministry's website and social media accounts. As an example, starting in 2006 and continuing until 2014, China's ENGO Friends of

20 The MEP disagreed with this choice and advocated for the introduction of a tax that would be administered alongside other environmental taxes.

21 David Shambaugh, 'Let a Thousand Democracies Bloom', *New York Times*, 6 July 2007, www.nytimes.com/2007/07/06/opinion/06iht-edsham.1.6530408.html.

Nature could edit annual China Environment Green Books (*Zhongguo huanjing lüpishu* 中国环境绿皮书) with the help of the Chinese Academy of Social Sciences, which gave unprecedented recognition to environmental activist voices.

From the mid-2000s onwards, the regime also acknowledged the right of citizens to participate in environmental governance. For example, SEPA's vice minister, Pan Yue, and Premier Wen Jiabao sided with protestors' demands in the landmark mobilisation against the construction of a PX plant in Xiamen in 2007. Subsequently, and more stringently under Xi Jinping, the party-state has striven to channel public participation by acknowledging certain environmental grievances and modes of action while delegitimising and repressing any politicised form of environmental activism. Legal instruments have featured prominently among the regime's favoured depoliticised participation channels. They include the public consultation requirements in the EIA law and the environmental information disclosure regulations of 2008. People's 'right to information, supervision, and participation' was enshrined in the revised EPL of 2014 (which was written in collaboration with several environmental lawyers and ENGOs). A central document on environmental governance issued in March 2020 further institutionalised these pathways for citizens to participate in environmental governance, which also includes the development of Environmental Public Interest Litigation (EPIL). Notwithstanding the opening of these official participation channels, most forms of public mobilisation and the public sphere have become significantly more controlled in the Xi era.

Xi Era: Growing Authoritarianism in Environmental Governance

In the Xi era, a noticeable change has been the increased use of 'sticks' and coercive supervisory mechanisms. Under the revised 2014 EPL, polluting companies face a stricter fine system with uncapped penalties, higher minimum fines and daily fines. Local government officials can be held criminally liable if they fail to punish polluters.[22] While it was once common for upper-level authorities to turn a blind eye to local officials' non-fulfilment of environmental targets and the manipulation of environmental data (Kostka 2016), such infractions now often result in severe punishment.

22 Environmental Protection Law (中华人民共和国环境保护法), as amended in April 2014, especially articles 67 and 68.

Consequently, the procuratorate-led EPIL has boomed, from 791 cases in 2016–17 to 3,454 in 2020. By contrast, Chinese courts have accepted a steady number of 50–60 lawsuits brought annually by ENGOs. Moreover, until 2018, the number of first instance judgements for these lawsuits was very small (less than 20 per year). While the number of judgements picked up to 100 in 2020, it remains small both in absolute terms and compared with procuratorate-led litigation, due both to the lukewarm attitude of some courts and to the very small number of NGOs that are able and willing to engage in EPIL (Ren and Liu 2020). The impact of procuratorate-led EPIL has been hotly debated. While it represents a sea change in the role that the judiciary branch can play in environmental governance, especially against local governments, which only procuratorates are allowed to sue, several authors have worried that procuratorates may be used for political gain or manipulated for bureaucratic infighting (Gao 2018). They are also suspected of concentrating on small and easy cases that boost their caseloads and meet their quantitative evaluation targets (Ren and Liu 2020).

In parallel, there has been more extensive use of planning and targets, along with campaigns and crackdowns. The Eleventh and Twelfth FYPs adopted under the Hu–Wen leadership significantly increased the number of environmental targets by upgrading them to a mandatory 'veto target' (*yi piao foujue* 一票否决) in the cadres' evaluation system. In the Xi era, binding environmental targets continue to play an important role. As before, these targets have often been neither scientifically nor fairly allocated, especially at the local level (Kostka and Goron 2021). In parallel, since 2016, the use of spatial planning for conservation has been expanded beyond the traditionally remote and less developed regions to the entire territory through the deployment of the ecological redlines (*shengtai hongxian* 生态红线) concept. While welcomed by those who have long requested more effective conservation and biodiversity protection measures, the top-down enforcement has also raised concerns regarding the potential adverse impacts on local economic development and communities.

Xi Jinping has also heavily relied on large political campaigns and crackdowns. Campaigns were sporadically used throughout the reform and opening-up era, but their use has been significantly increased under Xi. Typical examples of recent campaigns include the 2013 Action Plan for Air Pollution Prevention and Control (APAP), an ambitious effort to remedy severe air pollution in the Beijing–Hebei–Tianjin area, the 2016 clean-up of 'black and smelly waters' campaign (Hsu, Yi Yeo and Weinfurter 2020) and the 2018–20 blue sky war (Li and Shapiro 2020). Many of these campaigns have used drastic measures, including summarily closing polluting plants or cutting off factories' access to electricity and water (Kostka and Hobbs 2012). While such 'blunt-force regulation' (van der Kamp 2021a) may offer quick results in the short term (as shown in the rapid decline in PM2.5 pollution resulting from APAP measures), their ad hoc and arbitrary nature hinders the creation of long-term compliance and routine enforcement mechanisms, while also undermining the rule of law (Ma 2017; Van Rooij et al. 2017; van der Kamp 2021a). Moreover, many of these campaigns have focused narrowly on particular regions and pollutants (Kostka and Nahm 2017; Van Rooij et al. 2017). Van der Kamp (2021a) points to the considerable costs of such blunt-force regulations, as closing companies negatively affects local development and employment. In addition, with the sheer number of campaigns being launched every year, local bureaucracy has faced an 'over-mobilisation problem' that risks dampening cadres' enthusiasm and ability to implement future environmental campaigns with the same drive.

Another important new tool introduced in this period to contribute to the success of the campaigns is central environmental inspections, which have been rolled out in batches nationwide every year since 2016. While regional inspection centres were set up in various regions in 2006 to supervise the environmental law enforcement of local governments, it was under Xi that inspections were employed more systematically and forcefully than before. In 2016 and 2017 alone, national inspection teams punished more than 10,000 people for breaching environmental protection regulations.[23] In 2019, the central leadership adopted a central policy that made central environmental inspections a permanent mechanism of environmental governance rooted in the five-year terms of the Central Committee of the Communist Party.[24] Subsequently, in an unprecedented action, in December 2020, the central environmental inspectors used 'unusually trenchant and critical vocabulary'[25] when openly criticising the National Energy Agency for not limiting the country's expansion of coal power plants.

23 Mimi Lau and Frank Tang, 'China's Environmental Clean-up Campaign Hasn't Cost Jobs or Hit Economy, Minister Says', *South China Morning Post*, 23 October 2017, www.scmp.com/news/china/policies-politics/article/2116638/chinas-environmental-clean-campaign-hasnt-cost-jobs-or.

24 'Regulations on the Central Ecological Environmental Protection Supervision Work' (中共中央办公厅 国务院办公厅印发《中央生态环境保护督察工作规定》), General Office of the Central Committee of the Communist Party of China and the General Office of the State Council, 17 June 2019, www.gov.cn/zhengce/2019-06/17/content_5401085.htm.

25 'Q&A: Could an Environmental Inspector's Criticisms Accelerate China's Climate Policies?', *Carbon Brief*, 5 February 2021, www.carbonbrief.org/qa-could-an-environmental-inspectors-criticisms-accelerate-chinas-climate-policies.

Importantly, the central environmental inspectors' power has been significantly enhanced through support offered by the CCP Central Discipline and Inspection Commission (CDIC, *Zhongyang jiwei jiancha weiyuanhui* 中央纪律检查委员会). The new reliance on both environmental and CDIC inspections is seen as a strategic move to strengthen Party oversight and centralise control measures by leveraging the 'double responsibility' (*yigang shuangze* 一岗双责) of local officials under the state and Party.[26] These new top-down environmental inspections have been 'effectively above the law' and have created tremendous pressure on local governments, which sometimes choose to close local factories or entire industries in the expectation of upcoming environmental inspections (Li and Shapiro 2020; van der Kamp 2021a). Although the campaign was effective in curbing air pollution, the effectiveness of inspections in the long run and as a tool to address less visible and more complex sources of pollution, or climate change, is questionable. Li and Shapiro (2020, 55) note that:

> in the end, environmental enforcement becomes contingent on the arbitrary dictates of the central inspection team and the fears and ambitions of grassroots cadres, as opposed to transparent, accountable environmental laws and standards.

Recentralising Party supervision and reducing local discretion have, therefore, apparently emerged as new ways for leaders in Beijing to keep bureaucrats in check. While the CDIC's supervision of local officials is not new, since the start of Xi Jinping's Anti-Corruption Campaign in 2012, its use of disciplinary actions within the Party has increased dramatically. These actions tackle not only issues of corruption, but also and primarily the implementation of Party guidelines and priorities, of which the all-encompassing ecological civilisation is an integral part (Liao and Tsai 2020; van der Kamp 2021b). By looking at CDIC-led investigations and disciplinary actions taken against cadres in the environmental bureaucracy, van der Kamp (2021b) has found a sharp increase from a couple of hundred actions per year in 2012 to as many as 1,500 after 2016.

26 'Opinions of the CPC Central Committee and State Council on Accelerating the Construction of Ecological Civilization' (中共中央 国务院关于加快推进生态文明建设的意见), Document No. 12, CCP Central Office and State Council, 25 April 2015. Also see the follow-up: 'Comprehensive Plan for an Eco-Civilisation System' (生态文明体制改革总体方案), CCP Central Office and State Council, 21 September 2015.

Besides control on officials, control over society has also been tightened. Firstly, discursive space has shrunk. While critical voices and confrontational actions pointing out failures to solve environmental problems have been increasingly repressed, the Party has increased its capacity to disseminate 'correct' ideas and 'guide' online opinions about the environment (Hilton 2017). Ecological civilisation has been marshalled by the Party's propaganda organs in every corner of the public sphere, including in academia (Goron 2018), traditional and new media[27] (Goron and Bolsover 2019), and public spaces, encouraging the production of 'model environmental citizens' (Arantes 2020).

Secondly, the space for and recognition of social mobilisation for the environment has shrunk, even though formal channels of grassroots participation, such as through environmental impact assessments and environmental petitions, have been maintained (Fu and Distelhorst 2017). However, the number of environmental petitions has not appeared in the reports of the environmental ministry since 2015, and the large-scale environmental mobilisations of the 2000s have vanished. Under Xi Jinping, the Party control of civil society organisations has been significantly increased (Thornton, Chapter 2, this volume). Capitalising on mature horizontal networks (Wu 2013), Chinese grassroots ENGOs have shown resilience to the new environment. Some have been able to use public interest lawsuits (Ren and Liu 2020) and a series of other strategies to influence local environmental policies (Dai and Spires 2017). However, the 2017 foreign NGO law and the economic impact of the COVID-19 pandemic have significantly affected available funding sources, which severely constrains grassroots ENGOs' capacity. Li and Shapiro (2020, 38) point out that:

> mistrust and even fear of public participation, civil society organisation, and democratic processes mean that the public space for environmental activism is carefully delimited, even if the boundaries can be murky and changeable across time and space.

Finally, the Xi era has also seen the emergence of digital technologies to identify, analyse, report on and respond to polluting activities (Kostka, Zhang and Shin 2020). Advanced technologies such as geographic information systems, the global positioning system and remote sensing technologies have 'opened the door to new modes of monitoring and managing the

27 For example, Liu Youbin, 'Spokesperson of the Ministry of Ecology and Environment: Government Affairs New Media Must be Diligent' (生态环境部发言人刘友宾: 政务新媒体要勤政不能懒政), *China Environment*, 30 July 2018, www.nbd.com.cn/articles/2018-07-30/1239896.html.

environment' (Hsu et al. 2017, 2). For instance, Shanghai began to employ big data to manage different issues of urban governance as early as 2011, including the creation of a data platform for air quality monitoring and air pollution source management (Hsu et al. 2017; Kostka and Zhang 2018). Digitised governance has also gained ground in less developed western provinces such as Guizhou. By integrating and uploading hydrological, environmental, meteorological and biological data into the Caohai Big Data Monitoring and Management System under real-time surveillance, the province aims to improve the protection of the Caohai Grassland Reserve in the south-west.[28] The adoption of these new digital technologies in environmental management raises important new issues surrounding data sharing and data privacy practices, diverging interests between private tech firms and governments on the one hand, and government surveillance on the other.

To sum up, since the beginning of the reform and opening-up era, the CCP has pursued a regulatory governance style that was progressively enriched with the use of market-based instruments and participatory instruments in the 2000s. However, as these instruments failed to solve seemingly intractable implementation issues, they were supplemented and partly supplanted by Party-led authoritarian techniques of campaigns, crackdowns and inspections in the Xi era.

Conclusion

This chapter has looked at how the CCP has managed the environment since the founding of the PRC by providing a detailed review of the evolution of its environmental ideology, bureaucracy and governance. We found that major changes to how the CCP views the importance of environmental issues are reflected in the radical change to its environmental discourse and the way it has been woven into its vision of its developmental mission. We also showed how this environmental ideology integrated the CCP's changing vision of the appropriate way to govern the economy and society, from highly politicised campaigns in the Mao era to law- and market-based regulation in the reform era and, finally, a recentralisation and mobilisation of the structures of the CCP under Xi Jinping.

28 Cao Bin, Wang Jun, 'Cloud Chiefs Promote the Big Data Industry in Guizhou to a Higher Level' ("云长制"助推贵州大数据产业"冲上云霄"), *Xinhua News Agency New Media Line*, 25 September 2017, www.163.com/fashion/article/CV6H2RLI00264OPK.html.

This change is reflected in the evolution of the environmental bureaucracy, which was non-existent under Mao, developed into a regulatory state apparatus during the reform and opening-up era, and became recentralised in the Party under Xi Jinping. This shift occurred because, while the reform era saw a progressive build-up of legislative and regulatory capacity, it was not sufficient to overcome the focus on GDP growth that was rewarded, incentivised and sanctioned by the CCP political system. The CCP and Xi seem to have concluded that they need to overhaul the productivism logic through a realignment of the CCP's political reward and sanction system if they want to achieve the new developmental goal of ecological civilisation.

As these transformations have unfolded, the leadership has promoted different governance approaches and tools. For more than two decades, leaders in the reform era pursued Western-inspired neoliberal ideas – namely, that markets and the environment needed clear and solid laws and regulations and that society and markets had to be freed from direct state intervention but incentivised and supported in their efforts to protect the environment. However, starting in the 2000s, and with dramatic acceleration under Xi, the view that solving the environmental crisis and taming local bureaucrats' 'wild pursuit of economic growth'[29] required much more direct and political interventions from the party-state has become dominant. This has been pursued through an increased use of 'sticks', as well as the direct mobilisation of personalised CCP leadership and propaganda. While the regulatory institutions and participatory mechanisms of the reform era have been maintained under Xi, their performativity has been severely undermined.

References

Arantes, Virginie. 2020. 'From the Avoidable to the Desirable: The Chinese Communist Party "Green" Authoritarian Strategy. Shanghai as Case Study'. PhD thesis, Université Libre de Bruxelles.

Bell, Greenspan Ruth. 2003. 'Choosing Environmental Policy Instruments in the Real World'. OECD Global Forum on Sustainable Development. www.oecd.org/env/cc/2957706.pdf.

29 Li Jing, 'Ex-Minister Blames China's Pollution Mess on Lack of Rule of Law', *South China Morning Post*, 21 January 2013, www.scmp.com/news/china/article/1132566/ex-minister-blames-chinas-pollution-mess-lack-rule-law.

Bernstein, Steven. 2000. 'Ideas, Social Structure and the Compromise of Liberal Environmentalism'. *European Journal of International Relations* 6 (4): 464–512. doi.org/10.1177/1354066100006004002.

Biedenkopf, Katja, Sarah Van Eynde and Hayley Walker. 2017. 'Policy Infusion through Capacity Building and Project Interaction: Greenhouse Gas Emissions Trading in China'. *Global Environmental Politics* 17 (3): 91–114. doi.org/10.1162/GLEP_a_00417.

Bo, Hechuan. 1992. *China on the Edge: The Crisis of Ecology and Development.* China Books & Periodicals.

Carter, Neil T. and Arthur P. J. Mol. 2006. 'China and the Environment: Domestic and Transnational Dynamics of a Future Hegemon'. *Environmental Politics* 15 (2): 330–44. doi.org/10.1080/09644010600562294.

Chang, Yen-Chiang and Nannan Wang. 2010. 'Environmental Regulations and Emissions Trading in China'. *Energy Policy* 38 (7): 3356–64. doi.org/10.1016/j.enpol.2010.02.006.

Chen, Yanbin (陈延斌) and Zhou Bin (周斌). 2015. 'The Communist Party of China's Exploration of Ecological Civilisation Construction since the Founding of New China' (新中国成立以来中国共产党对生态文明建设的探索). *Zhongzhou Academic Journal* 6: 83–9.

Chien, Shiuh-Shen and Hong Dong-Li. 2018. 'River Leaders in China: Party-State Hierarchy and Transboundary Governance'. *Political Geography* 62: 58–67. doi.org/10.1016/j.polgeo.2017.10.001.

Dai, Jingyun and Anthony S. Spires. 2017. 'Advocacy in an Authoritarian State: How Grassroots Environmental NGOs Influence Local Governments in China'. *China Journal* 79: 62–83. doi.org/10.1086/693440.

Eaton, Sarah and Genia Kostka. 2017. 'Central Protectionism in China: The "Central SOE Problem" in Environmental Governance'. *China Quarterly* 231: 685–704. doi.org/10.1017/S0305741017000881.

Foster, John Bellamy. 2017. 'The Earth-System Crisis and Ecological Civilization: A Marxian View'. *International Critical Thought* 7 (4): 439–58. doi.org/10.1080/21598282.2017.1357483.

Fu, Diana and Greg Distelhorst. 2017. 'Grassroots Participation and Repression under Hu Jintao and Xi Jinping'. *China Journal* 79: 100–22. doi.org/10.1086/694299.

Gao, Qi. 2018. '"Public Interest Litigation" in China: Panacea or Placebo for Environmental Protection?' *China: An International Journal* 16 (4): 47–75. doi.org/10.1353/chn.2018.0038.

Goron, Coraline. 2018. 'Ecological Civilisation and the Political Limits of a Chinese Concept of Sustainability'. *China Perspectives* 4: 39–52. doi.org/10.4000/chinaperspectives.8463.

Goron, Coraline and Gillian Bolsover. 2019. 'Engagement or Control? The Impact of the Chinese Environmental Protection Bureaus' Burgeoning Online Presence in Local Environmental Governance'. *Journal of Environmental Planning and Management* 63 (1): 87–108. doi.org/10.1080/09640568.2019.1628716.

Goron, Coraline and Cyril Cassisa. 2017. 'Regulatory Institutions and Market-Based Climate Policy in China'. *Global Environmental Politics* 17 (1): 99–120. doi.org/10.1162/GLEP_a_00392.

Hilton, Isabel. 2017. 'Guidance and Transgression: The Contest for Narratives of Environment and Pollution in China'. Commentary. *International Journal of Communication* 11: 1323–41.

Hsu, Angel, Amy Weinfurter, Chendan Yan and Yaping Cheng. 2017. 'From Citizens to Satellites: Third-Wave Data Approaches in China'. *Yale Data-Driven*. datadrivenlab.org/wp-content/uploads/2017/01/Third_Wave_Exec_Summary_FINAL.pdf.

Hsu, Angel, Zhi Yi Yeo and Amy Weinfurter. 2020. 'Emerging Digital Environmental Governance in China: The Case of Black and Smelly Waters in China'. *Journal of Environmental Planning and Management* 63 (1): 14–31. doi.org/10.1080/09640568.2019.1661228.

Jahiel, Abigail R. 1997. 'The Contradictory Impact of Reform on Environmental Protection in China'. *China Quarterly* 149: 81–103. doi.org/10.1017/S0305741000043642.

Jahiel, Abigail R. 1998. 'The Organization of Environmental Protection in China'. *China Quarterly* 156: 757–87. doi.org/10.1017/S030574100005133X.

Jahiel, Abigail R. 2006. 'China, the WTO, and Implications for the Environment'. *Environmental Politics* 15 (2): 310–29. doi.org/10.1080/09644010600562666.

Jeffreys, Elaine and Su Xuezhong. 2016. 'Governing through Lei Feng: A Mao-Era Role Model in Reform-Era China'. In *New Mentalities of Government in China,* edited by David Bray and Elaine Jeffreys, 30–55. Abingdon: Routledge. doi.org/10.4324/9781315688848-3.

Ke, Jinhua. 2013. 'Introduction. Special Issue on Ecological Civilization and Beautiful China'. *Social Sciences in China* 34 (4): 139–42. doi.org/10.1080/02529203.2013.849092.

Kostka, Genia. 2016, 'Command without Control: The Case of China's Environmental Target System'. *Regulation and Governance* 10: 58–74. doi.org/10.1111/rego.12082.

Kostka, Genia and Coraline Goron. 2021. 'From Targets to Inspections: The Issue of Fairness in China's Environmental Policy Implementation'. *Environmental Politics* 30 (4): 513–37. doi.org/10.1080/09644016.2020.1802201.

Kostka, Genia and William Hobbs. 2012. 'Local Energy Efficiency Policy Implementation in China: Bridging the Gap between National Priorities and Local Interests. *China Quarterly* 211:765–85. doi.org/10.1017/S0305741012000860.

Kostka, Genia and Arthur Mol. 2013. 'Implementation and Participation in China's Local Environmental Politics: Challenges and Innovations'. *Journal of Environmental Planning and Policy* 15 (1): 3–16. doi.org/10.1080/1523908X.2013.763629.

Kostka, Genia and Jonas Nahm. 2017. 'Central–Local Relations: Recentralization and Environmental Governance in China' (Introduction to Special Section). *China Quarterly* 231: 567–82. doi.org/10.1017/S0305741017001011.

Kostka, Genia and Chunman Zhang. 2018. 'Tightening the Grip: Environmental Governance under Xi Jinping' (Introduction for Symposium). *Environmental Politics* 27 (5): 769–81. doi.org/10.1080/09644016.2018.1491116.

Kostka, Genia, Xuehua Zhang and Kyoung Shin. 2020. 'Information, Technology, and Digitalization in China's Environmental Governance' (Introduction to Special Issue). *Journal of Environmental Planning and Management* 63 (1): 1–13. doi.org/10.1080/09640568.2019.1681386.

Li, Yifei and Judith Shapiro. 2020. *China Goes Green: Coercive Environmentalism for a Troubled Planet.* Cambridge: Polity Press.

Liao, Xingmiu and Wen-Hsuan Tsai. 2020. 'Strengthening China's Powerful Commission for Discipline Inspection under Xi Jinping, with a Case Study at the County Level'. *China Journal* 84 (July): 29–50. doi.org/10.1086/708610.

Liebman, Adam. 2019. 'Reconfiguring Chinese Natures: Frugality and Waste Reutilization in Mao Era Urban China'. *Critical Asian Studies* 51 (4): 537–57. doi.org/10.1080/14672715.2019.1658211.

Lorentzen, Peter, Pierre Landry and John Yasuda. 2014. 'Undermining Authoritarian Innovation: The Power of China's Industrial Giants'. *Journal of Politics* 76 (1): 182–94. doi.org/10.1017/S0022381613001114.

Ma, Yun. 2017. 'Vertical Environmental Management: A Panacea to the Environmental Enforcement Gap in China?' *Chinese Journal of Environmental Law* 1: 37–68. doi.org/10.1163/24686042-12340004.

Marinelli, Maurizio. 2018. 'How to Build a "Beautiful China" in the Anthropocene: The Political Discourse and the Intellectual Debate on Ecological Civilization'. *Journal of Chinese Political Science* 23: 365–86. doi.org/10.1007/s11366-018-9538-7.

Pan, Jiahua. 2016. *China's Environmental Governing and Ecological Civilization*. Berlin and Heidelberg: Springer. doi.org/10.1007/978-3-662-47429-7.

Qi, Ye, Li Ma, Huanbo Zhang and Huimin Li. 2008. 'Translating a Global Issue into Local Priority: China's Local Government Response to Climate Change'. *Journal of Environment & Development* 17 (4): 379–400. doi.org/10.1177/1070496508326123.

Ran, Ran 冉冉. 2013. 'Political Incentives and Local Environmental Governance under a "Pressurised System"' ("压力型体制"下的政治激励与地方环境治理). *Jingji shehui tizhi bijiao* 3: 111–18.

Ren, Xiangyi and Lili Liu. 2020. 'Building Consensus: Support Structure and the Frames of Environmental Legal Mobilization in China'. *Journal of Contemporary China* 29 (121): 109–24. doi.org/10.1080/10670564.2019.1621533.

Shapiro, Judith. 2001. *Mao's War Against Nature: Politics and the Environment in Revolutionary China*. Cambridge: Cambridge University Press. doi.org/10.1017/CBO9780511512063.

Stern, Rachel. 2013. *Environmental Litigation in China: A Study in Political Ambivalence*. New York: Cambridge University Press. doi.org/10.1017/CBO9781139096614.

Tian, Xiaofei. 2011. 'The Making of a Hero: Lei Feng and Some Issues of Historiography'. In *The People's Republic of China at 60: An International Assessment*, edited by William C. Kirby, 293–305. Cambridge: Harvard University Asia Center. doi.org/10.2307/j.ctt1sq5tgr.25.

van der Kamp, Denise. 2021a. 'Blunt Force Regulation and Bureaucratic Control: Understanding China's War on Pollution'. *Governance* 34 (1): 191–209. doi.org/10.1111/gove.12485.

van der Kamp, Denise. 2021b. 'Can Police Patrols Prevent Pollution? The Limits of Authoritarian Environmental Governance in China'. *Comparative Politics* 53 (3): 403–33. doi.org/10.5129/001041521X15982729490361.

van der Kamp, Denise, Peter Lorentzen and Daniel Mattingly. 2017. 'Racing to the Bottom or to the Top? Decentralization and Governance Reform in China'. *World Development* 95: 164–76. doi.org/10.1016/j.worlddev.2017.02.021.

Van Rooij, Benjamin, Qiaoqiao Zhu, Na Li and Qiliang Wang. 2017. 'Centralizing Trends and Pollution Law Enforcement in China'. *China Quarterly* 231 (September): 583–606. doi.org/10.1017/S0305741017000935.

Wang, Alex L. 2013. 'The Search for Sustainable Legitimacy: Environmental Law and Bureaucracy in China'. *Harvard Environmental Law Review* 37: 365–440. doi.org/10.2139/SSRN.2128167.

Wang, Alex L. 2018. 'Symbolic Legitimacy and Chinese Environmental Reform'. *Environmental Law* 48 (4): 699–760.

Wang, Zhihe, Huili He and Meijun Fan. 2014. 'The Ecological Civilization Debate in China: The Role of Ecological Marxism and Constructive Postmodernism – Beyond the Predicament of Legislation'. *Monthly Review* 66 (6): 37–59. doi.org/10.14452/MR-066-06-2014-10_3.

Wu, Chenhui, Maosen Ju, Longfei Wang, Xiangyi Gu and Cuiling Jiang. 2020. 'Public Participation of the River Chief System in China: Current Trends, Problems, and Perspectives'. *Water* 12 (12): 3496. doi.org/10.3390/w12123496.

Wu, Fengshi. 2013. 'Environmental Activism in Provincial China'. *Journal of Environmental Policy & Planning* 15 (1): 89–108. doi.org/10.1080/1523908X.2013.763634.

Wu, Jian and Zhong Ma. 2011. 'What Role Can Public Expenditure Play in Meeting China's Environmental Protection Targets?'. In *Green China: Chinese Insights on Environment and Development*, edited by James Keeley and Yisheng Zheng, 184–90. London: International Institute for Environment and Development.

Zeng, Qinghong (曾庆红), Ma Shijiang (马石江), Wang Yuting (王雨亭), Wang Mingzhe (王明哲), Mao Fumin (毛福民), Lü Feng (吕丰), Li Rui (李锐), Li Junru (李君如), Li Tielin (李铁林), Zhang Quanjing (张全景), Chen Wei (陈威), Jin Shuwang (金树望), Zhao Zongnai (赵宗鼐), Meng Liankun (孟连崑), Jiang Zhenyun (蒋振云), Yu Yunyao (虞云耀). 2000. *Materials on the History of the Communist Party of China (Party List)* (中国共产党组织史资料(党卷)). Beijing: Editorial Board of Organization History of the Communist Party of China (中国共产党组织史资料编审委员会).

Zhang, Joy and Michael Barr. 2013. *Green Politics in China: Environmental Governance and State-Society Relations*. London: Pluto Press.

Zhang, Lianhui (张连辉). 2010. 'Early Exploration of Environmental Protection in New China – The Environmental Protection Efforts of the Chinese Government before the First National Environmental Protection Conference' (新中国环境保护事业的早期探索–第一次全国环保会议前中国政府的环保努力当代中国史研究). *Dangdai Zhongguoshi yanjiu* 17 (04): 40–47+126.

Zhang, Shuzhen (张淑珍). 2020. 'The Communist Party of China's Exploration and Research on the Construction of Socialist Ecological Civilisation before the Reform and Opening Up' (改革开放前中国共产党对社会主义生态文明建设的探索研究潍坊学院学报). *Weifang xueyuan xuebao* 20 (05): 67–72.

Zou, Jing (邹晶). 2008. 'Climate Change Leading Small Group' (国家应对气候变化领导小组). *World Environment* (世界绿报化) 2 (2): 96.

Appendix

Table A9.1: Career Tracks of Leaders in the Environmental Bureaucracy

Agency	Leader's name	Leader's position in the state	Term	Leader's position in the Party	Next appointment(s)
State Council Environmental Protection Leading Small Group (国务院环境保护领导小组), 1973–82	Yu Qiuli (余秋里) (1914–1999)	Vice premier of the State Council, director of the State Planning Commission, group leader of the Environmental Leading Group of the State Council	1973–82	1977–80: Member of the Politburo of the Central Committee 1980–82: Secretary of the Central Office of the CCP Central Committee Secretariat	1980–82: Director of the National Energy Commission 1982–83: State councillor and deputy secretary-general of the Central Military Commission of the CCP 1983–?: Member of the Central Military Commission
Environmental Protection Bureau under the Ministry of Urban and Rural Construction (城乡建设环境保护部内设环境保护局), 1982–88 Office of the State Council Environmental Commission, 1984–88	Qu Geping (曲格平) (1930–)	Deputy director of the Office of the State Council Environmental Protection Leading Small Group (absent a director)	1978–84	Party secretary of the National Environmental Protection Bureau	1988–93: UNEP China permanent representative, director of the Office of the Environmental Protection Commission of the State Council 1993–2002: Leader of the Environment and Resources Protection Committee of the National People's Congress and Member of its Standing Committee 2002– : Chairman of the China Environmental Protection Foundation
		Director of the Environmental Protection Bureau	1982–93		

Agency	Leader's name	Leader's position in the state	Term	Leader's position in the Party	Next appointment(s)
State Council Environmental Protection Commission (国务院环境保护委员会), 1984–98	Li Peng (李鹏) (1928–2019)	Vice premier of the State Council, director of the State Council Environmental Protection Commission	1984–88	Member of the Politburo of the CCP Central Committee and secretary of the Secretariat of the CCP Central Committee	1988–1998: Premier of the State Council
	Song Jian (宋健) (1931–)	State councillor, State Council Environmental Protection Commission, and director of the National Science and Technology Commission until 1993	1988–98	Member of the CCP Central Committee	1998–2002: President of the Chinese Academy of Engineering
National Environmental Protection Bureau (国家环境保护局), 1988–98 Office of the State Council Environmental Commission until 1998	Xie Zhenhua (解振华) (1949–)	Director of the National Environmental Protection Bureau, deputy director and secretary-general of the Environmental Commission of the State Council	1993–98	Party secretary of the National Environmental Protection Bureau	2006–15: Deputy director and secretary of the Party committee of the NDRC 2015–18: Member of the Twelfth National Committee of the Chinese People's Political Consultative Conference (CPPCC), deputy director of the Committee of Population, Resources and Environment 2015–22: China's special envoy for climate change
		Director of the State Environmental Protection Agency	1998–2005	Party secretary of the State Environmental Protection Agency	

Agency	Leader's name	Leader's position in the state	Term	Leader's position in the Party	Next appointment(s)
State Environmental Protection Agency (国家环境保护总局), 1998–2008	Zhou Shengxian (周生贤) (1949–)	Director of the State Environmental Protection Agency	2005–08	Party secretary of the State Environmental Protection	2015–18: Member of the Twelfth National Committee of the CPPCC, deputy director of the Population, Resources and Environment Committee of the CPPCC National Committee
		Minister of the Ministry of Environmental Protection	2008–15	Party secretary of the Ministry of Environmental Protection	
Ministry of Environmental Protection (环境保护部), 2008–18	Chen Jining (陈吉宁) (1964–)	Minister of the Ministry of Environmental Protection	2015–17	Party secretary of the Ministry of Environmental Protection	2017–18: Deputy secretary of the Beijing Municipal Committee, deputy acting mayor 2018– : Party secretary of the Beijing Municipal People's Government, mayor of Beijing
	Li Ganjie (李干杰) (1964–)	Minister of the Ministry of Environmental Protection	2017–18	Party secretary of the Ministry of Environmental Protection	2018–21: Deputy secretary of the CCP Shandong Provincial Committee and Governor 2021– : Secretary of the CCP Shandong Provincial Committee
		Minister of the Ministry of Ecology and Environment	2018–20	Party secretary of the Ministry of Ecology and Environment	
Ministry of Ecology and Environment (生态环境部), 2018–	Huang Runqiu (黄润秋) (1963–)	Minister of the Ministry of Ecology and Environment	2020–	Not a CCP member	NA
	Sun Jinlong (孙金龙) (1962–)	Secretary of the Ministry of Ecology and Environment	2020–	Party secretary of the Ministry of Ecology and Environment	NA

Source: Compiled by the authors from multiple sources, including online CVs and government websites (2022).

10

Adapting the *Hukou* to Modernise the Country While Maintaining Social Polarisation and Stratification

Chloé Froissart

Originating from the ancestral *baojia*[1] system (Dutton 1992; Wang 2005) and introduced during the Qing dynasty to register the population for the purposes of census, conscription, tax collection and maintaining social order, the *hukou* is the oldest extant institution in the history of China. Throughout the history of the People's Republic of China (PRC), the adaption and reform of this imperial institution has played a central role in the project for the modernisation of the Chinese Communist Party (CCP). The Party has used the *hukou* system to control and then plan the urbanisation of the country, and hence negotiate the difficult transition from a rural to an urban society while at the same time reducing the financial costs of this transition for the state. The *hukou* has also constantly been leveraged to support economic development, whatever strategy was employed by the CCP at different times, at great human cost.

Generating considerable inequality and injustice, the *hukou* has been the object of so much criticism, both in China and abroad, that Xi Jinping, focusing on 'common prosperity' (*gongtong fuyu* 共同富裕), promised to

1 System of surveillance and mutual responsibility of households that was codified in the Song dynasty.

accelerate reforms as early as 2013.[2] The notion of common prosperity, mentioned by Mao Zedong in a 1955 speech calling for the acceleration of collectivisation in order to improve the standard of living of poor peasants, was originally closely linked to the founder's ideals of equality (Mao 1955). When Deng Xiaoping took up the phrase in 1985, he was postponing it for a distant future, affirming that some should get rich first.[3] Xi Jinping, wishing to make common prosperity a reality during his reign to legitimise his authority, then associated it with justice and equity.[4]

While the CCP, following the line set out by Sun Yat-sen, has always emphasised the people's wellbeing, this chapter argues that the *hukou* has been the instrument of a socially polarising modernisation based on the exploitation and the exclusion of part of the population who possessed only their labour force, while mainstreaming a socioeconomic elite. The purpose of this institution during the Maoist regime, and the manner in which it has been reformed according to pragmatic criteria, serves as a reminder that the individual has always been considered a tool of the party-state, implying the sacrifice of part of the population for the benefit of the present prosperity of some and the supposed prosperity of all in the future.

This chapter traces this sacrifice's history, considering the manner in which features of the *hukou* have been perpetuated and adapted. By analysing the policies put in place to manage the integration of rural migrants in urban areas, it also outlines the main lines of the current social model and stresses how it recycles the principles of social citizenship as they were defined by the *hukou* in the Mao era. The long view favoured in the analysis of this institution allows us to explore the historical trajectory of the China development model upon which the definition of Xi Jinping's intended common prosperity model now depends.

This chapter highlights the recycling of Maoist principles of social citizenship in Xi's model of 'common prosperity' as embodied by the integration of migrant workers in urban eras through their access to public services. To do

2 'Decision on Major Issues Concerning Comprehensively Deepening Reforms in Brief', CCP Central Committee, *China Daily*, 16 November 2013, www.china.org.cn/china/third_plenary_session/2013-11/16/content_30620736.htm.

3 Yu Yongyue and Wang Shiming, 'Revisiting Deng Xiaoping's Thought on Common Prosperity' (重温邓小平共同富裕思想), *Guang'an Daily*, 24 October 2018, cpc.people.com.cn/n1/2018/1024/c69113-30359624.html.

4 'Xi Jinping's Report at the 19th National Congress of the Communist Party of China' (习近平在中国共产党第十九次全国代表大会上的报告), 28 October 2017, cpc.people.com.cn/n1/2017/1028/c64094-29613660.html.

so, it offers a three-step overview of the role played by the *hukou* system in the modernisation of China and its social consequences since the founding of the PRC. In the Mao era, the *hukou* was an instrument for organising labour and for controlling migration that enabled the exploitation of peasants to be used to benefit the development of heavy industry, and it established a localised, functional and stratified social citizenship.[5] The reforms redefined the features of the *hukou* to create an instrument for exploitation of migrants from the countryside for the benefit of the urban economy, particularly light industry, and for a system of urban planning favouring the integration of socioeconomic elites. Lastly, the point-record system, an avatar of the *hukou* regulating migrants' access to public services in the country's largest cities, has created an elitist and differentiated model for integration. Although it is more inclusive than during the Mao era or early reform era, the present social model – which started to be implemented in the second half of the 2000s – remains based on the principles of local, functional and stratified social citizenship. It still favours the integration of socioeconomic elites associated with urban development and continues to exclude the proletariat.

The Functions of the *Hukou* in the Socialist Development Project and Its Consequences on the Principles of Social Citizenship in the Mao Era

Originating under the imperial regime and modelled on the system of the Soviet *propiska*[6] (Dutton 1992; Wang 2005), the *hukou* system was an essential instrument for the organisation of labour and production, as well as for the collection and redistribution of resources all through the Mao era. Aiming to limit the labour market's instability and population growth in the urban areas where the inhabitants were supported by the state, it served as an auxiliary to industrialisation without urbanisation. It divided Chinese citizens into two distinct categories by attributing different rights and duties. But beyond the evident division between the rural and the urban

5 Although successive Chinese constitutions refer to the term 'citizenship', the 1958 PRC Household Registration Regulations have, as we will see in this chapter, established a social 'citizenship' with rights and duties that are not considered universal but are, rather, defined by the ascriptive characteristics of individuals.

6 System of registration of the population established in the Soviet Union in 1932 and also used for planning, redistribution of resources and control of migration.

population, the *hukou* system established a local, functionalist and stratified conception of social citizenship that has survived until the present in spite of numerous reforms.

A Tool for Organising the Labour and the Exploitation of Peasant Farmers

The formalisation of the *hukou* was one of the elements establishing the fundamental features of the PRC; that is, a Soviet-type regime based on economic planning. Formally established on 9 January 1958 in the PRC Household Registration Regulations, the *hukou* system was a specific element of socialist development in the Chinese context, encouraging rapid industrialisation, while prioritising the heavy industry sector, in the context of an agricultural labour surplus. Unlike the USSR, China had a very low level of urbanisation and a huge workforce, 85 per cent of which were peasants (Cheng 1991, 252). As during the revolution, Maoist dialectics transformed a Chinese weakness into an advantage, using the countryside to establish an unequal exchange between the agricultural and industrial sectors. In December 1953, the central government designed a system of mandatory sale to the state of grain quotas at very low prices. By heavily taxing the countryside in this way, the state managed to create a 'surplus' with which to finance industry and urban infrastructure, as well as providing 'iron rice bowls' to the urban population (Cheng and Selden 1994; Wang 2005).

The *hukou* system was intended to institutionalise this unequal exchange between the countryside and the cities by assigning to each citizen a position in the system of production – a position on which rights and duties depended. From 1958 onwards, this system covered the entire population of China and organised the workers into people's communes and works units, categorising them according to this registration as agricultural (*nongye* 农业) or non-agricultural (*fei nongye* 非农业). This categorisation established a hierarchy between the elite of the regime (mostly urban workers and employees in the state sector, cadres and army) and peasants. While the latter had to count on their own resources for food, housing, health care and education, the state took charge of the urban population from cradle to grave. The state allocated lifetime employment to urbanites and provided them with ration cards for food and clothing. The state also provided housing, education and social services, as well as public services such as water supply, sewage, transport and policing (Cheng 1991; Cheng and Selden 1994; Chan 1994; Wang 2005).

Designed as a 'mechanism of mass exploitation on a national scale', the *hukou* system created a state of internal colonisation in a context in which it was impossible for the CCP, because of its denunciation of capitalism and its links to imperialist expansion, to import from abroad the human resources and the raw materials necessary for its development as Western powers had done (Hayward 2022). Between 1949 and 1979, at least 600 billion yuan were transferred from rural communes to the urban state sector. While, in the early 1950s, the income of the urban population was twice that of the rural, in the late 1970s it had become four to six times greater thanks to state subsidies (Cheng 1991, 209–10, 247). However, at the time, this exploitation was not recognised as such. It wore the appearance of the egalitarianism dear to Mao, being disguised by the fact that the peasants were, in theory at least, the owners of their means of production within the people's communes.

An Instrument to Control Urbanisation: The End of Freedom of Movement

Although the PRC originally recognised freedom of movement and choice of place of residence (see the Common Program of 1949 and the PRC Constitution of 1954), the CCP was soon obliged to use travel authorisations and check points to strictly control migration. Such control was indeed necessary to limit public spending in urban areas and keep each individual in their assigned place in the production system in a context in which urban benefits were a strong pull factor for peasants. From the early 1960s, only two types of migration were allowed: temporary and permanent, both organised by the state via strict procedures. Temporary migration allowed for collective labour contracts between an agricultural production brigade and an urban enterprise, at the end of which the peasants were sent back to their villages. Living conditions for migrant workers in the city were different from those of urban workers in that they were considered temporary workers retaining their rural status (Walder 1986). Permanent migration was accompanied by a transfer of *hukou* from another location and implied a change of status when the move was from a rural to an urban location or vice versa. It was extremely rare to be granted non-agricultural status, which could occur only through strict administrative procedures (being recruited permanently by a state enterprise or the army, being promoted to an administrative post, attending university) and according to annual quotas set by the State Planning Commission. In all cases, any change in status had to be aligned with state objectives and did not take personal reasons into account, such as family regrouping (Chan and Zhang 1999; Chan and Buckingham 2008). According to a survey carried out in a village in Guangdong from 1964 to 1978, the annual probability for obtaining a non-agricultural status was 0.0228 per cent for a man and 0.0028 per cent for a woman (Potter 1983, 495).

Establishing a Complex Hierarchy between Chinese Citizens: A Local, Functionalist and Stratified Social 'Citizenship'

The *hukou* system reflected a functionalist conception of 'citizenship': the rights and duties of individuals were a function of their role in building socialism. This hereditary system (as the *hukou* was inherited from the mother until 1998)[7] gave rise to a status structure distinguishing a minority of privileged citizens (15 per cent of the population) from the vast majority of the peasants who had hardly any rights. But the consequence of the Maoist *hukou* was the establishing of a status system based on a complex categorisation of individuals extending far beyond the simple differentiation between the rural and the urban population. It introduced a status hierarchy across three criteria. First, the *hukou* introduced a functionalist classification of individuals as agricultural or non-agricultural. Second, within the latter category, it created differentiated treatment for urban dwellers based on the politico-spatial hierarchy of the cities where they lived. That the place of registration is mentioned in the *hukou* booklet underlines the importance of the local level in the Chinese system. Individuals belong to a given community, whether it is rural or urban, and their rights vary according to the economic and social resources of these communities. The Maoist regime established a strict spatial hierarchy favouring large urban centres. The village figured at the base of the ladder, then the township, the county, the city, the provincial capital, the autonomous municipality (Tianjin, Shanghai) and, right at the top, the national capital, Beijing. The higher up they lived on the ladder, the greater the state subsidies; the lower down, the higher the taxes they paid (Trolliet and Béja 1986, 154). Third, the *hukou* system determined status according to the hierarchy of the people's communes and the production units, among which a huge variation in living and working conditions prevailed, and to which individuals were

7 This is explained by the intention to reduce the burden of the state in the context of a majority of state sector employees being men and the transfer procedures of an agricultural to a non-agricultural *hukou* also favouring male workers.

bound by a relationship of 'organised dependence' (Walder 1986). From 1958 onwards, the work unit rather than the family defined the existence of a *hukou*, so that if husband and wife worked in two different production units (*danwei* 单位) or two different people's communes, or in an urban *danwei* and a people's commune (a frequent occurrence as the state assigned jobs), they each had a different *hukou* (Cheng and Selden 1994, 663).

In this way, the *hukou* fragmented the social body into a complex status system in order to facilitate administration and control, for production and allocation of resources, as well as for social control (Wang 2005). In complete contradiction to the notion of citizen equality stipulated in the 1954 and 1982 constitutions[8] and the egalitarianism intended by Mao, inequality was institutionalised in the bedrock of Chinese society by the *hukou* system. It imposed a particularising logic that endlessly subdivided society and, in practice, erased any aspect of equality between individuals. Thus it was the basis of a local, stratified and functionalist conception of social citizenship, whereas the concept of citizenship included in the PRC Constitution refers to a national citizenship and proceeds according to a universalist logic, insisting on what unites individuals rather than what differentiates them.

The *Hukou* under Reform: An Instrument for the Exploitation of Migrants and Urban Planning

The discontinuation of the socialist development project and the reintroduction of the market economy ran parallel with the redefinition of the functions of the *hukou*. From a system of exploitation of peasants for the development of heavy industry, the *hukou* was morphed into a system for the exploitation of migrants to the benefit of the urban economy, particularly the development of light industry geared to export. At the same time, from being a system for the control of urban development, the *hukou* became an urban planning tool that allowed the CCP to negotiate the difficult transition from a rural to an urban society, at the lowest cost to the state.

8 This notion of citizen equality before the law was removed from the 1975 and 1978 constitutions.

Retaining the *Hukou*, or the Creation of the Largest Proletariat in World History

The *hukou* constituted an efficient instrument for controlling migration as long as it remained a coherent part of a series of social and economic control mechanisms. However, these devices were challenged by the reintroduction of the market economy and by the partial withdrawal of the Party from the economic and social spheres from 1980 onwards. The disbanding of the people's communes freed the peasants from their shackles and provided a large supernumerary workforce that found employment first in small town businesses, then in the cantons and special economic zones, and then in the cities during the late 1980s when economic reforms were introduced there too. The year 1985 was a turning point: the creation of an identity card (a personal document, whereas the *hukou* booklet was collective) and temporary residence permit made movement easier, while renting out accommodation to the migrant population ceased to be illegal (Zhang, Chunhua and Ping 1998, 90). At the same time, the end of rationing in 1992 after the emergence of a grain market, and the monetisation of the economy, made it easier for migrants to stay in cities (Wang 1997, 159). The gradual removal of the obstacles to population movement and the development of the urban economy led to a steep rise in migration towards the cities. From 1991 to 2013, the urban workforce rose to 269 million, of whom 85 per cent were migrants from the countryside (Lin 2015, 38).

Table 10.1: Number of migrants from rural areas to urban areas (1980–2020)

Year	1980	1987	1989	1991	1999	2005	2010	2015	2020
Total number (by million)	2.5	28	30	42	209	230	242	277	286

Sources: China Statistical Yearbook; China Demographic Yearbook.

Keeping the *hukou* in place, and thus the agricultural status of the migrants moving from the countryside to the cities, as reflected in the neologism *nongmingong* (农民工, peasant workers), allowed the creation of a flexible reserve workforce that was cheap because deprived of rights. As social status was still attached to the place of *hukou* registration, city governments, as well as urban employers, were not responsible for the migrants' social protection, whether it involved health care, retirement pension or their children's education (Davin 1999; Pieke and Mallee 1999; Solinger 1999; Zhang 2001). Retaining the *hukou* also justified a segmentation of the employment market, keeping migrants in the most tiring and poorly paid jobs where their basic and essential rights (such as pay) were often not respected (Solinger 1999; Froissart 2013). In 2004, Vice Premier Zeng Peiyan revealed that 360 billion yuan were owed to migrant workers by their employers.[9] In general, the number and cost of the many different permits needed to stay, work and live legally in the city kept migrants in a state of illegality and effectively in a situation of lawlessness (Froissart 2013, 106–26).

The term 'peasant workers' did not necessarily refer only to those employed in industry. Such workers also played a crucial part in the development of the urban economy in general during the reform period, finding employment in local services, building and commerce; some also ran small businesses (*getihu* 个体户). A significant number were employed in the export-oriented manufacturing sector, often working for subcontractors of multinational businesses and allowing China to become the 'factory of the world' (Chan 2003; Pun 2005). Globalisation of the economy launched by the Chinese state in the absence of social protection, collective rights, trade unions, justice and independent civil society created a specific model of proletarisation of these migrants (Chan, Pun and Chan 2010; Kuruvilla, Lee and Gallagher 2011). Thus, while during the Mao era the exploitation of the peasants allowed the CCP to develop the Chinese economy without resorting to imperialist expansion, during the reform period, the exploitation of migrants to the benefit of the urban economy and world capital constituted one of the major contributing factors of the Chinese economic miracle.

Table 10.2: Distribution of employment of rural migrants by sector

Sector	Manufacturing	Construction	Services
Distribution of jobs in 2005	27%	26%	32%
Proportion of migrant employees in the sector in 2000	68%	80%	52%

Sources: Ministry of Labour and Social Security, 'A Series of Surveys: Number and Structural Characteristics of Current Floating Employment of Migrant Workers' (劳动和社会保障部, 系列调查: 当前农民工流动就业数量、结构特点), 14 February 2006, news.sohu.com/20060214/n241813280.shtml; *Bulletin on Main Data of the Fifth National Population Census in 2000* (2000年第五次全国人口普查主要数据公报), 28 March 2001, www.gov.cn/gongbao/content/2001/content_60740.htm.

9 Fu Jing, 'Zeng: Pay All Owed Wages to Migrants', *China Daily*, 26 August 2004.

Although social citizenship remained connected to the place of *hukou* registration, above all, it was land that served as social welfare for migrant workers, who supposedly returned home when they were no longer needed in the cities. However, illegal expropriations carried out by local governments aware of the market value of land became more frequent during the 1990s, depriving migrants of the only security from which they could benefit and effectively changing them into proletarians. According to official statistics, between 1990 and 2005, the surface area of arable land available nationally fell by 92 million mu (23,784,000 square miles) or 5 per cent of the total surface, reducing 50 million peasants to the state of 'three not-haves': no land, no training, no social security (He 2007, 120). As a result, from being individual and temporary, rural–urban migration became increasingly familial and permanent (Froissart 2013, 211–13). Family migration represented 14 per cent of migrations in 2000 and 21 per cent in 2004 (State Council Research Group 2006, 77). Many migrants hence became de facto urban residents, even if they did not have the full right to be.

The emergence of this new proletariat directly challenged the legitimacy of the Communist Party and pushed the Hu–Wen government to publish, in 2003, Document No. 1, 'Notice to Carry Out the Management of Urban Employment and Services to Peasant Workers in Cities'.[10] This document represented a political shift: it recognised for the first time that China's industrialisation should go hand in hand with urbanisation and invited the municipalities to guarantee equal rights to migrants and the urban population in terms of working conditions and access to employment, social welfare, training and education for their children. Without renouncing the control of migration, this document urged municipalities to work towards granting equal social and economic rights to migrants and urban residents. It clearly stated a new political priority: to integrate agricultural *hukou* holders into the cities. This document led to the implementation of public policies at the local level that directly modified the *hukou* system by allowing gradual integration of rural *hukou* holders into the cities, although still on an unequal basis.

10 'Notice to Carry Out the Management of Urban Employment of Peasants and Their Access to Public Services' (国务院办公厅关于做好进城务工就业管理服务工作通知), General Office of the State Council, 5 January 2003, www.gov.cn/gongbao/content/2003/content_62570.htm.

A Tool for Planning Urbanisation

From the 1980s onwards, the *hukou* system was reformed to allow China to manage its urban transition in a gradual and controlled manner, while also reducing the costs of this transition for the state. From the very start, *hukou* reforms demonstrated the CCP's intentions to promote balanced urbanisation by encouraging the development of lower-tier cities. They corresponded neatly to the slogan: 'Strictly control the development of cities, rationally develop cities and vigorously promote the development of towns and villages' (Davin 1999, 130).

The first reform of the *hukou* dates from 1984 with the establishment, only in small towns, of a 'self-supply grain *hukou*' (*zili kouliang chengzhen hukou* 自理口粮户口). Peasants could obtain an urban *hukou* for themselves and their immediate family on the condition that they could prove they had permanent lodging and employment and could supply themselves with food. Insofar as the state did not take charge of either their food rationing or their accommodation, and that there were far fewer social benefits for small town residents than for those in larger cities, the cost for the state of this sort of urbanisation was very low. The principle of an elitist urbanisation was subsequently set; those who had the means to finance their settlement in towns could acquire an urban status from then on.

The same model of integration at minimal cost for the state was gradually extended to small and medium-sized cities as the reforms enabled their economic growth. In 1997, a similar reform was launched in small cities (up to 200,000 inhabitants). Provincial authorities were asked to select a small number of urban units, below the level of the district administrative centre, where the economy and infrastructure were developed enough and financial resources were sufficient, and to fix quotas to accommodate migrants according to the city's capacity. This policy, at first limited to 450 pilot locations, was extended to all small cities in 2001, and quotas were removed (Wu 2013). In 2003, some provinces, such as Sichuan, extended this reform to medium-sized cities (Froissart 2008). But the hurdles in the way to obtaining an urban *hukou* in the largest and most dynamic municipalities, where the migrant workers possessing nothing but their labour – in other words, the proletarians – were mostly likely to go, remained very high and only accessible to the most well-off and most qualified migrants, who were usually urban residents from other cities (Froissart 2008; Chan and Buckingham 2008).

The National New-Type Urbanisation Plan published by the State Affairs Council in 2014 followed the same logic.[11] It planned to attribute an urban *hukou* to 100 million people by 2020, by further relaxing the restrictions in place in small (fewer than 500,000 inhabitants) and medium-sized (from 500,000 to 1 million inhabitants) cities, while maintaining strict control on migration to cities of more than 5 million inhabitants. The conditions for obtaining an urban *hukou* became stricter as the size of the city increased.

In small cities, the requirements remained minimal, yet to the condition of having stable work and accommodation was added that of contributing to the urban social security system. Requirements also included, depending on the size and attractiveness of the municipality, the time spent living in the city and contributing to social security, the type and length of employment, the amount of tax paid and the type of accommodation (new or old, surface area, ownership or tenant). Lastly, cities of more than 5 million inhabitants were authorised to use a points-record system (*jifen zhidu* 积分制度), enabling them to select and welcome immigrants whose presence reinforced the relative advantages of these major economic centres,[12] while also limiting access to public services in order to control state spending.

In 2016 and 2019, the central government published new directives instructing municipalities with a population of 1–3 million inhabitants to remove restrictions to the issuance of urban *hukou*, and those of 3–5 million to speed up the integration of priority groups, particularly families arriving from the countryside.[13] According to the National Development and Reform Commission, by the end of 2020, 100 million migrants from the countryside had transferred their *hukou* to a city. Also, municipalities of fewer than 3 million inhabitants had effectively abandoned their points-record system and were only taking into account the length of time an individual had been living in the city and their social security contributions when

11 'National New-Type Urbanisation Plan 2014–2020' (国家新型城镇化规划2014–2020), 16 March 2014, www.gov.cn/zhengce/2014-03/16/content_2640075.htm.

12 This permit endorsed practices that had been used voluntarily by the biggest cities in the country since 1980, particularly via the sale of the blue-stamp *hukou* (Froissart 2008).

13 'Notice on the Plan for Promoting the Settlement of 100 Million Non-Hukou Population in Cities' (国务院办公厅关于印发推动1亿非户籍人口在城市落户方案的通知), General Office of the State Council, 30 September 2016, www.gov.cn/zhengce/content/2016-10/11/content_5117442.htm; 'Key Tasks of New Urbanisation Construction in 2019' (国家发改委2019年新型城镇化建设重点任务), National Development and Reform Commission, www.ndrc.gov.cn/xxgk/zcfb/tz/201904/t20190408_962418.html.

issuing an urban *hukou*.[14] In February 2021, Jiangxi was the first province to announce the lifting of restrictions for the issue of an urban *hukou*, the only conditions retained being proof of employment, accommodation and a two- to three-year history of social insurance contributions according to the size of the city.[15]

By regularising migrants who had been living in urban settings for several years, these reforms aimed to extend the possibility for de facto residents to become fully-fledged residents in increasingly larger cities, while continuing to protect the largest cities. The reforms benefited a stable and well-off elite among rural migrants, particularly as obtaining an urban *hukou* implied giving up land in the countryside. However, in the big cities, which attracted most of the poorest migrants, central government policy allowed local development strategies to influence migration policy (Froissart 2008). As a result, while the urbanisation rate[16] in China had quadrupled since the Mao era, amounting to 64 per cent in 2020, the percentage of people holding an urban *hukou* only reached 45 per cent.[17]

An Elitist and Differentiated Integration Model: Point-Based Citizenship

The *hukou* system was also modified by policies concerning access to urban public services for migrants that were put in place from the early 2000s onwards. Similarly to the process of urbanisation, the integration of migrants in cities had been undertaken in a pragmatic way rather than in a spirit of justice and equity. I demonstrate here that the so-called social

14 Liu Yang, 'The Urbanisation Rate Is 44.38%: Our Country Has Completed the Goal of 100 Million People Settled in Ahead of Schedule' (城镇化率44.38%: 我国提前完成一亿人口落户目标), *Xinhua News Agency*, 7 October 2020, www.gov.cn/xinwen/2020-10/07/content_5549654.htm; Liu Meiling, 'Development and Reform Commission Major Official Announcement! These Cities Have Completely Lifted the Restrictions on Settlement' (发改委重磅官宣!这些城市全面取消落户限制), *Twenty-First New Economic Herald*, 13 April 2021, baijiahao.baidu.com/s?id=1696908360829549154&wfr=spider&for=pc.

15 'What's New about Jiangxi Household Registration Policy?' (江西上户口新政策有哪些方面?), 28 March 2021, www.64365.com/zs/1358059.aspx.

16 Calculated from the number of people who had been living in towns and cities for more than six months.

17 'Seventh National Census Report' (国家统计局第七次全国人口普查公报), National Bureau of Statistics, 2021, www.gov.cn/guoqing/2021-05/13/content_5606149.htm.

policies[18] (Qian, Hu and Su 2017) put in place by municipalities with a population exceeding 3 million inhabitants using a points-record system to control access to public services, and eventually to urban status, renew the principles of a functionalist and, therefore, stratified social citizenship. The nature of stratification is plural today. It extends a logic of status inherited from the *hukou* whereby 'long-stay residents' (*changzhu renkou* 常住人口)[19] who do not possess an urban *hukou* can access certain basic public services but are not treated as equal to those with urban roots and migrants who do not have such a permit remain irremediably excluded. Added to this are the socioeconomic inequalities linked to market forces, which local government policies only reinforce by favouring educated and qualified migrants who represent a socioeconomic elite within the 'long-stay resident' category. Finally, by stressing eligibility rather than rights (Zhang 2012), these policies determine different levels of access to urban public services in proportion to the value of the beneficiary in the eyes of the state, hence the idea of citizenship by points. In other words, these policies continue to exclude the poorest and most mobile migrants and, at the same time, to create new types of inequality among long-stay migrants already in the cities.

Development of Public Services and the Creation of New Social Stratifications

Following the publication of Document No. 1 in 2003, the central government continued to reiterate its intention to disconnect access to public services in cities from the granting of an urban *hukou*.[20] The creation in 2015 of a long-term residence permit was a major turning point.[21] It allowed access to public services, replacing the temporary residence permit that only established the legitimacy of staying in urban areas. However, the reforms were conducted in a decentralised manner,

18 CCP Central Committee, 'Decision on Major Issues Concerning Comprehensively Deepening Reforms in Brief', *China Daily*, 16 November 2013, www.china.org.cn/china/third_plenary_session/2013-11/16/content_30620736.htm.

19 Denoting migrants residing for more than six months in town and having acquired a residence permit (居住证). Only those with proof of both stable and legal employment and stable and legal accommodation could apply for a residence permit.

20 'Several Opinions of the State Council on Solving the Problem of Migrant Workers' (国务院关于解决农民工问题的若干意见), 2006, www.gov.cn/jrzg/2006-03/27/content_237644.htm; 'Opinions of the State Council on Promoting One Step Further the Work of Delivering Services to Migrant Workers' (国务院关于进一步做好为农民工服务工作的意见), State Council, 2014, www.gov.cn/zhengce/content/2014-09/30/content_9105.htm.

21 'Provisional Regulations on Residence Permits' (国务院令居住证暂行条例), State Council, 2015, www.gov.cn/zhengce/content/2015-12/12/content_10398.htm.

the municipalities implementing the directives from the centre according to their resources and needs, as the state bore no financial responsibility for the reforms. Even if from then on municipalities were required to take migrants into account in their spending – whereas previously the budget only took into account permanent residents – they undertook to limit the pressure on public finance. They were thus encouraged to select candidates for urban integration, to create different levels of integration and to favour the allocation of resources by the market.

From the early 2000s, the cities with the largest influx of migrants began to set up social protection systems. Each municipality developed its own model, but a common feature was that these systems were not based on taxation and redistribution. They were instead social insurance systems based on contributions indexed to salaries where the amount determined the benefits. Such systems strengthened the socioeconomic inequalities between city dwellers and migrants, with employers having less social responsibility towards migrants than their urban employees. In Shanghai, for example, employers contributed 5.5 per cent of the salary for their migrant employees and 12 per cent for urban *hukou* holders (Wu 2017, 132). Protection for these two categories of citizens remained very unequal, concerning both health and risk coverage, and the amount of eventual benefits received (Froissart 2013, 269–78). Also, even migrants covered by urban social insurance regimes were often obliged to return to the countryside for treatment or to forego treatment, as they lacked coverage for some conditions, in particular those requiring long-term treatment (Chan and O'Brien 2019; Müller 2016; Meng 2021). As they do not allow transfer of benefits, these localised contribution-based systems are not adapted for a mobile population, who lose their entitlement as soon as they move from the city where they have paid contributions. Moreover, these systems, with contributions based on salary, exclude most migrants who do not hold work contracts – 65 per cent of them in 2016.[22]

The social insurance schemes specifically designed for migrant workers enable the integration of the most stable and affluent, but at the price of a double discrimination based on their place of *hukou* registration and income (not only do migrant workers have less coverage than urban residents, but the poor have less coverage than the more affluent). This social policy certainly contributes to the integration of elite migrant workers

22 '2016 Migrant Workers Monitoring Survey Annual Report' (国家统计局2016年农民工监测调查报告), National Bureau of Statistics, 2017, www.gov.cn/xinwen/2017-04/28/content_5189509.htm#1.

but still stigmatises them as a specific social category and further stratifies within this category. Thus, an elite minority of migrant workers has the means to contribute to the urban social insurance scheme; a larger group is covered by the specific scheme for migrant workers; and the majority of those working in the informal sector, or who are too poor or too mobile, have no social insurance.

When it comes to access to education, the reforms have been taken further to create a proper public service available to some children of migrant workers. The doors of urban schools remained closed to these children until 1998, when they were admitted on condition that their parents had the required documents, stable employment and accommodation, and paid 'temporary schooling fees' that actually made them bear the full cost of tuition. Illegal private schools sprang up during the late 1990s to assist these children. As these schools were run with limited means, they provided mediocre teaching, could not issue state-recognised diplomas, and often did not respect the required conditions of hygiene and security. The consequence of the 2004 abolition of the temporary schooling fees was the integration of an elite, once again to the exclusion of the poorest. On the one hand, this measure encouraged the state schools to reinforce their selection procedures along socioeconomic lines to avoid overcrowding. On the other hand, the central government's instructions asking municipalities to prioritise the enrolment of these children in state schools was often used by local authorities as a pretext to shut down private schools, despite their efforts to gain recognition from the state (Froissart 2008). The repeated closures of private schools left tens of thousands of children without alternatives: either they separated from their parents and returned to the countryside or they put an end to their education. In 2006, 132 schools were closed in Beijing (of a total of 239 with 90,000 students) and 16 – some of which had more than 2,000 pupils – in Shanghai.[23]

This integration model created four categories of children of migrant workers with unequal rights of access to education: first, those receiving the same education as urban residents but entailing administrative (presentation of permits and documents not required by urban residents) and socioeconomic (children of more affluent and qualified parents were privileged) discrimination; second, those enrolled in lawful private schools with higher enrolment fees and lesser learning conditions; third, the

23 'Wave of Rectification Targets Migrant Children Schools' (打工子弟学校整顿风波), *Caijing*, 4 September 2006.

majority of children from poor mobile families who remained educated in illegal schools, which, in the absence of subsidies and adequate supervision, charged very high fees, could not issue qualifications and were constantly threatened with closure; last, the children separated from their parents and remaining in the countryside, where schooling was of even lesser quality (Froissart 2008, 2013). In 2017, roughly 45 per cent of migrant workers' children were still enrolled in country schools and could not join their parents in the cities.[24]

The Points-Record System: Greater Inclusion at the Cost of Increased Stratification

The creation of a points-record system in several cities in Guangdong around 2010 made it possible to systemise the logics of inclusion detailed above and to structure a coherent range of reforms. This system awarded points to all residence permit holders according to socioeconomic criteria and their respect of state directives. A migrant worker could obtain an urban *hukou* – and thus enjoy full citizenship in his city of residence – if he acquired sufficient points and if his application fell within the annual fixed quotas for each municipality. If he did not satisfy the criteria, he could obtain partial urban citizenship with access only to certain administrative and health services, education for his child, training and housing aid. Institutionalised at the provincial level in 2011, this system was gradually extended to cities with a population of between 1 and 3 million inhabitants from 2014 onwards, and to municipalities such as Shanghai (2014) and Beijing (2018). In other words, this system concerned cities where GDP per resident was the highest in China and enabled the control of the quantity and personal 'quality' (*sushi* 素质) of the migrant workers to reduce the cost to the state of their inclusion and to maximise their contribution to economic development.

Points were awarded according to a three-tiered system. The first level of criteria was common to all cities and corresponded to basic requirements: proof of a constant record of residence, long-term employment and accommodation, and uninterrupted contributions to social security. Young and healthy people were preferred as being less costly for the state and for social insurance; older people (men over 50 and women over 40) must have

24 '2017 National Education Development Statistical Report' (中华人民教育部2017年全国教育事业发展统计公报), Ministry of Education of the Republic of China, 2018, www.moe.gov.cn/jyb_sjzl/sjzl_fztjgb/201807/t20180719_343508.html.

contributed to social insurance for longer (a minimum of 10 years). Breaking the law in any way entailed points being removed, and any implication in criminal activity resulted in disqualification. The second and third levels of criteria, which could award more points, reflected the skills and qualifications required by each municipality according to economic priorities. The second level of criteria was related to the applicants' personal quality, mainly their level of education, qualifications and professional competences, and reputation (e.g. a healthy bank account and no debt). The application had to be sponsored by the employer, whose respect for employment law and corporate social responsibility were also considered. By awarding points according to the employer, municipalities used *hukou* attribution to strengthen industrial and business sectors in need of highly qualified personnel, to support projects that helped to increase the city's competitiveness, and to implement top-down plans and political directives. The third level of criteria (so-called merit-based) included how much had been invested in the local economy or the amount of tax paid, as well as the honours and awards received in local competitions. Bonus points could be won through voluntary participation in philanthropic activities or related donations.

While remaining within the logic of a selective immigration favouring a qualified socioeconomic elite among the migrants, this system represented a more inclusive policy through a tiered integration system based on the number of points gained. It allowed migrants who were not eligible for urban *hukou* to benefit from certain redistributive advantages, such as access to local schools. It also established a more predictable route for obtaining an urban *hukou*. While a very small elite group of highly qualified applicants obtained urban *hukou* each year (Zhang 2012; Losavio 2019), this system continued to exclude poor and mobile migrants without a residence permit and created new stratifications within the category of 'long-term residents' (*changzhu renkou* 常住人口). The number of points obtained determined the quality of accessible services.

Let us take the example of access to education. In 2016 in Zhuhai, three times as many points (118) were needed to enrol in a primary school in the most affluent area, where the quality of education was considered better, compared to the poorest district on the edge of town (42 points).[25] However, acquiring so many points remained beyond the reach of most migrants.

25 'The 2016 List of Migrant Workers Obtaining Zhuhai City's *Hukou* Based on the Points System Is Released!' (2016 年珠海市异地务工人员积分制入户人员名单出炉!), 25 October 2016, www.sohu.com/a/117152818_401403.

Between 2012 and 2015, the Dongguan municipality allotted annually between 20,200 and 28,300 places in local state schools for the 700,000 migrant children of school age (Guo and Liang 2017, 781). In other words, despite a slight increase over the period, the number of places in these schools remained clearly insufficient. Therefore, most migrant children in Dongguan remained enrolled in private schools. If we follow official figures, Dongguan is an exception, as, at the national level, 70 to 80 per cent of children of migrant workers were enrolled in local state schools during that time period (Friedman 2018).[26] However, as Friedman notes, these children had to win the *privilege* of being enrolled in such schools. Also, as cities only provided places to migrant workers' children for compulsory schooling years, to pursue secondary education they had to enrol in private schools or return to the countryside.

This system has made the *hukou* system more flexible while retaining its main features. First, it is a population management tool enabling the state to maintain its control over migrants by making the respect of their obligations a condition of their rights: for example, by registering with the police;[27] paying taxes, social contributions and debts; and conforming socially and becoming sedentary.[28] Second, this population management tool is intended to serve urban economic development strategies. As a means of selecting migrants, it is similar to systems put in place in Western countries regarding the nationalisation of foreign economic migrants (Zhang 2012). It allows the most prosperous cities in the country to further reinforce their competitiveness by selecting the human resources required to advance their position in the national, and international, economic race. Like the *hukou* under Mao, the points-record system favours a selected elite expected to carry urban economic development forward.

26 Zhang Ning, 'More than 80% of Migrant Workers' Children Who Moved with Them Attend Public Schools in the Importing Areas' (超过八成农民工随迁子女就读输入地公办学校), *People's Daily*, 21 February 2014, acftu.people.com.cn/n/2014/0221/c67502-24426047.html.

27 The condition for access to the points-record system is registration with the police to obtain a residence permit. The shortfall in registration of migrants remains a problem for the state. According to a national survey conducted in 2017, 66.4 per cent of migrant workers had a resident permit (Nie and Xia 2021, 92).

28 Any interruption in residence or in social security contributions for a period of three consecutive months entails exclusion from the local social security system and from the competition to obtain an urban *hukou*.

Although many cities with a population of 1–3 million have now abolished the points-record system,[29] the procedure to access public services remains the same. These services are divided into non-exclusive public services (*feipaitaxing gonggong fuwu* 非排他性公共服务) open to all, such as certain health care services (i.e. vaccination), culture or sport; and exclusive public services (*paitaxing gongong fuwu* 排他性公共服务) that remain conditional, such as education, accommodation, aid for starting businesses and services for the disabled.[30] As far as access to education is concerned, municipalities or employers pre-empt places in the local state schools for the children of 'workers coming from outside' (*wailai wugongrenyuan* 外来务工人员) whom they hope to attract. The remaining places are allocated to children whose parents satisfy certain criteria in terms of length of residence, employment and social security contributions (Wu and Li 2016). As outlined by Friedman (2018, 503), 'migrants are granted access to local citizenship and public education for their children if they can fulfil a specific, state-determined, need in the labour market'. Also, the available public housing rarely fits the needs of migrant workers, as they are often situated in areas on the edge of town, far from the migrants' workplace and the dormitories do not provide any privacy for families (Lou 2020). The unsuitability of the public services offered to migrants was also underlined in several studies addressing professional training (Guo and Liang 2017; Shi, Fang and Gao 2021).

The abolition of the points-record system does not imply greater access to public services for migrants. According to a 2018 study across 86 prefectural and provincial capitals, even if 82.42 per cent of public services were (theoretically) available for the migrant population, 45 per cent of rural migrants could not satisfy the conditions of access established by the municipalities and would, therefore, be excluded. This percentage rises to 55.85 per cent in one-quarter of these 86 cities where conditions were most strict. Also, judging from their GDP, the cities that have the greatest capacity to provide public services, and that also attract the greatest number of migrants, are those that provide the least (Qian and Song 2020). Thus, in the most dynamic cities in the country, migrants are still mostly considered necessary contributors to economic development without having the right to reap the benefices of growth. In these cities, far from promoting more

29 However, it remains in place in the biggest cities such as Beijing, Shanghai, Guangzhou, Shenzhen, Tianjin, Suzhou, Hangzhou, Wuhan and Chengdu.

30 'Thirteenth Five-Year Plan for Promoting the Equalisation of Basic Public Services' (十三五"推进基本公共服务均等化规划), State Council, 2017, www.gov.cn/zhengce/content/2017-03/01/content_5172013.htm.

justice and equity, reforms have contributed to the maintenance of a reserve of cheap labour for the urban economy, because the migrant labour force remains disenfranchised.

Conclusion

Throughout the history of the PRC, the maintenance and the adaption of the *hukou*, including reforms that modified and extended it, such as the points-record system, has played a crucial role in the modernisation of China. This system has allowed the CCP to control, plan and balance the urbanisation process by favouring the development of small towns and gradually promoting the urbanisation of larger cities, while keeping strict control of growth in the biggest cities. The *hukou* has constantly underpinned the economic development of the country, while allowing the state to limit spending. Development was built on the exploitation of peasants during the Mao era, and then on migrant workers in the reform period. At present, while the points-record system enables the most dynamic cities to attract, select and settle the migrants that suit their economic development strategy, and to regulate access to public services as they develop, the poorest, least educated and most mobile migrants continue to represent a cheap labour force in these same urban areas, where they are deprived of rights.

These reforms have not been implemented in a spirit of equity and social justice but of pragmatism and utilitarianism. To the extent that the state considers its resources limited, it has always sought to limit expenditure and to favour certain citizens, at present the affluent and competent because they contribute to the creation of wealth. These reforms, therefore, highlight the eligibility of migrant workers rather than their rights. Accommodation, employment and social security are not considered to be rights but rather the conditions of access to public services and, ultimately, to urban status that continues to favour a socioeconomic elite. Access to public services represents an award given by municipalities to individuals corresponding to their selection criteria. In the largest and most dynamic cities in the country, the extent and quality of the services are then proportional to the value of the beneficiary in the eyes of the local government. In this sense, the reforms re-established the logic of a functionalist social citizenship, whereby the advantages that individuals may enjoy depend on their contribution to urban economic development. Favouring the interests of the state over the rights of the individual, these reforms re-establish the principle of stratified social citizenship. At present, this stratification is both the product of the differences in status inherited from the Mao era (the native urban population continuing to be favoured over urban residents recently arrived from the countryside) and of socioeconomic inequalities that state policies reinforce rather than seek to correct.

In the end, these reforms do not challenge the principle of a local social citizenship. In urban areas, the amount of social insurance benefits and the quality of the care provided are conditioned by the place of residence registration. Moreover, the fact that migrant settlement policies are implemented at a local level and do not imply the transfer of entitlements constitutes a hindrance to individual mobility. As entitlements remain attached to the place of residence and not to individuals, migration always implies the loss of entitlements. Finally, the *hukou* remains a powerful tool for social control; apart from enabling the state to compel Chinese citizens to settle and migrants to register with the police, it also encourages them to socially conform by rewarding respect of the law and family planning rules, civic responsibility (paying taxes, joining in charity work, etc.), property ownership, education and qualifications. In other words, the logic of *hukou* attribution means that social citizenship is reserved for exemplary citizens.

The dynamic for access to social citizenship implemented by the CCP followed an inverse logic to that presiding over the creation of the welfare state. Based on the recognition of the intrinsic value of the individual, the final aim of the welfare state is, in theory, to guarantee the dignity of all members of a given society – that is, to ensure a modicum of economic welfare and security for all citizens according to the level of development of the society in which they are living (Marshall 1981). Integration proceeds from the base to the summit of the social pyramid: social policies apply first to the poorest and least educated. The state guarantees a level of equality – or a universal minimum – beyond which inequalities can develop. In China, conditional and elitist access to the urban *hukou* creates a quasi-Darwinian competition between individuals. Social inclusion proceeds from the top to the bottom of the social pyramid, the state reaching out to the most affluent according to a particularistic logic and creating exceptional statuses by granting privileges and excluding the poorest and the least educated. In this, far from correcting the existing inequalities, the action of the state contributes to their increase, thus enabling the creation of social classes.

It is true that these reforms have helped to improve the wellbeing of part of the population. In the cities, they tend to reduce the divide between urban *hukou* holders and long-term residents. But polarisation remains strong between those who have and have not been granted a residence permit. It is certain that migrants from the countryside in central and western China who have worked for years in the cities enjoy an improved standard of living when they are granted a *hukou* in a small or medium-sized city in an interior province. But those who still work in the 14 metropolises, where the conditions for access to public services and to the urban *hukou* remain most strict, have not seen substantial improvement in their daily life. The Party's promise is that, in the end, these inequalities can be levelled and that all Chinese will have access to prosperity, which will then be common to all. The sacrifice of the peasants and the migrants throughout the history of the PRC will then be justified. Yet, the practical challenges are considerable: improvements in the offer and the quality of public services; greater suitability of these services to needs; and harmonisation of the different urban social insurance systems, including between urban and rural settings. Beyond this, it is certain that the overwhelming challenge for the Party is to consider that rights are inherent to the individual, and not attached to particular qualities.

References

Chan, Alexsia and Kevin J. O'Brien. 2019. 'Phantom Services: Deflecting Migrant Workers in China'. *China Journal* 81: 103–22. doi.org/10.1086/699215.

Chan, Anita. 2003. 'A "Race to the Bottom": Globalization and China Labour Standards'. *China Perspectives* 46: 41–9. doi.org/10.4000/chinaperspectives.259.

Chan, Chris King-Chi, Pun Ngai and Jenny Chan. 2010. 'The Role of the State, Labour Policy and Migrant Workers' Struggles in Globalized China'. *Global Labor Journal* 1 (1): 132–51. doi.org/10.15173/glj.v1i1.1068.

Chan, Kam Wing. 1994. *Cities with Invisible Walls: Reinterpreting Urbanization in Post-1949 China.* Hong Kong: Oxford University Press.

Chan, Kam Wing and Li Zhang. 1999. 'The Hukou System and Rural–Urban Migration: Processes and Changes'. *China Quarterly* 160: 818–55. doi.org/10.1017/S0305741000001351.

Chan, Kam Wing and Will Buckingham. 2008. 'Is China Abolishing the Hukou System?' *China Quarterly* 195: 582–606. doi.org/10.1017/S0305741008000787.

Cheng, Jiejun. 1991. 'Dialectics of Control – The Household Registration (Hukou) System in Contemporary China'. PhD thesis, New York State University at Binghamton.

Cheng, Jietun and Mark Selden. 1994. 'The Origins and Social Consequences of China's Hukou System'. *China Quarterly* 139: 644–68. doi.org/10.1017/S0305741000043083.

Davin, Delia. 1999. *Internal Migration in Contemporary China*. New York: Saint Martin's Press. doi.org/10.1057/9780230376717.

Dutton, Michael. 1992. *Policing and Punishment in China: From Patriarchy to 'the People'*. Cambridge: Cambridge University Press.

Friedman, Eli. 2018. 'Just-in-Time Urbanization? Managing Migration, Citizenship and Schooling in the Chinese City'. *Critical Sociology* 44 (3): 503–18. doi.org/10.1177/0896920517695867.

Froissart, Chloé. 2008. 'Le système du *hukou*: pilier de la croissance chinoise et du maintien du PCC au pouvoir'. *Etudes du CERI*, no.149, Fondation nationale des sciences politiques.

Froissart, Chloé. 2013. *La Chine et ses migrants. La conquête d'une citoyenneté.* Rennes: Presses universitaires de Rennes. doi.org/10.4000/books.pur.71547.

Guo, Zhonghua and Liang Tuo. 2017. 'Differentiating Citizenship in Urban China: A Case Study of Dongguan City'. *Citizenship Studies* 21 (7): 773–91. doi.org/10.1080/13621025.2017.1353744.

Hayward, Jane. 2022. 'Reorganising Chinese Labour: The Establishment of the Household Registration System'. In *Proletarian China: A Century of Chinese Labour*, edited by Ivan Franceschini and Christian Sorace. London and New York: Verso Books.

He, Baochuan. 2007. 'La crise agraire en Chine: Données et réflexions'. *Etudes rurales* 179. doi.org/10.4000/etudesrurales.8453.

Kuruvilla, Sarosh, Ching Kwan Lee and Mary E. Gallagher. 2011. *From Iron Rice Bowl to Informalization: Markets, Workers and the State in a Changing China*. Ithaca: Cornell University Press. doi.org/10.7591/cornell/9780801450242.001.0001.

Lin, Chun. 2015. 'The Language of Class in China'. *Socialist Register* 51: 24–53.

Losavio, Cinzia. 2019. 'Building Wealth through a Stratified Inclusion: The Point-Based Hukou System in Zhuhai'. In *Pathways of Sustainable Urban Development across China*, edited by Natacha Aveline, 109–21. Imago Editor.

Lou, Wenlong (娄文龙). 2020. 'Study on the Institutional Dilemma of Migrant Worker Housing in China' (我国农民工住房的制度化捆紧研究). *Reform of Economic System* 1: 88–94.

Mao, Tse-tung (Mao Zedong). 1955. 'On the Co-operative Transformation of Agriculture'. *Selected Works of Mao Tse-tung*. www.marxists.org/reference/archive/mao/selected-works/volume-5/mswv5_44.htm.

Marshall, Thomas H. 1981. *Citizenship and Social Class and Other Essays*. London: Heinemann.

Meng, Fanqiang (孟凡强). 2021. 'Household Registration Discrimination and Generational Differences between Migrant Workers Participating in Basic Medical Insurance for Urban Workers' (户籍歧视与农民工参保职工基本医疗保险的差异). *Guangdong Social Sciences* 3: 35–43.

Müller, Armin. 2016. 'Hukou and Health Insurance Coverage for Migrant Workers'. *Journal of Current Chinese Affairs* 45 (2): 53–82. doi.org/10.1177/186810261604500203.

Nie, Wei (聂伟), Xia Zhike (贾志科). 2021. 'Transition or Substitution: The Impact of Residence Permits on the Willingness of Migrant Workers to Settle in Urban Areas' (过渡抑或替代: 居住证对农民工城镇落户意愿的影响). *Journal of Nantong University Social Science Edition* 37 (3): 89–99.

Pieke, Frank and Hein Mallee. 1999. *Internal and International Migration: Chinese Perspectives.* Surrey: Curzon.

Potter, Sulamith Heins. 1983. 'The Position of Peasants in Modern China's Social Order'. *Modern China* 9 (4): 465–99. doi.org/10.1177/009770048300900404.

Qian, Xueya (钱雪亚), Hu Qiong (胡琼) and Su Dongran (苏东冉). 2017. Observation on Access to Public Services, Residence Permit Points and Urbanisation of Migrant Workers' (公共服务享有、居住证积分与农民工市民化观察), *China's Economic Studies* 5: 47–57.

Qian, Xueya (钱雪亚) and Song Wenjuan (宋文娟). 2020. 'Study on the Measurement of the Openness of Urban Basic Public Services to Migrant Workers' (城市基本公共服务面向农民工开放度测量研究). *Statistical Research* 3: 33–47.

Shi, Xinjie (史新杰), Fang Shile (方师乐) and Gao Xuwen (高叙文). 2021. 'Preliminary Education, Vocational Training and Migrant Workers' Income' (基础教育、职业培训与农民工外出收入). *Journal of Finance and Economics* 47 (1): 153–68.

Solinger, Dorothy J. 1999. *Contesting Citizenship in Urban China: Peasant Migrants, the State, and the Logic of the Market*. Berkeley: University of California Press.

State Council Research Group (国务院研究室课题组). 2006. Chinese Migrant Workers Survey Report (中国农民工调研研究报道). Beijing: China Yanshi Press.

Trolliet, Pierre and Jean-Philippe Béja. 1986. *L'empire du milliard: populations et société en Chine*. Paris: Armand Collin.

Walder, Andrew G. 1986. *Communist Neo-Traditionalism Work and Authority in Chinese Industry*. Berkeley: University of California Press.

Wang, Fei-Ling. 2005. *Organizing through Division and Exclusion: China's Hukou System*. Stanford: Stanford University Press. doi.org/10.1515/9780804767484.

Wang, Feng. 1997. 'The Breakdown of the Great Wall: Recent Changes in the Household Registration System in China'. In *Floating Population and Migration in China: The Impact of Economic Reforms*, edited by Thomas Scharping. Hamburg: Institut für Asienkunde.

Wu, Jieh-min. 2017. 'Migrant Citizenship Regimes in Globalized China: A Historical-Institutional Comparison'. *Rural China: An International Journal of History and Social Science* 14: 128–54.

Wu, Ling. 2013. 'Decentralization and Hukou Reforms in China'. *Policy and Society* 32: 33–42. doi.org/10.1016/j.polsoc.2013.01.002.

Wu, Zhihui and Li Jingmei (邬志辉, 李静美). 2016. 'The Realistic Dilemma and Policy Choices of Children of Migrant Workers Receiving Education in Cities' (农民工随迁子女在城市接受教育的现实困境与政策选择). *Educational Research* 9: 19–31.

Zhang, Li. 2001. *Strangers in the City: Reconfigurations of Space, Power, and Social Networks within China's Floating Population*. Standford: Stanford University Press.

Zhang, Li. 2012. 'Economic Migration and Urban Citizenship in China: The Role of Points System'. *Population and Development Review* 38 (3): 503–33. doi.org/10.1111/j.1728-4457.2012.00514.x.

Zhang, Youyun, Ma Chunhua and Huang Ping. 1998. 'The Change of Regulations on Rural–Urban Migration in China'. In *Migration and Citizenship in the Asia Pacific: Legal Issues*, edited by Patrick Brownlee. Wollongong: APMRN Secretariat.

11

Capitalist Agrarian Change and the End of the Revolutionary Peasant Dialectic: Chinese Communist Party Rural Policies in Long-Term Perspective

Alexander F. Day

Introduction

Peasant incomes have risen considerably in Meitan County, Guizhou, since the late 1990s. The county government has promoted tea production for almost 20 years now, turning the county into one of China's top producers. In the process, many peasants have become commercial and entrepreneurial farmers, or have transferred their land to them through specialised cooperatives. The county now boasts more than 500 tea enterprises, mostly processers formed with local capital that contract with farmers for tea leaves, grow them on land they lease or buy them on the spot market. Rising incomes have led local producers to lease land in neighbouring counties to grow even more tea, and in turn peasants from those counties have begun to pick tea leaves as itinerant agricultural labourers in Meitan – class divisions somewhat aligning with administrative borders. The county has even published a book about how good it is to come to work as a 'peasant' labourer in Meitan.[1] Class differentiation, land markets, new spatial arrangements, poverty relief, new forms of cooperatives, agrobusiness and modern capitalist farming: these linked processes are transforming the Chinese Communist Party's (CCPs) relationship to the peasantry, and perhaps bringing about the end of the category itself.

This chapter puts contemporary rural policy into the long-term perspective of the Party's shifting relationship to the peasantry. The Party has always aimed to maintain and improve the livelihood of the peasantry through the transformation of rural society, ending debilitating poverty, usury, high rents and rural corruption while breaking it from feudal social relations. Yet, at the same time, the Party also intended to push China towards socialism, necessitating a release and development of the rural productive forces and their integration into wider, national developments. These changes in the structure of the People's Republic of China's (PRC) political economy meant that the social form of the peasantry – the particular social forms through which rural residents produced and reproduced themselves – had to be understood historically, and, more specifically, as a historically limited category. After the CCP came to rule in 1949, and as agriculture came to be structurally linked to national development though the institutionalisation of a rural–urban divide, the broader goals of political economy came to dominate the narrower goal of advancing peasant livelihoods, with rural residents having little power to challenge that dominance. Thus, this chapter questions the idea that there has been an enduring alliance between the Party and a sociological category of peasants.

While I develop the changing meaning of the category 'revolutionary peasant dialectic' throughout the chapter, it is important to note from the outset that there was neither a stable meaning for the category 'peasant' nor a simple or stable relationship between the Party and the peasantry as its social basis. Most basically, by 'dialectic' I am pointing to the historical movement and transformation of social classes and categories in relation to the changing political economy of production and social reproduction. How 'the peasantry' reacted to the rapid revolutionary social and political changes that China was undergoing in the twentieth century was complex because the category contained multiple unstable classes with differing social and political tendencies. 'The peasant', therefore, was always a contingent

1 The author is currently working on a history of tea production in Meitan County from the 1930s to the present. See Schneider (2021) and Day (2022).

political category. Instead of an enduring alliance with a social basis, from the beginning, Party politics and policy had to mediate the relationship between the Party's revolutionary and developmental goals on the one hand, and the complex social tendencies contained within the category of the peasantry on the other.

This chapter breaks the century-long relationship between the Party and the peasantry into four periods. In the first, the period of the civil war, the Party was forced into the countryside and developed a dialectical and revolutionary understanding of peasant tendencies, with an understanding that concrete analysis of peasant classes was crucial to the Party's victory against the Nationalists.

In the second, the socialist period of 1949 through to the 1970s, Party rural policy was guided by an understanding of the interaction between the overall political economy and the dialectical tendencies of agricultural producers. Thus, while the long-term historical goal of the Party was the transformation of China into a socialist industrial nation, attention always had to be paid to how various peasant classes reacted to rural policies that promoted the development along that historical line. Those reactions not only affected the rural legitimacy of the Party, clearly very important to the leadership, but also the development of the agrarian productive forces. Managing the Party's important relationship to rural dwellers meant analysis of potentially dangerous peasant tendencies that could block further progressive development. Collectivisation was to push rural society towards modern, scaled-up agriculture while it facilitated surplus extraction, though tensions rose as the Party often misread or ignored peasant interests in the process.

In the post-socialist reform period from the late 1970s, both the historical vision of the Party (Dirlik 1989) and its understanding of the peasant were transformed. For one, after 20-plus years of industrialisation, economic development was less reliant on rural surplus than in the past. Further, within the context of China's changing relationship to the world – a post-socialist relinking to global capitalism – the focus of China's political economy was shifting in two senses. First, there was a shift from increasing absolute production towards relative productivity, meaning greater attention to technological change and efficiency, under the rubric of the Four Modernisations. Second, attention to the development of the productive forces came to dominate the Party's vision, and the goal of a revolutionary transformation of social relations was shunted so far into the future that it receded beyond the horizon. With peasant developments playing a lesser role, agricultural production was returned to household management, and land, still owned by the village collective, was contracted to peasant families. This institutional compromise put agricultural modernisation on hold and restrained class differentiation while the Party focused on the technological development and expansion of the industrial economy along with its new connections to global capitalism. Throughout this period, the Party shifted its attention to a new, urban population for its legitimacy, and inequality between urban and rural residents grew through the 1990s.

From the perspective of rural China, this reform period is now over. In the post-reform period, beginning around 2008, the Party has renewed its focus on agricultural modernisation, but without any vision of a revolutionary transformation of social relations; rather, contemporary modernisation entails capitalist agrarian change, with class differentiation seen as playing a positive role in agricultural development. New rural institutions of capitalist agrarian change (land transfer with three-level property rights, specialised cooperatives, dragonhead agribusiness firms and more integrated value chains) together with urbanisation, a realignment of food security and the elimination of extreme rural poverty characterise this period. More rapid disintegration of the rural population into various classes means that, after almost a century of interaction with the peasantry, the Party is now bringing about its end as a pivotal political and sociological category.

Civil War

Li Dazhao and Chen Duxiu, the two main founders of the CCP, viewed the end of rural poverty, suffering and unequal landholdings as important goals of the Party; however, they had contrasting understandings of the peasantry. Li was more a populist, viewing the peasantry as a singular if distressed class, in need of organisation by China's progressive youth but potentially a powerful force. Not only that, Li tied the goals of the Party to the liberation of the peasantry: 'If they are not liberated, then our whole nation will not be liberated; their sufferings are the sufferings of our whole nation' (Meisner 1974, 81). Chen had a much more pessimistic view of the peasantry as backwards, feudal and petty bourgeois in class character, sustaining a consciousness that could not lead in a progressive, revolutionary direction. Chen was clear that 'the communist movement must rely on factory workers as its main force', asking: 'How can the communist movement become a mass movement in the owner-cultivator dominated Chinese countryside?' (Huang 1975, 279). Chen's view was dominant in the intellectual ferment of the May Fourth Movement, out of which the Party was formed.

But, thrown into the countryside in the late 1920s, the Party that Li and Chen had formed began to bring these two images of the peasant together in a new dialectical understanding of history (Huang 1975; Day 2013, 20). Mao's 1927 'Hunan Report' seemed to take Li's populism even further, arguing for the potential of spontaneous peasant revolt. Yet, conversely, Mao cautioned that the peasantry was not a singular class, but riven with class differences, and only deep investigations into the tendencies of peasant classes would allow the Party to understand how to mould sections of them into a revolutionary force. Peasants were neither spontaneously revolutionary nor inherently conservative; rather, peasant classes contained multiple tendencies that had to be analysed and carefully managed. Crucial were the middle peasants, who had a 'vacillating attitude', according to Mao, potentially going either way in support of the revolution or not, depending on many factors (Mao 1965a, 31). This was the 'dialectic of rural revolution', as Philip Huang has called it (Huang 1975, 292).

Over time, the Party came to see the complex tendencies of the peasant as crucial to revolutionary success and survival. Peasants exhibited a 'dual nature' (*liangchong xing* 两重性) (Kelliher 1994, 390); there was both a tendency towards rebellious activity and a conservative tendency towards petty-bourgeois protection of individual landholdings. For the revolutionary Party, the goal was to accentuate and direct the former into a powerful force while minimising the latter, which could dangerously lead towards class differentiation and block further socialist development. Thus, in 1937, Mao noted that peasants were the 'real motive force of historical development in Chinese feudal society', but that they could not transform rebellion into revolutionary change without the leadership of the proletariat and the CCP (Mao 1965b, 308–9). They were a force that needed directing, as they exhibited dual tendencies: rebellion against feudalism but without fomenting new relations or forces of production that could replace it. Thus, Mao (1965b, 324) declared:

> Only under the leadership of the proletariat can the poor and middle peasants achieve their liberation, and only by forming a firm alliance with the poor and middle peasants can the proletariat lead the revolution to victory.

Incorrectly analysing the dual nature of the peasantry during the revolution led to many policy mistakes, from which the Party had to backtrack. This was often a matter of the Party moving too fast, without attention to the interests of particular classes of peasants, especially the crucial middle peasants. For example, as both land reform and marriage reform moved into a more radical phase in the CCP base area of Jinggangshan at the end of the 1920s, it ran into trouble, leading to serious setbacks, as members of the lower-level local elite and intermediate classes resisted changes (Averill 1987; Huang 1975). In the Chinese Soviet Republic of the early 1930s, overly radical policies led to a 'class coalition [that] effectively excluded most of rural society' (Opper 2018, 45). A similar but more expansive story could be told of radical land reform in the years after the end of World War II but before 1949 (DeMare 2019, 12–18). More generally, as Qi Xiaolin (2015) has shown, peasants joined the CCP in the civil war for complex reasons, beyond class and nationalist logics, often just looking for better material conditions or seeing the army as a way to move up in status.

Socialist Period

Land reform, completed by the spring of 1953, was a first step in breaking the chains of rural poverty, and it was the most important process for building the Party's popularity and legitimacy with the peasantry. A crucial goal for the Party, therefore, was that peasant livelihoods not be negatively affected by the transformation of rural society (Shue 1980, 146). Further, from the Party's historical view, breaking feudal social relations would free up rural productive forces, allowing for an initial expansion of agricultural production. But the Party had always argued that land reform and the agrarian revolution should not be confused with a socialist revolution (Mao 1965b, 330). Land reform also created dangers for the Party, potentially reproducing a petty-bourgeois peasantry with an interest in maintaining their newly won economic positions as landholders. Such a peasantry could either form a block to socialist development – with the revolution stalling at a transitional stage – or, as economic differences re-emerged, produce the sprouts of a new rural capitalism. But there were twin dangers: the absolute egalitarianism of 'agrarian socialism', which would be a block to modernisation and economic advancement; and class differentiation, which would block the development of collectivisation.

In the early 1950s, the small peasant economy (*xiaonong jingji* 小农经济) was not simply judged along the lines of its effect on rural society and peasant livelihoods. More important still was the relationship between agriculture and the overall political economy of socialist development – the Party's developmental goals of extraction and agricultural modernisation – for agriculture was the only significant source of surplus to fuel the industrialisation process (Walker 1966, 2–4). How to mobilise the productive powers of the peasantry without the short-term, individual interests of peasants interfering with the long-term goal of industrialisation was a key problem for the Party. Some form of collectivisation was seen as a solution to these problems (Shue 1980; Teiwes and Sun 1993, 8; Walker 1966). Party leaders agreed on the long-term goal of agricultural modernisation, meaning the scale-up and eventual mechanisation of agricultural production and, therefore, also the end of the small peasant economy (Walker 1966) – implying the end of the peasant.

Gaining access to rural surplus would not be easy, however. At the time it commenced with its First Five-Year Plan (FYP), the Soviet Union had far larger per capita agricultural production than the PRC did as it began its First FYP (Tang 1967; see also Ash 2006). Despite 300 million peasants receiving over 40 per cent of total arable land during land reform (Ye 2015, 316), in China there simply was not enough land per capita, no matter how equally it was distributed, to create prosperous farming households (Hou 2016, 10–11). This placed a real material limit on industrialisation for the new Chinese state, as the rural surplus available to it was much smaller, and this further meant that the PRC had an even greater need to develop agriculture as it extracted surplus. In other words, it was not good enough to just take control over as large a surplus as possible, the overall production of agriculture had to be increased. By the early 1940s, it was clear to Mao that the development of agricultural production would rely on 'getting the peasants organised' (quoted in Hou 2016, 53).

These three goals – sustaining peasant livelihoods, extraction and development – thus implied a fourth: the revolutionary transformation of rural social relations. While a value in and of itself, how this fourth goal was related to the others – and the tension between them – was a key political question for the CCP, and one around which many disagreements formed. It was mainly a question of temporality: How fast should rural society be collectivised? How much would peasants have to sacrifice in current improvements for future gains, and how far off were those future gains?

Looking ahead, one long-term reading of these questions might suggest that peasant sacrifices never led to the imagined future gains, as the nation forgot its early promises as it returned to global capitalism.

Whatever one's political stance on these questions, peasant labour had to be mobilised, and peasant consciousness could make or break the developmental process. While a narrow focus on individual interests was seen as a conservative barrier to the Party's developmental goals, after 1949, the Party had to worry both about pushing the peasantry too fast towards socialism, leading to flagging incentives for production, and about allowing class differentiation and attendant social instability to re-emerge if socialist progress proved too weak. How to keep peasants producing as the state extracted heavily from the rural economy, while at the same time not allowing class differences to re-emerge, was a complex political question, and one that deeply shaped the Party's relationship to the peasantry. The 1953 introduction of the unified purchasing and sale system, creating a state monopoly on grain marketing, led to forms of peasant resistance to the extraction of grain, including the hiding of surpluses, attacks on cadre and manipulation of household classification (Wemheuer 2019, 105–6). Political campaigns, class labels and shifting remuneration policies were all attempts to mediate this tension, as were the use of supply and marketing and credit cooperatives, which were designed to help align peasant interests with collectivisation (Shue 1980, 275–8).

The factional mapping of political disagreements over rural policy has probably been overdrawn and overdetermined by the fractures of the late 1960s (Teiwes and Sun 1993, 1999). However, political disagreements did continually emerge during the socialist period. In 1950, for example, Gao Gang, Party secretary of the Northeast Bureau, had argued for rapid collectivisation, but Liu Shaoqi disagreed, arguing that conditions were not ripe and that gains made by the private agricultural economy should be consolidated first. Mechanisation was needed before collective farming (Hou 2016, 80; Bo 1991, 207). Here, Liu was following the then accepted Party theory of 'New Democracy', in which freedoms for the petty-bourgeois economy would be allowed for a period of time, though it was to remain somewhat 'restricted'. New Democracy implied that the Party had more to fear from 'agrarian socialism', a historical dead-end in which peasant egalitarian consciousness would infect collectivisation, blocking agricultural modernisation (Day 2013, 22). In this period, in other words, some differences between peasant households should be tolerated; egalitarianism was a greater danger than class differentiation. But, at the time, Mao had begun to shift away from this view. A new dispute involving Liu happened the next year. In response to the decline of mutual aid teams in some areas of rural Shanxi, the province sent a report to the North China Bureau, stating that, as land reform had allowed peasants to improve their livelihoods, some more well-off peasants were pushing not 'in the direction of modernisation and collectivisation that we demand, but in the direction of a rich peasantry' (quoted in Kuhn 2002, 104). The province argued that a greater push in the direction of mutual aid teams and collectivisation was needed. However, the North China Bureau and Liu disagreed, maintaining that class differentiation was less of a problem than excessive egalitarianism. Mao sided against Liu in this case, creating a greater space for collectivisation (Day 2013, 23–4; Hou 2016, 107–13).

Collectivisation was made a featured aspect of the Party's General Line in 1953, and, despite earlier disagreements, a Party consensus was developing that the collectivisation of agriculture before mechanisation was both possible and could aid the development of agriculture, although at a measured pace (Teiwes and Sun 1993, 8; Walker 1966). Amid rising tensions, peasant fears of the end of private ownership led to animal slaughter and other activities disruptive of agricultural production (Walker 1966, 20–1). Conversely, the agricultural sector was falling behind in its contribution to industrialisation during the First FYP (Walker 1966, 26–8; Shue 1980, 278–82). After a period of consolidation, the formation of agricultural producers' cooperatives accelerated from the summer of 1955 with higher-stage agricultural producers' cooperatives following in 1956 – a 'high tide' of collectivisation pushed forward by Mao. This high tide was followed by another period of consolidation and 'opposing rash advances' (*fan maojin* 反冒进) from 1956 to 1957, and then another, even greater, acceleration in the Great Leap Forward (GLF) (Teiwes and Sun 1999, ch. 1).

The GLF combined the rapid collectivisation of rural social and productive life into communes, a decentralisation of planning and industrialisation, and an expansion of extraction from the agricultural sector. It expressed a belief that peasant consciousness had been transformed, and the Party no longer had to fear backlash from a conservative peasantry; rather, according to Mao, it was the Party that had been acting more conservatively than the peasantry. The rapid collectivisation of 1955–56 proved that. As household reproduction, not just the household organisation of production, was collectivised, the rural family form itself was called into question. The socialisation of social reproduction, not just of production, briefly became the communist horizon (Day 2021). But this occurred just as extraction rose far beyond its sustainable material limits, and the socialisation of social reproduction was reduced to yet another form of self-reliant mobilisation of rural resources, of sacrifice for the greater good of socialism. Far from ending the peasant through the transformation of rural collectives – responsible for their own profits and losses, and built through self-reliance – into 'communist communes' (Teiwes and Sun 1999, 95) or state farms 'owned by the whole people', and far from ending the gendered division of labour through the socialisation of social reproduction, both social forms continued in often hidden forms as yet more sacrifice to the future (Hershatter 2011; Eyferth 2015, 134).

As is well known, the GLF and the collective system collapsed, taking a horrific human toll. The rural legitimacy of the Party was severely damaged, and peasants went their own way to survive, suspicious of collective approaches. Yet, as Felix Wemheuer (2019, 147) argues, 'neither the CCP nor Mao seem to have suffered terminal reputational damage even in rural areas'. In the short term, the supply system was rebalanced, and the famine subsided (Wemheuer 2019, 164). The more rapid urbanisation of the GLF period was reversed, with more than 20 million people moved back into the countryside in the early 1960s, and a firmer boundary between the rural and urban spheres constructed (Brown 2012, 79). In the early 1960s, a new 'workable system' (Unger 2002, 9) was built through political compromise, based on three levels of collective organisation: commune, brigade and production team. While Party centre documents formally discuss the devolution of power from the commune down to the brigade, then quickly amending the structure to place power at the level of the production team, the reality was that rural collective structures were being rebuilt from the ground up. The historical trajectory remained an evolution of power moving up to the brigade, as discussions in the late 1970s show (Teiwes and Sun 2016, 30–6), but now much more gradual than envisioned in the late 1950s, and ultimately the trend shifted in the other direction.

While this workable structure was a political compromise, now leaning towards a stress on incentives for production, the fear of class differentiation did not disappear. Rather than playing a central role in structuring the revolutionary transformation of rural social relations, however, that fear was, for a period, mainly relegated to the sphere of propaganda and political campaign. Mao, in particular, feared that as some did better and others worse, class differentiation and 'spontaneous capitalist tendencies' would re-emerge, and more well-off peasants would 'go it alone' (Baum 1975, 12). The conservative tendency of petty-bourgeois peasants would block collectivisation. Mao pushed for a 'bottom line', with limits on how far experiments with household responsibility systems could go (Wemheuer 2019, 179). At the same time, class differentiation led to the emergence of a rural constituency against household contracting (Unger 2002, 76). Nonetheless, in some rural areas, black markets emerged and private grain traders increased, as did other forms of peasant illegal activity for survival (Wemheuer 2019, 180, 189). The slower collectivisation of this new rural structure, and the problems that it engendered, needed a political complement: the Socialist Education Movement, which began in autumn 1962. It was difficult in this movement to know:

> where to draw the line between the legitimate (small-scale) private commercial undertakings of individual peasants and illegal speculation and profiteering by peasants with serious spontaneous capitalist tendencies; and how to classify, analyse, and deal with erroneous tendencies on the Party of members of various class strata in the countryside. (Baum 1975, 48)

In the early 1960s, at a moment of economic rebuilding in the wake of the GLF, most members of the Party leaned towards more liberal interpretations, in which the vast majority of peasants were to be seen as part of the productive forces, and to be educated but protected as such (Baum 1975, 49). As in the revolution, a class analysis of peasant tendencies, specifically focusing on the middle peasants, was vital. Care needed to be taken to make sure middle peasants were not 'pushed over to the side of the landlords and rich peasants' (Baum 1975, 51). During this period, however, as 'peasants learned the hard way that they could not rely on the state to survive', 'the state's ability to mobilize peasants for political campaigns of any kind seems to have been diminished' (Wemheuer 2019, 184, 186).

Yet, if a more 'liberal' line on peasant tendencies emerged in the early 1960s, this was to change with the Cultural Revolution in the second half of the decade, even if the weight of that movement was more urban than rural (Unger 2002, 51; Baum 1971). As I have argued elsewhere, the peasant dialectic reached a breaking point, in which more static images of the peasant as either a revolutionary carrier of socialism or a conservative class of small property owners contended with each other, and concrete material analysis suffered (Day 2019, 171). Even before the Cultural Revolution had begun in 1966, the developmental gains from the 'workable' collective system in the countryside were pushing against their limits. By the late 1960s, incentivising peasant production without giving producing class differentiation was increasingly difficult to maintain. The Dazhai system of remuneration, which worked by team members judging each other's attitude towards work, was one of the more developed systems. Yet, mutually judging attitudes led to contention between team members and, as Jonathan Unger (2002, 83–5) found in Chen Village, over time, teams moved away from carrying out such evaluations, allowing the system to become a rigid structure that no longer offered much incentive to work harder or better.

Likewise, political motivation largely channelled through the rural class status system did not prove effective. As Unger (2002, 48) puts it:

> The Party had been unable to live up to its economic promises of the collectivisation 'high tide' and Great Leap Forward; throughout the 1960s and 1970s most of the countryside remained impoverished. In lieu of prosperity, the Party could provide the majority of good-class peasants with marginal advantages (both material and nonmaterial) offered by the class line.

In the 1970s, policies increasingly shifted towards investments in mechanisation and farmland capital construction, with a 1975 goal of mechanising 70 per cent of agriculture by 1980 (Teiwes and Sun 2016, 21–3). This included the period of Hua Guofeng's leadership following Mao's death, with a big push towards mechanisation, irrigation and fertilisers; an increase in state investment; changes in agricultural pricing and taxation; and discussions of raising accounting from the team to the brigade level, leading in 1979 to big increases in agricultural production, especially for grain, and rising peasant incomes (Teiwes and Sun 2016, chs 1 and 3, 119 for production increases). But the Party continued to worry that raising the accounting level to the brigade would hurt peasant incentives to produce and the legitimacy of the Party in the countryside; likewise, while the Dazhai system advocated for the end of private plots, the Party cautioned against their removal (Wemheuer 2019, 248).

Reform Period

This big push proved unsustainable, politically if not economically, with the emergence of the reform period. In part to reduce the costs of agricultural modernisation and the state deficit, agriculture was de-collectivised and farming shifted back to household farming in the early 1980s: the 'burden' of agriculture on the state had to be reduced, with sharp decreases in state investment in agriculture in 1980 and 1981 (Teiwes and Sun 2016, 148–53, 203 for investment figures). While experiments in responsibility systems had existed for a long time, the main push towards de-collectivisation, despite narratives to the contrary, came from above (Teiwes and Sun 2016, 282; Unger 2002, 95–106). With an increasing use of markets to make economic decisions, a relinking to global capitalism, and the depoliticised developmentalism of the reform period, the historical dialectic of peasant tendencies was reversed. The petty-bourgeois focus on individual interests, and a degree of class differentiation, came to be seen as progressive, supposedly leading to entrepreneurial dynamism and economic development. Over time, this went even further than the rural developmentalism of early 1950s New Democracy. The individual land ownership of petty-bourgeois peasants was increasingly interpreted positively as a progressive force. Here, the fear of class differentiation largely fades from view, as does the goal of transforming rural social relations. For Wang Xiaoqiang and Bai Nansheng, the reform period was defined by the shift to a commodity economy with a focus on efficiency of production, instead of simple quantitative expansion. In their famous formulation of the time, peasants were differentiated by their 'quality' (*sushi* 素质), indicating 'the quality of engaging in commodity production and management' – the degree, in other words, to which they had an 'entrepreneurial spirit' (quoted in Day 2013, 41). This formulation aligned with a growing general discrimination against peasants, who were considered of 'low quality'; peasants were only to be valued when they broke from their peasantness and took on entrepreneurial qualities through class differentiation. Although Deng Xiaoping thought that class 'polarisation' could be avoided, he commented in 1985 that 'some people will become prosperous first, others later'.[2] Nonetheless, in the early 1980s rural poverty receded, but then rose again in the late 1980s.

After de-collectivisation, land remained owned by the village but contracted to households, with contracts growing in length over time. Thus, while this returned rural production to the household, without the sale of land, class differentiation was limited, effecting a compromise land policy that aimed at social stability, even as greater crop diversification and new rural markets opened a space for greater peasant profits. With this the 1980s saw the emergence of the celebrated 10,000-yuan households (*wanyuanhu* 万元户), with incomes far above the rural average. This de-collectivisation, together with higher prices for agricultural goods, also gave a one-off boost to agricultural production, and it further allowed surplus labour to work

2 'An Interview with Deng Xiaoping', *Time Magazine*, 4 November 1985, content.time.com/time/subscriber/article/0,33009,1050524-1,00.html.

outside of the household in burgeoning local industries (Unger 2002, 112). The rural economy was helped by the rapid expansion of these township and village enterprises (Oi 1999). But the new land system produced a block to the further scale-up of agriculture, with land fragmented into tiny plots worked by household labour, even if the Party continued to envision that future. As Du Runsheng, a key Party leader tied to the policy of the household responsibility system, said in 1983: 'We do not want to maintain petty production forever; we will move on to big modern production' (Xu 2014, 198). The institutional divide between the rural and urban spheres also remained in place, even if the movement of migrant labour into the cities was loosened. Through the early 2000s, the Party continued to use the rural–urban divide as a way to shift urban problems, whether economic, environmental or social, onto the rural population, most notably, the reproductive costs of a cheap manufacturing, assembly and construction workforce. In any case, with the initial boost to agricultural production in the early 1980s and the costs of a scaled-up, modernised agriculture on hold, the state shifted focus to reforming the urban, industrial economy.

The early 1990s was a period of rapid economic growth in the countryside that took on an independent dynamic, driven by rising farmgate prices and the development of rural industries. This period of economic growth again reduced rural poverty, and in the years of urban recession after the suppression of the 1989 protests, the resilience of the rural economy allowed the Party to lean on the peasantry for legitimacy. The question of scaling up agriculture also continued on hold as the Party extended land contracts to 30 years in 1993, even as Deng Xiaoping argued that, in the long run, agricultural modernisation and mechanisation was impossible without scaling up agriculture (Xu 2017). Yet both the rural and urban economies quickly began to overheat, leading to dangerous inflation and retrenchment from the central state (Keidel 2007, 55), which in turn led to a prolonged period of stagnation in the countryside from 1997 into the early 2000s. This period of stagnation made it hard for the state to modernise and scale-up the agricultural economy, as it would mean the loss of land for a large number of farming families and the production of a great deal of inequality, harming the legitimacy and popularity of the Party. In the process, the income differentials between the rural and urban spheres were exacerbated, and many villages came to be hollowed out as more and more rural workers migrated to cities for work (Day and Schneider 2018).

Further, this was a period in which the Party shifted problems of urban unemployment onto the rural sphere. Here we see the key tension within state policy towards the countryside during the reform period; the Party saw the countryside both as a site of potential capital accumulation (i.e. of profits) and as a place onto which the state could push urban social, economic and environmental problems. But it was hard to do both at the same time, and, in the 1990s, the Party leaned towards the latter in its treatment of the rural sphere. During periods of economic or political stress in China, this tension comes to the fore, and the autonomy of the rural sphere – the degree to which it was institutionally insulated from the rest of the economy – was a double-edged sword. In the late 1990s moment of stagnation, agrarian modernisation had to wait yet again; the compromise system of land property relations would hold. However, the general long-term aim of the Party remained to push towards modernisation and the scale-up of agriculture when the time was right, and experimentation in that direction was ongoing (Ye 2015, 320–1). In the process, the Party's relationship to the peasantry, especially for the local party-state, was in tatters and rural protest were on the rise (Day 2013). Yet peasant anger often focused on local governments, and as they protested against tax burdens and corrupt land expropriation, peasants often called on the Party and state to intervene on their behalf.

Responding to the rise in rural protests, the early 2000s – coinciding with the early years of the Hu–Wen administration – was a mixed period in rural reform. On the one hand, Party policy documents continued to push for agricultural modernisation and structural reform. On the other hand, the Party issued a series of 'number one documents' filled with pro-peasant ameliorative reforms and agricultural subsidies that aimed at stabilising rural society, leading to a renewed reduction of rural poverty but seeming to contradict the calls for a scaling up of agriculture. The latter held the day in the early 2000s, at least in terms of public pronouncements; seemingly, before it could turn back to agricultural modernisation, it first had to set about stabilising the rural scene with a series of reforms, including, most famously, the abolition of the agricultural tax by 2006. This new attention to the peasantry on the part of the party-state was partially in response to public criticism of the conditions of rural life coming from the countryside as well as pro-peasant activists and intellectuals, but it also opened space for more public debate on the conditions of the peasant (Day 2013; Day and Schneider 2018). However, this more open space was short-lived, and by around 2008 not only had Party policy shifted back towards agricultural modernisation, but the more open political environment was closed off as with the new Xi administration. While the compromising land policies of the household responsibility system, which placed limits on the transfer of land and thus the re-emergence of unequal landholding, was a check on class differentiation, the reform-period logic of the Party's relationship to the peasantry implied an eventual move in that direction, and, by the late 2000s, capitalist agrarian change (Zhang and Donaldson 2008) in China was clearly accelerating.

Post-Reform Period

By the late 1990s, the commodification of the urban and industrial workforce was largely complete, effecting the capitalist transformation of the urban sector, with China entering the World Trade Organization in 2001. But agrarian capitalism took a little longer, emerging more fully in the late 2000s. With that transition largely under way, from the perspective of rural China, the reform period is now over. In this time of capitalist agrarian change, while 'the peasant' remains a necessary political category for the CCP, if for no other reason than its importance to Party history and legitimacy, its original dialectical meaning has been lost.

The post-reform period emerged following the turn of the millennium with the weakening of the check on class differentiation that the household responsibility system provided and an embrace of capitalist agrarian change and scaled-up agriculture. With this latest shift, Party policy aims at pushing many less entrepreneurial peasants to give up control over their land and labour, becoming agricultural or urban workers, without the Party losing legitimacy. Conversely, rural and urban entrepreneurs alike are invited to invest in agricultural and rural industrial enterprises. Whether one works in agriculture in the countryside or as a migrant worker in the city, the category 'peasant' has less and less purchase.

In the new era of capitalist agrarian change, the structural self-containment of the rural sphere, which the state had used for crisis management and which rural activists of the early 2000s believed could be aligned to help protect peasants, is being significantly weakened. In its place, the state is in the process of transforming the rural sphere into another site of capitalist accumulation, one in which investments in efficiency and productivity are to lead to food security on the one hand, and in which class differentiation will lead to the divergent production of workers and capitalists on the other.

Since the ameliorative rural policies of the early Hu–Wen administration, especially the abolition of the agricultural tax in 2005–06, the Party has undertaken deeper structural and ideological changes that affect the countryside and the Party's relationship to the peasantry, expressed in a series of new rural policies and institutions. These changes can be grouped under four general categories, discussed below, with the capitalist agrarian change the main driving force of policy alteration: scaled-up capitalist agriculture, urbanisation and rural–urban integration, food security and poverty relief.

While many of these individual policies and institutions emerged at earlier times, they have become more coordinated and their implementation accelerated following the abolition of the agricultural tax, first under the umbrella of the New Socialist Countryside policy framework of the Hu–Wen administration (Looney 2020) and now under the framework of Rural Revitalisation for the Xi administration. The long-term strategy for realising capitalist agrarian change was most clearly announced in the 2018 National Strategic Plan for Rural Vitalisation (2018–22), with the aim of basically completing agricultural modernisation by 2035 and full rural revitalisation with wealthy farmers by 2050. With the Party finally completing this goal, the peasant and the rural sphere as separate categories would come to an end and rural land and labour would be more fully commoditised.

The central strategy for attaining these goals is the capitalist transformation of agriculture, producing scaled-up farming, although households remain the dominant farm operator. While reform-period agriculture was defined by the compromising land policy of the household responsibility system, which aimed at limiting class differentiation and maintaining the rural sphere as a place onto which urban problems could be shifted, the post-reform period is shaped by a new political economy of farming built around the transfer of land from smallholders to larger-scale commercial and entrepreneurial farmers (Zhang 2015).[3] Peasant farmers are being replaced by these 'new-style subjects of agriculture' (*xinxing nongye jingying zhuti* 新型农业经营主题). Because the fragmentation and abandonment of fields limits the development of agricultural productive forces, according to the Party, 'the form of dividing land to the households is unable to sustain agricultural modernisation' (Xu 2017). While village-owned and household-contracted

3 Note that it is important to analytically distinguish between commercial farms, which primarily rely on household labour and contracted land, and entrepreneurial farms, which rely on hired labour and leased land, although both produce for the market. Entrepreneurial farmers, although called 'big households', are often not household farmers at all. Further, these categories are not always easy to distinguish in state statistical or policy categorisation. For the CCP understanding, see Xu (2017).

agricultural land had been transferred to some extent since the 1980s, the process has accelerated dramatically from the late 2000s, clarifying three different levels of property rights: village collective ownership, household rights with long-term contracts and shorter-term leasing of managerial or use rights (Ye 2015). The transfer of agricultural land use rights occurs through several different mechanisms, managed individually by households, by the local state, village collectives or new specialised cooperatives. By 2018, the use rights of about 40 per cent of contracted farm land had been transferred, and transferred land is now responsible for about 10 per cent of rural income.[4] The construction of 'high-standard fields', irrigated land with good soil that allows for concentrated modern agriculture, has become a central priority for the state and its largest agricultural investment expense, mirroring somewhat the agricultural policies of Hua Guofeng in the late 1970s, but this time with capitalist social relations. Problems remain, however, as many large-scale operators enter farming at least in part for government subsidies, and land and bill abandonment abound when profits are not made.[5]

The modernisation and capitalisation of agriculture was further promoted by the expansion of dragonhead enterprises (Schneider 2017) and contract farming (Zhang 2012). Dragonheads, capitalist agricultural enterprises, are supposed to lead farmers to modern agriculture through a contracting relationship with households and specialised cooperatives, leading to the use of modern inputs, a focus on quality production as well as yields, increasing control over the labour process and the vertical integration of agricultural production. This last point is key. China is moving towards an agro-food system in which farming is integrated into value chains facilitating the production of higher-value food goods, and in which profits increasingly accrue in the food processing and marketing industries. Specialised cooperatives, which were codified by a 2007 law, further enable the integration of rural households into land, input and product markets; village land shareholding cooperatives have become an especially common way for villages to lease land to scaled-up farmers, with rent dividends then being paid to villagers, who also sometimes work for wages on the new farms. This was a defeat for early 2000s pro-peasant activists who hoped to use comprehensive cooperatives as a way to insulate peasants from the

4 'The China Dashboard: Land Policy Reform', Asia Society Policy Institute, Winter 2020, chinadashboard.gist.asiasociety.org/winter-2020/page/land.

5 'China's Large Farmers Abandon Land', 9 September 2019, dimsums.blogspot.com/2019/09/chinas-large-farmers-abandon-land.html.

market (Day and Schneider 2018). In the wake of these changes, the populist category of 'peasant', representing a unified category, is quickly losing its political efficacy. More rapid rural class differentiation has emerged among China's roughly 280 million people who work in farming (Zhang 2015), with commercial, contract and entrepreneurial farmers and semi-proletarian and proletarian farm workers increasingly taking the place of peasants.

Rural–urban integration has been promoted heavily since the early 2000s. The Third Plenary Session of the Seventeenth Party Congress in 2013, for example, specifically targeted the integration of rural and urban non-agricultural land markets while keeping agricultural land as a separate and protected category, with a red line at 120 million hectares of farmland. In other words, the real divide in land markets is increasingly between agricultural and non-agricultural land rather than between rural and urban land markets, although this has not stopped the requisitioning of agricultural land for urban and industrial uses, which also accelerated from 2008. The reform of the *hukou*, the resident permit system that separates agricultural and non-agricultural workers, continues, though at a slower pace than the reform of agricultural land use rights. Nonetheless, rapid urbanisation proceeds, facilitated by new policies since the beginning of the Xi administration. The urban population first surpassed that of the rural in 2011, and in 2020 it was 64 per cent of the total, up from less than 20 per cent at the beginning of the reform period.[6] During the COVID-19 pandemic, however, at least 50 million migrant workers were sent back or returned to the countryside, showing that the state still uses the rural–urban divided to maintain social stability, especially in the cities, when necessary,[7] even if the capacity to do this has weakened over time. Further, rapid urbanisation does not mean inclusive urbanisation, and rural migrants still face a lot of discrimination in cities, with larger cities even setting population caps. While rural migrants may shed the category of 'peasant' to take on new identities in the cities they move to – 'new workers' (*xin gongren* 新工人) or 'low-end population' (*diduan renkou* 低端人口) – these categories still express class differentiation and forms of discrimination (Day 2019, 173).

6 'Communique of the Seventh National Population Census, No. 7', National Bureau of Statistics, 11 May 2021, www.stats.gov.cn/english/PressRelease/202105/t20210510_1817192.html.

7 'China's Unemployed Disperse to Villages', 18 May 2020, dimsums.blogspot.com/search?updated-max=2020-07-01T20:31:00-04:00&max-results=7&start=14&by-date=false.

During the reform period, food security policies, which aim at largely maintaining China's self-sufficiency in food and, in particular, grain, often contradicted the Party's long-term goal of agricultural modernisation. For example, in the late 1990s, a time at which the urban economy was undergoing a painful transformation of state-owned enterprises encompassing massive layoffs, the rural economy was administratively made to compensate by producing cheap grain through the provincial governors' gain responsibility system (Hou and Liu 2010; Keidel 2007). In other words, at the time, food security impeded the shift to a profitable modern agrarian system. But this is changing in the post-reform period, in which food security is seen as premised upon the scale-up, mechanisation and technical modernisation of agriculture, and the state has allocated numerous incentives for these transformations. Further, in the contemporary moment, grain security 'has been used to empower and enrich large agrarian capital' at the expense of household farmers (Zhan 2017, 152).

Finally, poverty alleviation is a supplement to capitalist agrarian change, with the Chinese state announcing the elimination of extreme rural poverty by the end of 2020,[8] meeting its 2015 goal. With a sharp rural–urban divide in incomes, extreme poverty in China has been mostly situated in the rural sphere, and when the rural economy did well during the reform period – such as in the early 1980s, early 1990s and the 2000s – poverty was dramatically reduced there. The target set in 2015 announced a more activist response by the Party to rural poverty, leading up to the one-hundredth anniversary of the founding of the Party in 2021, and it comprised a sharp increase in state spending as well, raising the question of its sustainability. This entailed raising the poorest of China's farmers out of subsistence farming and integrating them into markets through road and infrastructure building, cash payments and subsidies, the provision of new social services and, in many cases, moving residents wholesale out of isolated villages and into new housing. It is important to note what 'extreme rural poverty' means. The United Nations (1995, ch. 2) characterises it as a 'severe deprivation of basic human needs, including food, safe drinking water, sanitation facilities, health, shelter, education and information'. By China's standards, it amounts to about $2.30 a day, higher than the World Bank's global standard for poor countries of $1.90, but somewhat low for an upper-middle-income

8 'China's Xi Declares Victory in Ending Extreme Poverty', *BBC News*, 25 February 2021, www.bbc.com/news/world-asia-china-56194622.

country such as China, for which the World Bank sets a standard of $5.50.[9] About 17 per cent of China's population remained under that higher UN standard as of 2018.[10] By this higher standard, the rural poor are supposed to disappear on China's road to fully modernised, wealthy farming by 2050. Following the elimination of extreme poverty, the State Council Leading Group Office of Poverty Alleviation and Development was replaced by the National Administration for Rural Vitalisation (*guojia xiangcun zhenxing ju* 国家乡村振兴局) in early 2021, pointing to those longer-range goals.[11] At the same time, as the Party began to celebrate overcoming extreme poverty and securing the basic welfare of rural residents (*wenbao* 温饱, indicating that people are clothed and have enough to eat), it increasingly focused on the construction of 'modern villages', with attention to the rural environment, a more 'civilized' rural living style, and cleaner and more hygienic villages. First proposed in the early 2000s under the framework of the New Socialist Countryside, this policy was also oriented towards developing the rural tourism market, with an aim of integrating agriculture, the processing industry and the rural service sector as rural capitalism advanced (Day 2022, 225). This integration is facilitated by a shift in rural governance, with lower levels, namely the village and the township, increasingly dominated by county or even city governments. Overall, this period entailed the weakening of the rural–urban dual-structure divide that has characterised PRC society since the 1950s, a state-directed process of capitalist agrarian change.

Conclusion

In some ways, the key principles shaping the Party's relationship to the peasantry seem to have remained remarkably stable over the last 100 years. On the one hand, improving rural livelihoods has persisted as a basic principle of Party rural policy. On the other hand, the peasant was a social form and political category that could only be understood in relationship to the historical trajectory of China's political economy and its directed transformation. Peasant surpluses would help determine the speed of the

9 The standard is also for absolute poverty, not relative poverty, a shifting line set in relation to the median income.

10 'Is China Succeeding at Eradicating Poverty?' *China Power*, 23 October 2020, chinapower.csis.org/poverty/.

11 'China Debuts New Government Body to Propel Rural Vitalization', *Xinhua*, 25 February 2021, www.xinhuanet.com/english/2021-02/25/c_139767216.htm.

national economy's development, but that development would, in the long run, lead to the transformation of the social relations of rural production, ending the small peasant social form. In other ways, however, *how* these two aspects – the improvement of peasant livelihoods and the social form's historical trajectory – relate has changed dramatically.

During the civil war, the Party connected peasant interests to national revolutionary interests through a peasant revolutionary dialectic. After 1949, that dialectic continued in modified form during the socialist period, with revolutionary transformation linking improving peasant livelihoods to progressive national development, industrialisation and agricultural modernisation. The temporality of improving livelihoods was linked to the trajectory of the developing political economy of the nation; both helped to determine each other as the social form of rural production moved through a series of transformations.

However, with industrialisation well underway and a relinking to global capitalism, that dialectical revolutionary link was replaced with a depoliticised developmentalism during the reform period. As household farming re-emerged, the clear link to national developments began to fade while a compromising land system put some restrictions on rural class differentiation for the time being. This was accompanied by a growing social discrimination against peasants. This system began to be restructured in the early 2000s, especially following the abolition of the agricultural tax in 2005–06, and a new set of rural institutions – in particular, dragonhead enterprises, specialised cooperatives and land transfer – now shape rural interests. The post-reform period thus entails the re-emergence of capitalist agrarian change, with a celebration of class differentiation and the complete disappearance of the Party's original aim of revolutionising rural social relations. In other words, while peasant livelihoods and extreme rural poverty relief are at the forefront of Party rural policy and propaganda, they have become a supplement to the Party's goal of modernising agriculture and the countryside. Instead of moving through a progressive series of social forms, rural producers are disintegrating into classes. Through this historical process, the potentiality of the peasant as a political figure, discovered in the revolutionary dialectic almost 100 years ago, melts away.

References

Ash, Robert. 2006. 'Squeezing the Peasants: Grain Extraction, Food Consumption and Rural Living Standards in Mao's China'. *China Quarterly* 188: 959–98. doi.org/10.1017/S0305741006000518.

Averill, Stephen C. 1987. 'Party, Society, and Local Elite in the Jiangxi Communist Movement'. *Journal of Asian Studies* 46(2): 279–303. doi.org/10.2307/2056015.

Baum, Richard. 1971. 'The Cultural Revolution in the Countryside: Anatomy of a Limited Rebellion'. In *The Cultural Revolution in China*, edited by Thomas Robinson, 367–476. Berkeley: University of California Press.

Baum, Richard. 1975. *Prelude to Revolution: Mao, the Party, and the Peasant Question, 1962–1966*. New York: Columbia University Press.

Bo, Yibo (薄一波). 1991. *Recollections of Several Important Political Decisions and Their Implementation* (若干重大决策与事件的回顾). Beijing: Zhonggong zhongyang dangxiao chubanshe.

Brown, Jeremy. 2012. *City versus Countryside in Mao's China: Negotiating the Divide*. Cambridge: Cambridge University Press. doi.org/10.1017/CBO9781139162197.

Day, Alexander F. 2013. *The Peasant in Postsocialist China: History, Politics, and Capitalism*. Cambridge: Cambridge University Press. doi.org/10.1017/CBO9781139626309.

Day, Alexander F. 2019. 'Peasant'. In *Afterlives of Chinese Communism*, edited by Christian Sorace, Ivan Franceschini and Nicholas Loubere, 169–73. Acton: ANU Press. doi.org/10.22459/ACC.2019.

Day, Alexander F. 2021. 'Breaking with the Family Form: Historical Categories, Social Reproduction, and Everyday Life in Late 1950s Rural China'. *positions: East Asian Cultures Critique* 29 (4): 869–94. doi.org/10.1215/10679847-9286740.

Day, Alexander F. 2022. 'State-Directed Capitalist Agrarian Change in the Creation of China's Biggest Tea County: Integrating Capital and Labor in Meitan County, Guizhou'. *Global Food History* 8 (3): 213–31. doi.org/10.1080/20549547.2022.2031792.

Day, Alexander F. and Mindi Schneider. 2018. 'The End of Alternatives? Capitalist Transformation, Rural Activism and the Politics of Possibility in China'. *Journal of Peasant Studies* 45 (7): 1221–46. doi.org/10.1080/03066150.2017.1386179.

DeMare, Brian. 2019. *Land Wars: The Story of China's Agrarian Revolution.* Stanford: Stanford University Press. doi.org/10.1515/9781503609525.

Dirlik, Arif. 1989. 'Postsocialism? Reflections on "Socialism with Chinese Characteristics"'. In *Marxism and the Chinese Experience,* edited by Arif Dirlik and Maurice Meisner. Armonk: M. E. Sharpe.

Eyferth, Jacob. 2015. 'Liberation from the Loom? Rural Women, Textile Work, and Revolution in North China'. In *Maoism at the Grassroots: Everyday Life in China's Era of High Socialism*, edited by Jeremy Brown and Matthew D. Johnson, 131–54. Cambridge: Harvard University Press. doi.org/10.4159/9780674287211-005.

Hershatter, Gail. 2011. *Gender of Memory: Rural Women and China's Collective Past.* Berkeley: University of California Press. doi.org/10.1525/california/9780520267701.001.0001.

Hou, Jack and Xuemei Liu. 2010. 'Grain Policy: Rethinking an Old Issue for China'. *International Journal of Applied Economics* 7 (1): 1–20.

Hou, Xiaojia. 2016. *Negotiating Socialism in Rural China: Mao, Peasants, and Local Cadres in Shanxi: 1949–1953.* Ithaca: Cornell University Press.

Huang, Philip. 1975. 'Mao Tse-Tung and the Middle Peasant, 1925—1928'. *Modern China* 1 (3): 271–96. doi.org/10.1177/009770047500100302.

Keidel, Albert. 2007. *China's Economic Fluctuations: Implications for its Rural Economy.* Washington: Carnegie Endowment for International Peace.

Kelliher, Daniel. 1994. 'Chinese Communist Political Theory and the Rediscovery of the Peasantry'. *Modern China* 20 (4): 387–415. doi.org/10.1177/009770049402000401.

Kuhn, Philip A. 2002. *Origins of the Modern Chinese State.* Stanford: Stanford University Press. doi.org/10.1515/9781503619661.

Looney, Kristen E. 2020. *Mobilizing for Development: The Modernization of Rural East Asia.* Ithaca: Cornell University Press. doi.org/10.7591/cornell/9781501748844.001.0001.

Mao, Zedong (毛泽东). 1965a. 'Report on an Investigation of the Peasant Movement in Hunan'. In *Selected Works of Mao Tse-tung.* Vol. 1, 23–59. Beijing: Foreign Languages Press.

Mao, Zedong. 1965b. 'The Chinese Revolution and the Chinese Communist Party'. In *Selected Works of Mao Tse-tung.* Vol. 2, 305–34. Beijing: Foreign Languages Press.

Meisner, Maurice. 1974. *Li Ta-chao and the Origins of Chinese Marxism*. New York: Atheneum.

Oi, Jean C. 1999. *Rural China Takes Off.* Berkeley: University of California Press.

Opper, Marc. 2018. 'Revolution Defeated: The Collapse of the Chinese Soviet Republic'. *Twentieth-Century China* 43 (1): 45–66. doi.org/10.1353/tcc.2018.0003.

Qi, Xiaolin (齐小林). 2015. *To Be a Soldier: How North China Base Area Peasants Went to the Battlefield* (当兵:华北根据地农民如何走向战场). Chengdu: Sichuan renmin chubanshe.

Schneider, Mindi. 2017. 'Dragon Head Enterprises and the State of Agribusiness in China'. *Journal of Agrarian Change* 17 (1): 3–21. doi.org/10.1111/joac.12151.

Schneider, Mindi. 2021. 'Working the Rural–Urban Divide: Alexander Day Traces a Century of Agricultural Modernisation in China's Present-Day Tea Capital'. *Commodity Frontiers* 2: 10–15. library.wur.nl/ojs/index.php/commodity-frontiers/article/view/18079.

Shue, Vivienne. 1980. *Peasant China in Transition: The Dynamics of Development towards Socialism, 1949–1956*. Berkeley: University of California Press.

Tang, Anthony M. 1967. 'Agriculture in the Industrialization of Communist China and the Soviet Union'. *Journal of Farm Economics* 49 (5): 1118–34. doi.org/10.2307/1236991.

Teiwes, Frederick C. and Warren Sun. 1993. 'Editors' Introduction'. *Chinese Law & Government* 26 (3–4): 5–27. doi.org/10.2753/CLG0009-46092603045.

Teiwes, Frederick C. and Warren Sun. 1999. *China's Road to Disaster: Mao, Central Politicians, and Provincial Leaders in the Unfolding of the Great Leap Forward: 1955–1959*. Armonk: M. E. Sharpe.

Teiwes, Frederick C. and Warren Sun. 2016. *Paradoxes of Post-Mao Rural Reform: Initial Steps towards a New Chinese Countryside, 1976–1981*. London: Routledge. doi.org/10.4324/9781315719498.

Unger, Jonathan. 2002. *The Transformation of Rural China*. Armonk: M. E. Sharpe.

United Nations. 1995. 'World Summit for Social Development 1995 Agreements'. Department of Economic and Social Affairs. www.un.org/development/desa/dspd/world-summit-for-social-development-1995/wssd-1995-agreements/pawssd-chapter-2.html.

Walker, Kenneth R. 1966. 'Collectivisation in Retrospect: The "Socialist High Tide" of Autumn 1955 – Spring 1956'. *China Quarterly* 26: 1–43. doi.org/10.1017/S0305741000013151.

Wemheuer, Felix. 2019. *A Social History of Maoist China: Conflict and Change, 1949–1976*. Cambridge: Cambridge University Press. doi.org/10.1017/9781316421826.

Xu, Junzhong (徐俊忠). 2017. 'Profoundly Grasping Comrade Xi Jinping's Important Treatise on Deepening the Reform of the Rural Land System' (深刻领会习近平同志关于深化农村土地制度改革的重要论述). *Hongqi* 5. www.qstheory.cn/dukan/hqwg/2017-08/09/c_1121455629.htm.

Xu, Zhun. 2014. 'Chinese Agrarian Change in World-Historical Context'. *Science & Society* 78 (2): 181–206. doi.org/10.1521/siso.2014.78.2.181.

Ye, Jingzhong. 2015. 'Land Transfer and the Pursuit of Agricultural Modernization in China'. *Journal of Agrarian Change* 15 (3): 314–37. doi.org/10.1111/joac.12117.

Zhan, Shaohua. 2017. 'Riding on Self-Sufficiency: Grain Policy and the Rise of Agrarian Capital in China'. *Journal of Rural Studies* 54: 151–61. doi.org/10.1016/j.jrurstud.2017.06.012.

Zhang, Qian Forrest. 2012. 'The Political Economy of Contract Farming in China's Agrarian Transition'. *Journal of Agrarian Change* 12: 460–83. doi.org/10.1111/j.1471-0366.2012.00352.x.

Zhang, Qian Forrest. 2015. 'Class Differentiation in Rural China: Dynamics of Accumulation, Commodification and State Intervention'. *Journal of Agrarian Change* 15 (3): 338–65. doi.org/10.1111/joac.12120.

Zhang, Qian Forrest and John A. Donaldson. 2008. 'The Rise of Agrarian Capitalism with Chinese Characteristics: Agricultural Modernization, Agribusiness and Collective Land Rights'. *China Journal* 60: 25–47. doi.org/10.1086/tcj.60.20647987.

12

The Chinese Communist Party and the Chinese Bourgeoisie (1949–present): From First Alliance to Repression and Contemporary Mutual Dependence

Gilles Guiheux

Introduction

In today's China, the private sector contributes more than 50 per cent to tax revenue and over 60 per cent to GDP. It also accounts for more than 70 per cent of technological innovation, over 80 per cent of urban employment and comprises more than 90 per cent of market players.[1] Nevertheless, the attitude of the party-state towards private entrepreneurs is ambiguous. Billionaires at the head of large companies are regularly criticised, and are sometimes prosecuted by the courts and imprisoned. At the same time, the contribution of private entrepreneurs to nation-building and prosperity is being praised.

1 'Private Sector's Development Key to Digital Economy Growth', *China Daily*, 7 September 2021, global.chinadaily.com.cn/a/202109/07/WS6136a6b1a310efa1bd66db60.html.

High-profile entrepreneurs in the tech industry have recently come under public and official scrutiny like never before. Several of the most prominent of them have retired from the management of their companies. Jack Ma, Alibaba co-founder, has kept an uncharacteristically low profile since October 2020, when the government began a regulatory crackdown on his companies. Colin Huang, founder of the Alibaba rival Pinduoduo, resigned as chairman in March 2021, less than a year after he stepped down as chief executive. In May 2021, Zhang Yiming, founder of TikTok's parent company, ByteDance, said he would hand over the chief executive post to focus on long-term strategy. In June 2021, Pan Shiyi and Zhang Xin, the husband and wife team that runs Soho China, a major national property developer, turned over their company to an investment firm.[2] This is not a new phenomenon and many other individual entrepreneurs, such as Sun Dawu and Ren Zhiqiang, have been forced to leave the stage over the years.

At the same time, the regime regularly praises private entrepreneurs for their unique role in bringing prosperity to the Chinese nation. In 2018, as the Chinese Communist Party (CCP) was celebrating the fourteenth anniversary of Deng Xiaoping' reforms, the All-China Federation of Industry and Commerce (AFIC), a key business association,[3] together with the United Front Work Department, the mission of which is to deal with people and entities that are outside of the Party proper, released a list of '100 Outstanding Private Entrepreneurs'.[4] The list aimed to show the significant achievements made in the development of China's private economy since reform and opening up, and:

> to vigorously promote the spirit of outstanding entrepreneurs, to create a good environment for the healthy growth of private entrepreneurs, and to better motivate the majority of non-public economic people to 'not forget the original spirit of entrepreneurship, to carry on the great work of reform'.[5]

---

2 'Jack Ma Shows Why China's Tycoons Keep Quiet', *New York Times*, 22 April 2021; 'As China Scrutinizes Its Entrepreneurs, a Power Couple Cashes Out', *New York Times*, 17 June 2021.

3 The All-China Federation of Industry and Commerce assists the government in managing the private sector economy and acts as a bridge between private sector entities and the government. It is supervised by the United Front Work Department.

4 'Here Is the List of 100 Outstanding Private Entrepreneurs to Celebrate the 40 Years of Reform and Opening Up! Take a Look at Who are There!' (改革开放40年百名杰出民营企业家名单来了!快看看都有谁), 24 October 2018, *Xinhuawang*, www.xinhuanet.com/fortune/2018-10/24/c_129978408.htm.

5 Ibid.

Over the past 40 years of reform and opening up, as the Chinese media reported, 'the private economy has developed rapidly, making a significant contribution to ushering in the great leap of the Chinese nation, standing up, getting rich and getting strong'.[6]

This chapter reviews the complex relationships between the CCP and private entrepreneurs over the last century. To explain today's ambiguous relationship between the CCP and private entrepreneurs, we look at the historical development of this relationship. Present practices of the Party as an organisation become less surprising if we look at how it behaved in the past. Historically, Chinese capitalists emerged as a social group during the first half of the twentieth century in the treaty ports. Together with merchants, craftsmen, bankers and officials involved in business, they were members of the emerging bourgeoisie extensively studied by Marie-Claire Bergère (2009). In the 1920s, they were not immune to social issues, nor to the interests of the working class; but, when it came to facing their social responsibilities, businessmen looked for inspiration in Christian values and in the traditional practices of guilds and chambers of commerce rather than in Marxism (Bergère 1969, 264). In 1927, the installation of a new government in Nanjing opened an era of difficult cooperation between the bourgeoisie and the Guomindang (GMD). Parks M. Coble (1980) has argued that Chiang Kai-shek's government actively and consistently opposed Shanghai capitalists, using a variety of techniques, both official and unofficial, to extract money from them. William C. Kirby (1995) has also shown how, for instance, modern forms of business organisations were adopted by the Nationalist government not for fostering wealth and independence for businessmen, but rather, quite the opposite, as a means to achieve state domination of the industrial sectors. In the 1940s, this gave way to open and mutual hostility. As a matter of fact, contrary to the hopes of the business community, the end of the war did not mean a return to more liberal economy policies. Entrepreneurs, whose daily activities were crippled by inflation, denounced the inconsistencies and brutalities of the government's policies, and the way in which the government was using the crisis to increase its control over industrial capacities – notably taking control of former Japanese companies (Bergère 1989). In 1946, Shanghai industrialists lost all confidence in the GMD's ability not only to resolve the economic and financial crisis, but also to govern the country and prevent the Communists from triumphing. They began to transfer capital and equipment out of China, mainly to Hong Kong.

6 Ibid.

In this chapter, we argue that the CCP policy towards capitalists since the reforms and opening up can be understood if we look at the mechanisms and techniques of governance used during the early People's Republic. The collaboration between the Party and private entrepreneurs over the last decades, like the recent tensions between the actual leadership and the entrepreneurs' class, look less exceptional if we acknowledge that red capitalists were creations of the Party itself in the 1950s.

The chapter starts with analysing how, after the establishment of the new regime, the CCP tried to rally some members of the so-called national bourgeoisie to its nation-building project. The alliance was temporary and was quickly followed by repression, all private businesses being nationalised in 1956. In the second part, we look at how, after the launch of the reform and opening-up policy in 1979, and especially after 1992, private entrepreneurs emerged again as a social group. Deng Xiaoping's call to 'let some people get rich first' (*rang yibufenren xian fuiqilai* 让一部分人先富起来) gave rise to a new social stratum of business owners. The chapter ends with a discussion of how capitalists may or may not be able to shape public policies in contemporary China. In the different periods of the history of the People's Republic considered here, the choice is made to use the terminology in force in China itself; thus, we talk about capitalists and bourgeoisie in the 1950s, and of the return of a social group of private entrepreneurs with the reforms.

The Chinese Bourgeoisie and the Founding Years of the People's Republic of China: An Opportunistic Alliance

In the 1920s, the CCP, which was founded by intellectuals under the guidance of the Comintern, tried to transform itself into a workers' party. In the 1930s, the double failure of its alliance with the GMD and its conquest of urban proletarians led it to take root in rural China. It is only when it moved into cities that the CCP had to consider what strategy to follow vis-a-vis the industrial and commercial bourgeoisie. That explains why we begin by looking at the founding years of the People's Republic of China (PRC).

If destroying capitalism was the ultimate target of the socialist revolution, during the first years of the PRC, businesspeople were the object of favours and leniency from the CCP. The main ideological justification of the relatively moderate policy of the CCP in its early years up to the Cultural Revolution was the united front policy. Most authors consider that the Party cooperated with the Chinese patriotic bourgeoisie out of opportunism and pragmatism. The CCP lured it to join the fight against the Japanese and then the civil war against Chiang Kai-shek, and finally to restore the productive capacity of industry after 1949. For Yang Kuisong (2007, 16), 'it was just a question of time before they [the Communists] would once again regard the Chinese national bourgeoisie as their political enemy'. Christian Henriot (2014, 160) argues, as well, that 'the Chinese bourgeoisie never had a chance'. Did the CCP cooperate with the bourgeoisie out of political expediency, and was the agenda set from the beginning? Other scholars argue that it would be a mistake to assume that the CCP and the Chinese capitalists definitively determined their relationship in 1949 and that it was the events that followed that were decisive (Chan 2014). Rather than speculating on what the Chinese leaders had in mind in the early 1950s, we can only observe what actually took place.

Rallying the 'National Bourgeoisie' to the Party: The New Democracy Policy

The idea of an alliance between the CCP and the bourgeoisie goes back to the Wayaobao meeting in December 1935, when the Party decided to renew cooperation with the GMD in a united national front against the Japanese invasion. A line was drawn between the 'national capitalists' (*minzu zibenjia* 民族资本家) who were true patriots, and the 'comprador bureaucratic capitalists' (*maiban guanliao zibenjia* 买办官僚资本家) who sold out to imperialist countries. The first group were invited to join the fight against the Japanese and, later, against Chiang Kai-shek. On the eve of the establishment of the People's Republic, Mao Zedong renewed the distinction: 'national capitalists' were welcome under socialism whereas 'bureaucratic capitalists' were the target of the revolution.

On 5 March 1949, in his report to the Second Plenary Session of the Seventh Central Committee of the CCP, Mao Zedong stated that 'private capitalism ranks second in modern industry; it is a great force that cannot be underestimated' (Zhao 2014, 263). Thus, after the takeover, the united front policy continued and justified continuing to grant privileges to the former capitalists. The CCP claimed that it wished to bring together and even accommodate all social classes, including the capitalists, under the political umbrella of the 'New Democracy' (*xin minzhu* 新民主). The section of the formal elites vetted by the CCP as 'national' had a role to play in China's democratic revolution. More pragmatically, the CCP was eager to mobilise and use the resources and skills of 'national capitalists' to rebuild the country. New Democracy, protecting private urban industry and commerce became the keynotes of the Party's policy on the bourgeoisie.

At the time of the founding of the PRC in 1949, the Central Committee of the CCP unambiguously proclaimed that 'the national bourgeoisie', along with workers, peasants and the petit bourgeoisie, enjoyed ownership in the new China. The priority was not to seize private assets, establish a planned economy or transform Chinese society, but to restore economic health and industrial production.

One reason why the CCP Central Committee took such a positive attitude in wooing the bourgeoisie was its understanding of the economic situation; the decrease of production and closure of many factories had led to a rapid increase in unemployment. For example, in Shanghai, in the spring of 1959, the unemployed accounted for more than 200,000 out of a population of 6 million (Yang 2007, 19).

New Democracy policies emphasised, among other things, labour–capital cooperation in private enterprise. China's economy did not come under state management with the Communist victory in 1949. During an initial period of transition, the CCP experimented with new forms of labour relations such as labour–capital consultative conferences (*laozi xieshang huiyi* 劳资协商会议), which were required by law in all privately owned factories. In some instances, such as in Shanghai's silk weaving industry, this novel form of consultative management achieved its goal of labour–capital cooperation and economic restoration (Cliver 2021). The labour–capital consultative conference benefited silk factory owners by reducing violence and disruption and granting them access to supplies, credit and markets. To Robert Cliver (2021, 53), this institution:

> reveals the complexities of the power relationship between the party-state and capitalist enterprises and demonstrates that most factory owners were not hapless victims of Communist revolution but were instead savvy and capable players.

Another example of this inclusive policy was the effort made by the CCP to persuade entrepreneurs who had fled the country to come back, especially the undecided big capitalists who had no history of supporting the GMD. Zhou Enlai wrote personal letters to some of the biggest capitalists with a promise that they would see their businesses grow rather than shrink under the new regime. One prominent example is Liu Hongsheng, who set off for Taiwan but decided not to move there and remained in Hong Kong, where he was assured that his business would not be affected by the regime. From Hong Kong, he moved back to Shanghai and, for the first two years, was strongly convinced that the new Communist regime was sincere in supporting capitalist enterprise and treating the capitalists well (Cochran 2007). Another famous example is Wu Yunchun, a major industrialist in the Republican period who manufactured monosodium glutamate. When the People's Liberation Army took over Shanghai, Wu had already taken refuge in the United States and was considering whether or not to return to China. Invited to come back, he arrived in Beijing in October 1949, where he met Zhou Enlai. In October 1950, Wu became a member of the Shanghai municipal government, a political position that seemed to uphold his economic status (Chen 2014).

Three years later, in October 1953, 640 delegates representing every sector of the Chinese economy attended a meeting of the Federation of Industry and Commerce. During the meeting, Li Weihan, the united front director, declared that:

> the period of transition extends from the founding of the PRC to the completion of socialist transformation … both [the public and private sectors] are essential and beneficial to the national economy of people's livelihood. (Zhao 2014, 267)

Despite these statements, the situation had already significantly deteriorated for private entrepreneurs by that time.

Repressing Capitalists: The Three-Anti and Five-Anti Movements

Two anti-corruption campaigns, the three-anti and five-anti movements, launched in 1951 and 1952, respectively, radically changed the social position of capitalists. The CCP gradually moved away from its original policy of cooperation with the national bourgeoisie. Aimed at the bourgeoisie as a whole, the campaigns succeeded in destroying the social basis for capitalist business; as a result, the socialisation of all private enterprises in 1955–56 would occur smoothly.

The Three-Anti Movement was launched in the winter of 1951 and was opposed to the three evils of corruption, waste and bureaucratism. It had initially been intended to combat corruption and waste by CCP cadres, but the three evils were rapidly linked with the so-called degenerate ideology of the bourgeoisie (Yang 2007, 23). As reports from the provinces claimed that bribery was rife and that public officials were acting in collusion with businesspeople, the leadership of the CCP leapt to the conclusion that this was a well-organised counter-revolutionary attempt by the bourgeoisie, 'a violent attack against our Party' (Yang 2007, 23).

The Three-Anti Movement was rapidly expanded into the Five-Anti Movement to deal with malpractices involving bribery, tax evasion, stealing of state assets, cheating on government contracts and theft of economic intelligence. It was a mass campaign, mobilising thousands of individuals to enter factories and shops and organise mass denunciations. Capitalists were humiliated, and ties of loyalty between employers and workers were severed. By May 1952, the final assessments for businesses under investigation were announced. According to the CCP's official data, the campaign scrutinised the business conduct of 999,707 firms nationwide. Business owners were investigated and then categorised into five groups: law-abiding business owners (10–15 per cent of the total), basically law-abiding (50–60 per cent), semi-law-abiding (25–30 per cent), serious lawbreakers (4 per cent) and total lawbreakers (1 per cent) (quoted in Lu 2018, 75).

Through these two successive campaigns, the Communist regime generated mass support for the social and financial destruction of the capitalist class. After 1953, the CCP began the socialisation of private firms by introducing public–private joint enterprises (*gongsi heying* 公私合营). From the second half of 1955, the government accelerated the process and within a year had rushed through the socialisation of all private enterprises.

As Christopher Leighton (2010) has shown, a distinction should be made between elite capitalists and smaller ones. The first were politically, economically and socially integrated into the new regime. United front institutions like the Democratic Construction Association and the Federation of Industry and Commerce drew prominent capitalists into collaboration with the Party, rewarding them with privilege and position in return for their networks and management expertise while preserving smaller capitalists to serve as targets for mass struggle. As Leighton (2010, 7) puts it, prominent 'red' capitalists were 'hybrid creations of the Party itself'.

Allowing Capitalist Lifestyles to Continue

While, by the mid-1950s, the CCP had deprived Chinese capitalists of their means of production, the socialisation of all private enterprises was carried out peacefully, an approach that differed from the confiscation of private enterprises in the Soviet Union and some Eastern European countries. The peaceful redemption included paying an indemnity in exchange for the property at a fixed rate of interest (*dingxi* 定息), assigning jobs to the private staff who were in active service and maintaining high wages for the owners of the enterprise. Government compensation was paid over seven years at 5 per cent fixed interest. By early 1956, 810,000 business owners and their agents had received payments nationwide (Lu 2018, 75). In 1962, the seven years of redemption ended. Following Chen Yun's and Zhou Enlai's suggestions, Mao Zedong agreed to extend the payment for three more years (Xiao-Planes 2014).

Another revealing fact is that capitalists were able to preserve their lifestyles (Lu 2018). After 1949, as far as material comfort was concerned, the long-time rich still lived an infinitely better life than most Chinese at the time. The persistence of bourgeois lifestyles under communism was an outcome of the CCP's United Front policy, as well as an ingenious use of government policy and programs by capitalists themselves to preserve a way of life that was politically condemned. After 1956, China's former capitalists, facing purges and political condemnation, were doomed as a class, but much of the lifestyle of the old capitalist class survived and persevered beneath the surface of Communist egalitarianism and asceticism. In Shanghai, former capitalists continued living in luxurious villas, throwing parties in their houses, organising lavish weddings and receptions in hotels, and banquets in high-end restaurants that were preserved notably to entertain foreign visitors. It is only with the Cultural Revolution in 1966 that the privileges the formerly wealthy still enjoyed after the 1949 revolution came to an end. Official records indicate that from August 1966 to the end of that year, the homes of more than 48,000 Shanghai capitalists were ransacked and the households' valuables confiscated (Lu 2018, 75).

From a comparative perspective with other socialist revolutions, China's case seems unique (Cochran 2014, 12–17). In China, the Party dispatched emissaries throughout the country and abroad to convince capitalists that they should serve their country under communism during the revolution; whereas during the Russian Revolution, the transition from capitalism to socialism was abrupt and violent – historians agree that pre-revolutionary private capitalists were virtually all killed or driven out of the country by 1920. Thus, the peaceful redemption of the means of production from private industrial enterprises contrasts with the confiscation of private enterprises in the Soviet Union and later in Eastern European countries.

The Re-emergence of Private Entrepreneurs (1979–2001)

One of the consequences of the reforms launched in the late 1970s was the reshaping of Chinese society and the re-emergence of private entrepreneurs. The formation of a new capitalist class was gradual. Once the party-state acknowledged their important contribution to the building of a prosperous nation, capitalists were not only encouraged but also portrayed as national heroes and incorporated within the system. Four decades later, private entrepreneurs form a socially diverse class.

The Gradual Development of the Private Sector's Legal Framework

The development of private enterprises since the end of the 1970s can be divided into several stages. The first decade (1978–88) was an informal entry stage during which entrepreneurs gained entry into the market in spite of the lack of a legal framework and were tolerated. With the opening-up policy, private enterprises developed first in the form of individual enterprises (*getihu* 个体户). In July 1981, the State Council issued a document making legal reference to such economic activities, stipulating that these enterprises could have no more than seven employees[7] and that their activities could only complement those of state-run and collective

7 The distinction may derive from Marx's discussion in *Das Kapital* (1867) of the non-exploitive character of household producing units (those with less than eight employees) versus capitalist producers (those employing more than eight employees).

enterprises. During the 1980s, the periodic political campaigns against spiritual pollution (1983–84), bourgeois liberalisation (1987), tax evasion and corruption regularly challenged the legitimacy of private entrepreneurs.

The second stage started in 1988 when the state legitimised private enterprises and permitted them to hire up to eight employees. From then on, the passing of new laws and successive revisions of the PRC Constitution contributed significantly to the development of a private sector. In April 1988, the National People's Congress modified article 11 of the PRC Constitution, which henceforth stipulated that 'the private economy is authorised to exist and develop within the framework as provided by law'. In June 1988, the State Council adopted new sets of regulations concerning what were now designated as private enterprises.

In early 1992, Deng Xiaoping travelled south to reinvigorate the national spirit for profit and encouraged the masses to 'jump into the sea' (*xiahai* 下海) of entrepreneurship. This call led many individuals to leave the security of state-owned enterprise work and to set up private businesses. But it took 10 more years for Chinese leaders to accord constitutional protection to the private economy. It was only in 2004 that the phrase 'the lawful private property of citizens is inviolable' was incorporated in the PRC Constitution.[8]

Private Entrepreneurs as Socialist Heroes

Not only has the structure of the Chinese economy changed with the private sector becoming a key player, but the Party and the state have also acknowledged this change and have revised their attitudes towards the individuals embodying it.

In post-reform China, the new subject promoted by the authorities is an entrepreneurial subject, autonomous from the state, at least in the economic and social arenas, and in that sense, entrepreneurs become the new symbolic figure, or hero, of the socialist market economy (Guiheux 2012). The entrepreneur, as a social category, epitomises some of the main values promoted by the Chinese state, because he embodies a new kind of autonomous subject. State dependency and supervision have been giving way to what may be called a post-Mao 'enterprise culture', a discourse that does not promote collective political action but 'individual and local

8 On the successive revision of the Chinese constitution since 1982, see Chen (2004).

calculations of strategies and tactics, costs and benefits' (Rose 1992, 145). Chinese citizens have been encouraged to draw on their own resources to compete in the open market, 'to conduct themselves with boldness and vigour, to calculate for their own advantage, to drive themselves hard and to accept risks in the pursuit of goals' (Rose 1992, 149).

At the end of the twentieth century, China's heroes, or model citizens, are those who have been able to start their own business. All kinds of rhetorical techniques are being used to praise entrepreneurs, whether they head small or large enterprises. In the case of formerly laid-off state workers, all kinds of titles and medals are being awarded to exemplary entrepreneurs: 'star of the re-employment policy', 'exemplary creator of enterprise', as well as 'model of excellence of the national youth' and 'model worker' (Guiheux 2007). Distributing honorific titles that are highly publicised in local media, state or Party agencies contributes to creating a new moral environment for business, legitimising the enrichment of a minority. Actually, there is a great similarity between the Mao-era call for self-dedication to the building of the country and the call for private entrepreneurship in terms of propaganda techniques, but the values promoted and the forms of self-achievement are not the same. In the earlier era, striving to be a model worker like Lei Feng meant selflessness and contributing to the community; now, becoming an entrepreneur means promoting reflexivity and autonomy.

Over the last 40 years of reform and opening up, entrepreneurs have moved from the fringe to the centre of the economic and political arenas. People engaging in independent economic endeavours were being blamed and socially marginalised in the late 1970s; a quarter of a century later, they are being praised for their contribution to the wellbeing of the whole Chinese society. Private entrepreneurs, previously persecuted, have been praised and courted by the CCP since the 1990s.

Incorporating Private Entrepreneurs within the CCP

In the 1980s, there were various answers to the question of what the role of entrepreneurs should be (Parris 1999). Hardliners argued that the official justification of the private sector did not conform to economic and political realities. Moderates wanted the private sector to remain marginal and transitional. For the reformers, the private sector was becoming a key part of the overall economy; private entrepreneurs and the newly rich needed to be presented as patriotic and hard-working innovators who enriched not only themselves but also the whole nation. Not unlike reformers in the late Qing dynasty, the reformers made the claim that the private was not inimical to the public but was a necessary part of it. They gained the upper hand during the 1997 Party congress.

On 1 July 2001, the eightieth anniversary of the founding of the CCP, Jiang Zemin introduced his Three Represents (*sange daibiao* 三个代表) theory. He made a controversial call for qualified members of the various social strata that had emerged over the reform period – including private entrepreneurs – to be admitted to the CCP.[9] According to Jiang, the Party represented the development requirements of China's advanced social productive forces, the progressive course of China's advanced culture and the fundamental interests of the majority of the Chinese people. Jiang's vision was clearly elitist: he recognised that technology, the domestic economy and globalisation were changing very quickly, and he wanted to incorporate those forces into the CCP. The Three Represents theory was later enshrined in the CCP Constitution at the Sixteenth Party Congress in autumn 2002 and in the preamble of the PRC Constitution in March 2004.

After the 1 July 2001 speech, Party leaders defended Jiang Zemin's call in practical terms. They agreed that it was necessary to admit to the Party the most dynamic social forces or face the same fate as the Communist parties of the former Soviet Union and the socialist countries of Eastern Europe. Party commentators repeatedly emphasised the rapid growth of the private economy and the Party's poor representation among that segment of society.

As a matter of fact, the inclusion of private entrepreneurs in the CCP was not a new phenomenon. Beginning in the mid-1980s, entrepreneurs were coopted into the Party in large numbers, but, fearing that 'bourgeois' influences were spreading into the Party, the CCP banned the new recruitment of private entrepreneurs after the imposition of martial law in 1989. According to a survey conducted in 1993, 13 per cent of private businessmen were members of the Party (Zhang and Liu 1995, 408). This jumped to 18 per cent in 1997, 19 per cent in 2000 and 30 per cent in 2002 (Zhang, Lizhi and Zhuanyun 2003, 31). However, these entrepreneurs were not necessarily directly recruited; a significant number of Party members had become private entrepreneurs (in 2002, 80 per cent of the entrepreneurs surveyed had become members of the Party before starting a business).

9 Though this has been widely reported as a call to admit 'capitalists' into the Party, Jiang never used the word 'capitalists', even if that was the intent of his remarks (Fewsmith 2001, 3).

The new legitimacy of private entrepreneurs in a still Communist China was made possible by a redefinition of the public good. Economic and social issues moved to the centre of the agenda of the CCP. Economic reform and the rise of the private economy had resulted in a struggle to redefine private interests as part of, rather than in opposition to, the public good. As the expansion of the private economy seemed inevitable, the public good was no longer identified with a revolutionary public spirit or Communist vision but, rather, with a more instrumental notion of material wellbeing and national power. Private entrepreneurialism, contributing not only to producing goods and services but also to creating jobs and solving unemployment issues, was therefore seen as an important force in the realisation of these goals.

Private Entrepreneurs as a Contested Social Class under Scrutiny

In this last part, we address the entrepreneurs' relationship to the state. We will first underline their social diversity, which helps explain why they should not be seen as a social and political force. Second, we will address the issue of their capacity for collective action. Third, we will give two examples of the recent increasing intrusion of the CCP into the private sector, looking at Party-building in the private sector and at state-driven philanthropy.

The Social Diversity of Chinese Entrepreneurs and Their Interaction with the State

In 40 years of development, the overall composition of private entrepreneurs has undergone major changes. In the early 2000s, Kellee Tsai argued that private entrepreneurs had a very heterogenous social constituency (Tsai 2005), underlining their differences in terms of company size, business significance and sociopolitical and geographical background. Twenty years later, whether or not private businesspeople altogether form a social class is still subject to debate.

The emergence of a group of private businesspeople over the last four decades is such an important social fact that one of the most enduring national-scale social surveys is dedicated to its study. The China Private Enterprise Survey (*zhongguo siyingqiye diaocha* 中国私营企业调查 or CPES) began in 1992, shortly after the Fourteenth Party Congress proposed the establishment of a socialist market economy; it has been conducted 14 times to date (Chen et al. 2019). The CPES is run by a research project team composed of members of the United Front Work Department of the CCP Central Committee, the AFIC, the State Administration for Market Regulation, the Chinese Academy of Social Sciences and the Chinese Private Economy Research Association.

Using data from the seventh CPES (1997–2014), Fan Xiaoguang and Lü Peng analysed the social background of private entrepreneurs in 2019. Two conclusions are particularly interesting. First, although the proportion of 'grassroots' entrepreneurs' (i.e. those who never worked for the state except at the village level) with limited education is still relatively high, the overall education level of entrepreneurs is rising, and the proportion of those with higher education has steadily increased. Among those who started their businesses in the early 1980s, the share of entrepreneurs with a bachelor's degree or higher accounted for only a single digit; by the end of the 1990s and early 2000s, they constituted about 20 per cent; and in the first half of the 2010s, they constituted more than 30 per cent. Unlike earlier entrepreneurs, those with a university education are increasingly entering the market directly, rather than joining government or state-owned enterprises before 'jumping into business'. Second, the origins of entrepreneurs from different social classes have maintained a diversified pattern. Whatever their type, entrepreneurs have a diversity of occupational experience before starting their businesses, and this diversity has persisted over time. This shows that China's private economy still maintains a certain degree of openness. Different social groups can join the private sector, and people from different social origins can become large and medium-sized entrepreneurs. In other words, economic expansion can still provide a stage for latecomers who have seized market opportunities (Fan and Lü 2019).

Isabela Nogueira and Hao Qi (2019) offer another typology built on the succession of accumulation regimes that have been the main engines of China's economic growth. They also argue that different types of entrepreneurs have distinct relationships with the state. The 'low road faction' dates back to the 1990s, when most capitalists accumulated wealth by relying on low wages, harsh management practices and access to cheap land. Such enterprises tended to be in labour-intensive, export-oriented industries, engaged in global value chains. Because of growing social protests against insufficient wages in the 2000s, and the will to upgrade the national economy, they have been in conflict with the state. The textile sector is a good example of this faction, with enterprises increasingly relying on subcontractors and informal workers, or moving their factories either inland or overseas, where they can pay lower wages.

Since the mid-2000s, in a context of rising wages, labour unrest and economic slowdown, and in order to lessen the economy's dependence on cheap labour and cheap land, the state has supported innovation. Thus an 'innovation faction' has emerged that relies on technical innovation and improved labour productivity for accumulation. The rapid growth of this faction is due to the state's supportive policies and, unlike the previous faction, expansion of domestic markets. Giant ecommerce enterprises are members of this faction.

Finally, as a result of the economic slowdown after the 2008 global financial crisis, rising wages in manufacturing and growing competition on the international market, Chinese capitalists have increasingly engaged in speculative financial activities. As a consequence of the decline in the profitability of capital accumulation, a 'finance faction' has emerged. A major challenge for the state is to regulate the activities of these entrepreneurs, both domestically and overseas. The HNA Group, founded in 2000 and involved in numerous industries including aviation, real estate, financial services, tourism and logistics, is one example of a diversified Chinese investment company; in 2021, after debt restructuring efforts failed, the corporation declared bankruptcy.

Beyond this diversity, Thomas Heberer and Gunter Schubert (2017, 101) argue that entrepreneurs, as the years go by, share a 'collective identity' resulting from belonging to the same networks, from having similar social backgrounds, social values and lifestyle patterns, and from their common exposure to the pressures and institutional constraints of China's political system. Again, comparatively, the Chinese configuration is quite unique, since the private sector has not emerged in opposition to the state, but as a result of its initiatives.

Private Entrepreneurs as Political Actors?

Political scientists have paid particular attention to the development of the Chinese private sector, inspired by seminal work on the links between economic and political modernisation (Lipset 1959). What could be the political role of the capitalist class, and could it be a social force for democratic change? In the case of China, the question is all the more difficult because the state is the main architect of economic and social transformation. After several decades, the debate is still open. Under Xi Jinping's mandate, the presence of the CCP in private enterprise has increased and entrepreneurs have been asked to join the Party's efforts to build a more socially and economically fair society; we argue that this illustrates the unequal alliance between capitalists and the CCP.

Most scholars have argued that Chinese private entrepreneurs form a largely atomised group of people focused on their individual interests and unable, or unwilling, to engage in collective action. According to Kellee Tsai (2007), since organising collective action and confronting a repressive regime carry huge costs and risks, Chinese private entrepreneurs understandably prefer other alternatives; they adopt various coping strategies, mostly relational, under China's relatively flexible formal institutional arrangements. In the early 2000s, Bruce Dickson (2003, 2008; Chen and Dickson 2010) argued that this social group that had emerged under the policy of reform and opening up favoured the political status quo and was, therefore, unlikely to bring about a shift towards more democracy. Private entrepreneurs are dependent on the party-state for their prosperity; coopted by the CCP, often from the apparatus (i.e. former Party or state cadres, or former managers or employees of state-owned enterprises), they are also its allies.

While most of the literature agrees that China's capitalists are politically coopted by the regime, Thomas Heberer and Gunter Schubert (2017) have recently argued that private entrepreneurs increasingly pursue their interests as a group in an uncoordinated and yet strategic way by working through formal and informal communication channels. The change of dynamics between the private sector and the state over the past decade suggests that private entrepreneurs could be considered a 'strategic group' (Heberer and Schubert 2017). While they do not openly challenge the CCP, they continuously alter the power balance within the current regime coalition. On the basis of surveys carried out between 2012 and 2016, Heberer and Schubert argue that private entrepreneurs hold increasing negotiating power vis-a-vis the party-state, though they are still not challenging the regime. Whereas previous authors underlined the incorporation of private entrepreneurs within the party-state, Heberer and Schubert emphasise the various forms of collective action and distinguish between formal and informal communication channels. Since the early 2000s, the CCP has been integrating emerging private business elites into the party-state through a variety of formal institutional arrangement: granting CCP memberships and allowing them to act as national- or local-level legislators.

At the local level, Zhang Changdong (2017) sees the same growing importance of private entrepreneurs. Over the years, private entrepreneur deputies have become the second largest deputy group in local people's congresses at the county and township levels in many regions. Zhang tries to assess if this change makes local congresses more representative and therefore makes local government more responsive. On the contrary, he finds that the cooption of economic elites generates patron–client relationships. In addition, direct elections are tightly controlled and sometimes deteriorate into personalised patronages, because private entrepreneurs purchase votes to win personal privileges, rather than to promote institutional reform (Zhang 2017, 17).

Obviously, private entrepreneurs are increasingly participating in legislative bodies at the national and local levels. The question of how they use their mandates is still open to debate. Yue Hou (2019) argues that private entrepreneurs actively seek opportunities within formal institutions to advance their business interests. By securing seats in the local legislatures, entrepreneurs use their political capital to deter local officials from demanding bribes, ad hoc taxes and other types of informal payments. In doing so, and in the absence of the rule of law, they create a system of selective, individualised and predictable property rights.

Business associations are another arena in which private entrepreneurs may forge their social identity and promote their interests. Examples are the AFIC, specialised trade and industry associations at the national level and associations established by local governments or set up by entrepreneurs themselves at the local level. Besides these formal institutions, there are an expanding number of information organisations where private entrepreneurs meet, such as clubs and circles of all kinds (Heberer and Schubert 2019, 488–92).

Party-Building in the Private Sector

While entrepreneurs are increasingly involved in formal arenas where public policies are debated, and are developing informal capacities to influence these policies, the CCP has deployed a variety of measures to expand into the private sector. Since the early 2000s, a major innovation has been the establishment of Party cells in private enterprises.

Xiaojun Yan and Jie Huang (2017) examine a campaign initiated in 2012 in Anhui Province by the CCP to extend its control over the increasingly powerful and influential private sector. The CCP used four key methods.

First, it created a new institution, an agency specifically dedicated to this task. Second, it sent down a group of 'party-building instructors' (*dangjian zhidaoyuan* 党建指导员), reminiscent of the 'work teams' deployed during the political campaigns of the Maoist era, when higher authorities sent external cadres to complete internal rectification tasks. Unlike China's traditional work teams, Party-building instructors today adopt a business-friendly approach and seek to facilitate and promote Party-building by providing their host firms with meaningful services and tangible benefits. Third, the CCP rewards private business elites with 'appointments to political positions' (*zhengzhi anpai* 整治安排), such as membership in local congresses or Party congresses. The Party is aware of the value of these prestigious appointments and uses them to incentivise private business elites to assist in local Party-building. Anhui's Party authorities have also encouraged private entrepreneurs and their family members to head the Party organisations within their businesses. As a result, the entrepreneurs targeted by government policies are transformed into guards of the CCP. Fourth, the CCP reorients the work of local Party organs to better serve the needs of the private sector; Party organisations within private firms are business-oriented and support production services and employees' welfare rather than intervening in day-to-day management and strategic planning. This is a striking example of the various techniques used by the CCP to penetrate private corporations. Daniel Koss (2021) has recently argued that the infiltration of firms by the CCP, from board rooms down to factory floors, has relied on the mobilisation of various recipes found in the organisation's history, calling it an 'institutional bricolage'. On one side, it is an innovation, since private firms disappeared in the 1950s; on the other side, the Party can build on its past experience, notably the establishment of committees in autonomously governed villages during the revolutionary era.

State-Driven Philanthropy

The increasing intrusion of the CCP into the private sector is one of the tools used by Xi Jinping to make China more socialist since 2012. During his first mandate, he increased Party discipline and asserted his commitment to promote the 'China Dream' and 'socialist core values'. Poised to begin a third term in 2022, Xi is now calling for China to achieve 'common prosperity' (*gongtong fuyu* 共同富裕), seeking to narrow a yawning wealth gap that threatens the country's economic ascent and the legitimacy of CCP rule. During the year 2021, Xi signalled a heightened commitment to delivering common prosperity, emphasising that it is not just an economic objective but core to the Party's governing foundation. To reach that goal, Xi explicitly encouraged high-income firms and individuals to contribute more to society via the so-called third distribution: charity and donations.[10]

Answering that call, several tech industry heavyweights, such as Alibaba and Tencent, announced major charitable donations and support for disaster relief efforts.[11] This is the latest avatar of a policy initiated more than 10 years ago, notably through the drafting of a charity law in 2016. Entrepreneurs' foundation's missions align with the state's core social welfare goals: disaster relief, poverty alleviation, assisting disadvantaged people and promoting education. Philanthropic action, understood within the framework of exchanges between capitalists and the party-state, is then similar to a more or less constrained redistribution of resources.

As in the United States at the end of the nineteenth century, philanthropy is being revived in contemporary China in an attempt to handle social issues. Private entrepreneurs are becoming agents of social justice, but, far from replacing state action, they are supportive of it. In so doing, private corporations join the efforts to build a new legitimacy for the party-state (Guiheux 2015). American donors refused to be confined to a role of complementing the state and insisted – and still insist today – on the innovative dimension of their philanthropic investments, including in the field of social or educational policies. In contemporary China, not only does the CCP still have a monopoly on defining public interest, but also private entrepreneurs and firms are confined to a complementary role vis-a-vis the party-state, forced to give back some of what they have gained from society in the shape of donations to government-recognised charity or assistance to government-backed projects.

After Jiang Zemin proposed the 'Three Represents' in 2001, the CCP and entrepreneurs entered a honeymoon period of more than 10 years. When Xi Jinping came to power in 2012, he began to strengthen the management of entrepreneurs and organisations. Recently, the government has pursued the 'common prosperity' agenda with a series of striking reforms, amounting to a major crackdown on tech, platform economy, private education, real

10 'China's "Common Prosperity" Goal to Evenly Distribute Wealth as Xi Jinping Sets Out Stall for Development', *South China Morning Post*, 18 August 2021, www.scmp.com/economy/china-economy/article/3145439/chinas-wealthy-urged-xi-jinping-give-back-society-ensure.

11 'Chinese Tech Giants Led by Alibaba and Tencent Donate Millions towards Flood Relief Efforts in Shanxi', *South China Morning Post*, 11 October 2021, www.scmp.com/tech/big-tech/article/3151924/chinese-tech-giants-led-alibaba-and-tencent-donate-millions-towards.

estate and financial capital. For some, this storm of new regulations aims to increase the size of middle-income groups, raise the earnings of low-income groups and reduce excessive incomes (Dunford 2022). But there is a high risk that the crackdown is killing the innovation, creativity and entrepreneurial spirit of the Chinese private sector. The state intervention has resulted in entrepreneurs' losing confidence in China's future.

Conclusion

In contemporary China, as the private sector is a major engine of economic growth, the authorities cannot do without private entrepreneurs. But, at the same time, at the local and national levels, the regime remains authoritarian; the party-state keeps its monopoly on the political agenda. This does not mean that it is not porous to certain interest groups, but it is still able to draw the line. The Party needs private entrepreneurs to create jobs, reduce poverty and create wealth, yet it is not ready to cede its leadership role, which helps explain why any individual who oversteps the boundaries is likely to fall. The party-state still directly controls a large state sector and access to loans, land and many material resources, and it monopolises legal and coercive resources. Collaboration between the party-state and the private sector is on an unequal footing and can be characterised as an 'asymmetric mutual dependence' (Zhang 2019).

Looking at today's relationship between the Party and private entrepreneurs from the perspective of the early years of the regime, the collaboration looks less exceptional than it might at first glance. We do not claim that post-Mao China is identical to China under Mao, but we argue that the CCP finds a useful repertoire of actions in the founding years of the regime. Although, ideologically, capitalism was the ultimate target of the revolution, within the first years after the CCP took power, under the broad strategy of the united front, it collaborated with 'national' capitalists. Our conclusion is in line with Sebastian Heilmann and Elizabeth Perry's (2011) argument that 'adaptive governance' – concrete mechanisms and techniques of governance that were shaped during the pre-1949 decades of guerrilla fighting and resistance, and, we argue, in the early 1950s – has continued to influence policymaking, providing the CCP with a unique resource of high resilience and adaptability.

References

Bergère, Marie-Claire. 1969. 'La bourgeoisie chinoise et les problèmes de développement économique (1917-1923)'. *Revue d'histoire moderne et contemporaine* 16 (2): 246–67. doi.org/10.3406/rhmc.1969.3204.

Bergère, Marie-Claire. 1989. 'Les capitalistes shanghaiens et la période de transition entre le régime Guomindang et le communisme (1948–1952)'. *Etudes chinoises* VIII-2: 7–30. doi.org/10.3406/etchi.1989.1107.

Bergère, Marie-Claire. 2009. *The Golden Age of the Chinese Bourgeoisie 1911–1937*. Cambridge: Cambridge University Press.

Chan, Kai Yiu. 2014. 'Think it through Three Times: Zhang Jianhui's Decisions in the 1950s'. In *The Capitalist Dilemma in China's Communist Revolution*, edited by Sherman Cocharan, 67–88. Cornell: Cornell University Press.

Chen, Guangjin, Peng Lu, Zeyan Lin and Na Song. 2019. 'Introducing Chinese Private Enterprise Survey: Points and Prospects'. *Nankai Business Review International* 10 (4): 501–25. doi.org/10.1108/NBRI-01-2019-0001.

Chen Jianfu. 2004. 'The Revision of the Constitution in the PRC: A Great Leap Forward or a Symbolic Gesture?' *China Perspectives* 53 (May–June): 15–32. doi.org/10.4000/chinaperspectives.2922.

Chen, Jie and Bruce Dickson. 2010. *Allies of the State: China's Private Entrepreneurs and Democratic Change*. Cambridge: Harvard University Press. doi.org/10.2307/j.ctv1r4xd8m.

Chen, Zhenqing. 2014. 'Socialist Transformation and the Demise of Private Entrepreneurs'. *European Journal of East Asian Studies* 13: 240–61. doi.org/10.1163/15700615-01302006.

Cliver, Robert. 2021. 'Factory Management in Chinese Capitalist Enterprises in the 1950s: The Case of the Shanghai Silk Weaving Industry Labour–Capital Consultative Conference'. *Entreprises et Histoire* 103: 36–53. doi.org/10.3917/eh.103.0036.

Coble, Parks M. 1980. *The Shanghai Capitalists and the Nationalist Government, 1927–1937*. Cambridge: Harvard University Press. doi.org/10.2307/j.ctt1tfjd17.

Cochran, Sherman. 2007. 'Capitalists Choosing Communist China: The Liu Family in Shanghai, 1948–56'. In *Dilemmas of Victory: The Early Years of the People's Republic of China*, edited by Jeremy Brown and Paul G. Pickowicz, 359–86. Cambridge: Harvard University Press. doi.org/10.4159/9780674033658-015.

Cochran, Sherman, ed. 2014. *The Capitalist Dilemma in China's Communist Revolution*. Ithaca: Cornell University Press.

Dickson, Bruce. 2003. *Red Capitalists in China: The Party, Private Entrepreneurs and Prospects for Political Change*. Cambridge: Cambridge University Press. doi.org/10.1017/CBO9780511510045.

Dickson, Bruce. 2008. *Wealth into Power: The Communist Party's Embrace of China's Private Sector*. Cambridge: Cambridge University Press. doi.org/10.1017/CBO9780511790706.

Dunford, Michael. 2022. 'The Chinese Path to Common Prosperity'. *International Critical Thought* 12 (1): 35–54. doi.org/10.1080/21598282.2022.2025561.

Fan, Xiaoguang and Lü Peng. 2019. 'The Social Composition of China's Private Entrepreneurs: Class and Cohort Differences'. *Social Sciences in China* 40 (1): 42–62. doi.org/10.1080/02529203.2019.1556472.

Fewsmith, Joseph. 2001. 'Rethinking the Role of the CCP: Explicating Jiang Zemin's Party Anniversary Speech'. *China Leadership Monitor* 1 (2) (December).

Guiheux, Gilles. 2007. 'The Promotion of a New Calculating Chinese Subject: The Case of Laid-Off Workers Turning into Entrepreneurs'. *Journal of Contemporary China* 16 (50): 149–71. doi.org/10.1080/10670560601026884.

Guiheux, Gilles. 2012. 'Chinese Socialist Heroes: From Workers to Entrepreneurs'. In *Towards a New Development Paradigm in Twenty-First Century China: Economy, Society and Politics*, edited by Eric Florence and Pierre Defraigne, 115–26. London: Routledge.

Guiheux, Gilles. 2015. 'Philanthropie d'entrepreneurs et construction d'un nouveau compromis social en Chine contemporaine'. In *Travail, luttes sociales et régulation du capitalisme dans la Chine contemporaine*, edited by Clément Sehier and Richard Sobel, 123–42. Lille: Presses Universitaires du Septentrion. doi.org/10.4000/books.septentrion.5804.

Heberer, Thomas and Gunter Schubert. 2017. 'Private Entrepreneurs as a "Strategic Group" in the Chinese Polity'. *China Review* 17 (2): 95–122.

Heberer, Thomas and Gunter Schubert. 2019. 'Weapons of the Rich: Strategic Behavior and Collective Action of Private Entrepreneurs in China'. *Modern China* 45 (5): 471–503. doi.org/10.1177/0097700418808755.

Heilmann, Sebastian and Elizabeth J. Perry. 2011. 'Embracing Uncertainty: Guerrilla Policy Style and Adaptive Governance in China'. In *Mao's Invisible Hand: The Political Foundations of Adaptative Governance in China*, edited by Sebastian Heilmann and Elizabeth J. Perry, 1–29. Cambridge: Harvard University Press. doi.org/10.2307/j.ctt1sq5tc6.7.

Henriot, Christian. 2014. 'The Great Spoliation: The Socialist Transformation of Industry in 1950s China'. *European Journal of East Asian Studies* 13: 155–62. doi.org/10.1163/15700615-01302002.

Kirby, William C. 1995. 'China Unincorporated: Company Law and Business Enterprise in Twentieth-Century China'. *Journal of Asian Studies* 54 (1): 43–63. doi.org/10.2307/2058950.

Koss, Daniel. 2021. 'Party Building as Institutional Bricolage: Asserting Authority at the Business Frontier'. *China Quarterly* 248: 222–43. doi.org/10.1017/S0305741021000692.

Leighton, Christopher. 2010. 'Capitalists, Cadres and Culture in 1950s China'. PhD thesis, Harvard University.

Lipset, Seymour. 1959. 'Some Social Requisites of Democracy: Economic Development and Political Legitimacy'. *American Political Science Review* 53 (1): 69–105. doi.org/10.2307/1951731.

Lu, Hanchao. 2018. 'Bourgeois Comfort under Proletarian Dictatorship: Home Life of Chinese Capitalists before the Cultural Revolution'. *Journal of Social History* 52 (1): 74–100. doi.org/10.1093/jsh/shx145.

Nogueira, Isabela and Hao Qi. 2019. 'The State and Domestic Capitalists in China's Economic Transition: From Great Compromise to Strained Alliance'. *Critical Asian Studies* 51 (4): 558–78. doi.org/10.1080/14672715.2019.1665469.

Parris, Kristen. 1999. 'The Rise of Private Business Interests'. In *The Paradox of China's Post Mao Reforms*, edited by Merle Goldman and Roderick MacFarquhar, 262–82. Cambridge: Harvard University Press.

Rose, Nikolas. 1992. 'Governing the Enterprising Self'. In *The Values of the Enterprise Culture: The Moral Debate*, edited by Heelas Paul and Morris Paul, 141–64. London and New York: Routledge.

Tsai, Kellee. 2005. 'Capitalists without a Class: Political Diversity Among Private Entrepreneurs in China'. *Comparative Political Studies* 38 (9): 1130–58. doi.org/10.1177/0010414005277021.

Tsai, Kellee S. 2007. *Capitalism without Democracy: The Private Sector in Contemporary China*. Ithaca: Cornell University Press.

Xiao-Planes, Xiaohong. 2014. '"Buy 20 Years": Li Kangnian Class Identity and the Controversy over the Socialisation of Private Business in 1957'. *European Journal of East Asian Studies* 13: 214–39. doi.org/10.1163/15700615-01302005.

Yan, Xiaojun and Huang Jie. 2017. 'Navigating Unknown Waters: The CCP's New Presence in the Private Sector'. *China Review* 17 (2): 37–63.

Yang, Kuisong. 2007. 'The Evolution of the Chinese Communist Party's Policy on the Bourgeoisie (1949–1952)'. *Journal of Modern Chinese History* 1 (1): 13–30. doi.org/10.1080/17535650701521049.

Yue, Hou. 2019. *The Private Sector in Public Office: Selective Property Rights in China*. New York: Cambridge University Press. doi.org/10.1017/9781108632522.

Zhang, Changdong. 2017. 'Reexamining the Electoral Connection in Authoritarian China: The Local People's Congress and Its Private Entrepreneur Deputies'. *China Review* 17 (1): 1–27.

Zhang, Changdong. 2019. 'Asymmetric Mutual Dependence between the State and Capitalists in China'. *Politics and Society* 47 (2): 149–76. doi.org/10.1177/0032329219833282.

Zhang, Houyi (张厚义) and Liu Wenpu (刘文璞). 1995. *Chinese Private Economy and Private Entrepreneurs* (中国的私营经济与私营企业主). Beijing: Zhishi chubanshe.

Zhang, Houyi (张厚义), Ming Lizhi (明立志) and Liang Zhuanyun (梁传运), eds. 2003. *Blue Book of Private Enterprises* (中国私营企业发展报告). Beijing: Shehuikexue wenxian chubanshe.

Zhao, Jin. 2014. '"A Helpless Choice": Liu Hongsheng's Zhanghua Company in the Throes of Socialist Transformation'. *European Journal of East Asian Studies* 13: 262–83. doi.org/10.1163/15700615-01302007.

IV. TERRITORIAL CONTROL AND NATION-BUILDING

13

'Unity within Diversity': The Chinese Communist Party's Construction of the Chinese Nation

Vanessa Frangville

When the Chinese Communist Party (CCP) took power in 1949, it inherited the territorial boundaries of the Qing dynasty and Republican China (excluding the northern part of Mongolia, which became an independent state after the 1910s). The inclusion of these territories and their populations into the newly established People's Republic of China (PRC) was not to be questioned, but how to integrate them was a core issue for the CCP. Indeed, beyond extending its administration and control over remote but crucial border areas, and to earn the loyalty of non-Han populations that largely inhabited them, the CCP had to define the Chinese nation in inclusive terms that could coincide with its political objectives and show a sharp difference from the Nationalist's assimilationist policies.

The objective of this chapter is to examine some key concepts and issues that shaped the CCP's vision and construction of the Chinese nation over the past century, starting from the late Qing when new narratives of the modern nation-state developed in China, with an emphasis on both the Republican era and the PRC. While I am aware that the implementation or content of ethnic policies may vary from one area to another to adjust to different geopolitical or economic situations (see Castets, Chapter 14, this volume, on the Uygur region; Bulag 2002 on Inner Mongolia), the main purpose of this chapter is to provide a broad picture of the CCP's discourse on China's ethnic diversity over the past century. By taking the concept of *minzu* (and its derivative) as a case in point, I identify trends and shifts in this nation-building process and try to link intellectual debates to policymaking. Through discourse analysis, I show that, up to now, different and sometimes antithetical perceptions of China's national identity coexist within the CCP, creating tensions and a longstanding oscillation between integration and assimilation. Considering recent developments in Tibet, Xinjiang and Mongolia (from the prohibition of local languages in schools to massive arrests and interments), this chapter argues that even though the CCP's policy after 1949 tried to use socialist affirmative strategy towards its minorities under the Soviet influence, the legacy of China's imperial occupation of non-Han border regions has remained its main drive. Such colonialist endeavours have resurfaced more overtly in the twenty-first century as securitisation has become a priority for Xi's government and have accelerated assimilationist trends by emphasising a Han-centred definition of the Chinese nation.

In this process of imagining and articulating a Chinese nation in the socialist era, the intellectual elite played an important role, from the late Qing and the Republican era to today's PRC. One key concept they have paid special attention to is *minzu* (民族), which refers to at least three different ideas: *minzu* as a national or ethnic group; *minzu* as a nation, here the Chinese nation (*Zhonghua minzu* 中华民族); and *minzu* as an informal shortcut for *shaoshu minzu* 少数民族 (minority ethnic groups), excluding the Han majority. The ambiguous meaning and inconsistent usages of *minzu* have been the objects of negotiations since the early stages of the formation of the PRC, and were at the heart of fiery debates in recent years, when the CCP policies in border areas were questioned following repeated uprisings in Tibet and Xinjiang in the late 2000s. Considering the symbiotic connection between academics and the government elites in this matter (Leibold 2013; Zhao and Tok 2021), looking into these discussions is essential to understand recent shifts in the CCP's delineation of the Chinese nation and their impact on policies towards non-Han populations. Indeed, as knowledge producers or 'actors of China's knowledge regime' (Zhao and Tok 2021, 167), public intellectuals and academics have been an important driving force for domestic change throughout China's modern history (Guo 2013b). In recent years, scholars have been increasingly called on to capitalise on their expertise to advise policymakers at local and national levels (Guo 2013a). Further, as institutional (or personal) connections between academics and policymakers are strong, it is not uncommon for an academic to be both a policy adviser and a decision-maker (Zhao and Tok 2021). This is particularly true for topics related to China's national identity and ethnic diversity management, for which academics are particularly active in the provision of recommendations to state actors (Zhao and Tok 2021). Thus, this chapter primarily looks at public academic debates to understand the extent to which they have influenced the CCP's approach to the Chinese nation and related policy in the last decade.

The first part of this chapter gives a brief overview of the emergence of *minzu*, defined here as a performative utterance that played a major role in the construction of a Chinese nation under the late-imperial and Republican periods. Ideas developed around *minzu* in the early twentieth century are indeed crucial to comprehending how the CCP positioned itself in its formative years. Although the Leninist model of the 'national question' is officially a main inspiration, the young CCP chiefly conceived its policies towards non-Han along imperial views of frontier management. Conversely, notions from the pre-1949 period have been recycled in present-day discourses and policies, as Xi Jinping's formulation of the Chinese nation, supported by academics-turned-policy-advisers calling for reforms in ethnic policies, borrows heavily from the imperial and Republican models more than from Marxist–Leninist concepts.

The second part looks at how the CCP at first attempted to step aside from previous assimilationist views and policies, and establish a more inclusive, though tightly framed, definition of the PRC as a unitary multinational state (*tongyi duo minzu de guojia* 统一多民族国家). Indeed, CCP leaders before 1949 were acutely aware of the dialectical relationship between the nation as a whole and its fragmented composition into several national groups, or what became the 'national question' (*minzu wenti* 民族问题, which can express both concerns for the nation and potential issues posed by non-Han integration). However, after 1949, the CCP was caught between the call for recognising and supporting diversity among its vast population and the imperative to maintain its territorial integrity, which resulted in a persistent gap between principles or regulations and practices, especially after the 1980s, when most measures discussed in the 1950s and 1960s were more systematically implemented.

The last part takes a close look at the gradual tightening around ethnic issues and the reshaping of the idea of the Chinese nation throughout the reform era, reaching an unprecedented point in the CCP's history when

Xi emphasised the need to build a sense of 'community of the Chinese nation' and introduced, for the first time, the idea of a 'Chinese nation' in the constitution in 2018. This assimilationist turn finds its roots in the aftermath of the 1989 Tiananmen protest and the collapse of the USSR in 1991, when national stability and territorial integrity became a priority in the CCP's agenda. At the same time, throughout the 1990s and 2000s, tensions dramatically increased in peripheral regions, where discrimination and social–economic marginalisation of non-Han had worsened. Consequently, the accommodationist approach that prevailed in the first few decades of the PRC was gradually questioned by scholars calling for a radical change. In influencing policymakers, these scholars competed with those in favour of a status quo in ethnic policies. *Minzu* thus became the subject of heated discussions about its implications and (mis)usage, leading to an ideological and political divide around the means of integrating non-Han groups into the Chinese nation – and, by essence, around the very definition of the Chinese nation.

The Formation of a Multinational/Multiracial China: From Federalism to Autonomy

Introduced by the Chinese elite in the 1890s, the concept of *minzu* has been constructed in the past century by borrowing Western, Japanese and Soviet ideas of nation. The term was imported from the Japanese *minzoku* (民族), a transfer generally attributed to thinker and essayist Liang Qichao (梁启超, 1873–1929), exiled in Tokyo after the failure of the Hundred Days' reform (1898). *Minzoku* was itself a translation from German to refer to the notions of *Volk* or nation in the civic sense, and *nation* in the ethnic sense (Burtscher 2012).[1] Within the Japanese context, *minzoku* supported both an ethno-racial division in response to the growing influence of Western powers in the East Asian region (Burtscher 2012), and the necessity of unifying the Japanese people under a racial imaginary during the period of territorial expansion in East Asia (Saito and Tsuboi 2015). This ethno-racial vision also dominated the importation of the *minzoku/minzu* concept to China, as Liang Qichao insisted on the historical

1 Brought over by Japanese jurists and philosophers returning from Germany, *minzoku* was a translation of concepts developed by German-speaking Swiss jurist Johann Caspar Bluntschli in his edited volume *Deutsche Staatslehre für Gebildete* (German Political Readings for the Educated), published in 1874.

connotation of *minzu*, in contrast to the political construction implied in other concepts that emerged in the same period, such as *kokumin/guomin* 國民 (civic nation, citizen).[2]

However, in contrast to Japan, which defined itself as mono-racial (under the 'Yamato race', *Yamato minzoku* 山本民族), the reality in China was one of an empire that integrated culturally diverse populations through conquests and annexations during the different periods of its history. Despite being perceived by imperial history as a civilising and superior people, the Han category was not forged on the idea of racial purity but remained flexible, without fixed borders, including the populations that submitted themselves to the rites and institutions of the emperor (Elliott 2012; Joniak-Luthi 2015). It was only at the end of the Qing dynasty that Han became a fixed and unified category (Joniak-Luthi 2015), and that a discourse synonymising Han with the legitimate inheritors of Chinese territories (Villard 2010), in opposition to the Manchus who then ruled the empire, emerged.

In this context, two opposing conceptions of the Chinese nation developed at the end of the Qing. On the one hand, part of the elite, such as the revolutionary philologist Zhang Bingling (张炳灵, 1869–1936), determined the Chinese nation in both geographical and cultural terms by introducing the terms *Zhonghua minzu* (literally, the nation of the central Hua region) and *Zhonghuaren* 中华人. Under this conception, only the 'Han race' (*hanzu* 汉族) were legitimate descendants of the Yellow Emperor to which power would legitimately return (Chow 1997). This narrow definition opened the possibility of abandoning the non-Han occupied territories, such as Tibet, Mongolia and Xinjiang, to establish a republic centred solely on historically Han territories (Leibold 2004).

On the other hand, reformists such as Liang Qichao, careful of preserving the entirety of the Chinese territories conquered by the Qing (of which the Han represented a limited portion), proposed a wider definition of the Chinese nation as an entity resulting from a merger or amalgamation (*ronghe* 融合) of different peoples, following the American 'melting pot' model (Leibold 2004, 176). The Manchus, and similarly the Hui (including the

2 In Japanese, *Minzoku* is a contraction of *ichizoku no jinmin* 一族ノ人民 (people of the same tribe or lineage). It is distinguished from *kokumin* 國民 (civic nation, citizen), which is a contraction of *ikkoku no jinmin* 一國ノ人民 (people of the same country/state). Liang Qichao emphasised this distinction when importing *minzoku/minzu* to China.

Turkic-speaking Muslim populations of the western regions)[3] as well as the Mongols and the Tibetans, were also pictured as descendants of the Yellow Emperor (Liang 1989) and could be part of the Chinese nation if only they assimilated into the Han.

By the time the Qing dynasty fell, the latter vision had been espoused. In 1912, the last emperor's abdication decree stipulated that it handed over to the new Republic of China 'the complete territorial integrity of the lands of the five races – Manchu, Han, Mongol, Hui and Tibetans – which shall combine to form a great Republic of China' (Gao 2016, 248).[4] A 'Republic of Five Races' (*wuzu gonghe* 五族共和) was thus established, assuring the integrity of the inherited national territory. The Han still remained the 'spine' (*gugan* 骨干) around which the other *minzu* would integrate themselves through a process of assimilation or *tonghua* 同化 (Leibold 2007, 32). Revolution leader and first president Sun Yat-sen (孙中山, 1866–1925) indeed favoured a discourse of integration of non-Han peoples, also called 'peoples of the borders' (*bianjiang minzu* 边疆民族), within the Han nation as being in their own interest; the adoption of the customs and institutions of the Han would allow their survival in a transforming world. At the centre of the question of survival was also the notion of blood (*xue* 血); the future of the non-Han depended on their capacity to biologically mix with the Han, thus stepping from a culturalist vision into a racialised representation of the Chinese nation.

Thus was set in motion an organic rhetoric concerning the relations between the Han and non-Han, presented in the speech Sun gave during the creation of the republic in 1912, which constituted the Chinese nation as 'one family' (*yijia* 一家), or 'one body' (*yiti* 一体) (Leibold 2004, 182; Sun 1982). Similarly, the ground was set for a nation imagined on two levels: the supra-nation or *zhonghua minzu*; and the infra-nation (or nations, *minzu*), also comprising the Han, which took the form of a group conceived as historically homogenous and unified. This conception of a Chinese nation likewise reveals an essential dichotomy in the formation and evolution of the discourse of national construction in China: the systematic opposition of Han versus an indistinct mass of numerous non-Han people. This distinction was embedded in the use of *shaoshu minzu* (literally, minority nation), a term that emerged in 1923 through the Comintern when Sun

3 In late imperial China, Hui or Huihui was a generic name for all Muslims in China. The CCP restricted the definition of Hui as sinophone Muslims in the 1930s and 1940s, in contrast with the first Republic, which encompassed all Muslims under the same term Hui.

4 In Chinese: '合滿、漢、蒙、回、藏五族完全領土爲一大中華民國'.

Yat-sen invited the CCP to form a united front; it was also put forward in Sun's speech at the opening of the first meeting of the Nationalist Party (Guomindang 国民党 or GMD) in 1924 (Liu 2001; Jin 1987). From then on, the term *shaoshu minzu* appeared regularly in speeches from both the GMD as well as the CCP.

The relation to territoriality was also primordial in juxtaposing state and national space. The loss of Mongolia in 1911,[5] as well as the threat that Japan presented to Manchuria and Russia in the north-west, confirmed the urgency of rethinking the Chinese nation in less exclusivist terms. Sun thus formed the connection between state and nation: 'One sole nation had founded one sole country' (*yige minzu zaocheng yige guojia* 一个民族造成一个国家). Although Sun and GMD leader Chiang Kai-shek (Jiang Jieshi 蒋介石, 1887–1975) did not necessarily share the same vision of the Chinese nation – China being multinational for Sun (who even supported self-determination in the 1920s) while Chiang conceived China as made up of only one nation – both advocated assimilationist policies (Grunfeld 1985; Zheng 2019).

The young CCP, on the other hand, in its 1922 Second National Congress, suggested a Chinese Federated Republic (*Zhonghua lianbang gongheguo* 中華聯邦共和國) including China proper, Mongolia, Tibet and Xinjiang (Brandt, Schwartz and Fairbank 1966), borrowing from Sun's idea of a multinational China. In its 1931 Soviet Constitution of Jiangxi,[6] article 14, the CCP even explicitly supported the idea of self-determination of its peoples and opened the possibility for the future independence of non-Han populations that did not historically identify with China (Villard 2010, 316–17; Zhu and Yu 2000, 48).[7] The unconditional adhesion of

5 The fall of the Qing empire was followed by a proclamation of independence by the northern half of Mongolia, which was a loss of 1.5 million square kilometres for the Republic of China along the Sino-Russian border. The People's Republic of Mongolia was proclaimed, under Soviet protection, in 1924.

6 The Soviet Republic of China (*Zhonghua suwei'ai gongheguo* 中华苏维埃共和国), whose central base was located in Jiangxi, was established in 1931 by Mao Zedong. It was dissolved in 1937, after the Nationalist Party retook control over the totality of the territories of the Republic of China.

7 This article states:

> The Soviet government of China recognises the *right of self-determination* of the national minorities in China, their *right to complete separation* from China, and to the formation of an independent state for each national minority. All Mongolians, Tibetans, Miao, Yao, Koreans, and others living on the territory of China shall enjoy the full right to self-determination, i.e. they may either join the Union of Chinese Soviets or secede from it and form their own state as they may prefer … The Soviet regime must encourage the development of the national cultures and of the respective national languages of these peoples.

Translation adapted from Brandt, Schwartz and Fairbank (1966, 223, emphasis added).

all non-Han groups to a Chinese multinational state was, however, taken for granted, and support for self-determination was rather rhetorical to be in line with Moscow (Leung 1981). Mixed experiences with non-Han populations along the Long March (1934–35) led CCP leaders to rethink their position, as they realised that non-Han were not natural allies and that Red Army bases in non-Han regions could face strong resistance from the local elite (Liu 2004, 79–81). The Yan'an period marked a definitive shift from Marxist–Leninist dogma on the national question. Subsequently, the inclusion of the non-Han people into a unified Chinese nation was stressed again, building more tightly on Han-centrism.

After the Long March ended, no further mention of independence was made in the CCP's official statements. The 'national question' was no longer framed in terms of a struggle for independence from the state, but in terms of class struggle under the soon-to-be Communist republic. *Quyu* or 'autonomous regional zones' (*minzu quyu zizhi* 民族区域自治) replaced the idea of 'national autonomy' (*minzu zizhi* 民族自治) for the regions primarily inhabited by non-Han groups. The primary connotation of the local in *quyu* thus placed the regions under a central authority while also putting in place a system of relative autonomy (Bulag 2020a). The autonomous region system, based on the entanglement between national diversity and territories, was obviously the legacy of both empire and Soviet principles.

Multiple Yet One: The CCP's Dialectical Process of Nation-Building

As the CCP began to implement new laws and rewrite its constitution after 1949, debates on the nature of the Chinese nation took place again. The CCP confirmed its vision of a Chinese nation composed of several groups in its 1954 constitution, of which article 3 stated that the PRC was a 'unitary multinational state' (*tongyi de duo minzu guojia* 统一的多民族的国家).[8] Nevertheless, not all agreed on the term *minzu*. Inspired by Soviet terminology, *minzu* was then used to refer to *nation* or *natsia* (Нация or the most advanced state of society) and determined according to Stalinist

8 Chinese and English versions of the 1954 constitution are available on the website of the Peking University Centre for Legal Information: en.pkulaw.cn/display.aspx?cgid=52993&lib=law. The same statements were moved to article 4 in the 1982 constitution.

criteria such as a community formed around a shared language, economy or territory as well as a sentiment of belonging to a common culture. For some, including historian and philologist Fan Wenlan (范文澜, 1893–1969), the Han had formed a nation/*minzu* corresponding to the four Stalinist criteria, without interruption, since the unification of China under the Qin (221 BC) (Fan 1954). Fan's vision was contradicted by intellectuals who reiterated that, according to Stalin, the nation was a product of capitalism, and it was therefore impossible to apply the term *minzu* to China before the Opium Wars in the mid-nineteenth century (Yang 2009; Liang 2016). On the other hand, 'nationality' (*narodnost,* Народность) was translated as *buzu* 部族 (from *buluo* 部落, tribe, not as advanced as *minzu*). Whether to qualify non-Han as a nation or as a nationality was debated. Eventually, *buzu* was rejected as too derogatory and in contradiction with the idea that all ethnic distinctions were to disappear with the enactment of socialism and the end of classes (Zhang 1997). Thus, the term *minzu* was finally adopted by the CCP for all the groups, Han and non-Han alike (Jin 1987; Thoraval 1990).

At the same time, Han chauvinism (*dahanzu zhuyi* 大汉族主义), a term coined by Mao,[9] was a constant concern up to the early years of the PRC, as a 'principal threat in … relationships among nationalities' (Nationalities Affairs Commission 1953; translation from Leung 1981), akin to 'bourgeois ideas' (Mao 1977). The 1954 constitution's preamble hence prohibited 'great nation chauvinism' (*daminzu zhuyi* 大民族主义) as well as 'local nationalisms' (*difang minzu zhuyi* 地方民族主义).

This does not mean than the Han versus non-Han divide disappeared. It was even reinforced by the vast state-launched campaigns of '*minzu* identification' (*minzu shibie* 民族识别), which led to the official recognition of 55 non-Han minority groups (*shaoshu minzu*) in the 1960s–70s. Officially based on Stalin's four criteria mentioned above, in practice, for most cases, *minzu* identities were assigned by the authorities, who gathered several different groups under state-constructed categories (Mullaney 2011; Yang 2009; Zhang 1997). Further, the identification project on the ground was rooted in colonialist modes of classification and transformation (Mullaney 2011, 99). Mullaney convincingly describes how, for instance, ethnologists and other social scientists sent by Beijing to Yunnan in the 1950s relied not

9 Mao Zedong (毛泽东), 'Anti-Japanese War and the New Stage of Development of the Anti-Japanese National United Front' (抗日民族战争与抗日民族统一战线发展的新阶段), 1938, www.marxists.org/chinese/maozedong/marxist.org-chinese-mao-19381012aa.htm.

so much on Soviet models but on the materials of Henry Rodolph Davis, a British army officer whose depiction of Yunnan peoples had become highly influential among scholars in the Republican era, thus valorising the British colonial episteme (Mullaney 2011, 54; Davies [1909] 2010). Such strategies allowed for a rapid, pragmatic and manageable taxonomy. The *minzu* category thus became fixed and exclusive. Up to today, this very recently constructed narrative of ethnic composition of China prevails, anchored within an ahistorical discourse of a millennia-old Chinese nation (Frangville 2007, 5; Pan 2016). In fact, the PRC's official discourse on a Chinese nation composed of 56 *minzu* including 55 minorities dates back to 1979, when the Jinuo were declared the fifty-fifth minority.

Within this process, the term *minzu* entered everyday official vocabulary, translated into English as 'nationality'. Even if all the groups that comprised China, both Han and non-Han, were described by the term *minzu* regardless of their social organisation or the state of their historical evolution, *minzu* slowly became associated with the non-Han. In the administrative language, all *minzu*-related affairs were, first and foremost, related to non-Han *minzu* and their relation to the majority or the state. For example, institutes of research and training were established for non-Han Party members (*minzu xueyuan* 民族学院). Other measures included the commencement of studies on the non-Han (*minzuxue* 民族学), reviews featuring the loyalty of the non-Han to state measures that were meant to instil 'national unity' (*minzu tuanjie* 民族团结) and policies reserved for the non-Han (*minzu zhengce* 民族政策). The semantic shift of *minzu* to *shaoshu minzu* had taken place while the usage of *minzu* to describe the totality of the nation weakened in favour of *renmin* or 'people' (人民) – the 1954 constitution, for instance, never mentioned *Zhonghua minzu* (Chinese nation) but stressed *Zhonghua renmin* (Chinese people). This is also true in the revised constitution of 1982, in which the concept of *Zhonghua minzu* does not appear at all and class prevailed over ethnicity.

In the decade following Mao's death, several university disciplines that had been labelled 'bourgeois' since 1950, such as ethnology, were re-established. A new generation of ethnologists and sociologists emerged who attempted to question the *minzu* classification carried out during the three decades prior, notably by pointing out the lack of coherence in its criteria (Mullaney 2011). Consequently, new campaigns were launched by the CCP in the 1980s to help people 'recover' (*huifu* 恢复) or 'change' (*gaibian* 改变) their minority identity, but no new minorities were identified. All self-reported new groups had to fit either into the Han category or into one of the 55 non-

Han groups (Wang 2019, 145). The official division between 56 *minzu*, of which 55 were 'minorities', was subsequently considered a classified affair, and this layout was eventually written in stone in 1987 as the state declared that the identification project was closed, and no other groups could claim to be a distinct *minzu* (Mullaney 2011; Yang 2009). The CCP's official (dichotomic) vision of the Chinese nation was, and remains, one of one Han majority and 55 minorities.

New contradictions also developed throughout the 1980s. On the one hand, there was a gust of liberalisation and a 'craze for culture' (*wenhua re* 文化热), whereby the accumulated interest for rethinking Chinese identity in cultural terms saw the light of day. The CCP re-established religious sites and created a positive discrimination policy favouring non-Han in terms of public employment, education, fertility and taxes. On the other hand, the overlap between Han culture and Chinese culture was strengthened in intellectual and popular discourses and permeated the CCP's policy towards non-Han. By the same token as *minzu* denoted non-Han only, Han-ness became, by default, a synonym for Chinese-ness. In fact, 'the PRC ideology also play[ed] a role in promoting Han chauvinism': non-Han were still considered 'backward' and their ways of life 'outmoded and unhealthy' (Sautman 1999, 291–2). The constant 'othering' of non-Han combined with discourses of Han superiority has been described as 'internal orientalism' (Schein 1997) or the result of an 'internal colonialism' (Gladney 1998) that arose from the Maoist area and developed after the 1980s. The Han continue to be seen as a normative, devoted and invisible majority, while the non-Han are constantly infantilised, instructed to be politically loyal and remain underrepresented in the highest political institutions (Li 2008). Even though the legislation established by the CCP provided, and still provides, instruments for recognising and condemning acts of discrimination against non-Han, very little effort has been made to implement them. As documented in scholarly literature, discrimination (and racism) against non-Han in employment (Mobius, Rosenblat and Wang 2016), earnings (MacDonald and Hasmath 2020; Zang 2011), criminal sentencing (Hou and Truex 2020) and everyday encounters (Chen 2019; Grose 2015) is not only ignored but denied in public speeches. As Deng Xiaoping (邓小平) (1904–1997) repeated on several occasions, 'there is no ethnic discrimination in the PRC' (Deng 1993; see also Sautman 1997, 80).[10]

10 In Chinese: '中华人民共和国没有民族歧视'.

Nevertheless, from the 1990s on, the CCP started to explicitly define the Chinese nation along the concept of race, reminiscent of the early twentieth century. The attachment to the state was increasingly formulated in terms of blood ties and other biological metaphors. Common ancestry of the Han and non-Han was stressed in official media, and several studies tried to demonstrate genetic similarities between, for instance, Tibetans and Han (Sautman 1997, 86; Meissner 2006), thus stressing national uniqueness and unity and representing Han as the main trunk of the 'yellow race' branched off to include the non-Han (Dikötter 2010, 9). Sustaining a 'scientific' framework, CCP leaders in the reform area constantly referred to the metaphor developed by renowned anthropologist Fei Xiaotong (费孝通) (1910–2005), who explained the subjugation of non-Han identities to an overarching Chinese national identity with the term *duoyuan yiti geju* (多元一体格局) or 'pluralistic and organic unity structure' (Fei 1989). Fei's attempt to balance ethnic diversity and national unity thus became a political framework for the CCP, especially after the fall of the Soviet bloc and the dismantlement of Yugoslavia in the early 1990s. His terminology was adopted by successive political leaders from Jiang Zemin to Hu Jintao and Xi Jinping (Zang 2015, 219).

However, tensions grew in non-Han areas as the result of the deployment of hundreds of thousands of People's Liberation Army officers and Han migrant workers sent by the state from the interior, the arrest of local leaders and religious figures, as well as increasingly race-based nationalism, with the Han at its core, supported by Beijing. While officially Han-centred nationalism was promoted by the state, non-Han nationalisms were suppressed, sometimes with much violence. This led to the fragmentation of Chinese identity (Gladney 2004) and the emergence of movements in non-Han regions to protest against CCP policies. While non-Han loyalties were expected to be overridden by the CCP's ideological enlightenment, ethno-nationalism rose in regions such as Tibet and Xinjiang. 'Splittism' and 'terrorism' were commonly used by the Chinese authorities to condemn such protests, leading to the implementation of martial law in Tibet in 1989 and 1990 and the 'strike-hard' campaign in Xinjiang from 1996. Increasingly, the CCP became torn between two main trends at the dawn of the twenty-first century to define the Chinese nation: assimilation and integration.

Turning towards Assimilationism: Forging a 'Collective National Consciousness'

In general, the necessity to stress unity over diversity became a priority from the 2000s onwards. A more 'ethnic' and 'depoliticised' approach to the national question was discussed by academics. Terminology was once again a hot topic. One main concern was that *minzu* as 'nationality' (in the Soviet sense) could create confusion and invite different non-Han groups to perceive themselves as entirely different and distinct nations, owing to their distinct social organisations and their own historical pasts, which predated the construction of a Chinese nation (Bulag 2010). This move towards a less political and more cultural categorisation was pursued through a re-translation of the term *minzu* according to various cases. In the mid-1990s, the English title of the official journal *Minzu tuanjie* (民族团结) became *Ethnic Unity* (in place of *National Unity*), and, during the 2000s, many state commissions were renamed with the word 'ethnic', such as the Commission on Ethnic Affairs (*guojia minzu shiwu weiyuanhui* 国家民族事务委员会), previously known as the 'State Commission on Nationalities' Affairs'. However, other intellectuals resisted this 'ethnicisation'. The anthropologist Pan Jiao (潘蛟), for example, argued for the retention of the translation as 'nationality' instead of 'ethnic group' to maintain the political position that *minzu* enjoyed in its formation and development, as well as to prevent the erasure of the achievements of minority groups that were connected to their 'nationality' status, such as regional autonomy (Pan 2003). Some preferred to avoid translating *minzu* in order to preserve the specificities tied to the concept; thus, in the 2000s, the Central University of Nationalities (*zhongyang minzu daxue* 中央民族大学) became the Minzu University of China (thus rendering its objective obscure to all non-Sinophones). This university was effectively revealed to be the home of an indigenisation of the concept, notably under the aegis of Zhang Haiyang (张海洋) and Hao Siyuan (郝时远) (Hao 2013).

A third option consisted of a complete revision of the notion of *minzu* and its replacement, in some cases, by *zuqun* (族群 literally *zu*, 'lineage' and *qun*, 'group'). *Zuqun* is also a term commonly used in Taiwan to conceptualise the island's diversity within the context of the democratisation of the 1990s (Schubert 1999). The term describes the 'sub-ethnicities' in the interior of the same nation. In the Chinese context of the 2000s, researchers who defended the double usage of *minzu* (that is as nation/nationality or ethnicity) agreed to use *zuqun* in place of *minzu*, relegating *minzu* to the ethnic sense of the term (thus specifically replacing *shaoshu minzu*). They also proposed to retain *minzu* solely to describe the Chinese nation in its entirety (*Zhonghua minzu*) (Leibold 2013; Elliott 2015). This proposal overlapped with the new debates as well as the search for an innovative conceptualisation of the Chinese nation of the twenty-first century. It is notably the result of the efforts of Ma Rong (马戎), a sociologist from Peking University, to rethink policies that, according to him, have led to divisions and conflicts in terms of Han–non-Han relations, as well as relations between the non-Han and the state, a dangerous situation for Chinese unity. This perception became more relevant after the revolts in the Tibetan and Uyghur regions during the period surrounding the Beijing Olympic Games in 2008. The turmoil in these regions, revealed to the world as it has been to the rest of China, aroused strong concern among certain leaders and university figures who, like Ma, warned of a dismantling of the Chinese state akin to the Soviet example (Ma 2007). Consequently, Ma (2014) proposed a 'depoliticisation' (*quzhengzhihua* 去政治化) of the domestic question of minority groups; specifically, he advocated for the abolition of the privileges associated with the *minzu* minority status and the levelling of relations through an American-style 'acculturation' or *wenhua hua* 文化化 (Ma 2017). The 'melting pot' model of a society harmoniously merging a variety of elements into one common culture, proposed by Liang Qichao a century prior, once again took centre stage among theoreticians who aimed to reform the conception of the Chinese nation after the year 2000.

Such proposals for a new terminology found resonance among policymakers, and it opened the path for more radical viewpoints that have significantly impacted CCP policy since 2010. Indeed, the necessity of accelerating this merging through a series of political measures was also supported by researchers at Tsinghua University, namely Hu Angang (胡鞍钢) and Hu Lianhe (胡联合). Typically, Hu Angang is a member of several CCP committees and activities at his Institute for Contemporary China Studies, one of China's main thinktanks involved in writing policy recommendations and reports commissioned by various governmental organs. Hu Lianhe, on the other hand, well known for his research on social stability, recently took on important roles under the CCP's United Front Work Department in charge of, among other things, managing ethnic and religious affairs and represented the Chinese state at the UN Committee on the Elimination of Racial Discrimination (Leibold 2018). Like Ma, the two Hus debated the terminology, advocating for the replacement of *minzu* with *zuqun* in terms of ethnic identification. But, more importantly, they also stressed a series of concrete political measures to favour the 'merging' (*jiarong* 交融) of the different communities under one monocultural state or *guozu* (国族 literally 'country' and 'lineage') (Hu and Hu 2011).[11] These measures included monolingual education in Mandarin, the abandonment of all privilege or special treatment for the non-Han (including the system of regional autonomy), as well as the promotion of interethnic marriages and celebrations labelled 'Chinese', and the radical reconfiguration of local practices that could be perceived as being in competition with national practices.

The most concrete examples of the application of these measures by the CCP happened from 2017 in the peripheric regions of Xinjiang, Tibet and Inner Mongolia, where the use of Mandarin in schools has been strictly enforced and the teaching of local languages largely marginalised. Outside schools, activities promoting Tibetan language in the Tibetan autonomous region were labelled 'illegal' in 2018 in a police statement (Roche 2021). In Inner Mongolia, from 2022, Mandarin will be the only language of instruction and Mongolian only a topic of instruction for a very limited time in school programs, a shift that triggered several protests when it was officially announced in 2020 (Atwood 2020; Bulag 2020b). In Xinjiang, since 2017 and the launch of massive internment campaigns, most schools at all levels have become residential, forcing children and university students to live in a Mandarin-speaking environment and separating them from Uyghur-speaking households.[12] Further, many textbooks in Tibetan or Uyghur have disappeared from library bookshelves and their authors have been condemned (Clarke 2021; Henry 2016), while new textbooks have been increasingly subjected to 'harmonisation'; often translated from Chinese, they intentionally omit cultural specificities or references to local history and characters (Mahmut and Smith Finley 2021).

11 This term, translated as 'race-state' or 'nation-state', connects the concepts of belonging to a country and a common lineage. The idea of such a congruence is not new, and the Hus borrowed the concept from the Republican period. Developed by thinkers such as Zhang Binlin and Liang Qichao at the start of the twentieth century, and afterwards picked up by Sun Yat-sen, *guozu* is often a substitute for *minzu* and *guojia* (国家 'country' and 'family'), notably by Liang, who, in a text from 1905, utilised it in a manner interchangeable with *Zhongguo minzu* (Chinese nation) and *Zhonghua guozu* (Chinese nation-state) (Matten 2012). For Liang, *guozu* defined a superior level of identification, that of the state, as compared to *buzu*, which allocated belonging to the level of the clan, or *jiazu* 家族 at the level of family.

12 Darren Byler, 'Xinjiang Education Reform and the Eradication of Uyghur-Language Books', SupChina, 2 October 2019, supchina.com/2019/10/02/xinjiang-education-reform-and-the-eradication-of-uyghur-language-books/.

In addition, Uyghur and Tibetan cultural heritage are increasingly reshaped and metamorphosed by local authorities to suit Chinese Han domestic taste, from transforming Uyghur domestic spaces to 'modernise' them (Grose 2020) to desacralising mosques or simply erasing major cultural spaces such as *mazars* (mausoleum) and cemeteries (Ruser et al. 2020; Thum 2020). Such radical changes have taken place alongside the implementation of mandatory celebrations of the Chinese Spring Festival – a holiday that brings many domestic tourists from inland China who are invited to enjoy 'Xinjiang tasty Spring Festival fried snacks'[13] – the Dragon Boat Festival (Grose 2021) and other events that are disconnected from Uyghur cultural practices and are artificially implemented in Xinjiang as part of a 'national culture' or a 'Chinafication' program (Castets, Chapter 14, this volume).

In the same region, bonus points in university entrance exams for Uyghur-language-educated prospective students have decreased, while children of Han and Uyghur mixed couples are given extra bonus points,[14] another measure to encourage mixed marriages (an idea that was already developed in the Republican era and linked to the idea of biological survival, as mentioned above). The promotion of interethnic marriages is indeed an important argument of the Hus and has been implemented in Tibet and Xinjiang, in particular, where local administrations offer various compensations to young mixed couples, from monthly allocations to housing and easier access to social services. Such incentives have been common in these regions since 2014.[15] The interethnic marriage trend has accelerated in Xinjiang since 2017, often at the expense of Uyghur women, who are increasingly coerced into marriages with Han migrants.[16]

In the meantime, special programs have been implemented to 'train' Tibetan and Uyghur rural labourers to engage in construction and manufacturing work across China. In 2020, no less than 543,000 Tibetans were trained

13 'Xinjiang's Tasty Spring Festival Fried Snacks', *People's Daily*, 20 February 2021, en.people.cn/n3/2021/0220/c90000-9820292-9.html.

14 Darren Byler, 'Uyghur Love in a Time of Interethnic Marriage', *SupChina*, 7 August 2019, supchina.com/2019/08/07/uyghur-love-in-a-time-of-interethnic-marriage/.

15 Eric Meyer, 'China Offers Work Placements and Mixed Marriage Incentives as Solutions for Its Xinjiang Problems', *Forbes*, 14 November 2014, www.forbes.com/sites/ericrmeyer/2014/11/13/chinas-newest-recipes-for-solving-its-xinjiang-problem-workplacements-and-mixed-marriage-incentives/; Cathy Wong, 'Mixed Marriages Get Cash Gifts in Xinjiang', *Global Times*, 3 September 2014, www.globaltimes.cn/content/879657.shtml.

16 Darren Byler, 'Uyghur Love in a Time of Interethnic Marriage', SupChina, 7 August 2019, supchina.com/2019/08/07/uyghur-love-in-a-time-of-interethnic-marriage/; Yi Xiaocuo, '"Saved" by State Terror: Gendered Violence and Propaganda in Xinjiang', SupChina, 14 May 2019, supchina.com/2019/05/14/saved-by-state-terror-gendered-violence-and-propaganda-in-xinjiang/.

as factory workers to be relocated, in part, to inland China.[17] Following the deployment of non-Han female factory workers to inland China in the 2010s, forced labour in Xinjiang has now been widely documented and includes specific schemes to send Uyghur workers to inland factories.[18]

These measures, which are implemented in their most extreme forms in the Uyghur region, demonstrate Xi Jinping's determination to strengthen the CCP's leadership over non-Han-related policy: under Xi, the CCP must play an active role in 'forging' (*zhulao* 铸牢) a unified Chinese nation.[19] Xi reaffirmed the CCP's current vision of a Chinese nation in which the national spirit 'integrated each *minzu* group in their blood and soul' (*ronjin le ge minzu renmin de xueye he lingyun* 融进了各族人民的血液和灵魂), or what he calls a 'communal consciousness of the Chinese nation' (*Zhonghua minzu gongtongti yishi* 中华民族共同体意识).[20] He also introduced, for the first time in the PRC's history, *Zhonghua minzu* into the preamble of the amended 2018 constitution.

Conclusion

Contradictory trends that already existed among policymakers in the 1960s are still manifest today, but those who oppose autonomy for non-Han seem to have won over those in favour of 'real' autonomy for non-Han. Consequently, although no official mention of further modifications in the CCP's ethnic policies has arisen in the past few years at a national level, the situation on the ground has changed dramatically through the systematic implementation of new laws and regulations at a local level.

17 '543,000 Tibetan Farmers and Herders to be Will Transferred for Employment between January and July 1–7' (月西藏农牧民转移就业54.3万人), Tibetan government official website, Government/Citizen interaction 12 August 2020, www.xizang.gov.cn/zmhd/hygq/202008/t20200812_165133.html.

18 Vicky Xiuzhong Xu, Danielle Cave, James Liebold, Kelsey Munron and Nathan Ruser, 'Uyghurs for Sale: "Re-Education", Forced Labor and Surveillance beyond Xinjiang', Australian Strategic Policy Institute, March 2020, www.aspi.org.au/report/uyghurs-sale.

19 James Leibold, 'China's Assimilationist Turn in Xi Jinping's China'. Asia Experts Forum, 18 March 2021, asiaexpertsforum.org/james-leibold-chinas-assimilationist-turn-xi-jinpings-china/; 'Deeply Understanding the Great Significance of Forging a Consciousness of the Community of the Chinese Nation – On the Study and Implementation of Xi Jinping's Important Talk at the Central Minzu Work Conference' (深刻认识铸牢中华民族共同体意识的重大意义——论学习贯彻习近平总书记中央民族工作会议重要讲话), *Xinhua*, 30 August 2021, www.gov.cn/xinwen/2021-08/30/content_5634055.htm.

20 'Xi Jinping: Speech at the National Conference for the Recognition of Ethnic Unity and Progress' (习近平: 在全国民族团结进步表彰大会上的讲话), *Xinhua*, 27 September 2019, www.xinhuanet.com/politics/leaders/2019-09/27/c_1125049000.htm.

The concretisation of a unified Chinese nation linked to indivisible territories is more than ever a priority for the CCP. The debates on the formation of a Chinese nation, and the methods to unify it according to foreign or indigenous models of integration and assimilation, have been pursued around the representation of a supra-nation (*minzu, guozu*) composed of sub-nations (*minzu, zuqun*). This ideology implies a necessary adhesion to a model of a supra-nation that was mainly defined in reference to the Han, a fragmented category but one considered unique and superior nonetheless. Yet, this model is not unanimous, and has triggered not only numerous conflicts in all the peripheral regions but also inspired within the Han a colonial irrationality that continues to produce inequalities, discrimination and stereotypes. The policies enacted these past years, whose climaxing form we currently see in the Uyghur region, does not inspire new and exciting political debates.

In this context, *minzu* still plays a major role in the CCP's rhetoric to produce a discourse on 'unity within diversity', and to shape an imaginary of a pacified and unified Chinese nation, described in biological and common ancestry terms. Indeed, *minzu* allows the CCP to continue to operate a narrative that can distinguish it from other colonial powers. Even though China formally supports the 2007 UN Declaration on the Rights of Indigenous Peoples, the CCP has never agreed to apply the concept of indigenous peoples or the rights of indigenous peoples within its borders; non-Han cannot in practice exercise their rights to prior consultation concerning any change in their territories. The terms 'indigenous' (*yuanzhumin*, *yuanjumin*, *xianzhumin* or *tuzhuren*) or indigeneity (*tuzhuxing*) are, in fact, conveniently understood as only applicable to Western colonial contexts (Wilson and Stewart 2008, 2), and are rarely, if ever, used in Chinese language to refer to China (Elliott 2015, 207). As we have observed, the PRC considers that China is not, and never was, a colonial power; the progressive 'fusion' of various peoples into today's Chinese nation is seen as a historical, natural and voluntary process. Since indigeneity is admittedly a political, non-natural category that implies rights and benefits, it is 'at odds with the concept of China as a "unified polyethnic state"' (Elliott 2015, 209) and consequently is rejected. For these reasons, the concept of *minzu* will certainly continue to prevail in the CCP's narrative of the Chinese nation.

References

Atwood, Christopher P. 2020. 'Bilingual Education in Inner Mongolia: An Explainer'. *Made in China*, 30 August. madeinchinajournal.com/2020/08/30/bilingual-education-in-inner-mongolia-an-explainer/.

Brandt, Conrad, Benjamin Schwartz and John K. Fairbank. 1966. *A Documentary History of Chinese Communism*. New York: Atheneum.

Bulag, Uradyn E. 2002. *The Mongols at China's Edge: History and the Politics of National Unity*. Lanham: Rowman and Littlefield.

Bulag, Uradyn E. 2010. 'Alter/native Mongolian Identity: From Nationality to Ethnic Group'. In *Chinese Society: Change, Conflict and Resistance*, edited by Elizabeth Perry and Mark Selden, 49–51. 3rd edition. London: Routledge. doi.org/10.1177/0306422020981275.

Bulag, Uradyn E. 2020a. 'Nationality/民族'. *Made in China*, 4 September. madeinchinajournal.com/2020/09/04/nationality-民族/.

Bulag, Uradyn E. 2020b. 'Dying for Their Mother Tongue: Why Have People in Inner Mongolia Recently Taken Their Lives?' *Index on Censorship* 49 (4): 49–51.

Burtscher, Michael. 2012. 'A Nation and a People? Notes toward a Conceptual History of the Terms Minzoku 民族 and Kokumin 國民 in Early Meiji Japan'. *Journal of Political Science and Sociology* 16: 47–106.

Chen, Yangbin. 2019. 'Uyghur Graduates' Ethnicity in Their Dislocated Life Experience: Employment Expectations, Choices and Obstacles'. *Asian Studies Review* 43 (1): 75–93. doi.org/10.1080/10357823.2018.1561652.

Chow, Kai-wing. 1997. 'Imagining Boundaries of Blood: Zhang Binglin and the Invention of the Han "Race" in Modern China'. In *The Construction of Racial Identities in China and Japan*, edited by Frank Dikötter, 34–52. Hong Kong: Hong Kong University Press.

Clarke, Donald. 2021. 'Chinese Government Imposes Suspended Death Sentence and Life Imprisonment for Writing Chinese Government-Approved Textbook'. *China Collection*, 3 April. thechinacollection.org/chinese-government-imposes-death-sentence-writing-chinese-government-approved-textbook/.

Davies, Henry Rodolph. [1909] 2010. *Yün-Nan: The Link between India and the Yangtze*. Cambridge: Cambridge University Press. doi.org/10.1017/CBO9780511707834.

Deng, Xiaoping (邓小平). 1993. *Selected Works*. Vol. 3 (文选第三卷). Beijing: People's Press.

Dikötter, Frank. 2010. 'Forging National Unity: Ideas of Race in China'. *Global Dialogue* 12 (2): 23–35.

Elliott, Mark. 2012. 'Hushuo: The Northern Other and the Naming of the Han Chinese'. In *Critical Han Studies: The History, Representation, and Identity of China's Majority*, edited by Thomas Mullaney, James Leibold, Stephane Gros and Eric Vanden Bussche, 173–90. Berkeley: University of California Press. doi.org/10.1086/679274.

Elliott, Mark. 2015. 'The Case of the Missing Indigene: Debate over a "Second-Generation Ethnic Policy"'. *China Journal* 73: 186–213.

Fan, Wenlan (范文澜). 1954. 'Reasons Why China Has Been a Nation since the Qin-Han Period' (自秦汉以来中国成为国家的原因). *Lishi Yanjiu*, 22–36.

Fei, Xiaotong (费孝通). 1989. *The Concept of Unity in Diversity in China* (中华民族多元一体格局). Beijing: Zhongyang minzudaxue chubanshe.

Frangville, Vanessa. 2007. 'L'unité dans la diversité: l'altérité en Chine, moteur de l'unité nationale'. *Discours sur l'autre, discours sur soi constructions identitaires face à l'altérité*. Lyon: Presses universitaires de Lyon.

Gao, Quanxi (高全喜). 2016. *Political Constitution and Future Constitutionalism* (政治憲法與未來憲制). Hong Kong: City University Press.

Gladney, Dru. 1998. 'International Colonialism and the Uyghur Nationality: Chinese Nationalism and its Subaltern Subjects'. *CEMOTI*, no. 25. doi.org/10.4000/cemoti.48.

Gladney, Dru. 2004. *Dislocating China: Muslims, Minorities and Other Subaltern Subjects*. Chicago: University of Chicago Press.

Grose, Timothy. 2015. 'Escaping "Inseparability": How Uyghur Graduates of the "Xinjiang Class" Contest Membership in the Zhonghua minzu'. In *Language, Education and Uyghur Identity in Urban Xinjiang*, edited by J. Smith Finley and Xiaowei Zang, 157–75. Abington: Routledge. doi.org/10.4324/9781315726588-8.

Grose, Timothy. 2020. 'If You Don't Know How, Just Learn: Chinese Housing and the Transformation of Uyghur Domestic Space'. *Ethnic and Racial Studies* 44: 1–22. doi.org/10.1080/01419870.2020.1789686.

Grose, Timothy. 2021. 'Dragon Boat Festival and Chinese Nation-Building in Xinjiang'. *Diplomat,* June. thediplomat.com/2021/06/dragon-boat-festival-and-chinese-nation-building-in-xinjiang/.

Grunfeld, Tom. 1985. 'In Search of Equality: Relations between China's Ethnic Minorities and the Majority Han'. *Bulletin of Concerned Asian Scholars* 17 (1): 54–67. doi.org/10.1080/14672715.1985.10414416.

Guo, Yingjie. 2013a. 'Discourse on Justice and Class: Impact on China's Intellectual Elites on Social Policy'. In *Elites and Governance in China*, edited by Xiaowei Zang and Chien-wen Kou, 12–33. Abington: Routledge.

Guo, Yingjie. 2013b. 'The Role of Intellectual Elites in China's Political Reform: The Discourse of Governance'. In *Elites and Governance in China*, edited by Xiaowei Zang and Chien-wen Kou, 34–53. Abington: Routledge.

Henry, Clémence. 2016. 'The Chinese Education System as a Source of Conflict in Tibetan Areas'. In *Ethnic Conflict and Protests in Tibet and Xinjiang*, edited by Ben Hillman and Gray Tuttle, 97–121. New York: Columbia University Press. doi.org/10.7312/columbia/9780231169981.003.0004.

Hou, Yue and Rory Truex. 2020. 'Ethnic Discrimination and Authoritarian Rule: An Analysis of Criminal Sentencing in China'. ssrn.com/abstract=3481448.

Hu, Angang (胡鞍钢) and Hu Lianhe (胡联合). 2011. 'The Second Generation of Minzu Policy: Promoting Ethnic Prosperity and Integration as One Body' (第二代民族政策：促进民族交融一体和繁荣一体). *Journal of Xinjiang Normal University* 5: 1–12.

Jin, Binggao (金炳镐). 1987. 'When Did the Term "National Minority" Appear in Our Country?' ('少数民族'一词在我国何时出现?). *Minzu tuanjie* 6: 47.

Joniak-Luthi, Agnieszka. 2015. *The Han: China's Diverse Majority*. Washington: University of Washington Press. doi.org/10.1353/cri.2015.0004.

Leibold, James. 2004. 'Positioning "Minzu" within Sun Yat-sen's Discourse of Minzuzhuyi'. *Journal of Asian History* 38: 163–211.

Leibold, James. 2007. *Reconfiguring Chinese Nationalism: How the Qing Frontier and Its Indigenes Became Chinese*. New York: Palgrave Macmillan. doi.org/10.1007/978-1-137-09884-9.

Leibold, James. 2013. *Ethnic Policy in China: Is Reform Inevitable?* Honolulu: East West Center.

Leibold, James. 2018. 'Hu the Uniter: Hu Lianhe and the Radical Turn in China's Xinjiang Policy'. *China Brief* 18 (16).

Leung, Edwin Pak-wah. 1981. 'Ethnic Compartmentalization and Regional Autonomy in the People's Republic of China'. *Chinese Law and Government* 14 (4).

Li, Cheng. 2008. 'Ethnic Minority in China's Party-State Leadership: An Empirical Assessment'. *China Leadership Monitor* 25.

Liang, Hongling. 2016. 'Chinese Anthropology and its Domestication Projects: Dewesternization, Bentuhua and Overseas Ethnography'. *Social Anthropology* 24 (4): 462–75. doi.org/10.1111/1469-8676.12307.

Liang, Qichao (梁启超). 1989. *The Complete Works of the Ice Drinker's Studio* (饮冰室文集). Beijing: Zhonghua shuju.

Liu, Xiaoyuan. 2001. 'Communism, Nationalism, Ethnicism, and China's "National Question" 1921–1945'. In *Chinese Nationalism in Perspective: Historical and Recent Cases*, edited by George Wei and Liu Xiaoyuan, 121–48. Westport: Greenwood Press.

Liu, Xiaoyuan. 2004. *Frontier Passages: Ethnopolitics and the Rise of Chinese Communism, 1921–1945*. Stanford: Stanford University Press.

Ma, Rong. 2007. 'A New Perspective in Guiding Ethnic Relations in the Twenty-First Century: "De-Politicization" of Ethnicity in China'. *Asian Ethnicity* 8 (3): 199–217. doi.org/10.1080/14631360701594950.

Ma, Rong. 2014. 'Reflections on the Debate on China's Ethnic Policy: My Reform Proposals and Their Critics'. *Asian Ethnicity* 15 (2): 237–46. doi.org/10.1080/14631369.2013.868205.

Ma, Rong. 2017. 'Reconstructing "Nation" (*minzu*) Discourses in China'. *International Journal of Anthropology and Ethnology* 1 (8). doi.org/10.1186/s41257-017-0003-x.

MacDonald, Andrew and Reza Hasmath. 2020. 'Discrimination in Ethnic Minority Earnings? Evidence from Urban China'. In *Ethnicity and Inequality in China*, edited by Björn A. Gustafsson, Reza Hasmath and Sai Ding, 216–32. Abingdon: Routledge. doi.org/10.4324/9781003082156-9.

Mahmut, Dilmurat and Joanne Smith Finley. 2021. 'Corrective "Re-education" as (Cultural) Genocide: A Content Analysis of the Uyghur Primary School Textbook Til-Ädäbiyat (2018, rev. 1st ed)'. In *The Xinjiang Emergency*, edited by Michael Clarke, 181–226. Manchester: Manchester University Press.

Mao, Zedong (毛泽东). 1977. 'Criticizing Han Chauvinism' (批判大汉族主义). *Selected Works of Mao Zedong*, vol. 5, 75–6. Renmin Press.

Matten, Marc A. 2012. '"China is the China of the Chinese": The Concept of Nation and its Impact on Political Thinking in Modern China'. *Oriens Extremus* 53: 63–106.

Meissner, Werner. 2006. 'China's Search for Cultural and National Identity from the Nineteenth Century to the Present'. *China Perspectives* 68 (November–December). doi.org/10.4000/chinaperspectives.3103.

Mobius, Markus, Tanya Rosenblat and Qiqi Wang. 2016. 'Ethnic Discrimination: Evidence from China'. *European Economic Review* 90: 165–177. doi.org/10.1016/j.euroecorev.2016.04.004.

Mullaney, Thomas. 2011. *Coming to Terms with the Nation, Ethnic Classification in Modern China*. Berkeley: University of California Press. doi.org/10.4000/chinaperspectives.5586.

Pan, Jiao (潘蛟). 2003. 'Ethnicity and Its Conceptual Changes in the West' (族群及其相关概念在西方的流变). *Guangxi minzu daxue xuebao*. doi.org/10.1163/9789004308886_015.

Pan, Jiao. 2016. 'Deconstructing Ethnic Minorities in China: Eliminating Orientalism or Re-orientalizing?' In *On China's Cultural Transformations*, edited by Keping Yu, 250–66. Leiden: Brill.

Roche, Gerald. 2021. 'Tibetan Language Rights and Civil Society in the People's Republic of China: Challenges of and for Rights'. *Asian Studies Review* 45(1): 67–82. doi.org/10.1080/10357823.2020.1758033.

Ruser, Nathan, Leibold James, Kelsey Munro and Tilla Hoja. 2020. 'Cultural Erasure: Tracing the Destruction of Uyghur and Islamic Spaces in Xinjiang'. Analysis and Policy Observatory, Policy Brief Report, no. 38. www.aspi.org.au/report/cultural-erasure.

Saito, Mino and Mutsuko Tsuboi. 2015. 'Translating "Nation" into Japanese during the Modernization of Japan: Dynamics of Translation as a Social and Interactional Practice'. *Meta* 60 (2): 369–70. doi.org/10.7202/1032920ar.

Sautman, Barry. 1997. 'Racial Nationalism and Chinese External Behaviour'. *World Affairs* 160 (2): 78–95.

Sautman, Barry. 1999. 'Ethnic Law and Minority Rights in China: Progress and Constraints'. *Law & Policy* 21 (3): 283–314. doi.org/10.1111/1467-9930.00074.

Schein, Louisa. 1997. 'Gender and Internal Orientalism in China'. *Modern China* 23 (1): 69–98. doi.org/10.1177/009770049702300103.

Schubert, Gunther. 1999. 'L'émergence d'une nouvelle nation? Le discours sur l'identité nationale dans le Taiwan de la fin du xxe siècle'. *Perspectives chinoises* 52: 58–70. doi.org/10.3406/perch.1999.3074.

Sun, Yat-sen. 1982. *Collected Works of Sun Yat-sen* (孙中山全集), vol. 2. Beiijng: Zhonghua Book Company.

Thoraval, Joël. 1990. 'Le concept chinois de nation est-il obscur ? À propos du débat sur la notion de minzu dans les années 1980'. *Bulletin de sinologie* 65: 24–41.

Thum, Rian. 2020. 'The Spatial Cleansing of Xinjiang: Mazar Desecration in Context'. *Made in China* 2. doi.org/10.22459/MIC.05.02.2020.04.

Villard, Florent. 2010. '"Class", "Race" and Language: Imagining China and the Discourse on the Category "Han" in the Writing of Marxist Revolutionary Qu Qiubai (1899–1935)'. *Asian Ethnicity* 11 (3): 311–24. doi.org/10.1080/1463 1369.2010.510873.

Wang, Linzhu. 2019. *Self-Determination and Minority Rights in China*. Leiden: Brill. doi.org/10.1163/9789004380578.

Wilson, Pamela and Michelle Stewart. 2008. 'Introduction: Indigeneity and Indigenous Media on the Global Stage'. In *Global Indigenous Media: Cultures, Poetics, and Politics*, edited by Pamela Wilson and Michelle Stewart, 1–36. New York: Duke University Press. doi.org/10.1215/9780822388692-001.

Yang, Bin. 2009. *Between Winds and Clouds: The Making of Yunnan (Second Century BCE–Twentieth Century CE)*. New York, Columbia University Press.

Zang, Xiaowei. 2011. 'Uyghur-Han Earnings Differential in Ürümchi'. *China Journal* 65: 141–55. doi.org/10.1086/tcj.65.25790561.

Zang, Xiaowei. 2015. *Ethnicity in China: A Critical Introduction*. Cambridge: Polity Press.

Zhang, Haiyang. 1997. 'Wrestling with the Connotation of Chinese "Minzu"'. *Economic and Political Weekly* 32 (30): 74–84.

Zhao, Taotao and Tok Sow Keat. 2021. 'From Academic Discourse to Political Decisions? The Case of the Xinjiang Ethnic Unity Education Textbook Reform'. *China Quarterly* 245: 165–85. doi.org/10.1017/S0305741020000119.

Zheng, Dahua. 2019. 'Modern Chinese Nationalism and the Awakening of Self-Consciousness of the Chinese Nation'. *International Journal of Anthropology and Ethnology* 3 (11). doi.org/10.1186/s41257-019-0026-6.

Zhu, Guobin and Yu Lingyun. 2000. 'Regional Minority Autonomy in the PRC: A Preliminary Appraisal from a Historical Perspective'. *International Journal on Minority and Group Rights* 7 (1): 39–57. doi.org/10.1023/A:1009953401939.

14

The Integration of Xinjiang into the Chinese Nation-State: Controlling Minority Representations and Fighting against Political Contestation

Rémi Castets

In memory of Dru

Introduction

Since its conquest, Xinjiang has been a restive territory where the authority of the Chinese central power is subject to challenge (Lattimore [1950] 1975; Forbes 1986; Benson 1990; Millward 2007). Understanding the ins and outs of the strategies pursued by the Chinese Communist Party (CCP) after its takeover of power in the area is not always an easy task since its decisions can be opaque. At the same time, its secretive decision-making process often masks diverging approaches among its cadres, especially between central and local levels.[1]

1 Interviews with former CCP members from the region living abroad. See also Jean-Pierre Cabestan, Chapter 1, this volume.

However, over the last three decades, the number of monographs, reports, PhD theses and scientific articles shedding light on the political history of Xinjiang have multiplied. This has fed a broader and deeper understanding of the origins of the strategic choices made by central and provincial administrations to reassert their control on the region (McMillen 1979; Teufel Dreyer 1986; Gladney 1996, 2003, 2004; Shichor 2003; Castets 2003, 2013; Zhu, Chen and Yang 2004; Millward 2007; Bovingdon 2010; Clarke 2011, 2022; Tobin 2020; Roberts 2020).

These studies on the political situation in Xinjiang make it clear that, over the past decades, the CCP has developed various strategies to cope with political opposition and ethnic minorities' demands for a less sinicising model of modernisation. These strategic changes, often linked to the evolution of the balance of power between Party factions, have unveiled CCP cadres' various sensibilities according to their ethnic or geographical origin and/or political supports/networks (McMillen 1979). However, the evolution of the balance of power between factions, and the evolution of the degree of autonomy given to local political and administrative levels, only partly explains the changing discourse and strategies mobilised since 1949.

This chapter aims to provide an overview of the mutations of the CCP's discourse and strategies deployed for controlling minority representations and fighting against political contestation in Xinjiang. Because of the opacity of CCP policies, some elements still remain unclear. However, we will try here to recontextualise those changes, relying on information provided in the academic literature, NGO reports and leaks from the Chinese administration, as well as interviews and data collected by the author over the last two decades in China, Xinjiang and among the Uyghur diaspora.

Chinese Communist Party's Production of Meaning, Nation-Building and Definition of the Right Modernisation Path

When the People's Liberation Army (PLA) took control of Xinjiang at the turn of the 1950s, the CCP cadres arrived in a territory where the Party had almost no base. In order to legitimise its rule, but also to implement its national and modernisation project, the CCP had to build and extend the scope of its new Chinese 'scientific state' – 'a political entity that seeks to homogenise the population within its borders for administrative purposes using the latest scientific techniques and methods in the name of efficiency (Smith 1971, 231).

First, the CCP had to establish a firm military presence and a ramification of CCP cells and administrative structures that would progressively assert its control on the people's lives and minds. Actually, the region's state administration and CCP apparatus were placed under the command of a hardliner, General Wang Zhen (王震) (1949–52), after General Peng Dehuai (彭德怀) had to take on other responsibilities. Wang Zhen was replaced in the early 1950s by another military man, Wang Enmao (王恩茂) (1952–67, 1981–85). This officer, having participated in the 'peaceful liberation of the region', eventually became a fine connoisseur of the local political context and would pilot the region through a mix of attentiveness and firmness. Both Wang Zhen and Wang Enmao mobilised PLA veterans to establish CCP and state authority in the region (Shichor 2003). They played a crucial role in pacifying and building the security architecture in the region, contributing to the structuration of what would become the Xinjiang Production and Construction Corps (*Xinjiang shengchan jianshe bingtuan* 新疆生产建设兵团).

At the same time, to enhance its stabilisation strategy (see below), the CCP initially promoted relatively moderate policies that sought to activate/reactivate[2] local political relays (McMillen 1979). On the right of the local political spectrum, the (moderate) former chairman of Xinjiang Province, Burhan Shahidi, and other pro-Guomindang (GMD) political or military cadres (such as Tao Zhiyue 陶峙岳[3]) were rallied. On the left, an alliance was secured with the Uyghur Communist cadres linked to the former East Turkestan Republic. In that field, Saïpidin Azizov[4] played a crucial role following the 'plane crash' that killed the ringleaders of the republic a few weeks before the arrival of PLA (McMillen 1979). However, the CCP's need for ideologised cadres was immense and pro-Soviet minority cadres were not fully reliable. Consequently, the Party had to send thousands of

2 Mao had tried to organise networks and connexions in the 1930s–40s, including by sending his brother to the area. Nevertheless, the small Maoist networks were largely dismantled after Sheng Shicai (盛世才) sided with the GMD in 1942 (Whiting and Sheng 1958).

3 He would become the first commander (1954–68) of the Xinjiang Production and Construction Corps.

4 After succeeding to Burhan Shahidi as chairman of the new autonomous region (1955–67), he will be the only Uyghur who served as Secretary of the Party in Xinjiang (1972–78). Considered a traitor by Uyghur anti-colonialists, he was a faithful follower of the Party lines of his time (McMillen 1979; Teufel Dryer 1986).

moderately skilled cadres to the area. They were supposed to be committed to its cause and had to try and win over Han[5] or minority elements who had to be socialised with CCP values to promote and diffuse its new systems of representations among the masses (McMillen 1979).

To use the hermeneutic metaphor of 'cable channels' (Gladney 2004, 28–50), just as broadcasting companies provide the means to decipher their programs through a decoding system, those CCP cadres had to deliver the 'deciphered' version of a national history,[6] economic relations and sociopolitical situations initially illegible or distorted by competing political forces trying to dominate the masses. Adjusted through the 'mass line' strategy,[7] the CCP's systems of interpretation, as we shall see, were destined to gather the assent of the national minorities (*shaoshu minzu* 少数民族), with varying degrees of authority, around the following idea: the CCP was the only legitimate political force able to guide an essentialised and unitary Chinese nation thanks to a scientific system of deciphering history and social relations capable of liberating the masses: Marxist–Leninist communism. In other words, the CCP's path of modernisation relied not only on socioeconomic teleologies aimed at freeing the masses, but also on a reinterpretation of the history of the peripheral regions aimed at integrating national minorities into the 'motherland' (*zuguo* 祖国).

In accordance with democratic centralism (*minzhu jizhongzhi* 民主集中制),[8] the production of meaning on key issues such as class struggle and nation-building but also the control of the state and its monopoly of legitimate violence were to be the prerogatives of the Party. The Party set the political line. In other words, it mobilised a teleology that no one was allowed to question. Given this mission, in contrast to liberal democracies that do not fundamentally challenge the capitalist system, the Party's relationship to alternative ideologies and thoughts implied a strong security dimension in order to avoid any 'backsliding'. This certainty that there is no other way forward stemmed from the assumption that 'scientific socialism'/ Marxism was not an ideology but a scientific framework for uncovering the march of history. As mentioned above, the Party was the bearer of a system of deciphering social, economic and political facts that would restore a 'truth' that it alone had the means to distil. The Party, by virtue of its

5 In this context, former cadres or allies of the GMD or demobilised soldiers of the Nationalist army.

6 On this issue, see Vanessa Frangville, Chapter 13, this volume.

7 On this issue, see Jean-Pierre Cabestan, Chapter 1, this volume.

8 Ibid.

capacity to mobilise the analytical prism of historical materialism, held a sort of monopoly on the production of 'truth', and through the objectives set by the Politburo in particular, it also held a monopoly on defining the margins of interpretations and arrangements that should be made to fit with the context.

In other words, as the agent of class struggle, the CCP saw itself as the spearhead of a nation that it alone was entitled to define and protect. Mobilising a policy of national categorisation derived from that of Moscow, the Party became the guardian of an indivisible unitary Chinese nation with the mission of embracing the populations that had emerged from the multiethnic Qing Empire. This multiethnic but unitary national model (*tongyi duo minzu de guojia* 统一多民族国家) was accompanied by a theoretical recognition of the particularities of these populations, a system of autonomy (however bogus, as we will see later in this chapter), and a series of material and statutory benefits.[9] Recognising the particularities of national groups, the Chinese nationalities policy aimed to get them to accept identities and histories that justified their belonging to the 'motherland' in exchange for material and symbolic benefits. In Xinjiang, as in the rest of China, to serve its ideological goals and manufacture consent, the Party at the same time pushed forward its egalitarian, progressive project and the dismantling of 'feudal' and capitalist systems of economic domination in response to the frustrations or aspirations of some left-wing elites and the most impoverished masses.

However, the CCP found Xinjiang to be a territory where systems of representation antagonistic or difficult to reconcile with Communist ideology and the Chinese nation had taken root among the masses and elites. The attachment to local interpretations of Islam and their accompanying principles and value systems complicated matters. The supporters of the traditional Islamic order[10] as well as supporters of a reformist Islam, despite their division and lack of political structuring, defended alternative value systems and sociopolitical orders (Castets 2013).

In addition, during the first half of the twentieth century, the region witnessed the structuring of two rival anti-colonial ideological nebulae that gradually spread their systems of representation and their project of national

9 National minorities were given quota points for easier access to university, were entitled to one more child under the one-child policy and so on.

10 Particularly relevant to the Sufi world.

construction among the elites. The spread of Jadid/Pan-Turkist reformism (Forbes 1986; Hamada 1990; Klimeš 2015) as well as the development of pro-Soviet anti-colonial Communist circles (Lattimore [1950] 1975; Whiting and Sheng 1958; Benson 1990; Wang 1999; Brophy 2016) were likely to weaken the CCP's projects and Chinese sovereignty. The first, viscerally anti-Communist, promoted a discourse on the modernisation of local societies and the nation that inscribed them with a Turkic and Islamic character outside of Chineseness. The second circle was mainly established in the territory of the former Republic of East Turkestan and in the north. It was nourished by Marxist–Leninist thought disseminated by Stalin's USSR (Wang 1999; Brophy 2016). However, for many of Turkic-speaking militants, their Marxist ideological background was backed up by an anti-colonial perspective feeding defiance towards the Chinese nation-state.

Even if the local anti-Chinese political forces were ideologically divided and were not in a position to threaten the PLA militarily, the entrenchment of the systems of representation that they promoted or defended was likely to fuel defiance of the CCP's policies and national model. In the same way, the entrenchment in the society of their ideological systems and of the systems of representations they mobilised rendered part of the population impervious to the Party's discourse and ideology.[11] In other words, these forces and the systems of representation they relied on weakened the legitimacy of the Party and the acceptance of its modernisation project.

Faced with the persistence of this more or less vigorous defiance fed by the verticality and sinicising dimension of centre–periphery relations in the Chinese Communist state, the Party used various strategies to impose its model of modernisation and the integration of minorities into the Chinese nation. In spite of fundamental changes in the management of minority issues and the perspectives and goals of policymaking in Xinjiang, the last decades of CCP rule have been marked by a more or less exacerbated security approach to alternative opinions and thought against the backdrop of the fundamental question of defining the degree and spectrum of control of representations that are supposed to guarantee national cohesion in Xinjiang.

11 Following Andrew Vincent (2010, 18), we will consider here ideologies as:

> bodies of concepts, values, and symbols which incorporate conception of human nature and thus indicate what is possible and impossible for humans to achieve; critical reflections on the nature of human interaction; the values which humans ought either to reject or aspire to; and the correct technical arrangements for social, economic, and political life which will meet the needs and interests of human beings.

Strategies for Countering Political Forces and Alternative Systems of Representation in Maoist China

A key issue for the CCP was to legitimise itself and to accelerate Xinjiang's integration into the Chinese nation through ideological work and the diffusion of a new interpretation of local history. CCP cadres had to deploy propaganda work to familiarise CCP recruits and the masses with those systems of representation. As in the rest of China, the Party took control of school curricula and the media, and ensured the establishment of associations to monitor religious communities, such as the Islamic Association of China (*Zhongguo Yisilanjiao xiehui* 中国伊斯兰教协会) (IAC).[12] In other words, the CCP started propagating interpretations of history linking the destiny of the minorities to the Chinese nation while simultaneously discrediting historical figures, anti-Communist politicians, and readings of Islam that went against the Party's modernisation and nation-building efforts. Historical actors and events were viewed through a prism analysing their 'separatist/loyalist' and 'feudal/modernist' dimension. This approach to history led to a denunciation of separatist figures and anyone who upheld the 'reactionary order' (Qi and Qian 2004; Zhang 1997).

Concerning the fight against potentially hostile political forces, the as yet fragile CCP initially targeted the most antagonistic elites, in other words the Jadids and the most anti-Communist Islamic elites. Jadid Pan-Turkists[13] had made the pragmatic choice of allying themselves with the GMD (Forbes 1986) to avoid the region falling under Communist rule. To avoid execution or jail, many Jadid militants (Mohammad Emin Bughra, Isa Yusuf Alptekin) went into exile. However, in southern Xinjiang, the establishment of Communist authority was made more complicated by the religious ties between religious leaders[14] and their followers, as well as by the entrenchment of anti-colonial Jadid reformism among the intellectual and economic elites. The CCP was counting on its redistributive and egalitarian project to gain

12 Created in May 1953, a local branch was set up in Xinjiang in 1956 as part of a strategy to coopt Muslim figures who would simultaneously supervise clerics and transmit CCP policies. Nevertheless, due to the anti-religious movements that began in 1958, the IAC's activity was reduced and it was completely disbanded at the start of the Cultural Revolution, when the Party took over responsibility for religious affairs.

13 A reformist movement aimed at importing modernity into Turkic-speaking societies to avoid their acculturation and eventually led to the end of colonial rule in the areas concerned.

14 Mostly Sufis.

the support of the poorest Uyghur peasants. However, this project required undermining a strong attachment to Islam and the influence of the most anti-Communist fringes of Uyghur society (i.e. the landowners, the Islamic elites, the traders, etc.). The more remote, restive oases of the Tarim Basin were not part of a multiethnic world like the north or east of Xinjiang, and the people were mindful of what had happened in neighbouring Soviet Central Asia two decades prior. The fear of experiencing the same repression and of living in a de-Islamised and collectivised order were strong tools for mobilisation.

Between 1950 and 1952, in the context of the campaign to suppress counter-revolutionaries and the three- and five-antis campaigns, and later in the context of agrarian reform, dominant classes and former anti-Communist militants were targeted. With the Agrarian Reform Law of June 1950, followed by collectivisation in the mid-1950s, land was redistributed and later nationalised. At the same time, the elites' economic power and the ties of dependence that bound the masses to them were gradually eroded. However, the lack of knowledge of local culture and the clumsy zeal of many Han Party cadres frequently led them to offend the population. They sometimes alienated the support of the masses on whom they could have relied to bring down the power of the traditional and capitalist anti-Communist elites. Southern Xinjiang was thus riven by insurrectionary movements, particularly in the region between Kashgar and Khotan. They brought together Jadid cadres, landowners and certain Sufi networks before being gradually eradicated in the second half of the 1950s at the turn of the Great Leap Forward (Zhang 1997, 266–7; Castets 2013, 313–18).

At the same time, the state banned religious institutions from withholding taxes and progressively eliminated the economic power of the Islamic elites and landlords through the same measures aimed at redistributing property inheritance. A law to reform the management of the national minorities' religions came into force in 1958. It confirmed the dismantling of the system of autonomous mosques and of mortmain properties possessed by the clergy (Zhu, Chen and Hong 2004, 55–65). Having lost some of their sources of income, the religious elites lost their economic power and thereby their influence over persons whose income depended upon them. In turn, these elites became dependent on the benefits distributed by a Chinese state that only compensated the most conciliatory clerics.

In the north and east, insurrections launched by the Kazakh Osman Batur and the Uyghur Yulbar Khan were quickly crushed in the early 1950s. There, the CCP could rely on a larger Han presence[15] and political allies. In the north, the CCP had to rely on the former pro-Soviet cadres of the Republic of East Turkestan who had recently been rallied thanks to pressure from the USSR. The pro-Soviet Communist circles of the Association for the Defence of Peace and Democracy in Xinjiang, the former sole party of the East Turkestan Republic (1944–49), remained powerful; in the summer of 1950, it still had more than 77,000 members. However, the CCP was rightly suspicious of them. Among the Turkic-speaking members of the Union, the Communist systems of representation covered up the anti-colonial and anti-Chinese sentiment that was ready to resurface. Many were deeply pro-Soviet, and distrust of the Chinese was widespread.

The province of Xinjiang was transformed into an autonomous region in 1955 partly to meet their aspirations. However, the largely symbolic autonomy fell far short of the genuine political autonomy or federal republic that many had hoped for.[16] In spite of a theoretical recognition of the particularities of these populations and a series of material and statutory advantages, the shortcomings of this system prevented the transcription of numerous aspirations of Uyghur society, as well as the questioning of policies that were massively rejected, the most resented undoubtedly being the colonisation of the region and control of the local Party organisation by cadres from the centre. In addition, the Uyghurs, who were still the majority at the beginning of the 1950s, felt that the Party was playing other minorities against them through its policy of cooption and administrative division of the region.[17]

In short, disappointed by the limits of the Chinese system of autonomy, some took advantage of the Hundred Flowers Movement (*baihua yundong* 百花运动) to denounce Han chauvinism (*dahan zhuyi* 大汉注意) and to voice their disappointment. In the 1957 Anti-Rightist Movement (*fanyoupai yundong* 反右派运动) that followed the Hundred Flowers

15 Around 7 per cent of the regional population according 1953 Census.

16 It is true that the chairmen of the People's Government, autonomous prefectures and autonomous townships of the Xinjiang Uyghur Autonomous Region were often members of the nationality of the administrative unit in question. But, as in the rest of China, these autonomous political institutions were subject to CCP control. Up to now, the most important Party positions in the autonomous regions have been held by Han nationals loyal to Beijing.

17 Interviews in the early 2000s with former Uyghur intellectuals who had fled to the diaspora (Kazakhstan).

Movement, critical pro-Soviet cadres were subject to repression. By the end of 1957, more than 2,700 Party cadres were sent to the countryside as part of the Rectification Movement (McMillen 1979, 90) as a massive campaign against local nationalism (*difang minzuzhuyi* 地方民族主义) was launched between December 1957 and April 1958. The exodus to the USSR or withdrawal of these cadres from political life accelerated as the Sino-Soviet conflict and the Cultural Revolution worsened during the 1960s. Any political affinity with the Soviets could lead to serious problems. Moreover, at this time, Sino-Soviet tensions led the Party to be vigilant against any destabilising intent. Members of pro-Soviet circles participated in a secret network supported by the KGB, the People's Party of East Turkestan (PPTO) (*Shärkiy Türkistan Xälq Partiyisi*). The PPTO attempted to mobilise Xinjiang's Turkic-speaking population and cadres in preparation for a general insurrection against Beijing. It is said to have instigated various local uprisings and engaged in guerrilla acts (sabotage, skirmishes with the Chinese police and army, etc.) (Zhang 1997, 267–71). However, it was gradually weakened by the arrest of its leaders and by the end of Soviet support as tensions with China waned.

During the 1950s, the collectivisation drive pushed along by the Great Leap Forward (1958–60) fundamentally altered modes of life and favoured the immersion of minorities in the Party's new systems of representation. Madrasas and places of worship were closed down one after the other.[18] Islam henceforth became excluded from life within the people's communes (*renmin gongshe* 人民公社). Despite a relative reprieve after the Great Leap Forward in some areas of Xinjiang, repression increased with the launch of the Cultural Revolution in 1966. While cadres considered to be too pragmatic were evicted from CCP or PLA top positions in the region (such as Wang Zhen or Tao Zhiyue) (Teufel Dreyer 1986), radical Maoists or opportunist cadres endorsed the eradication of religion and the rapid assimilation of the national minorities.[19] This repression reached its height during the campaign against the 'Four Olds' (*po si jiu* 破四旧).[20] Promotion of atheism, the banning of Islam and cultural assimilation became the rule. Along with figures suspected of 'local nationalism', many clerics, Shaykhs, Ishans and their disciples were sent to work camps, decimating the elite of the Turkic-speaking population. At the same time, the legitimacy of the

18 Interviews with Uyghur clerics who fled abroad in the 1990s (Turkey, 2007).

19 On the issue of cadres' pragmatism, see Jérôme Doyon and Long Yang, Chapter 5, this volume.

20 That is to say, 'old ideas, old culture, old customs, and old habits'.

Party had been weakened by the disastrous image of bullying and excesses generated by the harshest periods of the Cultural Revolution (McMillen 1979, 181–307).

1980s: Opening New Spaces of Freedom and an Informal Process of Conflict Mediation

After the dark years of the Cultural Revolution, in the 1980s, the Party, at the initiative of reformist cadres such as Hu Yaobang (胡耀邦), reviewed its policy on minorities in order to regain a certain legitimacy (Clarke 2011, 72–91). This change of line gave hope to anti-colonial circles. Hu Yaobang's visit[21] to Tibet at the beginning of the 1980s was followed by reforms. In 1982, through the revision of the People's Republic of China (PRC) Constitution, and in 1984, through the Law of the People's Republic of China on Regional National Autonomy[22] (*Zhonghua renmin gongheguo minzu quyu zizhi fa* 中华人民共和国民族区域自治法), the Chinese state signalled that it would make the system of autonomy more effective, particularly in the cultural, educational and economic fields in areas inhabited by minorities.[23] While economic reform and economic development were seen as essential tools for the resolution of ethnic tensions, the reformists around Deng Xiaoping chose at the same time to reopen spaces for cultural (art. 10, 37, 38) and religious freedom (art. 11), as stated in the Law of the PRC on Regional National Autonomy. Without abandoning the repression of ideas or activities that questioned Chinese sovereignty, the authorities chose to build trust and cohesion through cooption. Han and minority intellectuals sympathetic to the Party's cause continued to distil its discourse on society and the nation, but, as censorship was relaxed, alternative discourses could once again be expressed in the social sphere and even published as long as they did not engage in direct confrontation with the Party (Clarke 2011, 79–91).

At the same time, with de-collectivisation and the disappearance of the people's communes, control was less easy, and the Party had to find new relays to prevent the masses from straying too far from the path it

21 Hu Yaobang visited Xinjiang three times: 1983, 1985 and 1986.

22 Amended in 2001.

23 Chapters 1 and 3 of the Law of the People's Republic of China on Regional National Autonomy, 1984.

had traced. The Party, in this case the autonomous region's general Party secretary, Wang Enmao, resumed a united front policy: in short, rallying actors outside the Party in order to achieve the CCP's political goals. Purged cadres were rehabilitated while some of the Han people sent to the region during the Cultural Revolution were authorised to return to inland China. The Party incorporated or called upon individuals to serve as its relays, for example in religious associations. These minority cadres were sometimes recruited in spite of their political past and sometimes even in spite of their actual degree of loyalty to the Party. Apart from careerists, some believed that greater autonomy could be achieved by reforming the Party from within. In a way, the indulgence and even collaboration of some of those local cadres with the regenerating anti-colonial forces contributed to expanding the space for alternative ideas and political action. However, these minority cadres and intellectuals also acted as mediators when conflicts with the state emerged (Castets 2013, 205–54, 308–36). They were the vectors of the subjectivity of the local populations, allowing a better understanding of the Party and easing bursts of tension.

In a territory in which most minorities were Muslim, the Party also relied on the Islamic Association of China. The IAC's activities were reaffirmed by the Party Central Committee on 31 March 1982. While the new constitution solemnly declared freedom of religious belief[24] without abandoning the promotion of atheism, the Central Committee in its Document 19 of 1982 developed a framework regulating relations between the state and religion after the long period of trouble:

> The basic task of these patriotic religious organisations is to assist the Party and the government to implement the policy of freedom of religious belief, to help the broad mass of religious believers and persons in religious circles to continually raise their patriotic and socialist awareness, to represent the lawful rights and interest of religious circles, to organise normal religious activities, and to manage religious affairs well. All patriotic religious organisations should follow the Party's and government's leadership. Party and government cadres in turn should become adept in supporting and helping religious organisations to solve their own problems.[25]

24 Article 35 of the 1982 constitution.

25 For an entire translation of the document, see MacInnis (1989, 8–26).

According to the official rhetoric, the IAC thus acted as a 'bridge' (*qiaoliang* 桥梁) and as a 'link' (*niudai* 纽带) with the Muslim communities (Zhang, Li and Wang 2008; Doyon 2014). The IAC was supposed to transmit the religious policies of the Party and, at the same time, represent the Muslim masses. Its revival was part of a series of reforms intended to forge channels of dialogue between Muslims and the state. It also contributed to the creation of a climate of confidence and trust. However, the Party's trust was not boundless. In Document 19, the Central Committee stipulated that places of worship were to remain under the dual supervision of the Religious Affairs Bureau (RAB, *Zongjiao shiwu ju* 宗教事务局) and the religious associations in charge of running them. Thus, through the RAB, the state maintained the direct right to oversee places of worship. However, without a precise legal codification of what constituted illegal religious activities, certain clerics were able to mobilise networks at various levels, bypassing the instructions of the administration. In some areas, RAB surveillance could be lax in order to avoid problems outside periods of tensions, while in other situations their zeal could exacerbate tensions.[26]

1990s–2000s: Increased Surveillance, Repression and the Introduction of Legal Measures to Regulate Society

After the waves of anti-colonial student protests in 1985 and 1988 and then the protests against the book *Sexual Customs* (*xing fengsu* 性风俗),[27] which again degenerated into anti-colonial protests in May 1989 (Castets 2013, 221–8), the conservative faction of the CCP, which had taken over the reins of power in Beijing, called for control over the region to be strengthened. Conservatives believed that the looser control that had prevailed during the previous decade had allowed the restructuring of opposition forces and led society to retreat from the principles and values advocated by the Party. A report from Xinjiang Social Academy Research group on Pan-Turkism

26 Interviews with Uyghur clerics who fled abroad in the 1990s (Turkey, 2007).

27 The book contained blasphemous statements dealing with the sexual habits of Chinese Muslims. Demonstrations involving religious leaders and members of the main Muslim national minorities were organised throughout the country (Beijing, Xining, Xian, Kunming, etc.). The Party addressed the demands of protestors in China proper, but in Urumqi, protesters attacked official buildings and shouted anti-colonial slogans, resulting in multiple arrests and convictions.

and Pan-Islamism diffusion and countermeasures (反伊斯兰主义反突厥注义在新疆的转播及对策研究)[28] is indicative of the Party's concerns in the 1990s:

> In some places of southern Xinjiang, religious activities have reached a fever peak and a small number of ethnic separatists under the banner of religion are spreading separatism and fighting for ideological strongholds, seizing grassroots political power and the younger generation, and openly interfering with administration, the judicial system, and marriage. (Zhang 1997, 274)

The strategy of relying on mediators proved to be ineffective or even dangerous due to some cadres' lack of loyalty to the Party or insufficient ideological conviction. For example, the religious practices of some Party members raised concerns that the Party might become ideologically infiltrated and its ideological line distorted. The concerns of the Party leadership were confirmed by the outbreak of an aborted jihad that mobilised security forces and the army for a few days in the Akto district near Kashgar in April 1990. It was launched by talips[29] from an underground network called the East Turkestan Islamic Party (PITO) (*Shärkiy Türkistan Xälq Partiyisi*) (Zhang 1997, 271–3; Castets 2013, 321–8). The event was indicative of the complacency of some members of the CCP and patriotic organisations such as the IAC. In this case, a large proportion of PITO members came through the madrasas that Ablikim Makhsum Damolla had set up in the Karghilik oasis. This literate cleric, a supporter of the reformist current of Uyghur Islam, was also known to have been one of the protagonists of the uprisings against the Party in the 1950s in southern Xinjiang. However, after spending 20 years in custody, he had become vice-president of the regional branch of the IAC (Castets 2013, 275–7).

Moreover, at the time, the reopening of the borders between Xinjiang and neighbouring Muslim territories and the political events that shook Central Asia aroused the Party's vigilance. For some, the defeat of the Soviets in Afghanistan showed that hardened Muslim fighters could drive the army of a Communist empire, however powerful, from their territory. The fall of Communist totalitarianism in Europe, the collapse of the USSR and the independence of the Central Asian Republics galvanised an anti-colonial

28 This book, for internal use in Party and administration circles, is a collection of chapters bringing together the analysis of researchers and internal sources on the history of modern and pre-modern political opposition in Xinjiang from the Party's perspective.

29 Students in religion.

and pro-democracy sentiment that took advantage of the looser political climate of the 1980s to find expression in Xinjiang. After 1991, the militant circles mentioned above, and even some of the masses, saw the emergence of national states that included other major Turkic peoples of Central Asia as legitimising their independence aspirations.

In addition, the Uyghur diasporas in Central Asia and Turkey were reconnecting to Xinjiang. They were home to militant nationalist circles (Castets 2011) that were taking advantage of the reopening of the region to forge links, in particular the policies to open up Xinjiang to trade with Central Asia (Clarke 2011, 98–122). Thus, at the turn of the 1990s, while the majority of organisations in the Uyghur diaspora in the West began to unite around lobbying for the protection of the fundamental rights of Uyghurs, in Xinjiang, small groups with a sometimes short-life expectancy adopted more radical modes of action. In the early 1990s, while hopes for a greater autonomy vanished, violence rose in an attempt to destabilise China's sovereignty and alert the international community. Sabotage, arson, attacks on police barracks and military bases, the assassination of Han officials and Uyghur collaborators and bomb attacks revealed that radicalised anti-colonialist and Islamist elements were veering towards a terrorist strategy (Castets 2013, 229–40, 321–37).

In response to this situation, the Party gradually re-established tight control of the population based on several instructions and 'strike-hard' (*yanda* 严打) campaigns[30] aimed at targeting national splittism (*minzu fenlie* 民族分裂). At a special meeting on maintaining security in Xinjiang in 1996, the Politburo resurrected several priorities to re-establish firm control over the region and its minorities (CCP Central Committee Document 1996).[31]

First, although the issue was already mentioned in Document 19 and in the preamble of the Regional Ethnic Autonomy Law, the Party was making a priority of effectively reinforcing ideological homogeneity between the leading circles and the base in Xinjiang and to rely on reliable Party cadres:

30 This increasingly repressive approach would be embodied during his terms by the XUAR's new CCP secretary Wang Lequan (王乐泉) (1994–2010).

31 'Document No. 7 of the Politburo of the Central Committee from the meeting on Maintaining Stability in Xinjiang' (关于维护新疆稳定的会以纪要 中央政治局委员会7号文件), Chinese Communist Party Central Committee Document Central, 19 March 1996, trans. Turdi Ghoja. The minutes of this meeting are better known as 'Secret Document No 7'.

> On every level, Party committees and the people's government and concerned branches have to adhere to Deng Xiaoping's theory of building Chinese-style socialism and the Party's basic principles and guiding policy. On every level, Party and government leaders need to create a responsible order in defending ethnic unity and social stability and perfecting it while holding high the banner of defending ethnic unity and respect of the law with great political sensitivity and pride, unifying to the greatest level the cadres and people of every nationality and depending on them to alienate as much as possible the very small number of ethnic separatists and criminals who commit serious crimes, and strike hard against them, thus reinforcing the work of defending stability in all fields … The chairmen of village Party branches and the heads of neighbourhood districts have to be chosen carefully … At the same time, take real measures to train a large number of Han cadres who love Xinjiang and who will adhere to the Party's basic theories, principles, and guiding policies to correctly implement the Party's ethnic and religious policies and relocate them to Xinjiang.[32]

According to the Politburo Standing Committee, regional authorities also had to 'stabilise the ideological and cultural stronghold against separatism through strong propaganda' addressing 'the Party's ethnic and religious policies, laws and decrees … and patriotic and socialist ideas'. This implied, for example in the field of religion belief, that Communist Party members and cadres should be Marxist materialists, and therefore should not be allowed to believe in and practice religion. The Politburo also underlined the necessity of 'implementing comprehensively and correctly the Party's ethnic and religious policies' through the strengthening of 'legal control of ethnic and religious affairs'. This recommendation confirmed another major trend.

Between the end of the 1980s and the 1990s, regional authorities, with support from the central government, started paving the way for a system of judicial control designed to define the spectrum of discourses and religious activities that were tolerated. This framework aimed in particular to characterise as unlawful any activities and discourses that were detrimental to the modernisation model and the national construction efforts of the Party. This move was also supposed to provide a framework for the administrative bodies in charge of implementing these new rules.

32 Ibid.

The juridisation (*fazhihua* 法制化) in this respect indicates the basic trend. During the Maoist period, the state relied on cadres and activists to launch rectification campaigns. Until then, there was no real legislation in this area: the degree of state control over society was primarily determined by the political directives of the CCP Politburo. In an attempt to counteract the rise of subversive discourse in Islamic circles, the government of the Xinjiang Uyghur Autonomous Region issued, from the late 1980s and early 1990s onwards, a series of religious regulations targeting several aspects of religious practice and organisation in the area. A wider framework was established in 1994 through the Xinjiang Uighur Autonomous Region Regulations on Religious Affairs (*Xinjiang weiwuer zizhi qu zongjiqo shiwu guanli tiaolie* 新疆维吾尔自治区宗教事务管理条例). From that time onward, religious regulations were constantly widened and tightened (Castets 2015). The registration of places of worship was implemented, and religious activities within them were monitored with increasing strictness. While Xinjiang served as a kind of laboratory for experimenting with these measures, national and regional regulations were to follow over the years. Little by little, imams were purged and placed under close control of the Religious Affairs bureaus, which strictly relayed the instructions of the State Administration of Religious Affairs. While religious influence was closely monitored, or even proscribed in the administration and the school system, the teaching of Islam was placed under the close control of the Party with a view to transforming the new generation of imams into faithful relays of Party ideology. This work of regulating the spectrum of religious activities was supported by a takeover of the religious education systems. With regard to the teaching of Islam, the new legislation outlawed underground Koranic schools/classes (*siban jingwen xuexiao / ban* 私办经文学校/班). They were closed down one after the other, and those that continued illegally were severely punished from the 1990s onwards. Imams were no longer allowed to give 'catechism' classes without authorisation. To be accredited, young imams had to graduate from official Islamic Institutes (*Yisilanjiao jingxuexiao* 伊斯兰教经学校).

This move went hand in hand with a relative marginalisation of the IAC in the monitoring and regulation of religious life. The Party decided to rely on administrative structures it could control more directly (Castets 2015). However, the management of religious issues and ethnic affairs was still taking place in a complex ecosystem whose balances could vary locally according to the networks, zeal or reluctance of the parties involved.[33] The few testimonies we collected[34] seemed to indicate different configurations, depending on the charisma and networks of religious personnel and the attitude of the local government or administration. Other elements were indicative of this short-circuiting of the IAC and increasingly close surveillance of the administration. The fact that the IAC branches in some of Xinjiang's sensitive oases operated on a shoestring budget, or that their offices were integrated squarely into the CCP's United Front Work Department or the RAB, was also revealing (Zhang, Li and Wang 2008).

The Politburo document also recommended drastically reinforcing the public security and national security apparatus and 'fully utilising their functions in fighting separatism and sabotage activities'. By then it was already encouraging the creation of systematic records of 'unpatriotic elements'. Another preoccupation of the Party was to wield diplomatic actions and other means to deactivate Uyghur ethnic separatist organisations operating abroad, especially in Central Asia, Turkey and the West, a policy that has been fruitful mainly in Central Asia (Castets 2011).

After the 2001 terrorist attacks on the United States, a major inflection occurred in the lexicon and the international dimension of the struggle against the Uyghur political opposition (Clarke 2008). China decided to capitalise on the capture of elements of the East Turkistan Islamic Party by US forces in the Af-Pak area after the fall of the Taliban to try to insert the fight against the Uyghur political opposition into the fight against international jihadism. From the 1980s onwards, separatism had become an increasingly decried evil in the discourse of Party cadres. However, from the early 2000s, opponents or critics in Xinjiang were quite systematically assimilated into the 'three forces' (*san gu shili* 三股势力): terrorism, separatism and (religious) extremism. This repackaging defended the idea that Uyghur non-violent anti-colonial nationalist circles, non-violent Islamists and Salafi jihadists formed a sort of nebula with vague outlines, called East Turkistan (*dongtu* 东突). In short, this new terminology assimilating distinct political networks made it possible to lump them together and to legitimise, in the name of the fight against terrorism, the repression of any form of challenge to the authority of the CCP.

33 About how these processes unfolded differently outside Xinjiang, see for example Jérôme Doyon's work on the Nanjing region (Doyon 2014).

34 Interviews conducted in the diaspora between 2003 and 2008.

The Turning Point of the 2010s: The Projection of Xinjiang into the Ultra-Controlled Society of the 'Chinese Dream' (中国梦)

As we have seen above, from the 1990s onwards, the Party returned to a logic of social control, based on recurrent security campaigns and on a legal framework that was to be constantly reinforced and implemented. At the same time, it relied on an accelerated economic growth boosted by transfers from the central state and investments by public companies in infrastructure, the exploitation of natural resources and tourism (Shan and Wei 2010). The economic opening up of the region, towards Central Asia in particular, was deepened with growing interconnection in transport networks (road, rail, hydrocarbons, etc.) to stimulate trade and attract investment. The Xinjiang region has also been one of the areas favoured by the Great Western Development Plan, the main objective of which is to speed the growth of the provinces concerned through public investment and the attraction of foreign direct investment.

Thus, the low-intensity terrorism that emerged in the 1990s almost completely disappeared (Castets 2003, 2013, 318–36). Despite occasional large-scale outbreaks of rioting, such as in Khotan and Ghulja (Yining) in 1995 and 1997, the political situation was quite stabilised by the end of the 1990s; however, it deteriorated again from the end of the decade. In the months leading up to the Beijing Olympics, the Turkestan Islamic Party, which at that time belonged to an Al-Qaeda affiliates network in Waziristan, began to threaten the Chinese authorities. By the late 2000s, the measures mentioned above had destroyed the ability of minority Party members, intellectuals or imams to mediate in conflicts or tensions (Castets 2015). While the sinicisation of the school system in particular was increasingly presented as a corollary of modernisation and economic development (Tobin 2020, 59–86), previously isolated incidents began multiplying as levels of control and repression rose further following the riots in the regional capital, Urumqi, in July 2009. In southern Xinjiang, attacks and violence carried out by young people denouncing colonial policies started shaking the Uyghur majority areas (Julienne 2021, 166–92). The constant tightening of control, the sanctioning of an ever-broader range of opinions, and the zeal and even abuses of certain Han officials who felt protected by a hierarchy under pressure from the central government to stabilise the region started feeding a vicious circle.

In July 2009, demonstrations by the Uyghur population to demand more equality and consideration from the authorities degenerated in the regional capital in the face of repression. Hans were targeted before retaliating in turn. The riots officially claimed 197 lives, three-quarters of whom were Hans. Arrests were massive; some people disappeared, and dozens of Uyghurs were sentenced to death. The internet was cut off for several months, video surveillance became widespread and Xinjiang became a testing ground for various technological surveillance devices.[35]

A few months after those events, in May 2010, the first Xinjiang work conference (a joint conference of the CCP Central Committee and PRC State Council) was held. The group of leaders[36] participating in the conference decided to deepen economic support from the central government and other provinces while continuing policies aimed at maintaining stability and fighting against ethnic separatism. Among those policies, the Partner Assistance Programme was to provide increased personnel and financial support from 19 provinces and cities from the rest of China. Another decision was to modify the implementation of taxes on natural resources and to reallocate them to the regional government as a means of boosting government investment.[37] One major decision of the group was to reallocate some of these funds to improve living standards in the poorest minority areas, while the regional government was to develop vocational training and new jobs benefiting minorities (Shan and Wei 2010, 63–4).

However, minorities felt more than ever the weight of Chinese state control and repression. While the sinicisation of the school system was accelerating (Zhang and McGhee 2014, 32–9), a portion of the youth and of the wider Uyghur population felt increasingly alienated, and also frustrated on a daily basis by restrictions on freedoms and the abuses of a security apparatus under pressure to obtain results. The administration was pushed after 2009 to identify and eradicate the 'three forces' and to sanction more widely any

35 For a more detailed analysis of the event and its aftermath, see Tobin (2020, 114–38).

36 Among these were President Hu Jintao (胡锦涛) and Vice-President Xi Jinping (习近平).

37 Investment in fixed assets was to increase drastically through this system during the 2011–15 Five-Year Plan (Shan and Weng 2010, 63; Zhang and McGhee 2014, 28–32). This adjustment went hand in hand with hardliner Wang Lequan's departure as Xinjiang Party secretary and the arrival of Zhang Chunxian (张春贤), a cadre mostly focused on developmental and social issues.

unpatriotic behaviour.[38] The general situation, but also police malpractice and administration intransigence, fuelled in return growing frustrations within society, and premeditated and unpremeditated acts of violence proliferated. Together, the rejection of the Chinese state's verticality, abuses and brutally sinicising model of modernisation exacerbated despair and fuelled increasing acts of violence and attacks in the south. Whereas between 2008 and 2012, casualties of what the authorities described as terrorist acts[39] did not exceed a few dozen per year, they numbered several hundred in 2014. Several violent actions were aimed at striking Chinese and foreign public opinion and media. These included a vehicle-ramming attack on Tiananmen Square in autumn 2013, a knife attack at the Kunming railway station in March 2013 and the spring 2014 attacks in Urumqi. While smaller-scale attacks took place in the following months, 2014 was a black year for China, with more than 300 victims of 'terrorism' compared to a handful of victims each year in the 2000s according to official figures (Julienne 2018, 82).

President Xi Jinping, visiting Xinjiang at the time of the 2014 attacks, promised to eradicate the terrorist threat at its roots and, more broadly, to ensure the stability of the region.[40] A second Central Xinjiang Work Conference was held in May 2014 to solve the problem. The issue of addressing the question of national minorities through economic development and measures for improving minority living standards became overshadowed by a security prism aimed at annihilating any opposition to CCP rule through unprecedented surveillance, control and coercion over Xinjiang's minorities. A new Special Strike-Hard against Violent Terrorism Campaign (*yanli da ji baoli kongbu huodong zhuanxiang xingdong* 严厉打击暴力恐怖活动专项行动) opened the way to a vast policy of categorisation of individuals as 'trustworthy', 'average' or 'untrustworthy'.[41] It also launched a hunt inside Party and administrative organs against 'two-faced' cadres who had criticised Party policies (*liangmian ren* 两面人).[42]

38 Human Rights Watch, '"Eradicating Ideological Viruses": China's Campaign of Repression against Xinjiang's Muslims', 9 September 2018, www.hrw.org/report/2018/09/09/eradicating-ideological-viruses/chinas-campaign-repression-against-xinjiangs.

39 Not all acts defined as terrorism in China are covered by anti-terrorist legislation in the West.

40 For a wider view of Xi Jinping's discourse following the 2014 events, see Austin Ramzy and Chris Buckley, '"Absolutely No Mercy": Leaked Files Exposed How China Organized Mass Detention Among Muslims', *New York Times*, 16 November 2019, www.nytimes.com/interactive/2019/11/16/world/asia/china-xinjiang-documents.html.

41 Human Rights Watch, '"Eradicating Ideological Viruses"'.

42 Heike Holberg, 'Xi Jinping and the Self-Fulfilling Prophecy of "Two-Faced Individuals"', *China Trends*, 7, October 2020, www.institutmontaigne.org/en/publications/china-trends-7-shrinking-margins-debate.

This turn to a zero-tolerance attitude was affirmed at a time when China's president had begun to reorganise the bodies in charge of minority issues, religious issues and the fight against terrorism. The aim was to rationalise their organisation by placing them under closer supervision of the Party and the circles of power affiliated with the president (Kam and Clarke 2021, 630–2).[43] The management of national minorities and religious affairs, formerly in the hands of various administrations but also of the so-called 'representative' patriotic associations, was to some extent questioned. They were not considered reliable enough, even if in official discourse they were still considered the CCP's main partners. The supervision of these tasks had been entrusted to the Party's United Front Work Department (UFWD),[44] itself more than ever in resonance with the president's lines after being placed under the control of his allies (Zhao and Leibold 2019, 41; Kam and Clarke 2021, 630–2). Thus, the State Ethnic Affairs Commission, the State Administration for Religious Affairs Commission and, a fortiori, the IAC were now effectively bypassed/short-circuited by Party organs such as the UFWD (Doyon 2018) and the National Security Commission created in late 2013. The establishment of a dedicated Xinjiang office within the UFWD in 2017 under the supervision of security officials indicated the intention to handle Xinjiang policy through a security perspective (Kam and Clarke 2021).

In addition, increasingly narrow legal frameworks continue to be refined to combat what the Chinese authorities label as 'terrorism' and 'extremism' and, more broadly, all opinions and political or religious thinking that does not fit within the Party lines. In November 2014, the Assembly of the Xinjiang Autonomous Region passed a new law updating the 1994 regional religious regulations. One of the main threats identified by this new regional law was religious extremism.[45] The law provided an extended frame for extremism's juridical characterisation as well as sanctions to eliminate 'extremist' content that could circulate via new media such as the internet or social media. In December 2015, the National People's Congress passed China's first antiterrorism law (*Zhonghua renmin gongheguo fankongbuzhuyi*

43 Max Oitdmann, 'The Xi Jinping Cohort and the Chinafication of Religion', *Berkeley Forum*, 16 March 2020, berkleycenter.georgetown.edu/responses/the-xi-jinping-cohort-and-the-chinafication-of-religion.

44 See Emmanuel Jourda, Chapter 6, this volume.

45 The latter is defined as 'activities or comments that twist the doctrines of a religion and promote thoughts of extremism, violence and hatred'. See 'Religious Extremism Law Imposes New Restrictions on China's Uyghurs', *Radio Free Asia*, 12 October 2014, www.rfa.org/english/news/uyghur/religious-extremism-law-12102014160359.html?searchterm:utf8:ustring=extremism+xinjiang.

fa 中华人民共和国反恐怖主义法). This law, which came into force in 2016, gives an extensive definition of terrorism, criminalising a large range of activities. It is also aimed at coordinating the political, economic, legal, cultural, educational, diplomatic and military struggle against 'terrorist activities' through the establishment at different administrative levels of 'counterterrorism work steering agencies' (*fankongbuzhuyi lingdao jigou* 反恐怖主义工作领导机构), the fight against 'terrorist activities' being supervised at the national level by the National Counter-Terrorism Working and Coordinating Small Group (*Guojia fankongbu gongzuo lingdao xiaozu* 国家反恐怖工作领导小组) (Julienne 2021, 199–204). Those structures can rely on the information provided by the National Counterterrorism Intelligence Centre (*Guojia fankongbuzhuyi zhongxin* 国家反恐怖主义情报中心). This national centre's goal is to rationalise the collection and use of information in order to better anticipate and strengthen the efficiency of the counterterrorism apparatus.

The frame provided by these new sets of laws, new bodies and reorganisations, and the use of traditional and high-tech tools of surveillance has generated a kind of Orwellian world. The strengthening of police forces has played a crucial role in increasing security, surveillance and data collection. One main policy in this field in 2014 was the establishment of public security offices in every village or hamlet in the region, using regular and auxiliary staff. Special police forces and anti-riot equipment has been strengthened, and police recruitment reached a peak[46] after Chen Quanguo (陈全国) replaced Zhang Chunxian as Xinjiang's Party secretary. This tendency is also revealed by the explosion in security budgets.[47] While the security situation was deteriorating in 2013, Zhang Chunxian's '*fang hui ju* 访惠聚' (visit, benefit, gather) program was presented as the reinvigoration of the Maoist practice of the 'mass line'.[48] Two hundred thousand Party cadres and administrators were sent to visit mostly Uyghur families in southern Xinjiang, sometimes staying for several days to interview adults and children in order to provide patriotic education and identify disloyal

46 Adrian Zenz and James Leibold, 'Xinjiang's Rapidly Evolving Security State', *Jamestown Foundation*, 14 March 2017, jamestown.org/program/xinjiangs-rapidly-evolving-security-state/.

47 Adrian Zenz, 'Domestic Security Budgets Reveal Scope of China's Actions in Xinjiang', *New Lens*, 14 November 2018, international.thenewslens.com/article/108116.

48 This trend is visible in Hong Kong too: see Samson Yuen and Edmund Cheng, Chapter 15, this volume.

subjects.[49] In October 2016, the initiative was expanded through the Becoming Family Campaign mobilising more than 1 million cadres visiting mainly families in rural areas (Grose and Leibold 2022).

One main feature of surveillance in Xinjiang and in China generally is the massive use of technology. Various devices and practices are commonly mobilised. Internet and phone telecommunications are massively monitored. Smartphones and computers are subject to verification and data can even be siphoned off by the police at any time at the multiple checkpoints that dot the roads or through wi-fi sniffers.[50] As in the rest of China today, a vast video surveillance system with facial recognition has been developed since 2009, while QR codes are affixed to the entrances of houses to better access the data of those who live there. Vehicles are fitted with GPS systems to make them trackable, and automatic number plate recognition systems scan vehicles on the road. A vast regional health campaign has already registered the DNA of the population. This campaign goes hand in hand with retinal scans, fingerprinting and even voice recordings.[51] This level of mass surveillance reveals another change in China's security philosophy. It is no longer only a question of monitoring society and punishing harshly those who do wrong. The new devices are part of a logic of constant control and even predictive mass control against 'extremism'. The most advanced data collection and cross-referencing system is undoubtedly the famous 'Integrated Joint Operations Platform' (*yitihua lianhe zuozhan pingtai* 一体化联合作战平台).[52] Developed by a subsidiary of the China Electronics Technology Group Corporation, its fine-mesh surveillance net aims to capture all seeds of dissent before they take root while at the same time flushing out 'two-faced' individuals[53] – that is, those who hide their true political views. The system is able to analyse a considerable amount of data according to a grid of arbitrary criteria[54] making it possible to flag 'unusual' behaviour and to classify individuals according to the degree of supposed risk they present.

49 Human Rights Watch, '"Eradicating Ideological Viruses"'.

50 Human Rights Watch, 'China's Algorithms of Repression Reverse Engineering a Xinjiang Police Mass Surveillance App', May 2019, www.hrw.org/sites/default/files/report_pdf/china0519_web5.pdf.

51 Ibid.

52 Ibid.

53 On this notion, see Jérôme Doyon and Long Yang, Chapter 5, this volume.

54 Such as 'Reciting the Quran', 'Wearing religious clothing or having a long beard', 'Having more children than allowed by family planning policy', 'Having returned from abroad', 'Acting suspiciously', 'Having complex social ties or unstable thoughts', 'Having improper [sexual] relations', 'Using suspicious software'. See Human Rights Watch, 'China's Algorithms of Repression'.

In this perspective, once refractory people and, more generally, people supposedly exposed to extremist thought are identified by these surveillance devices, they are to be treated within a vast re-education system designed to fight against 'extremism' in Xinjiang. This system was developed from the extrajudicial 'transformation through education work' (*jiaoyu zhuanhua gongzuo* 教育转化工作) system developed in China in the 1990s to re-educate followers of the Falun Gong sect. The system was reinvigorated in Xinjiang under Zhang Chunxian's guidance in 2014 and was considerably expanded when Chen Quanguo became the CCP secretary for Xinjiang in 2016 (Grose and Leibold 2022). According to Adrian Zenz's analysis of satellite data and government contracts, more than 10 per cent of the Uyghur population is believed to have passed through the system (Zenz 2018; Zhao and Leibold 2019). The re-education system in Xinjiang employs a vast network of education/re-education/de-extremification devices and structures aimed at reforming minds in order to build a society of loyal citizens sharing common views, beliefs and values with the Party. Those devices range from patriotic education classes to infrastructure meant to mobilise processes of re-education adapted to their degree of 'radicalisation' and 'dangerousness' (Grose and Leibold 2022). Following criticism by international human rights organisations and Uyghur diasporic organisations, a new set of regulations revised in 2018 (*Xinjiang weiwuer zizhiqu jiduanhua tiaolie* 新疆维吾尔自治区极端化条列) provide a kind of legal framework to justify the re-education system, presenting a portion of it as vocational boarding schools.[55]

Conclusion

Since the 'peaceful liberation of Xinjiang', the CCP, relying in particular on state structures, as well as united front and mass organisations, has waged a struggle that is still ongoing to eradicate anti-colonial political forces and any form of expression questioning the verticality of centre–periphery relations in China.

55 'Vocational Education and Training in Xinjiang', State Council of the People's Republic of China, 17 August 2019, english.www.gov.cn/archive/whitepaper/201908/17/content_WS5d57573cc6d0c6695ff7ed6c.html#:~:text=The%20vocational%20education%20and%20training,influence%20of%20religious%20extremist%20teachings.

To eliminate intellectuals, activists or discourses defending alternative ideological or value systems, but also to take control of representations to legitimise the appropriation of its own ideological representation systems, the Party has implemented a range of strategies over the last few decades. They include counter-insurgency; united front work;[56] mass mobilisations and mass line campaigns; re-education; juridical definitions of unpatriotic activities and attitudes; and, now, counterterrorism and mass surveillance mobilising information communications technology. The discourse on threats (securitisation) has also greatly evolved. The Party legitimised its strategies of eliminating competing political forces and ideas through a discourse of threat that, depending on the period, assimilated the enemy in Xinjiang into the major threats identified by the Politburo Standing Committee. In other words, local securitisation discourse has been subjected to the national discourse on threats in spite of the specificities of local political configurations. Over the years, an evolving, and often broad, lexical field has qualified the underground political opposition, the proponents of alternative ideologies and even critical elements within the Party. Initially, the terms 'feudal' or 'counter-revolutionary' forces were used; however, in the second half of the 1950s, these terms expanded to 'rightists' or 'local nationalists', and then, during the 1960s–70s, included (pro-Soviet) 'revisionists' to denounce disloyal elements of the Party. At the turn of the 1990s and the implementation of the 'three forces' (*sangu shili* 三股势力) rhetoric, counter-revolutionaries and local nationalists became 'terrorists' or 'extremists' – notions that have been placed in the second half of the 2010s under the seal of counterterrorism, de-extremification and re-education.

As a defender of a non-negotiable national model, the Party has rejected the identification of possible colonial issues. It has also rejected any further political autonomy or the implementation of a modernisation model that is less sinicising and more respectful of the sociocultural aspirations of minorities. Under Xi Jinping's guidance, it promotes, on the contrary, an accelerated 'Chinafication' (*zhongguohua* 中国化) of their culture and religion.[57]

56 On the history of the notion, see Emmanuel Jourda, Chapter 6, this volume. On the evolving practices of the united front work, see Samson Yuen and Edmund Cheng, Chapter 15, this volume.

57 This process should lead to the 'creation of a new supra-ethnic identity animated by the loyalty to the PRC state and the messianic world-historical mission of the CCP'. See Oitdmann, 'The Xi Jinping Cohort'.

For the Party, the causes of protest and violence in Xinjiang cannot be associated with its model of modernisation but are linked to the spread of subversive ideas, 'ideological viruses' distorting an idealised social reality and instilled by malevolent external political forces. In short, the Party has chosen to reject any dialogue on the redefinition of its policies in Xinjiang and pathologises alternative thinking (Grose and Leibold 2022).

Now, at the time of the 'Chinese Dream', Xi Jinping's Party promotes a social order that, through social credit and the devices mentioned above, is intended to ensure the security of the population, increase its moral quality (*suzhi* 素质) and homogenise its representations to structure a stronger nation-state.

In other words, what Xinjiang is going through is nothing more than a litmus test revealing an increasingly securitarian drift and the building of a new high-tech form of 'scientific state' (Smith 1971). This new tentacular state control, unlimited by the democratic right of citizen scrutiny, rule of law or the separation of powers, capitalises on technologies and a pool of high-tech, state-supported companies that could proliferate abroad through Chinese cooperation with other authoritarian states. This scientific state, increasingly 'total' in its aspirations, would, according to its supporters in the Party, surpass Western liberal states weakened by values and systems of homogenisation and control that are too lax and too protective of individual rights, leading them towards long-term decline.

References

Benson, Linda. 1990. *The Ili Rebellion: Muslim Challenge to Chinese Authority in Xinjiang, 1944–49*. 1st edition. New York: Routledge. doi.org/10.4324/9781003069737.

Bovingdon, Gardner. 2010. *The Uyghurs in Xinjiang: Strangers in Their Own Land.* New York: Colombia University Press.

Brophy, David. 2016. *Uyghur Nation. Reform and Revolution on the Russian-China frontier*. Cambridge: Harvard University Press. doi.org/10.4159/9780674970441.

Castets, Rémi. 2003. 'The Uyghurs in Xinjiang. The Malaise Grows'. *China Perspectives* 49: 34–48. doi.org/10.3406/perch.2003.3490.

Castets, Rémi. 2011. 'Les recompositions de la scène politique ouïghoure dans les années 1990-2000'. *Relations Internationales* 45: 87–104. doi.org/10.3917/ri.145.0087.

Castets, Rémi. 2013. 'Nationalisme, Islam et politique: les trajectoires idéologiques de l'opposition politique ouïghoure'. PhD thesis, Institut d'Etudes politiques de Paris (Sciences Po).

Castets, Rémi. 2015. 'The Modern Chinese State and Strategies of Control over Uyghur Islam'. *Central Asian Affairs* 2 (3): 221–45. doi.org/10.1163/22142290-00203001.

Clarke, Michael. 2008. 'China's "War on Terror" in Xinjiang: Human Security and the Causes of Violent Uighur Separatism'. *Terrorism and Political Violence* 20 (2): 271–301. doi.org/10.1080/09546550801920865.

Clarke, Michael. 2011. *Xinjiang and China's Rise in Central Asia. A History of National Integration in Xinjiang*. New York: Routledge.

Clarke, Michael. 2022. '"Round the Clock, Three Dimensional Control": The Evolution and Implications of the "Xinjiang Mode" of Counterterrorism'. In *The Xinjiang Emergency: Exploring the Causes and Consequences of China's Mass Detention of Uyghurs*, edited by Michael Clarke, 275–305. Manchester: Manchester University Press. doi.org/10.4324/9780203831113.

Doyon, Jérôme. 2014. *Négocier la place de l'islam chinois. Les associations islamiques de Nankin à l'ère des réformes*. Paris: L'Harmattan.

Doyon, Jérôme. 2018. 'Actively Guiding Religion under Xi Jinping'. *Asia Dialogue*, 21 June. theasiadialogue.com/2018/06/21/actively-guiding-religion-under-xi-jinping/.

Forbes, Andrew D. 1986. *Warlords and Muslims in Chinese Central Asia, A Political History of Republican Xinjiang 1911–1949*. Cambridge: Cambridge University Press.

Gladney, Dru. 1996. 'L'expansion du colonialisme intérieur en Chine'. *Pouvoirs* 81: 59–69.

Gladney, Dru. 2003. 'Responses to Chinese Rule: Patterns of Cooperation and Opposition'. *Mongolian Journal of International Affairs* 10: 102–19. doi.org/10.5564/mjia.v0i10.122.

Gladney, Dru. 2004. *Dislocating China, Muslims, Minorities and Other Subaltern Subjects*. London: Hurst & Company.

Grose, Timothy and James Leibold. 2022. 'Pathology, Inducement and Mass Incarceration of Xinjiang's "Targeted Populations"'. In *The Xinjiang Emergency: Exploring the Causes and Consequences of China's Mass Detention of Uyghurs*, edited by Michael Clarke, 127–53. Manchester: Manchester University Press.

Hamada, Masami. 1990. 'La transmission du mouvement nationaliste au Turkestan Oriental (Xinjiang)'. *Central Asian Survey* 9 (1): 29–48. doi.org/10.1080/02634939008400688.

Julienne, Marc. 2018. 'Du Xinjiang à la Syrie, la Chine face au terrorisme transnational', *Diplomatie* 91: 81–5.

Julienne, Marc. 2021. 'Les stratégies chinoises de lutte contre le terrorisme: reflet de la montée en puissance de l'Etat sécuritaire'. PhD thesis, Institut National des Langues et Civilisations orientales.

Kam, Stephanie and Michael Clarke. 2021 'Securitization, Surveillance and "De-extremization" in Xinjiang'. *International Affairs* 97 (3): 625–42. doi.org/10.1093/ia/iiab038.

Klimeš, Ondrej. 2015. *Struggle by the Pen: The Uyghur Discourse on Nation and National Interest c.1900–1949*. Leiden: Brill. doi.org/10.1163/9789004288096.

Lattimore, Owen. [1950] 1975. *Pivot of Asia: Xinjiang and the Inner Frontiers of China and Russia*. New York: AMS Press.

MacInnis, Donald. 1989. *Religion in China Today: Policy and Practice*. New York: Orbis.

McMillen, Donald. 1979. *Chinese Communist Power and Policy in Xinjiang 1949–1977*. Boulder: Westview Press.

Millward, James. 2007. *Eurasian Crossroads: A History of Xinjiang*. New York: Columbia University Press.

Qi, Qingshun (齐清顺) and Weijiang Qian (田卫疆). 2004. *Studies on Chinese Central Dynasties Governance Policies of Xinjiang* (中国历代中央王朝治理新疆政策研究). Urumqi: Xinjiang People's Publisher.

Roberts, Sean. 2020. *The War on the Uyghurs. China's Campaign against Xinjiang's Muslims*. Manchester: Manchester University Press. doi.org/10.1515/9780691202211.

Shan, Wei and Cuifen Weng. 2010. 'China's New Policy in Xinjiang and Its Challenges'. *East Asian Policy* 2 (3): 58–66.

Shichor, Yitzhak. 2003. 'The Great Wall of Steel: Military and Strategy in Xinjiang'. In *Xinjiang: China's Muslim Borderland*, edited by S. Starr Frederick, 120–62. Armonk: M. E. Sharpe.

Smith, Anthony. 1971. *Theories of Nationalism*. London: Gerald Duckworth.

Teufel Dreyer, June. 1986. 'The Xinjiang Uyghur Autonomous Region at Thirty. A Report Card'. *Asian Survey* 26 (7): 721–44. doi.org/10.2307/2644208.

Tobin, David. 2020. *Securing China's Northwest Frontier: Identity and Insecurity in Xinjiang*. Cambridge: Cambridge University Press. doi.org/10.1017/9781108770408.

Vincent, Andrew. 2010. *Modern Political Ideologies*. Oxford: Wiley-Blackwell.

Wang, David. 1999. *Under the Soviet Shadow: The Yining Incident: Ethnic Conflicts and International Rivalry in Xinjiang, 1944–1949*. Hong Kong: Chinese University Press.

Whiting, Allen and Shicai Sheng. 1958. *Xinjiang: Pawn or Pivot?* East Lansing: Michigan University Press.

Zenz, Adrian. 2018. '"Thoroughly Reforming Them towards a Healthy Heart Attitude": China's Political Re-education Campaign in Xinjiang'. *Central Asian Survey* 38 (1): 102–28. doi.org/10.1080/02634937.2018.1507997.

Zhang, Jingquan (张敬全), Li Jinxin (李进新) and Wang Wei (王伟). 2008. 'The Role of the Islamic Association as a Bridge and Link: Survey and Reflection on Xinjiang Islamic Association Levels' (试论伊斯兰教协会的桥梁纽带作用. 对新疆个及伊斯兰教协会的调查与思考). *Gansu Social Sciences* 5: 85–9.

Zhang, Shaoying and Derek McGhee. 2014. *Social Policies and Ethnic Conflict in China: Lessons from Xinjiang*. Basingstoke: Palgrave Macmillan. doi.org/10.1057/9781137436665.

Zhang, Yuxi (张玉玺). 1997. 'The Struggle against Separatism and Its Historical Lessons in Xinjiang since the Liberation' (新疆解放以来反对民族分裂主义的斗争及其历史经验题). In *Research on Pan-Turkism and Pan-Islamism* (泛伊斯兰主义泛突厥注意研究), edited by Yang Faren (杨发仁), Li Ze and Dong Cheng, 264–79. Urumqi: Xinjiang Academy of Social Sciences.

Zhao, Taotao and James Leibold. 2019. 'Ethnic Governance under Xi Jinping: The Centrality of the United Front Work Department and Its Implications'. *Journal of Contemporary China* 29 (124): 487–502. doi.org/10.1080/10670564.2019.1677359.

Zhu, Peiming (朱培民), Chen Hong (陈宏) and Yang Hong (杨红). 2004. *The Chinese Communist Party and the National Minorities Issue in Xinjiang* (中国共产党与新疆民族问题). Urumqi: Xinjiang Renmin Chubanshe.

15

From Making Friends to Countering Threats: The Changing Contours of United Front Work in Hong Kong

Samson Yuen and Edmund W. Cheng

Introduction

Hong Kong has been a Special Administrative Region (SAR) of the People's Republic of China since 1997. However, long before the semi-autonomous city was handed over from the British, the Chinese Communist Party (CCP), since its birth, had sought to establish its presence in the territory. The capitalist city, despite being a stark ideological opposite to the socialist ideal, has served as a useful and relatively safe haven for the CCP to conduct revolutionary and political work, and as a strategic outpost to communicate, interact and trade with the outside world. These activities strengthened the Party's survival in its nascent years and have also enabled it to meet its political needs at different periods of time. Facilitating these activities is the idea of the united front, a Leninist invention that originally sought to unite all workers from non-socialist parties against the capitalist class. Adopted by the CCP to bring friends and sympathisers in line against its political opponents, and credited by Mao Zedong as one of the CCP's 'three great magic weapons' (*sanda fabao*), united front work has been an – if not the most – important tool to expand and consolidate political influence in

Hong Kong, both before and after the sovereignty handover. It has allowed the party-state to build up an extensive pro-Beijing following to ensure its dominion over the city. To a large extent, one could say that united front work was simply the 'basis and starting point of various tasks' for the local CCP (Loh 2010, 88).

Given the centrality of the united front in China's policy towards Hong Kong, the topic has aroused substantial interest among scholars. Numerous studies have been published about the history of united front work in Hong Kong (Chan Lau 1999; Loh 2010), the target of such work (Chu 2010), the role of key united front actors (Burns 1990; Lee 2019), the strategies involved (Lam and Lam 2013) and its impact on local politics (Lo, Hung and Loo 2019). But despite their contribution to the field, these works have several limitations. First, these studies often put the attention on state actors that are formally responsible for carrying out united front work, usually the Central Liaison Office and its predecessor. This focus neglects the fragmented nature of China's authoritarianism (Lieberthal and Lampton 1992; Mertha 2009) in that many local government actors are also actively involved in developing their line of united front work in Hong Kong. Second, these studies tend to adopt a state-centric perspective, portraying the united front as a top-down, hierarchical structure. Although they do recognise the relational nature of united front work, the analytical attention is tilted towards state actors and their policies, which understates their interaction with myriad social actors. Third, because of the clandestine nature of the united front, these studies have mostly relied on archival and anecdotal data, which makes the findings rather descriptive and unidimensional. This has undermined the actual scale, scope and rhythm of united front work on an empirical level.

This chapter seeks to unravel the dynamics of China's united front work in post-handover Hong Kong. Based on publicly available reports and an original event dataset, we use a social network approach to delineate the changing landscape of the united front and the interactions between myriad state and non-state actors that are taking place under united front work. Besides showing the steady organisational proliferation of pro-Beijing social organisations, we also demonstrate their increasingly frequent interaction with the SAR government and different levels of government in mainland China. By doing so, we argue that united front work has become more decentralised and multilayered in its structure, and that its objective has been shifting from elite cooption to counter-mobilisation against pro-democracy threats.

Our findings seek not only to highlight the continual salience of united front tactics that the Leninist party-state relies on to control a peripheral territory, but also to cast it under a different analytical light. By utilising a rich set of event data that have not been explored by scholars, we are able to visualise and, to some extent, quantify united front work in a relational and temporal manner. Moreover, by showing the multitude of state and non-state actors involved in the united front, the results indicate that state power in post-handover Hong Kong does not solely belong to the remit of governmental institutions; it is increasingly exercised through the nexus between state and society.

The Political Art of Making Friends

The CCP's united front work has a long history in Hong Kong. As soon as the Party was established in the early 1920s, it began to operate in the then British-ruled colonial city, using it as a revolutionary base to build up power against the Nationalist government. Although by the mid-1930s the Communist activities had almost come to a complete halt due to the Long March (Chan Lau 1999), Japanese invasion provided an opportunity for the Party to re-establish itself and expand its united front in the city (Loh 2010, 56–63). After the Party captured political power in the mainland, Hong Kong continued to serve as an important outpost. Despite its ideological aversion to imperialism, the CCP decided to leave Hong Kong in the hands of the British for strategic purposes. It adopted a policy known as 'making full use of Hong Kong in the interest of long-term planning' (*changqi liyong, chongfen dasuan*), which would remain in place for the next few decades until the handover (Loh 2010, 84). Under this policy, Hong Kong became both a window through which the CCP communicated and engaged with the outside world, and an ideological battlefield against the Guomindang (GMD) and the US-led 'Free World'. The city's unequivocal capitalism also provided a stable source of foreign currency and other essential supplies for the Leninist party-state to sustain itself through its economic turmoil and international sanctions.

To achieve these objectives and make full use of Hong Kong, the CCP developed an extensive united front that spanned a wide range of sectors. Apart from aligning with the working class, its traditional base of support, the party-state – represented by the New China News Agency (NCNA, also known as *Xinhua*) in the territory – cultivated supporters and friends among the capitalists, professionals and politicians, while extending its influence into education, media and cultural circles. This extensive united front, known locally as the 'leftists', was mobilised en masse during the 1967 riots due to the influence of the Cultural Revolution, when pro-Beijing groups organised a Struggle Committee to coordinate strike actions and violent protests against the colonial authorities (Cheung 2009). However, because of its increasing radicalisation, coupled with the hardline responses from the colonial authorities (Yep 2008), the leftists lost public sympathy. Many citizens instead opted to throw their support behind the colonial government. As a result, the united front was forced to go underground through the 1970s (Ma 2007, 35).

It was not until the negotiation of Hong Kong's sovereignty in the 1980s that the united front re-emerged from the dark. After the Sino-British Joint Declaration was signed in 1984, the local CCP, led by the newly appointed head of the NCNA, Xu Jiatun, became very active in rebuilding the united front. Xu particularly focused on the tycoons, the business elites and the middle class in order to solicit their support for the 1997 handover (Chu 2010, 77–94; Loh 2010, 145–68). New political institutions, such as the Basic Law Drafting Committee and the Basic Law Consultative Committee, were established, not only for managing the transition but also for coopting social and professional elites under the CCP's sphere of influence. Promises and assurances that Hong Kong would be reunited with China under 'democratic reunification' were also made to an emerging group of student activists and pro-democracy advocates to gain their support. Although the charm offensive was suspended by the Tiananmen crackdown in 1989, many elites soon realigned themselves with the party-state either because of the lure of the lucrative Chinese market or because of the guarantee of official appointments in the post-handover administration. Thereafter, pro-Beijing groups remained active in politics, occasionally mobilising against the electoral and legal reforms introduced by the last governor, Chris Patten (Ma 2007, 42, 131).

Two main features characterised China's united front work in pre-handover Hong Kong. First, united front work was conducted under a relatively centralised system and through a hierarchical command-and-control structure featuring 'statist corporatism' (Lam and Lam 2013). The apparatus was directed at the top by the Central Foreign Affairs Leading Small Group headed by Premier Zhou Enlai, whose orders were implemented locally by the NCNA (Burns 1990). Although there were, at times, subtle tensions between central government agencies (e.g. Hong Kong and Macao Affairs

Office) and the NCNA, and although personalistic features were salient in united front work, the united front apparatus was, to a great extent, centrally coordinated by a limited number of actors. Second, the primary objective of united front tactics in the pre-handover era was cooption. Given that the CCP did not enjoy any formal power in the colonial city, united front work needed to remain discreet and underground. Its scope had to be limited to building alliances with elites and masses through which to achieve the Party's strategic objectives and to build up a significant base of social support after the handover. Even though the underground front mobilised in some particular instances, such as the 1967 riots or the Patten reforms, it generally refrained from participating openly in local politics. Making friends remained its principal task.

To some extent, these features are still relevant after the 1997 handover. On the one hand, united front work remains the precinct of the Central Liaison Office (CLO) of the Central People's Government in the Hong Kong SAR, which has replaced the NCNA as a local Party branch since 2000. The CLO has expanded the size, operation and scope of work over the years. It has actively engaged with many social sectors and has assisted pro-Beijing political parties to campaign in elections. Its role has grown so significantly that Lee (2019) has characterised it as a quasi-ruling party. On the other hand, cooption still constitutes an important component of united front work. Business and professional elites continue to pack national political institutions (Wong 2012), namely the National People's Congress (NPC) and the Chinese People's Political Consultative Conference (CPPCC), which provide them with direct access to Beijing (Fong 2014). Mass line work has expanded substantially through a wide range of social organisations and residential associations, which enable penetration into the grassroots (Ma 2007, 151–3). Lam and Lam (2013, 322) argue that united front work in post-handover Hong Kong reflects 'a more inclusionary version of state corporatism', and relies on a variety of tactics that revolve around cooption, depending on 'whether the central government regards its targets as friends, valuable potential co-optees or enemies'.

However, there have also been significant changes. First and foremost is that united front work has surfaced from the underground and become more conspicuous, even though the Party does not operate formally in the territory.[1] The objectives of united front work have also diversified:

1 The CCP has not been formally registered as a legal entity in Hong Kong, even after the 1997 handover, and has not publicly declared local members.

rather than being limited to coopting supporters, the united front has become a crucial vehicle of electoral mobilisation for the pro-Beijing camp (Kwong 2007; Lo, Hung and Loo 2019). Moreover, pro-Beijing grassroots organisations have been increasingly involved in contentious activities against the political opposition, ranging from signature campaigns, to rallies in support of unpopular government policies, to counter-protests (Lee 2019, 10; Cheng 2020). In short, united front work has evolved from a transitional and preparational strategy in the colonial period into a routinised governing approach in the post-handover era. Nevertheless, although some of these changes have been captured by the existing scholarship, these works have largely followed the framework of statist-corporatism, focusing on the role of the CLO and its line of authority. This analytical lens has neglected the involvement of many central and local government agencies that are increasingly salient in the united front work in Hong Kong, and the relational dynamics of these state actors with social organisations. The secretive nature of united front work also means that we still know little about its scale, scope and rhythm, as well as the relative importance of different actors, on an empirical level.

Methods and Data

This chapter aims to delineate the dynamics of China's united front work in post-handover Hong Kong using an original event-organisational dataset. Much of the data were extracted from the social organisation news section (*shetuan xinwen*) of *Wenweipo* (社团新闻), a state-owned newspaper and the CCP's mouthpiece in Hong Kong. Since 2003, the section has reported events involving pro-Beijing social organisations as well as various governmental actors in mainland China and Hong Kong, providing an invaluable record of united front activities. We scraped the reports between 2003 and 2019 from the newspaper's website using computer programming techniques. After removing the reports that had an unusually long length (which were likely to be long lists of names), we collected a total of 30,174 reports. Given that the large amount of data rendered manual coding impossible, we utilised the same computer program to identify the organisations present in each report, based on an organisational list that we prepared. The list consisted of 3,869 organisations, spanning five different types: 1) central Party agencies (e.g. United Front Department, Propaganda Department and Organisation Department); 2) local government agencies (i.e. agencies on or under the provincial level, including local united front bureaus);

3) Hong Kong government agencies (e.g. Chief Executive's Office, Home Affairs Bureau, and Constitutional and Mainland Affairs Bureau); 4) the CLO and its various subdivisions; and 5) pro-Beijing social and political organisations (e.g. hometown associations and community organisations). The first four types were collected through government websites and the list of China's administrative divisions, while the last was compiled through the lists of organisations from various pro-government signature campaigns.

The list allowed us to identify how many organisations, and which type of organisations, were present in a single report, each of which was assumed to represent an event.[2] To analyse the co-occurrence of different actors, we excluded events that had fewer than two actors, leaving us with 14,503 events (on average, 853 events per year). Based on the assumption that events allow multiple organisations to interact with one another (and, therefore, perform united front work), we performed a co-occurrence analysis on the events, using the five different types of actors as analytical units. We only counted the co-occurrence of any two different types of actors as interactions, ignoring the co-occurrence of the same type.

Co-occurrence of different actors in each event does not *always* imply that these actors had built tangible and meaningful relationships through that event. After all, actors need not interact or mingle with one another even if they are attending an event together. However, co-occurrence helps to reflect the potentiality of interactions, which, we believe, offers a useful proxy to gauge the possible scale of united front activities, given the relational nature of such work. It also gives researchers a quantifiable basis to compare the volume of possible united front activities across time periods. To strengthen our co-occurrence analysis, we also collected the background data of the major pro-Beijing grassroots organisations in Hong Kong, based on the same list that we collated. We used Wisenews, online search engines and newspaper advertisements to find out their year of establishment, membership size and affiliated organisations. Finally, we relied on annual financial reports and participant observations to delineate the resources and activities of these grassroots organisations.

2 Examples of events include ceremonies, banquets, exhibitions and meetings.

The Organisational Proliferation of the United Front

During the revolutionary era, the CCP's united front involved an alliance of non-Party social forces, or, in some cases, secondary enemies, in order to defeat the Party's primary enemies. This strategy often targeted the educated class and the nationalistic capitalists before the founding of the People's Republic. However, once the party-state established formal state power and extended its tentacles into the peripheral territory, the strategy of united front work also needed to be adapted (U 2012). Since the CCP did not directly and formally exercise political power in the colonial enclave, it had to depend on a range of local intermediaries, primarily social organisations, to penetrate society and channel its influence. Moreover, under Mao Zedong's indigenisation of Marxism–Leninism, which emphasised the principle of 'mass line' (*qunzhong luxian*), the united front apparatus in capitalist Hong Kong had to ensure close ties with the grassroots, rather than just the bourgeois professionals. These two strategic considerations laid the foundation for a multilayered and decentralised structure of the united front later in post-handover Hong Kong, even though it remained rather centralised and unitary for much of the colonial era (Burns 1990).

Given the changing state-society relations in post-handover Hong Kong discussed earlier, the united front's operational dynamics and cooption targets have shifted accordingly. During the early post-handover period, the primary aim of the united front was to contain the contradiction between socialism and capitalism under 'One Country, Two Systems'. To earn support from the capitalist class for ensuring stable transition and effective governance, business elites were thus the principal targets of cooption. Coopted business elites often gained representation in the national political institutions in the mainland as well as statutory bodies in the SAR. Nominations to different levels of people's congresses and people's political consultative conferences were mostly handled by the CCP's United Front Department after taking into account advice from the Hong Kong and Macau Office and the CLO.[3] In return, the capitalist class made use of its standing and influence in professional and business organisations to support the SAR government. However, the massive 1 July rally in 2003 against a proposed

3 Chen Chu Chu (陳楚楚), 'Demystifying the Rule of the HKMAO and CLO: Who Is Hong Kong's Future Ruler?' (解密「兩辦」治港: 誰才是香港未來的管治者?), *Initium*, 19 May 2020, theinitium.com/article/20200519-hongkong-the-liaison-office-new-boss/.

national security law prompted Beijing to adopt a more organised effort to control the territory. As the party-state saw the societal challenges as a form of national security threat, business alliances and underground operations were seen as insufficient for containing the pro-democracy opposition. The united front needed to expand its reach and deepen its penetration into the masses, much more so than it had done during colonial times, to strengthen the patriotic force.

The result has been a gradual shift from statist-corporatism to political clientelism, in which the majority of social organisations are no longer subsumed under the SAR government's framework of governance but are instead leveraged by the CLO as vehicles to expand its influence at the grassroots. Lee's (2019) recent study suggested that the uniqueness of clientelism in Hong Kong is that its political machine is adapted from the party-state's united front infrastructure of indirect rule over Hong Kong. Under the new united front ecology, business elites become clients under the political patronage of the CLO, and they in turn sponsor social organisations and increase the dependency of the masses on the political machine.

After 2008, the CLO significantly expanded its internal structure and boosted its public visibility, not only to make friends but also to combat enemies. Its internal bureaus increased from nine to 25, which, in turn, are territorially divided according to district boundaries and functional roles (Lee 2017). Each regional bureau oversees several electoral constituencies. Further, its social work, external relations and public affairs bureaus are given the responsibility to unite business and grassroots associations, liaise with the local and mainland authorities regarding economic, educational and cultural exchanges, and supervise propaganda mouthpieces and pro-Beijing political parties. The united front's organisational proliferation can be measured by its ability to coopt and revamp three types of social organisations, including local federations, hometown associations and non-governmental organisations (NGOs).

Figure 15.1 illustrates the hierarchical and relational structure of the united front apparatus for Hong Kong. The Central Committee's Central Leading Group on Hong Kong and Macau Affairs commands at the top as the highest decision-making body on matters related to Hong Kong. Like other leading small groups, it is headed by a committee or standing committee member of the Politburo and is responsible for advising the Politburo on policy matters and coordinating policy implementation decisions.

To ensure a chain of command and effective policy implementation, the heads of relevant Party departments and government committees serve as either deputies or members.

Established in 1958 and reshuffled in 2003, the Hong Kong – Macau Leading Small Group is one of many primary leading small groups within the Central Committee (Miller 2008, 3). The leading small group coordinates two important implementation bodies: 1) the United Front Work Department, a Party organ; and 2) the State Council's Hong Kong and Macau Affairs Office (HKMAO), a government unit. The United Front Work Department is tasked with making loyal friends among a broad spectrum of social elites (Wang and Groot 2018, 570). Along with its provincial branches, it is responsible for vetting and recommending elites to be coopted into the national and local assemblies (i.e. the people's congresses and consultative conferences). The HKMAO, meanwhile, is tasked with mobilising state resources to coordinate actions at local-level authorities. It also develops working relations with the SAR government and other business and professional organisations and elites in the semi-autonomous city.

In terms of hierarchy, the CLO is supposed to be half a level below the HKMAO, whose status is equivalent to a ministry. But, in terms of its status, the CLO could be as powerful as the HKMAO because its head was ranked as the Party secretary of the Hong Kong Work Committee, which is the highest-level Party organ in Hong Kong.[4] Moreover, past leaders of the CLO were always members of the Central Committee who were members of the Central Leading Group and enjoyed access to the Politburo, and they also possessed extensive organisational and social connections in local society. As a result, the CLO has direct control of the leftist groups that have served as the subsidiaries or extended arms of the party-state since the founding of the People's Republic. Apart from the old patriots, the CLO is also coopting an increasing number of grassroots social organisations to expand its patron–client networks with the support of pro-Beijing business elites. On the other hand, although the SAR government is supposed to be highly autonomous from the united front work organisations, in recent years its interactions with the mainland authorities and social organisations have also significantly increased, indicating the organisational proliferation of united front work.

4 The Hong Kong Work Committee is the top Party branch in Hong Kong. It shares the same personnel as the Central Liaison Office, under the principle of 'a single organisation, two signboards' (*yige jigou liangkuai paizi*).

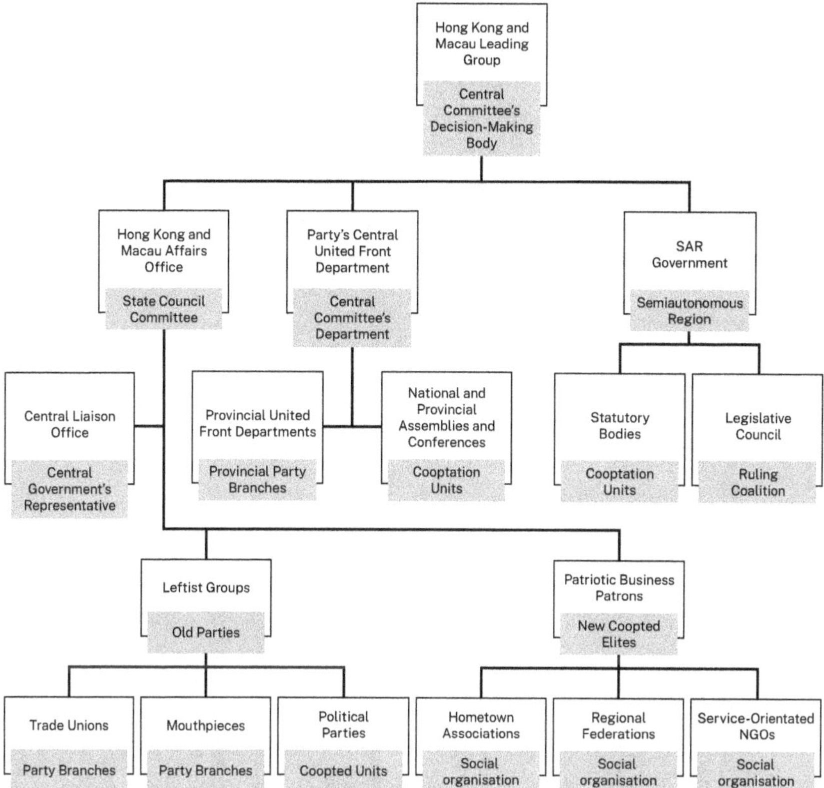

Figure 15.1: The Structure of the United Front in Hong Kong.

Source: Author's research.

Three types of social organisations are prioritised as targets under the post-handover united front. The first, and arguably most important, type of social organisations being coopted are Chinese hometown associations. Formed organically by people who share the same lineage or ancestral connections, hometown associations aim to provide mutual aid to Chinese migrants from the same places or bloodlines and to serve as their business networks. They have a long history in Hong Kong and Southeast Asia (Sinn 1997; Liu 1998). Most of the early hometown associations were county or city-based, serving migrants from different parts of Guangdong Province and coastal regions such as Xiamen, Quanzhou, Ningbo and Shanghai. In the post-handover period, particularly after 2003, many new hometown associations from lesser-known localities and regions have been established (see Figure 15.2). Many of these received support from the local governments of the respective region in the mainland, which sought to establish their economic and political clout in the semi-autonomous city. Meanwhile, a rising number of province-based 'federations of hometown associations', such as those representing Guangdong, Guangxi, Fujian and Hainan, have also been established to serve as an umbrella platform to consolidate the local-level hometown associations, which used to be disconnected from one another. They were often set up by established or nouveau pro-Beijing business and professional elites, who would, in turn, receive positions from national political institutions such as the NPC and the CPPCC.

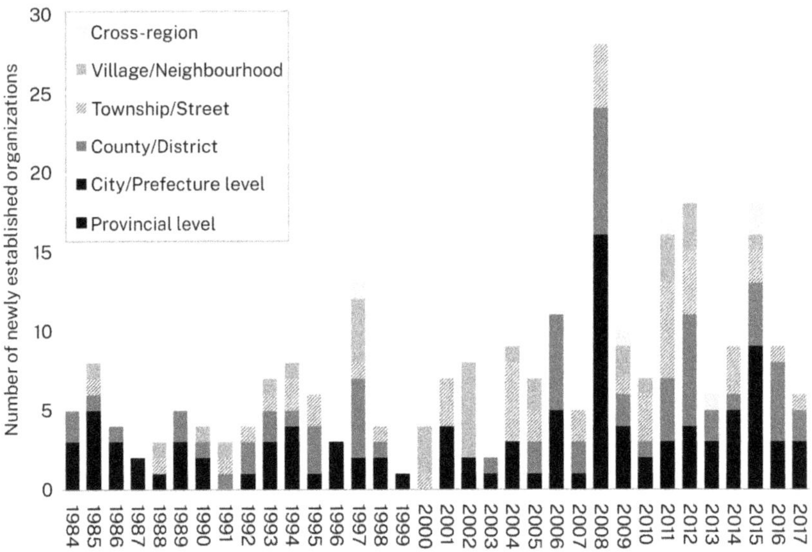

Figure 15.2: The Growth of Hometown Associations in Hong Kong, 1984–2017.

Source: Annual reports and official websites.

The primary goal of these new umbrella platforms is to ensure better coordination and the building of ties among the pro-Beijing forces. Each of these federations claimed to have at least hundreds of thousands of members and dozens of city- or prefecture-based hometown associations. Federations of hometown associations constitute the top layer of each provincial community, whereas all lower-level associations within each province are designated as second- or third-layer member units. Leaders of the city or prefectural-level associations are often appointed as senior board directors, whereas leaders of associations at the county and village level become the rank and file directors. This arrangement has created a pyramid-like, multilayered and interconnected structure to bridge class, dialect and geographical divisions in each native-place community

(Choi 2006). They are no longer simply welfare providers for migrants as they increasingly take on the function of an overt broker for united front work. For instance, the annual report of the Federation of Hong Kong Guangxi Community Organisations indicated that the hometown association was established under the support of the Guangxi Committee United Front Work Department to promote the spirit of 'Love the Nation, Love Hong Kong' and to consolidate the patriotic forces in Hong Kong.[5]

The second prime target in the united front strategy is the three local federations in Hong Kong Island, Kowloon and the New Territories, respectively. For instance, the Kowloon Federation of Associations was formed in 1997 and reportedly has 220,000 members, 191 affiliated associations and hundreds of community branches corresponding to different districts and neighbourhoods as of 2019.[6] Members of these federations include women's associations, youth groups, cultural societies, neighbourhood associations and mutual aid committees. The neighbourhood associations and mutual aid committees were formed by the colonial government in the 1970s to encourage public participation in neighbourhood affairs, help organise community activities and government campaigns, and offer advice on local matters (Ma 2007). Since the handover, while these committees are supposed to be self-governing and represent the interests of grassroots citizens, they have become heavily dependent on the funding and directives of the government through the Home Affairs Bureau (HAB). In this connection, it is not surprising that the successive secretaries of the HAB since 2007 have been former members of the two largest pro-Beijing parties in Hong Kong, even though most of the principal officials of the Hong Kong government did not previously have any Party affiliation. Each year, the HAB allocated tens of millions of dollars to these federations and their member associations, which would in turn organise a dizzying range of mega-cultural and community events to reach out to grassroots residents. As the opposition seldom apply for such funding (and would likely be rejected if they did), public resources have thus been effectively channelled into these pro-Beijing organisations and their extended arms.

The third target for cooption is the service-oriented NGOs, which advance the Party's social reach through professional service provision. The New Home Association is a notable example. Established in 2010 and sponsored

5 Federation of Guangxi Community Association, *2013 Annual Report of Federation of Guangxi Community Association* (香港廣西社團總會2013年年報), 4.

6 Kowloon Federation of Associations, accessed 1 May 2023, 2019, klnfas.hk/tc/.

by numerous pro-Beijing tycoons, it has become highly competitive in the social work sector, which is a stronghold of the democratic opposition. With an enormous annual budget, the New Home Association has recruited hundreds of social workers to serve new immigrants from China and the grassroots. The one-stop services and extensive networks helped to establish a relationship of dependency between providers of patronage goods and their grassroots clients (Lee 2019). Often registered as charities, such social organisations serve as important intermediaries to build new ties in the community and advance the state agenda. Another example is the business chambers, which financed hundreds of exchange tours to China each year for students of different ages through groups such as the Future Star Federation of Students and the Hong Kong Youth Exchange Promotion Association. Their charity status ensures that donations from patrons are tax exempt. The SAR government is another major source of funding for these activities. A government audit report revealed that HAB spending for mainland exchange tours quadrupled from HK$26.4 million to HK$112.7 million between 2012 and 2017.

The organisational proliferation of the united front has created an extensive and multilayered patron–client network that is highly dependent on the party-state directives but less regulated by administrative protocols. Unlike in the late colonial and the early SAR period, many social organisations are no longer regulated by professional ethics and funding rules but are increasingly facilitated by relational networks and political connections. Hometown associations, federations of community organisations and serviced-oriented NGOs were either created on purpose or systematically revamped to serve political tasks. Their activities have also been increasingly subsumed under a united front logic, much unlike in the pre-handover period when they were organically set up as a social hub through which natives or co-workers could mingle and maintain connections with their community and professions. Meanwhile, although business elites continue to be a target of cooption, they are now expected to play a more proactive role in brokering organisational proliferation. Their most important function is not so much to offer their professional expertise, but to provide the financial resources and social networks in creating these organisations from scratch, managing the registration process, recruiting members, drafting the constitution, donating money and sponsoring properties to serve as office spaces.

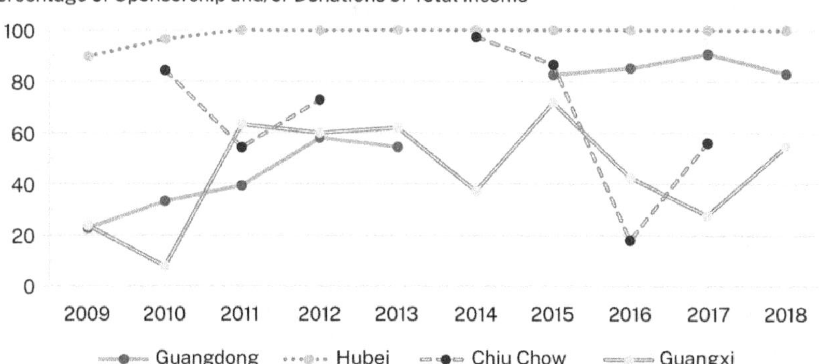

Figure 15.3. Income Source of Representative Hometown Associations in Hong Kong, 2009–18.

Source: Annual financial reports of the Federation of Hong Kong Guangdong Community Organizations Ltd, Federation of Hong Kong Hubei Associations Ltd, Federation of Hong Kong Chiu Chow Community Organizations Ltd and Federation of Hong Kong Guangxi Community Organizations Ltd, 2009–18.

Figure 15.3 shows the size of donations and sponsorship as a proportion of total income of four representative hometown federations from 2009 to 2018. The size of their funding has dramatically increased over time, corresponding to the new united front initiative to proactively penetrate the grassroots. For example, the total income of the Guangdong federation increased from HK$15.2 million in 2009 to HK$29.9 million in 2018. Despite the overall increase, their main source of income remained dependent on donations. Take 2017 for example: on average, more than 68.6 per cent of their income came from donations from local tycoons or sponsorships from the HAB or district councils. In contrast, membership subscription and event income were highly insignificant and in 2017 accounted for only 6.5 and 11.3 per cent, respectively. Moreover, their large-scale events often incurred deficits. For example, for the Chiu Chow federation, both the Chiu Chow Festival and the Yu Lan Festival ran a deficit of HK$3.34 million and HK$0.99 million, respectively, in 2017. Overall, only the events in 2009 and 2010 for Guangdong, and those in 2012 for Chiu Chow, were in surplus. Hence, it is highly unlikely that these organisations would be able to sustain themselves under either the market model or the charity model. Given that their operations are highly dependent on the support of state apparatuses and pro-regime elites, they thus resemble social organisations in China more than conventional civil society organisations. What makes them different from the state-dependent model in mainland China is that they are not merely extended arms of the state but are horizontally connected through an extensive patron–client network and are often financed by patriotic business tycoons.

The Multilayered Structure of the United Front

To promote and coordinate the Party's political agenda in Hong Kong, the CLO has become the organisational nexus to connect different levels of government in the mainland, the Hong Kong authorities and local social organisations. However, although its political role has been strengthened notably after the 2003 rally, it was not until the second decade of the SAR that this was materialised by a concerted policy directive with institutional implications (Cheng 2016). In 2008, a CLO ranking officer published an article in *Study Times*, the mouthpiece of the Central Party School, advocating the creation of a 'second governing team' to 'fully, openly, and legally' assist the SAR government.[7] Although the official was relatively junior in the hierarchy, this publication has proven to be a reflection of top-level policy formation. This was partly revealed by the restructuring of the CCP's Leading Small Group on Hong Kong and Macau Affairs in the same year. It also coincided with the appointment of Xi Jinping, then Politburo Standing Committee member, to head the leading small group in 2008, shortly before he became Party general secretary in 2012. During his tenure as the top policymaker on Hong Kong matters, Xi reportedly prescribed a more proactive approach and the mass line principle for pro-Beijing social organisations to participate in local affairs (Li 2019, 10).

Apart from a more active CLO, governmental actors from the mainland have also become increasingly involved in united front work. The most salient, perhaps, are different levels of local governments, ranging from the provincial to the street/prefecture level. To develop ties with fellow natives from their localities who live in Hong Kong for both economic and political objectives, local governments from across the mainland have been visibly active in encouraging native elites to establish hometown associations. As a result, local officials are frequently invited to Hong Kong as officiating guests for the various activities of these hometown associations, such as inauguration ceremonies and annual celebrations of key political dates. Their travel tours to their hometowns in the mainland are often accompanied by meetings with local government officials and learning sessions (Yuen 2021).

7 Cao Er Bao (曹二宝), 'Governing Force in Hong Kong under the Condition of "One Country, Two Systems"' ("一国两制"条件下香港的管治力量), *Xuexi Shibao,* 28 January 2008.

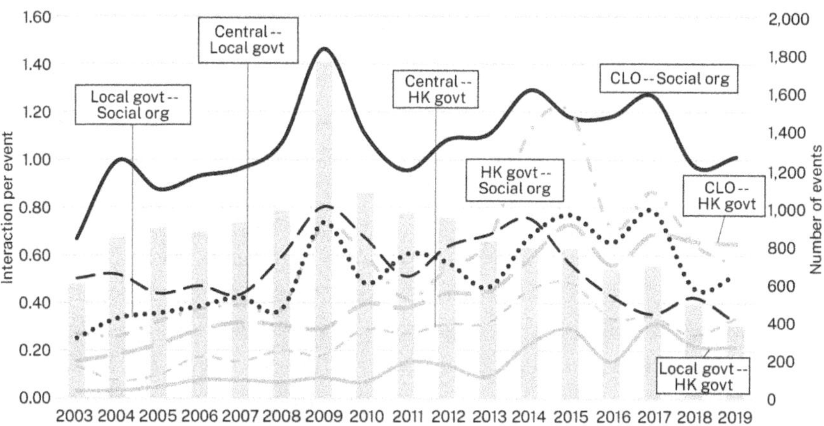

Figure 15.4. Interactions between State Agencies and Social Organisations in Hong Kong, 2003–19.

Source: Wenweipo.

Figure 15.4 shows the interaction between the five types of organisational actors as briefly discussed in the methods section. Overall, there have been increasing interactions between any two types of actors from 2003 to 2019. Interactions that involved social organisations were particularly frequent, and they all suddenly surged in 2009, which was likely because many new social organisations, particularly hometown associations, were established in that year, as suggested by Figure 15.2. The increased interactions between different levels of party-state institutions and social organisations also corresponds to the suggestion of a second ruling team run by the CLO to assist with the governance process.

The most visible trend in Figure 15.4 is the salient role of the CLO. Among its relationships, the most frequent interactions take place between the CLO and local social organisations. On average, the two types of actors have more than one interaction per event, which means that, for any one event, one expects to find more than one co-occurrence of the CLO and a local social organisation. The frequency of interactions is also growing. This pattern serves as a proxy to illustrate the organisational proliferation of social organisations through united front work. Recent studies show that leaders of social organisations tend to interact with CLO officials because these officials are responsible for nominating seats in national and regional people's congresses and consultative conferences (Yuen 2021). Their business interests in the mainland are also better protected with these official titles, which explains why they are interested in being coopted and often try to use sponsorship of these social organisations and community events to strengthen their ties with mainland officials.

Another important trend concerns the increased interactions between local governments in the mainland and social organisations in Hong Kong, which indicates the former's growing local presence. As noted earlier, local officials were frequently invited to Hong Kong as honoured guests in a wide range of activities, during which they could mingle with local actors. Interestingly, the line closely correlates with that between the CLO and local social organisations (a 0.82 correlation), even though the former has a lower magnitude. Conversely, interactions between central government agencies and local social organisations rose from 2003 to 2014 but dropped afterwards (only a 0.39 correlation with the interaction between CLO and local social organisations). One possible explanation is the gradual institutionalisation of the role of the CLO. After rapid expansion in the late 2000s, the CLO has become the primary nexus between mainland authorities and Hong Kong's community actors. Local government officials needed to 'go through' the CLO when interacting with the local actors, as indicated by the high correlation. In comparison, the central government agencies have become less relevant in everyday united front work.

The third notable trend is the increasingly salient role of the Hong Kong government under the multilayered united front work. Interaction between the Hong Kong government and social organisations is not only rising, but also there was a sudden jump between 2013 and 2015. Similarly, there are also substantially more interactions between the CLO and the Hong Kong government. Those between central government agencies and the Hong Kong government, and those between mainland local governments and the Hong Kong government, have slightly increased as well. The ups and downs illustrate two operational dynamics of the united front. On the one hand, united front activities are driven by important events. The dramatic spike between 2013 and 2015 was most likely associated with the counter-mobilisation towards the Umbrella Movement in 2014. On the other hand, the SAR government has also taken a more proactive role to build ties with various community actors. In the late colonial and early post-handover period, it tended to adopt a consultative model that mainly regulated the funding source but gave organisational autonomy to grassroots actors. In the post-2008 period, it has played an increasingly active role in united front work by cultivating the grassroots networks.

The Counter-Mobilisation Tactics of the United Front

Counter-mobilisation is another new tactic of the pro-Beijing forces in post-handover Hong Kong, which reflects a change in both the targets and tactics of united front work. We consider counter-mobilisation as 'a form of state mobilised contention that arises in response to a formidable threat to the prevailing order' (Cheng 2020, 4). It is a common tactic used by hybrid or authoritarian regimes around the world (Robertson 2010; Hellmeier and Weidmann 2020). In Hong Kong, the rise of counter-mobilisation was set against the background of the increase in the scale and interval of protest events since 2003. The old united front tactic that emphasised building government–business alliances and grassroots networks were seen as inadequate for coping with these societal threats. This prompted the regime to proactively counteract the oppositional forces by relying on the pro-Beijing grassroots networks as the organisational basis. These networks have long been mobilised to support the pro-Beijing political parties during elections. Such experiences facilitated their swift mobilisation once the arena moved from institutional politics to street politics. Moreover, with the proliferation of patron–client networks between the state and social organisations, united front directives from above become easily channelled into pro-Beijing groups to perform counter-mobilisation.

The first massive counter-protest in post-handover Hong Kong occurred in 2010, when pro-Beijing political parties and social organisations took the lead to organise rallies in support of the Hong Kong government's constitutional reform bill. Initiated by renowned public figures, the pro-government rally largely emulated the repertoire of pro-democracy protests and managed to create some level of social support for the passing of the bill. Inspired by the success, a number of pro-Beijing political groups were later established to follow the counter-mobilisation playbook. Notable examples include Caring Hong Kong Power, Voice of Loving Hong Kong and the Defend Hong Kong Campaign. Although some of their initiators and organisers were former personnel in various pro-Beijing social organisations, these political groups fashioned themselves as citizen-based organisations. They were also referred to as 'satellite groups' to indicate their network linkage but physical distance with the regime (Cheng 2020). The naming of their organisations reflected their loyalty and political beliefs, symbolising the idea that they were self-mobilised to take to the streets out of their love towards the nation and the city, which had been threatened by the chaos produced by pro-democracy activism.

This top-down initiative found a new life alongside the rise of pro-democracy protests and gradually evolved into a multilayered and decentralised network of counter-protests. Unlike electoral mobilisation, which is more institutionalised and regulated by electoral rules, counter-mobilisation is event-driven and situationally induced. Indeed, many of the counter-protest groups were established before or during the large-scale pro-democracy protests such as the Umbrella Movement in 2014 and the Anti-Extradition Bill Movement in 2019. For instance, in August 2014, a group known as the Alliance of Peace and Democracy, which brought together numerous pro-Beijing grassroots organisations, initiated a petition campaign that collected signatures from nearly 1,600 organisations and 1.8 million individuals in one month. It was followed by a march that claimed to have rallied 130,000 people. Our analysis of the signatories suggested that a wide range of grassroots organisations were involved – more than one-fourth were hometown associations, along with community organisations, resident associations, alumni groups, youth and women's groups, as well as cultural and sports associations. This unprecedented parade of pro-Beijing forces would not have been possible without the pre-existing grassroots networks, indicating how the social capital cultivated through organisational proliferation can be readily activated in crisis situations.

Counter-protests against pro-democracy forces continued after the end of the Umbrella Movement with the main targets shifting to the pro-autonomy localist movements (Veg 2017). Meanwhile, grassroots organisations – such as the Alliance of Peace and Democracy and its member units – replaced the satellite groups as the new leading forces. This was likely because, first, satellite groups often adopted overly dramatic and coercive protest tactics that created embarrassment for the pro-Beijing camp; and, second, grassroots organisations have greater legitimacy because of their organic connections with the masses and are thus in a better position to appeal to their nationalistic sentiments.

The Anti-Extradition Bill Movement in 2019 further highlighted the role of pro-Beijing grassroots organisations in mobilising counter-protests. After the SAR government failed to suppress the movement through heavy-handed police tactics, and right before the central government put forward the official rhetoric of 'stop violence and restore order' on 7 August, pro-Beijing groups were swiftly mobilised. Two mass rallies were organised on 20 July and 3 August, respectively, to indicate that 'a silent majority' was in support of the government. In both protests, pro-Beijing grassroots organisations, particularly the hometown associations, became the core units of mobilisation. During the 20 July rally, which claimed a turnout of 310,000, we counted 75 grassroots organisations, 39 of which were hometown associations. In some cases, lower-level associations were tasked by their high-level associations to recruit a certain minimum number of protestors, which they had to fill by mobilising through their grassroots networks and social media tools. Participant observation at that rally also showed that these organisations often came in large groups, distinguished by large banners indicating their affiliations. Such practices have long been adopted during electoral mobilisation, which aimed to cultivate group solidarity, demonstrate organisational capacity and display loyalty to state directives.

However, it is important to note that the counter-mobilisation strategy is not always successful in curbing opposition, as reflected by the anti-extradition protests. Not only did the overwhelming public support for the protests make it difficult for counter-mobilisation to be effective, but also public outrage against police brutality meant that pro-Beijing forces could not come up with a rightful frame to justify their counteractions, unlike during the Umbrella Movement (Yuen and Cheng 2017). Moreover, the multilayered and diffused structure of counter-mobilisation implied that some of its frontline actions could not be properly restrained, as indicated by the 21 July Yuen Long incident. The landslide defeat of the pro-Beijing camp in the November 2019 District Council Election was also an indication that the grassroots penetration and social mobilisation of the pro-Beijing forces were not as effective as expected.

The drastic reform of the electoral system, which came after the introduction of the National Security Law in July 2020, represented an important turning point for China's united front work in Hong Kong. Under the newly promulgated principle of 'patriots ruling Hong Kong', candidates for the Legislative Council are to be nominated by the Election Committee, a powerful body that until now elected only the chief executive. The Election Committee has also expanded from 1,200 to 1,500 members, with the inclusion of representatives of native-place associations in the third sector, as well as a new fifth sector that comprises Hong Kong members of the NPC and the CPPCC and representatives of Hong Kong members of relevant national organisations. The changes imply the promotion of key elites in the united front to official positions of power, unlike before when they could only wield informal influence on electoral matters.

In addition, any prospective legislative member, member of the Election Committee, or candidate for the chief executive has to be vetted by a separate screening committee. Meanwhile, although the overall seats increase from 70 to 90, the number of directly elected members fall from 35 to 20. Out of the 90 seats, 40 are now chosen by the Election Committee. The Legislative Council election held in December 2021 adopted this arrangement for the first time, leading to the landslide victory of the pro-Beijing camp, with many new faces elected as legislative members. While the long-term effects of the reform are still too early to tell, what is certain is that the united front is no longer simply an underground front.

Conclusion

As an integral component of China's policy towards Hong Kong, united front work has been a widely researched topic among scholars. However, due to the opaque nature of such work, existing research has mostly relied on historical and anecdotal data, which makes it difficult to delineate the evolution of united front work in terms of its structure and objectives. This chapter is an attempt to fill this empirical gap. By making use of organisational reports and an original event dataset, we have shown how post-handover united front work, particularly since the mid-2000s, has involved a steady organisational proliferation of social organisations and increasingly frequent interactions between these social organisations, different levels of the mainland authorities and the Hong Kong government. The result is a more decentralised and multilayered structure of the united front apparatus, involving multiple state and social actors. Also witnessed are the shifting objectives of united front work. Rather than adhering to elite cooption, united front work has become more proactive in organising the pro-Beijing forces in the semi-autonomous territory and counter-mobilising against the pro-democracy opposition whenever opportunities arise. Due to the changing roles and relationships between the party-state and grassroots actors, and between the central and local governments, the governance model of post-handover Hong Kong has gradually shifted from regulatory statist-corporatism to collaborative political clientelism.

Our findings thus contribute to a better understanding of China's united front work in a peripheral region over which it has yet to gain complete political control despite its sovereignty status. Although the findings are by no means completely new, they have provided empirical support to the perceived trend of increasing united front activities through the first two decades of the handover. More importantly, the findings have indicated that the remit of united front work is not limited to a conventional set of government organisations, such as the CLO or the United Front Work Department. The analytical scope should be broadened to include other governmental units, such as local governments in the mainland and the Hong Kong government. Moreover, because of the relational nature of united front work, analysts must focus on the interaction between these state actors and various social actors. In other words, the united front should be considered an extensive network comprising both state and social actors, rather than just an extended arm of the state.

References

Burns, John P. 1990. 'The Structure of Communist Party Control in Hong Kong'. *Asian Survey* 30 (8): 748–65. doi.org/10.2307/2644496.

Chan, Lau, Kit-ching. 1999. *From Nothing to Nothing: The Chinese Communist Movement and Hong Kong 1921–1936*. Hong Kong: Hong Kong University Press. doi.org/10.1353/cri.2000.0071.

Cheng, Edmund W. 2016. 'Street Politics in a Hybrid Regime: The Diffusion of Political Activism in Post-colonial Hong Kong'. *China Quarterly* 226: 383–406. doi.org/10.1017/S0305741016000394.

Cheng, Edmund W. 2020. 'United Front Work and Mechanisms of Countermobilization in Hong Kong'. *China Journal* 83: 1–33. doi.org/10.1086/706603.

Cheung, Gary Ka-wai. 2009. *Hong Kong's Watershed: The 1967 Riots*. Hong Kong: Hong Kong University Press.

Choi, Susanne Y. P. 2006. 'Association Divided, Association United: The Social Organization of Chaozhou and Fujian Migrants in Hong Kong'. In *Voluntary Organizations in the Chinese Diaspora*, edited by Khun Eng Kuah-Pearce and Evelyn Hu-Dehar, 121–40. Hong Kong: Hong Kong University Press.

Chu, Cindy Yik-yi. 2010. *Chinese Communists and Hong Kong Capitalists: 1937–1997*. New York: Palgrave Macmillan. doi.org/10.1057/9780230113916.

Fong, Brian Chi Hang. 2014. 'The Partnership between the Chinese Government and Hong Kong's Capitalist Class: Implications for HKSAR Governance, 1997–2012'. *China Quarterly* 217: 195–220. doi.org/10.1017/S0305741014000307.

Hellmeier, Sebastian and Nils B. Weidmann. 2020. 'Pulling the Strings? The Strategic Use of Pro-Government Mobilization in Authoritarian Regimes'. *Comparative Political Studies* 53 (1): 71–108. doi.org/10.1177/0010414019843559.

Kwong, Bruce Kam-kwan. 2007. 'Patron–Client Politics in Hong Kong: A Case Study of the 2002 and 2005 Chief Executive Elections'. *Journal of Contemporary China* 16 (52): 389–415. doi.org/10.1080/10670560701314222.

Lam, Wai-man and Kay Chi-yan Lam. 2013. 'China's United Front Work in Civil Society: The Case of Hong Kong'. *International Journal of China Studies* 4 (3): 301–25.

Lee, Ching Yan. 2017. 'Sai Wan Ruling Hong Kong, CLO Out of Darkness' (西環治港, 中聯辦化暗爲明). *Hong Kong Economic Journal Monthly*, March.

Lee, Eliza W. Y. 2019. 'United Front, Clientelism, and Indirect Rule: Theorizing the Role of the "Liaison Office" in Hong Kong'. *Journal of Contemporary China* 29 (125): 1–13. doi.org/10.1080/10670564.2019.1704996.

Li, Xiaohui. 2019. *Social Organisations in Hong Kong: Theory and Practice* (香港社團: 理論與實務). Hong Kong: The Commercial Press. doi.org/10.12809/hkmj187855.

Lieberthal, Kenneth G. and David M. Lampton. 1992. *Bureaucracy, Politics, and Decision Making in Post-Mao China.* Berkeley: University of California Press.

Liu, Hong. 1998. 'Old Linkages, New Networks: The Globalization of Overseas Chinese Voluntary Associations and Its Implications'. *China Quarterly* 155: 588–609. doi.org/10.1017/S0305741000050001.

Lo, Sonny Shiu-hing, Steven Chung-fun Hung and Jeff Loo Hai-chi. 2019. *China's New United Front Work in Hong Kong: Penetrative Politics and Its Implications.* Singapore: Palgrave Macmillan. doi.org/10.1007/978-981-13-8483-7.

Loh, Christine. 2010. *Underground Front: The Chinese Communist Party in Hong Kong.* Hong Kong: Hong Kong University Press. doi.org/10.4000/chinaperspectives.5321.

Ma, Ngok. 2007. *Political Development in Hong Kong: State, Political Society, and Civil Society.* Hong Kong: Hong Kong University Press. doi.org/10.5790/hongkong/9789622098107.001.0001.

Mertha, Andrew. 2009. 'Fragmented Authoritarianism 2.0: Political Pluralization in the Chinese Policy Process'. *China Quarterly* 200: 995–1012. doi.org/10.1017/S0305741009990592.

Miller, Alice. 2008. 'The CCP Central Committee's Leading Small Groups'. *China Leadership Monitor* 26: 1–21.

Robertson, Graeme B. 2010. *The Politics of Protest in Hybrid Regimes: Managing Dissent in Post-Communist Russia*. Cambridge: Cambridge University Press. doi.org/10.1017/CBO9780511921209.

Sinn, Elizabeth. 1997. 'Xin Xi Guxiang: A Study of Regional Associations as a Bonding Mechanism in the Chinese Diaspora: The Hong Kong Experience'. *Modern Asian Studies* 31 (2): 375–97. doi.org/10.1017/S0026749X00014347.

U, Eddy. 2012. 'Dangerous Privilege: The United Front and the Rectification Campaign of the Early Mao Years'. *China Journal* 68: 2–32. doi.org/10.1086/666579.

Veg, Sebastien. 2017. 'The Rise of "Localism" and Civic Identity in Post-Handover Hong Kong: Questioning the Chinese Nation-State'. *China Quarterly* 230: 323–47. doi.org/10.1017/S0305741017000571.

Wang, Ray and Gerry Groot. 2018. 'Who Represents? Xi Jinping's Grand United Front Work, Legitimation, Participation and Consultative Democracy'. *Journal of Contemporary China* 27 (112): 569–83. doi.org/10.1080/10670564.2018.1433573.

Wong, Stan Hok-wui. 2012. 'Authoritarian Co-optation in the Age of Globalization: Evidence from Hong Kong'. *Journal of Contemporary Asia* 42 (2): 182–209. doi.org/10.1080/00472336.2012.668348.

Yep, Ray. 2008. 'The 1967 Riots in Hong Kong: The Diplomatic and Domestic Fronts of the Colonial Governor'. *China Quarterly* 193: 122–39. doi.org/10.1017/S0305741008000076.

Yuen, Samson. 2021. 'Native-Place Networks and Political Mobilization: The Case of Post-Handover Hong Kong'. *Modern China* 47 (5): 510–39. doi.org/10.1177/0097700420934093.

Yuen, Samson and Edward W. Cheng. 2017. 'Neither Repression nor Concession? A Regime's Attrition against Mass Protests'. *Political Studies* 65 (3): 611–30. doi.org/10.1177/0032321716674024.

16

The Chinese Communist Party's Unfulfilled 'Taiwan Dream'

Gunter Schubert

Introduction

The Chinese Communist Party (CCP)'s Taiwan policy, driven by the quest for eventual 'unification' (*tongyi* 统一) of the two sides of the Taiwan Strait, has served as a major cornerstone of the Party's ruling legitimacy argument, in which it portrays itself as the creator and perfector of the modern Chinese nation. Since the end of the Maoist era, and particularly after Taiwan's transition to democracy in the late 1980s, CCP-driven Chinese nationalism has increasingly found itself challenged by Taiwan's pro-independence forces and the gradual formation of a distinct Taiwanese national identity (*guojia rentong* 国家认同) (Wachman 1994; Lin 2016). While post-authoritarian Guomindang (GMD)-led governments, at least at a declaratory level, adhered to the 'One China' principle and were thus seen in Beijing as partners of the CCP in a joint effort to bring about 'peaceful unification' of whatever sort, the return to power of the Democratic Progressive Party (DPP) in 2016 has made a cross-strait political rapprochement on the CCP's terms a dim possibility at best. Since the days of former Party secretary Jiang Zemin (江泽民), the CCP has maintained a carrot-and-stick approach to Taiwan, hoping to bring the island back into its fold. However, as the political tide changed in Taiwan over the years and fomented the idea of a 'community of destiny' based on an implicit consensus that a Taiwanese nation exists and should continue to exist, the CCP's invocation of Taiwan being an 'inalienable part of the great Chinese nation' has become anachronistic and meaningless for most Taiwanese.[1]

The CCP's Taiwan policy has quite obviously failed to achieve 'peaceful unification', having underestimated, or intentionally ignored, how much the island's democratisation and the 'China impact' (Schubert 2016; Wu 2016), which has loomed large behind all friendly gestures by Beijing, has driven Taiwanese nationalism. Today, under the leadership of strongman Xi Jinping (习近平), the CCP is forced to increasingly display its full range of 'hard power' to keep Taiwan's quest for sovereignty – the code word of de jure independence – at bay and discourage international support for the island. In the context of China's neo-imperial rise, Taiwan arguably embodies one of the most serious contemporary challenges to CCP legitimacy, a fact that has been further aggravated by Beijing's recent suppression of Hong Kong 'localism' (Kwong 2016) and rising tensions in the US–China relationship.

This chapter traces the CCP's Taiwan policy, focusing on developments since the early reform years, as there arguably existed no such policy in the Mao era when Beijing's approach to Taiwan was frozen into the formula of 'liberating Taiwan' and the constant denigration of the 'Chiang clique' as lackeys of US imperialism. Since its conception in the early 1980s, then, Beijing's Taiwan policy has remained relatively consistent, perhaps even 'immovable', but it has failed to adequately understand and constructively respond to Taiwan's rising national identity – slowly evolving under the Republic of China (ROC) nameplate. The CCP has stuck to its long-time policy approach, relying on a two-pronged strategy of applying 'hard power' – military might and political 'strangulation' – alongside continuing policy efforts to lure the owners of Taiwan's capital and the brightest Taiwanese minds to the mainland, where they may prosper but will have to bow to China's irredentism. This strategy, however, has only reinforced the CCP's

1 This has been documented by countless surveys over the years, regularly conducted by the National Chengchi University's Election Study Center. According to recent figures (June 2021), 63.3 per cent of those questioned think of themselves as being 'Taiwanese', but only 2.7 as 'Chinese'; 31.4 per cent think they are both. Only 7.1 per cent opt for 'unification asap' or 'maintain status quo, move to unification', while most respondents either opted for 'independence asap' (a minority of 5.7 per cent) or 'maintaining the status quo' either indefinitely, for the time being or with an inclination to move towards 'independence' (81.5 per cent). See 'Taiwan Independence vs. Unification with the Mainland (1994/12–2022/12)', Education Study Center, National Chengchi University, accessed 6 October, 2021, esc.nccu.edu.tw/PageDoc/Detail?fid=7801&id=6963.

reputation, both in Taiwan and the international community, as a revisionist and nationalist state with no sense for compromise and a determination to do whatever it takes to safeguard its 'territorial integrity'.

In the remainder of this chapter, I briefly address China's Taiwan policy in the Maoist era and then build on Chen Chien-Kai's (陳建凱) (2012) analytical framework to distinguish between the periods of leadership by CCP general secretaries Jiang Zemin (1989–2002), Hu Jintao 胡锦涛 (2002–12) and, in greater detail, Xi Jinping (since 2012) to explain the relationship between their 'patience' – or 'impatience' – with solving the 'Taiwan issue'. In accordance with Chen, I define two factors as critical for a Party leader's (im)patience with Taiwan, which would induce him to convey messages of increasing urgency to solve the 'Taiwan issue', maybe even announcing timetables for achieving eventual 'unification': 1) his perception of Taiwanese domestic politics and of Taiwan's China policy; and 2) his perception of the US–Taiwan relationship. The focus on perception related to these two factors on the part of the CCP's general secretaries to explain the vicissitudes of China's Taiwan policy is foremost methodological, as I do not claim that this is the major explanatory variable with no other players (e.g. the Chinese military or the CCP's United Front Work Department) or perceptions having significant impact. However, given the superior position of the general secretary in the CCP's hierarchy and this chapter's focus on the Xi Jinping era, which involves a Party leader of exceptional clout and resolve, it makes at least some sense to probe this perspective.[2] While I do agree in most parts with Chen's analysis of Jiang Zemin as displaying increasing impatience while Hu Jintao appears more patient with Taiwan, my assessment of the Xi Jinping era is one of rising and, arguably, irreversible impatience. This is driven by a dangerous 'lock-in' of the two factors determining perception – a situation that did not, at least not to this extent, exist in the previous two periods. Taiwan's steadfast rejection of the 'One China' principle and the '1992 Consensus' has resulted in deep alienation and a demonstrated readiness by the Xi Jinping regime

2 There is an alternative perspective argued by Edward Friedman that the most important factor determining China's Taiwan policy has always been the CCP's quest for domestic legitimacy, and that it has been 'militarised' for purely domestic reasons in the aftermath of the crisis years (1989–91) when:

> the nation-wide democratic mobilization headquartered in Beijing's Tiananmen Square in 1989 led to a major shift in how Chinese rulers imagined the world, suddenly leading them to interpret democratic Taiwan as a threat to the survival of the CCP Regime. (Friedman 2007, 125)

to militarily threaten Taiwan, feeding into the deteriorating relationship between the US and China that, again, drives the conflict across the Taiwan Strait, arguably making Taiwan one of the most dangerous place on earth.[3]

The CCP's Taiwan Policy under Deng Xiaoping, Jiang Zemin and Hu Jintao

Taiwan Policy in the Mao Era

The CCP's Taiwan policy after the founding of the People's Republic of China (PRC) was foremost determined by the Cold War and, in this regard, by the Beijing–Moscow relationship and Washington's protection of the exiled Nationalist government in Taiwan. Beijing was mute on the Taiwan issue during the Korean War (1950–53), which had triggered the dispatchment of the Seventh US fleet to the Taiwan Strait to protect Taiwan from any attack by PRC forces. However, the Communist Party propaganda machine drummed up a public campaign to 'liberate Taiwan' in the summer of 1954, just before the signing of the ROC–US Mutual Defense Treaty on 2 December of that year.[4] This treaty was a consequence of the First Taiwan Straits Crisis, which began in August 1954 when Chiang Kai-shek (蔣介石) sent some 63,000 soldiers to Kinmen and Matsu to fortify the military installations there. The message to Beijing was one of clear belligerence. The shelling of both islands by People's Liberation Army (PLA) forces provoked an official note by the US Joint Chiefs of Staff on 12 September that nuclear weapons may be used against the PRC – a threat that was, however, not sustained by President Eisenhower. The PLA seized the Yijiangshan and Dachen Islands in January and February 1955, respectively, encouraging Mao Zedong (毛泽东) to ponder a military invasion of Taiwan. This only induced the US government to repeat their threat of nuclear attack, forcing Mao to back down and declare his willingness to negotiate by April 1955. This terminated the First Taiwan Strait Crisis but did not settle the problem (Garver 1997).

3 See 'The Most Dangerous Place on Earth', cover page of the 1 May 2021 edition of the *Economist*.

4 This treaty did not include the protection of the islands of Kinmen and Matsu but just covered the main island of Taiwan and the Pescadores. For that reason, the US did not directly interfere in the Second Taiwan Straits Crisis in 1958.

With the radicalisation of domestic politics during the Great Leap Forward, the CCP leadership, and Mao Zedong in particular, confident in his observation that the 'East Wind prevails over the West Wind', provoked a Second Taiwan Straits Crisis only three years later. After PRC landing forces were repelled by the Nationalists without taking Dongding Island south of Kinmen in August 1958, the shelling of Kinmen and Matsu began again. However, Moscow was as disinterested as the US in risking a large-scale war over Taiwan with another superpower. However, the latter intervened by assisting the Nationalists with naval escort operations to the islands to protect supply lines and with modern missiles that gave the ROC air force a decisive edge over Chinese fighter planes. Mao did not dare to attack US forces and eventually had to back down again; a ceasefire was declared on 6 October, and by the end of the year the crisis itself had fizzled out, though a strange ritual of mutual and limited (but still dangerous) shelling on alternating even and odd days would last until the late 1970s (Szonyi 2008).[5]

After this, the CCP gave up on military invasion and restricted itself to mechanically calling for Taiwan's 'liberation'. The sentiment, however, was soon swallowed up in Mao's Cultural Revolution and faced a GMD government in Taiwan that celebrated its mission to uphold traditional Chinese culture against the self-destructing ideological iconoclasm on the mainland. In fact, cross-strait relations ossified during the 1960s and 1970s as a composite result of uncompromising nationalisms pursued in Beijing and Taipei (Deans 2005), the breakdown of the Sino-Soviet alliance, and Washington's concurrent determination to keep things stable in the Taiwan Strait to allow for a US–China rapprochement. The latter materialised in the early 1970s, paving the way for a new chapter in the CCP's history and Taiwan policy.

5 On 27 September 1958, Moscow sent a letter to Beijing telling Mao that 'attacking China means attacking the Soviet Union'. Khrushchev pondered assistance to increase the PLA's air and naval fighting power, mirroring the US strategy of indirect support for the Nationalist forces. But Mao declined, which could have been connected to his unfolding rivalry with Khrushchev and the Kremlin concerning leadership of the Socialist bloc (Sheng 2008).

Reorientation from 'Liberation' to 'Peaceful Unification' under Deng

When Deng Xiaoping (邓小平) transmitted his 'Message to the Compatriots in Taiwan' on New Year's Eve 1979,[6] it seemed to usher in a new era of cross-strait relations after decades of sabre-rattling and non-communication between Beijing and Taipei. Henceforth, a strategy of 'peaceful unification' replaced the threat of 'liberating Taiwan', the latter much more strongly suggesting the use of force. In reality, Premier Zhou Enlai (周恩来) had already announced the Party's intention to 'liberate Taiwan by peaceful means under possible conditions' in May 1955, and in a document issued on 6 October 1956, the PRC's Defence Ministry delivered a 'Message to Compatriots in Taiwan' written by Mao Zedong proposing to 'conduct negotiation' to 'achieve peaceful resolution'. However, concrete policy steps never emerged. Moreover, the Quemoy crisis in 1958 and the continued, symbolic bombardment of Kinmen from then until the day of Deng Xiaoping's 'Message' on 1 January 1979, when he ordered a stop to this ritualised practice, were evidence enough that 'unification' was still primarily thought of in terms of enforced liberation (Lee 2020).

In historical hindsight, the 'Message' can be read as a corollary to Deng's turn to economic reforms, inviting Taiwan's people to participate in the project of rebuilding China after the disastrous Cultural Revolution (and much of what had happened before that), and at the same time relieving some of the pressure on the Chinese leadership to solve the 'Taiwan issue'. Instead, all efforts could be focused on 'reform and opening up' (*gaige kaifang* 改革开放). At the same time, the text of the 'Message' highlights the strong connection between regime legitimacy and 'unification'. The promise to modernise China – or 'rejuvenate' the Chinese nation, in Xi Jinping's terms – can only be fulfilled by incorporating Taiwan into the party-state, which represents both China and the Chinese nation. With Deng's 'Message', an explicit link was established between China's reform trajectory and 'unification' with Taiwan, whereby the quest for 'unification' would feed into China's modernisation project, and 'unification' could be postponed for the time being. Deng's 'Message' abstained from using the phrase 'liberating Taiwan' and, for the first time, proposed cross-strait talks: 'To create the necessary prerequisites and a secure environment for the two sides to make contacts and exchanges in whatever area' (cf. Xin 2020).

6 For an English translation of Deng's 'Message', see www.china.org.cn/english/7943.htm.

The new policy approach towards Taiwan was backed up by Marshal Ye Jianying's (叶剑英) 'Nine-Point Proposal' announced on 1 October 1981, and Deng Xiaoping's 'Six-Point Proposal' of 26 June 1983. Both documents spelled out, though did not explicitly mention, the 'one country, two systems' formula as constituting the model for Taiwan's political future in a 'reunified' China.[7] However, as Deng reiterated repeatedly during the early 1980s, there was no hurry in bringing about 'reunification' when rebuilding China economically was of primary importance. Deng's priorities were clearly set, which meant he did not need to be impatient about solving the 'Taiwan issue', nor did the US–Taiwan relationship at the time necessitate impatience. Diplomatic relations had been established between both countries on 1 January 1979, seven years after the Shanghai Communique was signed and the US–China relationship 'normalised'. Although Washington reassured Taipei – by promulgating the Taiwan Relations Act on 1 April 1979 – that stability in the Taiwan Strait was of 'grave concern' to the US and that the 'Six Assurances' of 1982[8] would hold, Deng and the CCP could be certain of overall international support for their 'One China Policy'. Further, in Taiwan, GMD leader and ROC president Chiang Ching-kuo (蔣經國) led a government that also stuck to that principle, although already under 'democratic pressure' from indigenous forces. Put differently, Taiwan's domestic politics and the international situation were advantageous enough for Deng to be patient and put 'reunification' on the backburner, while focusing on the immediate necessity of reconsolidating one-party rule through economic reform. This situation endured until the mid-1990s, when a legitimacy crisis at home coincided with political developments in Taiwan and a shift in the US–China relationship, producing new uncertainty on the 'Taiwan issue' for the Communist Party.

Crisis Awareness and 'Impatience' under Jiang Zemin

Jiang Zemin was installed as CCP general secretary in 1989 to deal with the aftermath of the Tiananmen Square incident, which had damaged the ruling legitimacy of the Communist Party considerably. The focus in the first years

7 For an English translation of Ye's 'Nine-Point Proposal' that was published in the *Renmin Ribao* on 1 October 1981, see en.wikisource.org/wiki/Nine-Point_Proposal. The 'Six-Point Proposal' is included in vol. 3 of Deng Xiaoping's *Selected Works*. See also 'Deng Liutiao', Wikipedia, accessed 13 October 2021, zh.wikipedia.org/zh-tw/邓六条.

8 The 'Six Assurances' were proposed to the US government by Taiwan and officially promulgated by the former as guiding Washington's Taiwan policy in July 1982. See 'The "Six Assurances" to Taiwan', July 1982, accessed 13 October 2021, www.taiwandocuments.org/assurances.htm.

of his reign was, therefore, placed on domestic reconsolidation of the one-party rule in China (Chu 2000). In Taiwan at the same time, Lee Teng-hui (李登輝), who had succeeded Chiang Ching-kuo in early 1988 as the first Taiwan-born GMD leader and ROC president, pushed for democratisation and initiated a new China policy to bring about a cross-strait détente and gain Taiwan more political manoeuvring space in the regional and international arena. By building a whole new institutional edifice for cross-strait policymaking and sub-official relations between Taipei and Beijing, Lee encouraged his Chinese counterparts to acknowledge, inexplicitly at least, the so-called 1992 Consensus by which both the PRC and the ROC governments would recognise that there was only 'One China', though they accepted different interpretations of its state representation (Hsieh 2003).[9] This pragmatic turn in cross-strait relations allowed for a number of talks between non-official entities of both sides culminating in the first cross-strait summit held in Singapore in April 1993.[10] Cross-strait relations thus seemed to have entered a new era in which 'peaceful unification', at some undetermined date in the future, remained a common objective of both sides.

In 1995, Jiang Zemin officially spoke out for the first time, giving the CCP Taiwan policy a personal imprint. His 'Eight Points' announced on 30 January of that year reiterated the official stance on Taiwan following Deng Xiaoping's 1979 'Message', but also confirmed the CCP's willingness to 'continually encourage exchange and contacts across the Taiwan Straits which promote mutual understanding', invoking the possibility of establishing direct postal, transport and trade links across the Taiwan Strait.[11] Soon afterwards, however, he was confronted with an unexpected setback that had been building in the background for some time. A white paper on

9 As is standard knowledge now, the '1992 Consensus' was invented by former chairman of the Mainland Affairs Council Su Qi in 2000, after the election of Chen Shui-bian to the ROC presidency, to rationalise the awkward avoidance of the sovereignty issue by Beijing and Taipei during their rapprochement in the 1990s (Su 2009).

10 The 'Wang-Koo Summit', named after the presidents of the two semi-official organisation holding cross-strait talks since 1992, China's Association for Relations across the Taiwan Strait (ARATS) and Taiwan's Strait Exchange Foundation (SEF) took place on 'neutral ground' in Singapore from 27 to 29 April as a result of preceding talks between officials of both sides in Hong Kong one year before when an implicit agreement, later called the '1992 Consensus' was, in one way or the other, achieved (Xu 2001).

11 'Jan 30, 1995: President Jiang Zemin Puts Forward Eight Propositions on Development of Relations between Two Sides of Taiwan Straits', *China Daily*, 30 January 2011, www.chinadaily.com.cn/china/19th cpcnationalcongress/2011-01/30/content_29715090.htm. Jiang's 'Eight Points' were countered by Lee Teng-hui's 'Six Points', made in a speech on 5 April 1995, which reiterated ROC sovereignty and were read as an immediate rebuff of Jiang. See 'Lee Teng-hui Responds to Jiang Zemin', *Taiwan Communique*, no. 66, June 1995, www.taiwandc.org/twcom/66-no4.htm.

cross-strait relations published in 1994 announced Lee Teng-hui's strategy of pragmatic or flexible diplomacy, and spelled out Taiwan's future position of a 'divided government' along the lines of Germany and Korea after World War II. Henceforth, the ROC government would no longer compete with its Chinese counterpart for international representation of China, would abolish its policy of establishing official relations only with those countries supporting Taipei's claim, and would strive for internationally recognised statehood.[12] One year later, Lee was allowed to enter the United States to visit his alma mater, Cornell University, after considerable bickering between the Oval Office and Congress, and gave a public speech in which he told his audience the story of democratic Taiwan and joined the chorus of the time in declaring that 'Communism is dead or dying'.[13] Although he was travelling in a private capacity, this was seen as a provocation by Beijing and led to what then became known as the 'Second Taiwan Strait Crisis', lasting from late 1995 until Taiwan's presidential elections in March 1996.

Lee Teng-hui's (re-)election was a blow to the CCP and pointed towards a Taiwanese determination to resist any Chinese pressure to vote for a political leader favoured by Beijing. Jiang Zemin was alarmed by this development and interrupted cross-strait talks. They briefly resumed in 1998, while the state media in China pounded Lee Teng-hui as a traitor of the Chinese nation as he increasingly displayed an independentist line. This regression in cross-strait relations then culminated in Lee's sudden move to spell out a 'Two States Theory' in an interview with German radio channel Deutsche Welle in May 1999, suggesting that relations across the Taiwan Strait were of a special state-to-state nature.[14] Even though this ostensible break with the GMD's China policy eventually led to Lee Teng-hui's expulsion from the ruling party, the damage to cross-strait relations was done.

12 The key passage in this text concerning international representation goes as follows:

> The experience of East and West Germany shows us that joint participation by the two halves of a divided nation in the international community by no means damages the prospects for unification; indeed, it can have the effect of easing tension and creating conditions favourable to unification as well as safeguarding the interests of the entire people. Not so long ago, North and South Korea adopted a similar course of action.

For an English translation see the archives of the ROC's Mainland Affairs Council, accessed 8 October 2021, www.mac.gov.tw/en/News.aspx?n=8A319E37A32E01EA&sms=2413CFE1BCE87E0E&_CSN=E6436B9A96D5AEE5.

13 See 'Pres. Lee Teng-hui, Cornell University Commencement Address, June 9, 1995', china.usc.edu/pres-lee-teng-hui-cornell-university-commencement-address-june-9-1995.

14 According to Jacobs and Liu (2007), Lee Teng-hui made this statement to prevent a scheduled visit of the then president of China's Association Across the Taiwan Strait, Wang Daohan, from being exploited by Jiang Zemin as a 'breakthrough to the reunification of China on the 50th anniversary of the founding of the People's Republic'.

In 1998, Jiang began speaking in terms of 'unification' timetables. In the months following Lee's Deutsche Welle interview, he referred on various occasions to the possible use of force against Taiwan and suggested that the 'Taiwan issue' may be resolved by the middle of the twenty-first century (Shirk 2007, 191; Cheng 2005, 352).[15] The State Council's 2000 white paper on Taiwan arguably highlighted Jiang's impatience by stating that Taiwan's rejection of 'reunification' negotiations would result in the use of military force. In his work report to the Sixteenth CCP National Congress in November 2002, Jiang's farewell speech again insisted that resolution of the 'Taiwan issue' could not be delayed indefinitely (Chen 2012, 957). At this point, Taiwan had already been governed for two years by an independence-minded president from the DPP, Chen Shui-bian (陳水扁), who had come to power in May 2000 after the first change of government since Taiwan's democratic transition. After some tactical reservations, Chen had publicly claimed in August 2002 that Taiwan and China were two countries on each side of the Taiwan Strait.[16] Jiang Zemin had reason to be worried, but it was not only Taiwan's domestic political development that nurtured this sense of urgency in him.

The United States had carefully observed Taiwan's democratic transition throughout the late 1980s and early 1990s; indeed, Washington had been an important driving force of democratisation. As mentioned above, Lee Teng-hui was granted a visa to visit the United States in May 1995, giving him unprecedented international status and a public platform to praise Taiwan's economic and political development, and to publicly promote ROC sovereignty. In December 1995, the US government dispatched an aircraft carrier, the Nimitz, and in March 1996 two aircraft carrier battle groups were sent into the Taiwan Strait to deter China from further threatening the island with military exercises close to its coastline ahead of Taiwan's 1996 presidential elections. Even though President Clinton tried to de-escalate the situation between the two countries during his state visit to China in June 1998 by assuring Jiang that the US did not support Taiwan independence, his successor George W. Bush claimed publicly only a year

15 However, the Chinese government rejected any inference made from Jiang's public statements on Taiwan that he had spoken in terms of timetables, and stated that Beijing's general policy line vis-a-vis Taiwan had not changed.

16 For an extracted Chinese text summarising Chen's statement in his telecast to the annual conference of the World Federation of Taiwanese Associations meeting in Tokyo on 3 August 2002, see Russell Hsiao, 'Hu Jintao's "Six-Points" Proposition to Taiwan', *China Brief*, 12 January 2009, jamestown.org/program/hu-jintaos-six-points-proposition-to-taiwan/.

later that the US would do 'whatever it took to help Taiwan defend herself'.[17] This did little to help assuage Jiang Zemin's distrust that Washington would stick to its Taiwan policy approach of 'strategic ambiguity' and opposing Taiwan independence. Impatience and distrust brought cross-strait relations to an all-new low at the end of Jiang Zemin's term, by which point he had obviously lost confidence in a peaceful solution of the 'Taiwan issue'. However, there was little he could do besides reiterating the CCP's official stance that Taiwan independence was a no-go and that there was no leeway for cross-strait talks, and continuing to patrol the international arena to make sure that most states toed Beijing's line.

Reassurance and Patience under Hu Jintao

Hu Jintao replaced Jiang as CCP general secretary in November 2002 and took up the state presidency one year later. Interestingly, he seemed, from the outset, to be less troubled about the 'Taiwan issue' than Jiang was in his final years as the CCP's paramount leader. Taiwan seemed to be on a stiff trajectory of 'de-sinicisation' (*quzhongguohua* 去中國化), referring to government policies aiming to weaken or eradicate Taiwan's links to Chinese history or cultural symbols and the National People's Congress. In a move raising eyebrows worldwide, Hu promulgated an 'Anti-Secession Law' in March 2005 to deter Taiwan's pro-independence forces. However, despite these tensions, Hu remained rather moderate in his public statements and emphasised at various occasions that cross-strait relations needed stability and perseverance to achieve 'unification' by peaceful means.[18] Starting in the same year, he and GMD leader Lien Chan (連戰) met several times in China and set up regular party-to-party talks as a channel for circumventing the DPP government and cross-strait parallel diplomacy to demonstrate to the Taiwan people how much they could expect to gain once the GMD was back in power. This process was accompanied by the establishment of a CCP–GMD platform for cross-strait economic and cultural exchange that foremost targeted Taiwanese elites, encouraging them to interact

17 'Bush Pledges Whatever It Takes to Defend Taiwan', CNN, 25 April 2001, edition.cnn.com/2001/ALLPOLITICS/04/24/bush.taiwan.abc/.

18 The promulgation of the Anti-Secession Law was probably more of a symbolic act to reassure Hu Jintao's critics within the Communist Party of his steadfast stance on Taiwan rather than anything else, but it puts all CCP leaders under pressure if the political tide in China turns sharply against Taiwan. Article 8 of the law stipulates that 'the state shall employ non-peaceful means and other necessary measures to protect China's sovereignty and territorial integrity' if, among others, 'possibilities of a peaceful reunification should be completely exhausted'. For an English translation of the Anti-Secession Law, see www.china-embassy.org/eng/zt/999999999/t187406.htm.

with their Chinese counterparts and thereby bring about more cross-strait interaction, if not integration, and build trust (Beckershoff 2014). The 'peaceful development' of cross-strait relations, which was first proposed in 2004 and then further endorsed by the CCP's national congresses in 2007 and 2012 (Gang 2016), could be seen as the manifestation of Hu Jintao's demonstrative patience with the 'Taiwan issue'. He was confident that the GMD, which retook the government in 2008, would help the CCP's cause. 'Peaceful development' did not only mean harmonious party-to-party relations, however, but also winning the Taiwan people's hearts and minds by accentuating the promising possibilities of cross-strait economic integration and downplaying China's military threat – an approach formalised in Hu's December 2008 'Six-Point-Proposal' celebrating the thirtieth anniversary of Deng Xiaoping's 'Message to the Compatriots of Taiwan'.[19]

At this point, the GMD under Ma Ying-jeou (馬英九) had indeed returned to power after an astounding electoral victory in January 2008, when it gained both the presidency and an absolute majority in the Legislative Yuan, bringing home the point that the Taiwan people had been convinced of the GMD's China-friendly policy approach and had realised the dead-end into which DPP-sponsored Taiwanese nationalism had led them. In fact, Ma did not hesitate to make good on his promise to turn the wheel in cross-strait relations, and, based on the agreements made in the CCP–GMD Party talks of the foregoing years, he negotiated the restoration of the 'three links' – direct trade, transport and communication – before the end of his first year in office. In 2010, both sides negotiated an 'Economic Framework Agreement', which was particularly advantageous for Taiwan, and more cross-strait agreements were signed.[20] Thus, Hu Jintao had many reasons to be patient, as his moderate policy approach to the 'Taiwan issue' seemed to be bearing fruit. Until the end of his term, he did not mention a timeframe for 'unification', and Ma Ying-jeou's re-election in 2012 allowed for further confidence in this focus on cooperation with the Taiwan government, under the auspices of the 'One China' principle, even though Ma's mandate was weaker than it had been four years before.

---

19 Hu's six points on China's Taiwan policy were: 1) firm adherence to the 'one China' principle; 2) strengthening commercial ties, including negotiating an economic cooperation agreement; 3) promoting personnel exchanges; 4) stressing common cultural links between the two sides; 5) allowing Taiwan's 'reasonable' participation in global organisations; and 6) negotiating a peace agreement. For an English translation, see Hsiao, 'Hu Jintao's "Six-Points" Proposition to Taiwan'.

20 Overall, cross-strait talks during the Ma Ying-jeou era resulted in 21 formal agreements, three memoranda of understanding and two joint statements (Sullivan and Smyth 2018).

At the same time, the US government's behaviour since Hu's coming to power was more reassuring than disheartening for China's 'unification' ambitions. In December 2003, President Bush, who had claimed that the US would do what it took to defend Taiwan, expressed his stern opposition to Chen Shui-bian's plan to hold a referendum for a new Taiwanese constitution by stating, in the presence of Chinese premier Wen Jiabao (温家宝), that 'the comments and actions made by the leader of Taiwan indicate that he may be willing to make decisions unilaterally to change the status quo – which we oppose'.[21] The Bush administration also openly rejected: Chen's efforts to rename Taiwan's representative offices abroad and its state-owned enterprises from 'ROC' to 'Taiwan'; his efforts to 'rectify the country's name' campaign and 'Taiwanisation' policy; his hidden move to abolish the 'National Unification Council', established in the early days of the Lee Teng-hui presidency; and the revitalisation of Chen's project of constitutional reform.[22] It seemed Washington was not in favour of Taiwan rocking the boat of Sino-US relations, again reassuring Hu Jintao that solving the 'Taiwan issue' was not urgent. Hu could feel even more relaxed as the US government repeatedly expressed its optimism for the future of cross-strait relations after the election of a 'China-friendly' ROC president in 2008. Clearly, Washington was relieved that there would be no further sidestepping of US demands to coordinate Taiwan's China policy with Washington's prerogatives on Taipei's part.

During his state visit to China in 2009, President Obama, newly elected, declared in a joint statement with Hu Jintao that the US 'applauded the steps that the People's Republic of China and Taiwan had already taken to relax tensions and build stable ties across the Taiwan Strait'.[23] During his eight years in office, Obama and his leading officials remained very cautious on Taiwan and constantly uttered support for the cross-strait rapprochement that had set in after Ma Ying-jeou took office. The US would not waver in its arms sales to Taiwan, however, which served to reassure Taiwan that Washington's general policy line concerning the 'Taiwan issue' had not changed. When Tsai Ing-wen (蔡英文), the DPP's candidate for the 2012

---

21 'Remarks Following Discussions with Premier Wen Jiabao of China and an Exchange With Reporters', US Government Publishing Office, 9 December 2003, www.govinfo.gov/content/pkg/PPP-2003-book2/html/PPP-2003-book2-doc-pg1700.htm.

22 'Chen Pledges to Change Names', *Taipei Times*, 5 December 2004, www.taipeitimes.com/News/front/archives/2004/12/06/2003213954.

23 'Joint Press Statement by President Obama and President Hu of China', The White House, 17 November 2009, obamawhitehouse.archives.gov/the-press-office/joint-press-statement-president-obama-and-president-hu-china.

presidential elections, visited Washington in September 2011 to make herself, and her prospective China policy, known to US officials, her efforts did not prove particularly convincing. One US official publicly stated that 'she left us with distinct doubts about whether she is both willing and able to continue the stability in cross-Strait relations the region has enjoyed in recent years' (Tiezzi 2015). And the following November, during the APEC Economic Leader's Meeting held in Honolulu, Obama told Hu Jintao that 'the U.S. is glad to see continuous progress made in cross-Strait relations' and that it would 'continue to pursue the one-China policy based on the three China-U.S. joint communiqués and does not support Taiwan independence'.[24]

With Taiwan's domestic politics following a course to China's liking and US support for cross-strait rapprochement continuing on the basis of the '1992 Consensus', Hu Jintao obviously saw no reason for impatience when it came to solving the 'Taiwan issue'. In contrast to Jiang Zemin's negative perception of the 'Taiwan' and 'US factor' in cross-strait relations in his final years as CCP general secretary, Hu's perception was more positive, even though he chose to ignore the changing tide within Taiwanese society, and the increasing resistance to Ma Ying-jeou's China policy (Sullivan and Smyth 2018). Assured of sound US–China relations at the time and confident that the GMD would carry the day in Taiwan, he could probably not have foreseen the nationalist turn that his successor would bring to Chinese politics, which would prove potentially as important a factor impacting the cross-strait relationship as Taiwanese domestic politics and US–Taiwan relations.

Growing Impatience under Xi Jinping

Xi Jinping was elected CCP general secretary in November 2012 and president of the PRC in March 2013. During the first years of his reign as China's paramount leader, he seemed to be willing to continue Hu Jintao's policy of accentuating 'peaceful development' in cross-strait relations within the overall framework of China's carrot-and-stick approach to Taiwan. This visibly changed after the 2016 national elections in Taiwan and the return to power of the DPP, which both seized the presidential office and gained an

24 See 'Chinese, U.S. Presidents Pledge to Advance Cooperative Partnership', Embassy of the PRC, 14 November 2011, ca.china-embassy.org/eng/zt/APEC123/t876627.htm.

absolute majority in the Legislative Yuan. Since then, China's Taiwan policy has become increasingly uncompromising, if not belligerent, both in terms of language and action – though perhaps not in overall strategy. Arguably, Xi Jinping's perception of the 'Taiwan issue' has taken a pessimistic turn, in response to the DPP's strategy of institutionalising de facto independence by rejecting the 'One China' principle and the '1992 Consensus' on the one hand, and decreasing Taiwan's economic dependency on China on the other. These developments also coincide with a new China policy consensus in Washington aiming to push back against China's rise and global ambitions.

Xi Jinping's Taiwan Policy before 2016: Patience, but a Rising Sense of Urgency

During his first years in office, with a 'pro-China' GMD politician as Taiwan's leader, Xi Jinping was foremost interested in incorporating Taiwan, on the discursive level, into his narrative of the 'rejuvenation of the great Chinese nation', itself the centrepiece of his so-called 'China Dream'. This narrative was part of an ideological project to recount the CCP's story of China's rise to national pride, prosperity and global power, accompanied by measures to recalibrate the political system and develop a blueprint for geo-economical influence-building in China's 'periphery': the 'Belt and Road Initiative'. In April 2013, at the occasion of the Twelfth Boao Forum, Xi met Taiwan's representative Vincent Siew and called for both Taiwan and China to 'work hard towards realising the great rejuvenation of the Chinese nation' and to foster closer economic cooperation.[25] Several months later, in October 2013, Xi met Siew again at the APEC meeting in Bali, Indonesia, pronouncing that both China and Taiwan 'are of one family' and that, in referring to the 'Taiwan issue', they 'cannot hand those problems down from generation to generation'.[26] This indicated a sense of urgency that had not been articulated so explicitly at any point in the Hu Jintao era.

This sense of urgency came to the fore again in September 2014 when Xi Jinping told a visiting delegation of pro-unification groups from Taiwan that 'the basic guideline to solve the Taiwan question is "peaceful reunification; one country, two systems" and it is also the best way to realize

25 'Twelfth Boao Forum for Asia Concludes', CNTV, 9 April 2013, www.china.org.cn/video/2013-04/09/content_28485945.htm.

26 'Problems Should Not Be Handed down to Later Generations: Xi', *China Daily*, 7 October 2013, english.sina.com/china/2013/1006/634689.html.

national reunification' – language that had not been heard in many years.[27] At this time, the CCP and Xi were already aware of a serious downturn in cross-strait relations, as Taiwan's 'Sunflower Movement' in March–April 2014 had unmistakably demarcated the limits of Ma Ying-jeou's China policy by successfully mobilising against the Cross-Strait Trade in Service Act (Ho 2019; Jones 2017). When this development culminated in the election of a new independence-minded DPP president, Tsai Ing-wen, in January 2016, after eight years of relatively stable cross-strait relations, Xi's perception of the 'Taiwan issue' changed from increasingly sceptical to utterly pessimistic. It quickly became clear that 'peaceful unification' negotiated with a Taiwan government committed to the '1992 Consensus' and the 'One China' principle was no longer a realistic option, at least not in the medium term.

This assumption is also supported by the CCP's earlier frustration with the Ma administration's hesitant response to any effort to push cross-strait talks beyond issues of economic integration. With all the low-hanging fruits already having been harvested, cross-strait relations were getting into the deep water of politics. Even if Ma Ying-jeou and his government felt bound by rising domestic opposition against the government's 'pro-China' policies and accusations of 'selling out' Taiwan to China, or if these policies had just always been tactically framed by 'unificationist' terminology, the CCP could not make any headway in its efforts to achieve its ultimate objective. After 2016, Taiwan's responses to the CCP's Taiwan policy thus became increasingly irrelevant as Xi embarked on a refurbished approach that would no longer bet on cross-strait negotiations nor on the GMD as a political force that could help the CCP's goal of 'unification'.

After 2016: Impatience and Intensifying Sabre-Rattling

It is not far-fetched to assume that Tsai Ing-wen's approach to the cross-strait relationship has proven incredibly frustrating for Xi Jinping and the CCP, as it combines political restraint in provoking China with an unwavering strategy to solidify Taiwan's de facto independence with a resolute project aiming to 'de-sinicise' Taiwan, aptly summarised by Lee Wei-chin (李偉欽):

27 'Xi Steadfast on Reunification', *People's Daily*, 26 September 2014, www.globalsecurity.org/wmd/library/news/taiwan/2014/taiwan-140926-pdo01.htm.

> In order to fulfill its independence vision, the DPP government has discreetly adopted a persistently constructive approach to identity indigenization through the change of educational contents and name rectification schemes as part of social engineering. It has been a deliberate effort to de-legitimize the China-oriented cultural identification and historical genealogy for the expansion of the 'Taiwan-centered' social construct and a collective history without 'China' in cultural and political reference. Given time, such a constructive movement would quietly transform public conviction and cultural identification and convince future generations of the irrelevancy of China in Taiwan's democratic politics through elections and public referendums. (Lee 2020, 207)

Against this background, Xi Jinping recalibrated the CCP's Taiwan policy by both sweetening the carrots and strengthening the sticks. The platform for this track change was the Nineteenth CCP Congress held in October 2017, when Xi maintained the general tone of the CCP's long-term Taiwan policy of 'peaceful development' but also used stern language in his lengthy report to make sure that nobody misunderstood China's resolve to deter 'Taiwan independence' and achieve 'national unification'.[28] In his report to the Twentieth CCP Congress held in October 2022, he addressed what had been discussed within the CCP as the 'Overall Policy Framework for Resolving the Taiwan Question in the New Era' (*Xin shidai dang jiejue Taiwan wenti de zongti fanglüe* 新时代党解决台湾问题的总体方略) since the Sixth Meeting of the Nineteenth CCP Central Committee in November 2021. This is not a strategy put down in a formal Party document but rather a comprehensive set of ideas and 'axiomatic thinking' that make the CCP's Taiwan policy and informs all official statements on Taiwan, including the latest white paper, entitled 'The Taiwan Question and China's Reunification in the New Era', released in August 2022.[29]

Xi explicitly subscribed to the '1992 Consensus' as the embodiment of the 'One China' principle but omitted any hint of the 'two interpretations' formula, which was foundational for the GMD's Taiwan policy whenever it had governed Taiwan. Xi also emphasised that Taiwan's future was firmly linked to the 'One Country, Two Systems' model, deliberately ignoring an

28 'Secure a Decisive Victory in Building a Moderately Prosperous Society in All Respects and Strive for the Great Success of Socialism with Chinese Characteristics for a New Era', Report delivered at the Nineteenth National Congress of the Chinese Communist Party, accessed 18 October, 2021, www.xinhuanet.com/english/download/Xi_Jinping's_report_at_19th_CPC_National_Congress.pdf.

29 See Chen (2022) who traces the historical formation, academic discussion in China and major content of the 'Framework'.

overarching consensus in Taiwan that this arrangement is a no-go. In his speech on 2 January 2019 commemorating the fortieth anniversary of Deng's 'Message to Compatriots in Taiwan', Xi Jinping dispersed all remaining hopes, particularly within the GMD, that there was still some leeway to return to the ambiguous understanding of the '1992 Consensus', in which both sides had agreed to disagree on what 'One China' means.[30] Though Xi did not mention a timeframe for 'reunification' in his Taiwan-related speeches, he certainly transmitted a sense of urgency and impatience with solving the 'Taiwan issue' that was well noticed in Taiwan. Interestingly, as GMD chairman Jiang Chi-chen (江啓臣) told me in May 2020, Xi Jinping had taken the '1992 Consensus' away from the GMD, so that no such thing exists anymore. The moment had, therefore, come for the GMD to take a stand, either by giving up on the consensus or adhering to it against all odds, signalling to China that dialogue with Taiwan would not be possible without it and that legitimate sovereignty for the ROC under the auspices of the 'One China' principle is indispensable. However, since the recent election of a new GMD Party chairman, Chu Li-lun (朱立倫), in September 2021, the '1992 Consensus' has been revitalised – obviously because the GMD has nothing else it could otherwise offer to the CCP. Tsai Ing-wen issued a resolute statement in the afternoon of the same day, in which she first rejected Xi's implication that the '1992 Consensus' was equal to subscribing to 'One County, Two Systems', a suggestion unacceptable for the vast majority of the Taiwan people. Future cross-strait negotiations, she continued, must be led by governments or government-authorised agencies.[31]

Since 2016, pressure on Taiwan has heightened considerably in both political and military terms. For instance, in May 2018, China forced 44 international airlines to revise their website identifications of Taiwan to indicate Taiwan's subjugation to the 'One China' principle.[32] Airlines now have to identify the territory as 'China Taiwan' or 'China Taiwan region'. Moreover, Beijing snatched away seven of Taiwan's few diplomatic allies after the DPP came to power, so that, at the end of 2023, no more than

30 Xi's speech is available on YouTube, see www.youtube.com/watch?v=not9jASVHds.

31 'President Tsai Issues Statement on China's President Xi's Message to Compatriots in Taiwan', Office of the President of the Republic of China, 2 January 2019, english.president.gov.tw/News/5621.

32 'Foreign Airlines Make Changes to Reflect One-China Principle', *Xinhua*, 13 October 2018, www.shine.cn/news/nation/1807269416/.

13 countries have stayed in Taiwan's camp.[33] Chinese aircraft and naval operations in the Taiwan Strait have increased progressively since November 2016, resulting in the highest-ever density of Chinese fighter planes entering Taiwan's airspace and warships crossing the medium line in the Taiwan Strait in spring 2021. Chinese intrusions into Taiwan's airspace continued for the rest of the year. This, among other issues pertaining to great power politics, has induced a number of US officials and high-ranking military officers to predict that a Chinese military invasion of Taiwan is imminent and will materialise over the course of the next few years (Roy 2021). These voices argue that China's increasing military capabilities and sharp power assertiveness,[34] against a background of deteriorating US–China relations and unperturbed Taiwanese nationalism, will progressively strengthen China's sense of urgency and impatience, pushing the Xi administration to solve the 'Taiwan issue' as soon as possible. At the very least, China will continue posturing under Xi, displaying willingness and capability at the possibility of a showdown, so that those who feel the US must intervene to prevent a Chinese invasion of Taiwan will perhaps think twice.

At the same time, Xi Jinping has added new carrots to his Taiwan policy, exclusively targeting the 'hearts and minds of the Taiwan people' and accentuating China's focus on people-to-people relations. In February 2018, the State Taiwan Affairs Office promulgated a package of 31 preferential policies (PPs) (*huitai zhengce* 惠台政策) to be granted to Taiwanese businesses: 12 policies promised the equal treatment of Taiwanese and domestic Chinese companies concerning access to government procurement and infrastructure projects, but also to sectors previously banned for Taiwanese (and foreign) companies, for instance, private medical clinics and solicitors; the remaining 19 announced the opening up of the Chinese job market for high-skilled Taiwanese labour and university graduates.[35] These central policies have been taken up quickly at the local level and, in the course of adaption, have been expanded by provincial and city governments, resulting in, for instance, 66 PPs in Fujian Province and 68 PPs in Fuzhou

33 Since 2016, Taiwan has lost, successively, São Tomé and Principe (December 2016), Panama (June 2017), Dominican Republic (May 2018), Burkina Faso (May 2018), El Salvador (August 2018), the Solomon Islands and Kiribati (September 2019), Nicaragua (December 2021) and Honduras (March 2023).

34 'Sharp power' foremost refers to China's united front efforts to manipulate public opinion in Taiwan by disseminating fake news in cyberspace, steering pro-Chinese media reporting and mobilising pro-Chinese radical groups to protest against the government (Hsu and Cole 2020).

35 For details concerning the 31 PP package see 'State Council Taiwan Affairs Office: The 31 Taiwan preferential measures will be quickly put in place' (国台办: '31条惠台措施'将很快全部落实到位), 30 May 2018, www.gov.cn/xinwen/2018-05/30/content_5294812.htm.

City. On the surface, the 31 PPs and their lower-level specifications have ushered in a new era for China's 'united front' strategy, as they promise to do away with almost all restrictions for Taiwanese people and entities on the Chinese mainland. This extends into the realm of residency rights,[36] market access (including investment opportunities in sectors so far controlled by Chinese state-owned enterprises) and occupational freedom. In fact, there is some demand for these 'goodies'. A sluggish economy, low wages and the expected consequences of recent pension reforms are important push factors for Taiwanese businesspeople and professionals, but also young university graduates and even high school students, to leave Taiwan, while China's vast market and its new policy incentives arguably make for strong pull factors.[37] All Taiwanese are invited to equally share the benefits of a prospering Chinese economy with their mainland 'compatriots' – at least, this is the message sent across the Taiwan Strait.[38] The Western media also reported on Xi Jinping's trip in March 2021, when he visited Fujian, the mainland province directly opposite Taiwan, telling officials that they should explore new forms of cross-strait economic development and integration.[39] It is clear that the DPP government faces increasing pressure to come up with convincing policy responses that could revitalise the Taiwanese economy and thereby incentivise its citizens to stay.

However, Xi Jinping must be worried by the changing US–China relationship, which will likely reinforce Taiwan's determination to withstand China's quest for unity. If Washington increasingly regards Taiwan as the focal point of a great power conflict that will decide the future global order, Taiwan could benefit from this renewed attention. As the Chinese expected, the Biden administration has so far continued its predecessor's

36 In August 2018, the Chinese government announced that mainland residents from Taiwan (as well as from Hong Kong and Macao) would be offered a new residence card (旧居证) to replace the old 'certificate of Taiwan compatriots' (台胞证), making it easier for Taiwanese to get access to certain public services and comply with numerous registration requirements. See 'New ID Card Will Give Hong Kong, Macau and Taiwan Residents Same Access to Public Services as Mainland Chinese Counterparts', *South China Morning Post*, 16 August 2018, www.scmp.com/news/hong-kong/politics/article/2159989/new-id-card-will-give-hong-kong-macau-and-taiwan-residents; 'President Tsai: New "Residence Permits" for Taiwanese in China Do Not Determine "Identity"', *Taiwan News*, 20 August 2018, www.taiwannews.com.tw/en/news/3510495.

37 Other measures are meant to facilitate the everyday life of Taiwanese on the Chinese mainland. For example, senior managers from Taiwan can apply for Chinese credit cards, and academic certificates from Taiwan are fully recognised.

38 This migration has come on top of Taiwan's massive outflow of investment and human capital since the late 1980s, resulting in some 3 million Taiwanese 'compatriots' permanently residing in the Chinese mainland today (see Lee 2020; Rigger and Schubert 2017).

39 'China's Growing Military Confidence Puts Taiwan at Risk', *Economist*, 1 May 2021.

policies of strengthening the US–Taiwan relationship in both words and deeds, most notably in having maintained the Taiwan Travel Act and the National Defense Authorization Act for US naval port calls to Taiwan, both promulgated in 2018, and sales of modern weapon systems fiercely opposed by China. Such measures certainly intensify Xi Jinping's sense of urgency to solve the 'Taiwan issue' sooner rather than later, and, although a timeframe has never been publicly mentioned, Xi has implicitly linked 'unification' to the centennial goal of the People's Republic becoming a 'developed country' and attaining great power status by 2049. Some pundits even contend that he is personally willing to do whatever it takes to bring Taiwan back to the motherland before he steps down, which would be much earlier than 2049. To what extent such alarmism should be taken seriously is anybody's guess, but it is obvious that – alongside the Taiwan and US factors in Xi Jinping's Taiwan policy – the continuous modernisation of the PLA, Xi's refusal to disconnect the 'Taiwan issue' from Chinese ethno-nationalism and the CCP's continuous quest for legitimacy in ruling China – which is, in itself, connected to the idea of a unified Chinese nation-state – do not bode well for a peaceful solution of the conflict in the Taiwan Strait.

Conclusion

Despite the CCP's hollow threat to 'liberate Taiwan' throughout the Mao era, for much of the early reform era, the CCP seemed confident in its goal of 'peaceful unification' by adjusting the 'One County, Two Systems' model to Taiwan. The island's increasing economic dependence on the Chinese mainland coupled with rational calculation on the part of the Taiwanese people – many of whom migrated to and pursued a career on the mainland – seemed to suggest that achieving unification was a question of when, not if. Accordingly, 'peaceful unification' was the buzzword of China's Taiwan policy from Deng Xiaoping to Hu Jintao and into the first years of the Xi Jinping era. Despite periodic friction, successive Chinese leaders' overall patience with Taiwan was based on positive assessments of Taiwan's political development on the one hand and the US factor in China–Taiwan relations on the other. Even facing an independence-minded president, Chen Shui-bian, who ruled Taiwan throughout most of the 2000s, Hu Jintao remained patient with Taiwan as the US was willing to rein in the DPP government, thereby supporting the CCP's Taiwan policy, which relied primarily on deterring independence. Besides, China was focused on its domestic problems and reform requirements, and was not yet ready to assume a more assertive role in the Taiwan Strait.

Under Xi Jinping, however, it seems that the CCP has finally come to realise that the expectation of 'peaceful unification' was largely based on a miscalculation. The assumption was that a common Chinese historical and cultural heritage, economic gain and the promise of enduring peace across the Taiwan Strait would eventually lead the Taiwanese towards political subservience – or, to put it in more positive terms, that it would foster a growing enthusiasm for being 'unified'. With the 'Sunflower Movement', the CCP understood that Taiwan – with a rising, though not uncontested, national identity of its own – would never subscribe to 'peaceful unification'. At the same time, the US, now feeling threatened by China's 'rightful rise', would prove to be an obstacle rather than a helping hand holding 'creeping Taiwan independence' at bay. Xi Jinping has, therefore, become observably impatient on the 'Taiwan issue' and, backed by impressive military clout, is arguably more willing to press for 'unification' by force. An even more disturbing indicator of a regressing cross-strait relationship is the irrelevance of the GMD – or any Taiwan government for that matter – as a factor in the CCP's Taiwan policy. Carrots are still offered to attract Taiwanese investment and human capital to China under the banner of deepening people-to-people relations, but these policies suffer from the usual implementation gap in China's political system. At the same time, these policies cannot turn the tide in Taiwan's public perception of the 'China threat', a perception in itself caused by Xi Jinping's reinforced focus on the stick-side of this method, both in terms of words and deeds.

For all its credit as an adaptive and pragmatic, problem-solving party that has secured regime survival against all odds in the previous four decades since the launching of the reform and opening-up policy (Shambaugh 2008), the inflexibility and ideological narrow-mindedness of the CCP's Taiwan policy is striking. The link chaining regime legitimacy to 'unification' has never been critically assessed by the CCP leadership. Retrieving Taiwan is foundational for Chinese nationalism and its current narrative of the 'rejuvenation of the great Chinese nation'. At the same time, 'unification' is of geo-economical and geopolitical significance, because Taiwan is a production and innovation hub of the global semiconductor industry and a gateway to military control over the Western Pacific. In this context, creative solutions towards some form of 'shared sovereignty' have never made it to the agenda-setting stage of the CCP's Taiwan policy. On the contrary, by erasing the ambiguous '1992 Consensus with different interpretations' once and for all, Xi Jinping has effectively told the Taiwanese that they must give up any hope for a deal with China beyond a modified version of the Hong Kong 'One Country, Two System' model, which would mean abandoning their current de facto sovereignty as well as their democratic system. Xi Jinping's Taiwan policy arguably exhibits a degree of impatience not seen since the later days of Jiang Zemin's reign, or even since Mao's last efforts to test the waters of military invasion, culminating in the 1958 Quemoy crisis.

Taiwan has become so critical for the maintenance of the CCP's legitimacy that the slightest retreat from the claim to 'unification', or any effort to creatively redefine what 'unification' could mean in terms of 'shared sovereignty', would be interpreted, both within and outside China, as the beginning of the end of one-party rule. Having boxed itself into a corner of nationalist and ideological petrification, the CCP under Xi Jinping's leadership can now only threaten Taiwan (and the Taiwanese) with military invasion to force submission. This serves to confirm to the world, and particularly to the US, that China is ready not only to fulfil its holy mission to rescue the Chinese nation from Taiwanese 'separatism', but also, putting it very simply, to go to war for Taiwan and thereby end American hegemony in the Asia-Pacific. This perception, though it may sound alarmist, can only strengthen the belief of the Taiwanese people that their country's sovereignty must be defended, no matter the cost. It also nurtures an anti-China sentiment around the world, strengthening those voices who predict a violent showdown between the US and China, with Taiwan arguably one of the most likely places where such a clash will happen. This again can only drive Xi Jinping's impatience to solve the 'Taiwan issue' as soon as possible, because time is no longer on Beijing's side. Thus, the CCP's Taiwan policy under Xi Jinping has reached a dead-end, equating to a formidable failure, as the costs of deterring independence rise while the probability of 'peaceful unification' becomes proportionally smaller and smaller.[40] This failure may, over time, not only be detrimental to the CCP's ruling legitimacy but also, in the worst of all cases, to regional and global peace as well.

40 However, Shelley Rigger (2018) contends that the CCP's Taiwan policy has not failed, as it has 'avoided the worst-case scenario' of Taiwan independence. Whether Xi Jinping thinks that way is debatable, as avoiding Taiwan independence does not help 'unification' but rather diminishes its 'market value' over time.

References

Beckershoff, André. 2014. 'The KMT–CCP Forum: Securing Consent for Cross-Strait Rapprochement'. *Journal of Current Chinese Affairs* 43 (1): 213–41. doi.org/10.1177/186810261404300108.

Chen, Chien-kai. 2012. 'Comparing Jiang Zemin's Impatience with Hu Jintao's Patience Regarding the Taiwan Issue, 1989–2012'. *Journal of Contemporary China* 21 (78): 955–72. doi.org/10.1080/10670564.2012.701034.

Chen, Guiqing (陈桂清). 2022. '新时代党解决台湾问题的总体方略: 历史形成与核心内涵' (Overall Policy Framework for Resolving the Taiwan Question in the New Era). 统一战线研究 (Journal of United Front Science) 6: 81–93.

Chu, Yun-han. 2000. 'Making Sense of Beijing's Policy toward Taiwan: The Prospect of Cross-Strait Relations during the Jiang Zemin Era'. In *China under Jiang Zemin*, edited by Hung-mao Tien and Yun-han Chu, 139–212. Boulder: Lynne Rienner. doi.org/10.1515/9781685859220-012.

Deans, Phil. 2005. 'Cross-Strait Relations since 1949: From Radicalism to Conservatism and Back Again'. *China aktuell* 3: 25–35.

Friedman, Edward. 2007. 'China's Changing Taiwan Policy'. *American Journal of Chinese Studies* 14 (2): 119–34.

Gang, Lin. 2016. 'Beijing's New Strategies toward a Changing Taiwan'. *Journal of Contemporary China* 25 (99): 321–35. doi.org/10.1080/10670564.2015.1104863.

Garver, John W. 1997. *The Sino-American Alliance: Nationalist China and American Cold War Strategy in Asia*. Armonk: M. E. Sharpe.

Ho, Ming-Sho. 2019. *Challenging Beijing's Mandate of Heaven: Taiwan's Sunflower Movement and Hong Kong's Umbrella Movement*. Philadelphia: Temple University Press.

Hsieh, John Fu-sheng. 2003. 'Taiwan's Mainland China Policy under Lee Teng-hui'. In *Sayonara to the Lee Teng-hui Era: Politics in Taiwan, 1988–2000*, edited by Wei-chin Lee, T. Y. Wang, 185–99. Lanham: University Press of America.

Hsu, Szu-chien and J. Michael Cole. 2020. *Insidious Power: How China Undermines Global Democracy*. Manchester: East Bridge.

Jacobs, Bruce J. and Ben I-hao Liu. 2007. 'Lee Teng-hui and the Idea of "Taiwan"'. *China Quarterly* 190: 375–93. doi.org/10.1017/S0305741007001245.

Jones, Brian Christopher. 2017. *Law and Politics of the Taiwan Sunflower and Hong Kong Umbrella Movements*. London: Routledge. doi.org/10.4324/9781315575063.

Kwong, Ying-ho. 2016. 'The Growth of "Localism" in Hong Kong'. *China Perspectives* (3): 63–8. doi.org/10.4000/chinaperspectives.7057.

Lee, Wei-chin. 2020. 'Multiple Shades of China's Taiwan Policy after the 19th Party Congress'. *Journal of Asian and African Studies* 55 (2): 201–20. doi.org/10.1177/0021909620905063.

Lin, Shirley Syaru. 2016. *Taiwan's China Dilemma: Contested Identities and Multiple Interests in Taiwan's Cross-Strait Economic Policy.* Stanford: Stanford University Press. doi.org/10.1515/9780804799300.

Rigger, Shelley. 2018. 'Has China's Taiwan Policy Failed? And If So, What Next?' In *A New Era in Democratic Taiwan: Trajectories and Turning Points in Politics and Cross-Strait Relations*, edited by John Sullivan and Chun-yi Lee, 142–55. London: Routledge. doi.org/10.4324/9781315161648-8.

Rigger, Shelley and Gunter Schubert. 2017. 'Taiwan's Development Experience for the Chinese Mainland: The Perspective of Chinese Intellectuals'. In *Taiwan's Impact on China: Why Soft Power Matters More than Economic or Political Inputs*, edited by Steve Tsang, 95–123. Basingstoke: Palgrave MacMillan.

Roy, Denny. 2021. 'Rumors of War in the Taiwan Strait'. *Diplomat*, 20 March. thediplomat.com/2021/03/rumors-of-war-in-the-taiwan-strait/.

Schubert, Gunter, ed. 2016. *Taiwan and the China Impact: Challenges and Opportunities*. London: Routledge. doi.org/10.4324/9781315671116.

Shambaugh, David. 2008. *China's Communist Party: Atrophy and Adaptation*. Berkeley: University of California Press. doi.org/10.4000/chinaperspectives.4755.

Sheng, Michael M. 2008. 'Mao and China's Relations with the Superpowers in the 1950s: A New Look at the Taiwan Strait Crisis and the Sino-Soviet Split'. *Modern China* 34 (4): 477–507. doi.org/10.1177/0097700408315991.

Shirk, Susan L. 2007. *China: Fragile Superpower: How China's Internal Politics Could Derail Its Peaceful Rise*. Oxford: Oxford University Press.

Su, Chi. 2009. *Taiwan's Relations with Mainland China: A Tail Wagging Two Dogs.* London: Routledge. doi.org/10.4000/chinaperspectives.4959.

Sullivan, Jonathan and James Smyth. 2018. 'The KMT's China Policy: Gains and Failures'. In *Assessing the Presidency of Ma Ying-jiu in Taiwan: Hopeful Beginning, Hopeless End?*, edited by André Beckershoff and Gunter Schubert, 17–36. London: Routledge. doi.org/10.4324/9781351045117-2.

Szonyi, Michael. 2008. *Cold War Island: Quemoy at the Front Line*. Cambridge: Cambridge University Press.

Tiezzi, Shannon. 2015. 'Cross-Strait Relations: The DPP's Tightrope Walk'. *Diplomat,* 11 June. thediplomat.com/2015/06/cross-strait-relations-the-dpps-tightrope-walk/.

Wachman, Allan M. 1994. *Taiwan: National Identity and Democratization.* Armonk-London: M. E. Sharpe.

Wu, Jieh-min. 2016. 'The China Factor in Taiwan: Impact and Response'. In *Routledge Handbook of Contemporary Taiwan,* edited by Gunter Schubert, 426–46. London: Routledge. doi.org/10.4324/9781315769523-29.

Xin, Qiang. 2020. 'Having Much in Common? Changes and Continuity in Beijing's Taiwan Policy'. *Pacific Review* 34 (6): 926–45. doi.org/10.1080/09512748.2020.1773908.

Xu, Shiquan. 2001. 'The 1992 Consensus: A Review and Assessment of Consultations between the Association for Relations across the Taiwan Strait and the Straits Exchange Foundation'. *American Foreign Policy Interests* 23 (3): 121–40. doi.org/10.1080/10803920131705766l.

www.ingramcontent.com/pod-product-compliance
Lightning Source LLC
Chambersburg PA
CBHW030855270326
41929CB00008B/433

* 9 7 8 1 7 6 0 4 6 6 2 3 7 *